CONSTITUTIONAL REVIEW SYSTEMS AROUND THE WORLD

Constitutional Review Systems Around the World

Arne Marjan Mavčič, P.E, editor

Published by:

Vandeplas Publishing, LLC – April 2018

801 International Parkway, 5th Floor
Lake Mary, FL. 32746
USA

www.vandeplaspublishing.com

ISBN 978-1-60042-297-3

CONSTITUTIONAL REVIEW SYSTEMS AROUND THE WORLD

ARNE MARJAN MAVČIČ, P.E, EDITOR

Preface

The present study contains a comparative constitutional analysis of the constitutional/judicial review systems in 208 countries. It gives a broader overview and deeper knowledge of such systems around the world. The study was created by the students research group of the European Law School to the New University in Slovenia, conducted by professor Arne Marjan Mavčič.

The institutional and functional comparative method is making readers familiar with constitutional systems of different countries, drawing on features for individual world regions and considering specific types of constitutional and judicial review. Using a special systemic presentation model, the researchers treat different systems and institutions that hold their exclusive decision-making power on constitutional matters. Their review quite often covers legislative acts that are the highest legal instruments of a specific legal and political system. This gives each constitutional/judicial review institution a special status with power to provide constitutional and/or review under the system of the separation of powers, especially in relation to the legislative power in that it may even annul statutes adopted by the legislative body.

Each systemic presentation model is completed depending on the currently available data (sources).

Arne Mavčič, Professor Emeritus, completed his graduated and post-graduated law studies at the University of Ljubljana (Slovenia) and Zagreb (Croatia). He was head of the Information and International Department of the Slovenian Constitutional Court and the liaison officer for Slovenia to the Venice Commission under the Council of Europe, the national correspondent for Slovenia to ACCPUF Paris, a member for Slovenia in different international research groups and a Fulbright Scholar. As Senior Expert Counsellor to the University of Ljubljana Law School, Professor of Human Rights Law, Constitutional Law and Comparative Constitutional Law at the School of Government and European Studies and at the European Law School to the New University of Ljubljana, he specialises in legal information systems, (comparative) constitutional law and human rights law. As the author and editor of several publications in the field of constitutional law as well as the author of over 300 papers and reports of a national and international character, Dr Mavčič has largely been engaged in practical and promotional activities in the fields of comparative constitutional review and human rights law.

Arne Marjan Mavčič, P.E: amavcic@gmail.com or amavcic@concourts.net

MEMBERS OF THE RESEARCH GROUP:

Erazem Bohinc, M.Law: erazem.bohinc@gmail.com

Tina Debeljak, B.Law: tdstinatina@gmail.com

Andreja Friškovec, undergraduate student of law: andreja.friskovec@gmail.com

Nejc Goršič, B.Law: n.gorsic@gmail.com

Teja Živec Kavčič, undergraduate and postgraduate student of law: teja.kavcic79@gmail.com

Sabina Lukač Homjak, undergraduate student of law: sabina.homjak@hotmail.com

Tjaša Peternel, B.Law: tjasa.peternel@gmail.com

Aleksandra Samac, B.Law: samac.aleksandra@gmail.com

INTRODUCTION

This research presents a comparative constitutional analysis of the constitutional/judicial review systems in 205 countries.

Based on an uniform systemic presentation model (from www.concourts.net), there are presented current national systems of constitutional/judicial review and bodies that hold this special and exclusive decision-making power on constitutional matters. Individual country models are completed differently, depending on the available sources.

DOSSIER OF THE CONSTITUTIONAL COURT OR OTHER EQUIVALENT COURT............................

STATE:
TITLE:
YEAR OF FOUNDATION:
SEAT:

I. CHRONICLE

1. **Date and context of establishment**
2. **Position in the hierarchy of courts**

II. STANDARD LEGAL REFERENCE

3. **The Constitution of.....................**
4. **The Constitutional Court Act......................**
5. **The Rules of Procedure........................**
6. **Other Internal Rules...........................**

III. COMPOSITION AND ORGANIZATION

1. **Composition**
   1. The number of judges:
   2. Electoral/appointment body:
      1. Appointment based system (Without the Participation of a Representative Body):

2. **Other powers**
    1. Constitutional complaints:
    2. Jurisdictional disputes:
    3. The unconstitutionality of acts and activities of political parties:
    4. Charges against the President of the Republic:
    5. Charges against the Prime Minister or against any Minister of State:
    6. Electoral matters:
    7. Referendums:
    8. Other matters with which the Court is charged by the Constitution or statute:
3. **Standing before the Constitutional Court**
    1. State bodies:
    2. Individuals:

V. NATURE AND EFFECTS OF DECISIONS

1. **Finality**:
2. **Binding force**:
    1. Erga omnes:
    2. Inter partes:
3. **Ex officio**:
4. **The temporary order**:
5. **Abrogation in whole or in part**:
    1. Effectiveness immediately or within a certain period of time:
6. **Annulment in whole or in part**:
7. **The consequences of decisions, damage claims**
8. **The declaration of unconstitutionality and illegality**:
9. **The legislative omissions**:
10. **The abrogation, retroactive or prospective, of a general act while deciding on a constitutional complaint**:
11. **The final decision on a contested human right or freedom based on a constitutional complaint**:
12. **Stating the competent body**:
13. **Impeachment**:
    1. Finding the proposal for impeachment to be unfounded:
    2. Decision on the basis for impeachment/decision on the termination of the Presidents/Prime Ministers/Ministers office:
14. **The annulment of an unconstitutional act/activity of a political party act/activity or the ordering of a deletion from the register of legal political parties**:

15. **The annulment of decisions of the National Assembly and rulings on the election of representatives:**
16. **Obligatory opinions on the conformity of international treaties with the Constitution:**
17. **Declarations on the constitutionality of a proposal to call a referendum:**
18. **Other forms of decisions:**

VI PUBLICATION OF CONSTITUTIONAL COURT DECISIONS

1. **The Official Gazette:**
2. **The Official Digest:**
3. **Legal Journals:**
4. **Electronic Publishing:**
5. **Other forms:**

The research comprises the the structure and powers of constitutional courts or other equivalent courts as special bodies responsible for protecting the constitutionality for which they hold a certain legal superiority in relation to other branches of power. Their review quite often covers legislative acts that are the highest legal instruments of a specific legal and political system. This gives the particular constitutional court or other equivalent court a special status with a power to perform constitutional/judicial review in accordance with the principle of the separation of powers.

This research is based on the constitutional documents in their English version available on the Internet. Additionally, some relevant sources of comparative character are available on http://www.concourts.net/comparison.php

CONTENTS:

(1)

DOSSIER OF THE CONSTITUTIONAL COURT OF THE REPUBLIC OF ABKHAZIA

STATE: Republic of Abkhazia
TITLE: The Constitutional Court
YEAR OF FOUNDATION:

- 2016 (not in power due to unsuccessful election of judges)
- Constitution of the Republic of Abkhazia of 26.11.1994 (amended 3.10.1999, No. 146-IV 30.1.2014)

SEAT: Sukhumi

I. CHRONICLE

Date and context of establishment:
Adopted by the 12th session of the Supreme Council of the Republic of Abkhazia on the 26.11.1994 and approved by the national voting on the 3.10.1999 with amendment adopted by the national voting (referendum) on the 3.10.1999 and project No. 146-IV of the Constitutional law of the Republic of Abkhazia on amendment to the Constitution of the Republic of Abkhazia on the 30.1.2014.

Position in the hierarchy of courts:
Article 68 of the Constitution states that judicial power in the Republic of Abkhazia is exercised through constitutional, civil, criminal and administrative proceedings. Article 72.1 stipulates that the Constitutional Court of the Republic of Abkhazia is a judicial body of constitutional control, independently exercising judicial power through constitutional legal proceedings. Article 73 of the Constitution states that the Supreme Court of the Republic of Abkhazia shall be the highest judicial body in civil, criminal, administrative and other cases within the competence of the courts of general jurisdiction of the Republic of Abkhazia.

II. STANDARD LEGAL REFERENCE

The Constitution of the Republic of Abkhazia 1994
The Constitutional Law of the Republic of Abkhazia On the Judiciary (As amended on July 22, 1997, № 348-c-XIII, May 31, 1999 № 510-c-XIII, May 27, 2005 № 1045-c-XIV, February 22, 2007 № 1659-c-XIV, November 5, 2010 № 2753-c-IV, January 30, 2014 No. 146-IV)

III. COMPOSITION AND ORGANIZATION

Composition
The number of judges:
5 judges (as stipulated by the Law on the Constitutional Court);

Electoral/appointment body: Mixed system:
Article 71 of the Constitution stipulated that the Judges of the Constitutional Court of the Republic of Abkhazia are elected by the Parliament of the Republic of Abkhazia on the proposal of the President of the Republic of Abkhazia by a qualified majority of the total number of deputies of the Parliament of the Republic of Abkhazia. The right to propose to the President of the Republic of Abkhazia the candidature of the judges of the Constitutional Court of the Republic of Abkhazia belongs to a group of deputies constituting not less than one third of the total number of deputies of the Parliament of the Republic of Abkhazia and the highest judicial self-government body.

The Constitutional Court members:
The term of office: 15 years

The qualifications and the required professional experience of constitutional court judges:
Article 69, para. 3 and 4 of the Constitution: The judges of the Constitutional Court of the Republic of Abkhazia may be citizens of the Republic of Abkhazia who have reached the age of 40 years, have a higher legal education and have worked for at least 15 years in the legal profession. The Constitutional Law may establish additional requirements for judges.

Incompatibilities:
Article 70 para. 1 of the Constitution: Judges cannot occupy a different position in public authorities and local self-government bodies, engage in entrepreneurial or other paid activities, except for teaching, scientific and other creative activities. Judges can not belong to political parties.

Proceedings

Public hearing:

Article 72: Court examinations in all courts shall be open to the public except in cases established by the law. The legal procedure shall be adversarial with both sides having equal rights.

Organization

Administrative autonomy:

Article 72.1 of the Constitution: The Constitutional Court of the Republic of Abkhazia is a judicial body of constitutional control, independently exercising judicial power through constitutional legal proceedings.

Budget: Article 70, para. 2 of the Constitution: Judges receive in due time the monetary compensation paid by the Republic of Abkhazia for their service.

IV. POWERS

Constitutional Court Review

Preventive review:

Article 72.1 of the Constitution: The Constitutional Court of the Republic of Abkhazia:

1) resolve cases on compliance with the Constitution of the Republic of Abkhazia:

[...] B) international treaties of the Republic of Abkhazia that have not entered into legal force;

[...] 6) gives a conclusion on the conformity of the proposal for amendments or revision of the Constitution of the Republic of Abkhazia to the requirements of Chapter 7 of this Constitution;

A posteriori review:

Article 61 of the Constitution: Legal acts of the President of the Republic of Abkhazia that do not comply with the Constitution of the Republic of Abkhazia shall be subject to abolition by the Constitutional Court of the Republic of Abkhazia.

Article 72.1 of the Constitution: The Constitutional Court of the Republic of Abkhazia:

1) resolve cases on compliance with the Constitution of the Republic of Abkhazia:

A) constitutional laws, laws, legal acts of the President of the Republic of Abkhazia, the Parliament of the Republic of Abkhazia, the Cabinet of Ministers of the Republic of Abkhazia and local self-government bodies;

Abstract review:

The Constitutional Court of the Republic of Abkhazia:

[...] 4) at the request of the President of the Republic of Abkhazia, the Parliament of the Republic of Abkhazia, the Cabinet of Ministers of the Republic of Abkhazia gives an interpretation of the Constitution of the Republic of Abkhazia;

Concrete review:

Other powers

Constitutional complaints:

Article 72.1 of the Constitution: The Constitutional Court of the Republic of Abkhazia:

[...] 3) on complaints of violation of constitutional rights and freedoms of citizens and upon the requests of courts, verify compliance of the law applied or to be applied in a concrete case to the Constitution of the Republic of Abkhazia.

Jurisdictional disputes:

Article 72.1 of the Constitution: The Constitutional Court of the Republic of Abkhazia:

2) resolve disputes about competence:

A) between public authorities;

B) between state authorities and local self-government bodies;

Charges against the President of the Republic:

Article 64 of the Constitution: Should the President violate his oath or breach the Constitution and the laws of the Republic of Abkhazia, he can be relieved of his duties. Such decisions are taken by the Parliament of the Republic of Abkhazia - on the basis of Constitutional Court of the Republic of Abkhazia findings - by a two-thirds majority of its Deputies voting by secret ballot.[1]

Article 72.1 of the Constitution: The Constitutional Court of the Republic of Abkhazia:

[...] 5) at the request of the Parliament of the Republic of Abkhazia, issue an opinion on the observance of the established procedure for the nomination of the prosecution for removal from office of the President of the Republic of Abkhazia;

Referendums:

Other matters with which the Court is charged by the Constitution or statute:

According to Article 72.1 the Constitutional Court of the Republic of Abkhazia:

[...] 7) exercise other powers conferred on him by the constitutional law.

1 AN: word 'deputies' should be replaced by 'judges' according to the amendment of the Constitution No. 146-IV 30.1.2014

Standing before the Constitutional Court

State bodies: X

Individuals: X

Article 72.1: The Constitutional Court of the Republic of Abkhazia:

[...] 3) on complaints of violation of constitutional rights and freedoms of citizens and upon the requests of courts, verify compliance of the law applied or to be applied in a concrete case to the Constitution of the Republic of Abkhazia;

V. NATURE AND EFFECTS OF DECISIONS

Obligatory opinions on the conformity of international treaties with the Constitution:

Article 72.1 of the Constitution: The Constitutional Court of the Republic of Abkhazia:

1) resolve cases on compliance with the Constitution of the Republic of Abkhazia:

[...] B) international treaties of the Republic of Abkhazia that have not entered into legal force.

SOURCES:

https://en.wikipedia.org/wiki/Constitutional_Court_of_Abkhazia

http://abkhazinform.com/item/4919-valerij-bganba-sozhaleet-chto-konstitutsionnyj-sud-ne-sformirovan

https://en.wikipedia.org/wiki/Constitution_of_Abkhazia#cite_note-agov25488-1

http://gazeta-ra.info/index.php?ELEMENT_ID=8928

http://www.kapba.de/Constitution.html

(2)

DOSSIER OF THE SUPREME COURT OF THE ISLAMIC REPUBLIC OF AFGHANISTAN

STATE: Islamic Republic of Afghanistan
TITLE: Supreme Court (Afg. Stera Mahkma)
YEAR OF FOUNDATION: 2004
SEAT: Kabul

I. CHRONICLE

Date and context of establishment:
The Supreme Court of Afghanistan was created by the Constitution of Afghanistan, which was approved on January 4, 2004. Its creation was called for by the Bonn Agreement (Agreement on Provisional Arrangements in Afghanistan Pending the Re-Establishment of Permanent Government Institutions, 2001)

Position in the hierarchy of courts:
Article 116 of the Constitution states that the Supreme Court shall be the highest judicial organ, heading the judicial power of the Islamic Republic of Afghanistan.

II. STANDARD LEGAL REFERENCE

The Constitution of Afghanistan 2004
The Rules of Procedure: Law of the Organization and Authority of the Courts of Islamic Republic of Afghanistan (2005)

Composition

The number of judges: 9

Electoral/appointment body:

Mixed Systems (Appointment and Election):

Article 17 of the Law of the Organization and Authority of the Courts of Islamic Republic of Afghanistan: he Supreme Court shall be composed of nine persons appointed by the president in an agreement with Wolusi Jirga (house of people) in accordance with Article 117 and 118 of the Constitution. The president shall appoint one of the members as the chief of the Supreme Court.

The Court members: /

The term of office: /

Article 117 of the Constitution: Three members for a period of four years, three members for seven years, and three members for ten years. Later appointments shall be for period of ten years. Appointment of members for a second term shall not be permitted.

The Court President: /

The term of office:

Article 117 of the Constitution: The President shall appoint one of its members as Chief Justice of the Supreme Court. Members of the Supreme Court, except under circumstances stated in Article One Hundred Twenty Seven of this Constitution, shall not be dismissed till the end of their term.

The qualifications and the required professional experience of constitutional court judges:

Article 118 of the Constitution: Supreme Court members shall have the following qualifications:

1. At time of appointment the age of the Chief Justice of the Supreme Court and its members shall not be less than forty year.
2. Shall be a citizen of Afghanistan.
3. Shall have higher education in legal studies or Islamic jurisprudence as well as expertise and adequate experience in the judicial system of Afghanistan.
4. Shall have good character as well as good reputation.
5. Shall not have been convicted, by a court, for crimes against humanity, crimes, or deprivation of civil rights.
6. Shall not be a member of any political party during his term of duty.

Incompatibilities:
Article 118 of the Constitution: (...) 6. Shall not be a member of any political party during his term of duty.

Release from office prior to the expiration of the term:
Article 127 of the Constitution: If more than one third of the members of the House of People demand the trial of the Chief Justice of the Supreme Court or any of its members accused of a crime related to job performance or committing a crime, and, the House of People approves this demand by two thirds majority of all members, the accused shall be dismissed and the issue referred to a special court. The formation of the court and procedure of the trial shall be regulated by law.

Proceedings
The Dissenting/Concurring opinion:
Public hearing:
Article 8 of the Law of the Organization and Authority of the Courts of Islamic Republic of Afghanistan: Trials in the Afghanistan courts shall happen in open procedure in which everybody may attend, subject to law. The court may convene the trials in a close procedure only if they are legally required or that it is deemed necessary. Making notice of the final decision shall always be open to public.

Organization
Administrative autonomy:
The budget:
Article 125 of the Constitution: The budget of the judiciary shall be prepared by the Supreme Court in consultation with the Government, and shall be presented to the National Assembly as part of the national budget. The Supreme Court shall implement the budget of the judiciary.

Administrative services:
Article 29 of the Law of the Organization and Authority of the Courts of Islamic Republic of Afghanistan: Article 29: (1) The Supreme Court shall have the following duties and jurisdictions in its relevant administration affairs:

1. Prepare the budget for the judiciary in consultation with the government
2. lead and control the administrative activities of courts of Islamic Republic of Afghanistan
3. Approve rules and regulations to regulate matters concerning judicial and administration of courts.
4. Evaluate the results of judicial scrutiny and studies and taking measures to remove defects and coordinate courts' procedures.

5. Propose on the appointment of judges and judicial advisors to the president's office according to provisions of this law.
6. Propose on the appointment, transfer, upgrading, extension of the appointments' duration and retirement of judges according to the provisions of this law.
7. Propose on the establishment of courts and legal document registration directorates, and their specification of judicial and administration jurisdiction to the president's office.
8. Implement the budget of the judiciary.
9. Providing necessary facilities for the courts' activities.
10. Holding judicial practice course.
11. Taking appropriate measures for enhancing the knowledge and experiences of judges.
12. Monitor performances and activities of employees of judicial authority.
13. Prepare annual statistic report of all courts judicial activities.
14. Other duties and jurisdictions which are delegated to Supreme Court according to this law and all other laws.

(2) The powers set forth in clause one of this Article shall be implemented through the General Administration Office of the Judiciary.

Article 132 of the Constitution: Judges are appointed at the proposal of the Supreme Court and approval of the President. Appointment, transfer, promotion, punishment and proposals for retirement of judges, carried out according to provisions of the laws, shall be within the authority of the Supreme Court. To better regulate judicial as well as judicial administrative matters and attain necessary reforms, the Supreme Court shall establish the Office of General Administration of the Judiciary.

IV. POWERS

Constitutional Court Review

Preventive review:
A posteriori review:
Abstract review:

Article 121 of the Constitution: At the request of the Government, or courts, the Supreme Court shall review the laws, legislative decrees, international treaties as well as international covenants for their compliance with the Constitution and their interpretation in accordance with the law.

Concrete review:

Article 24 of the Law of the Organization and Authority of the Courts of Islamic Republic of Afghanistan: The Supreme Court shall have the following jurisdictions and duties within the scope of interpretation of laws and judicial issues: (...) 3) Revising the rulings of courts due to presence of new reasons based on complaint by the AGO or by party to the claim according to the mentioned provisions and arrangement in the law.

Article 26 of the Law of the Organization and Authority of the Courts of Islamic Republic of Afghanistan: 1. If a Supreme Court Dewan determines that the lower court ruling was contrary to the law, fails to conform or interpret or contrary to the Articles 130 and 131 of the Constitution, it shall overturn the ruling and remand it to the lower court for issuance of ruling. The Supreme Court Dewan may overturn a ruling which it observes as contrary to the law even if the breach is not mentioned in the appeal. 2. If the failure in consistency or interpreting the law does not substantially affect the ruling and the ruling is accurate and agrees to the law, the relevant Dewan may confirm it.

Article 130 of the Constitution: In cases under consideration, the courts shall apply provisions of this Constitution as well as other laws. If there is no provision in the Constitution or other laws about a case, the courts shall, in pursuance of Hanafi jurisprudence, and, within the limits set by this Constitution, rule in a way that attains justice in the best manner.

Article 131 of the Constitution: The courts shall apply the Shia jurisprudence in cases involving personal matters of followers of the Shia sect in accordance with the provisions of the law. In other cases, if no clarification in this Constitution and other laws exist, the courts shall rule according to laws of this sect.

Other powers

Jurisdictional disputes:

Article 24 of the Law of the Organization and Authority of the Courts of Islamic Republic of Afghanistan: The Supreme Court shall have the following jurisdictions and duties within the scope of interpretation of laws and judicial issues: (...) 4) resolving Courts' Conflict of Jurisdiction and submitting jurisdiction of resolving a case from one court to the other based on proposal by the AGO or party to the claim when reasonable grounds arise.

Other matters with which the Court is charged by the Constitution or statute:

Article 24 of the Law of the Organization and Authority of the Courts of Islamic Republic of Afghanistan: The Supreme Court shall have the following jurisdictions and duties within the scope of interpretation of laws and judicial issues: (...) 2) Propose for draft law on regulating the judicial affairs to the national assembly through government.

5) Studying reasons and making decision on extraditing criminals to foreign states in accordance with law

6) Studying reasons of a charge made and making decision on submitting the Afghan citizen to the foreign state in the light of Article 28 of the Constitution.

7) Ensuring uniformity in judicial treatment.

8) Taking measures on criminal and disciplinary offences by judges.

9) Evaluating the courts inquiries on judicial issues and providing responses accordingly.

Article 133 of the Constitution: When a judge is accused of a crime, the Supreme Court shall, in accordance with the provisions of the law, consider the case. After hearing the defense, if the Supreme Court considers the accusation valid, it shall present a proposal to the President for dismissal of the judge. After Presidential approval, the accused judge shall be dismissed and punished according to the provisions of the law.

Standing before the Constitutional Court

State bodies and Individuals:

Article 120 of the Constitution: The authority of the judicial organ shall include consideration of all cases filed by real or incorporeal persons, including the state, as plaintiffs or defendants, before the court in accordance with the provisions of the law.

V. NATURE AND EFFECTS OF DECISIONS

Finality:

Article 116 of the Constitution: The judiciary shall be an independent organ of the state of the Islamic Republic of Afghanistan. The judiciary shall be comprised of one Supreme Court, Courts of Appeal as well as Primary Courts whose organization and authority shall be regulated by law. The Supreme Court shall be the highest judicial organ, heading the judicial power of the Islamic Republic of Afghanistan.

Binding force:

Article 28 (Enforceability of orders and Rulings(Qarar)) of the Law of the Organization and Authority of the Courts of Islamic Republic of Afghanistan: The orders and Qarars by the higher court shall be enforceable on the lower courts on newly resolving of cases.

Annulment in whole or in part:

Article 26 of the Law of the Organization and Authority of the Courts of Islamic Republic of Afghanistan: 1. If a Supreme Court Dewan determines that the lower court ruling was contrary to the law, fails to conform or interpret or contrary to the Articles 130 and 131 of the Constitution, it shall overturn the ruling and remand it to the lower court for issuance of ruling.

The Supreme Court Dewan may overturn a ruling which it observes as contrary to the law even if the breach is not mentioned in the appeal.

Article 27 (Remand for invalidity) of the Law of the Organization and Authority of the Courts of Islamic Republic of Afghanistan: 1. If the Supreme Court Dewan overturns the appealable ruling due to invalidity in the order or invalidity in the basic procedures of the order, it shall remand the case to the relevant court by mentioning the reasons for a decision. In the event the case is remanded to the first court, majority of the judges who consider the case shall not have decided the case before the appeal. 2. If there is a second appeal against the decision of the court for which the case was previously remanded and the appeal is based on the previous reasons and grounds and the referred court has issued the previous ruling (overturned by Supreme Court) with the same (first) reasons, the Supreme Court shall take the issue into further study. If the appealed case is overturned by the majority vote of the Court for related cases, the court for which the remanded ruling was referred shall resolve and issue ruling and in this case the referred court shall be duty bound to respect the instructed resolution by the Supreme Court and their ruling at this stage shall be final.

The legislative omissions:

Article 26 of the Law of the Organization and Authority of the Courts of Islamic Republic of Afghanistan: (...) 2. If the failure in consistency or interpreting the law does not substantially affect the ruling and the ruling is accurate and agrees to the law, the relevant Dewan may confirm it.

Stating the competent body:

Article 24 of the Law of the Organization and Authority of the Courts of Islamic Republic of Afghanistan: The Supreme Court shall have the following jurisdictions and duties within the scope of interpretation of laws and judicial issues: (...) 4) resolving Courts' Conflict of Jurisdiction and submitting jurisdiction of resolving a case from one court to the other based on proposal by the AGO or party to the claim when reasonable grounds arise.

SOURCES:

The Constitution of Afghanistan, http://www.afghanembassy.com.pl/afg/images/pliki/TheConstitution.pdf

Law of the Organization and Authority of the Courts of Islamic Republic of Afghanistan (2005), http://supremecourt.gov.af/content/media/documents/law_on_org_juris_courts_english112011121448474.pdf

http://supremecourt.gov.af/en

http://supremecourt.gov.af/Content/files/Brochure%20final%20with%20edit(1).pdf

(3)

DOSSIER OF THE CONSTITUTIONAL COURT OF REPUBLIC OF ALBANIA

STATE: Republic of Albania
TITLE: The Constitutional Court
YEAR OF FOUNDATION: 1992
SEAT: Tirana

I. CHRONICLE

Date and context of establishment:
The process of transformation of Albania into a functioning democratic State[2] indispensably included the adoption of the Constitution of Republic of Albania (Albanian: Kushtetuta e Shqipërisë) (Constitution currently in force was adopted by the Parliament on 28 November 1998 and ratified by a popular referendum) and establishment of the Constitutional Court of Republic of Albania on 29 April 1992.

Position in the hierarchy of courts:
Article 124 of the Constitution: 2. The Constitutional Court is subject only to the Constitution.

Article 2 of the Law on the organisation and functioning of the Constitutional Court of the Republic of Albania (Functioning of the Constitutional Court): The Constitutional Court is the highest authority, which guarantees the respecting of the Constitution and provides its final interpretation.

Article 3 of the Law on the organisation and functioning of the Constitutional Court of the Republic of Albania (Independence of the Constitutional Court): 1. The Constitutional Court is dependent only on the Constitution.

2. The Constitutional Court enjoys complete organizational, administrational and financial independence in fulfilling the tasks provided by the Constitution and this Law.

2 History, http://www.gjk.gov.al/web/History_97_2.php

II. STANDARD LEGAL REFERENCE

The Constitution of Republic of Albania 1992 with amendments
The Law on the organisation and functioning of the Constitutional Court of the Republic of Albania (Nr. 8577, 10.2.2000);

III. COMPOSITION AND ORGANIZATION

Composition
The number of judges:
Article 125 of the Constitution: 1. The Constitutional Court shall consist of 9 (nine) members. (...)

Electoral/appointment body:
Mixed Systems (Appointment and Election):
Article 125 of the Constitution: (...) Three members shall be appointed by the President of the Republic, three members shall be elected by the Assembly and three members shall be elected by the High Court. The members shall be selected among the three first ranked candidates by the Justice Appointments Council, in accordance with the law.

The Court members:
The term of office:
Article 125 of the Constitution: 3. The judges of the Constitutional Court shall hold office for a 9 year mandate without the right to re-appointment. (...) 6. The composition of the Constitutional Court shall be renewed every 3 years to one- third thereof, in accordance with the procedure determined by law. (...) 7. The Constitutional Court judge shall continue to stay in office until the appointment of the successor, except for the cases provided for in Article 127, paragraph 1, subparagraph c, ç), d), and dh).

Article 127 of the Constitution: 1. The mandate of Constitutional Court judges shall end, when:

a) Reaching the age of 70 years;
b) The 9 year mandate expires;
c) He/she resigns;
ç) Dismissed in accordance with the provisions of Article 128 of the Constitution;
d) Establishing the conditions of inelectability and incompatibility in assuming the function;
dh) Establishing the fact of incapacity to exercise the duties;

2. The end of the mandate of the Constitutional Court judge shall be declared upon the decision of the Constitutional Court.

3. Where the position of a judge remains vacant, the appointing body shall appoint a new judge, the latter staying in office until the expiry of the mandate of the outgoing judge.

Article 8 of the Law on the organisation and functioning of the Constitutional Court of the Republic of Albania (Start of tenure): 1. The tenure of the judge of the Constitutional Court starts after his/her swearing in to the President of the Republic of Albania. 2. The oath wording is: I solemnly swear to be always loyal to the Constitution of the Republic of Albania in fulfilling my duties . 3. The tenure of the judge of the Constitutional Court starts on the day of his/her swearing in and terminates on the same date of that month, unless otherwise provided by the Constitution. 4. The judge of the Constitutional Court sits in his/her seat until the appointment of his/her successor.

The Court President:

Article 11 of the Law on the organisation and functioning of the Constitutional Court of the Republic of Albania (Conduct of Constitutional Court): The activity of the Constitutional Court is organized and lead by the President of the court and in his/her absence by any judge He/She assigns to, unless when this Law provides it to the power of the meeting of the judges.

Article 12 of the Law on the organisation and functioning of the Constitutional Court of the Republic of Albania (Powers of the President of the Court): "The President of the Constitutional Court has the following powers:

a. Prepares, convenes and leads the plenary sessions of the Constitutional Court,

b. Represents the Court to the relations with third parties,

c. Coordinates the work among the judges,

d. Signs the acts of the Constitutional Court, except the decisions of the court, which are signed by all judges,

e. Nominates and dismisses the administrative staff and issues disciplinary measures to it.

The qualifications and the required professional experience of constitutional court judges:

Article 124 of the Constitution: 4. The judges of the Constitutional Court shall have a law degree, at least 15 years of experience as judges, prosecutors, advocates, law professors or lectors, senior employees in the public administration, with a renowned activity in the constitutional, human rights or other areas of law.

Incompatibilities:

Article 124 of the Constitution: 5. The judge should not have held political posts in the public administration or leadership positions in a political party in the last past 10 years before running as a candidate. Further criteria and the procedure for the appointment and election of judges of the Constitutional Court shall be regulated by law.

Article 130 of the Constitution. Being a Constitutional Court judge shall not be compatible with any other political, state activity, as well as any other professional activity exercised against payment, except for teaching, academic and scientific activities, in accordance with the law.

Immunities:

Article 128 of the Constitution: 1. The Constitutional Court judge shall be disciplinary liable under the law.

Article 16 (Chapter III – Status of the judge of the Constitutional Court) of the Law on the organisation and functioning of the Constitutional Court of the Republic of Albania (Immunity): 1. The judges of the Constitutional Court enjoy immunity due to their seat. The judge of the Constitutional Court are not legally responsible for opinions or his/her voting provided for the case under review.

The judge of the Constitutional Court cannot be investigated without the consent of the Constitutional Court. The judge of the Constitutional Court may be detained or arrested only if caught in the act of committing the crime or immediately after it. The respective organ provides immediate notification to the Constitutional Court. The respective organ releases the judge unless the Constitutional Court provides its consent to present the case to an ordinary court within 24 hours.

The decision of the Constitutional Court, which is taken on the majority of votes should be reasoned. The said judge, after being heard of, does not participate in the voting.

Article 18 of the Law on the organisation and functioning of the Constitutional Court of the Republic of Albania (Other rights of the judge of the Constitutional Court): 1. The judge of the Constitutional Court should:

a. have special individual, family and property protection, when thus requested by him/her under serious circumstances or so is considered necessary. Respective organs in charge of protection of senior personalities are obliged to respond to every request of this kind.

b. enjoy the right of annual paid holidays of 40 days. The annual holidays are during August – September.

c) be provided free of charge the Official Gazette and juridical newspapers and magazines,

d) enjoy equal rights with members of the Assembly of Albania as provided in Article 16, point 1, 19, 20, 23, 25 and 26 of Law Nr. 8550, date 18.11.1999 On the Status of the deputy .

The tenure of the judge of the Constitutional Court may not be limited, unless thus provided in the Constitution and this Law.

After normal termination of the tenure, unless dismissed through the procedures provided in the Law, the judge of the Constitutional Court is appointed to another job equal or similar and providing the transitional remuneration of the judge of the Constitutional Court and/or supplementary retirement according to the legislation in power.

Release from office prior to the expiration of the term:

Article 128 of the

Constitution: (...) 2. The disciplinary proceedings against the judge shall be carried out by the Constitutional Court, which decides on his/her dismissal when:

a) It finds serious professional and ethical misconduct which discredit the position and the image of a judge in exercising the mandate;

b) Sentenced by a final court decision for commission of a crime.

The Constitutional Court judge shall be suspended from duty by decision of the Constitutional Court when

a) Upon him/her is imposed the personal security measure of "arrest in prison" or "house arrest" for commission of a criminal offence;

b) He/she obtains the capacity of the defendant for an offence committed intentionally;

c) Disciplinary proceedings being initiated under the law.

Article 9 of the Law on the organisation and functioning of the Constitutional Court of the Republic of Albania (Termination of tenure): 1. The tenure of the judge of the Constitutional court terminates when:

a. sentenced by a final decision for a committed crime,

b. is absent for more than 6 (six) months without any justification,

c. reaches the age of 70 years old,

d. offers his/her resignation,

e. a final judicial decision declares him/her incapable to act.

Termination of tenure of the judge is declared by decision of the Constitutional Court. Theapplication to declare the termination of tenure of a judge is presented by the President of the Constitutional Court.

In case of vacancy seats, the President of the Republic appoints a new judge upon the consent of the Assembly within one month. The newly appointed judge seats until the termination of the tenure ofthe judge he/she sits instead.

Article 10 of the Law on the organisation and functioning of the Constitutional Court of the Republic of Albania (Dismissal of the judge): 1. The judge of the Constitutional Court may be dismissed by the Assembly through two thirds of its complete members if he/she violates the Constitution, commits a crime, becomes mentally or physically incapable, commits other acts that incriminate the position and personality of the judge. The decision of the Assembly is reviewed by the Constitutional Court, which upon verification of the above causes, declares the dismissal of the members of the Constitutional Court.

2. The reviewing of the procedure of the Assembly on the dismissal of the judges of the Constitutional Court, for one of the causes provided in point 1 of this Article, commences upon a motivated request of no less than half of the entire number of the members of the Assembly.

Proceedings

Hearing in plenum:

A quorum:

Article 20 of the Law on the organisation and functioning of the Constitutional Court of the Republic of Albania (Discussion in Panel): Cases at the Constitutional Court are collegially discussed. The decision is taken by the judges present at the session the said case has been discussed.

The Dissenting/Concurring opinion:

Article 72 of the Law on the organisation and functioning of the Constitutional Court of the Republic of Albania (Decision taking and its proclamation):

1. Discussions on and voting for the decision are not public.
2. The decisions of the Constitutional Court are taken on the majority of votes the judges present at the plenary hearing session. Abstaining from is not allowed.
3. The decision is signed by all the judges present at the plenary hearing session.
4. Parties in the process are notified about the date of the proclamation of the decision. Their absence makes no justification to post pone the proclamation of the decision.
5. The decision is proclaimed on the name of the Republic.
6. The decision of the Constitutional Court should be reasoned and read by the Presider of the plenary hearing session or any other judge as decided by him.
7. The decision of the Constitutional Court is obligatory to all and final.
8. The judge in descenting opinion enjoys the right to reason his opinion and thus it is attached to and published together with the court decision.
9. Copies of the decision are liable to be handed to the involved parties if thus requested by them and upon the respective fee.

Public hearing:

Article 21 of the Law on the organisation and functioning of the Constitutional Court of the Republic of Albania (Public hearing): 1. Cases are heard at the Constitutional Court at open plenary sessions.

2. The Constitutional Court may void the public from the whole or part of the session, justifying on the public moral, public order, national security and the right of private life or personal rights.

Organization

Administrative autonomy:

Article 3 of the Law on the organisation and functioning of the Constitutional Court of the Republic of Albania (Independence of the Constitutional Court): (...) 2. The Constitutional Court enjoys complete organizational, administrational and financial independence in fulfilling the tasks provided by the Constitution and this Law.

The budget:

Article 124 of the Constitution: (...) 3. The Constitutional Court shall have a separate budget, which it administers independently.

Article 6 of the Law on the organisation and functioning of the Constitutional Court of the Republic of Albania (Financial means): 1. The Constitutional court administers its own budget, which as part of the state budget is drafted by the Court and presented for approval to the Assembly of the Republic of Albania. 2. Any other income not prohibited by law is included at the financial means. 3. The High State Audit does the audit of the Constitutional Court.

IV. POWERS

Constitutional Court Review:

Article 124 of the Constitution:1. The Constitutional Court settles constitutional disputes and makes the final interpretation of the Constitution.

Preventive review:

Article 131 of the Constitution: The Constitutional Court decides on: (...) b) compatibility of international agreements with the Constitution, prior to their ratification; (...)

The Constitutional Court shall, when recourse being sought for examining a law on the revision of the Constitution approved by the Assembly according to Article 177, control only the compliance with the procedural requirements foreseen in the Constitution.

A posteriori review:

Abstract review:

Article 131 of the Constitution: The Constitutional Court decides on: a) compatibility of the law with the Constitution or with international agreements as provided for in Article 122;

(...) c) compatibility of normative acts of the central and local bodies with the Constitution and international agreements;

Concrete review:
Article 131 of the Constitution: The Constitutional Court decides on:
(...) d) constitutionality of the parties and other political organizations, as well as their activity, according to Article 9 of this Constitution;
f) final examination of the complaints of individuals against the acts of the public power or judicial acts impairing the fundamental rights and freedoms guaranteed by the Constitution, after all effective legal means for the protection of those rights have been exhausted, unless provided otherwise by the Constitution.

Constitutional complaints:
Jurisdictional disputes:
Article 131 of the Constitution: The Constitutional Court decides on: (...) ç) conflicts of competencies between powers, as well as between central government and local government;

The unconstitutionality of acts and activities of political parties:
Article 131 of the Constitution: The Constitutional Court decides on: (...) d) constitutionality of the parties and other political organizations, as well as their activity, according to Article 9 of this Constitution;

Charges against the President of the Republic:
Article 131 of the Constitution: The Constitutional Court decides on: (...) dh) dismissal from duty of the President of the Republic and verification of his inability to exercise his functions;

Charges against the Prime Minister or against any Minister of State:
Article 131 of the Constitution: The Constitutional Court decides on: (...) e) the issues bearing a connection to the electability and compliance in assuming the functions of the President of the Republic, MPs, functionaries of bodies foreseen in the Constitution, as well as to the verification of their election.

Electoral matters:
Article 131 of the Constitution: The Constitutional Court decides on: (...) e) the issues bearing a connection to the electability and compliance in assuming the functions of the President of the Republic, MPs, functionaries of bodies foreseen in the Constitution, as well as to the verification of their election.

Referendums:

Article 131 of the Constitution: The Constitutional Court decides on: (...) ë) constitutionality of the referendum and verification of its results;

Other matters with which the Court is charged by the Constitution or statute:

Article 12 of the Law on the organisation and functioning of the Constitutional Court of the Republic of Albania (Powers of the President of the Court): The President of the Constitutional Court has the following powers:

a. Prepares, convenes and leads the plenary sessions of the Constitutional Court,

b. Represents the Court to the relations with third parties,

c. Coordinates the work among the judges,

d. Signs the acts of the Constitutional Court, except the decisions of the court, which are signed by all judges,

e. Nominates and dismisses the administrative staff and issues disciplinary measures to it.

Standing before the Constitutional Court

State bodies and Individuals:

Article 134 of the Constitution: 1. Recourse to the Constitutional Court shall be sought upon the request of:

a) President of the Republic;

b) Prime Minister;

c) Not less than one-fifth of the members of Assembly;

ç) People's Advocate;

d) Head of High State Audit;

dh) Any court, in the event of Article 145, point 2, of this Constitution;

e) Any commissioner established by law for the protection of the fundamental rights and freedoms guaranteed by the Constitution;

ë) High Judicial Council and High Prosecutorial Council;

f) Local governance units;

g) Religious communities' forums;

gj) Political parties;

h) Organizations;

i) Individuals.

2. The entities provided for in sub-paragraphs d, dh, e, ë, f, g, gj, h, and i of paragraph 1 of this Article may file a request only regarding the issues connected to their interests.

Finality:

Article 132 of the Constitution:1.The decisions of the Constitutional Court shall be final and binding for enforcement.

Article 80 of the Law on the organisation and functioning of the Constitutional Court of the Republic of Albania (Interpretation and completion of the decision):

1. The Constitutional Court cannot annul or change its own decisions, but it can:

a. interpret the decision in case of doubts or disputes concerning its
understanding, but never changing its content,

b. complete the decision or correct any possible mistake in calculating or
any other evident inaccuracy in it within 2 (two) months from the date of its proclamation.

2. The review of the above-mentioned cases is made at plenary hearing session with the participation of involved parties.

Abrogation in whole or in part:

Effectiveness immediately or within a certain period of time:

1. Article 132 of the Constitution:

2. The decisions of the Constitutional Court shall enter into force on the day of their publication in the Official Journal. The Constitutional Court may decide that its decision, which has examined the act, gives effect on another date.

3. The dissenting opinion shall be published along with the final decision

Article 76 of the Law on the organisation and functioning of the Constitutional Court of the Republic of Albania (Juridical effects of the decisions of the Constitutional Court): 1. The decision of the Constitutional Court, which has abrogated a law or normative act as incompatible with the Constitution or International Agreements, as a rule will have its juridical effects from the date of its enforcement.

The decision is retroactive only in case:

a. it concerns a criminal sentencing and such a decision is under execution, if directly related with the implementation of the abrogated law or normative act,

b. it concerns case under review by the courts, unless their decisions have is final,

c. of effects of unimplemented law or normative act.

The consequences of decisions, damage claims:

Article 77 of the Law on the organisation and functioning of the Constitutional Court of the Republic of Albania (Juridical effects of the judicial decision): Decisions of courts of any instance, which are abrogated by the Constitutional Court have no juridical effect since their proclamation. The case is delivered to be reviewed to the court which decision has been abrogated.

Article 79 of the Law on the organisation and functioning of the Constitutional Court of the Republic of Albania (Interpreting decision): The decision of the Constitutional Court, which provides the interpretation of the Constitution is retrospective.

Stating the competent body:

Article 81 of the Law on the organisation and functioning of the Constitutional Court of the Republic of Albania (Execution of the decisions):

1. The execution of the decisions of the Constitutional Court is obligatory.
2. The execution of the decisions of the Constitutional Court is secured by the Council of Ministers of the Republic of Albania through the respective state administration.
3. The Constitutional Court may assign another organ to execute its decision and the means of execution, if thus necessary.
4. Persons, who do not implement or hinder the execution of the decisions of the Constitutional Court, unless the case provides a criminal offence, are fined with 100 (one hundred) thousand Lek by the President of the Constitutional Court and this decision is final and comprise an executive title.

Impeachment:

Decision on the basis for impeachment/decision on the termination of the Presidents/Prime Ministers/Ministers office:

Article 131 of the Constitution: The Constitutional Court decides on: (...) dh) dismissal from duty of the President of the Republic and verification of his inability to exercise his functions;

VI PUBLICATION OF CONSTITUTIONAL COURT DECISIONS

The Official Gazette:

Article 26 of the Law on the organisation and functioning of the Constitutional Court of the Republic of Albania (Publication of final decision): 1. Decisions of the Constitutional Court are final. They are published at the Official Gazette and enter into force on the day of their publication. The Court may decide to have its decision enforced on the day of its proclamation when decision concerns the protection of constitutional rights of the person.

2. The organ, which publishes the Official Gazette is obliged to publish the decisions of the Constitutional Court no later than 15 days after the decision is presented at said organ.

The Official Digest:

Article 26 of the Law on the organisation and functioning of the Constitutional Court of the Republic of Albania (Publication of final decision): (...) 3. The Constitutional Court prepares annual summary of its decisions.

SOURCES:

The Constitution of Republic of Albania (1998 as amended), http://www.gjk.gov.al/web/constitution_of_albania_1722.pdf

On the organization and functioning of the Constitutional Court of the Republic of Albania (Nr. 8577, 10.2.2000), http://www.gjk.gov.al/web/law_nr_8577_date_10_02_2000_84.pdf

Constitutional Court of Republic of Albania, http://www.gjk.gov.al/web/Constitutional_Court_1_2.php

Albania 1998, https://www.princeton.edu/~pcwcr/reports/albania1998.html

(4)

DOSSIER OF THE CONSTITUTIONAL COUNCIL OF PEOPLE'S DEMOCRATIC REPUBLIC OF ALGERIA

STATE: People´s Democratic Republic of Algeria
TITLE: The Supreme Court and Constitutional Council
YEAR OF FOUNDATION: 2016
SEAT: Algiers

I. CHRONICLE

Date and context of establishment:
The Algerian Constitution adopted in 2016 is the fundamental law of Algeria. The proposed constitution was presented on 4 February 2016 and then adopted on 7 February 2016. The 2016 Constitution replaces the 1996 Constitution.

Position in the hierarchy of courts:
The Supreme Court and Constitutional Council are the two heads of judiciary of Algeria, while the Constitutional Council addresses all matters of constitutional interpretation and review.[3]

II. STANDARD LEGAL REFERENCE

The Constitution of the People's Democratic Republic of Algeria of 7 February 2016

3 Constitutionnet - Constitutional history of Algeria, http://www.constitutionnet.org/country/constitutional-history-algeria

Composition

The number of judges:

Article 183 of the Constitution: The Constitutional Council shall consist of twelve (12) members: (...)

Electoral/appointment body: Mixed System (Appointment and Election):

Article 183 of the Constitution: (...) four (4) shall be appointed by the President of the Republic, including the President of the Council and the Vice President, two (2) shall be elected by the People's National Assembly, two (2) shall be elected by the Council of the Nation, two (2) shall be elected by the Supreme Court, and two (2) shall be elected by the Council of the State.

In the case of a tie between the members of the Constitutional Council, the President of the Council shall have the casting vote.

The Council members:

The term of office:

Article 183 of the Constitution: (...) The other members of the Constitutional Council shall serve a single term of eight (8) years; the membership of the Council shall be renewed by one-half (1/2) every four (4) years.

The Court President:

The term of office:

Article 183 of the Constitution: (...) The President of the Republic shall appoint the President and vice president of the Constitutional Council for a single eight-year (8) term.

The qualifications and the required professional experience of constitutional court judges:

Article 184 of the Constitution: The elected or designated members of the Constitutional Council shall: Be aged forty (40) on the day of their appointment or election. Have a professional experience of no less than fifteen (15) years in the higher education of legal sciences, in magistracy and as a lawyer at the Supreme Court, at the Council of State or in one of the State's higher positions.

Incompatibilities:

Article 183 of the Constitution: (...) As soon as they are elected or designated, the members of the Council shall cease any other mandate, function, task or mission, as well as any other liberal activity or profession.

Immunities:

Article 185 of the Constitution: During their mandate, the President, Vice-President and the members of the Constitutional Council shall be granted jurisdictional immunity in criminal matters. They shall not be subject to legal actions, arrest for any felony or offence, unless the concerned person expressly waivers his immunity or upon an authorisation from the Constitutional Council.

Organization

Administrative autonomy and the budget:

Article 182 of the Constitution: The Constitutional Council shall have administrative and financial autonomy.

IV. POWERS

Constitutional Court Review

Preventive review:

Article 190 of the Constitution: When the Constitutional Council rules that a treaty, agreement or convention is unconstitutional, it shall not be ratified.

The Constitutional Council may be requested by the President or either of the two Presidents of Parliament to review the constitutionality of organic laws and the internal regulation of the Parliament.[4]

A posteriori review:

Abstract review:

Article 182 of the Constitution: The Constitutional Council is an independent institution in charge of monitoring the observance of the Constitution. (...)

Article 186 of the Constitution: Aside from the other functions which are expressly conferred upon it by other provisions of the Constitution, the Constitutional Council shall rule on the constitutionality of treaties, statutes and regulations.

4 Ibid.

Upon request by the President of the Republic, the Constitutional Council shall issue a binding opinion on the constitutionality of the organic laws after their adoption by Parliament.

The Constitutional Council shall also rule in the same form, as specified in the preceding paragraph, on the conformity of the rules of procedure of each Chamber of Parliament with the Constitution.

Concrete review:

Other powers

Constitutional complaints:

Article 188 of the Constitution: The Constitutional Council shall be called upon based on the exception of unconstitutionality pursuant to a request by the Supreme Court or the Council of the State when one of the parties in a trial claims before the jurisdiction that the legislative provision upon which the issue of litigation relies may adversely affect the rights and freedoms granted by the Constitution.

The conditions and modalities of implementing the paragraph above shall be determined by an organic law.

Charges against the President of the Republic, charges against the Prime Minister or against any Minister of State:

Article 187 of the Constitution: The Constitutional Council might be called upon by the President of the Republic, the President of the Council of the Nation, the President of the People's National Assembly or the Prime Minister.

It might also be called upon by fifty (50) of the deputies or thirty (30) of the members of the Council of the Nation.

The referral to the Constitutional Council specified in the two preceding paragraphs shall not apply to a referral based on the exception of unconstitutionality stipulated by Article 188 below.

Article 188 of the Constitution: The Constitutional Council shall be called upon based on the exception of unconstitutionality pursuant to a request by the Supreme Court or the Council of the State when one of the parties in a trial claims before the jurisdiction that the legislative provision upon which the issue of litigation relies may adversely affect the rights and freedoms granted by the Constitution.

The conditions and modalities of implementing the paragraph above shall be determined by an organic law.

Electoral matters:

Article 103 of the Constitution: If a candidacy for the presidential election has been validated by the Constitutional Council, the withdrawal can only occur in cases of serious impediment duly noted by the Constitutional Council or death of the candidate concerned. If one of the two candidates for the second round withdraws, the electoral process shall continue without taking the withdrawal into account.

In case of death or legal incapacity of one of the two candidates in the second round, the Constitutional Council shall declare that the whole electoral process must be held again. It shall extend, in this case, the period for the organisation of new elections for a maximum of sixty (60) days.

When applying the provisions of this Article, the President of the Republic in office or who assumes the function of Head of State shall remain in office until the President of the Republic takes the oath.

An organic law shall determine the conditions and modalities of implementation of these provisions.

Article 104 of the Constitution: The Government in office at the time of the impediment, death or resignation of the President of the Republic cannot be dismissed or reshuffled until the new President of the Republic undertakes his duties.

If the Prime Minister in office becomes a candidate for the Presidency of the Republic, he shall resign de jure. The function of the Prime Minister shall be assumed by another member of the Government appointed by the Head of State.

During the periods stipulated in Articles 102 and 103 above, the provisions in paragraphs 7 and 8 of Article 91 and Articles 93, 142, 147, 154, 155, 208, 210 and 211 of the Constitution may not be applied.

During these same periods, the provisions of Articles 105, 107, 108, 109 and 111 of the Constitution cannot be implemented without the approval of Parliament, convened in a joint session of both Chambers. The Constitutional Council and the High Council of Security ought to be consulted beforehand.

Article 182 of the Constitution: (...) 3. It shall review, in their substance, the appeals it receives on the provisional results of the presidential and legislative elections and shall announce the final results of all the operations provided in the preceding paragraph.

Referendums:

Article 182 of the Constitution: (...) 2.The Constitutional Council shall monitor, among other matters, the proper conduct of referendum operations, (...).

Other matters with which the Court is charged by the Constitution or statute:

Article 182 of the Constitution: 1. The Constitutional Council is an independent institution in charge of monitoring the observance of the Constitution. (...)

Article 102 of the Constitution: When the President of the Republic, because of a serious and lasting illness, is totally unable to perform his functions, the Constitutional Council shall meet de jure and, after having verified the reality of the impediment by all appropriate means, it shall propose, unanimously, to Parliament to declare the state of impediment.

Parliament, convened in a joint session of both Chambers, shall declare the state of impediment of the President of the Republic, by a majority of two thirds (2/3) of its members and assign, as an acting Head of State, for a period of forty-five (45) days, the President of the Council of the Nation who shall exercise his prerogatives in accordance with the provisions of Article 104 of the Constitution.

If the impediment continues at the expiry of the period of forty five (45) days, there shall be a declaration of vacancy by a resignation de jure, in pursuance to the procedure referred to in the paragraphs above and the provisions of the following paragraphs of this Article.

In case of resignation or death of the President of the Republic, the Constitutional Council shall meet de jure and declare the permanent vacancy of the Presidency of the Republic.

It shall immediately communicate the act of declaration of definitive vacancy to Parliament, which shall meet de jure.

The President of the Council of the Nation shall assume the function of the Head of State for a maximum period of ninety (90) days, during which presidential elections shall be organized.

The Head of State, so designated, may not be a candidate for the Presidency of the Republic.

In case of coincidence of the resignation or death of the President of the Republic with the vacancy of the Presidency of the Council of the Nation, for any reason whatsoever, the Constitutional Council shall meet de jure and declare unanimously the permanent vacancy of the Presidency of the Republic and the incapacity of the President of the Council of the Nation. In this case, the President of the Constitutional Council shall assume the function of the Head of State, in pursuance to the terms provided in the preceding paragraphs of this Article and Article 104 of the Constitution.

He cannot be candidate for the Presidency of the Republic.

Article 105 of the Constitution: In case of urgent necessity, after convening the High Council of Security, and consulting the President of the Council of the Nation, the President of the People's National Assembly, the Prime Minister and the President of the Constitutional Council, the President of the Republic shall decree the state of emergency or the state of siege, for a definite period, and take all necessary measures to restore the situation.

The duration of the state of emergency or the state of siege can be extended only after approval of Parliament, convened in joint session of both Chambers.

Article 107 of the Constitution: When the country is threatened by an imminent danger to its institutions, its independence or its territorial integrity, the President of the Republic shall decree the state of exception.

Such a measure shall be taken after consulting the President of the Council of the Nation, the President of the people's National Assembly and the President of the Constitutional Council, and after hearing the High Council of Security and the Council of Ministers.

The state of exception shall empower the President of the Republic to take exceptional measures that are fundamental to safeguarding the independence of the Nation and the institutions of the Republic.

Parliament shall be convened de jure.

The state of exception shall be terminated according to the same aforementioned forms and procedures that led to its proclamation.

Article 109 of the Constitution: The President of the Republic shall declare war in case of actual or imminent aggression, in accordance with the relevant provisions of the United Nations Charter, after having convened the Council of Ministers, having heard the High Council of Security and having consulted the President of the Council of the Nation, the President of the People's National Assembly and the President of the Constitutional Council.(...)

Article 110 of the Constitution: During the period of the state of war, the Constitution shall be suspended; the President of the Republic shall assume all the powers.

When the mandate of the President of the Republic comes to expiry, it shall be extended de jure until the end of the war.

In case the President of the Republic resigns or dies or any other impediment, the President of the Council of the Nation shall assume, as Head of State and within the same conditions as that of the President of the Republic, all the prerogatives required by the state of war.

In case there is a conjunction of the vacancy of the Presidency of the Republic and the Presidency of the Council of the Nation, the President of the Constitutional Council shall assume the functions of the Head of State within the conditions provided for above.

Article 111 of the Constitution: The President of the Republic shall sign armistice agreements and peace treaties.

He shall obtain the opinion of the Constitutional Council on the relevant agreements.

He shall submit the agreements immediately to be approved explicitly by each Chamber of Parliament.

V. NATURE AND EFFECTS OF DECISIONS

Finality:
Article 191 of the Constitution: The opinions and decisions of the Constitutional Council are irrevocable. (...)

Binding force:
Erga omnes:
Article 191 of the Constitution: (...) They shall be binding upon all public authorities as well as the administrative and jurisdictional authorities.

Abrogation in whole or in part:
Effectiveness immediately or within a certain period of time:
Article 191 of the Constitution:
When the Constitutional Council rules that a statutory or regulatory provision is unconstitutional, it ceases to be effective from the day of the decision of the Council. When a statutory provision is ruled unconstitutional based on Article 188 above, it ceases to be effective from the day of the decision of the Constitutional Council.

VI PUBLICATION OF CONSTITUTIONAL COURT DECISIONS

The Official Gazette:
The Journal Officiel (Government Gazette) website provides direct free access to the published issues of the Official Journal of the People's Democratic Republic of Algeria. The information is updated every Wednesday and dates back to 1962. The Codes are also available on the website. The site's information is available in both Arabic and French.

SOURCES:

Constitutionnet - Constitutional history of Algeria, http://www.constitutionnet.org/country/constitutional-history-algeria

The People's Democratic Republic of Algeria, Constitutional Council, http://www.conseil-constitutionnel.dz/indexAng.htm

The Official Journal of the People's Democratic Republic of Algeria, http://www.joradp.dz/HAR/Index.htm

(5)

DOSSIER OF THE CONSTITUTIONAL COURT OF PRINCIPALITY OF ANDORRA

STATE: Principality of Andorra
TITLE: The Constitutional Court
YEAR OF FOUNDATION: 1993
SEAT: Andorra la Vella

I. CHRONICLE

Date and context of establishment:
The Constitution was signed by Andorra's two co-princes, the President of France François Mitterrand, and the Bishop of Urgell Joan Martí Alanis who are Andorra's heads of state. Llei qualificada del Tribunal Constitucional (Qualified Act of 3 September 1993 on the Constitutional Court) imposes on this Court the obligation to send to the General Council an annual report on the state of justice.[5]

Position in the hierarchy of courts:
The Constitution of Andorra (Catalan: Constitució d'Andorra) is the supreme law of the Principality of Andorra. Article 95 of the Constitution: The Tribunal Constitucional is the supreme interpreter of the Constitution, functions jurisdictionally, and its decisions bind public authorities and individuals alike.

II. STANDARD LEGAL REFERENCE

The Constitution of the Principality of Andorra, of April 28, 1993
Qualified Law on the Constitutional Court, dated September 3, 1993, and its modification of April 22, 1999
Regulation concerning the functioning of the Constitutional Court during the holiday period, of July 10, 1997

5 Annual Reports of the Constitutional Court, http://www.tribunalconstitucional.ad/memories

Composition

The number of judges:

Article 96 of the Constitution: The Tribunal Constitucional is composed of four Constitutional magistrates, (...)

Electoral/appointment body:

Mixed System (Appointment and Election):

Article 96 of the Constitution: (...) appointed among persons of known juridical or institutional experience, one by each of the Coprinces and two by the General Council. (...)

The Court members:

The term of office:

Article 96 of the Constitution: (...) They may not hold office for more than two consecutive eight-year terms. The renewal of the Tribunal Constitucional will be partial. The system of incompatibility shall be regulated by the Qualified Law mentioned in the preceding Article.

The Court President:

The term of office:

Article 96, para. 2 of the Constitution: The Tribunal Constitucional is presided over by the Magistrate to whom the post corresponds, on the basis of a two-year rotation system.

The qualifications and the required professional experience of constitutional court judges:

Article 10 of the Qualified Law on the Constitutional Court: 1. The Constitutional Court comprises four judges, one of whom is nominated by each Coprince and two by the General Council from among persons over the age of 25 years with recognized knowledge of legal and institutional matters.

Incompatibilities:

Article 11 of the Qualified Law on the Constitutional Court: Where, of necessity, a person who does not possess Andorran nationality is appointed a judge, that person enjoys the status of ex officio nationality throughout his term of office in accordance with the provisions of the Qualified Law on Nationality.

Article 12 of the Qualified Law on the Constitutional Court:

The office of constitutional judge is incompatible with:

a. The exercise of any other public office attached to a State or Parish institution, irrespective of whether it is an elective office, a post in the civil service or a contractual office.

b. The exercise of activities associated with the representation, management or defense of, or the provision of advice in connection with, the private interests of third parties in Andorran territory.

c. Any office associated with the direction of political parties, trade unions or associations, whether national or foreign.

d. Any other activity susceptible of posing a threat to independence and impartiality in the performance of their duties.

Immunities: Article 16 of the Qualified Law on the Constitutional Court: Constitutional judges shall be subject to civil, criminal and disciplinary liability.

Article 17 of the Qualified Law on the Constitutional Court: Cases involving civil and criminal liability for acts or omissions in the performance of their duties are brought before the Higher Court of Justice in accordance with the substantive and procedural laws applicable to members of the ordinary judiciary.

Article 18 of the Qualified Law on the Constitutional Court: 1. In respect of serious and very serious offenses disciplinary liability is determined by the Constitutional Court in plenary session and the unanimous votes of the other members. In respect of slight offenses liability is determined by the president of the Court or, where appropriate, the vice president.

2. The following are slight offenses:

- Lack of consideration and respect towards other members of the Court, the Court staff or persons appearing in the proceedings, in whatever capacity.
- Imprudent delay in performing the duties arising out of their office.

3. The following are serious offenses:

- Failure to observe the requirement of secrecy of the deliberations.
- Failure by reporting judges to state the reasons for the opinions which they submit.
- Manifest and repeated negligence in the resolution of the cases within their jurisdiction.
- Public criticism of or disagreement with the decisions and judgments of the Court.
- Issuing warnings, compliments or rebukes to the bodies and authorities of the State.
- Unwarranted absence from two or more plenary sessions of the Court or from two or more sessions formally called by the president.
- Infringement of the parties' right to conduct the proceedings at any stage thereof.
- Repetition of slight offenses where the penalty imposed has not yet lapsed.

4. The following shall be very serious offenses:

- Failure to observe the grounds for disqualification provided for in this Law.
- Unwarranted dereliction of judicial duties for more than two months.
- Repeated or further commission of serious offenses.

Release from office prior to the expiration of the term:
Article 13 of the Qualified Law on the Constitutional Court: While in office constitutional judges are independent and irremovable and are not liable to any penalty except on the grounds and in the form provided for in this Law. Any judge who considers that his independence is threatened or his duties disrupted by the action of a public body or by individuals shall inform the president of the Court and the latter seeks the assistance of the ordinary courts in order to deal with the threat or disruption.

Proceedings
Hearing in camera:
A quorum:
Article 97 of the Constitution: 1. The Tribunal Constitucional takes its decisions by a majority vote. Its votes and its debates are secret. The chairman, always chosen by drawing lots, has the deciding vote in case of a tie (...)

Organization
Administrative autonomy:
Article 95, para. 2 of the Constitution: The Tribunal Constitucional decides on its own rules of procedure and carries out its functions subject only to the Constitution and the corresponding Qualified Law regulating it.

The budget:
Article 20 of the Constitution: Judges' remuneration shall be paid by the State budget.(...)

IV. POWERS

Constitutional Court Review

Preventive review:

Article 98 of the Constitution: The Tribunal Constitucional tries: (...) b. Requests of preliminary opinion of unconstitutionality about international laws and treaties. (...)

Article 101 of the Constitution: 1. The Coprinces, under the provisions of Article 46.1.f), the Head of Government or a fifth of the General Council, may request an opinion about the constitutionality of international treaties prior to their ratification. The proceedings with that intent shall take priority. 2. The judgment admitting the unconstitutionality of the treaty shall prevent its ratification. In all cases the conclusion of an international treaty including stipulations contrary to the Constitution shall require the previous revision of the latter.

A posteriori review:

Abstract review:

Article 98 of the Constitution: The Tribunal Constitucional tries: a. Appeals of unconstitutionality against laws, executive regulations and the Rules of Procedure of the General Council. (...)

Concrete review:

Article 98 of the Constitution: The Tribunal Constitucional tries: (...) c. Processes of constitutional appeal. (...)

Article 85 of the Qualified Law on the Constitutional Court: "By the appeal for protection the Constitutional Court, in its capacity as supreme judicial authority, guarantees the rights recognized in Chapters III and IV of Title II of the Constitution other than the right laid down in Article 22.

Constitutional complaints:

Article 98 of the Constitution: The Tribunal Constitucional tries: (...) c. Processes of constitutional appeal. (...)

Jurisdictional disputes:

Article 98 of the Constitution: The Tribunal Constitucional tries: (...) d. Conflicts of jurisdiction between constitutional organs. To this effect the Coprinces, the General Council, the Govern, the High Court of Justice and the Local Councils are considered as constitutional organs.

Other matters with which the Court is charged by the Constitution or statute:

Article 52 of the Qualified Law on the Constitutional Court: In the exercise of their judicial functions, the Batlles (judges of first instance), the Court of Batlles, the Tribunal de Corts (criminal court) and the Higher Court of Andorra are entitled to apply for interlocutory proceedings to be opened in respect of laws, legislative decrees and regulations having statutory force on the ground that they are unconstitutional, irrespective of the date on which they entered into force.

Standing before the Constitutional Court

State bodies:

Only qualified state bodies as mentioned in Articles above.

Individuals:

Yes, corresponding to the right for the appeal for protection by the Constitutional Court.

V. NATURE AND EFFECTS OF DECISIONS

Finality and Binding force:

Erga omnes:

Article 95 of the Constitution: 1. The Tribunal Constitucional is the supreme interpreter of the Constitution, functions jurisdictionally, and its decisions bind public authorities and individuals alike.

The temporary order:

Article 58 of the Qualified Law on the Constitutional Court: (...) Save in cases of favourable retroactive application, the existing effects produced by this law or regulation before they were declared null and void endure until new laws and regulations have been created to regulate the pre-existing legal situations.

VI PUBLICATION OF CONSTITUTIONAL COURT DECISIONS

The Official Gazette:

Article 58 of the Qualified Law on the Constitutional Court: (...) 2. Decisions declaring the law or regulation referred to the Constitutional Court unconstitutional in whole or in part take effect on the date on which they are published in the Official Gazette of the Principality of Andorra.

SOURCES:

Annual Reports of the Constitutional Court, http://www.tribunalconstitucional.ad/memories

The Constitution of the Principality of Andorra, of April 28, 1993, https://www.constituteproject.org/constitution/Andorra_1993.pdf?lang=en

Qualified Law on the Constitutional Court, dated September 3, 1993, and its modification of April 22, 1999, https://www.google.si/url?sa=t&rct=j&q=&esrc=s&source=web&cd=1 &cad=rja&uact=8&ved=0ahUKEwj547rI44PWAhXD6xQKHRSXCUkQFggm MAA&url=http%3A%2F%2Fwww.legislationline.org%2Fdownload%2Faction%2Fdownload%2Fid%2F6934%2Ffile%2FAndorra_law_Constitutional_Court_1993_am2006_en.pdf&usg=AFQjCNGIRDDLHP1wbFGTd6BaF92Tan6QVA

(6)

DOSSIER OF THE CONSTITUTIONAL COURT OF REPUBLIC OF ANGOLA

STATE: Republic of Angola
TITLE: Constitutional Court of Angola (Tribunal Constitucional de Angola)
YEAR OF FOUNDATION: 2010
SEAT: Luanda

I. CHRONICLE

Date and context of establishment:
Constitutional history of Angola coincides with its tumultuous history heavily influenced by a recovery from a 27 year civil war which ended in 2002 after independence from Portugal in 1975. After the signing of peace accord in 2002 process of drafting the new constitution begun. The Constitution in force was approved on January 21, 2010 by the National Assembly of Angola.[6]

Position in the hierarchy of courts:
Article 176 (System of jurisdiction) of the Constitution: 1. The High Courts of the Republic of Angola shall be the Constitutional Court, the Supreme Court, the Court of Auditors and the Supreme Military Court.

Article 180 (Constitutional Court) of the Constitution: 1. The Constitutional Court shall, in general be responsible for the administration of justice in legal and constitutional matters, under the terms of the Constitution and the law. (...)

II. STANDARD LEGAL REFERENCE

The Constitution of Republic of Angola, Friday, 5 February 2010, Official Gazette of Angola, I Series - No 23

6 Constitutional history of Angola, http://www.constitutionnet.org/country/constitutional-history-angola

Composition

The number of judges:

Article 180 of the Constitution stipulates that the Constitutional Court is comprised of 11 members serving non-renewable 7 year terms: 4 judges nominated by the President, including the President of the Court, 4 judges elected by the National Assembly by a two-thirds majority, including the Vice-President of the Court, 2 judges elected by the Supreme Judicial Council, and 1 judge elected by the other judges.[7]

Electoral/appointment body:

Mixed System (Appointment and Election):

Article 119 (Responsibilities as Head of State) of the Constitution: As Head of State, the President of the Republic shall be responsible for: (...) f. Appointing the Presiding Judge of the Constitutional Court and the other judges of the said court; (...)

Article 163 (Competence in relation to other bodies) of the Constitution: With regard to other bodies, the National Assembly shall be responsible for: a. Electing judges to the Constitutional Court, under the terms of the Constitution; (...)

Incompatibilities:

Article 179 (Judges) of the Constitution: (...) 5. Serving judges may not exercise any other public or private duties except teaching or academic research of a legal nature.

Serving judges may not become affiliated to political parties or political associations or become involved in party political activities.

It shall be recognised that judges have the right to social and professional associations, but are forbidden the right to strike. (...)

Immunities: Article 179 (Judges) of the Constitution: 1. In the exercise of their duties, judges shall be independent and shall owe obedience only to the Constitution and the law.

> 2. Judges shall not be removed from office, nor transferred, promoted, suspended, retired or dismissed unless under the terms of the Constitution and the law.
>
> 3. Judges shall not be responsible for the decisions they make during the course of their duties, except for the restrictions imposed by law.
>
> 4. Judges may only be imprisoned after being charged when the infraction is punishable with a prison sentence of more than two years, except in the case of flagrante delito involving a felony punishable with the same sentence. (...)

7 Ibid.

Article 180 of the Constitution: (...) 3. Judges of the Constitutional Court shall be appointed for a non-renewable seven-year term and shall enjoy the same guarantees of independence, irremovability from office, impartiality and non-liability as judges from the other courts.

Release from office prior to the expiration of the term:
Article 179 (Judges) of the Constitution: 2. Judges shall not be removed from office, nor transferred, promoted, suspended, retired or dismissed unless under the terms of the Constitution and the law.

Organization

Administrative autonomy:
Article 105 (Sovereign bodies) of the Constitution: 1. The President of the Republic, the National Assembly and the courts shall be sovereign bodies. (...)

Article 178 (Administrative and financial autonomy of the courts) of the Constitution: The courts shall enjoy administrative and financial autonomy and the law must define mechanisms to enable the judiciary to contribute towards drawing up their budget.

The budget:
Article 178 (Administrative and financial autonomy of the courts) of the Constitution: The courts shall enjoy administrative and financial autonomy and the law must define mechanisms to enable the judiciary to contribute towards drawing up their budget.

IV. POWERS

Constitutional Court Review:
Article 227 (Objective of review) of the Constitution: All acts which constitute violations of constitutional principles and norms shall be subject to a review of their constitutionality, specifically: a. Legislation;

b. International treaties, conventions and agreements;

c. Revisions of the Constitution;

d. Referenda.

Preventive review:

Article 180 (Constitutional Court) of the Constitution: (...) 2. The Constitutional Court shall be responsible for: (...) b. Providing a prior review of the constitutionality of the laws of parliament; (...)

Article 228 (Prior review of constitutionality) of the Constitution: 1. The President of the Republic may ask the Constitutional Court to conduct a prior review of the constitutionality of any rule contained in legislation that has been submitted for enactment, any international treaty submitted to him for ratification or any international agreement sent to him for signature.

2. One tenth of the Members of the National Assembly in full exercise of their office may also request a prior review of the constitutionality of any rule contained in legislation that has been submitted for enactment.

3. A prior review of constitutionality must be requested within twenty days of reception of the legislation in question.

4. The Constitutional Court must pronounce within forty-eight days, which may be reduced due to urgency if so requested by the President of the Republic or one tenth of the Members of the Assembly in full exercise of their office.

Article 229 (Effect of prior review) of the Constitution: 1. Legislation for which a prior review of constitutionality has been requested from the Constitutional Court may not be enacted, signed or ratified before the Constitutional Court has delivered its ruling.

2. If the Constitutional Court declares that any rule contained in a piece of legislation, treaty, convention or international agreement is unconstitutional, it must be vetoed by the President of the Republic and returned to the body which had approved it.

3. In cases provided for under the previous point, the legislation, treaty, convention or international agreement may not be enacted, ratified or signed, as appropriate, unless the body that passed it expunges the rule that has been deemed unconstitutional.

4. If the legislation, treaty, convention or international agreement is reformulated, the President of the Republic or the Members who had contested its constitutionality may request a prior review of the constitutionality of any of its rules.

A posteriori review:

Abstract review:

Article 180 (Constitutional Court) of the Constitution: (...) 2. The Constitutional Court shall be responsible for: a. Assessing the constitutionality of any rules and other acts of the state; (...)

Article 231 (Effects of abstract review) of the Constitution: 1. A declaration of unconstitutionality with generally binding force shall be effective from the date on which the rule that has been declared unconstitutional came into force and shall lead to the revalidation of the rule that has been revoked.

2. However, in the case of unconstitutionality due to an infraction of a subsequent constitutional rule, the declaration shall only be effective from the date on which the latter comes into force.

3. Rulings in cases that have already been tried shall stand, save when the Constitutional Court rules to the contrary in relation to rules concerning penal or disciplinary matters or administrative offences and their contents were less favourable to the defendant.

4. When required for the purposes of legal certainty, reasons of fairness or matters of exceptionally important public interest, which must be duly justified, the Constitutional Court may rule that the scope of the effects of the unconstitutionality or illegality shall be more restricted than those provided for in Points 1 and 2 of this Article.

Concrete review: No.

Constitutional complaints:
Article 180 (Constitutional Court) of the Constitution: (...) d. Assessing appeals against the constitutionality of the decisions of the various courts which have refused to apply particular rules on the grounds that they are unconstitutional; (...)

e) Assessing appeals against the constitutionality of rulings made by the various courts that have applied rules whose constitutionality has been questioned during the relevant proceedings; (...)

Jurisdictional disputes:
The unconstitutionality of acts and activities of political parties:
Article 180 (Constitutional Court) of the Constitution: (...) 2. The Constitutional Court shall be responsible for:

(...) c. Exercising jurisdiction in other legal and constitutional, electoral and party political matters, under the terms of the Constitution and the law; (...)

Charges against the President of the Republic:

Article 129 (Removal from office of the President of the Republic) of the Constitution: 1. The President of the Republic may be removed from office in the following circumstances:

a. For the crimes of treason and espionage;
b. For the crimes of subordination, fraudulent conversion of public money and corruption;
c. Due to permanent physical and mental incapacity;
d. As the holder of an acquired nationality;
e. For heinous and violent crimes, as defined in this Constitution;

2. The President of the Republic may also be removed from office for the crime of violating the Constitution when a serious threat is made against:

a. The democratic state and the rule of law;
b. State security;
c. The regular functioning of institutions.

3. The Supreme Court shall be responsible for hearing and ruling on the criminal procedures referred to in Point 1(a), (b) and (e) of this Article which are instigated against the President of the Republic.

4. The Constitutional Court shall be responsible for hearing and ruling on the procedures for the removal of a President of the Republic from office which are referred to in Point 1(c) and d) and Point 2 of this Article.
5. The procedures for criminal liability and removal of a President of the Republic from office referred to in the previous points shall observe the following:

a. The initiation of proceedings must be duly justified and shall be the responsibility of the National Assembly;

b. The proposal to initiate proceedings shall be presented by one third of the Members in full exercise of their office;

c. The decision shall be approved by a two-thirds majority of Members in full exercise of their office and the respective communication or application for proceedings must afterwards be sent to the Supreme Court or Constitutional Court, as appropriate.

6. These proceedings must take absolute priority over all others and must be heard and decided within a maximum period of one hundred and twenty days commencing on the date on which the appropriate application is received.

Article 130 (Vacant office) of the Constitution: 1. The office of President of the Republic shall become vacant in the following circumstances:

a. Resignation from office, under the terms of Article 116;

b. Death;

c. Removal from office;

d. Permanent physical or mental incapacity;

e. Abandonment of duties.

2. The vacancy shall be verified and declared by the Constitutional Court, under the terms of the Constitution and the law.

Article 132: (Substitution of the President of the Republic) of the Constitution: 1. If the office of the elected President of the Republic elect becomes vacant, the duties shall be performed by the Vice-President, who shall complete the term of office with full powers.
2. Should the situation referred to in the previous point arise or should the office of Vice-President become vacant, the President of the Republic shall appoint an individual elected to Parliament by the list of the political party or coalition of political parties which receives the most votes to perform the duties of the Vice-President, having consulted the political party or coalition of parties which presented the candidate for President of the Republic, under the terms of Articles 109 and 142 onwards of this Constitution.
3. Should both the President of the Republic and the Vice-President become permanently and simultaneously unable to perform their duties, the President of the National Assembly shall assume the duties of the President of the Republic until new general elections are held, which must happen within one hundred and twenty days of verification of their inability to serve.

4. Should the President of the Republic elect become permanently unable to perform his duties before his inauguration, he shall be replaced by the Vice-President elect, and a substitute Vice-President shall be appointed under the terms of point 2 of this Article.
5. Should both the President of the Republic elect and the Vice-President elect become permanently and simultaneously unable to perform their duties prior to taking up office, the political party or coalition of political parties whose list elected the President and Vice-President so impeded shall be responsible for appointing their substitutes from among Members elected by the same list, to take up office.
6. The Constitutional Court shall be responsible for verifying the cases of permanent inability to serve, as prescribed in this Constitution.

Article 234 (Passage and enactment) of the Constitution: 1. Alterations to the Constitution shall be approved by a two-thirds majority of Members in full exercise of their office. 2. The President of the Republic shall not refuse to enact the Constitutional revision law, although he shall have the authority to request a prior review by the Constitutional Court. (...)

Electoral matters:
Article 180 (Constitutional Court) of the Constitution: (...) 2. The Constitutional Court shall be responsible for:

(...) c. Exercising jurisdiction in other legal and constitutional, electoral and party political matters, under the terms of the Constitution and the law; (...)

Referendums:
Article 227 (Objective of review) of the Constitution: All acts which constitute violations of constitutional principles and norms shall be subject to a review of their constitutionality, specifically:

(...) d. Referenda.

Other matters with which the Court is charged by the Constitution or statute:
Article 114 (Inauguration) of the Constitution: 1. The President of the Republic elect shall be inaugurated by the President of the Constitutional Court. (...)

Article 232 (Unconstitutionality by omission) of the Constitution: 1. The President of the Republic, one fifth of the Members in full exercise of their office and the Attorney-General may request the Constitutional Court to rule on unconstitutionality by omission.

2. Whenever the Constitutional Court determines unconstitutionality by omission it shall inform the appropriate legislative body in order to enable it to amend the omission.

Standing before the Constitutional Court

State bodies:

Article 230 (Legitimacy) of the Constitution: 1. The Constitutional Court shall consider and shall declare with generally binding force the unconstitutionality or otherwise of any rule.

2. The following may request a declaration of unconstitutionality from the Constitutional Court: a. The President of the Republic;

b. One tenth of the Members of the Assembly of the Republic in full exercise of their office;

c. Parliamentary Groups;

d. The Attorney-General;

e. The Ombudsman;

f. The Bar Association of Angola.

Individuals: Yes.

V. NATURE AND EFFECTS OF DECISIONS

Finality and Binding force:

Article 229 (Effect of prior review) of the Constitution: 1. Legislation for which a prior review of constitutionality has been requested from the Constitutional Court may not be enacted, signed or ratified before the Constitutional Court has delivered its ruling.

2. If the Constitutional Court declares that any rule contained in a piece of legislation, treaty, convention or international agreement is unconstitutional, it must be vetoed by the President of the Republic and returned to the body which had approved it.

3. In cases provided for under the previous point, the legislation, treaty, convention or international agreement may not be enacted, ratified or signed, as appropriate, unless the body that passed it expunges the rule that has been deemed unconstitutional.

4. If the legislation, treaty, convention or international agreement is reformulated, the President of the Republic or the Members who had contested its constitutionality may request a prior review of the constitutionality of any of its rules.

VI PUBLICATION OF CONSTITUTIONAL COURT DECISIONS

Electronic Publishing:

Publicly available on official webpage of the Constitutional Court of Angola http://www.tribunalconstitucional.ao/

SOURCES:

Constitution of Republic of Angola, (English version), https://www.constituteproject.org/constitution/Angola_2010.pdf?lang=en

Constitutional history of Angola, http://www.constitutionnet.org/country/constitutional-history-angola

(7)

DOSSIER OF THE EASTERN CARIBBEAN SUPREME COURT (ANTIGUA AND BARBUDA)

STATE: Antigua and Barbuda
TITLE: The High Court of Antigua and Barbuda
YEAR OF FOUNDATION: 1981
SEAT: St Lucia (headquarters)

I. CHRONICLE

Date and context of establishment:
Antigua and Barbuda islands became an independent state within the Commonwealth of Nations on November 1, 1981, with Elizabeth II as the first Queen of Antigua and Barbuda. The Antigua and Barbuda Constitutional Order was adopted on July 31, 1981 and came into force on October 31, 1981.

Position in the hierarchy of courts:
The legal system of Antigua and Barbuda is based on English Common Law. The Eastern Caribbean Supreme Court, is responsible for the administration of justice in its member states, which includes Antigua and Barbuda. The Eastern Caribbean Supreme Court consists of two divisions, a Court of Appeal and a High Court of Justice. The High Court has 16 judges, two of whom are permanently resident in the country and sit in the court of summary jurisdiction. The High Court's jurisdiction includes fundamental rights and freedoms, and constitutional issues.[8]

Article 2 (Constitution is supreme law) of the Constitution:This Constitution is the supreme law of Antigua and Barbuda and, subject to the provisions of this Constitution, if any other laws is inconsistent with this Constitution, this Constitution shall prevail and the other law shall, to the extent of the inconsistency, be void.

Article 119 (Original jurisdiction of High Court in constitutional questions) of the Constitution: 1. Subject to the provisions of sections 25(2), 47(8)(b), 56(4), 65(5), 123(7)(b) and 124 of this Constitution, any person who alleges that any provision of this Constitution (other than

8 Nexus, Commonwealth Network, Legal System, http://www.commonwealthofnations.org/sectors-antigua_and_barbuda/business/legal/.

a provision of Chapter II) has been or is being contravened may, if he has a relevant interest, apply to the High Court for a declaration and for relief under this section. (...)

II. STANDARD LEGAL REFERENCE

The Antigua and Barbuda Constitution Order 1981. Antigua and Barbuda Statutory Instruments. 1981 No. 1106.

III. COMPOSITION AND ORGANIZATION

Composition

The number of judges:

The Eastern Caribbean Supreme Court is composed of the Chief Justice, who is the Head of the Judiciary, five (5) Justices of Appeal, High Court Judges; and High Court Masters, who are primarily responsible for procedural and interlocutory matters. The Court of Appeal judges are based at the Court's Headquarters in Castries, Saint Lucia where administrative and legal support is provided under the supervision of the Court Administrator and Chief Registrar respectively. The High Court Judges are each assigned to, and reside in, the various Member States. The High Court Registry is headed by a legally trained Registrar who coordinates the provision of the necessary administrative and legal support for the functioning of the High Court.[9]

The High Court has 16 judges, two of whom are permanently resident in the country and sit in the court of summary jurisdiction.[10]

IV. POWERS

Constitutional Court Review

Preventive review:

A posteriori review:

Abstract review and Concrete review:

Article 120 (Reference of constitutional questions to High Court) of the Constitution: 1. Where any question as to the interpretation of this Constitution arises in any court of law

9 The Eastern Caribbean Supreme Court, https://www.eccourts.org/.

10 Nexus, Commonwealth Network, Legal System, http://www.commonwealthofnations.org/sectors-antigua_and_barbuda/business/legal/.

established for Antigua and Barbuda (other than the Court of Appeal, the High Court or a court-martial) and the court is of the opinion that the question involves a substantial question of law, the court may, and shall if any party to the proceedings so requests, refer the question to the High Court.

2. Where any question is referred to the High Court in pursuance of this section, the High Court shall give its decision upon the question and the court in which the question arose shall dispose of the case in accordance with that decision or, if the decision is the subject of an appeal to the Court of Appeal or Her Majesty in Council, in accordance with the decision of the Court of Appeal or, as the case may be, Her Majesty in Council.

Other powers

Constitutional complaints:

Article 119 (Original jurisdiction of High Court in constitutional questions) of the Constitution: 1. Subject to the provisions of sections 25(2), 47(8)(b), 56(4), 65(5), 123(7)(b) and 124 of this Constitution, any person who alleges that any provision of this Constitution (other than a provision of Chapter II) has been or is being contravened may, if he has a relevant interest, apply to the High Court for a declaration and for relief under this section. (...)

Article 121 (appeals to Court of Appeal) of the Constitution: Subject to the provisions of section 44 of this Constitution, an appeal shall lie from decisions of the High Court to the Court of Appeal as of right in the following cases:

a. final decisions in any civil or criminal proceedings on questions as to the interpretation of this Constitution;

b. final decisions given in exercise of the jurisdiction conferred on the High Court by section 18 of this Constitution (which relates to the enforcement of the fundamental rights and freedom); and

c. such other cases as may be prescribed by Parliament.

Article 122 (appeals to her Majesty in Council) of the Constitution: 1. An appeal shall lie from decisions of the Court of Appeal to Her Majesty in Council as of right in the following cases:

a. final decisions in any civil proceedings where the matter in dispute on the appeal to Her Majesty in Council is of the prescribed value or upwards or where the appeal involves directly or indirectly a claim to or question respecting property or a right of the prescribed value or upwards;

b. final decisions in proceedings for dissolution or nullity of marriage;

c. final decisions in any civil or criminal proceedings which involve a question as to the interpretation of this Constitution; and

d. such other cases as may be prescribed by Parliament.

2. Subject to the provision of section 44(8) of this Constitution, an appeal shall lie from decisions of the Court of Appeal to Her Majesty in Council with the leave of the Court of Appeal in the following cases:

a. decisions in any civil proceedings where in the opinion of the Court of Appeal the question involved in the appeal is one that, by reason of its great general or public importance or otherwise, ought to be submitted to Her Majesty in Council; and

b. such other cases as may be prescribed by Parliament.

3. An appeal shall lie to Her Majesty in Council with the special leave of Her Majesty from any decision of the Court of Appeal in any civil or criminal matter.

4. Reference in this section to decisions of the Court of Appeal shall be construed as references to decisions of the Court of Appeal in exercise of the jurisdiction conferred upon that court by this Constitution or any other law for the time being in force.

5. In this section the prescribed value means the value of fifteen hundred dollars or such other value as may be prescribed by Parliament.

Jurisdictional disputes:

Article 119 (Original jurisdiction of High Court in constitutional questions) of the Constitution: (...) 2. The High Court shall have jurisdiction on an application made under this section to determine whether any provision of this Constitution (other than a provision of Chapter II) has been or is being contravened and to make a declaration accordingly. (...)

Other matters with which the Court is charged by the Constitution or statute:

Article 119 (Original jurisdiction of High Court in constitutional questions) of the Constitution: (...) 4. The Chief Justice may make provision, or authorise the making of provision, with respect to the practice and procedure of the High Court in relation to the jurisdiction and powers conferred on the court by or under this section, including provision with respect to the time within which any application under this section may be made. (...)

Standing before the Constitutional Court

State bodies:

Individuals:

Article 119 (Original jurisdiction of High Court in constitutional questions) of the Constitution: 1. Subject to the provisions of sections 25(2), 47(8)(b), 56(4), 65(5), 123(7)(b) and 124 of this Constitution, any person who alleges that any provision of this Constitution (other than a provision of Chapter II) has been or is being contravened may, if he has a relevant interest, apply to the High Court for a declaration and for relief under this section. (...)

5. A person shall be regarded as having a relevant interest for the purpose of an application under this section only if the contravention of this Constitution alleged by him is such as to affect his interests.

6. The rights conferred on a person by this section to apply for a declaration and relief in respect of an alleged contravention of this Constitution shall be in addition to any other action in respect of the same matter that may be available to that person under any other law or any rule of law.

7. Nothing in this section shall confer jurisdiction on the High Court to hear or determine any such question as is referred to in section 44 of this Constitution.

V. NATURE AND EFFECTS OF DECISIONS

SOURCES:

The Eastern Caribbean Supreme Court, https://www.eccourts.org/

Nexus, Commonwealth Network, Legal System, http://www.commonwealthofnations.org/sectors-antigua_and_barbuda/business/legal/

(8)

DOSSIER OF THE SUPREME COURT OF THE ARGENTINE REPUBLIC

STATE: Argentine Republic
TITLE: The Supreme Court of Argentina (Sp. Corte Suprema de Justicia de la Nación)
YEAR OF FOUNDATION: 1863
SEAT: Buenos Aires

I. CHRONICLE

Date and context of establishment:
The Argentine Constitution was adopted in 1853 and served as an attempt to unite the unstable and young country of the United Provinces of the Rio de la Plata under a single law. It was then reformed in 1860, 1866, 1898, 1949, 1957 (which mainly repealed the 1949 reform), and the current version is the reformed text of 1994. It was inaugurated on January 15, 1863.[11] However, during much of the 20th century, the Court and, in general, the Argentine judicial system, has lacked autonomy from the executive power. The Court has recently been reformed by the decree 222/03 which addressed the appointment of judges of the Supreme Court (see *infra*).[12]

Position in the hierarchy of courts:
The Supreme Court of Justice is the highest court of law of the Argentine Republic.

Article 108 of the Constitution: The Judicial Power of the Nation shall be vested in a Supreme Court of Justice, and in such lower courts as the Congress may establish in the territory of the Nation.

Article 109 of the Constitution: In no case may the President of the Nation exercise judicial functions, assume jurisdiction over pending cases, or reopen those decided.

11 El tribunal, http://www.csjn.gov.ar/institucional/historia-de-la-corte-suprema/el-tribunal.

12 Los jueces de la corte suprema, http://www.csjn.gov.ar/institucional/historia-de-la-corte-suprema/los-jueces-de-la-corte.

II. STANDARD LEGAL REFERENCE

The Constitution of Argentina, enacted 1853, amend. 1860, 1866, 1898, 1957 and 1994; text according to Law 24430, published in the Official Bulletin in the Supplement of 10/1/1995 (Promulgated by Decree 3/1995).

III. COMPOSITION AND ORGANIZATION

Composition

The number of judges: 5

The Court has recently been reformed (in 2003) by the decree 222/03 which addressed the appointment of judges of the Supreme Court. Regarding the composition and residence of the Court, the National Constitution of 1853 provided, in Article 91, that the Judicial Power of the Nation would be exercised by a Supreme Court composed of nine judges and two prosecutors. In 1862, the amendment which was adopted determined that the Court would consist of five members and a procurator general. In 1960, by law of the Congress, the number of judges has been changed to seven, and in 1990 this number changed again to nine (Law 23,774). Law 26.183, passed in both Chambers and promulgated on December 15, 2006, provides for the reduction of the number of judges of the Supreme Court to five.[13]

Electoral/appointment body:

Mixed System (Appointment and Election):

Article 99 of the Constitution: The President of the Nation has the following powers: (...) 4. He appoints the judges of the Supreme Court, with the consent of the Senate by two-thirds of its members present, in a public session convened for that purpose.

This power has been regulated by decree 222/03 of the Executive Power of the Nation, which establishes certain criteria for the selection of the proposed candidate. Among them, it has to take into account the circumstances regarding the general composition of the Court in terms of gender diversity, professional specialties and regional and federal integration, as well as the requirements regarding moral integrity and technical suitability and commitment to democracy and the defense of the human rights that the candidates must meet.[14]

13 Ibid.

14 Ibid.

The Court members:

The term of office:

Article 110 of the Constitution states that the judges of the Court retain their employment for the duration of their good conduct. The Argentine constitutional system enshrines, as guarantees of the independence of the Judiciary - and consequently, of the legal security of the people of the Republic - the irremovability of the judges and the irreducibility of their remunerations. The constitutional reform of 1994 introduced a modification to Article 99 of the Constitution, whereby a new agreement will be necessary for judges - whether from the Supreme Court or lower courts - once they reach the age of seventy-five. Such appointment shall be made for five years and may be repeated indefinitely.[15]

Article 99 of the Constitution: The President of the Nation has the following powers: (...) 4. (...) A new appointment, preceded by the same consent, shall be necessary in order to maintain in office any of these magistrates once they attain the age of seventy-five. All appointments of magistrates whose age is that indicated or greater shall be made for five years and may be repeated indefinitely following the same procedure.

Article 110 of the Constitution: "The judges, both of the Supreme Court and of the inferior courts of the Nation, shall hold their offices during their good behavior, and shall receive for their services a compensation that the law shall determine and that shall not be diminished in any way while they remain in office.

The Court President:

The term of office:

The President of the Court and the Vice-President shall be elected by absolute majority of the Ministers of the Court and shall serve for three years in the exercise of their functions (Article 79 of the Rules of Procedure for National Justice).[16]

The qualifications and the required professional experience of constitutional court judges:

In order to be a judge of the Court, a minimum age of 30 years is required to be a lawyer, with a minimum of eight years of practice in the profession, and the other qualities necessary to be a senator (Article 111 of the Constitution), to which are added the conditions established by decree 222/03. The name and the background of whoever is considered suitable for the coverage of the vacancy must be published within a maximum period of 30 days produced in the Official Gazette and in at least two newspapers of national circulation for three days, as well as in the page official of the Ministry of Justice. The applicant must submit an affidavit of his assets in the terms indicated in the Law on the Ethics of Public Function (Law 25.188). It will

15 Ibid.

16 Ibid.

also reveal certain aspects of your professional performance with the limitations imposed by the current ethical standards. All citizens are entitled to submit comments on candidates, as well as non-governmental organizations, professional associations, academic and human rights entities, who submit them to the Ministry of Justice and can be addressed at the public hearing held. carried out in the Senate after the proposal formulated by the Executive Power. As for its removal, according to Article 53 of the Constitution, it is the Chamber of Deputies that exercises the right to indict the members of the Supreme Court before the Senate for reasons of poor performance, for committing crimes in the exercise of their functions or for common crimes, for vote of a two-thirds majority of its members present. In turn the Article 59 of the Constitution states that it is up to the Senate to try the accused for a public trial by the Chamber of Deputies. The ruling also requires two-thirds of the majority of the members present and has as its sole effect the dismissal of the accused whom he may declare incapable of occupying any job of honor, trust or salary in the Nation (Article 60 of the Constitution).[17]

Article 111 of the Constitution: No one shall be able to be a member of the Supreme Court of Justice without being a lawyer of the Nation, with eight years of practice, and possessing the qualifications required to be a Senator.

Immunities and Release from office prior to the expiration of the term:

Article 53 of the Constitution:

Only the Chamber of Deputies has the right to bring charges before the Senate against the President, the Vice President, the Chief of the Cabinet of Ministers, the Ministers, and the members of the Supreme Court, in cases where they are allegedly responsible for poor performance or for committing an offense in carrying out their duties, or for common crimes, after being apprized of [the charges] and having declared by a two-thirds majority of the members present that there is cause for bringing an action.

IV. POWERS

Constitutional Court Review

A posteriori review:

Abstract review:

Article 39 of the Constitution: Citizens have the right of initiative in presenting bills in the Chamber of Deputies. Congress must give them express treatment within the period of twelve months.

17 Ibid.

Other powers

Constitutional complaints:

Article 39 of the Constitution: Citizens have the right of initiative in presenting bills in the Chamber of Deputies. Congress must give them express treatment within the period of twelve months.

Charges against the President of the Republic:

Article 59 of the Constitution: The Senate is charged with trying in public trial the persons impeached by the Chamber of Deputies, and its members shall take an oath when sitting for that purpose. When the person accused is the President of the Nation, the Senate shall be presided over by the President of the Supreme Court. No person shall be declared guilty except by a two-thirds majority of the members present.

Article 60 of the Constitution: The judgment shall go no further than to remove the accused person from office, and in addition declare him incapable of holding any employment of honor, trust, or pay of the Nation. But the party convicted shall, nevertheless, be subject to indictment, trial, and punishment according to law before the ordinary courts.

Other matters with which the Court is charged by the Constitution or statute:

Article 116 of the Constitution (Chapter II. The Powers of the Judiciary): The Supreme Court of Justice and the lower courts of the Nation have jurisdiction over and decide all cases that deal with matters governed by the Constitution and the laws of the Nation, except as provided in clause 12 of Article 75, and over treaties with foreign nations, in cases concerning ambassadors, public ministers and foreign consuls, in cases of admiralty and maritime jurisdiction, in suits in which the Nation is a party, in cases arising between two or more Provinces, between one province and the citizens of another, between citizens of different Provinces, and between a Province or its citizens against a foreign State or citizen.

Article 117 of the Constitution: In these cases the Supreme Court shall exercise appellate jurisdiction, according to the rules and exceptions that Congress may prescribe; but in all matters concerning ambassadors, foreign ministers and consuls, and those in which a Province shall be a party, the Court shall exercise original and exclusive jurisdiction.

Article 127 of the Constitution: No Province may declare or wage war against another Province. Their complaints must be submitted to and settled by the Supreme Court of Justice. Their de facto hostilities are acts of civil war, characterized as sedition or rebellion, which the Federal Government must suppress and punish in accordance with the law.

Standing before the Constitutional Court

Individuals:

Article 39 of the Constitution: Citizens have the right of initiative in presenting bills in the Chamber of Deputies. Congress must give them express treatment within the period of twelve months.

VI PUBLICATION OF CONSTITUTIONAL COURT DECISIONS

The Official Gazette: Yes.

Other forms:

Judicial Informaton Center (http://www.cij.gov.ar/inicio.html) adds to transparency of judicial system in Argentina where judgements and public hearings are accessible online and depending on importance also broadcasted through CIJ TV (Sp. Centro de Información Judicial)

SOURCES:

The Constitution of Argentina, enacted 1853, amend. 1860, 1866, 1898, 1957 and 1994; text according to Law 24430, published in the Official Bulletin in the Supplement of 10/1/1995 (Promulgated by Decree 3/1995), https://www.constituteproject.org/constitution/Argentina_1994.

El tribunal, http://www.csjn.gov.ar/institucional/historia-de-la-corte-suprema/el-tribunal.

Los jueces de la corte suprema, http://www.csjn.gov.ar/institucional/historia-de-la-corte-suprema/los-jueces-de-la-corte.

(9)

DOSSIER OF THE CONSTITUTIONAL COURT OF THE REPUBLIC OF ARMENIA

STATE: Republic of Armenia
TITLE: The Constitutional Court
YEAR OF FOUNDATION: 1995
SEAT: Yerevan

I. CHRONICLE

Date and context of establishment:
In December 1988, a Constitutional Control Committee was set up under an amendment to the Constitution of the Soviet Union. The Law of the Union relating to this Committee also provided for creating a Constitutional Control Committee in each Republic of the Union, which never actually happened. In 1991, moreover, the Armenian legislative had considered setting up a Constitutional Court, although it never actually did so (two laws, namely the Law on the President of the Republic of 1 October 1991 and the Law on the Supreme Council of the Republic of Armenia of 19 November 1991, simply alluded to such a Constitutional Court). However, no law or amendment to the Constitution of the Armenian SSR was ever adopted to put this declaration of intention into effect. The new Constitution promulgated by referendum on 5 July 1995 finally set up the Armenian Constitutional Court. The Law on the Constitutional Court was adopted by the National Assembly on 20 November 1995 and signed by the President of the Republic on 6 December 1995. On 5 and 6 February 1996 the members of the Constitutional Court were appointed and the Court began operating on 6 February 1996, when its members were sworn in before the National Assembly.[18]

Position in the hierarchy of courts:
Article 93 of the Constitution: The Constitutional Court administers the constitutional justice in the Republic of Armenia.

18 The description of the Constitutional Court of the Republic of Armenia, http://concourt.am/english/cc/history.htm

II. STANDARD LEGAL REFERENCE

The Constitution of the Republic of Armenia, adopted 1995, amended 2005, 2015.
The law of the Republic of Armenia on the Constitutional court, Adopted on 1 June, 2006

III. COMPOSITION AND ORGANIZATION

Composition

The number of judges:

Article 99 of the Constitution: The Constitutional Court shall be composed of nine members.

Electoral/appointment body:

Mixed System (Appointment and Election):

Article 55 of the Constitution: The President of the Republic: (...) 10. shall appoint four members of the Constitutional Court, and, if the National Assembly fails to appoint the President of the Constitutional Court in the timeframe outlined in Article 83(2) of the Constitution, shall appoint the President of the Constitutional Court. He may, on the basis of a conclusion of the Constitutional Court terminate the powers of any of his appointees in the Constitutional Court or give his consent to name the member as an accused, detain, authorize the institution of a court proceeding to subject the member to administrative responsibility; (...)

Article 83 of the Constitution: The National Assembly shall:

1. appoint five members of the Constitutional Court upon the recommendation of the President of the National Assembly;
2. within thirty days after the post of the President of the Constitutional Court is vacant, upon the recommendation of the President of the National Assembly, appoint the President from among the members of the Constitutional Court;
3. by a majority vote of the total number of Deputies and on the basis of a conclusion of the Constitutional Court, terminate the powers of any of its appointees in the Constitutional Court, or give its consent to name the member as an accused, detain him/her, authorize the institution of a court proceeding to subject the member to administrative responsibility; (...)

The Court members:

The term of office:

Article 96 of the Constitution: The Judge and the members of the Constitutional Court shall be irremovable. The Judge and the member of the Constitutional Court shall hold their offices until the age of 65. They may be removed from office only in the cases and in a manner prescribed by the Constitution and the law.

Incompatibilities:

Article 97 of the Constitution

When administering justice, judges and members of the Constitutional Court shall be independent and shall only be subject to the Constitution and the law.

The guarantees for the exercise of their duties and the grounds and procedures of the legal responsibility applicable to judges and members of the Constitutional Court shall be prescribed by law.

The Judge and the members of the Constitutional Court may not be arrested, named as an accused, as well as subjected to administrative liability through the judicial process except with the consent of the Council of Justice or Constitutional Court.

The Judge and the members of the Constitutional Court shall not be detained save for cases when caught in flagrante delicto. In such cases, the President of the Republic and the President of the Cassation Court or Constitutional Court, accordingly, shall be notified immediately of the arrest.

Article 98 of the Constitution Judges and members of the Constitutional Court may not go into business, hold office unrelated to his/her duties in a state or local self-administration body or in a commercial enterprise, or perform other paid work, save for academic, pedagogical and creative work. Judges and members of the Constitutional Court may not be members of any political party nor engage in any political activity.

Article 9 of the Constitution Independence of the Constitutional Court member

1. The Constitutional Court member shall be independent and only subject to the Constitution and to the Law while administering constitutional justice.
2. The Constitutional Court member has no right to seek for instructions or receive those in the course of its activities.
3. Any exerting of influence on a Member of the Court in relation to his/her activities is prohibited and shall be persecuted by Law.
4. In case of interference or any other influence on a Member of the Court in relation to his/her activities shall be immediately reported to the Constitutional Court, which can request with its decision from an authorized body to hold liable the person who interfered and (or) organized the interference.

Immunities:

Article 10 of the Constitution Irremovability of the Constitutional Court member

1. The Constitutional Court member shall be irremovable.
2. The powers of the Constitutional Court member are revoked on the grounds and by the procedures stipulated by Article 14 of this Law.

Article 11 of the Constitution The immunity of the Constitutional Court member

The Constitutional Court member shall have immunity.

2. The Constitutional Court member shall not be detained, involved as an accused or subjected to administrative liability through the judicial process except with the consent of the Constitutional Court and the body that has appointed him/her, i.e. the National Assembly and the President. The consent of the Constitutional Court is given as a Resolution, the consent of the National Assembly is provided as a Decision of the National Assembly and the consent of the President as a Decree.

3. The Member of the Constitutional Court shall not be arrested except for cases when caught in the act immediately or after that. In this case the President of the Republic and the President of the Constitutional Court shall be notified immediately about the arrest. The decision on the arrest shall be sent to the President and to the Constitutional Court not later then in 24 hours. The arresting authority and its officials are obligated to provide the free entrance of the President of the Constitutional Court in the area where the Member of the Constitutional Court is kept and assure his/her meeting with the arrested Member of the Constitutional Court.

4. The Member of the Constitutional Court can not be summoned. The authorized person who summoned a person without documents shall release the person as soon as he/she finds out that the summoned person is the Constitutional Court member.

5. The entrance to the office buildings for search, examination, seizure of any documents or objects can be done after informing the President of the Constitutional Court.

6. The Constitutional Court member shall be charged with criminal offence only with the warrant of the Prosecutor-General.

7. The Constitutional Court member shall not be prosecuted or held liable for actions arising from his/her status during and after his/her term of office.

8. If martial law or emergency state is declared the guarantees of immunity prescribed in this Article are not abolished.

9. A diplomatic passport shall be issued for the Constitutional Court member.

Release from office prior to the expiration of the term:

Chapter 3 of the Constitution

Termination of power of the member of the Constitutional Court

Article 14 of the Constitution Grounds for termination and suspension of power of the Constitutional Court member

1. The power of the Constitutional Court member shall be terminated when he/she:

1) has reached the age of 65;

2) has died;

3) has had his/her citizenship withdrawn or has been granted a foreign citizenship;

4) has applied in writing to the body that has appointed him/her, requesting to terminate his powers and has informed the Constitutional Court of that appeal and at least in 10 days has reiterated his/her resignation.

5) is determined by a Court of Law to be unable to work, missing or dead;

6) has been found guilty by a Court of Law.

7) has been appointed with a violation of Constitution, which was proved by a Court of Law.

2. In the case described by point 1 of Paragraph 1 of this Article, if the Constitutional Court Member is involved in the case hearing of one or more cases at a time of reaching the age limit of remaining in power, then his/her power is terminated the day when the case(s) is completed, but no later than six months after the day when he/she reaches the age limit.

3. The membership in the Constitutional Court shall be terminated on the basis of a ruling of the Constitutional Court by the appointing body when the Member:

1) has been absent for three times within one year from the sessions of the Court without an excuse;

2) has been unable to fulfill his/her powers as the Constitutional Court for six months member because of some temporary disability or other lawful reason;

3) violates the rules of incompatibility related to the Constitutional Court Member that are prescribed by this Law.

4) expressed an opinion in advance on the case being reviewed by the Constitutional Law or otherwise raised suspicion in his/her impartiality or released information on the proceess of the closed door consultation or broke the oath of the Constitutional Court Member in any other way.

5) is affected by a phisical desease or illness, which affected the fulfilment of the duties of a Constitutional Court Member.

4. In the cases described by Paragraph 3 of this Article the powers of the Constitutional Court Member appointed by the National Assembly are terminated by the order prescribed by the Law Charter of the National Assembly.

5. In the cases described by Paragraph 3 of this Article the President applies to the Constitutional Court for Resolution on the termination of the power of the Constitutional Court Member appointed by the President. On the basis of Resolutions of the Constitutional Court finding grounds of termination the President can remove the Constitutional Court Member from the position with his/her decree.

If the power of the Constitutional Court Member is not terminated within three days after the release of the Resolution of the Constitutional Court the same grounds can not be later used for such termination.

6. After the approval of the request of involving the Constitutional Court Member as an accused in a criminal case the power of the Constitutional Court Member is suspended in an order determined for the suspension of the power of a judge.

7. In cases when the membership in the Constitutional Court has been terminated because of the reasons envisaged by this Article, the President of the Constitutional Court, in the term of

two days after the vacancy has occurred, shall apply respectively either to the President of RA or the National Assembly, requesting to appoint a new Member.

Proceedings

Public hearing:

Article 22 of the Constitution Publicity

1. The court hearing is open for public with the exceptions provided in Paragraph 3 of this Article.

2. The court hearing can be written down, recorded.

The court hearing can be videotaped and broadcast by the decision of the Constitutional Court.

3. By a majority vote, the Constitutional Court shall decide to hold a session or part of a session in the absence of the media and the public for the interest of community morals, public order and state security, and for the privacy of the parties and the case.

4. With the initiation of the Constitutional Court or with the motion of any party of the trial the issue of the close-door court hearing is also examined and solved in the closed session.

5. The parties of the trial, their representatives, and in the case of need the witnesses, as well as the experts and interpreters have the right to be present at the closed session.

The parties present at the closed session are notified by the Constitutional Court about the liability for disclosure of the information acquired during the closed session.

6. The decision of the Constitutional Court on the substance of the case as well as the final part of the Resolution in any case is announced at the open session.

IV. POWERS

Constitutional Court Review

Preventive review:

Article 100 of the Constitution: The Constitutional Court shall, in conformity with the procedure defined by law: (...) 2. prior to the ratification of international agreements determine the compliance of the commitments stipulated therein with the Constitution; (...)

A posteriori review:

Abstract review:

Article 100 of the Constitution: The Constitutional Court shall, in conformity with the procedure defined by law: 1. determine the compliance of the laws, decisions of the National Assembly, decrees and orders of the President of the Republic, decisions of the Prime Minister and bodies of the local self-government with the Constitution; (...)

Other powers

Constitutional complaints:

Article 25. (the Right to Appeal to the Constitutional Court) of the Law of the Republic of Armenia on the Constitutional Court: The bodies and persons determined by Article 101 of the Constitution shall appeal to the Constitutional Court in the order prescribed by the Constitution and this Law. Moreover, in the cases determined in Paragraph 6 of Article 101 legal persons are also eligible to appeal to the Constitutional Court according to Article 42.1 of the Constitution. Article 26 (the Cause of Case Review in the Constitutional Court) of the Law of the Republic of Armenia on the Constitutional Court: The Constitutional Court reviews the case only if a relevant application exists.

The unconstitutionality of acts and activities of political parties:

Article 100 of the Constitution: The Constitutional Court shall, in conformity with the procedure defined by law: (...) 9. in cases prescribed by law adopt a decision on suspending or prohibiting the activities of a political party.

Charges against the President of the Republic:

Article 100 of the Constitution: The Constitutional Court shall, in conformity with the procedure defined by law: (...) 5. provide a conclusion on the existence of grounds for impeaching the President of Republic; 6. provide a conclusion on the incapacity of the President to discharge his/her responsibilities; (...)

Electoral matters:

Article 100 of the Constitution: The Constitutional Court shall, in conformity with the procedure defined by law: (...) 3.1. resolve all disputes arising from decisions adopted with regard to the elections of the President of the Republic and Deputies; 4. declare insurmountable or eliminated obstacles for a candidate for the President of the Republic; (...)

Referendums:

Article 100 of the Constitution: The Constitutional Court shall, in conformity with the procedure defined by law: (...) 3. resolve all disputes arising from the outcomes of a referendum; (...)

Other matters with which the Court is charged by the Constitution or statute:

Article 100 of the Constitution: The Constitutional Court shall, in conformity with the procedure defined by law: (...) 7. provide a conclusion on terminating the power of a member of the Constitutional Court, on detaining the member, on agreeing to name the member as an accused, as well as instituting a court proceeding to subject the member to administrative responsibility; 8. provide the conclusion which serves as a basis for the removal of the Community head; (...)

Standing before the Constitutional Court

State bodies: YES.

Individuals: YES.

The proceedings before the Constitutional Court are governed by the Law on the Constitutional Court. According to the Constitution, the following are entitled to apply to the Constitutional Court:

1) the President of the Republic - in cases stipulated in es 1, 2, 3, 7 and 9 of Article 100 of the Constitution;

2) the National Assembly – in cases stipulated in Paragraphs 3, 5, 7 and 9 of Article 100 of the Constitution;

3) at least one-fifth of the total number of the deputies - in cases stipulated in Paragraph 1 of Article 100 of the Constitution;

4) the Government - in cases stipulated in Paragraphs 1, 6, 8 and 9 of Article 100 of the Constitution;

5) bodies of the local self-governance on the issue of compliance to the Constitution of the state bodies' normative acts violating their constitutional rights;

6) every person in a specific case when the final judicial act has been adopted, when the possibilities of judicial protection have been exhausted and when the constitutionality of a law provision applied by the act in question is being challenged;

7) courts and the Prosecutor General on the issue of constitutionality of provisions of normative acts related to specific cases within their proceedings;

8) the Human Rights' Defender – on the issue of compliance of normative acts listed in Paragraph 1 of Article 100 of the Constitution with the provisions of Chapter 2 of the Constitution;

9) candidates for the President of the Republic and Deputies – on matters listed in Paragraphs 3.1 and 4 of Article 100 of the Constitution. The Constitutional Court issues decisions and conclusions on application only: it is not empowered to consider cases on its own initiative. Applications are transmitted to the Constitutional Court in writing and presented to the President of the Constitutional Court.[19]

Article 25 (the Right to Appeal to the Constitutional Court) of the Law of the Republic of Armenia on the Constitutional Court: "The bodies and persons determined by Article 101 of the Constitution shall appeal to the Constitutional Court in the order prescribed by the Constitution and this Law. Moreover, in the cases determined in Paragraph 6 of Article 101 legal persons are also eligible to appeal to the Constitutional Court according to Article 42.1 of the Constitution.

19 Ibid.

V. NATURE AND EFFECTS OF DECISIONS

Finality:
Article 102 of the Constitution: The Constitutional Court shall adopt decisions and conclusions in conformity with the procedure and terms stipulated in the Constitution and the Law on the Constitutional Court. The decisions of the Constitutional Court shall be final and shall come into force following the publication thereof. (...)

VI PUBLICATION OF CONSTITUTIONAL COURT DECISIONS

The Official Gazette:
Yes

Electronic Publishing:
Yes. Official webpage of Constitutional Court of Armenia: http://www.concourt.am/english/decisions/common/index.htm

SOURCES:

The Constitutional Court of the Republic of Armenia, History, http://concourt.am/english/cc/history.htm

The law of the Republic of Armenia on the constitutional court, Adopted on 1 June, 2006, http://www.concourt.am/english/law_cc/index.htm#2

The Constitution of the Republic of Armenia, as amended, http://concourt.am/english/constitutions/index.htm

(10)

DOSSIER OF THE HIGH COURT OF AUSTRALIA

STATE: Commonwealth of Australia
TITLE: High Court of Australia
YEAR OF FOUNDATION: 1903
SEAT: Canberra

I. CHRONICLE

Date and context of establishment:
The genesis of the court can be traced back to the middle of the 19th century. By 1906, the High Court had become established as a viable, effective and necessary part of the Australian judicial system. The increasing demands on the High Court led to the number of justices being increased to five in 1906, and then to seven in 1913. The primary registry of the High Court was initially located in Melbourne, and from 1973 in Sydney. When the High Court building was finished in 1980 the administration was transferred to Canberra.[20]

Position in the hierarchy of courts:
The High Court of Australia represents the apex in Australian court hierarchy and is the ultimate court of appeal on matters of both federal and State law. The High Court exercises both original jurisdiction (cases that originate in the High Court) and appellate jurisdiction (appeals made to the High Court from other courts). The High Court is the court of final appeal with the ability to interpret the common law for the whole of Australia, not just the state or territory in which the matter arose.

Article 71 of the Constitution: The judicial power of the Commonwealth shall be vested in a Federal Supreme Court, to be called the High Court of Australia, and in such other federal courts as the Parliament creates, and in such other courts as it invests with federal jurisdiction. (...)

II. STANDARD LEGAL REFERENCE

Commonwealth of Australia Constitution Act, 1901

20 High Court of Australia – Fact sheet 221, http://www.naa.gov.au/collection/fact-sheets/fs221.aspx.

Composition

The number of judges:

Article 71 of the Constitution: (...)The High Court shall consist of a Chief Justice, and so many other Justices, not less than two, as the Parliament prescribes.

Electoral/appointment body:

Mixed System (Appointment and Election):

They are appointed by the Governor-General of Australia, on the advice of the federal government, and under the constitution must retire at age 70.

Article 72 of the Constitution: The Justices of the High Court and of the other courts created by the Parliament: i.shall be appointed by the Governor-General in Council; (...)

The Court members:

The term of office:

Article 72 of the Constitution: (...) The appointment of a Justice of the High Court shall be for a term expiring upon his attaining the age of seventy years, and a person shall not be appointed as a Justice of the High Court if he has attained that age. (...)

Incompatibilities:

Article 72 of the Constitution: (...) The appointment of a Justice of the High Court shall be for a term expiring upon his attaining the age of seventy years, and a person shall not be appointed as a Justice of the High Court if he has attained that age. (...)

Immunities:

Article 72 of the Constitution: The Justices of the High Court and of the other courts created by the Parliament: (...) ii:shall not be removed except by the Governor-General in Council, on an address from both Houses of the Parliament in the same session, praying for such removal on the ground of proved misbehaviour or incapacity; (...)

Release from office prior to the expiration of the term:

Article 72 of the Constitution: (...) A Justice of the High Court or of a court created by the Parliament may resign his office by writing under his hand delivered to the Governor-General. (...)

Constitutional Court Review

A posteriori review:

Abstract and Concrete review:

Article 73 (Appellate Jurisdiction of High Court) of the Constitution: The High Court shall have jurisdiction, with such exceptions and subject to such regulations as the Parliament prescribes, to hear and determine appeals from all judgments, decrees, orders, and sentences:

i. of any Justice or Justices exercising the original jurisdiction of the High Court;

ii.of any other federal court, or court exercising federal jurisdiction; or of the Supreme Court of any State, or of any other court of any State from which at the establishment of the Commonwealth an appeal lies to the Queen in Council;

iii.of the Inter-State Commission, but as to questions of law only; (...)

Article 75 (Original Jurisdiction of High Court) of the Constitution: In all matters: i. arising under any treaty; (...) the High Court shall have original jurisdiction.

Article 76 (Additional Original Jurisdiction) of the Constitution: The Parliament may make laws conferring original jurisdiction on the High Court in any matter: i. arising under this Constitution, or involving its interpretation; (...)

Other powers

Constitutional complaints:

Article 73 (Appellate Jurisdiction of High Court) of the Constitution: The High Court shall have jurisdiction, with such exceptions and subject to such regulations as the Parliament prescribes, to hear and determine appeals from all judgments, decrees, orders, and sentences:

i. of any Justice or Justices exercising the original jurisdiction of the High Court;

ii.of any other federal court, or court exercising federal jurisdiction; or of the Supreme Court of any State, or of any other court of any State from which at the establishment of the Commonwealth an appeal lies to the Queen in Council;

iii.of the Inter-State Commission, but as to questions of law only; (...)

Jurisdictional disputes:

Article 77 (Power to Define Jurisdiction) of the Constitution: With respect to any of the matters mentioned in the last two sections the Parliament may make laws: i. defining the jurisdiction of any federal court other than the High Court;

ii. defining the extent to which the jurisdiction of any federal court shall be exclusive of that which belongs to or is invested in the courts of the States;

iii. investing any court of a State with federal jurisdiction.

Other matters with which the Court is charged by the Constitution or statute:
Article 75 (Original Jurisdiction of High Court) of the Constitution: In all matters: (...) ii. affecting consuls or other representatives of other countries;

iii. in which the Commonwealth, or a person suing or being sued on behalf of the Commonwealth, is a party;

iv. between States, or between residents of different States, or between a State and a resident of another State;

v. in which a writ of Mandamus or prohibition or an injunction is sought against an officer of the Commonwealth;

the High Court shall have original jurisdiction.

Article 76 (Additional Original Jurisdiction) of the Constitution: The Parliament may make laws conferring original jurisdiction on the High Court in any matter: (...) ii. arising under any laws made by the Parliament;

iii. of Admiralty and maritime jurisdiction;

iv. relating to the same subject-matter claimed under the laws of different States.

Standing before the Constitutional Court
State bodies: Yes
Individuals: Yes

V. NATURE AND EFFECTS OF DECISIONS

Finality:
Article 73 (Appellate Jurisdiction of High Court) of the Constitution: (...) and the judgment of the High Court in all such cases shall be final and conclusive. (...)

VI PUBLICATION OF CONSTITUTIONAL COURT DECISIONS

Legal Journals:
Annual Reports, http://www.hcourt.gov.au/publications/annual-reports/annual-reports

Electronic Publishing:
Yes. Judgments are available on the Court website at http://eresources.hcourt.gov.au.

Other forms:

Records held by the Archives about the High Court date from 1901, and include judges' notebooks, correspondence between High Court members, reports on issues involving the High Court, records of Court judgements and a range of images of the High Court. A selection of records created by the High Court, and records created by other Commonwealth departments and agencies about the High Court, are listed below.

SOURCES:

Official webpage of High Court of Australia, http://www.hcourt.gov.au/

Official webpage of High Court of Australia, About the Justices; http://www.hcourt.gov.au/justices/about-the-justices

Commonwealth of Australia Constitution Act, http://www.aph.gov.au/About_Parliament/Senate/Powers_practice_n_procedures/Constitution.aspx

Judicial Review, Administrative Appeals Tribunal, http://www.aat.gov.au/about-the-aat/engagement/speeches-and-papers/the-honourable-justice-garry-downes-am-former-pre/judicial-review

(11)

DOSSIER OF THE CONSTITUTIONAL COURT OF AUSTRIA

STATE: Republic of Austria
TITLE: Constitutional Court
YEAR OF FOUNDATION: 1919
SEAT: Vienna

I. CHRONICLE

Date and context of establishment:
The Imperial Court (1867-1919) of the Constitutional Monarchy was a precursor of the Constitutional Court. In 1919, in the republican era, the German-Austrian Constitutional Court was established. It took over the functions of the Imperial Court and the State Court. It was furnished with the power to review laws, i.e. laws adopted by a provincial assembly, upon the request of the state government. Pursuant to the Constitution (Federal Constitutional Law – B-VG) adopted on 10 November 1920, the Constitutional Court, which had been established in 1919, was entrusted with all the functions formerly exercised by the Imperial Court and the State Court. At the same time, the Court was given a whole range of new tasks: the power to review the lawfulness of regulations and the constitutionality of federal laws upon application by a provincial government (the German-Austrian Constitutional Court already had the power to review provincial laws), to review federal and provincial laws in an ex-officio capacity, to review the lawfulness of elections, and to rule on violations of international law. Moreover, the provisions regarding the constitutional responsibility of supreme authorities of the state were expanded. The Constitution of 1934 was also adopted through a regulation based on the 1917 War Powers Act. In order to "sanction" the new Constitution, a "rump parliament" was convened by decree on the day of its promulgation. Since the delegates of the Social Democratic Party were all absent, their mandates were declared terminated by decree. This Constitution provided for a High Federal Court, which was called upon to ensure the constitutionality of legislation and the lawfulness of the public administration, essentially exercising the functions of the former Administrative Court and the former Constitutional Court. The president, the vice-president, and the other members of the court – the Constitution did not specify their number – were appointed by the federal president upon proposals made by the federal government. After the annexation of Austria to the German Reich, the High Federal Court lost its constitutional powers.

The court itself continued to exist, but was converted into a Reich authority called the Vienna Administrative Court in 1940. In 1941, the court was merged with other administrative courts of the German Reich, operating as the "Vienna External Senate" as part of the Administrative Court of the German Reich. The Constitutional Court was re-established and restored to its pre-1933 powers in 1945; it resumed its activities in 1946. In the course of the following decades, the powers of the Court were repeatedly extended and some of the legal provisions pertaining to its organization were modified.[21]

Position in the hierarchy of courts:

Article 137 (Establishment of constitutional court) of the Constitution: The Constitutional Court pronounces on pecuniary claims against the Federation, the Laender, the municipalities and municipal associations which cannot be settled by ordinary legal process nor be liquidated by the ruling of an administrative authority.

II. STANDARD LEGAL REFERENCE

The Constitution of Republic of Austria, Gazette No. 1/1930, as amended by Gazette I No. 102/2014
The Constitutional Court Act, Federal Law Gazette No. 85/1953, Federal Law Gazette I No. 90/2016

III. COMPOSITION AND ORGANIZATION

Composition

The number of judges:

Article 147 of the Constitution: 1. The Constitutional Court consists of a President, a Vice-President, twelve additional members and six substitute members. (...)

Electoral/appoinment body:

Mixed Systems (Appointment and Election):

Article 147 of the Constitution: (...) 2. The President, the Vice-President, six additional members and three substitute members are appointed by the Federal President on the recommendation of the Federal Government; these members and the substitute members shall be selected from among judges, administrative officials, and professors holding a chair in law. The remaining six members and three substitute members are appointed by the Federal President on the basis

21 VFGH, The History of the Constitutional Court: An Overview, https://www.vfgh.gv.at/verfassungsgerichtshof/geschichte/history_overview.en.html

of proposals submitted by the National Council for three members and two substitute members and by the Federal Council for three members and one substitute member. Three members and two substitute members must have their domicile outside the Federal capital, Vienna. Administrative officials on active service who are appointed members or substitute members shall be exempted, with their pay terminating, from all official duties. This shall not apply to administrative officials appointed substitute members who for the term of such exemption have been freed from all activities in the pursuit of which they are bound by instructions.

The qualifications and the required professional experience of constitutional court judges:

Article 147 of the Constitution: (...) 3. The members and substitute members of the Constitutional Court must have completed legal studies or studies in law and political science and have had ten years of professional experience. (...)

Incompatibilities:

Article147 of the Constitution: (...) 4. The following cannot belong to the Constitutional Court: members of the Federal Government, or a Land Government furthermore members of a general representative body or of the European Parliament; for members of a general representative body or of the European Parliament; who have been elected for a fixed term of legislation or office such incompatibility continues until the expiry of that term of legislation or office. Finally persons who are in the employ of or hold office in a political party cannot belong to the Constitutional Court.

5. Anyone who during the preceding five years has exercised one of the functions specified in para 4 above cannot be appointed President or Vice-President of the Constitutional Court.

6. Article 87 paras 1 and 2 and Article 88 para 2 of the Constitution apply to members and substitute members of the Constitutional Court; detailed provisions will be prescribed in the Federal law to be promulgated pursuant to Article 148 of the Constitution.

The 31 December of the year in which the member or the alternate member completes his seventieth year of life is fixed as the age limit on whose attainment his term of office ends. (...)

Release from office prior to the expiration of the term:

Article 147 of the Constitution: (...) 7. If a member or substitute member disregards without satisfactory excuse three successive requests to attend a hearing of the Constitutional Court, the Court shall formally establish the fact after listening to his testimony. Establishment of the fact entails loss of membership or the status of substitute membership. (...)

Constitutional Court Review

Preventive review:

Article 139a of the Constitution: The Constitutional Court pronounces on the illegality of proclamation of the republication of a law (state treaty). Article 139 of the Constitution shall apply mutatis mutandis.

Article 140a of the Constitution: The Constitutional Court pronounces whether state treaties are contrary to law. Art 140 shall apply to political, to law-modifying and to law-amending state treaties and to state treaties modifying the contractual bases of the European Union, Art 139 to all other state treaties with the following proviso, 1. A state treaty of which the Constitutional Court establishes, that it is contrary to law or unconstitutional shall not be applied any more by the authorities competent for its execution from the expiry of the day of the judgment's publication unless the Constitutional Court determines a deadline prior to which the state treaty shall continue to be applied; such deadline must not exceed two years for the political, law-modifying and law-amending state treaties and the state treaties modifying the contractual bases of the European Union and one year in the case of all other state treaties. 2. In addition, a provision, that the state treaty is to be implemented by issuing ordinances or a resolution, that the state treaty is to be implemented by the issuance of laws, becomes ineffective upon expiration of the day of the judgment's publication.

A posteriori review:

Abstract and Concrete review:

Article 139 of the Constitution: The Constitutional Court pronounces on illegality of ordinances: 1. on application by a court; (...) 2. ex officio insofar as the court will have to apply the ordinance in a suit pending before him; (...) 5. of a Federal authority also upon application by a Land Government or the Ombudsman; 6. in the case of ordinances of an authority of a province also at the request of the Federal Government or, to the extent the constitutional law of a province has declared competent the Ombudsman also for the sphere of competence of the administration of the respective province, the Ombudsman or an institution pursuant to Article 148i para 2.; 7. in the case of ordinances of a supervisory authority according to Article 119a para 6 also on application of the municipality whose ordinance has been rescinded. (...)

Other powers

Constitutional complaints:

Article 139 of the Constitution: The Constitutional Court pronounces on illegality of ordinances: (...) III. on application by a person who alleges to have been violated in her rights directly by the illegality, if the ordinance has become effective without a judicial decision having been rendered or a ruling having been rendered has become effective for this person; 4. upon application of a person, who claims to be hurt as a party in its rights because of a legal issue decided by a general court in first instance with the application of an illegal ordinance, on the occasion of an appeal against this decision; (...)

1. of laws

a. on application of a court;

b. ex officio in so far as he will have to apply such a law in a suit pending before him;

c. on application by a person who alleges to have been violated in her rights directly by unconstitutionality, if the ordinance has become effective without a judicial decision having been rendered or a ruling having been rendered has become effective for this person;

d. upon application of a person, who claims to be hurt as a party in its rights because of a legal issue decided by a general court in first instance with the application of an unconstitutional law, on the occasion of an appeal against this decision

2. of Federal Laws also on application by the government of a Land, a third of the members of the National Council or a third of the members of the Federal Council.

3. of Laws of a Land also on application by the Federal Government or, if the Constitutional Law of a Land so provides, on application of a third of the members of the Diet. (...)

Jurisdictional disputes:

Article 138 of the Constitution: (1) The Constitutional Court pronounces on conflicts of competence:

1. between courts and administrative authorities;

2. between Courts of Justice and Administrative Courts or between the (Federal) Administrative Court as well as between the Constitutional Court itself and all other Courts;

3. between the Federation and a Land or between the Laender amongst themselves.

(2) The Constitutional Court furthermore determines at the application of the Federal Government or a Land Government whether an act of legislation or execution falls into the competence of the Federation or the Laender.

Charges against the President of the Republic:

Article 142 of the Constitution: 1. The Constitutional Court pronounces on suits which predicate the constitutional responsibility of the highest Federal and Land authorities for legal contraventions culpably ensuing from their official activity.

2. Suit can be brought: a. against the Federal President, for contravention of the Federal Constitution: by a vote of the Federal Assembly;

b. against members of the Federal Government and the authorities placed with regard to responsibility on an equal footing with them, for contravention of the law: by a vote of the National Council; (...)

Article 143 of the Constitution: A suit can be brought against the persons mentioned in Article 142 also on the score of actions involving penal proceedings connected with the activity in office of the individual to be arraigned. In this case competence lies exclusively with the Constitutional Court; any investigation already pending in the ordinary criminal courts devolves upon it. The Court can in such cases, in addition to Art icle142 para 4, apply the provisions of the criminal law.

Charges against the Prime Minister or against any Minister of State:
Art icle142 of the Constitution: 1. The Constitutional Court pronounces on suits which predicate the constitutional responsibility of the highest Federal and Land authorities for legal contraventions culpably ensuing from their official activity. 2. Suit can be brought: a. against the Federal President, for contravention of the Federal Constitution: b. against members of the Federal Government and the authorities placed with regard to responsibility on an equal footing with them, for contravention of the law: by a vote of the National Council; (...)

Electoral matters:
Article 141 of the Constitution: 1. The Constitutional Court pronounces upon a. challenges to the election of the Federal President and elections to the general representative bodies, the European Parliament and the constituent authorities (representative bodies) of statutory professional associations; b. challenges to elections to a Land Government and to municipal authorities entrusted with executive power; c. application by a general representative body for the loss of seat by one of its members; application by at least the half of the members of the European Parliament having been elected in Austria for a loss of seat by such a member of the European Parliament; d. application by a Municipal Council for loss of seat of a member of the organ of the municipality, in charge of execution, and by a constituent organ (representative body) of a statutory professional association for loss of seat by one of the members of such organ; e. on the challenge of the result of referenda, plebiscites, public opinion polls and European Citizen Action Groups; f. on the registration of persons in electoral registers and deletion of persons from electoral registers; g. on the challenge of individually appealable rulings and decisions of administrative authorities and as far as established by federal or Laender law – of the administrative courts in the cases of subpara a to f. The challenge according to subpara a, b, e, f and g can be based on the alleged illegality of the procedure, the application according to subpara c and d on a reason provided by law for the loss of membership in a general representative body, in the European Parliament, in a municipal authority entrusted with executive power, or in a constituent authority (representative body) of a statutory professional association. The

Constitutional Court shall allow challenge if the alleged illegality has been proven and was of influence on the result of the procedure. In proceedings before the administrative authority the general representative body and the statutory organ (representative body) of the statutory professional association has litigant status. 2. If a challenge pursuant to para 1 subpara a above is allowed and it thereby becomes necessary to hold the election to a general representative body, to the European Parliament or to a constituent authority of a statutory professional association in whole or in part again, the representative body's members concerned lose their seat at the time when it is assumed by those elected at the ballot which has to be held within a hundred days after delivery of the Constitutional Court's decision. (...)

Other matters with which the Court is charged by the Constitution or statute:
Article 126a of the Constitution: Should divergences of opinion arise between the Public Audit Office and a legal entity (Article 121 para 1) on interpretation of the legal provisions which prescribe the competence of the Public Audit Office, the Constitutional Court decides the issue upon application by the Federal Government or a Land Government or the Public Audit Office. All legal entities must in accordance with the legal opinion of the Constitutional Court render possible a scrutiny by the Public Audit Office.

Article 140 of the Constitution: (...) 3. The Constitutional Court may rescind a law as unconstitutional only to the extent that its rescission was expressly requested or the Court would have to apply the law in the suit pending with it. If however the Court concludes that the whole law was enacted by a legislative authority unqualified in accordance with the allocation of competence or published in an unconstitutional manner, it shall rescind the whole law as unconstitutional. This does not hold good if rescission of the whole law manifestly runs contrary to the legitimate interests of the litigant who has filed an application pursuant to para 1 sentence 1 subpara c or d above or whose suit has been the occasion for the ex officio initiation of examination proceedings into the law.

4. If the law has at the time of the Constitutional Court's delivery of its judgment already been repealed and the proceedings were initiated ex officio or the application filed by a court or an applicant alleging infringement of personal rights through the law's unconstitutionality, the Court must pronounce whether the law was unconstitutional. Para 3 above applies analogously. (...)"

Art icle144 of the Constitution: "1. The Constitutional Court pronounces on rulings by an Administrative Court in so far as the appellant alleges an infringement by the ruling of a constitutionally guaranteed right or on the score of an illegal ordinance, an illegal pronouncement on the republication of a law (state treaty), an unconstitutional law, or an unlawful treaty."

Article 145 of the Constitution: "The Constitutional Court pronounces judgment on contraventions of international law in accordance with the provisions of a special Federal law.

Standing before the Constitutional Court
State bodies: Yes.
Individuals: Yes.

V. NATURE AND EFFECTS OF DECISIONS

Finality and Binding force:
Erga omnes:
Article 140 of the Constitution: (...) 7. If a law has been rescinded on the score of unconstitutionality or if the Constitutional Court has pursuant to para 4 above pronounced a law to be unconstitutional, all courts and administrative authorities are bound by the Court's decision. The law shall however continue to apply to the circumstances effected before the rescission the case in point excepted, unless the Court in its rescissory judgment decides otherwise. If the Court has in its rescissory judgment set a deadline pursuant to para 5 above, the law shall apply to all the circumstances effected, the case in point excepted till the expiry of this deadline.

VI PUBLICATION OF CONSTITUTIONAL COURT DECISIONS

The Official Gazette:
Yes.

Electronic Publishing:
Yes.

SOURCES:

VFGH, The History of the Constitutional Court: An Overview, https://www.vfgh.gv.at/verfassungsgerichtshof/geschichte/history_overview.en.html

The Constitution of Republic of Austria, Gazette No. 1/1930, as amended by Gazette I No. 102/2014

- https://www.ris.bka.gv.at/Dokument.wxe?ResultFunctionToken=f759f3b4-71a6-46fe-982c-8f1797baf651&Position=1&Abfrage=Erv&Titel=&Quelle=&ImRisSeit=Undefined&ResultPageSize=100&Suchworte=Federal+Constitutional+Law&Dokumentnummer=ERV_1930_1

The Constitutional Court Act, Federal Law Gazette No. 85/1953,
Federal Law Gazette I No. 90/2016, https://www.ris.bka.gv.at/Dokument.

wxe?ResultFunctionToken=b19a3ec6-eb4f-48da-84e9-bea09ee30799&Position=1&Abfrage=Erv&Titel=&Quelle=&ImRisSeit=Undefined&ResultPageSize=100&Suchworte=Constitutional+Court+Act&Dokumentnummer=ERV_1953_85

(12)

DOSSIER OF THE HIGH COURT OF AZAD KASHMIR

STATE: Jammu and Azad Kashmir
TITLE: High Court
YEAR OF FOUNDATION: 1928
SEAT: Srinagar/Jammu

I. CHRONICLE

Date and context of establishment

The full-fledged High Court of Judicature for the Jammu and Kashmir State was established in the year 1928. Prior to the establishment of High Court of Judicature. The Ruler of the State (Maharaja) was the final authority in the administration of justice. http://jkhighcourt.nic.in/

Position in the hierarchy of courts

Supreme Court of Azad Jammu and Kashmir.- (1) There shall be constituted a Supreme Court of Azad Jammu and Kashmir to be the highest Court of appeal.

II. STANDARD LEGAL REFERENCE

The present constitution was adopted on 17 November 1956, and came into effect on 26 January 1957. As of 2002, 29 amendments have been affected to the Constitution

III. COMPOSITION AND ORGANIZATION

Composition

The number of judges:

There shall be a High Court for the State, consisting of a Chief Justice and two or more other Judges. Article 93 of the Constitution

Electoral/appointment body:

The Chief Justice of Azad Jammu and Kashmir shall be appointed by the President on the advice of the Council and each of the other Judges of the Supreme Court of Azad Jammu and Kashmir shall be appointed by the President on the advice of the Council after consultation with the said Chief Justice.

Every Judge of the High Court shall be appointed by the President by warrant under his hand and seal after consultation with the Chief Justice of India... Article 95 of the Constitution

The Court members:

The term of office:

A Judge of the Supreme Court of Azad Jammu and Kashmir shall hold office until he attains the age of sixty-five years.

IV. POWERS

Constitutional Court Review :

The High Court shall have superintendence and control over all courts for the time being subject to its appellate or revisional jurisdiction and all such courts shall be subordinate to the High Court. (Para.1) Article 104 of the Constitution

If the High Court is satisfied that a case pending in a court subordinate to it involves a substantial question of law as to the interpretation of this Constitution or the Constitution of India the determination of which is necessary for the disposal of the case, it shall withdraw the case and may (a) either dispose of the case itself, or (b) determine the said question of law and return the case to the court from which the case has been so withdrawn together with a copy of its judgment on such question and the said court shall on receipt thereof proceed to dispose of the case in conformity with such judgment. Article 105 of the Constitution

Other forms of human rights protection

The High Court shall have power to issue to any person or authority, including in appropriate cases any Government within the State, directions, orders or writs, including writs in the nature of habeas corpus, mandamus, prohibition, quo warranto and Certiorar, or any of them, for any purpose other than those mentioned in clause (2-A) of Article 32 of the Constitution of India. Article 103 of the Constitution

Standing before the Constitutional Court

State bodies: X

Individuals: X

SOURCES:

https://www.hrw.org/reports/2006/pakistan0906/4.htm

http://www.ajkassembly.gok.pk/ajkinterimconstitutionact1974.html

(13)

DOSSIER OF THE CONSTITUTIONAL COURT OF AZERBAIJAN REPUBLIC

STATE: Republic of Azerbaijan
TITLE: Constitutional Court
YEAR OF FOUNDATION: 1998
SEAT: Baku

I. CHRONICLE

Date and context of establishment:
The Constitutional Court was set up on 14 July 1998. The legal basis for the activity of the Constitutional Court is the Constitution of the Republic of Azerbaijan adopted on 12 November 1995 (with modifications introduced as a result of referendum held on 24 August 2002), inter-state agreements that Azerbaijan Republic is a party to, Law "On Constitutional Court" adopted on 23 December 2003, other laws and the Rules of Procedure of the Constitutional Court.[22]

Position in the hierarchy of courts:
The Constitutional Court of the Republic of Azerbaijan is the supreme body of constitutional justice on the matters attributed to its jurisdiction by the Constitution of the Republic of Azerbaijan. Basic objectives of the Constitutional Court are the ensuring of the supremacy of the Constitution of the Republic of Azerbaijan and protection of individual's fundamental rights and freedoms.[23]

II. STANDARD LEGAL REFERENCE

The Constitution of Republic of Azerbaijan, adopted on 12 November 1995
The Constitutional Law on Normative Legal Acts of the Republic of Azerbaijan

22 The Constitutional Court of the Republic of Azerbaijan, About CC, http://www.constcourt.gov.az/cat/1

23 Ibid.

Composition

The number of judges:

Article 130 (Constitutional Court of the Republic of Azerbaijan) of the Constitution: I. Constitutional Court of the Republic of Azerbaijan consists of 9 judges. (...)

Electoral/appointment body:

Mixed System (Appointment and Election):

Article 130 (Constitutional Court of the Republic of Azerbaijan) of the Constitution: II. Judges of Constitutional Court of the Republic of Azerbaijan are appointed by Milli Majlis of the Republic of Azerbaijan on recommendation by the President of the Republic of Azerbaijan. (...)

The Court members:

The term of office:

The judges are appointed for a period of 15 years. After expiration of his/her term of office a judge of the Constitutional Court may not be re-appointed to the same post. Chairman and Deputy Chairman of Court shall be appointed by the President of the Republic of Azerbaijan.[24]

Proceedings

Hearing in plenum:

A quorum:

Constitutional Court shall examine the cases at the sessions of Chambers and Plenum.[25]

Organization

Administrative autonomy, the budget:

Constitutional Court is an independent state body and does not depend in its organizational, financial or any other form of activity on any legislative, executive and other judicial bodies, local self-government bodies as well as legal and physical persons.[26]

Services:

In the Staff of the Constitutional Court are department for constitutional rights; Department of Criminal and Administrative Law; Department of International Law and International Cooperation; Department of Protocol and Public Relations; Department of Human Rights; the organization and analysis; Civil Law Department; Department for Reception of Citizens and

24 Ibid.

25 Ibid.

26 Ibid.

Complaints; General Department; Department of Legal Support and systematization of legislation; Sector for Supervision for Execution of Court Decisions; Sector for Organization of Court Sessions; Assistants and Advisors to Chairman and Judges. The current supervision of staff is implemented by Head of Staff and his/her Deputy. Besides, the material technical, financial and economical maintenance is realized by Logistics Department.[27]

IV. POWERS

Constitutional Court Review

Preventive review:

Article 130 (Constitutional Court of the Republic of Azerbaijan) of the Constitution: (...) 6. correspondence of interstate agreements of the Republic of Azerbaijan, which have not yet become valid, to Constitution of the Republic of Azerbaijan; correspondence of intergovernmental agreements of the Republic of Azerbaijan to Constitution and laws of the Republic of Azerbaijan; (...)

A posteriori review:

Abstract review:

Article 130 (Constitutional Court of the Republic of Azerbaijan) of the Constitution: (...) III. Constitutional Court of the Republic of Azerbaijan based on inquiry of the President of the Republic of Azerbaijan, Milli Majlis of the Republic of Azerbaijan, Cabinet of Ministers of the Republic of Azerbaijan, Supreme Court of the Republic of Azerbaijan, Prosecutor s Office of the Republic of Azerbaijan, Ali Majlis of Nakhichevan Autonomous Republic takes decisions regarding the following: 1. correspondence of laws of the Republic of Azerbaijan, decrees and orders of the President of the Republic of Azerbaijan, resolutions of Milli Majlis of the Republic of Azerbaijan, resolutions and orders of Cabinet of Ministers of the Republic of Azerbaijan, normative-legal acts of central bodies of executive power to Constitution of the Republic of Azerbaijan;

2. correspondence of decrees of the President of the Republic of Azerbaijan, resolutions of Cabinet of Ministers of the Republic of Azerbaijan, normative-legal acts of central bodies of executive power to the laws of the Republic of Azerbaijan;

3. correspondence of resolutions of Cabinet of Ministers of the Republic of Azerbaijan and normative-legal acts of central bodies of executive power to decrees of the President of the Republic of Azerbaijan;

27 Ibid.

4. in cases envisaged by law, correspondence of decisions of Supreme Court of the Republic of Azerbaijan to Constitution and laws of the Republic of Azerbaijan;

5. correspondence of acts of municipalities to Constitution of the Republic of Azerbaijan, laws of the Republic of Azerbaijan, decrees of the President of the Republic of Azerbaijan, resolutions of Cabinet of Ministers of the Republic of Azerbaijan (in Nakhichevan Autonomous Republic - also to Constitution and laws of Nakhichevan Autonomous Republic and resolutions of Cabinet of Ministers of Nakhichevan Autonomous Republic); (...)

7. correspondence of Constitution and laws of Nakhichevan Autonomous Republic, resolutions of Ali Majlis of Nakhichevan Autonomous Republic, resolutions of Cabinet of Ministers of Nakhichevan Autonomous Republic to Constitution of the Republic of Azerbaijan; correspondence of laws of Nakhichevan Autonomous Republic, resolutions of Cabinet of Ministers of Nakhichevan Autonomous Republic to laws of the Republic of Azerbaijan; correspondence of resolutions of Cabinet of Ministers of Nakhichevan Autonomous Republic to decrees of the President of the Republic of Azerbaijan and decrees of Cabinet of Ministers of the Republic of Azerbaijan; (...)

V. Constitutional Court of the Republic of Azerbaijan gives interpretation of the Constitution and laws of the Republic of Azerbaijan based on inquiries of the President of the Republic of Azerbaijan, Milli Majlis of the Republic of Azerbaijan, Cabinet of Ministers of the Republic of Azerbaijan, Supreme Court of the Republic of Azerbaijan, Prosecutor s Office of the Republic of Azerbaijan and Ali Majlis of Nakhichevan Autonomous Republic. (...)

Concrete review:

Article 130 (Constitutional Court of the Republic of Azerbaijan) of the Constitution: (...) VI. In accordance with the procedure provided by the laws of the Republic of Azerbaijan, courts may apply to the Constitutional Court of the Republic of Azerbaijan for an interpretation of the Constitution and the laws of the Republic of Azerbaijan with regard to issues arising out of the implementation of rights and liberties of a person and citizen.

VII. The Commissioner for human rights of the Republic of Azerbaijan shall apply to the Constitutional Court of the Republic of Azerbaijan in cases where the rights and liberties of a person have allegedly been violated by legislative acts in force, normative acts of the executive or of municipalities, or court decisions in accordance with the procedure provided for by the laws of the Republic of Azerbaijan on the adjudication of the cases and applications listed in items 1-7 in section III of the present Article. (...)

Other powers

Constitutional complaints:

According to Article 34 para 1 of the Law On Constitutional Court of the Republic of Azerbaijan any person who alleges that his/her rights and freedoms have been violated by the normative legal act of the Legislative and Executive, the acts adopted by municipality or a court may submit a complaint to Constitutional Court in order to restore his/her human rights and freedoms. Constitutional Court can examine individual complaints in following cases: if the normative legal act which should have been applied was not applied by a court; if normative legal act which should not have been applied was applied by a court; if normative legal act was not properly interpreted by a court. Complaints can be submitted to Constitutional Court after exhaustion of all remedies within six months from the date of entrance of the decision of the court of last instance into force or within three months from the date of violation of complainant's right to apply to court. In accordance with the procedure specified in the legislation of the Republic of Azerbaijan the Ombudsman of the Republic of Azerbaijan shall apply to the Constitutional Court in cases where the rights and freedoms of a person had been violated by legislative acts in force, normative acts of executive power, the acts adopted by municipality or a court.[28]

Article 130 (Constitutional Court of the Republic of Azerbaijan) of the Constitution: (...) V. Everyone who claims to be the victim of a violation of his/her rights or liberties by a decision of the legislative, executive and judiciary or by one of the municipal acts set forth in the items 1-7 of section III of this Article may appeal, in accordance with the procedure provided for by law, to the Constitutional Court of the Republic of Azerbaijan with the view of the restoration of his/her violated human rights and liberties. (...)

Jurisdictional disputes:

Article 130 (Constitutional Court of the Republic of Azerbaijan) of the Constitution: III. Constitutional Court of the Republic of Azerbaijan based on inquiry of the President of the Republic of Azerbaijan, Milli Majlis of the Republic of Azerbaijan, Cabinet of Ministers of the Republic of Azerbaijan, Supreme Court of the Republic of Azerbaijan, Prosecutor s Office of the Republic of Azerbaijan, Ali Majlis of Nakhichevan Autonomous Republic takes decisions regarding the following: (...) 8.settlement of disputes connected with division of authority between legislative, executive and judicial powers.

Charges against the President of the Republic:

Article 104 (Inability of the President of the Republic of Azerbaijan to carry out his/her powers) of the Constitution: "I. The President of the Republic of Azerbaijanis considered having left his/her position ahead of time on resignation, complete inability to fulfil his/her powers due to illness, dismissal from his/her post in cases and in via the order envisaged in the present Constitution.

> II. When the President of the Republic of Azerbaijan is going to resign, his/her application concerning resignation is presented to Constitutional Court of the Republic of Azerbaijan. Constitutional Court of the Republic of Azerbaijan, having confirmed that the President of

28 Ibid.

the Republic of Azerbaijan himself sent in his/her resignation adopts the decision to accept such resignation. From that moment the President is considered having left his/her post due to resignation.

III. Having received notifications about complete inability of the President of the Republic of Azerbaijan to fulfil his/her powers due to poor health, Milli Majlis of the Republic of Azerbaijan applies to the Constitutional Court of the Republic of Azerbaijan for clarification of this fact. The Constitutional Court of the Republic of Azerbaijan makes a decision on this matter by a majority of six votes. Should the Constitutional Court of the Republic of Azerbaijan confirm this fact the issue is settled.

Article 107 (Dismissal of the President of the Republic of Azerbaijan from his/her post) of the Constitution: I. In case of grave crime done by the President of the Republic of Azerbaijan the question of dismissal of the President may be submitted to Milli Majlis of the Republic of Azerbaijan on initiative of Constitutional Court of the Republic of Azerbaijan based on conclusions of Supreme Court of the Republic of Azerbaijan presented within 30 days.

II. The President of the Republic of Azerbaijan may be dismissed from his/her post by resolution of Milli Majlis of the Republic of Azerbaijan taken by majority of 95 votes of deputies. This resolution is signed by the Chairman of Constitutional Court of the Republic of Azerbaijan. If Constitutional Court of the Republic of Azerbaijan fails to sign said resolution within one week it shall not come into force.

III. Resolution about dismissal of the President of the Republic of Azerbaijan from his/her post must be adopted within 2 months from the date of application of Constitutional Court of the Republic of Azerbaijan to Milli Majlis of the Republic of Azerbaijan. If said resolution is not taken within said term, then accusation against the President of the Republic of Azerbaijan is considered rejected.

Electoral matters:

Article 86 (Inspection and approval of results of elections of deputies of Milli Majlis of the Republic of Azerbaijan) of the Constitution: Accuracy of results of elections is checked and approved by Constitutional Court of the Republic of Azerbaijan as specified in the law.

Article 102 (Results of elections of the President of the Republic of Azerbaijan) of the Constitution: "Results of elections of the President of the Republic of Azerbaijan are officially announced by Constitutional Court of the Republic of Azerbaijan within 14 days from the day of voting."

Other matters with which the Court is charged by the Constitution or statute:

Article 88 (Sessions of Milli Majlis of the Republic of Azerbaijan) of the Constitution:

I. Every year, Milli Majlis of the Republic of Azerbaijan holds two regular, spring and autumn, sessions. The first session of Milli Majlis of the Republic of Azerbaijan is called no later than one week from the day of confirmation of the authority of 83 deputies of Milli Majlis of the Republic of Azerbaijan. If after the confirmation of the authority of 83 deputies of Milli Majlis of the Republic of Azerbaijan is not confirmed by the 10th of March, then the Constitutional Court of the Republic of Azerbaijan determines the time of the first session of Milli Majlis of the Republic of Azerbaijan.

II. Extraordinary sessions of Milli Majlis of the Republic of Azerbaijan will be summoned by the Chairman of Milli Majlis of the Republic of Azerbaijan at request of the President of the Republic of Azerbaijan or 42 deputies of Milli Majlis of the Republic of Azerbaijan.

III. Agenda of extraordinary session will be prepared by those who summoned said session. After the questions of agenda have been discussed extraordinary session ends.

IV. The assemblies of the sessions of the Milli Majlis of the Republic of Azerbaijan shall be open to the public. An assembly of the session of the Milli Majlis may be closed to the public upon the claim of 83 members of parliament or the proposal by the President of the Republic of Azerbaijan.

Article 103 (Oath of a person elected the President of the Republic of Azerbaijan) of the Constitution: "I. A person elected the President of the Republic of Azerbaijan, within 3 days from the day when results of elections of the President of the Republic of Azerbaijan have been announced, with participation of judges of Constitutional Court of the Republic of Azerbaijan takes an oath: Carrying out powers of the President of the Republic of Azerbaijan I swear to follow the Constitution of the Republic of Azerbaijan, protect sovereignty and territorial integrity of the state, to serve people.

II. It is considered that the President of the Republic of Azerbaijan began carrying out his/her official powers from the day when he/she took his/her oath.

Article 103 (Vice-presidents of the Republic of Azerbaijan) of the Constitution: I. The First Vice-President and Vice-Presidents of the Republic of Azerbaijan are appointed and dismissed by the President of the Republic of Azerbaijan.

II. A citizen of the Azerbaijani Republic, having voting right and university decree and having no obligations in other states can be appointed to the post of Vice-President of the Republic of Azerbaijan.

Article 130 (Constitutional Court of the Republic of Azerbaijan) of the Constitution: (...) VIII. Constitutional Court of the Republic of Azerbaijan exercises also other authorities envisaged in the present Constitution.

Standing before the Constitutional Court

State bodies:

Yes. Article 130 (Constitutional Court of the Republic of Azerbaijan) of the Constitution: (...) III. Constitutional Court of the Republic of Azerbaijan based on inquiry of the President of the Republic of Azerbaijan, Milli Majlis of the Republic of Azerbaijan, Cabinet of Ministers of the

Republic of Azerbaijan, Supreme Court of the Republic of Azerbaijan, Prosecutor s Office of the Republic of Azerbaijan, Ali Majlis of Nakhichevan Autonomous Republic takes decisions regarding the following: (...)

Yes. According to the Constitution the following entities may apply to Constitutional Court: President of the Republic of Azerbaijan; Milli Majlis of the Republic of Azerbaijan (Parliament); Cabinet of Ministers of the Republic of Azerbaijan; Supreme Court of the Republic of Azerbaijan; Prosecutor's Office of the Republic of Azerbaijan; Ali Majlis of Nakhichevan Autonomous Republic; Courts;

Individuals:
İndividuals; Ombudsman.[29]

V. NATURE AND EFFECTS OF DECISIONS

Finality and Binding force:
Erga omnes:
Decisions of the Constitutional Court are final and cannot be cancelled, changed or officially interpreted by any body or official.

Article 130 (Constitutional Court of the Republic of Azerbaijan) of the Constitution: (...) IX. Constitutional Court of the Republic of Azerbaijan takes decisions as regards the questions of its competence. Decisions of Constitutional Court of the Republic of Azerbaijan are obligatory all over the territory of the Republic of Azerbaijan. The decisions of the Constitutional Court of the Republic of Azerbaijan shall be published. (...)

Abrogation in whole or in part:
Effectiveness immediately or within a certain period of time:
Article 130 (Constitutional Court of the Republic of Azerbaijan) of the Constitution: (...) X. Laws and other acts, individual provisions of these documents, intergovernmental agreements of the Republic of Azerbaijan cease to be valid in term specified in the decision of Constitutional Court of the Republic of Azerbaijan, and interstate agreements of the Republic of Azerbaijan do not come into force.

29 Ibid.

Electronic Publishing:

Yes – on the official webpage of the Constitutional Court of Azerbaijan: http://www.constcourt.gov.az/cat/1

Article 130 (Constitutional Court of the Republic of Azerbaijan) of the Constitution: (...) IX. Constitutional Court of the Republic of Azerbaijan takes decisions as regards the questions of its competence. Decisions of Constitutional Court of the Republic of Azerbaijan are obligatory all over the territory of the Republic of Azerbaijan. The decisions of the Constitutional Court of the Republic of Azerbaijan shall be published. (...)

SOURCES:

The Constitutional Court of the Republic of Azerbaijan, About CC, http://www.constcourt.gov.az/cat/1

The Constitution of Republic of Azerbaijan, adopted on 12 November 1995, http://www.constcourt.gov.az/laws/26

(14)

DOSSIER OF THE SUPREME COURT OF THE COMMONWEALTH OF BAHAMAS [JURISDICTION OF PRIVY COUNCIL]

STATE: Commonwealth of the Bahamas
TITLE: Supreme Court
YEAR OF FOUNDATION: 1973
SEAT: Freeport

I. CHRONICLE

Date and context of establishment
Position in the hierarchy of courts
Article 93 para of the Constitution: There shall be a Supreme Court for The Bahamas which shall have such jurisdiction and powers as may be conferred upon it by this Constitution or any other law.

II. STANDARD LEGAL REFERENCE

The Constitution of the >Commonwealth of Bahamas 1973

III. COMPOSITION AND ORGANIZATION

Composition
Artile 93 para 2 of the Constitution: The Justices of the Supreme Court shall be the Chief Justice and such number of other Justices as may be prescribed by Parliament.

The number of judges:

Electoral/appointment body:

Article 93 para 4 of the Constitution: The Supreme Court shall be a superior court of record and, save as otherwise provided by Parliament, shall have all the powers of such a court.

Article 94 para 1 of the Constitution: The Chief Justice shall be appointed by the Governor-General by instrument under the Public Seal on the recommendation of the Prime Minister after consultation with the Leader of the Opposition.

Article 94 para 2 of the Constitution: The other Justices of the Supreme Court shall be appointed by the Governor-General by instrument under the Public Seal acting on the advice ofthe Judicial and Legal Service Commission.

IV. POWERS

Part III of the Constitution

Appeals relating to fundamental rights and freedoms.

Article 104 para 1 of the Constitution: An appeal to the Court of appeal shall lie as of right from final decisions of the Supreme Court given in exercise of the jurisdiction conferred onthe Supreme Court by Article 28 of this Constitution (which relates to the enforcement of fundamental rights and freedoms).

Article 104 para 2 of the Constitution: An appeal shall lie as of right to the Judicial Committee of Her Majesty's Privy Council or to such other court as may be prescribed by Parliament under Article 105 para 3 of this Constitution form any decisions given by the Court of Appeal in any such case.

Article 105 para 1 of the Constitution: Parliament may provide for an appeal to lie from decisions of the Court of Appeal established by Part 2 of this Chapter to the Judicial Committee of Her Majesty's Privy Council or to such other court as may be prescribed by Parliament under this Article, either as of right or with the leave of the said Court of Appeal, in such cases other than those referred to in Article 104(2) of this Constitution as may be prescribed by Parliament.

Article 105 para 2 of the Constitution: Nothing in this Constitution shall affect any right of Her Majesty to grant special leave to appeal from decisions such as are referred to in paragraph 1 of this Article.

Article 105 para 3 of the Constitution: Parliament may by law provide for the functions required in this Chapter to be exercised by the Judicial Committee of Her Majesty's Privy Council to be exercised by any other court established for the purpose in substitution for the Judicial Committee.

SOURCES:

https://www.oas.org/juridico/mla/en/bhs/en_bhs-int-text-const.pdf

(15)

DOSSIER OF THE CONSTITUTIONAL COURT OF THE KINGDOM OF BAHRAIN

STATE: The Kingdom of Bahrain
TITLE: The Constitutional Court
YEAR OF FOUNDATION: 2002
SEAT: Manama

I. CHRONICLE

Date and context of establishment
The Constitutional Court of The Kingdom of Bahrain was established by Constitution of The Kingdom of Bahrain from the year 2002. On August 15, 2012, the King of Bahrain issued a Royal Decree containing Law 38-2012, which amends Law 27-2002 concerning the establishment of the Constitutional Court.

Position in the hierarchy of courts
Article 106 of the Constitution: The court's area of competence is to watch over the constitutionality of laws and statutes.

II. STANDARD LEGAL REFERENCE

The Constitution of the Kingdom of Bahrain 2002

III. COMPOSITION AND ORGANIZATION

Composition
Article 106 of the Constitution The number of judges: President and 6 memebrs (Law 38-2012 covers the structure of the Court and the duration of its terms of office. It declares that the Court shall consist of a chief justice, a deputy chief, and five other justices)

Electoral/appointment body:
appointed by a Royal Order (with Law 38-2012 – The King)

The Court members:
The term of office:
...' for a period specified by the law (Constitution); 5 yers, renewable once) (Law 38-2012)

Organization
The budget:
Article 8 of the Constitution: The court shall have its own independent annual budget which commences with the beginning of the official financial year and ends by the end thereof. (Law 38-2012)

IV. POWERS

SOURCES:

https://www.constituteproject.org/constitution/Bahrain_2012?lang=en
http://www.bna.bh/portal/en/news/520904?date=2012-09-10
http://www.loc.gov/law/foreign-news/ Article/
bahrain-royal-decree-amends-provisions-on-constitutional-court/

(16)

DOSSIER OF THE SUPREME COURT OF PEOPLE'S REPUBLIC OF BANGLADESH

STATE: People's Republic of Bangladesh
TITLE: Supreme Court of Bangladesh
YEAR OF FOUNDATION: 1972
SEAT: Dhaka ("The permanent seat of the Supreme Court, shall be in the capital, but sessions of the High Court Division may be held at such other place or places as the Chief Justice may, with the approval of the President, from time to time appoint." Article 100 of the Constitution)

I. CHRONICLE

Date and context of establishment

The Supreme Court of People's Republic of Bangladesh was established by Constitution of People's Republic of Bangladesh from the year 1972.

Position in the hierarchy of courts

The High Court shall have superintendence and control over all courts and tribunals subordinate to it. (Article 109 of the Constitution)

II. STANDARD LEGAL REFERENCE

The Constitution of the Peoples Republic of Bangladesh 1971..................

III. COMPOSITION AND ORGANIZATION

Composition

The number of judges:

As of June 2017, there are 7 Justices in Appellate Division and 85 (all are permanent) in High Court Division

Electoral/appointment body:

The Chief Justice shall be appointed by the President, and the other Judges shall be appointed by the President after consultation with the Chief Justice. The Court members:

The term of office:

Subject to the other provisions of this Article, a Judge shall hold office until he attains the age of sixty seven years. (Article 96 of the Constitution)

The qualifications and the required professional experience of constitutional court judges:

A person shall not be qualified for appointment as a Judge unless he is a citizen of Bangladesh and-

a. has, for not less than ten years, been an advocate of the Supreme Court; or

b. has, for not less than ten years, held judicial office in the territory of Bangladesh; or

c. has such other qualifications as may be prescribed by law for appointment as a Judge of the Supreme Court.

Release from office prior to the expiration of the term:

A Judge shall not be removed from his office except by an order of the President passed pursuant to a resolution of Parliament supported by a majority of not less than two-thirds of the total number of members of Parliament, on the ground of proved misbehaviour or incapacity.

A Judge may resign his office by writing under his hand addressed to the President. (Article 96 of the Constitution)

SOURCES:

http://www.lexadin.nl/wlg/courts/nofr/oeur/lxctbah.htm

http://www.supremecourt.gov.bd/web/

https://www.constituteproject.org/constitution/Bangladesh_2014?lang=en

https://en.wikipedia.org/wiki/Supreme_Court_of_Bangladesh

(17)

DOSSIER OF THE SUPREME COURT OF JUDICATURE OF BARBADOS

STATE: Barbados
TITLE: The Supreme Court of Judicature of Barbados
YEAR OF FOUNDATION: 1982
SEAT: St. Michael

I. CHRONICLE

Position in the hierarchy of courts
The Supreme Court shall be a superior court of record and, save as otherwise provided by Parliament, shall have all the powers of such a court.
The Supreme Court of Judicature of Barbados is the highest judicial body in the country of Barbados. It is made up of the High Court and the Court of Appeals.
Appeals from the Supreme Court can be further referred to the jurisdiction of the Caribbean Court of Justice (CCJ).

The Caribbean Court of Justice (CCJ), (based in Port Of Spain, Trinidad and Tobago), is the court of last resort (final jurisdiction) for Barbados. It replaced the London-based Judicial Committee of the Privy Council (JCPC) in 2003, upon the passage of both the *Caribbean Court of Justice Act* and the *Constitution (Amendment) Act* by the Parliament of Barbados. These acts were brought into force by Proclamation on April 8, 2005; allowing the CCJ to supersede the Privy Council as the court of final Appellate Jurisdiction. The CCJ is also entrusted with the power to resolve disputes dealing with the Caribbean (CARICOM) Single Market and Economy (CSME).

II. STANDARD LEGAL REFERENCE

The Constitution of Barbados 1966

III. COMPOSITION AND ORGANIZATION

Composition
It is made up of the High Court and the Court of Appeals.

Electoral/appointment body:
Justices are appointed by the Service Commissions for the Judicial and Legal Services.

IV. POWERS

The High Court consists of Civil, Criminal, and Family branches.

The Court of Appeals handles appeals from the High Court and Magistrate Courts, and hears appeals in both the civil and criminal branches of law. It may consist of a single Justice of Appeal sitting in Chambers, or as a Full Court of three Justices of Appeal.

SOURCES:

www.lexadin.nl/wlg/courts/nofr/oeur/lxctbar.htm

https://www.constituteproject.org/constitution/Barbados_2007?lang=en

(18)

DOSSIER OF THE CONSTITUTIONAL COURT OF THE REPUBLIC OF BELARUS

STATE: Republic of Belarus
TITLE: The Constitutional Court of the Republic of Belarus
YEAR OF FOUNDATION: 1994
SEAT: Minsk

I. CHRONICLE

Date and context of establishment
The Constitutional Court of the Republic of Belarus was established in April 1994 according to the Constitution of the Republic of Belarus

II. STANDARD LEGAL REFERENCE

The Constitution of the Republic of Belarus 1994

III. COMPOSITION AND ORGANIZATION

Composition
The number of judges: 12
Electoral/appointment body:
Six Judges of the Constitutional Court shall be appointed by the President of the Republic of Belarus and six elected by the Council of the Republic. The Chairperson of the Constitutional Court shall be appointed by the President with the consent of the Council of the Republic.

The Court members:

The term of office:
The term of the members of the Constitutional Court shall be 11 years, and the permissible age limit shall be 70 years.

The qualifications and the required professional experience of constitutional court judges:
As a Judge of the Constitutional Court of the Republic of Belarus may be appointed (elected) a citizen of the Republic of Belarus with the knowledge of Belarusian and Russian languages having a higher legal education and being a highly qualified specialist in the field of law, who, as a rule, has a scientific degree and possesses high moral standards. (Code of the Republic of Belarus on Judicial System and Status of Judges, Article 91 of the Constitution).

Release from office prior to the expiration of the term:
The powers of a Judge of the Constitutional Court of the Republic of Belarus may be ceased upon:

the resignation;

his submission of an application for unsolicited dismissal;

reaching the retirement age of a Judge of the Constitutional Court of the Republic of Belarus;

the expiration of the term of office;

the refusal to take an oath;

the termination of citizenship of the Republic of Belarus as a result of the renunciation of citizenship or its forfeiting;

the appointment (election) to another post or transfer to another position;

carrying out the activity that is incompatible with the post of a judge, non-compliance with restrictions pertaining to the public service;

the gross violation of professional duties, committing a misconduct incompatible with the public service;

the entry into legal force of judgement of conviction;

the entry into legal force of judgement of a court on recognition of a Judge as having limited legal capacity or legally incapable;

the recognition of a Judge, under the established procedure, as incapacitated for work or his inability, certified by medical conclusion, to perform functions of a Judge for a long term (not less than one year) due to the state of health;

the death of a Judge, declaring him to be dead or recognising to be missing by judgement of a court entered into legal force – without making a specific decision. (Code of the Republic of Belarus on Judicial System and Status of Judges, Article 124 of the Constitution)

Proceedings
Hearing in plenum:

A quorum:
The Constitutional Court is entitled to considerate cases in a court session in the presence of at least eight Judges of the Constitutional Court (quorum of Judges of the Constitutional Court). (Law of the Republic of Belarus on the constitutional proceedings, Article 4)

Organization
Administrative autonomy:
The organisational, material and technical support of functioning of the courts within arranged powers shall be carried out:

in relation to the Constitutional Court of the Republic of Belarus – by the Secretariat of the Constitutional Court of the Republic of Belarus. (Code of the Republic of Belarus on Judicial System and Status of Judges, Article 183)

IV. POWERS

Supervision of the constitutionality of enforceable enactments of the state shall be exercised by the Constitutional Court of the Republic of Belarus.

Constitutional Court Review

A posteriori review:

Abstract review:

The Constitutional Court on the recommendations of the President of the Republic of Belarus, the House of Representatives, the Council of the Republic, the Supreme Court of the Republic of Belarus, the Supreme Economic Court of the Republic of Belarus, the Cabinet of Ministers of the Republic of Belarus shall produce a ruling on:

[...] the conformity of laws, decrees and edicts of the President, international agreements and other obligations of the Republic of Belarus to the Constitution and other instruments of international law ratified by the Republic of Belarus;

Standing before the Constitutional Court

State bodies:

The President of the Republic of Belarus, the Houses of Parliament – the National Assembly (the House of Representatives and the Council of the Republic), the Supreme Court, the Government – the Council of Ministers are entitled to address the Constitutional Court.

Individuals:

Other state bodies, other organisations as well as individuals, including individual entrepreneurs, shall address officials and bodies entitled to make proposals to the Constitutional Court with the initiative of making proposals that shall be considered within the jurisdiction of the Constitutional Court.

V. NATURE AND EFFECTS OF DECISIONS

The final decision on a contested human right or freedom based on a constitutional complaint:

The Constitutional Court is empowered: [...]to give the official interpretation of decrees and edicts of the President of the Republic of Belarus concerning constitutional rights, freedoms and duties of individuals;

The Official Gazette:

The Official Digest:

The Bulletin of the Constitutional Court of the Republic of Belarus Vestnik Konstitutsionnogo Suda Respubliki Belarus is the regular official quarterly publication of the Constitutional Court of the Republic of Belarus since 1994.

SOURCES:

https://www.constituteproject.org/constitution/Belarus_2004?lang=en

http://www.kc.gov.by/en/main.aspx

https://en.wikipedia.org/wiki/Constitutional_Court_of_Belarus

(19)

DOSSIER OF THE CONSTITUTIONAL COURT OF THE KINGDOM OF BELGIUM

STATE: Kingdom of Belgium
TITLE: Constitutional Court
YEAR OF FOUNDATION: 1980
SEAT: Brussels

I. CHRONICLE

Date and context of establishment

Founded as the Court of Arbitration, the court owes its existence to the development of the Belgian unitary state into a federal state. The original name that had been given to the Court already says a lot about its mission, which is to supervise the observance of the constitutional division of powers between the federal state, the communities and the regions.

The Court of Arbitration was officially inaugurated in the Belgian Senate on 1 October 1984. On 5 April 1985 it delivered its first judgment. In May 2007, upon a change of the Belgian Constitution, the court was renamed Constitutional Court as this name is more in keeping with the actual jurisdiction of the court.

Position in the hierarchy of courts

II. STANDARD LEGAL REFERENCE

The Constitution of the Kingdom of Belgium 1994 as amended

III. COMPOSITION AND ORGANIZATION

Composition

The number of judges: 12

Electoral/appointment body:
by the King from a list of two candidates proposed alternately by the House of Representatives and the Senate by a majority of at least two-thirds of the members present.

The Court members:
The term of office: for life
The Court President:
The term of office:
1 year (The judges of each linguistic group elect a president, who preside in turn over the Court for a term of one year, commencing on 1 September.)

The qualifications and the required professional experience of constitutional court judges:
Six judges belong to the Dutch language group, six to the French language group. One of the judges must have an adequate knowledge of German. Each linguistic group is composed of three judges appointed on the basis of their legal experience (professor of law at a Belgian university, judicial officer at the Supreme Court or the Council of State, legal secretary at the Constitutional Court) and three judges who have had at least five years' experience as Members of Parliament. The Court is composed of judges of both genders, at the rate of at least one third for the least numerous group, on the understanding that this group must be represented in both the aforementioned professional categories.

Candidates must be at least forty years old. The judges may hold office until the age of seventy.

Incompatibilities:
There are strict rules of incompatibility with other offices, posts and professional activities.

Organization
Administrative autonomy:
The budget:
Administrative services:
The Court is assisted by legal secretaries (maximum 24), of whom half are Dutch-speakers and the other half French-speakers. They have a university degree in law and are selected on the basis of an open competition, the terms and conditions of which are determined by the Court.

Constitutional Court Review

A posteriori review:

Abstract review:

Article 142 of the Constitution

This Court rules by means of judgments on:

1°. those conflicts referred to in Article 141 ("The law organises a procedure to prevent conflicts between laws, federate laws and rules referred to in Article 134, as well as between federate laws themselves and between the rules referred to in Article 134 themselves.");

2°. the violation of Articles 10, 11 and 24 by a law, a federate law or a rule as referred to in Article 134; (human rights – for example free education, equality,...)

3°. the violation of constitutional Articles that the law determines by a law, a federate law or by a rule as referred to in Article 134.

Other powers

Electoral matters:

In the cases, under the conditions and according to the terms that it specifies, the law can give the Court competence to pronounce by a judgment on appeals lodged against decisions made by legislative assemblies or bodies thereof regarding the control of electoral expenditure incurred in the elections for the House of Representatives.

Referendums:

The Court pronounces by a ruling, under the conditions and according to the terms specified by the law, on every referendum described in Article 39bis before it is organised.

Standing before the Constitutional Court

State bodies:

A matter may be referred to the Court by any authority designated by the law, by any person that can prove an interest or, pre-judicially, by any court.

Individuals:

Yes

Finality:

Judgments of the Constitutional Court are enforceable by law and not open to appeal.

SOURCES:

http://www.const-court.be/en/common/home.html

https://www.constituteproject.org/constitution/Belgium_2014?lang=en

https://en.wikipedia.org/wiki/Constitutional_Court_(Belgium)

www.legislationline.org/documents/id/9045

(20)

DOSSIER OF THE SUPREME COURT OF BELIZE

STATE: Belize
TITLE: Supreme Court of Belize
YEAR OF FOUNDATION: 1981
SEAT: Corozal Town

I. CHRONICLE

Date and context of establishment
The Supreme Court of Belize is duly constituted under section 94 of the Constitution of Belize: "There shall be for Belize a Supreme Court of Judicature and Court of Appeal."

Position in the hierarchy of courts
The Supreme Court shall be a superior court of record and, save as otherwise provided by any law, shall have all the powers of such a court.

II. STANDARD LEGAL REFERENCE

The Constitution of Belize 1981

III. COMPOSITION AND ORGANIZATION

Composition
The number of judges:
The Court is headed by the Chief Justice and currently consists of 8 other Justices

Electoral/appointment body:
The Chief Justice shall be appointed by the Governor-General, acting in accordance with the advice of the Prime Minister given after consultation with the Leader of the Opposition.

Justices of the Supreme Court other than the Chief Justice shall be appointed by the Governor-General, acting in accordance with the advice of the Judicial and Legal Services Commission and with the concurrence of the Prime Minister given after consultation with the Leader of the Opposition. (Article 97 of the Constitution)

The Court members:

The term of office:

A justice of the Supreme Court shall hold office until he attains the age of sixty-five years

The qualifications and the required professional experience of constitutional court judges:

A person shall not be qualified to be appointed as a justice of the Supreme Court unless-

a. he is qualified to practise as an attorney-at-law in a court in Belize or as an advocate in a court in any other part of the Commonwealth having unlimited jurisdiction either in civil or criminal causes or matters; and

b. he has been qualified for not less than five years so to practise in such a court. (Article 97 of the Constitution)

Release from office prior to the expiration of the term:

A justice of the Supreme Court may be removed from office only for inability to perform the functions of his office (whether arising from infirmity of body or mind or from any other cause) or for misbehaviour, and shall not be so removed except in accordance with the provisions of this section.

IV. POWERS

Constitutional Court Review

Article 79 of the Constitution: There shall be a Supreme Court of Judicature for Belize and a Court of Appeal. The Supreme Court shall have unlimited original jurisdiction to hear and determine any civil or criminal proceedings under any law. Any question concerning the interpretation of the Constitution arising in a lower court shall be referred by it to the Supreme Court. The Supreme Court shall be a superior court of record and shall have all the powers of such a court, including all the powers that are vested in the Supreme Court of Belize immediately before the Constitution comes into effect.

SOURCES:

http://www.belizejudiciary.org/web/supreme-court/

https://www.constituteproject.org/constitution/Belize_2011?lang=en

(21)

DOSSIER OF THE CONSTITUTIONAL COURT OF THE REPUBLIC OF BENIN

STATE: Benin
TITLE: Constitutional Court of Benin
YEAR OF FOUNDATION: 1990
SEAT: Porto Novo

I. CHRONICLE

Date and context of establishment
Constitution of the Republic of Benin, 1990

Position in the hierarchy of courts
The Constitutional Court shall be the highest jurisdiction of the State in constitutional matters. It shall be the judge of the constitutionality of the law and it shall guarantee the fundamental human rights and the public liberties. It shall be the regulatory body for the functioning of institutions and for the activity of public authorities.

II. STANDARD LEGAL REFERENCE

The Constitution of the Republic of Benin 1990.
The Constitutional Court Act.
The Rules of Procedure.
Other Internal Rules.

III. COMPOSITION AND ORGANIZATION

Composition
The number of judges: 7

Electoral/appointment body:
four shall be appointed by the Office of the National Assembly and three by the President of the Republic (Article 115)

The Court members:
The term of office:
or a term of five years renewable only one time

The Court President:
The term of office:
5 years

The qualifications and the required professional experience of constitutional court judges:
In order to be a member of the Constitutional Court, besides the condition of professional competence, one must have good morals and great honesty. (Article 115 of the Constitution)

Incompatibilities:
The duties of a member of the Constitutional Court are incompatible with the position of a member of the Government, with the exercise of any elective mandate, with all public employment-civil or military, with any other professional activity as well as with any office of national representation except in the situation provided for in Article 50 paragraph 3 of the Constitution.

Immunities:
The members of the Constitutional Court shall be irremovable for the duration of their term of office. They may not be prosecuted or arrested without the authorization of the Constitutional Court and the Office of the Supreme Court sitting in joint session except in cases of flagrant offence. In these cases the matter must be referred to the President of the Constitutional Court and to the President of the Supreme Court immediately and within forty-eight hours at the latest.

IV. POWERS

Constitutional Court Review

Preventive review:
The Constitutional Court shall

Rule obligatorily on:

- The constitutionality of organic laws and of laws in general in advance of their promulgation;

The organic laws in advance of their promulgation; the Rules of Procedure of the National Assembly, of the High Authority of Audio-Visuals and of Communications, and of the Economic and Social Council before their enforcement must be submitted to the Constitutional Court which shall give its decision on their conformity to the Constitution. (Article 123 of the Constitution)

A posteriori review:

Abstract review:

The Constitutional Court shall

Rule obligatorily on:

- The Rules of Procedure of the National Assembly, of the High Authority of Audio-Visuals and Communications, and of the Economic and Social Council in advance of their enforcement with regard to their conformity to the Constitution;
- The constitutionality of laws and regulatory acts deemed to infringe on fundamental human rights and on public liberties, and in general on the violation of the rights of the individual;
- The conflicts of prerogatives between the institutions of the State.

Concrete review:

Other powers

Electoral matters:

The Constitutional Court shall rule, in contested cases, on the regularity of legislative elections;

The Constitutional Court shall oversee the regularity of the election of the President of the Republic; examine the objections; rule on the irregularities that it may have found itself, and proclaim the results of the balloting (Article 117 of the Constitution)

Referendums:

The Constitutional Court shall rule on the regularity of the referendum and proclaim its results (Article 117 of the Constitution)

Standing before the Constitutional Court

State bodies:

Individuals:

Yes: Any citizen may complain to the Constitutional Court about the constitutionality of laws whether directly or whether by the procedure of the exception of unconstitutionality invoked in a matter which concerns him before a court of law. (Article 122 of the Constitution)

V. NATURE AND EFFECTS OF DECISIONS

Finality:
The decision of the Constitutional Court shall not be subject to any appeal.
(Article 124 of the Constitution)

Binding force:
A provision declared unconstitutional may not be promulgated or enforced. (Article 124 of the Constitution)

VI PUBLICATION OF CONSTITUTIONAL COURT DECISIONS

The Official Gazette:
The Official Digest: X
Legal Journals:
Electronic Publishing: X

SOURCES:

https://www.slideshare.net/AnnaRotman/281-benins-constitutional-court
https://www.constituteproject.org/constitution/Benin_1990?lang=en

(22)

DOSSIER OF THE CONSTITUTIONAL COURT OF THE KINGDOM OF BHUTAN

STATE: The Kingdom of Bhutan
TITLE: Supreme Court of Bhutan
YEAR OF FOUNDATION: 2008
SEAT: Thimphu

I. CHRONICLE

Date and context of establishment
Position in the hierarchy of courts
The Supreme Court shall be the guardian of this Constitution and the final authority on its interpretation.

The Supreme Court is the highest in the hierarchy, followed by the High Court, Dzongkhag, and Dungkhag Courts.

The Supreme Court of Bhutan, which shall comprise the Chief Justice and four Drangpons, shall be the highest appellate authority to entertain appeals against the judgments, orders, or decisions of the High Court in all matters and shall have the power to review its judgments and orders. (Article 21 of the Constitution)

II. STANDARD LEGAL REFERENCE

The Constitution of the Kingdom of Bhutan 2008

III. COMPOSITION AND ORGANIZATION

Composition
The number of judges:
The Supreme Court consists of one Chief Justice and four Drangpons (Associate Justices)

The Court members:

The term of office:

ten years or until attaining the age of sixty-five years, whichever is earlier

The Court President:

The term of office:

five years or until attaining the age of sixty-five years, whichever is earlier

IV. POWERS

Constitutional Court Review

Preventive review:

The Supreme Court may, on its own motion or on an application made by the Attorney General or by a party to a case, withdraw any case pending before the High Court involving a substantial question of law of general importance relating to the interpretation of this Constitution and dispose off [sic] the case itself. (Article 21 of the Constitution)

Standing before the Constitutional Court

State bodies:

Individuals:

Every person has the right to approach the courts in matters arising out of the Constitution or other laws subject to section 23 of Article 7 of the Constitution (Article 21 of the Constitution)

SOURCES:

https://www.constituteproject.org/constitution/Bhutan_2008?lang=en

http://www.judiciary.gov.bt/index.php

https://en.wikipedia.org/wiki/Supreme_Court_of_Bhutan

(23)

DOSSIER OF THE PLURINATIONAL CONSTITUTIONAL TRIBUNAL OF PLURINATIONAL STATE OF BOLIVIA

STATE: Plurinational State of Bolivia
TITLE: Plurinational Constitutional Tribunal
YEAR OF FOUNDATION: 2009
SEAT: Sucre

I. CHRONICLE

Date and context of establishment
Constitution of Plurinational State of Bolivia, 2009
The 1994 reform of Bolivia's Constitution authorized a Constitutional Tribunal. However, the body did not begin to function until 1999.

Position in the hierarchy of courts

II. STANDARD LEGAL REFERENCE

The Constitution of Plurinational State of Bolivia, 2009

III. COMPOSITION AND ORGANIZATION

Composition
The number of judges: 7
Electoral/appointment body:
APPOINTMENT BASED SYSTEM (Without the Participation of a Representative Body):

Election Based System:

The Pluri-National Constitutional Court shall consist of Judges elected on the basis of pluri-nationality, with representation from the ordinary system and the rural native indigenous system. (Article 197 of the Constitution)

Members of the Tribunal are chosen by national nonpartisan election

The qualifications and the required professional experience of constitutional court judges:

To become a Judge of the Pluri-National Constitutional Court, in addition to the general requisites to become a public servant, one must be thirty five years of age and have specialized or credited experience of at least eight years in the disciplines of Constitutional law, Administrative law or Human Rights law. For purposes of determining merit, experience as a native authority under its system of justice shall be taken into account. (Article 199 of the Constitution)

IV. POWERS

Constitutional Court Review

Preventive review:

A posteriori review:

Abstract review:

In addition to those established by law, the powers of the Pluri-National Constitutional Court, are to hear and resolve the following:

1. As the court of jurisdiction in the matters of pure law concerning the unconstitutionality of laws, Autonomous Statutes, Constitutional Charters, decrees and every type of ordinance and non-judicial resolution. If the case is of abstract character, only the President of the Republic, Senators, Deputies, Legislators and the maximum authorities of the autonomous territorial entities may present it to the court.
2. The conflicts of jurisdiction and powers among the organs of popular power.
3. The conflicts of jurisdiction between the Pluri-National government and the autonomous and decentralized territorial entities, and between the latter.
4. The appeals of fees, taxes, rates, licenses, rights or contributions that are created, modified or suppressed in violation of that set forth in the Constitution.
5. The appeals of resolutions of the Legislative Organ, when its resolutions affect one or more rights, regardless of who might be affected.

6. The review of the actions of Liberty, Constitutional Protection, Protection of Privacy, Popular actions and those for Compliance. This review shall not impede the immediate and obligatory application of the resolution that decided the action.
7. The legal consultations of the President of the Republic, of the Pluri-National Legislative Assembly, the Supreme Court of Justice or the Agro-Environmental Court on the constitutionality of proposed bills. It is obligatory to comply with the decision of the Constitutional Court.
8. The legal consultations of the rural native indigenous authorities on the application of their juridical norms as applied in a concrete case. Compliance with the decision of the Constitutional Court is obligatory.
9. The review of the constitutionality of international treaties prior to their ratification.
10. The constitutionality of the procedure of partial reform of the Constitution.
11. The conflicts of authority between the rural native indigenous jurisdiction and ordinary and agro-environmental jurisdiction.
12. The direct appeals of nullity.

(Article 202 of the Constitution)

V. NATURE AND EFFECTS OF DECISIONS

Finality:
no subsequent ordinary appeal is allowed

Binding force:
The decisions and sentences of the Pluri-National Constitutional Court are binding and of obligatory compliance, and no subsequent ordinary appeal of them is allowed. (Article 203 of the Constitution)

SOURCES:

https://www.constituteproject.org/constitution/Bolivia_2009?lang=en
https://www.revolvy.com/main/index.php?s=Plurinational%20Constitutional%20Tribunal&item_type=topic
https://en.wikipedia.org/wiki/Plurinational_Constitutional_Tribunal

(24)

DOSSIER OF THE CONSTITUTIONAL COURT OF BOSNIA AND HERZEGOVINA

STATE: Bosnia and Herzegovina
TITLE: Constitutinal Court of Bosnia and Herzegovina
YEAR OF FOUNDATION: 1964
SEAT: Sarajevo

I. CHRONICLE

Date and context of establishment

The Constitutional Court of Bosnia and Herzegovina was established for the first time on 15 February 1964 pursuant to the Constitution of 1963. Its existence was confirmed in the Constitution of 1974. The role and jurisdiction of the Constitutional court was redefined in the Dayton Peace Agreement (Annex IV - Constitution of Bosnia and Herzegovina, Article VI). The Constitution of Bosnia and Herzegovina (Annex 4 of the General Framework Agreement for Peace in Bosnia and Herzegovina), which entered into force on 14 December 1995, now provides the legal framework for the organization and functioning of the Constitutional Court. This gives it a completely new political and legal foundation as compared with that of the previous period.

The Court was established following the election and appointment procedures in May 1997 when the first session of the Constitutional Court was held. The basic task of that session was to establish procedures enabling the Court to function. Rules of Procedure were adopted at the session held on 29 July 1997.

Position in the hierarchy of courts

It is considered to be the second-highest judicial authority, since it has the appellate jurisdiction over issues under the Constitution arising out of a judgment of any other court in Bosnia and Herzegovina, and is subjected to abiding decisions by a foreign High Representative (Article VI, paragraph 3.b of the Constitution).

Beside the Constitutional Court of Bosnia and Herzegovina there are separately established the Constitutional Court of the Federation BiH and the Constitutional Court of the Republika Srpska as constitutional courts of two entities (more on www.concourts.net).

II. STANDARD LEGAL REFERENCE

The Constitution:
Dayton Peace Agreement (Annex IV - Constitution of Bosnia and Herzegovina, Article VI). The Constitution of Bosnia and Herzegovina (Annex 4 of the General Framework Agreement for Peace in Bosnia and Herzegovina) entered into force on 14 December 1995

III. COMPOSITION AND ORGANIZATION

Composition
The number of judges: 9
Electoral/appointment body:
Four members shall be selected by the House of Representatives of the Federation, and two members by the Assembly of the Republika Srpska. The remaining three members shall be selected by the President of the European Court of Human Rights after consultation with the Presidency. (Article VI., paragraph 1a of the Constitution)

The Court members:
The term of office:
5 years, until the age of 70

The Court President:
The term of office:
The qualifications and the required professional experience of constitutional court judges:
Judges shall be distinguished jurists of high moral standing. Any eligible voter so qualified may serve as a judge of the Constitutional Court. The judges selected by the President of the European Court of Human Rights shall not be citizens of Bosnia and Herzegovina or of any neighboring state. (Article VI., paragraph 1b of the Constitution)

Immunities:
Release from office prior to the expiration of the term: they can resign or are removed for cause by consensus of the other judges. (Article VI., paragraph 1c of the Constitution)

Proceedings
Hearing in plenum:

A quorum:
A majority of all members of the Court shall constitute a quorum. (Article VI., paragraph 2a of the Constitution)

IV. POWERS

Constitutional Court Review

Preventive review:
A posteriori review:
Abstract review:

The Constitutional Court shall have jurisdiction over issues referred by any court in Bosnia and Herzegovina concerning whether a law, on whose validity its decision depends, is compatible with this Constitution, with the European Convention for Human Rights and Fundamental Freedoms and its Protocols, or with the laws of Bosnia and Herzegovina; or concerning the existence of or the scope of a general rule of public international law pertinent to the court's decision. (Article VI., paragraph 3c of the Constitution)

Other powers
Jurisdictional disputes:
The Constitutional Court shall have exclusive jurisdiction to decide any dispute that arises under this Constitution between the Entities or between Bosnia and Herzegovina and an Entity or Entities, or between institutions of Bosnia and Herzegovina, including but not limited to:

- Whether an Entity's decision to establish a special parallel relationship with a neighboring state is consistent with this Constitution, including provisions concerning the sovereignty and territorial integrity of Bosnia and Herzegovina.
- Whether any provision of an Entity's constitution or law is consistent with this Constitution. (Article VI., paragraph 3a of the Constitution)

Standing before the Constitutional Court
State bodies:
Disputes may be referred only by a member of the Presidency, by the Chair of the Council of Ministers, by the Chair or a Deputy Chair of either chamber of the Parliamentary Assembly, by one-fourth of the members of either chamber of the Parliamentary Assembly, or by one-fourth of either chamber of a legislature of an Entity. (Article VI., paragraph 3a of the Constitution)

Individuals: X

V. NATURE AND EFFECTS OF DECISIONS

Finality:
Decisions of the Constitutional Court shall be final and binding. (Article VI., paragraph 5 of the Constitution)

Binding force:
Decisions of the Constitutional Court shall be final and binding.

VI PUBLICATION OF CONSTITUTIONAL COURT DECISIONS

The Official Gazette: X
The Official Digest: X
Legal Journals: X
Electronic Publishing: X

SOURCES:

https://www.constituteproject.org/constitution/Bosnia_Herzegovina_2009?lang=en
http://www.ustavnisud.ba/
https://en.wikipedia.org/wiki/Constitutional_Court_of_Bosnia_and_Herzegovina

(25)

DOSSIER OF HIGH COURT OF THE REPUBLIC OF BOTSWANA

STATE: Republic of Botswana
TITLE: High Court
YEAR OF FOUNDATION: 1966
SEAT: Lobatse

I. CHRONICLE

Date and context of establishment
Position in the hierarchy of courts
The highest court of Botswana is the Court of Appeal, which is constituted under section 99 of the Constitution and consists of a President and such number of Justices of Appeal as may be prescribed by Parliament.

II. STANDARD LEGAL REFERENCE

The Constitution of the Republic of Botswana 1966

III. COMPOSITION AND ORGANIZATION

Composition
The judges of the Court of Appeal shall be—

a. the President of the Court of Appeal;
b. such number, if any, of Justices of Appeal as may be prescribed by Parliament; and
c. the Chief Justice and the other judges of the High Court:

The number of judges:
There are currently eight judges of the Court of Appeal, who are all expatriates drawn from different parts of the Commonwealth.

Electoral/appointment body:
The President of the Court of Appeal shall, unless that office is held ex-officio by the Chief Justice, be appointed by the President. The Court members:

The qualifications and the required professional experience of constitutional court judges:
A person shall not be qualified to be appointed as a judge of the Court of Appeal unless—

a. he or she holds, or has held office as, a judge of a court having unlimited jurisdiction in civil and criminal matters in Botswana, in a Commonwealth country or in any country outside the Commonwealth that may be prescribed by Parliament or a court having jurisdiction in appeals from such a court; or
b. he or she is qualified to practise as an advocate or attorney in such a court and has been qualified for not less than ten years to practise as an advocate or attorney in such a court; or
c. he or she is qualified to practise as an advocate or attorney and he or she has had experience in the teaching of law in a recognised university for not less than ten years.

IV. POWERS

Interpretation of the Constitution (ss 105-106 of the Constitution)

Section 105 of the Constitution. Reference to High Court of cases involving interpretation of Constitution

(1) Where any question as to the interpretation of this Constitution arises in any proceedings in any subordinate court and the court is of the opinion that the question involves a substantial question of law, the court may, and shall, if any party to the proceedings so requests, refer the question to the High Court.
(2) Where any question is referred to the High Court in pursuance of this section, the High Court shall give its decision upon the question and the court in which the question arose shall, subject to any appeal, dispose of the case in accordance with that decision.

Section 106 of the Constitution. Appeal to Court of Appeal

An appeal shall lie as of right to the Court of Appeal from any decision of the High Court which involves the interpretation of this Constitution, other than a decision of the High Court under section 69(1) of this Constitution:

Provided that no appeal shall lie from a determination of the High Court under this section dismissing an application on the ground that it is frivolous or vexatious.

SOURCES:

https://www.constituteproject.org/constitution/Botswana_2005?lang=en

http://www.nyulawglobal.org/globalex/Botswana.html#_Establishment_of_the_High%20Court%20of%20

http://www.commonlii.org/bw/legis/const/1966/1.html#Ch6P1

(26)

DOSSIER OF THE SUPREME FEDERAL TRIBUNAL OF THE FEDERATIVE REPUBLIC OF BRAZIL

STATE: Federative Republic of Brazil
TITLE: Supreme Federal Tribunal (Brazilian Federal Supreme Court (Supremo Tribunal Federal – STF)
YEAR OF FOUNDATION: 1829
SEAT: Brasília

I. CHRONICLE

Date and context of establishment

The court was inaugurated during the colonial era in 1808, the year that the royal family of Portugal (the House of Braganza) arrived in Rio de Janeiro. It was originally called the House of Appeals of Brazil (Casa de Suplicação do Brasil).

The proclamation of the Brazilian Declaration of Independence and the adoption of the Imperial Constitution in 1824 preceded the establishment of the Supreme Court of Justice (Supremo Tribunal de Justiça) in 1829. With the first Constitution of the Republic, the current Court was established.

Position in the hierarchy of courts

The Federal Supreme Court (STF) is the highest body of the Judiciary Branch and the protection of the Constitution is incumbent upon it, as defined by Article 102 of the Federal Constitution (CF).

II. STANDARD LEGAL REFERENCE

The Imperial Constitution of 1824, article 163, and organized by the Imperial Law of September 18th, 1828.

III. COMPOSITION AND ORGANIZATION

Composition

The Federal Supreme Court is composed by eleven native Brazilian Justices (Article 12, § 3°, IV, of the CF/88), chosen among citizens with more than 35 and less than 65 years of age, with Remarkable legal knowledge and unblemished reputation (Article 101 of the CF/88), nominated by the President of the Republic after the approval of the election by the absolute majority of the Federal Senate.

The number of judges: 11
Electoral/appointment body:
APPOINTMENT BASED SYSTEM (Without the Participation of a Representative Body):
nominated by the President of the Republic after the approval of the election by the absolute majority of the Federal Senate
The Court members:
The term of office:
until retirement
The Court President:
The term of office: 2
The qualifications and the required professional experience of constitutional court judges:
One-fifth of the seats on the Federal Regional Tribunals and the Tribunals of the States, Federal District and Territories, shall be occupied by members of the Public Ministry with over ten years of service and by lawyers of notable legal knowledge and unblemished reputations, with over ten years of actual professional activity, nominated in a list of six names by the entities that represent the respective groups. (Article 94)
Incompatibilities:
they are not allowed to exercise another function or position, receive compensations for their participation in lawsuits, exercise partisan activities, practice law in the court she belong after three years of removal.

IV. POWERS

Constitutional Court Review

The main role of the Supreme Federal Court is to guard and interpret the Constitution. Due to such competence, STF is responsible for deciding matters related to the Constitution or about which there is doubt or controversy through special legal actions that work as instruments to evaluate the constitutionality of laws and matters. These instruments are:

- Direct Unconstitutionality Action (ADI): it is an action directed to uphold a law or normative act contrary to the Constitutional text.
- Declaratory Action of Constitutionality (ADC): it is an instrument directed to declare constitutional any law or federal norm about which there is controversy or relevant doubt as to the interpretation of the Constitution.
- Action of Unconstitutionality (ADO): it is directed to gauging of unconstitutionality in face of an omission from lawmakers to legislate, limiting, thus the exercise of certain rights due to lack of regulamentation.
- Claim of Breach of Fundamental Precept (ADPF): It is an action directed to protect fundamental precepts, mostly guidelines and principles present in the Constitution, from contrary laws or normative acts in case of relevant constitutional controversy.

The Supreme Federal Court also decides appeals in last instance and matters of its jurisdiction such as:

- Habeas Corpus: it is originally an action destined to guarantee the right of freedom of movement. It is the competence of the Federal Supreme Court when the constrained party is the President of the Republic, the Vice-President, members of the National Congress, the Court's own Justices and the Procurator-General of the Republic, or when it is to be decided as an appeal in last instance.
- Writ of security and habeas data: the writ of security is an action designed to protect any liquid an certain right and the habeas data guards the right to knowledge of personal information in records or databasis. The Supreme Court shall decide such action when they are issued against acts of the President of the Republic, Executive Committees of the Chamber of Deputies and Federal Senate, Tribunal of Accounts of the Union, Attorney-General of the Republic and the Supreme Court itself. It will be also in the competence of STF to decide such actions as appeals in last instance.
- Extradition requests from foreign Nations.

Preventive review:

A posteriori review:

Abstract review:

In the Brazilian system, the abstract constitutional control is concentrated in the Supreme Federal Court, which is responsible for the process and ruling of the autonomous actions involving constitutional controversies (direct action of unconstitutionality, declaratory action of constitutionality, direct action of unconstitutionality by omission and allegation of disobedience of fundamental precept, which are typical of the abstract constitutional control, as defined in Article 103 of 1988`s Federal Constitution).

Standing before the Constitutional Court

State bodies:

According to the Constitution, the following authors are legitimate to file the cited actions: the President of the Republic, the Executive Committee of the Federal Senate, the Executive Committee of the Chamber of Deputies, the Executive Committee of the Legislative Assemblies of the States or of the Legislative Chamber of the Federal District, the Governors of the States and of the Federal District, the Advocate-General of the Union, the Federal Council of the Brazilian Bar Association, political parties with representation in the National Congress and trade union confederations or national class entities.

Individuals: X

V PUBLICATION OF CONSTITUTIONAL COURT DECISIONS

The Official Gazette: X
The Official Digest: X
Legal Journals: X
Electronic Publishing: X

SOURCES:

https://www.constituteproject.org/constitution/Brazil_2015?lang=en
https://en.wikipedia.org/wiki/Supreme_Federal_Court
http://www2.stf.jus.br/portalStfInternacional/cms/verPrincipal.php?idioma=en_us
http://www.nyulawglobal.org/globalex/Brazil1.html#_Toc448767057

(27)

DOSSIER OF THE SUPREME COURT OF BRUNEI DARUSSALAM

STATE: Brunei Darussalam
TITLE: Supreme Court
YEAR OF FOUNDATION:
SEAT: Darussalam

I. CHRONICLE

Date and context of establishment

Position in the hierarchy of courts

There are two parallel justice systems, one presided over by the Supreme Court and the other by the Sharia courts. The Supreme Court comprises the Court of Appeal and the High Court. Criminal cases that do not carry a death sentence and less serious civil cases are conducted by the intermediate courts before judges or the subordinate courts before magistrates.

Appeals are heard by the Court of Appeal, which in criminal cases is the final court of appeal. In civil cases, however, appeals may be made to the Privy Council in the UK. Judges are appointed by the Sultan for three-year terms.

II. STANDARD LEGAL REFERENCE

(Constitution) Laws of Brunei (rev. 2013)

III. COMPOSITION AND ORGANIZATION

Composition

The Supreme Court shall consist of the President, the Chief Justice, the Judges and the Judicial Commissioners of the Supreme Court.

The number of judges:

Electoral/appointment body:

APPOINTMENT BASED SYSTEM (Without the Participation of a Representative Body):
The Judges shall be appointed by His Majesty the Sultan and Yang Di-Pertuan by instrument under His Majesty Sign Manual and the State Seal.

The Court members:

The term of office:

Subject to the provisions of this section, a person holding the office of a Judge shall vacate that office on attaining the age of 65 years or such later time as His Majesty the Sultan and Yang Di-Pertuan may approve.

IV. POWERS

Article 84C of the 'Constitution of Brunei Darussalam' states that: There is and shall be no judicial review in any court of any act, decision, grant, revocation or suspension... any exercise of or refusal or omission to exercise any power, authority or discretion by His Majesty the Sultan and Yang Di-Pertuan, or any party acting on his behalf or under his authority.

SOURCES:

https://www.constituteproject.org/constitution/Brunei_2006?lang=en
https://en.wikipedia.org/wiki/Politics_of_Brunei#Judicial_branch
http://www.commonlii.org/bn/legis/sc5226/
http://www.judiciary.gov.bn/Theme/Home.aspx
http://www.agc.gov.bn/AGC%20Images/LAWS/ACT_PDF/cap005.pdf

(28)

DOSSIER OF THE CONSTITUTIONAL COURT OF THE REPUBLIC OF BULGARIA

STATE: Republic of Bulgaria
TITLE: Constitutional Court of the Republic of Bulgaria
YEAR OF FOUNDATION: 1991
SEAT: Sofia

I. CHRONICLE

Date and context of establishment
The Constitutional Court was established by the new Bulgarian Constitution, 1991
Position in the hierarchy of courts

II. STANDARD LEGAL REFERENCE

The Constitution of the Republic of Bulgaria 1991

III. COMPOSITION AND ORGANIZATION

Composition
The number of judges: 12
Electoral/appointment body:
one third shall be elected by the National Assembly, one third shall be appointed by the President, and one-third shall be elected by a joint meeting of the judges of the Supreme Court of Cassat (Article 147 of the Constitution)
The Court members:
The term of office:
9 years The judges of the Constitutional Court shall be elected or appointed for a period of nine years and shall not be eligible for re-election or re-appointment. (Article 147, paragraph 2))

The Court President:

The judges of the Constitutional Court shall elect by secret ballot a Chairman of the Court for a period of three years. (Article 147, paragraph 4 of the Constitution)

The term of office:

3 years

The qualifications and the required professional experience of constitutional court judges:

The judges of the Constitutional Court shall be lawyers of high professional and moral integrity and with at least fifteen years of professional experience. (Article 147, paragraph 3 of the Constitution)

Incompatibilities:

The status of a judge of the Constitutional Court shall be incompatible with a representative mandate, or any state or public post, or membership in a political party or trade union, or with the practicing of a free, commercial, or any other paid occupation (Article 147, paragraph 5 of the Constitution)

Immunities:

A judge of the Constitutional Court shall enjoy the same immunity as a Member of the National Assembly. (Article 147, paragraph 6 of the Constitution)

Release from office prior to the expiration of the term:

The mandate of a judge of the Constitutional Court shall expire upon any of the following occurrences:

1. The expiry of the term of office;
2. Resignation submitted before the Constitutional Court;
3. Entry into force of a final sentence imposing imprisonment for an intentional criminal offence;
4. Permanent de facto inability to perform his duties for more than a year;
5. Incompatibility with an office or activity referred to in Article 147 para 5.
6. Death.

(Article 148, paragraph 1 of the Constitution)

IV. POWERS

Constitutional Court Review

Preventive review:

A posteriori review:

Abstract review:

The Constitutional Court shall:

[...] 1. Provide binding interpretations of the Constitution;

[...] 2. Rule on constitutionality of the laws and other acts passed by the National Assembly and the acts of the President;

Concrete review:

Other powers

Constitutional complaints: NO

Jurisdictional disputes:

The Constitutional Court shall: [...] 3. Rule on competence suits between the National Assembly, the President and the Council of Ministers, and between the bodies of local self-government and the central executive branch of government;The unconstitutionality of acts and activities of political parties: The Constitutional Court shall: [...] 5. Rule on challenges to the constitutionality of political parties and associations;

Impeachment:

The Constitutional Court shall: [...] 8. Rule on impeachments by the National Assembly against the President or the Vice President.

Electoral matters:

The Constitutional Court shall:

[...] 6. Rule on challenges to the legality of the election of the President and Vice President;

[...] 7. Rule on challenges to the legality of an election of a Member of the National Assembly;

Standing before the Constitutional Court

State bodies:

The Constitutional Court shall act on an initiative from not fewer than one-fifth of all Members of the National Assembly, the President, the Council of Ministers, the Supreme Court of Cassation, the Supreme Administrative Court or the Prosecutor General. (Article 150, paragraph 1 of the Constitution)

The Ombudsman may approach the Constitutional Court with a request for declaring as unconstitutional a law which infringes human rights and freedoms. (Article 150, paragraph 3 of the Constitution)

The Supreme Judicial Council may approach the Constitutional Court with a petition to establish unconstitutionality of any law whereby any rights and freedoms of citizens are violated. (Article 150, paragraph 4 of the Constitution)

Individuals: NO

V. NATURE AND EFFECTS OF DECISIONS

Obligatory opinions on the conformity of international treaties with the Constitution:

The Constitutional Court shall: [...] 4. Rule on the compatibility between the Constitution and the international treaties concluded by the Republic of Bulgaria prior to their ratification, and on the compatibility of domestic laws with the universally recognized norms of international law and treaties

VI PUBLICATION OF CONSTITUTIONAL COURT DECISIONS

The Official Gazette: x
The Official Digest: x
Legal Journals: x
Electronic Publishing: x

SOURCES:

https://www.constituteproject.org/constitution/Bulgaria_2015?lang=en
https://en.wikipedia.org/wiki/Constitutional_Court_of_Bulgaria
http://www.constcourt.bg/en/Home/AboutCourt
http://www.cecl.gr/RigasNetwork/databank/REPORTS/r1/Bu_R1_konstantinov.htm

(29)

DOSSIER OF THE CONSTITUTIONAL COUNCIL OF BURKINA FASO

STATE: Burkina Faso
TITLE: Constitutional Council
YEAR OF FOUNDATION: 1989
SEAT: Ouagadougou

I. CHRONICLE

Date and context of establishment
The Constitutional Council (Conseil Constitutionnel) was estabished by the Constitution of 23 February 1989. It normally performs control for constitutionality and conformity of some legal texts with the Constitution as well as certain functions with respect to electoral matters.

Position in the hierarchy of courts

II. STANDARD LEGAL REFERENCE

The Constitution of burkina Faso 1989

III. COMPOSITION AND ORGANIZATION

Composition
The number of judges:
Constitutional Council or Conseil Constitutionnel (consists of the council president and 9 members)

Electoral/appointment body:
APPOINTMENT BASED SYSTEM (Without the Participation of a Representative Body):

Constitutional Council judges appointed by the president of Burkina Faso upon the proposal of the minister of justice and the president of the National Assembly

IV. POWERS

Constitutional Court Review

Article 152 of the Constitution: The Constitutional Council is the institution that deals with constitutional and electoral matters. It shall be responsible for giving rulings on the constitutionality of laws and decrees, as well as on the conformity of international treaties and agreements to the Constitution. It shall interpret the provisions of the Constitution. It shall monitor the legality, transparency and impartiality of referendums and presidential and legislative elections, and shall be the judge of electoral litigations. It shall announce the final results of presidential, legislative and local elections. The monitoring of the legality and transparency of local elections shall fall under the jurisdiction of the administrative courts.

...

Preventive review:

Article 155 of the Constitution: The laws of government organs and the regulations of the National Assembly and those of the Chamber of Representatives must be submitted to the Constitutional Council, before being promulgated or implemented. To the same end, ordinary laws and treaties submitted for ratification may be referred to the Constitutional Council before promulgation.

Standing before the Constitutional Court

State bodies:

Article 157 of the Constitution: The following may submit matters to the Constitutional Council:

- the President of Faso;
- the Prime Minister;
- the President of the National Assembly;
- the President of the Chamber of Representatives;
- at least one-fifth of the members of the National Assembly.

Article 158 of the Constitution: The submission of a matter to the Constitutional Council shall defer the promulgation of the texts submitted to it.

Individuals:

V. NATURE AND EFFECTS OF DECISIONS

Finality:
Binding force:
Erga omnes:
Article 159 of the Constitution: A provision declared unconstitutional may not be promulgated nor implemented. There is no possible appeal against the decisions of the Constitutional Council. These decisions shall be mandatory for government authorities and all administrative and jurisdictional authorities.

The annulment of an unconstitutional act/activity of a political party act/activity or the ordering of a deletion from the register of legal political parties:
Article 156 of the Constitution: The Constitutional Council is also charged with the control of the respect by the political parties of the provisions of article 13, line 5 of the Constitution.

VI PUBLICATION OF CONSTITUTIONAL COURT DECISIONS

The Official Gazette:
The Official Digest:
Legal Journals: X
Electronic Publishing: X

SOURCES:

https://www.constituteproject.org/constitution/Burkina_Faso_2012?lang=en
http://www.nationsencyclopedia.com/Africa/Burkina-Faso-JUDICIAL-SYSTEM.html
http://www.conseil-constitutionnel.gov.bf/index.php/les-textes-fondamentaux/la-constitution
https://www.africanlii.org/links/weblink/70

(30)

DOSSIER OF THE CONSTITUTIONAL COURT OF THE REPUBLIC OF BURUNDI

STATE: Republic of Burundi
TITLE: Constitutional Court of Burundi
YEAR OF FOUNDATION: 1992
SEAT: Bujumbura

I. CHRONICLE

Date and context of establishment
The court was established in 1992 as the authority on the new constitution adopted the same year. Previously, the Supreme Court had exercised jurisdiction over constitutional questions.

Position in the hierarchy of courts
The Constitutional Court deals with the interpretation of the Constitution of 2005 and is considered the country's second highest court. In conjunction with the Burundian Supreme Court (Cour Suprême), the Constitutional Court can sit en banc as a High Court of Justice (Haute Cour de Justice) with special prerogatives, such as the power to try an incumbent president.

II. STANDARD LEGAL REFERENCE

The Constitution of the Republic of Burundi 2005

III. COMPOSITION AND ORGANIZATION

Composition
The number of judges: 7
Electoral/appointment body:
nominated by the President of the Republic and after approval of the Senate.

The Court members:

The term of office:

six years nonrenewable

The Court President:

The term of office:

The President, Vice-President and the career magistrates are permanent.

The qualifications and the required professional experience of constitutional court judges:

At least three members of the Constitutional Court are career magistrates. The members of the Constitutional Court are chosen among jurists recognized for their moral integrity, their impartiality and their independence.

Proceedings

Hearing in plenum:

A quorum:

The Constitutional Court may only sit validly if at least five of its members are present. Its decisions are taken with the absolute majority of the sitting members, the voice of the President being decisive in the case of equal sharing of the voices. (Article 227 of the Constitution)

Hearing in camera:

IV. POWERS

Constitutional Court Review

Preventive review:

The organic laws before their promulgation, the internal regulations of the National Assembly and of the Senate before their application, are submitted obligatory to the control of constitutionality. (Article 228 of the Constitution)

Other powers

Electoral matters:

The Constitutional Court is competent to: [...]Decide on the regularity of the presidential and legislative elections and of the referenda and to proclaim the definitive results of them;

Standing before the Constitutional Court

State bodies:

The Constitutional Court is referred to a matter by the President of the Republic, the President of the National Assembly, the President of the Senate, by one-quarter of the members of the National Assembly or one-quarter of the members of the Senate, or by the Ombudsman. (Article 230 of the Constitution)

Individuals:

Yes; Every natural or legal person interested, including the Public Ministry, may refer the Constitutional Court to a matter of the constitutionality of the laws, either directly by way of an action or indirectly by the procedure of exception of unconstitutionality invoked in a matter submitted to another jurisdiction. (Article 230 of the Constitution)

V. NATURE AND EFFECTS OF DECISIONS

Finality:

The decisions of the Constitutional Court are not susceptible to any recourse. (Article 231 of the Constitution)

Binding force:

A provision declared unconstitutional may not be promulgated or implemented. (Article 231 of the Constitution)

SOURCES:

https://www.constituteproject.org/constitution/Burundi_2005?lang=en

https://en.wikipedia.org/wiki/Constitutional_Court_of_Burundi

(31)

DOSSIER OF THE CONSTITUTIONAL COUNCIL OF THE KINGDOM OF CAMBODIA

STATE: Kingdom of Cambodia
TITLE: The Constitutional Council
YEAR OF FOUNDATION: 1993
SEAT: Phnom Penh

I. CHRONICLE

Date and context of establishment

The 1993 Constitution was adopted to guarantee the respect of the Constitution. The Constitutional Council has been effectively functioning since June 15, 1998 , the first time in the history of Cambodia .

Position in the hierarchy of courts

II. STANDARD LEGAL REFERENCE

The Constitution of the Kingdom of Cambodia 1993

III. COMPOSITION AND ORGANIZATION

Composition

The number of judges: 9

Electoral/appointment body:

Three members shall be appointed by the King, three by the National Assembly and three by the Supreme Council of the Magistracy. The Chairperson shall be elected by the members of the Constitutional Council. (Article 137 of the Constitution)

The Court members:

The term of office:

9 years

The Court President:

The term of office:

3 years

The qualifications and the required professional experience of constitutional court judges:

Members of the Constitutional Council shall be selected from among dignitaries with a higher-education degree in law, administration, diplomacy or economics and who have considerable work experience. (Article 138 of the Constitution)

Members of the Constitutional Council shall be chosen among dignitaries who :

- are Khmer by birth,
- have at least 45 year of age,
- have at least 15 years of professional experiences,
- Possess degree of higher education in the areas of law, administration, diplomacy or economics.

(http://www.ccc.gov.kh/composition_en.php)

Incompatibilities:

A member of the Constitutional Council must not be a Senator, a Member of the National Assembly, a Member of the Royal Government, a sitting Judge, a public servant, the president or vice-president of a political party or the president or vice-president of a union. (Article 139 of the Constitution)

Immunities:

Members of the Constitutional Council shall not be liable to civil or penal sanctions for decisions taken while fulfilling their functions of members of the Council.

Release from office prior to the expiration of the term:

The decision for the dismissal of any member of the Council shall be taken by a vote by 2/3 majority of the whole members of the Council in closed door hearing with his/her presence. The Constitutional Council can dismiss any member whose activity is incompatible with his/her function or who does not attend over 3 consecutive meetings without prior notification or cannot fulfill his/her duties due to physical or mental disabilities.

IV. POWERS

Constitutional Court Review

Preventive review:

The King, the Prime Minister, the President of the National Assembly, one tenth of the members of the National Assembly, the President of the Senate, or one quarter of the Senators may send laws adopted by the National Assembly to the Constitutional Council for review before promulgation.

The Internal Regulations of the National Assembly, the Internal Regulations of the Senate and organic laws must be sent to the Constitutional Council for review before promulgation. The Constitutional Council shall decide within 30 days whether the laws, the Internal Regulations of the National Assembly or the Internal Regulations of the Senate are constitutional. (Article 140 of the Constitution)

A posteriori review:

Abstract review:

After any law is promulgated, the King, the President of the Senate, the President of the National Assembly, the Prime Minister, one quarter of the Senators, one tenth of Members of the National Assembly, or the Courts, may request the Constitutional Council to review the constitutionality of that law. (Article 141 of the Constitution)

Standing before the Constitutional Court

State bodies:

Individuals:

Yes - People shall have the rights to appeal against the constitutionality of any law through Members of the National Assembly, or the President of the National Assembly, or Senators, or the President of the Senate as stipulated in the above paragraph. (Article 141 of the Constitution)

V. NATURE AND EFFECTS OF DECISIONS

Finality:

Decisions of the Constitutional Council are final. (Article 142 of the Constitution)

Binding force:

Any provision of any Article declared by the Constitutional Council to be unconstitutional shall not be promulgated or implemented. (Article 142 of the Constitution)

Erga omnes:

Inter partes:

Ex officio:

As a principle, the Constitutional Council cannot examine any matter on its own initiative.

SOURCES:

https://www.constituteproject.org/constitution/Cambodia_2008?lang=en

http://www.ccc.gov.kh/index_en.php

(32)

DOSSIER OF THE CONSTITUTIONAL COUNCIL OF THE REPUBLIC OF CAMEROON

STATE: Republic of Cameroon
TITLE: Constitutional Council
YEAR OF FOUNDATION: 1996
SEAT: Yaoundé

I. CHRONICLE

Date and context of establishment

Until 1990, though the situatuion is not much different now, Cameroon has had a higly centralized, autocratic political system with a strong executive, a judiciary under the control of the executive, and a National Assembly dominated by the ruling party. Economic mismanagement, pervasive corruption, a harsh and authoritarian system of government, and a challenging business environment retarded the economy of Cameroon. This led to discontent and frustartion among the citizens and exploded into series of strikes (ghost town campaigns), killings, and a nationwide call for constitutional and political reforms. A Constitutional Council was introduced in Cameroon in 1996 by Law No. 9676 of 18 January 1996 which amended the Constitution of 2 June 1972 with juristiction over constitutionality of laws. (*www.etd.ceu.hu/2009/malah_anna.pdf)*

Position in the hierarchy of courts

The Supreme Court is the highest judicial body in Cameroon. As defined in Article V of the Constitution of Cameroon, the Supreme Court is above the courts of appeal and the tribunals.

The Supreme Court shall perform the duties of the Constitutional Court until the latter is set up. (Article 67, paragraph 4 of the Constitution)

The Constitutional Council is one of the newest institutions created by Law N° 96 /06 of 18th January 1996 on constitutional revision of 2nd June 1972.

In Section 46, the Constitution defines the said institution as competent authority as regards constitutional matters it rules on the constitutionality of laws. It is the regulatory organ for institution's functioning.

II. STANDARD LEGAL REFERENCE

The Constitution of the Republic of Cameroon 1972

III. COMPOSITION AND ORGANIZATION

Composition

The number of judges: 11

Electoral/appointment body:

Members of the Constitutional Council shall be appointed by the President of the Republic.

They shall be designated as follows:

- three, including the President of the Council, by the President of the Republic;
- three by the President of the National Assembly after consultation with the Bureau;
- three by the President of the Senate after consultation with the Bureau;
- two by the Higher Judicial Council. Besides the eleven members provided for above, former presidents of the Republic shall be ex officio members of the Constitutional Council for life. In case of a tie, the President of the Constitutional Council shall have the casting vote. (Article 51, paragraph 2 of the Constitution)

The Court members:

The term of office:

6 years (eventually renewable)

The qualifications and the required professional experience of constitutional court judges:

These members shall be chosen from among personalities of established professional renown.

They must be of high moral integrity and proven competence.

(Article 51, paragraph 1 of the Constitution)

IV. POWERS

Constitutional Court Review

Preventive review:

The Constitutional Council shall give a final ruling on:

[...]

- the constitutionality of the standing orders of the National Assembly and the Senate prior to their implementation;

(Article 47, paragraph 1 of the Constitution)

Laws as well as treaties and international agreements may, prior to their enactment, be referred to the Constitutional Council by the President of the Republic, the President of the National Assembly, the President of the Senate, one-third of the members of the National Assembly, one-third of the Senators, or the Presidents of the regional executives pursuant to the provisions of paragraph (2) above. (Article 47, paragraph 3 of the Constitution)

A posteriori review:

Abstract review:

The Constitutional Council shall give a final ruling on:

- the constitutionality of laws, treaties and international agreements;

(Article 47, paragraph 1 of the Constitution)

Other powers

Jurisdictional disputes:

The Constitutional Council shall give a final ruling on:

[...]

- conflict of powers between State institutions; between the State and the Regions, and between the Regions. (Article 47, paragraph 1 of the Constitution)

Electoral matters:

The Constitutional Council shall ensure the regularity of presidential elections, parliamentary elections and referendum operations. It shall proclaim the results thereof. (Article 48, paragraph 1 of the Constitution)

Referendums:

Any challenges in respect of the regularity of a referendum may be referred to the Constitutional Council by the President of the Republic, the President of the National Assembly, the President of the Senate, one-third of the members of the National Assembly or one-third of the Senators. (Article 48, paragraph 3 of the Constitution)

Standing before the Constitutional Court

State bodies:

Matters may be referred to the Constitutional Council by the President of the Republic, the President of the National Assembly, the President of the Senate, one-third of the members of the National Assembly or one-third of the Senators. (Article 47, paragraph 2 of the Constitution)

V. NATURE AND EFFECTS OF DECISIONS

Finality:
Rulings of the Constitutional Council shall not be subject to appeal. They shall be binding on all public, administrative, military and judicial authorities, as well as all natural persons and corporate bodies. (Article 50, paragraph 1 of the Constitution)

Binding force:
Rulings of the Constitutional Council shall not be subject to appeal. They shall be binding on all public, administrative, military and judicial authorities, as well as all natural persons and corporate bodies. (Article 50, paragraph 1 of the Constitution)

VI PUBLICATION OF CONSTITUTIONAL COURT DECISIONS

The Official Gazette:
The Official Digest:
Legal Journals:
Electronic Publishing: X

SOURCES:

https://www.constituteproject.org/constitution/Cameroon_2008?lang=en
https://www.prc.cm/en/cameroon/institutions/171-constitutional-council
http://www.nyulawglobal.org/globalex/Cameroon1.html#_Current_Court_System
www.etd.ceu.hu/2009/malah_anna.pdf

(33)

DOSSIER OF THE SUPREME COURT OF CANADA

STATE: Canada
TITLE: Supreme Court
YEAR OF FOUNDATION: 1875 (1949 - became the highest court in the country)
SEAT: Ottawa

I. CHRONICLE

Date and context of establishment

The creation of the court was provided for by the British North America Act, 1867, renamed in 1982 the Constitution Act, 1867. The first bills for the creation of a federal Supreme Court, introduced in the Parliament of Canada in 1869 and in 1870, were withdrawn. It was not until 8 April 1875 that a bill was finally passed providing for the creation of a Supreme Court of Canada.

Prior to 1949, however, the Supreme Court did not constitute the court of last resort; litigants could appeal to the Judicial Committee of the Privy Council in London. As well, some cases could bypass the court and go directly to the Judicial Committee from the provincial courts of appeal.

The Supreme Court of Canada formally became the Court of last resort for criminal appeals in 1933 and for all other appeals in 1949. The last decisions of the Judicial Committee on cases from Canada were made in the mid-1950s, as a result of their being heard in a court of first instance prior to 1949.

Position in the hierarchy of courts

The highest court of Canada, the final court of appeals in the Canadian justice system

II. STANDARD LEGAL REFERENCE

8 April 1875 that a bill was finally passed providing for the creation of a Supreme Court of Canada

III. COMPOSITION AND ORGANIZATION

Composition

The number of judges: 9

Electoral/appointment body:

All judges are appointed by the Governor in Council

The Court members:

The term of office:

A judge holds office during good behaviour until he or she retires or attains the age of 75 years

The qualifications and the required professional experience of constitutional court judges:

must have been either a judge of a superior court or a member of at least ten years' standing of the bar of a province or territory; minimum of three judges coming from Quebec.

Incompatibilities:

The judges must devote themselves exclusively to their judicial duties. No judge may hold any other remunerative office or engage in any business enterprise.

Release from office prior to the expiration of the term:

A judge holds office during good behaviour until he or she retires or attains the age of 75 years, but is removable for incapacity or misconduct in office before that time by the Governor General on address of the Senate and House of Commons

IV. POWERS

Constitutional Court Review

Preventive review:

In addition to being Canada's court of final appeal, the Supreme Court performs a unique function. It can be asked by the Governor in Council to hear references, that is, to consider important questions of law such as the constitutionality or interpretation of federal or provincial legislation and to give its opinion on the question.

A posteriori review:

Abstract review:

In addition to being Canada's court of final appeal, the Supreme Court performs a unique function. It can be asked by the Governor in Council to hear references, that is, to consider important questions of law such as the constitutionality or interpretation of federal or provincial legislation and to give its opinion on the question.

Constitutional questions may also be raised by the parties in appeals involving individual litigants or governments or government agencies. In such cases, the federal and provincial governments must be notified of the constitutional questions and can intervene to present arguments with respect to them.

The Supreme Court has the ultimate power of judicial review over Canadian federal and provincial laws' constitutional validity. If a federal or provincial law has been held contrary to the division of power provisions of one of the various constitution acts, the legislature or parliament must either live with the result, amend the law so that it complies, or obtain an amendment to the constitution.

Constitutional questions may, of course, also be raised in the normal case of appeals involving individual litigants, governments, government agencies or crown corporations. In such cases the federal and provincial governments must be notified of any constitutional questions and may intervene to submit a brief and attend oral argument at the court. Usually the other governments are given the right to argue their case in the Court, although on rare occasions this has been curtailed and prevented by order of one of the court's judges.

V. NATURE AND EFFECTS OF DECISIONS

VI PUBLICATION OF CONSTITUTIONAL COURT DECISIONS

The Official Gazette:

The Official Digest:

Legal Journals:

Electronic Publishing: x

SOURCES:

https://en.wikipedia.org/wiki/Supreme_Court_of_Canada

https://www.constituteproject.org/constitution/Canada_2011?lang=en

http://www.scc-csc.ca/home-accueil/index-eng.aspx

(34)

DOSSIER OF THE SUPREME COURT OF JUSTICE OF THE REPUBLIC OF CAPE VERDE

STATE: Cape Verde (Republic of Cabo Verde)
TITLE: Supreme Court of Justice
YEAR OF FOUNDATION: 1992
SEAT: Praia

I. CHRONICLE

Date and context of establishment 1992
Position in the hierarchy of courts
The Supreme Court of Justice shall be the supreme body in the hierarchy of courts and shall have jurisdiction over all the national territory. (Article 229, paragraph 1 of the Constitution)

Cabo Verde has no constitutional court even though the 1999 constitutional amendments provide for its creation. This is because the PAICV and the MpD could not reach consensus on the members of the court.

II. STANDARD LEGAL REFERENCE

The Constitution of the Republic of Cape Verde of 1992 with amendments

III. COMPOSITION AND ORGANIZATION

Composition
The number of judges:
minimum of five judges

Electoral/appointment body:

a. One judge appointed by the President of the Republic;

b. One judge elected by the National Assembly;

c. Other judges designated by the Superior Council of Magistrates.

The Court members:

The term of office:

5 years

The qualifications and the required professional experience of constitutional court judges: ...

2. The judge appointed by the President of the Republic must be selected from among the Judicial Magistrates or from the Public Prosecutor's Office.

3. The judge elected by the National Assembly may be selected from among the Judicial Magistrates, the Public Prosecutor's Office, or national jurists.

4. The judges designated by the Superior Council of Magistrates must be judicial magistrates. (Article 230 of the Constitution)

1. Judges of the Supreme Court of Justice must be national citizens of good reputation, law graduates in possession of their civic and political rights who, at the time they are designated, have functioned in a professional activity in the magistrature or other legal activity or law teaching for at least five years.

2. In addition to the requirements established in the preceding paragraph, others may be established by law for the designation of judges by the Superior Council of Magistrates. (Article 231 of the Constitution)

Release from office prior to the expiration of the term:

1. Except for the expiration of their term, the duties of judges of the Supreme Court of Justice shall cease only in the following instances:

a. Death or permanent physical or mental disability;

b. Resignation;

c. Dismissal or compulsory retirement as a result of disciplinary or criminal proceedings;

d. Acceptance of a position or responsibility which is constitutionally or legally incompatible with the exercise of his duties. (Article 236 of the Constitution)

Constitutional Court Review

Preventive review:

A posteriori review:

Abstract review:

The Supreme Court of Justice in plenary session shall have the following responsibilities:

a. To consider the constitutionality of regulations and resolutions in their overall guidelines or concrete effects; (Article 237 of the Constitution)

Other powers

The Supreme Court of Justice shall also have the following responsibilities:

[...]

d. To accept requests for registration from political parties, coalitions, and associations in the register created especially for this purpose in the Court, and to keep records on these parties as required by law, and to annul registrations by cancellation or dissolution;

e. To consider the legality of the names and symbols of political parties, coalitions, and associations and their similarity to other parties and coalitions already registered;

f. To declare the illegality of political and partisan organizations which may not be constituted and to decree their abolition. (Article 238 of the Constitution)

Electoral matters:

The Supreme Court of Justice shall also have the following responsibilities:

a. To receive and admit candidates for the Presidency of the Republic;

b. To judge appeals in cases of protest and grievances presented during the verification of election results for the Presidency of the Republic;

c. To judge appeals in the area of candidacies and contested elections for the National Assembly and for local bodies; (Article 238 of the Constitution)

SOURCES:

https://www.constituteproject.org/constitution/Cape_Verde_1992?lang=en

(35)

DOSSIER OF THE CONSTITUTIONAL COUNCIL OF THE REPUBLIC OF CHAD

STATE: The Republic of Chad
TITLE: Constitutional Council
YEAR OF FOUNDATION: 1996
SEAT: N'Djamena

I. CHRONICLE

Date and context of establishment 1996
It was established by Title VII of the Constitution of Chad of 1996

Position in the hierarchy of courts

II. STANDARD LEGAL REFERENCE

The Constitution of the Republic of Chad of 1996

III. COMPOSITION AND ORGANIZATION

Composition
The number of judges:
composed of nine (9) members including three (3) magistrates and six (6) jurists

Electoral/appointment body:

two (2) magistrates and three (3) jurists by the President of the Republic;
one (1) magistrate and three (3) jurists by the President of the National Assembly;

The Court members:
The term of office:
9 years non-renewable (The Constitutional Council is renewed by thirds (1/3) every three (3) years.)

The Court President:
The term of office:
3 years renewable

The qualifications and the required professional experience of constitutional court judges:
The members of the Constitutional Council must be of a recognized professional competence, of good morals and of grand probity. (Article 160 of the Constitution)

Incompatibilities:
The functions of member of the Constitutional Council are incompatible with the character of member of the Government, the exercise of any elective mandate, of any public employment and of any other lucrative activity. (Article 162 of the Constitution)

Release from office prior to the expiration of the term:
The members of the Constitutional Council are irremovable for the duration of their mandate, except in cases of condemnation for misdemeanors and crimes, of resignation or of definitive impediment. (Article 160 of the Constitution)

IV. POWERS

Constitutional Court Review

Preventive review:

It decides obligatorily on the constitutionality of the organic laws before their promulgation[,] and of the Internal Regulations of the National Assembly before their implementation. (Article 161 of the Constitution)

The Constitutional Council, at the demand of the President of the Republic, of the Prime Minister, of the President of the National Assembly or of at least one-tenth [1/10] of the members of the National Assembly, decides on the constitutionality of a law before its promulgation. (Article 165 of the Constitution)

A posteriori review:

Abstract review:

The Constitutional Council is the judge of the constitutionality of the laws, of the treaties and international agreements. (Article 161 of the Constitution)

Other powers

Jurisdictional disputes:

It rules [on] the conflicts of attribution between the institutions of the State. (Article 161 of the Constitution)

Electoral matters:

It takes cognizance of the disputes [concerning] the presidential [and] legislative elections. (Article 161 of the Constitution)

Referendums:

It sees to the regularity of the operations of the referendum and proclaims the results of it. (Article 161 of the Constitution)

Other matters with which the Court is charged by the Constitution or statute:

It receives the oath of the elected President of the Republic. (rticle 161 of the Constitution)

Standing before the Constitutional Court

State bodies:

The Constitutional Council, at the demand of the President of the Republic, of the Prime Minister, of the President of the National Assembly or of at least one-tenth [1/10] of the members of the National Assembly, decides on the constitutionality of a law before its promulgation. (Article 165 of the Constitution)

Individuals:

Any citizen can raise the pleadings of unconstitutionality before a jurisdiction in a matter which concerns them. (Article 166 of the Constitution)

V. NATURE AND EFFECTS OF DECISIONS

Finality:

The decisions of the Constitutional Council are not susceptible to any recourse. (Article 169 of the Constitution)

Binding force:

They are binding on the public powers and on all the administrative, military and jurisdictional authorities. (Article 169 of the Constitution)

SOURCES:

https://www.constituteproject.org/constitution/Chad_2005?lang=en

(36)

DOSSIER OF THE CONSTITUTIONAL COURT OF THE REPUBLIC OF CHILE

STATE: Republic of Chile
TITLE: The Constitutional Court of Chile
YEAR OF FOUNDATION: 1970
SEAT: Santiago-Chile

I. CHRONICLE

Date and context of establishment
The Constitutional Court was created in 1970, under the Constitution of 1925 rule. In 1973, after the coup d'état, is dissolved, but the 1980 Constitution reinstated it.

Position in the hierarchy of courts

II. STANDARD LEGAL REFERENCE

The Constitution of Chile of 1980

III. COMPOSITION AND ORGANIZATION

Composition
The number of judges: 10
Electoral/appointment body:
APPOINTMENT BASED SYSTEM (Without the Participation of a Representative Body):
There will be a Constitutional Court composed by ten members, designated as follows:

a. Three designated by the President of the Republic.

b. Four elected by the National Congress. Two shall be appointed directly by the Senate and two shall be previously proposed by the Chamber of Deputies for approval or rejection by the Senate.

The designations, or the proposals, in their case, shall be made in single votes and will require will require for their approval of the favorable vote of two thirds of the senators or active deputies, as appropriate.

c. Three elected by the Supreme Court in a secret ballot that shall be celebrated in a session specially convened for that purpose.

(Article 92 of the Constitution)

The Court members:

The term of office:

9 years

The qualifications and the required professional experience of constitutional court judges:

They must have held the degree of lawyer for at least fifteen years, must have excelled in professional, academic or public activity, must not have any ineligibility that renders them unfit to hold the office of judge (Article 92 of the Constitution)

Incompatibilities:

[...]will be subjected to the norms of Articles 58, 59 and 81 of the Constitution, and will not be able to exercise the profession of lawyer, including the judicature, or any other act of those established in the second and third paragraphs of Article 60 of the Constitution (Article 92 of the Constitution)

Release from office prior to the expiration of the term:

The members of the Constitutional Court are irremovable and may not be re-elected, except in the case of the one that has been a replacement and has held the position for less than five years. They will cease to hold office once they turn 75 years old. (Article 92 of the Constitution)

Proceedings

Hearing in plenum:

The Court will function in plenum or divided into two chambers.

A quorum:

at least 8 members

Hearing in camera:

The Court will function in plenum or divided into two chambers.

A quorum:

at least 4 members

Constitutional Court Review

Preventive review:

The powers of the Constitutional Court are:

1. To exercise the control of constitutionality of the laws that interpret any provision of the Constitution, of the constitutional organic laws and of the norms of a treaty which are related to matters belonging to the latter, before their promulgation; (Article 93 of the Constitution)

[...]

3. To resolve questions of constitutionality that appear during the processing of bills law or of constitutional reform projects and of the treaties subject to congressional approval;

A posteriori review:

Abstract review:

The powers of the Constitutional Court are:

[...]

2. To resolve matters of constitutionality of agreed orders [autos acordados] issued by the Supreme Court, the Courts of Appeal and the Electoral Court;

[...]

4. To resolve questions that appear regarding the constitutionality of a decree with force of law;

[...]

6. To resolve, by the majority of its active members, the inapplicability of a legal rule, in the case that the application of the rule in any procedure to be followed before a regular or special court is contrary to the Constitution;

7. To resolve, by the majority of four-fifths of its active members, the unconstitutionality of a legal rule declared inapplicable in accordance with the provisions of the preceding paragraph;

8. To resolve complaints in the case that the President of the Republic does not promulgate a law when required to do so or enacts a different text than the one that is constitutionally appropriate;

9. To resolve on the constitutionality of a decree or order issued by the President of the Republic that the Office of the Comptroller General of the Republic has objected to [representado] because it deems it unconstitutional, when it is required by the President in accordance with Article 99 of the Constitution;

Other powers

Jurisdictional disputes:

The powers of the Constitutional Court are:

[...]

12. To resolve the jurisdictional disputes that arise between the political or administrative authorities and the courts of justice, which do not correspond to the Senate;

The unconstitutionality of acts and activities of political parties:

The powers of the Constitutional Court are:

[...]

10. To declare the unconstitutionality of organizations and movements or political parties, as well as the responsibility of persons who have been involved in the events that led to the declaration of unconstitutionality, in accordance with the provisions of the sixth, seventh and eighth paragraphs of number 15 Article 19 of this Constitution. However, if the person affected was to be the President of the Republic or the elected President, the aforementioned declaration will also require the agreement of the Senate adopted by the majority of its active members;

V. NATURE AND EFFECTS OF DECISIONS

Finality:

Against decisions of the Constitutional Court no recourse whatsoever will proceed; without prejudice that the Court itself may, in accordance to law, rectify the factual errors in which it could have incurred. The provisions that the Court declares unconstitutional may not become law in the bill or decree with force of law in question. (Article 94 of the Constitution)

VI PUBLICATION OF CONSTITUTIONAL COURT DECISIONS

The Official Gazette:

The Official Digest:

Legal Journals:

Electronic Publishing: X

SOURCES:

https://www.constituteproject.org/constitution/Chile_2015?lang=en

https://en.wikipedia.org/wiki/Constitutional_Court_of_Chile

https://en.wikipedia.org/wiki/Judiciary_of_Chile

http://www.tribunalconstitucional.cl/

(37)

DOSSIER OF THE STANDING COMMITTEE OF THE NATIONAL PEOPLE'S CONGRESS OF THE PEOPLE'S REPUBLIC OF CHINA

STATE: People's Republic of China
TITLE: Standing Committee of the National People's Congress
YEAR OF FOUNDATION: The NPC Standing Committee is the permanent body of the National People's Congress.
SEAT: Beijing

I. CHRONICLE

Date and context of establishment
Position in the hierarchy of courts
The National People's Congress of the People's Republic of China is the highest organ of state power. Its permanent body is the Standing Committee of the National People's Congress. (Article 57 of the Constitution)

II. STANDARD LEGAL REFERENCE

The Constitution of the People's Republic of China

III. COMPOSITION AND ORGANIZATION

The Standing Committee of the 12th NPC has 150 members.

Electoral/appointment body:
Election Based System:
National People's Congress

The term of office: 5 years

The National People's Congress exercises the following functions and powers:

To amend the Constitution;

To supervise the enforcement of the Constitution;

Constitutional Court Review

A posteriori review:

Abstract review:

The Standing Committee of the National People's Congress exercises the following functions and powers:

To interpret the Constitution and supervise its enforcemen

SOURCES:

https://www.constituteproject.org/constitution/China_2004?lang=en

https://en.wikipedia.org/wiki/Judicial_system_of_China

https://en.wikipedia.org/wiki/Standing_Committee_of_the_National_People%27s_Congress

http://www.npc.gov.cn/englishnpc/Organization/node_2846.htm

(38)

DOSSIER OF THE CONSTITUTIONAL COURT OF THE UNION OF THE COMOROS

STATE: Union of the Comors
TITLE: Constitutional Court
YEAR OF FOUNDATION: 1977 (Supreme Court)
SEAT: Moroni

I. CHRONICLE

Date and context of establishment:
The Comorian legal system rests on Islamic law and an inherited French legal code. Village elders or civilian courts settle most disputes. The judiciary is independent of the legislative and the executive. First judicial entity with powers to interpret constitution was the Supreme Court which has been introduced in 1977 Constitution. Subsequent amendments to the Constitution introduced the Constitutional Court of Comoros as the highest court in the hierarchy of Comoros judicial system.

Position in the hierarchy of courts:
Article 36 of the Constitution: The Constitutional Court shall rule on the constitutionality of the statutes of the Union and the islands. The Constitutional Court shall guarantee the distribution of powers between the Union and the islands. (...)

II. STANDARD LEGAL REFERENCE

The Comoros's Constitution of 2001 with Amendments through 2009

III. COMPOSITION AND ORGANIZATION

Composition

The number of judges:

Electoral/appointment body:

APPOINTMENT BASED SYSTEM (Without the Participation of a Representative Body):

Article 37 of the Constitution: The President of the Union, the Vice Presidents of the Union, the President of the Assembly of the Union, and the heads of the island executives shall each appoint one member to the Constitutional Court.

The Court members:

The term of office:

Article 38 of the Constitution: (...) They shall be appointed for a renewable six-year term. (...)

The Court President:

The term of office:

Article 38 of the Constitution: (...) The President of the Constitutional Court shall be designated by his peers for a term of six years, renewable once. (...)

The qualifications and the required professional experience of constitutional court judges:

Article 38 of the Constitution: The members of the Constitutional Court shall be persons of great morality and honesty and shall have recognized standing in legal, administrative, economic or social matters. They must be able to point to a professional experience of at least fifteen years. (...)

Incompatibilities:

Article 38 of the Constitution: (...) The functions of a member of the Constitutional Court shall be incompatible with the membership in the institutions of the Union or the islands, as well as with any public employment or professional activity.

Immunities:

Article 38 of the Constitution: (...) The members of the Constitutional Court shall be irremovable from office. They may not be prosecuted or arrested without authorization of the Court, except in the case of committing a crime or offense flagrante delicto. (...)

Constitutional Court Review:
Article 36 of the Constitution: (...) Finally, it shall guarantee the fundamental rights of the individual and public liberties. (...)

Preventive review:

Article 10 of the Constitution: Peace Treaties, Trade agreements, treaties or agreements relating to international organization, those committing the finances of the State, those modifying provisions which are the preserve of statute law, those relating to the status of persons, and those involving the ceding, exchanging or acquiring of territory, may be ratified or approved only by an Act of Parliament. They shall not take effect until such ratification or approval has been secured. If the Constitutional Court, upon referral by the President of the Union, by the President of the Assembly of the Union or by the Heads of the island executives has held that an international undertaking contains a clause contrary to the Constitution, authorization to ratify or approve the international undertaking involved may be given only after amending the Constitution. Treaties or agreements duly ratified or approved shall, upon publication, prevail over Acts of the Union or the islands, subject, with respect to each agreement or treaty, to its application by the other party.

A posteriori review:
Abstract review:
Yes

Other powers
Constitutional complaints:
Article 36 of the Constitution: (...) Every citizen may request a ruling a ruling of the Constitutional Court on the constitutionality of statutes, either directly or by way of objecting to the application of an allegedly unconstitutional statute before a court of the Union or of an island in a case involving him. The court shall stay the proceedings until the Constitutional Court has given its ruling, which it shall do within thirty days.

Jurisdictional disputes:
Article 36 of the Constitution: (...) It shall be competent to rule on the conflicts of jurisdiction between two or several institutions of the Union, between the Union and the islands, and among the islands themselves. (...)

Electoral matters and referendums:
Article 36 of the Constitution: "(...) It shall monitor the proper conduct of the electoral operations in the islands as well as at Union level, including referendums; it shall rule on electoral disputes. (...)

Other matters with which the Court is charged by the Constitution or statute:
Article 36 of the Constitution: (...) The Constitutional Court shall guarantee the distribution of powers between the Union and the islands. (...)

Standing before the Constitutional Court
State bodies: Yes.
Individuals: Yes.

V. NATURE AND EFFECTS OF DECISIONS

Finality and Binding force
Erga omnes:
Article 40 of the Constitution: (...) The decisions of the Constitutional Court shall not be subject to appeal. They shall be binding on all public authorities and courts in the territory of the Union.

Abrogation in whole or in part:
Article 40 of the Constitution: A provision which has been declared unconstitutional shall be void and shall cease to apply. (...)

SOURCES:

The Comoros's Constitution of 2001 with Amendments through 2009, https://www.constituteproject.org/constitution/Comoros_2009.pdf

(39)

DOSSIER OF THE CONSTITUTIONAL COURT OF THE REPUBLIC OF CONGO (BRAZZAVILLE)

STATE: Democratic Republic of Congo
TITLE: Constitutional Court
YEAR OF FOUNDATION: 20/1-2002
SEAT: Brazzaville

I. CHRONICLE

Date and context of establishment 2002
Position in the hierarchy of courts

II. STANDARD LEGAL REFERENCE

The Constitution of the Republic of Congo

III. COMPOSITION AND ORGANIZATION

Article 144 of the Constitution
A Constitutional Court is instituted.

Composition

The Constitutional Court includes nine members whose mandate is of nine years and renewable. It is renewed by thirds every three years.

The number of judges:
Electoral/appointment body:
APPOINTMENT BASED SYSTEM (Without the Participation of a Representative Body):
Three members of the Constitutional Court are appointed by the President of the Republic. The other members are appointed by the President of the Republic on the basis of two members

on a proposal from the President of each chamber of the Parliament and of two members on a proposal from the Bureau of the Supreme Court from among the members of that jurisdiction.

The Court President:

The President of the Constitutional Court is appointed by the President of the Republic from among its members. He has a preponderant voice in the case of equal division of the voices.

Incompatibilities:

Article 145 of the Constitution

The functions of member of the Constitutional Court are incompatible with those of member of the Government, of the Parliament or of the Supreme Court. The notable persons condemned for forfeiture, high treason, perjury, economic crimes, war crimes, genocide or for any other crime against humanity, may not be members of the Constitutional Court.

The other incompatibilities are established by the law.

Organisation:

Article 151 of the Constitution

An organic law determines the rules of organization, of composition and of the functioning of the Constitutional Court, the procedure to be followed and, notably, the time periods for referring a matter to it.

IV. POWERS

Constitutional Court Review

Article 146 of the Constitution

The Constitutional Court is given the charge of the control of the constitutionality of the laws, of the international treaties and agreements.

Other powers

Electoral matters:

Article 146 of the Constitution

The Constitutional Court is given the charge of the control of the constitutionality of the laws, of the international treaties and agreements.

It sees to the regularity of the election of the President of the Republic. It examines the claims and proclaims the results of the ballot.

Article 147 of the Constitution

With the exception of the local elections and the preparatory acts for the elections, the Constitutional Court, in the case of dispute, decides on the regularity of the legislative and senatorial elections.

It sees to the regularity of the operations of the referendum and proclaims the results.

The electoral law determines the jurisdiction competent to take cognizance of the disputes concerning the local elections and of the preparatory acts of the elections.

Referendums:

Other matters with which the Court is charged by the Constitution or statute:

Standing before the Constitutional Court

State bodies:

Article 148 of the Constitution

The Constitutional Court is referred to a matter by the President of the Republic, by the President of the National Assembly, by the President of the Senate or by a third of the members of each chamber of the Parliament.

The Constitutional Court is referred to a matter, for opinion of conformity, before the promulgation of the organic laws or the implementation of the Internal Regulations of each chamber of the Parliament.

In this case, the Constitutional Court decides within a time period of one month. However, on the express demand of the petitioner, this time period can be reduced to ten days, if there is urgency.

The referral to a matter of the Constitutional Court suspends the time period for the promulgation of the law or for the implementation of the Internal Regulations.

Individuals:

Article 149 of the Constitution

Any person can, either directly, or by the procedure of the plea of unconstitutionality invoked before a jurisdiction in a matter that concerns him, refer the Constitutional Court to a matter concerning the constitutionality of the laws.

In the case of a plea of unconstitutionality, the referred jurisdiction postpones its decision and grants the petitioner a time period of one month from the notification of the decision.

V. NATURE AND EFFECTS OF DECISIONS

Finality:

Article 150of the Constitution

A provision, declared unconstitutional, cannot be, promulgated or implemented. The decisions of the Constitutional Court are not susceptible to any recourse. They impose themselves on the public powers, on all the administrative, jurisdictional and individual authorities.

Binding force:

Article 150 of the Constitution

A provision, declared unconstitutional, cannot be, promulgated or implemented. The decisions of the Constitutional Court are not susceptible to any recourse. They impose themselves on the public powers, on all the administrative, jurisdictional and individual authorities.

SOURCES:

https://www.constituteproject.org/constitution/Congo_2001.pdf

(40)

DOSSIER OF THE COURT OF APPEAL OF COOK ISLANDS [JURISDICTION OF PRIVY COUNCIL OF THE UNITED KINGDOM]

STATE: Cook Islands
TITLE: Court of Appeal
YEAR OF FOUNDATION: 1965
SEAT: Avarua

I. CHRONICLE

Date and context of establishment 1981

In 1965 the Cook Islands became self-governing in free association with New Zealand, adopting its own Constitution and developing its own government. The free association agreement with New Zealand has meant that the Cook Islands Government has had full executivepowers to make its own laws, whilst Cook Islanders have been able to retain New Zealand citizenship.

Position in the hierarchy of courts

The Constitution establishes a *Court of record, to be called the High Court of the Cook Islands, for the administration ofjustice throughout those islands* (Article 47(1) of the Constitution). The High Court has Civil, Criminal and Land Divisions (Article 47(2) of the Constitution), with jurisdiction to: *hear and determine ...[s]uch proceedings as are, under or by virtue of any enactment, to be heard and determined by that Division [and s]uch other proceedings as may from time to time be determined by the Chief Justice, either generally or in any particular proceedings or classes of proceedings* (Article 48(1) of the Constitution).

II. STANDARD LEGAL REFERENCE

The Constitution of 1965, amendment 1981

III. COMPOSITION AND ORGANIZATION

The Chief Justice of the High Court is appointed by the Queen's Representative, *acting on the advice of the Executive Council tendered by the Prime Minister*, other Judges, *by the Queen's Representative, acting on the advice of the Executive Council tendered by the Chief Justice of the High Court and the Minister of Justice* (Article 52 of the Constitution).

IV. POWERS

Constitutional Court Review

Because of the costs involved and the shortage of requisite human and other resources in the Cook Islands at the time, the Constitution in 1965 recognised a right of appeal from the High Court of the Cook Islands to the Court of Appeal of New Zealand. By the early 1980s, however, the domestic resource situation had improved and Constitution Amendment (No 9) Act 1980-81 did away with the initial arrangement. Established was a Court of Appeal of the Cook Islands as a *superior Court of record* (Article 56(1) of the Constitution). Article 59 of the Constitution provides that *the determination of the Court of Appeal shall be final, and there shall be no appeal to the High Court of New Zealand or to the Court of Appeal of New Zealand from any judgment of the Court of Appeal of the Cook Islands. [However, t]here shall be a right of appeal to Her Majesty the Queen in Council, with the leave of the Court of Appeal, or, if such leave is refused, with the leave of Her Majesty the Queen in Council, from judgments of the Court of Appeal in such cases and subject to such conditions as are prescribed by Act*.

PRIVY COUNCIL

the case involves a substantive question of law as to the interpretation or effect of the Constitution of Cook Islands;.............

COURT OF APPEAL

- has jurisdiction to hear appeals from the High Court as of right where:_
- the High Court certifies that a substantive question of law is involved; ....
- may also determine a question of law by way of case stated, either on pplication by a party or the High Court's own motion

SOURCES:

http://www.paclii.org/ck/courts.html

(41)

DOSSIER OF THE SUPREME COURT OF JUSTICE OF THE REPUBLIC OF COSTA RICA

STATE: Republic of Costa Rica
TITLE: The Supreme Court of Justice
YEAR OF FOUNDATION: 1825
SEAT: San José

I. CHRONICLE

Date and context of establishment:
In 1871 a new constitution has been written. It established that the Judicial Power of Costa Rica would be operated by the Supreme Court of Justice and other courts that the law established.

Position in the hierarchy of courts:
Article 152 of the Constitution: "The judicial power is exercised by the Supreme Court of Justice and by the other tribunals that the law establishes."

Article 156 of the Constitution: "The Supreme Court of Justice is the superior tribunal of the Judicial Power, and the tribunals, functionaries and employees in the judicial branch [ramo] are dependent of it, without prejudice to that provided by this Constitution concerning [the] civil service."

II. STANDARD LEGAL REFERENCE

The Constitution of Costa Rica of 1949 with Amendments through 2011

Composition

The number of judges:

The Supreme Court has 22 proprietary magistrates, 25 substitute magistrates in three first chambers and 12 substitute magistrates in the Constitutional Chamber. They are distributed of the following way: five in each one of the three Chambers of Annulment and seven in the Constitutional Chamber.

Electoral/appointment body:

Election Based System:

They are nominated by the Legislative Assembly of Costa Rica every eight years.

Article 158 of the Constitution: (...) by the votes of the two-thirds part of the totality of the members of the Legislative Assembly. In the performance of their functions, they must act with efficiency and will be considered re-elected for equal periods, unless the contrary is agreed in a vote of no less than the two-thirds part of the totality of the members of the Legislative Assemble. The vacancies will be filled for complete periods of eight years.

The Court members:

The term of office:

Article 158 of the Constitution: The Magistrates of the Supreme Court of Justice will be elected for a period of eight years (...)

The qualifications and the required professional experience of constitutional court judges:

Article 159 of the Constitution: [The following] is required to be [a] Magistrate: 1. To be [a] Costa Rican by birth, [or] by naturalization, with domicile in the country for no less than ten years after obtaining the respective letter. Nevertheless, the President of the Supreme Court of Justice must be Costa Rican by birth;

2. To be a citizen in exercise;
3. To belong to the secular status;
4. To be older than thirty-five years of age;
5. To posses a degree of lawyer, issued or legally recognized in Costa Rica, and to have exercised the profession for ten years at least, unless it concerns judicial functionaries with judicial practice of no less than five years. The Magistrates must, before entering into possession of the office, render the guarantee that the law establishes.

Incompatibilities:

Article 160 od the Constitution: Whoever is bound by kinship within the third degree of consanguinity or affinity inclusive, to a member of the Supreme Court of Justice[,] may not be elected as a Magistrate.

Immunities:

Article 165 of the Constitution: The Magistrates of the Supreme Court of Justice may not be suspended except by declaration that there should be the formation of [a] cause or for the motives that the law expresses in the chapter corresponding to the disciplinary regime. In this last case, the agreement has to be taken by the Supreme Court of Justice, in [a] secret vote of no less than two-thirds of the total of its members.

IV. POWERS

Constitutional Court Review

Preventive review:

Article 10 of the Constitution: (...) b. To take cognizance of the consultations on bills of constitutional reform, of approval of international agreements or treaties and of other bills of law, as provided in the law.

Article 128 of the Constitution: If the veto is founded on reasons of unconstitutionality not accepted by the Legislative Assembly, it will send the legislative decree to the Chamber indicated in Article 10, for it to resolve the dispute within the following thirty calendar days from the date on which it receives the file [expediente]. The provisions declared unconstitutional will be considered rejected and the others will be sent to the Legislative Assembly for the corresponding proceedings. The same will be done with the bill of law approved by the Legislative Assembly, when the Chamber declares that it does not contain unconstitutional provisions.

A posteriori review:

Abstract review:

Article 10 of the Constitution: It will correspond to a specialized Chamber of the Supreme Court of Justice to declare, by absolute majority of its members, the unconstitutionality of the norms of any nature and of the acts subject to the Public Law. (...)

Concrete review:

Other powers

Jurisdictional disputes:

Article 10 of the Constitution: (...) a. To settle the conflicts of competence between the powers of the State, the Supreme Tribunal of Elections included, as well as with the other entities or organs that the law indicates. (...)

Other matters with which the Court is charged by the Constitution or statute:

Article 167 of the Constitution: For the discussion and approval of bills of law that refer to the organization or functioning of the Judicial Power, the Legislative Assembly must consult [with] the Supreme Court of Justice; to divert from the criteria of this, the vote of the two-thirds part of the total of the members of the Assembly will be required.

SOURCES:

The Constitution of Costa Rica of 1949 with Amendments through 2011

DOSSIER OF THE CONSTITUTIONAL COUNCIL OF THE REPUBLIC OF CÔTE D'IVOIRE

STATE: Republic of Cote d'Ivoire
TITLE: Constitutional Council
YEAR OF FOUNDATION: 1995
SEAT: Abidjan

I. CHRONICLE

Date and context of establishment:
The Constitutional Council of Ivory Coast is a judicial body in the government of Ivory Coast that is patterned after the Constitutional Council of France. The Council was created by law in 1994 and began its operations in 1995. There were three Constitutions in the history of Ivory Coast. The Constitution currently in force was approved by referendum on October 30, 2016 and officially adopted on November 8, 2016. The referendum was also approved by the Constitutional Council.[30]

Position in the hierarchy of courts:
Article 126 of the Constitution: The Constitutional Council is a constitutional court. It is independent and impartial. The Constitutional Council is the regulating body of the functioning of government. The Constitutional Council shall determine the compliance of the law as a constitutional principle. The Constitutional Council is judicial review of presidential and parliamentary elections.

Article 138 of the Constitution: Constitutional Council's decisions are not subject to appeal. They are binding on public authorities to any administrative authority, judicial, military and any natural or legal person.

30 Ivory Coast court validates referendum on new constitution, https://www.reuters.com/ Article/us-ivorycoast-referendum/ivory-coast-court-validates-referendum-on-new-constitution-idUSKBN12Z2NC.

II. STANDARD LEGAL REFERENCE

The Constitution of Côte d'Ivoire, the third constitution of November 8, 2016

III. COMPOSITION AND ORGANIZATION

Composition
The number of judges: 8.
Article 128 of the Constitution: The Constitutional Council consists of: • a President; • former Presidents of the Republic, except express waiver of their hand; • six councilors, (...)

Electoral/appointment body:
Article 128 of the Constitution: (...) three appointed by the President of the Republic, two by the President of the National Assembly and the President of the Senate. (...)

The Court members:
The term of office:
Article 128 of the Constitution: (...) The Constitutional Council is renewed by half every three years.
Article 130 of the Constitution: The Councilors are appointed for a term of six years non renewable by the President of the Republic from among persons of recognized competence and expertise proven in legal or administrative matters. Before taking office, they take an oath on the Constitution before the President of the Constitutional Council, saying: I am committed to fully and faithfully discharge my duties, to exercise independently and impartially in compliance of the Constitution, to keep secret the deliberations and votes, even after the termination of my functions, to take no public position on legal, political, economic or social, to any consultation privately on issues within the jurisdiction of the constitutional Council. The first Constitutional Council include:

- three members, two appointed by the Presidents of the Assembly National and Senate, appointed for three years by the President of the Republic;
- three members including one nominated by the President of the National Assembly, appointed for six years by the President of the Republic.

The Court President:
The term of office:
6 years.

Article 129 of the Constitution: The President of the Constitutional Council is appointed by the President of the Republic for a term of six years non renewable among the personalities known for their competence and expertise proven in legal or administrative matters. Before taking office, an oath on the Constitution before the President of the Republic, in these words: I am committed to fully and faithfully discharge my duties, to exercise independently and impartially in accordance with the Constitution, to keep secret the deliberations and votes, even after the termination of my functions, take no public position on legal, political, economic or social, to any consultation privately on matters within the jurisdiction of the constitutional Council.

The qualifications and the required professional experience of constitutional court judges:

Article 129 of the Constitution: The President of the Constitutional Council is appointed by the President of the Republic for a term of six years non renewable among the personalities known for their competence and expertise proven in legal or administrative matters. (...)

Article 130 of the Constitution: The Councilors are appointed for a term of six years non renewable by the President of the Republic from among persons of recognized competence and expertise proven in legal or administrative matters. (...)

Incompatibilities:

Article 131 of the Constitution: The member of the Constitutional Council are incompatible with the exercise of any political function, any public employment or elected office and of any professional activity. Is removed from any member of the Constitutional Council office located in one of the cases of incompatibility. In case of death, resignation or absolute impediment for any reason whatsoever, the President and councilors are replaced within a period of eight days for the term of office still to run.

Immunities:

Article 132 of the Constitution: No member of the Constitutional Council may not, during his term of office, be prosecuted, arrested, detained or tried in a criminal or correctional matter without the authorization of the Council, except in cases of flagrante delicto.

IV. POWERS

Constitutional Court Review:

Article 126 of the Constitution: The Constitutional Council is a constitutional court. It is independent and impartial. The Constitutional Council is the regulating body of the functioning of government. The Constitutional Council shall determine the compliance of the law as a constitutional principle. The Constitutional Council is judicial review of presidential and parliamentary elections.

Preventive review:

Article 72 of the Constitution: Draft laws and ordinances may be submitted by the President of the Republic to the Constitutional Council before being examined by the Council of Ministers. The draft decrees may be submitted by the President of the Republic to the Council of State for an opinion before being examined by the Council of Ministers.

Article 113 of the Constitution: Laws may, before their promulgation, be referred to the Constitutional Council by the President of the Republic, President of the National Assembly or the President of the Senate or at least one tenth of the deputies or senators or by the parliamentary groups. The associations defending human rights legally constituted may also refer to the Constitutional Council, before their promulgation, laws relating to public freedoms. The laws relating to public freedoms are, before their promulgation, transmitted to the organization responsible for the defense of human rights. The referral to the Constitutional Council shall suspend the time limit for promulgation. The Constitutional Council shall within fifteen days of referral.

Article 120 of the Constitution: Peace treaties, treaties or agreements relating to the creation of international organizations, those that modify the internal laws of the State may be ratified only after a law. The enabling legislation for the ratification is subject to the Constitutional Council.

Article 122 of the Constitution: If the Constitutional Council, the President of the Republic, the Speaker of the National Assembly or the Senate or at least one tenth of the deputies or senators, said that a treaty or an international agreement contains a clause contrary to the Constitution, authorization to ratify it may only occur after the revision of the Constitution.

Article 134 of the Constitution: International commitments under Article 120 before ratification, constitutional laws passed through parliament, organic laws before their promulgation, rules of parliamentary assemblies before their application should be referred to the Constitutional Council, which rules on their compliance with the Constitution. The referral to the Constitutional Council suspends the period of enactment or enforcement.

A posteriori review:

Abstract review and Concrete review:

Article 133 of the Constitution: On notification by the President of the Republic, projects or bills can be submitted for review to the Constitutional Council. Upon notification by the President of the National Assembly or the President of the Senate, projects or bills can be submitted for review to the Constitutional Council.

Other powers

Constitutional complaints:

Article 135 of the Constitution: Any litigant may, by way of exception, raise the unconstitutionality of a law before any court. The court before which the challenge to the law is raised stays proceedings and shall specify the litigant within fifteen days to appeal to the Constitutional Council. At the end of that period, if the applicant does not report evidence of referral to the Council, the court ignores.

Charges against the President of the Republic:

Article 62 of the Constitution: In the event of the vacancy of the Presidency of the Republic by death, resignation or absolute impediment of the President of the Republic, the Vice-President of the Republic becomes, as of right, President of the Republic. Before taking office, he takes the oath before the Constitutional Council, meeting in solemn audience. The functions of the new President of the Republic cease at the end of the current presidential term. The absolute impediment of the President of the Republic for incapacity to exercise his functions shall be immediately established by the Constitutional Council, which shall be seized for this purpose by a motion of the Government approved by a majority of its members. In the event of the death, resignation or absolute incapacity of the Vice-President of the Republic, the President of the Republic shall appoint a new Vice-President after the Constitutional Council has verified his eligibility. The Vice-President of the Republic shall take the oath, under the conditions laid down by law, before the Constitutional Council, meeting in solemn audience. In the event of the death, resignation or absolute incapacity of the Vice-President of the Republic, when the vacancy of the Presidency of the Republic arises, the functions of President of the Republic shall be exercised by the Prime Minister. It may not make use of Articles 70, 75 (1) and 177 of the Constitution.

Article 166 of the Constitution: The Ombudsman is appointed by the President of the Republic for a term of six years non renewable, after consulting the President of the National Assembly and the President of the Senate. In case of death, resignation or absolute impediment noted by the Constitutional Council, the President of the Republic, he shall be replaced, within eight days.

Electoral matters and referendums:

Article 51 of the Constitution: The people exercise their sovereignty through the referendum and by their elected representatives. The conditions for the referendum as well as the procedure for the election of the President of the Republic and the members of Parliament are determined by the Constitution and specified by an organic law. The Independent Commission responsible for organizing the referendum, the presidential, legislative and local elections, under the conditions provided for by law, is an independent administrative authority. A law determines its powers, its mode of organization and functioning. The Constitutional Council reviews the regularity of the operations of the referendum, the election of the President of the Republic and members of Parliament.

Article 127 of the Constitution: The Constitutional Council rules on: • the eligibility of candidates for the presidential election. The Council Constitutional adopts and publishes the final list of candidates for the presidential election two weeks before the first round of voting, after the Independent Commission of Elections has verified records of the various candidates and published the provisional list of candidates;

- the eligibility of candidates for parliamentary elections. The list final nominations for the election of deputies and senators is prepared and published by the Independent Commission on Elections;
- disputes relating to the election of the President of the Republic, deputies and senators;
- disqualification of MPs and senators.

The Constitutional Council announces the final results of the presidential election. It controls the regularity of referendums and proclaim the results.

Other matters with which the Court is charged by the Constitution or statute:

Article 57 of the Constitution: If before the first ballot one of the candidates from a list of candidates selected by the Constitutional Council is prevented or dies, the Constitutional Council may defer the election within seventy-two hours, starting from referral by the Independent Electoral Commission. In the event of the death or absolute impediment of the candidate for the presidency of the Republic from one of the two lists of candidates leading at the end of the first round, the President of the Independent Electoral Commission shall immediately refer the matter to the Council Constitutional Court, which decides, within seventy-two hours of its referral, to postpone the election. In both cases, the election of the President of the Republic and the Vice President of the Republic shall be held within a period not exceeding thirty days from the decision of the Constitutional Council.

Article 58 of the Constitution: After the final proclamation of the results by the Constitutional Council, the elected President of the Republic takes an oath on the Constitution before the Constitutional Council, meeting in solemn audience. The Vice-President of the Republic shall attend the swearing-in ceremony. The swearing-in of the elected President of the Republic shall take place on the second Monday of December in the fifth year of office of the current President of the Republic. During this public ceremony, he receives the attributes of his function and delivers on this occasion a message to the Nation.

Article 179 of the Constitution: The President of the Republic in office at the date of the promulgation of this Constitution shall appoint the Vice-President of the Republic, after verification of his eligibility by the Constitutional Council. The President of the Republic shall terminate his functions. The Vice-President of the Republic named oath, as provided by law, to the Constitutional Council, meeting in solemn audience.

Standing before the Constitutional Court
State bodies: Yes.
Individuals: Yes.

V. NATURE AND EFFECTS OF DECISIONS

Finality and Binding force:
Erga omnes:
Article 137 of the Constitution: In case of referral to the Constitutional Council by action, law or provision declared unconstitutional may not be promulgated or implemented. Law or otherwise to the Constitution is void with regard to all. In case of referral to the Constitutional Council by way of exception, the decision of the Constitutional Council are binding on all, beyond the parties to the trial. Law or provision declared unconstitutional by the Constitutional Council is repealed.

Article 138 of the Constitution: Constitutional Council's decisions are not subject to appeal. They are binding on public authorities to any administrative authority, judicial, military and any natural or legal person.

SOURCES:

The Constitution of Côte d'Ivoire, the third constitution of November 8, 2016
Ivory Coast court validates referendum on new constitution, https://www.reuters.com/ Article/us-ivorycoast-referendum/ivory-coast-court-validates-referendum-on-new-constitution-idUSKBN12Z2NC

DOSSIER OF THE CONSTITUTIONAL COURT OF THE REPUBLIC OF CROATIA

STATE: Republic of Croatia
TITLE: Constitutional Court
YEAR OF FOUNDATION: 1963 (reonstruction 1990)
SEAT: Zagreb

I. CHRONICLE

Date and context of establishment:
The first multi-party elections in Croatia were held on 22 and 23 April 1990, at a time when Croatia was still a federal unit (republic) within the former SFRY. At that time the Constitution of SR Croatia from 1974 and its amendments were still in force. The first multi-party Parliament of SR Croatia (with three chambers) was constituted on 30 May 1990. On 29 June 1990, the new multi-party Croatian Parliament, at a sitting of all the three chambers, passed the Decision to Commence Discussion on Changing the Constitution of the Socialist Republic of Croatia, on the grounds that the provisions expressing ideological single-mindedness should be removed from the Constitution of SR Croatia and should be replaced by constitutional provisions that will adequately express the democratic, multi-party and republican form of state organisation (...) . On 25 July 1990, the Parliament passed the decision to enact the Constitution of the Republic of Croatia at a sitting of all the three chambers. On the same day the Decision on Proclaiming Amendments LXIV to LXXV of the Constitution of the Socialist Republic of Croatia was also passed. Amendment LXIV provided that the word socialist would be deleted before the words Republic of Croatia in the title of the Constitution and in its provisions, so that from 25 July 1990 the national parliament has been called the Parliament of the Republic of Croatia. On 25 July 1990, the earlier name of the Constitutional Court of the Socialist Republic of Croatia was changed to the Constitutional Court of the Republic of Croatia. On 22 December 1990, the Parliament of the Republic of Croatia passed a new Constitution of the Republic of Croatia, which - with revisions and amendments - is still in force.[31]

31 Creating the Republic of Croatia and establishing the constitutional court of the Republic of Croatia, https://www.usud.hr/en/history-and-development-croatian-constitutional-judicature.

Position in the hierarchy of courts:
Article 5 of the Constitution: In the Republic of Croatia, laws shall comply with the Constitution. Other regulations shall comply with the Constitution and law. All persons shall be obliged to abide by the Constitution and law and respect the legal order of the Republic of Croatia.

II. STANDARD LEGAL REFERENCE

The Constitution of Republic of Croatia, Narodne novine, No. 56 of 22 December 1990. The revisions and amendments of the Constitution of the Republic of Croatia were published in Narodne novine, Nos. 135/97 (8/98 - consolidated wording), 113/2000 (124/2000 - consolidated wording) and 28/2001 (41/2001 - consolidated wording, 55/2001 - correction) and the Amendments to the Constitution of the Republic of Croatia published in Narodne novine, no. 76/2010, in which the date of their entry into force is indicated.

The Constitutional Act on the Constitutional Court of the Republic of Croatia, consolidated text, Official Gazette No. 49/02 of May 3, 2002

III. COMPOSITION AND ORGANIZATION

Composition
The number of judges: 13.
Article 122 of the Constitution: The Constitutional Court of the Republic of Croatia shall consist of thirteen judges (...)

Electoral/appointment body:
Election Based System:
Article 122 of the Constitution: (...) elected by a two-thirds majority of the deputies of the Croatian Parliament (...) The committee of the Croatian Parliament in charge of constitutional issues shall conduct the procedure for the nomination and proposal of candidates for justices of the Constitutional Court of the Republic of Croatia to the Croatian Parliament. (...)

The Court members:
The term of office:
8 years.

Article 122 of the Constitution: (...) The term of office of a Constitutional Court justice shall be eight years, to be extended, in exceptional cases up to six months, where upon expiry of an incumbent's term of office a new justice has not been elected or has not assumed office. (...)

Court President:

The term of office:

4 years.

Article 122 of the Constitution: (...) The Constitutional Court of the Republic of Croatia shall elect its Chief Justice for a term of four years. (...)

The qualifications and the required professional experience of constitutional court judges:

Article 122 of the Constitution: (...) elected by a two-thirds majority of the deputies of the Croatian Parliament from among notable jurists, especially judges, public prosecutors, attorneys and university law professors pursuant to the procedure and method set forth by a constitutional act. (...)

Incompatibilities:

Article 123 of the Constitution: The justices of the Constitutional Court of the Republic of Croatia may not perform any other public nor professional duty. (...)

Immunities:

Article 123 of the Constitution: (...) The justices of the Constitutional Court of the Republic of Croatia shall enjoy same immunity as members of the Croatian Parliament.

Release from office prior to the expiration of the term:

Article 124 of the Constitution: A justice of the Constitutional Court of the Republic of Croatia may be relieved of office prior to the expiry of the term for which he has been elected at his/her own request, if he/she is sentenced to imprisonment, or if he/she is permanently incapacitated from the performance of duties, which is to be ascertained by the Court itself.

IV. POWERS

Constitutional Court Review

Preventive review:

Article 89 of the Constitution: Laws shall be promulgated by the President of the Republic within eight days from the date of their enactment by the Croatian Parliament. If the President of the Republic holds that a promulgated law does not conform with the Constitution, he/she may institute proceedings to review the constitutionality of such law before the Constitutional Court of the Republic of Croatia.

A posteriori review:

Abstract review:

Article 125 of the Constitution: The Constitutional Court of the Republic of Croatia: – shall decide upon the compliance of laws with the Constitution,

– shall decide upon the compliance of other regulations with the Constitution and laws, – may decide on the constitutionality of laws and the constitutionality and legality of other regulations which are no longer valid, provided that less than one year has elapsed from the moment of such cessation until the filing of a request or a proposal to institute proceedings, (...)

– shall monitor compliance with the Constitution and laws and shall report to the Croatian Parliament on detected violations thereof, (...)

Article 126 of the Constitution: "The Constitutional Court of the Republic of Croatia shall repeal a law if it finds it to be unconstitutional. The Constitutional Court of the Republic of Croatia shall repeal or annul any other regulation if it finds it to be unconstitutional or illegal. In the cases specified in Article 125, paragraph (1), sub-paragraph 3 of the Constitution, if the Constitutional Court of the Republic of Croatia finds that a law is non-compliant with the Constitution and law or that another regulation is non-compliant with the Constitution and law, it shall hand down a decision pronouncing non-compliance with the Constitution or law.

Other powers

Constitutional complaints:

Article 125 of the Constitution: The Constitutional Court of the Republic of Croatia: (...) – shall decide on constitutional petitions against individual decisions taken by governmental agencies, bodies of local and regional self-government and legal persons vested with public authority where such decisions violate human rights and fundamental freedoms, as well as the right to local and regional self-government guaranteed by the Constitution of the Republic of Croatia, (...)

urisdictional disputes:

Article 125 of the Constitution: The Constitutional Court of the Republic of Croatia: (...) – shall decide upon jurisdictional disputes between the legislative, executive and judicial branches, (...)

The unconstitutionality of acts and activities of political parties:

Article 6 of the Constitution: The right to establish political parties shall be unrestricted. The internal structure of political parties shall comply with fundamental constitutional democratic principles. Political parties shall publicly disclose the sources of their finances and assets. Political parties which, in their platforms or by violent action, intend to undermine the free democratic order or threaten the existence of the Republic of Croatia shall be deemed unconstitutional. The Constitutional Court of the Republic of Croatia shall decide on such unconstitutionality. The status and financing of political parties shall be regulated by law.

Article 125 of the Constitution: The Constitutional Court of the Republic of Croatia: (...) – shall supervise compliance of the platforms and activities of political parties with the Constitution and may, in compliance with the Constitution, ban non-compliant parties, (...)

Charges against the President of the Republic:

Article 105 of the Constitution: The President of the Republic shall be impeachable for any violation of the Constitution that he/she has committed while discharging his/her duties. Proceedings for the impeachment of the President of the Republic may be instituted by the Croatian Parliament by a two-thirds majority vote of all deputies. The Constitutional Court of the Republic of Croatia shall decide on the impeachment of the President of the Republic by a two-third majority vote of all of its judges. The Constitutional Court shall make its decision on the impeachment of the President of the Republic within 30 days from the date on which it receives the proposal to impeach the President of the Republic for a violation of the Constitution. If the Constitutional Court of the Republic of Croatia sustains the impeachment, the President of the Republic shall be relieved of his/her duty by virtue of the Constitution.

Article 125 of the Constitution: The Constitutional Court of the Republic of Croatia: (...) – shall decide, in conformity with the Constitution, on the impeachment of the President of the Republic, (...)

Electoral matters and referendums:

Article 125 of the Constitution: "The Constitutional Court of the Republic of Croatia: (...) – shall monitor whether elections and referenda are conducted in compliance with the Constitution and laws and shall resolve electoral disputes falling outside the jurisdiction of the courts, (...)

Other matters with which the Court is charged by the Constitution or statute:

Article 97 of the Constitution: In case the President of the Republic is prevented from discharging his/her duties for a shorter period as a result of his/her absence, illness or use of annual leave, he/she may entrust the Speaker of the Croatian Parliament to discharge his/her duties on his/her behalf. The President of the Republic shall decide on the resumption of his/her duties.

In case the President of the Republic is prevented from discharging his/her duties for a longer period as a result of illness or incapacity and, in particular, if he/she is incapable of making the decision to entrust somebody to discharge his/her duties on a temporary basis, the Speaker of the Parliament shall assume the office of President pro tempore of the Republic pursuant to the decision of the Constitutional Court. The Constitutional Court shall decide thereon at the proposal of the Government.

In the event of the death of the President of the Republic, his/her resignation, which is to be tendered to the Chief Justice of the Constitutional Court of the Republic of Croatia and disclosed to the Speaker of the Croatian Parliament, or when the Constitutional Court finds any grounds for the termination of his/her term of office, the Speaker of the Croatian Parliament shall assume the office of President pro tempore of the Republic by virtue of the Constitution.

When the Speaker of the Croatian Parliament, acting as the President pro tempore of the Republic, makes a decision promulgating a law, such a decision shall be countersigned by the Prime Minister of the Republic of Croatia.

Elections for a new President of the Republic shall be held within 60 days from the date when the President pro tempore of the Republic assumed office under paragraph (3) of this Article.

Article 105a of the Constitution: The President of the Republic shall enjoy immunity. The President of the Republic shall not be detained nor shall any criminal prosecution be instigated against him/her without prior approval by the Constitutional Court. The President of the Republic may be detained without approval from the Constitutional Court only if he/she has been caught in the perpetration of a criminal offence carrying a sentence of imprisonment exceeding five years. In such a case, the governmental agency which has detained the President of the Republic shall forthwith notify the Chief Justice of the Constitutional Court thereof.

Article 120 of the Constitution: Judges shall have life tenure. A judge shall be relieved of office: – at his/her own request,

- if permanently incapacitated from performance of duties,
- if sentenced for a criminal offence making him/her unworthy of holding judicial office,
- if, in conformity with law, the National Judicial Council so decides due to the perpetration of grave infringement of discipline,
- when reaching seventy years of age.

A judge shall have the right to lodge an appeal against a decision relieving him/her of judicial duty with the Constitutional Court within 15 days after the date on which the decision has been served. The Constitutional Court shall rule on the appeal applying such procedure and being of such composition as determined by the Constitutional Act on the Constitutional Court of the Republic of Croatia.

A judge shall have the right to lodge an appeal against a decision by the National Judicial Council on disciplinary accountability with the Constitutional Court within 15 days after the date on which the decision has been served. The Constitutional Court shall decide on the appeal in the manner and by applying the procedure as determined by the Constitutional Act on the Constitutional Court of the Republic of Croatia.

In the cases specified in paragraphs (4) and (5) of this Article, the Constitutional Court shall rule within no more than 30 days from the day the appeal has been lodged. Such ruling of the Constitutional Court shall exclude the right to a constitutional petition.

A judge shall not be transferred against his/her will except in cases when the court is abolished or reorganized in compliance with law. A judge shall not hold an office or perform work defined by law as being incompatible with his/her judicial office.

Article 125a of the Constitution: Insofar as the Constitutional Court finds that a competent body charged with enacting a regulation needed for the application of the Constitution, law or other regulation has failed to do so, it shall notify the Government thereof, and shall notify the Croatian Parliament when the Government has been charged with enacting such regulation and failed to do so.

Standing before the Constitutional Court
State bodies: Yes.
Individuals: Yes.

V. NATURE AND EFFECTS OF DECISIONS

Finality and Binding force:
Erga omnes:
Article 126 of the Constitution: The Constitutional Court of the Republic of Croatia shall repeal a law if it finds it to be unconstitutional. The Constitutional Court of the Republic of Croatia shall repeal or annul any other regulation if it finds it to be unconstitutional or illegal. In the cases specified in Article 125, paragraph (1), sub-paragraph 3 of the Constitution, if the Constitutional Court of the Republic of Croatia finds that a law is non-compliant with the Constitution and law or that another regulation is non-compliant with the Constitution and law, it shall hand down a decision pronouncing non-compliance with the Constitution or law.

VI PUBLICATION OF CONSTITUTIONAL COURT DECISIONS

Electronic Publishing:
Yes. Official webpage of the Constitutional Court of the Republic of Croatia, https://www.usud.hr/en/case-law

SOURCES:

Creating the Republic of Croatia and establishing the constitutional court of the Republic of Croatia, https://www.usud.hr/en/history-and-development-croatian-constitutional-judicature.
The Constitution of Republic of Croatia, Narodne novine, No. 56 of 22 December 1990 as amended, https://www.usud.hr/sites/default/files/dokumenti/THE_CONSTITUTION_OF_THE_REPUBLIC_OF_CROATIA_-_consolidated_text.pdf

(44)

DOSSIER OF THE PEOPLE'S SUPREME COURT OF THE REPUBLIC OF CUBA

STATE: Republic of Cuba
TITLE: People´s Supreme Court (Sp. Tribunal Supremo Popular)
YEAR OF FOUNDATION: 1976
SEAT: Havana

I. CHRONICLE

Date and context of establishment:
Even before attaining its independence from Spain, Cuba had several constitutions either proposed or adopted by insurgents as governing documents for territory they controlled during their war against Spain. Cuba has had several constitutions since winning its independence. Between 1952 till 1976 parts of the Constitution were suspended and eventually the Constitution was completely abolished after the Cuban revolution. The current constitution was drafted in 1976 and has since been amended. Cuba is one of the few remaining Marxist–Leninist socialist states, where the role of the vanguard Communist Party is enshrined in the Constitution. Independent observers have accused the Cuban government of numerous human rights abuses, including arbitrary imprisonment.[32]

Position in the hierarchy of courts:
The People's Supreme Court (Tribunal Supremo Popular) is the highest body of judicial power in Cuba.

Article 75 of the Constitution: The National Assembly of People's Power is invested with the following powers: (...) q. keeping informed of, evaluating, and adopting pertinent decisions on the reports on the rendering of accounts submitted by the Council of State, the Council of Ministers, the People's Supreme Court, the Office of the Attorney General of the Republic and the Provincial Assemblies of People's Power; (...)

32 Cuban Memories: the Cuban Constitution of 1940, then and today. Cuban Heritage Collection. University of Miami Libraries, http://library.miami.edu/chc/2010/10/14/cuban-memories-the-cuban-constitution-of-1940-then-and-today/.
Haken Ted, Celaya Miriam, Castellanos Dimas, Cuba, ABC-CLIO, 2013, p. 100-103.

Article 90 of the Constitution: The Council of State is invested with the power to: (...)h. issue general instructions to the courts through the Council of Government of the People's Supreme Court; (...)

Article 120 of the Constitution: "The function of imparting justice emanates from the people, and is exercised in their name by the People's Supreme Tribunal and the other Tribunals that the law institutes. (...)

II. STANDARD LEGAL REFERENCE

The Constitution of the Republic of Cuba of 1967, amended 2002

III. COMPOSITION AND ORGANIZATION

Composition
The number of judges:
Electoral/appointment body:
Election Based System:
Article 75 of the Constitution: The National Assembly of People's Power is invested with the following powers: (...) m. electing the President, Vice President and other judges of the People's Supreme Court; (...)

The Court members: 43.
People's Supreme Court consists of court president, vice president, 41 professional justices, and an unknown number of lay judges.[33]

The term of office:
Professional judges elected by the National Assembly are not subject to a specific term; lay judges nominated by workplace collectives and neighborhood associations and elected by municipal or provincial assemblies; lay judges appointed for 5-year terms and serve up to 30 days per year.[34]

33 CIA, The World Factbook, https://www.cia.gov/library/publications/the-world-factbook/fields/2094.html

34 Ibid.

The qualifications and the required professional experience of constitutional court judges:

The requirements to be a judge include age, citizenship, and a requisite amount of legal experience that varies depending upon which court one is to serve on (10 years for Supreme Court; Five years for Provincial Courts; Two years for municipal courts.) Membership in the Cuban Communist Party is not required to be a judge. In 1988, 43% of the judges were not members of the Party.[35]

Incompatibilities:

Article 122 of the Constitution: Judges, in their function of imparting justice, are independent, and owe obedience solely to the law.

Release from office prior to the expiration of the term:

Article 126 of the Constitution: The power to recall judges is incumbent on the organ that elects them.

Organization

Administrative autonomy:

Article 121 of the Constitution: The tribunals constitute a system of State organs, structured with functional independence from any other, and subordinate hierarchically to the National Assembly of the People's Power and the Council of State. (...)

Special services:

Article 121 of the Constitution: The tribunals constitute a system of State organs, structured with functional independence from any other, and subordinate hierarchically to the National Assembly of the People's Power and the Council of State. The People's Supreme Tribunal exercises the maximum judicial authority, and its decisions in this respect are definitive. Through its Council of Government, it exercises legislative initiative and regulatory power; it makes decisions and issues rules for mandatory compliance by all tribunals and, based on the experience of the latter, issues instructions of a mandatory nature for the establishment of a uniform judicial practice in the interpretation and application of the law.

IV. POWERS

While Cuba's Supreme Court is the country's foremost judicial unit, it does not in fact constitute an independent branch of government, with the leverage and autonomy to act as a check

35 Judicial system of Cuba, https://en.wikipedia.org/wiki/Judicial_system_of_Cuba

on potential excess of the legislative and executive branches, or the 15-member Politburo of the Communist Party. Such "adversarial" relations among different branches of government are a threat to the overriding principle of national unity. In short, Cuban courts are not designed to limit the power of the government and protect individual right and liberties (del Aguila 1994: 165). Likewise, the formal separation of powers and the investing of legal, institutional pre-eminence to the National Assembly cannot hide the fact that it does not exercise de fact rule.[36]

Other matters with which the Court is charged by the Constitution or statute:

Article 88 of the Constitution: The proposal of laws is the responsibility of: (...) e. the People's Supreme Court, in matters related to the administration of justice; (...)

V. NATURE AND EFFECTS OF DECISIONS

Finality and Binding force:

Erga omnes:

Article 121 of the Constitution: (...) The People's Supreme Tribunal exercises the maximum judicial authority, and its decisions in this respect are definitive.

Through its Council of Government, it exercises legislative initiative and regulatory power; it makes decisions and issues rules for mandatory compliance by all tribunals and, based on the experience of the latter, issues instructions of a mandatory nature for the establishment of a uniform judicial practice in the interpretation and application of the law.

Article 123 of the Constitution: The sentences and other decisions of the tribunals, pronounced or enacted within the limits of their jurisdiction, must be obeyed and implemented by State agencies, economic and social institutions and citizens, by those directly affected and by those who do not have a direct interest in their implementation but have the duty to participate in it.

SOURCES:

The Constitution of the Republic of Cuba of 1967, amended 2002, https://www.constituteproject.org/constitution/Cuba_2002.pdf?lang=en

Haken Ted, Celaya Miriam, Castellanos Dimas, Cuba, ABC-CLIO, 2013, p. 100-103.

Judicial system of Cuba, https://en.wikipedia.org/wiki/Judicial_system_of_Cuba

CIA, The World Factbook, https://www.cia.gov/library/publications/the-world-factbook/fields/2094.html

36 Haken Ted, Celaya Miriam, Castellanos Dimas, Cuba, ABC-CLIO, 2013, p. 102.

(45)

DOSSIER OF THE SUPREME CONSTITUTIONAL COURT OF THE REPUBLIC OF CYPRUS

STATE: Republic of Cyprus
TITLE: The Supreme Constitutional Court
YEAR OF FOUNDATION: Constitution of Cyprus: 1960, rev. 2013
SEAT: Nicosia

I. CHRONICLE

Date and context of establishment:
The 1960 Constitution by which the Republic of Cyprus was established, provided for the existence of both a High Court as well as a Supreme Constitutional Court.[37]

Position in the hierarchy of courts:
The Supreme Court is the highest court in the Republic.[38]

II. STANDARD LEGAL REFERENCE

Constitution of Cyprus: 1960, rev. 2013

III. COMPOSITION AND ORGANIZATION

Composition
Electoral/appointment body:
Para. 2 Article 133 of the Constitution: The President and the other judges of the Supreme Constitutional Court shall be appointed jointly by the President and the Vice-President of the Republic: Provided that in the case of a vacancy solely in the post of either the Greek or the

37 http://www.supremecourt.gov.cy/judicial/sc.nsf/DMLfaq_en/DMLfaq_en?OpenDocument

38 http://www.supremecourt.gov.cy/judicial/sc.nsf/DMLSCourt_en/DMLSCourt_en?OpenDocument

Turkish judge the proposal of the President or the Vice-President of the Republic to whose Community the judge to be appointed shall belong shall prevail if the President and the Vice-President of the Republic do not agree on the appointment within a week of such proposal.

The Court members:

The term of office:

Para. 7.7 Article 133 of the Constitution:The Greek and the Turkish judge of the Court shall be permanent members of the judicial service of the Republic and shall hold office until they attain the age of sixty-eight.

The Court President:

The term of office:

Para. 6.1. Article 133 of the Constitution: six years.

IV. POWERS

Constitutional Court Review

A posteriori review:

Abstract review:

- Para. A Article 149 of the Constitution:To determine any conflict between the two texts of this Constitution by reference to the text of the draft of this Constitution signed at Nicosia on the 6th April, 1960, in the Joint Constitutional Commission together with the schedule of amendments thereto signed by representatives of the Kingdom of Greece, the Republic of Turkey and the Greek and Turkish Cypriot communities, due regard being had to the letter and spirit of the Zurich Agreement dated the 11th February, 1959, and of the London Agreement dated the 19th of February, 1959;
- Para. B Article 149 of the Constitution: To make, in case of ambiguity, any interpretation of this Constitution, due regard being had to the letter and spirit of the Zurich Agreement dated the 11th February, 1959, and of the London Agreement dated the 19th February, 1959.

Other powers

Charges against the Prime Minister or against any Minister of State:

- Article 139 of the Constitution: The Supreme Constitutional Court shall have jurisdiction to adjudicate finally on a recourse made in connexion with any matter relating to any conflict or contest of power or competence arising between the House of Representatives and the Communal Chambers or any one of them and between any organs of, or authorities in, the Republic.

Electoral matters:

- Para. 1 Article146 of the Constitution: The Supreme Constitutional Court shall have exclusive jurisdiction to adjudicate finally on any election petition, made under the provisions of the Electoral Law, with regard to the elections of the President or the Vice President of the Republic or of members of the House of Representatives or of any Communal Chamber.
- Article 85 of the Constitution: Any question with regard to the qualifications of candidates for election and election petitions shall be finally adjudicated by the Supreme Constitutional Court.

Other matters with which the Court is charged by the Constitution or statute:

Para. 3 Article 44 of the Constitution: The Supreme Constitutional Court shall decide on any question arising out of sub-paragraph (d) of paragraph I of this Article on a motion by the Attorney-General and the Deputy Attorney-General of the Republic upon a resolution of the Representatives belonging to the same Community as the President or the Vice-President of the Republic respectively, carried by a simple majority.

V. NATURE AND EFFECTS OF DECISIONS

Finality:

Article 136 of the Constitution: The Supreme Constitutional Court shall have exclusive jurisdiction to adjudicate finally on all matters as provided in the ensuing Articles.

SOURCES:

http://www.kypros.org/Constitution/English/

DOSSIER OF THE CONSTITUTIONAL COURT OF THE CZECH REPUBLIC

STATE: Czech Republic
TITLE: The Constitutional Court
YEAR OF FOUNDATION: Constitution of the Czech Republic: 1993, rev. 2013
SEAT: Brno[39]

I. CHRONICLE

Date and context of establishment:
Following the dissolution of the Czechoslovak federation, the existence of a constitutional court was also provided for in the Constitution of the independent Czech Republic, of 16 December 1992. The first Constitutional Court of the Czech Republic began its work on 15 July 1993.[40]

Position in the hierarchy of courts:
Article 92 of the Constitution: The Supreme Court is the highest judicial body in matters that fall within the jurisdiction of courts, with the exception of matters that come under the jurisdiction of the Constitutional Court or the Supreme Administrative Court.

III. COMPOSITION AND ORGANIZATION

Composition
The number of judges:
Para. 1 Article 84 of the Constitution: Fifteen judges.

Electoral/appointment body:
Para. 2 Article 84 of the Constitution: The Justices of the Constitutional Court shall be appointed by the President of the Republic with the consent of the Senate.

39 http://www.usoud.cz/en/history/

40 http://www.usoud.cz/en/history/

The Court members:
The term of office:
Para 1. Article 84 of the Constitution: Ten years.

The Court President:
The term of office:
Para. 1 Article 84 of the Constitution: Ten years.

Organization
Administrative autonomy:
The budget:
Para 2. Article 62 of the Constitutional Court Act: The costs of a proceeding arising from the taking of evidence before the Court and the costs of interpreting shall be charged to the budget of the Court. The Court shall pay the attorney's fees from its budget. The amounts paid as reimbursed expenses of such proceedings shall become revenue of the state budget.

IV. POWERS

Constitutional Court Review
Preventive review:
Para. 2 Article 87 of the Constitution: Prior to the ratification of a treaty under Article 10a or Article 49 of the Constitution, the Constitutional Court shall further have jurisdiction to decide concerning the treaty's conformity with the constitutional order. A treaty may not be ratified prior to the Constitutional Court giving judgment.

A posteriori review:

Abstract review:
Para. 1a Article 87 of the Constitution: The Constitutional Court has jurisdiction to annul statutes or individual provisions thereof if they are in conflicts with the constitutional order and to annul other legal enactments or individual provisions thereof if they are in conflict with the constitutional order, a statute.

Other powers
Constitutional complaints:
Para. 1c and 1d Article 87 of the Constitution: The Constitutional Courts has jurisdiction over constitutional complaints by the representative body of a self-governing region against an

unlawful encroachment by the state and over constitutional complaints against final decisions or other encroachments by public authorities infringing constitutionally guaranteed fundamental rights and basic freedoms;

Jurisdictional disputes:
Para. 1k Article 87 of the Constitution: The Constitutional Court has to decide jurisdictional disputes between state bodies and bodies of self-governing regions, unless that power is given by statute to another body.

The unconstitutionality of acts and activities of political parties:
Para. 1j Article 87 of the Constitution: The Constitutional Court has a jurisdiction to determine whether a decision to dissolve a political party or other decisions relating to the activities of a political party is in conformity with constitutional acts or other laws.

Charges against the President of the Republic:
Para. 1g Article 87 of the Constitution: The Constitutional Court has jurisdiction over a constitutional charge brought by the Senate against the President of the Republic.

Electoral matters:
Para. 1e Article 87 of the Constitution: The Constitutional Court has a jurisdiction over remedial actions from decisions concerning the certification of the election of a Deputy or Senator.

Other matters with which the Court is charged by the Constitution or statute:
Para. 1f and 1i Article 87 of the Constitution: The Constitutional Court has a jurisdiction to resolve doubts concerning a Deputy or Senator's loss of eligibility to hold office or the incompatibility under Article 25 of some other position or activity with holding the office of Deputy or Senator. The Constitutional Court also has a jurisdiction to decide on the measures necessary to implement a decision of an international tribunal which is binding on the Czech Republic, in the event that it cannot be otherwise implemented.

V. NATURE AND EFFECTS OF DECISIONS

Binding force:
Erga omnes:
Para. 2 Article 89 of the Constitution: Enforceable decisions of the Constitutional Court are binding on all authorities and persons.

Obligatory opinions on the conformity of international treaties with the Constitution:

Para. 2 Article 87 of the Constitution: Prior to the ratification of treaty under Article 10a or Article 49 of the Constitution, the Constitutional Court shall further have jurisdiction to decide concerning the treaty's conformity with the constitutional order. A treaty may not be ratified prior to the Constitutional Court giving judgment.

SOURCES:

http://www.usoud.cz/en/history/

https://www.constituteproject.org/constitution/Czech_Republic_2013?lang=en

(47)

DOSSIER OF THE CONSTITUTIONAL COURT OF THE DEMOCRATIC REPUBLIC OF CONGO (CONGO KINSHASA)

STATE: Democratic Republic of Congo
TITLE: Constitutional Court
YEAR OF FOUNDATION: 18/2-2006
SEAT: Kinshasa

I. CHRONICLE

Date and context of establishment 2006
Position in the hierarchy of courts
Article 157 of the Constitution
A Constitutional Court (*Cour Constitutionnelle*) is established.

II. STANDARD LEGAL REFERENCE

The Constitution of the Democratic Republic of Congo

III. COMPOSITION AND ORGANIZATION

Composition
The number of judges: 9
Electoral/appointment body:
Mixed Systems (Appointment and Election):
The Constitutional Court consists of nine members appointed by the President of the Republic; he appoints three of them on his own initiative, three who have been designated by the Parliament assembled as Congress and three designated by the High Council of the Judiciary.

The Court members:

The term of office:

The non-renewable term of office of the members of the Constitutional Court is nine years.

A third of the membership of the Constitutional Court is renewed every three years. However, on the occasion of each renewal, one member of each group will be determined by the drawing of lots.

The Court President:

The term of office:

The President of the Constitutional Court is elected by his peers for a term of three years, renewable once. He is invested by ordinance of the President of the Republic.

The qualifications and the required professional experience of constitutional court judges:

Article 159 of the Constitution

No one may be appointed as member of the Constitutional Court who

a) is not Congolese;

b) cannot show practical experience of fifteen years in the judicial or political sphere.

No one may be appointed as member of the Constitutional Court who

a) is not Congolese;

b) cannot show practical experience of fifteen years in the judicial or political sphere.

Article 158 of the Constitution: Two-thirds of the members of the Constitutional Court must be lawyers from the ranks of judges or prosecutors, from the Bar or from university education.

Incompatibilities:

Article 145 of the Constitution

IV. POWERS

Article 160 of the Constitution

The Constitutional Court is charged with the control of the constitutionality of laws and of measures having the force of law.

Constitutional Court Review

Preventive review:

Article 160 of the Constitution: Organic laws prior to their promulgation and the internal regulations of the parliamentary Chambers and of Congress, of the Independent National Electoral Commission as well as of the High Council for Audiovisual Media, prior to their application, have to be submitted to the Constitutional Court which rules on their conformity with the Constitution.

For the same purpose of examining their constitutionality, statutes may be referred to the Constitutional Court prior to their promulgation by the President of the Republic, the Prime Minister, the President of the National Assembly, the President of the Senate or a tenth of the Deputies or Senators.

The Constitutional Court must decide within the period of one month. However, in cases of urgency, this delay is reduced to eight days at the request of the Government.

A posteriori review:

Concrete review:

Article 162 of the Constitution

The Constitutional Court rules on the objection of unconstitutionality raised by or before a court.

Other powers

Jurisdictional disputes:

Article 160 of the Constitution

It examines conflicts of jurisdiction between the Executive Power and the Legislative Power as well as between the State and the Provinces.

It examines the appeals against the judgments of the Court of Cassation and the Council of State, but only insofar as they decide on the reference of the dispute to the general or the administrative jurisdiction. This appeal is only admissible if an objection of denial of jurisdiction has been raised by or before the Court of Cassation or the Council of State.

The details and the effects of the remedies referred to in the preceding paragraphs are determined by law.

Charges against the President of the Republic:

Article 163 of the Constitution

The Constitutional Court is the criminal court for the Head of the State and the Prime Minister in the cases and conditions provided by the Constitution.

Article 164 of the Constitution

The Constitutional Court is the criminal court for the President of the Republic and the Prime Minister with regard to the offenses of high treason, contempt of Parliament, failings in matters of honor and integrity as well as insider crimes and all the other common law offenses committed in the exercise or on the occasion of the exercise of their functions. It is equally competent to try their co-authors and accomplices.

Article 165 of the Constitution

Without prejudice to the other provisions of the Constitution, high treason is established if the President of the Republic has deliberately violated the Constitution or if he or the Prime Ministers are identified authors, co-authors or accomplices of grave and specific human rights violations, or of the transfer of a part of the national territory.

Failings in matters of honor and integrity are established particularly if the conduct of the President of the Republic or the Prime Minister is contrary to morality or if they are identified as authors, co-authors or accomplices of embezzlement of funds, corruption or unjustified enrichment.

An insider crime of the President of the Republic or the Prime Minister is established if they conduct commercial operations with regard to immovable assets or goods on which they possess privileged information that they use for their benefit before it is known by the public.

The insider crime covers the purchase and the selling of shares based on information which would never be disclosed to the shareholders.

Contempt of Parliament is established if the Prime Minister does not provide any response to questions asked by either of the Parliamentary Chambers concerning the activities of the Government within a time period of thirty days.

Article 166 of the Constitution

The decision to prosecute and the bringing of charges against the President of the Republic and the Prime Minister are voted by a two-thirds majority of the members of Parliament assembled as Congress in accordance with the procedure provided for by the internal regulations.

The decision to prosecute as well as the bringing of charges against members of the Government are voted by an absolute majority of the members of the National Assembly in accordance with the procedures provided for by the internal regulations.

The members of the Government against whom charges have been brought tender their resignation.

Article 167 of the Constitution

In case of a conviction, the President of the Republic and the Prime Minister are relieved of their functions. The termination of their functions is pronounced by the Constitutional Court.

With regard to the offenses committed outside the exercise of their functions, the prosecution of the President of the Republic and the Prime Minister is suspended until the end of their terms of office. During this period, the statute of limitations does not apply.

Electoral matters:

Article 160 of the Constitution

It settles disputes relating to the presidential and parliamentary elections as well as to referendums.

Standing before the Constitutional Court

State bodies:

Article 161 of the Constitution

The Constitutional Court examines the applications for interpretation of the Constitution upon request by the President of the Republic, the Government, the President of the Senate, the President of the National Assembly, a tenth of the members of each Parliamentary chamber, the provincial Governors and the Presidents of the Provincial Assemblies.

Individuals:

Article 162 of the Constitution

The Constitutional Court rules on the objection of unconstitutionality raised by or before a court.

Any individual may appeal to the Constitution Court for unconstitutionality of a statutory or regulatory measure.

In addition, he/she may appeal to the Constitutional Court by way of raising an objection of unconstitutionality in a matter affecting him/her before a court.

The former court suspends the proceedings and submits the matter to the Constitutional Court, by giving it preference over all its other work.

V. NATURE AND EFFECTS OF DECISIONS

Finality:

Article 168 of the Constitution

The judgments of the Constitutional Court cannot be appealed and are enforceable immediately.

Binding force:

Article 168 of the Constitution

The judgments of the Constitutional Court cannot be appealed and are enforceable immediately. They are binding and have to be observed by the public institutions, by all administrative, jurisdictional, civil and military authorities and by the individuals.

Any measure declared to be not in conformity with the Constitution is automatically void.

SOURCES:

http://www.constitutionnet.org/sites/default/files/DRC%20-%20Congo%20Constitution.pdf

DOSSIER OF THE SUPREME COURT[41] OF THE KINGDOM OF DENMARK

STATE: Kingdom of Denmark
TITLE: The Supreme Court
YEAR OF FOUNDATION: The Supreme Court 1661[42], the Constitution of the Kingdom of Denmark: 1953
SEAT: Copenhagen[43]

I. CHRONICLE

Date and context of establishment:
The Danish Supreme Court was set up by King Frederik the Third in 1661 in connection with the introduction of absolute monarchy.[44]

Position in the hierarchy of courts:
The highest instance in the Danish legal system is the Supreme Court.[45]

II. STANDARD LEGAL REFERENCE

Constitution of the Kingdom of Denmark: 1953

41 The Danish Supreme Court is not mentioned in its constitution.

42 http://www.supremecourt.dk/about/history/Pages/default.aspx

43 http://www.domstol.dk/om/otherlanguages/english/thedanishjudicialsystem/thesupremecourt/Pages/default.aspx

44 http://www.supremecourt.dk/about/history/Pages/default.aspx

45 http://www.domstol.dk/om/publikationer/HtmlPublikationer/Profil/Profilbrochure%20-%20UK/kap03.html

III. COMPOSITION AND ORGANIZATION

Composition

The number of judges:

Eighteen judges and one president.[46]

Electoral/appointment body:

They are appointed by the Minister of Justice on recommendation from the independent Judicial Appointments Council. The president is elected by and from among the justices and appointed by the Minister of Justice.[47]

IV. POWERS

Other matters with which the Court is charged by the Constitution or statute:

The Supreme Court is a court of appeal that reviews judgments and orders delivered by the High Court of Eastern Denmark, the High Court of Western.

SOURCES:

http://www.supremecourt.dk/about/history/Pages/default.aspx

http://www.domstol.dk/om/otherlanguages/english/thedanishjudicialsystem/thesupremecourt/Pages/default.aspx

http://www.domstol.dk/om/publikationer/HtmlPublikationer/Profil/Profilbrochure%20-%20UK/kap03.html

http://www.supremecourt.dk/about/history/Pages/default.aspx

46 http://www.supremecourt.dk/about/staff/Pages/default.aspx

47 http://www.supremecourt.dk/about/staff/Pages/default.aspx

(49)

DOSSIER OF THE CONSTITUTIONAL COUNCIL OF THE REPUBLIC OF DJIBOUTI

STATE: Republic of Djibouti
TITLE: The Constitutional Council
YEAR OF FOUNDATION: 1992
SEAT: Djibouti

I. CHRONICLE

Position in the hierarchy of courts:
Article 75 of the Constitution: The Constitutional Council sees to respect for the constitutional principles.

II. STANDARD LEGAL REFERENCE

The Constitution of the Republic of Djibouti: 1992, rev. 2010

III. COMPOSITION AND ORGANIZATION

Composition
The number of judges:
Article 76 of the Constitution: Six judges.

Electoral/appointment body:
Article 76 of the Constitution: They are designated as follows: two appointed by the President of the Republic; two appointed by the President of the National Assembly; two appointed by the Superior Council of the Magistrature. The President of the Constitutional Council is appointed by the President of the Republic from among its members.

The Court members:

The term of office:

Article 76 of the Constitution: Eight years.

The Court President:

The term of office:

Article 76 of the Constitution: Eight years.

IV. POWERS

Constitutional Court Review

Preventive review:

Article 66 of the Constitution: The laws to which Constitution confers the character of organic laws may only be adopted with the absolute majority of members of the National Assembly, and may only be promulgated after declaration by the Constitutional Council of their conformity with the Constitution.

A posteriori review:

Abstract review:

- Article 78 of the Constitution: The organic laws, before their promulgation, and the internal regulations of the National Assembly, before their implementation, must be submitted to the Constitutional Council which decides on their conformity with the Constitution.
- Article 79 of the Constitution: To the same end, the laws may be deferred to the Constitutional Council before their promulgation by the President of the Republic, the President of the National Assembly or ten Deputies.
- Article 35 of the Constitution: The President of the Republic refers the Constitutional Council to a matter when he deems that a law is contrary to this Constitution.

Other powers

Electoral matters:

- Article 77 of the Constitution: The Constitutional Council sees to the regularity of all the elections and proclaims the results of them. It examines the complaints and decides on them. The Constitutional Council is referred to the matter in case of dispute concerning the validity of an election by any candidate or any political party.
- Article 47 of the Constitution: The Constitutional Council decides in case of dispute concerning the regularity of the election of the Deputies and concerning their eligibility.

- Article 27 of the Constitution: If, in the seven days preceding the deadline of deposit of the candidatures, one of the persons having, less than thirty days before this date, publicly announced their decision to be a candidate, dies or is found to be incapacitated, the Constitutional Council can decide to postpone the election. If, before the first round, one of the candidates dies or is found to be incapacitated, the Constitutional Council orders the postponement of the election. In the case of death or of incapacity of one of the two candidates most favored in the first round, before any eventual withdrawals, or that of one of the two candidates remaining following any such withdrawals, the Constitutional Council can decide on the repetition of the whole of the electoral operations.

Referendums:

- Article 77 of the Constitution: The Constitutional Council sees to the regularity of the operations of referendum and proclaims the results of them. It examines the complaints and decides on them.
- Article 33 of the Constitution: The President of the Republic can, after consultation of the President of the National Assembly and of the President of the Constitutional Council, submit any Bill of law to referendum.

Other matters with which the Court is charged by the Constitution or statute:

- Article 79 of the Constitution: The referral to the matter of the Constitutional Council by the President of the Republic must intervene within the six days following the transmission that is made to him of the law definitively adopted; the referral to the matter by the President of the National Assembly or the Deputies must intervene within the time of six days from the definitive adoption of the law.
- Article 75 of the Constitution: It controls the constitutionality of the laws. It guarantees the fundamental rights of the human person and the public freedoms. It is the regulatory organ of the functioning of the institutions and of the activity of the public powers.
- Article 29 of the Constitution: In case of vacancy of the Presidency of the Republic, for any cause that may be, or of definitive incapacity determined by the Constitutional Council, referred to the matter by the Prime Minister or by the President of the National Assembly, the interim is assured by the President of the Supreme Court, who may not be a candidate for the Presidency during the interim.
- Article 57 of the Constitution: The texts of legislative form intervening in these matters can be modified by decree if the Constitutional Council, at the demand of the President of the Republic, declares that they have a regulatory character by virtue of the preceding paragraph.
- Artcile 59 of the Constitution: The proposals, Bills and amendments which are not of the domain of the law are irreceivable. The irreceivability is declared by the President of the National Assembly after the deliberation of the Bureau. In case of dispute, the Constitutional Council,

referred to the matter by the President of the National Assembly or the President of the Republic decides in a time of twenty days.

V. NATURE AND EFFECTS OF DECISIONS

Finality:
Article 81 of the Constitution: The decisions of the Constitutional Council are not susceptible to any recourse.

Binding force:
Erga omnes:
Article 81 of the Constitution: The decisions of the Constitutional Council establish authority concerning the matter judged.

SOURCES:
https://www.constituteproject.org/constitution/Djibouti_2010?lang=en

(50)

DOSSIER OF THE EASTERN CARIBBEAN SUPREME COURT OF THE COMMONWEALTH OF DOMINICA

STATE: Commenwealth of Dominica
TITLE: The Eastern Caribbean Supreme Court[48]
YEAR OF FOUNDATION: The Eastern Caribbean Supreme Court: 1967[49],
the Constitution of the Commonwealth of Dominica: 1978, rev. 1984
SEAT: Santa Lucia[50]

I. CHRONICLE

Date and context of establishment:
In 1967, the Organization of Eastern Caribbean States – namely Antigua, Anguilla, Dominica, Grenada, Saint Vincent, Saint Kitts & Nevis, and Saint Lucia – joined in a new "status of association" with the United Kingdom, in accordance with the West Indies Act of 1967. The Act provided for Her Majesty by Order in Council to establish common courts for the Associated States with "such jurisdiction and powers as may be so specified or determined." The West Indies Associated States Supreme Court Order duly followed and gave effect to Section 6 of the West Indies Act, permitting the establishment of common courts for the Associated States – "West Indies Associated States Supreme Court[51]".

II. STANDARD LEGAL REFERENCE

Constitution of the Commonwealth of Dominica: 1978, rev. 1984

48 Commonwealth of Dominica is a part of the Eastern Caribbean Supreme Court. (https://www.eccourts.org/structure-of-the-court/)

49 https://www.eccourts.org/brief-history-of-the-court/

50 https://www.eccourts.org/brief-history-of-the-court/

51 https://www.eccourts.org/brief-history-of-the-court/

Composition

The number of judges:

The Eastern Caribbean Supreme Court consists of two divisions, a Court of Appeal and a High Court of Justice. The Court of Appeal judges are based at the Court's Headquarters in Castries, Saint Lucia where administrative and legal support is provided under the supervision of the Court Administrator and Chief Registrar respectively.

The High Court Judges are each assigned to, and reside in, the various Member States. The High Court Registry is headed by a legally trained Registrar who coordinates the provision of the necessary administrative and legal support for the functioning of the High Court. The Eastern Caribbean Supreme Court is composed of the Chief Justice, who is the Head of the Judiciary, four (4) Justices of Appeal, nineteen (19) High Court Judges; and three (3) Masters.[52]

SOURCES:

https://www.eccourts.org/brief-history-of-the-court/

https://www.eccourts.org/structure-of-the-court/

52 https://www.eccourts.org/structure-of-the-court/

(51)

DOSSIER OF THE CONSTITUTIONAL COURT OF THE DOMINICAN REPUBLIC

STATE: Dominican Republic
TITLE: Constitutional Court
YEAR OF FOUNDATION: 2015
SEAT: Santo Domingo

I. CHRONICLE

Position in the hierarchy of courts:
Article 184 of the Constitution: There shall be a Constitutional Court to guarantee the supremacy of the Constitution, the defense of the constitutional order and the protection of fundamental rights.

II. STANDARD LEGAL REFERENCE

The Constitution of the Dominican Republic: 2015

III. COMPOSITION AND ORGANIZATION

Composition
The number of judges:
Article 186 of the Constitution: Thirteen members.

The Court members:
The term of office:
Article 187 of the Constitution: Nine years.

The Court President:

The term of office:

Article 187 of the Constitution: Nine years.

Organization

Administrative autonomy:

Article 184 of the Constitution: The Constitutional Court shall enjoy administrative autonomy.

The budget:

Article 184 of the Constitution: The Constitutional Court shall enjoy budgetary autonomy.

IV. POWERS

Constitutional Court Review

Preventive review:

Para. 2 Article 185 of the Constitution: The preventative control of international treaties before their ratification by the legislative organ.

A posteriori review:

Abstract review:

Para. 1 Article 185 of the Constitution: Direct actions of unconstitutionality against the laws, decrees, rules, resolutions and ordinances at the instance of the President of the Republic, of one third of the members of the Senate or of the Chamber of Deputies and any person with legitimate and juridically protected interest.

Other powers

Other matters with which the Court is charged by the Constitution or statute:

Para. 3 Article 185 of the Constitution: Conflicts of responsibility between the public powers at the instance of one of their heads.

Para. 4 Article 185 of the Constitution: Any other matter that the law provides.

V. NATURE AND EFFECTS OF DECISIONS

Binding force:

Erga omnes:

Article 184 of the Constitution: Its decisions are definitive and irrevocable and constitute binding precedents for the public powers and all the organs of the State.

SOURCES:

https://www.constituteproject.org/constitution/Dominican_Republic_2015?lang=en

(52)

DOSSIER OF THE CONSTITUTIONAL COURT OF THE REPUBLIC OF ECUADOR

STATE: The Republic of Ecuador
TITLE: Constitutional Court
YEAR OF FOUNDATION: 2008
SEAT: Quito

I. CHRONICLE

Position in the hierarchy of courts:
Article 429 of the Constitution: Constitutional Court is the supreme body for controlling, constitutionally interpreting and administering justice in this matter.

II. STANDARD LEGAL REFERENCE

Constitution of the Republic of Ecuador: 2008, rev. 2015

III. COMPOSITION AND ORGANIZATION

Composition
The number of judges:
Article 432 of the Constitution: Nine judges.

Electoral/appointment body:
Article 434 of the Constitution: The members of the Constitutional Court shall be designated by a qualification commission comprised of two persons appointed by each one of the following branches of government: the legislative, the executive, and transparency and social monitoring. Members shall be elected from among the candidates submitted by the above-mentioned

branches of government, through a public examination process, with citizen oversight and option for challenging the process.

The Court members:

The term of office:

Article 432 of the Constitution: Nine years.

The Court President:

The term of office:

Article 432 of the Constitution: Three years.

Organization

Administrative autonomy:

Article 430 of the Constitution: The Constitutional Court shall enjoy administrative autonomy.

The budget:

Article 430 of the Constitution: The Constitutional Court shall enjoy financial autonomy.

IV. POWERS

Constitutional Court Review

Preventive review:

Para. 1 Article 438 of the Constitution: The Constitutional Court shall issue a prior and binding ruling of constitutionality of the International treaties, prior to their ratification by the National Assembly. Article 245 of the Constitution: The proposed bylaws shall be submitted to the Constitutional Court to rule whether they violate or not the Constitution. The respective ruling shall be issued within a maximum of forty-five (45) days; should it not be issued within this period, the ruling shall be taken as favorable. Following the favorable ruling from the Constitutional Court and the passing of the bill for the organic law, the inhabitants of the provinces comprising the potential region shall be called to vote in a referendum to take position on the regional bylaws.

- Para. 3 Article 438 of the Constitution: The Constitutional Court shall issue a prior and binding ruling of constitutionality in the following cases, in addition to those stipulated by the law: Objections of unconstitutionality presented by the President of the Republic in the processing of drafting laws.

A posteriori review:

Abstract review:

- Para. 2 Article 436 of the Constitution: To hear and resolve public claims of unconstitutionality, based either on substantive or procedural grounds, filed against general regulatory acts issued by authorities of the State. The declaration of unconstitutionality shall lead to invalidation of the challenged regulatory act.
- Para. 3 Article 436 of the Constitution: To declare, by virtue of its office, unconstitutional those norms that are related, when in those cases submitted to its examination it concludes that one or various of them are contrary to the Constitution.
- Para. 4 Article 436 of the Constitution: To hear and resolve, at the request of a party, claims of unconstitutionality against general administrative acts issued by all public authorities. The declaration of unconstitutionality shall lead to the invalidity of the challenged administrative act.
- Para. 5 Article 436 of the Constitution: To hear and resolve, at the request of the party, claims of noncompliance that are filed to guarantee enforcement of general administrative regulations or acts, regardless of their nature or hierarchy, as well for enforcement of rulings or reports from international organizations for the protection of human rights that are not enforceable through regular judiciary channels.
- Para. 8 Article 436 of the Constitution: To ensure, by virtue of its office and immediately, monitoring of the constitutionality of the declarations of state of emergency, when this involves the suspension of constitutional rights.
- Para. 9 Article 436 of the Constitution: To hear and sanction failure to comply constitutional rulings and decisions.

Other powers

Jurisdictional disputes:

Para. 7 Article 436 of the Constitution: To arbitrate conflicts of jurisdictions or attributions among the branches of government or bodies established by the Constitution.

The unconstitutionality of acts and activities of political parties:

Para. 10 Article 436 of the Constitution: To declare the unconstitutionality incurred by State institutions or public authorities that fail to observe, either totally or partially, the mandates contained in constitutional norms, within the time-limits set by the Constitution or within the time-limits deemed to be reasonable by the Constitutional Court. If this failure persists, after this time-limit has elapsed, the Court shall provisionally issue the regulation or enforce the observance, in accordance with the law.

Referendums:

Para. 2 Article 438 of the Constitution: The Constitutional Court shall issue a prior and binding ruling of constitutionality to those stipulated by the law regarding the calls to referendums nationwide or of decentralized autonomous governments.

Other matters with which the Court is charged by the Constitution or statute:

- Para. 6 Article 436 of the Constitution: To issue judgments that constitute binding case law with respect to actions of protection, enforcement, habeas corpus, habeas data, access to public information and other constitutional processes, as well as those cases selected by the Court for review.
- Para. 5 Article 86 of the Constitution: All final judgments shall be referred to the Constitutional Court for their development in case law.
- Article 94 of the Constitution: The special proceedings for protection shall be admissible against those rulings or definitive judgments where there has been a violation, by deed or omission, of the rights enshrined in the Constitution, and they shall be filed with the Constitutional Court. This appeal shall be admissible when regular and special appeals have been exhausted within the legal framework, unless the failure to file these resources was not attributable to the negligence of the person bearing the constitutional right that was infringed.

Standing before the Constitutional Court

Individuals:

Article 437 of the Constitution: Citizens individually or collectively shall be entitled to file a special petition for protection against judgments, final writs or resolutions that have the force of sentencing.

V. NATURE AND EFFECTS OF DECISIONS

Finality:

Article 400 of the Constitution: The rulings and decisions by the Constitutional Court shall be final and without recourse to appeal.

SOURCES:

https://www.constituteproject.org/constitution/Ecuador_2015?lang=en

https://www.corteconstitucional.gob.ec/

(53)

DOSSIER OF THE SUPREME CONSTITUTIONAL COURT OF THE ARAB REPUBLIC OF EGYPT

STATE: Arab Republic of Egypt
TITLE: The Supreme Constitutional Court
YEAR OF FOUNDATION: 1979[53],
SEAT: Article 191 of the Constitution: It is based in Cairo. If necessary, it may convene anywhere else in the country with the approval of the Court's General Assembly.

I. CHRONICLE

Position in the hierarchy of courts:
Article 192 of the Constitution: The Supreme Constitutional Court is exclusively competent to decide on the constitutionality of laws and regulations, interpret legislative texts, and adjudicate in disputes pertaining to the affairs of its members, in disputes between judicial bodies and entities that have judicial mandate, in disputes pertaining to the implementation of two final contradictory rulings, one of which is issued by any judicial body or an agency with judicial mandate and the other issued by another body, and in disputes pertaining to the implementation of its rulings and decisions.

II. STANDARD LEGAL REFERENCE

Constitution of the Arab Republic of Egypt: 2014

53 http://www.sis.gov.eg/En/Templates/ Articles/tmp Articles.aspx?CatID=250#

III. COMPOSITION AND ORGANIZATION

Composition

The number of judges:

Article 193 of the Constitution: The Court is made up of a president and a sufficient number of deputies to the president.

Electoral/appointment body:

Article 193 of the Constitution: The General Assembly chooses the Court's President from among the most senior three vice-presidents of the court. It also chooses the vice-presidents and the members of its Commissioners Authority, who are appointed by a decree from the President of the Republic.

Organization

The budget:

Article 185 of the Constitution: It has an independent budget whose items are all discussed by the House of Representatives. After it is approved, it is incorporated in the state budget as a single figure.

IV. POWERS

Constitutional Court Review

A posteriori review:

Abstract review:

Article 192 of the Constitution: To decide on the constitutionality of law and regulations.

Other powers

Charges against the President of the Republic:

Para. 2 Article 159 of the Constitution: The President of the Republic is tried before a special court headed by the president of the Supreme Judicial Council, and with the membership of the most senior deputy of the president of the Supreme Constitutional Court, the most senior deputy of the president of the State Council, and the two most senior presidents of the Court of Appeals; the prosecution to be carried out before such court by the Prosecutor General. If an impediment exists for any of the foregoing individuals, they are replaced by order of seniority. The court verdicts are irrevocable and not subject to challenge.

Other matters with which the Court is charged by the Constitution or statute:

- Article 185 of the Constitution: The President of the Republic may submit his resignation to the House of Representatives. If the House is dissolved, he submits it to the General Assembly of the Supreme Constitutional Court.
- Article 192 of the Constitution: The Supreme Constitutional Court is exclusively competent to adjudicate in disputes pertaining to the affairs of its members, in disputes between judicial bodies and entities that have judicial mandate, in disputes pertaining to the implementation of two final contradictory rulings, one of which is issued by any judicial body or an agency with judicial mandate and the other issued by another body, and in disputes pertaining to the implementation of its rulings and decisions and to interpret legislative texts.

SOURCES:

http://www.sis.gov.eg/En/Templates/ Articles/tmp Articles.aspx?CatID=250#

https://www.constituteproject.org/constitution/Egypt_2014?lang=en

(54)

DOSSIER OF THE SUPREME COURT OF JUSTICE OF THE REPUBLIC OF EL SALVADOR

STATE: Republic of El Salvador
TITLE: The Supreme Court of Justice
YEAR OF FOUNDATION: 1983
SEAT: San Salvador[54]

I. CHRONICLE

Position in the hierarchy of courts:
Article 21 of the Constitution: The Supreme Court of Justice will always have the authority to determine, within its competence, if a law is or is not of public order (Sala de lo Constitucional).

II. STANDARD LEGAL REFERENCE

Constitution of the Republic of El Salvador: 1983, rev. 2014

III. COMPOSITION AND ORGANIZATION

Composition
Electoral/appointment body:
Article 173 of the Constitution: The Supreme Court of Justice shall be made up of the number of Magistrates determined by the law, who will be elected by the Legislative Assembly, and one of them shall be the President. He shall be the President of the Judicial Organ.

54 http://www.csj.gob.sv/idioma.html

Constitutional Court Review

Preventive review:

- Article 138 of the Constitution: When a bill of law is returned because the President of the Republic considers it to be unconstitutional and the Legislative Organ ratifies it in the manner established in the preceding Article, the President of the Republic shall present it to the Supreme Court of Justice within three business days, so that the latter may, after hearing the arguments of both sides, decide whether it is or is not constitutional, within fifteen business days at the latest. If the Court decides that the bill is constitutional, the President of the Republic shall be obligated to sanction it and to order its publication as law.

A posteriori review:

Abstract review:

- Para. 2 Article 21 of the Constitution: The Supreme Court of Justice will always have the authority to determine, within its competence, if a law is or is not of public order.

Other powers

Jurisdictional disputes:

Para. 2 Article 182 of the Constitution: To settle competitions that arise among the tribunals of any jurisdiction (fuero) or nature.

Charges against the Prime Minister or against any Minister of State:

Para. 6 Article 182 of the Constitution: To take cognizance of the responsibility of public functionaries in those cases indicated by the laws.

Other matters with which the Court is charged by the Constitution or statute:

- Para. 2 Article 182 of the Constitution: To take cognizance of prize cases (causas de presa), and of those not reserved to another authority; to order the issuance of letters or commissions rogatory created to perform proceedings outside the Republic and to demand compliance with those proceeding from other countries, without prejudice to the provisions of existing treaties; and to grant extradition;
- Para. 4 Article 182 of the Constitution: to grant, according to the law and when necessary, permission for the execution of sentences pronounced by foreign courts;
- Para. 5 Article 182 of the Constitution: To see that justice is promptly and faithfully administered, for which it shall adopt the measures it deems necessary; Para. 7 Article 182: To hear cases of suspension or loss of the rights of citizenship in the cases included in numbers 2 and

4 of Article 74, and in numbers 1, 3, 4, and 5 of Article 75 of this Constitution, as well as of the corresponding rehabilitation;

- Para. 8 Article 182: To issue reports and opinions on applications for pardon and change of punishment;
- Para. 9 Article 182 of the Constitution: To appoint Magistrates of the Chambers of Second Instance, Judges of First Instance, and Justices of Peace from the lists of three candidates (ternas) proposed by the National Council of the Judicature; as well as Forensic Physicians and the employees of their dependent offices; to remove them, to recognize their resignations, and to grant them leave;
- Para. 10 Article 182 of the Constitution: To appoint associate justices in those cases provided by the law;
- Para. 11 Article 182 of the Constitution: To receive, personally or through functionaries it designates, the constitutional oath of office of the functionaries appointed by it;
- Para. 12 Article 182 of the Constitution: To admit lawyers and authorize them to practice their profession; to suspend them for nonfulfillment of professional obligations, for grave negligence or ignorance, unethical professional conduct, or for notoriously immoral private conduct; to disqualify them for venality, bribery, fraud, deceit, and others, and to reinstate them for legal reasons. In cases of suspension and disqualification it shall proceed in the manner prescribed by law and render decisions only on the moral force of the evidence. The same powers shall be exercised with respect to notaries;
- Para. 13 Article 182 of the Constitution: to prepare the budget bill for salaries and expenditures in the administration of justice and send it to the Executive Organ for inclusion, without modifications, in the bill for the General Budget of the State. The Legislative Assembly shall consult with the Supreme Court of Justice for the budgetary adjustments that it may deem necessary to this proposed budget.

Other forms of human rights protection:

Para 1. Article 182 of the Constitution: To hear cases on amparo.

SOURCES:

- http://www.csj.gob.sv/idioma.html
- https://www.constituteproject.org/constitution/El_Salvador_2014?lang=en

(55)

DOSSIER OF THE CONSTITUTIONAL COURT OF THE REPUBLIC OF EQUATORIAL GUINEA

STATE: Republic of Equatorial Guinea
TITLE: The Constitutional Court
YEAR OF FOUNDATION: 2010
SEAT:Malabo

I. CHRONICLE

Position in the hierarchy of courts:
Article 93 of the Constitution: The Constitutional Court is the competent jurisdiction in constitutional, [and] electoral matters and in [matters] of the fundamental rights and freedoms.

II. STANDARD LEGAL REFERENCE

Constitution of the Republic of Equatorial Guinea: 2010

III. COMPOSITION AND ORGANIZATION

Composition
The number of judges:
Article 100 of the Constitution: Nine judges.

Electoral/appointment body:
Article 101 of the Constitution: The President of the Constitutional Court is elected by his peers

The Court members:
The term of office:
Article 101 of the Constitution: Nine years.

The Court President:

The term of office:

Article 101 of the Constitution: Nine years.

IV. POWERS

Constitutional Court Review

Preventive review:

- Article 80 of the Constitution: Within the eight clear [francs] days that follow the adoption of a law, the President of the Republic, at least one-tenth of the Deputies or the Independent National Institution for Human Rights, may refer the Constitutional Court to [the matter] of a recourse looking to [visant] have it control the conformity of the law with the Constitution. The time period for promulgation is then suspended. The Constitutional Court decides within the thirty days that follow its referral or if the President of the Republic so demands, within eight days. The Order [Arrêt] of the Constitutional Court is published in the Journal Officiel [Official Gazette]. A provision of a law declared non-conforming with the Constitution may not be promulgated or applied. The Order of the Constitutional Court imposes itself on all. The time period for promulgation runs counting from the publication of the Order of the Constitutional Court which declares the law conforming to the Constitution.
- Article 94 of the Constitution: The Constitutional Court decides on the constitutionality of the laws before their promulgation.

Posteriori review

- Article 94 of the Constitution: The Constitutional Court decides on: the Internal Regulations of the National Assembly, of the Economic and Social Council, of the High Authority of Communication, of the Independent National Electoral Commission, of the National Institution of Human Rights, of the Mediator of the Republic, [and] of the High Council of the Local Collectivities regarding their conformity to the Constitution.
- Article 93 of the Constitution: It judges the constitutionality of the laws, [and] of the ordinances as well as the conformity of the international treaties and agreements to the Constitution.

Concrete review:

Article 94 of the Constitution: The Constitutional Court decides on the exception [pleadings] of unconstitutionality raised before the jurisdictions.

Other powers

Jurisdictional disputes:

- Article 94 of the Constitution: The Constitutional Court decides on the conflicts of attributions between the constitutional organs.

Charges against the President of the Republic:

Article 94 of the Constitution:The Constitutional Court decides on the recourses formed against the acts of the President of the Republic taken in application of Articles 2, 45, 74 and 90 of the Constitution, as well as the recourses formed against the Ordinances taken in application of Article 82 of the Constitution, under reserve of their ratification.

Electoral matters:

- Article 94 of the Constitution: The Constitutional Court decides on Court the electoral disputes of the national elections. It sees to the regularity of the national elections and of the referendums of which [dont] it proclaims the definitive results.
- Article 30 of the Constitution: In the case of death or of definitive incapacity declared by the Constitutional Court of a candidate figuring on the list specified in Article 29 of the Constitution, the Constitutional Court decides, if there is need, to reopen the time periods during which new candidatures can be deposited. In this case a new date of the ballot is established within the conditions specified in Article 28 of the Constitution.
- Article 32 of the Constitution: The Constitutional Court sees to the regularity of the electoral campaign and to the equality of the candidates for the utilization of the means of propaganda, within the conditions determined by an organic law.
- Article 33 of the Constitution: If no objection [contestetion] relative to the regularity of the electoral operations has been presented by one of the candidates to the Greffe of the Constitutional Court within the eight days that follow the day when the first global totalization has been rendered public, the Constitutional Court proclaims the President of the Republic elected. In the case of dispute [contestation], the Constitutional Court decides within the three days that follow its referral [to the matter]. Its order carries [emporte] proclamation or annulment of the election.
- Article 34 of the Constitution: In the case of death or of definitive incapacity of one of the candidates to the second round, before the proclamation of the definitive results, if the deceased candidate is he who obtained the greater number of votes, the Constitutional Court decides on the reprise of the whole [ensemble] of the electoral operations. In the case of death, of definitive

incapacity or of withdrawal of one of the two candidates arriving ahead between the ballot of the first round and the provisional proclamation of the results, or between this provisional proclamation and the definitive proclamation of the results of the first round by the Constitutional Court, the candidate following in the order of the votes is admitted to present himself to the second round.

- Article 51 of the Constitution: Before convoking the electors by decree, the President of the Republic obtains the opinion [avis] of the Constitutional Court on the conformity of the bill or the proposal of law to the Constitution.
- Article 62 of the Constitution: The Constitutional Court sees to the regularity of the ballot and of the electoral campaign that precedes it. It receives and judges the eventual challenges [contestations].

Referendums:

Article 51 of the Constitution: The Constitutional Court sees to the regularity of the operations of the referendum.

Other matters with which the Court is charged by the Constitution or statute:

- Article 39 of the Constitution: During his mandate, the President of the Republic may not, by himself, by a member of his family and even by others, purchase or lease an asset that belongs to the domain of the State, without the authorization of the Constitutional Court within the conditions established by the law.
- Article 41 of the Constitution: The vacancy of the function of President of the Republic consecutive to death, to resignation, or to any other cause of definitive incapacity is declared by the Constitutional Court.
- Article 90 of the Constitution: The state of siege, as the state of urgency, is decreed by the President of the Republic, after the opinion [après avis] of the President of the National Assembly and of the President of the Constitutional Court. These opinions are published in the Journal Officiel [Official Gazette].

SOURCES:

https://www.constituteproject.org/constitution/Guinea_2010?lang=en

(56)

DOSSIER OF THE SUPREME COURT OF THE STATE OF ERITREA

STATE: The State of Eritrea
TITLE: The Supreme Court
YEAR OF FOUNDATION: 1997
SEAT: Asmara

I. CHRONICLE

Position in the hierarchy of courts:
Article 49 of the Constitution: The Supreme Court shall be the court of last resort.

II. STANDARD LEGAL REFERENCE

Constitution of the State of Eritrea: 1997

III. COMPOSITION AND ORGANIZATION

Composition
The number of judges and the term of office:
Para. 4 Article 49 of the Constitution: The tenure and number of justices of the Supreme Court shall be determined by law.

Constitutional Court Review

A posteriori review:

Abstract review:

Para. 2a Article 49 of the Constitution:The Supreme Court has a sole jurisdiction of interpreting this Constitution and the constitutionality of any law enacted or any action taken by government.

Other powers

Charges against the President of the Republic:

Para. 2a Article 49 of the Constitution: The Supreme Court has a sole jurisdiction of hearing and adjudicating upon charges against a President who has been impeached by the National Assembly pursuant to the provisions of Article 41(6) a) and b).

Other matters with which the Court is charged by the Constitution or statute:

Para. 2c Article 49 of the Constitution: The Supreme Court has the power of hearing and adjudicating cases appealed from lower courts pursuant to law.

SOURCES:

https://www.constituteproject.org/constitution/Eritrea_1997?lang=en

(57)

DOSSIER OF THE SUPREME COURT OF THE REPUBLIC OF ESTONIA

STATE: Republic of Estonia
TITLE: Supreme Court of Estonia
YEAR OF FOUNDATION: 1992
SEAT: Tartu[55]

I. CHRONICLE

Date and context of establishment:
The foundations for the restoration of the activities of the Supreme Court were laid by the Constitution of the Republic of Estonia, adopted by a referendum on 28 June 1992. The Constitution vested with the Supreme Court the functions of a court of cassation and of a court of constitutional review.[56]

Position in the hierarchy of courts:
Article 149 of the Constitution: The Supreme Court is the highest court in Estonia and shall review court judgements by way of cassation proceedings. The Supreme Court is also the court of constitutional review.

II. STANDARD LEGAL REFERENCE

The Constitution of the Republic of Estonia: 1992, rev. 2011

55 http://www.nc.ee/?id=181

56 http://www.nc.ee/?id=181

III. COMPOSITION AND ORGANIZATION

Composition

Electoral/appointment body:

Article 150 of the Constitution: The Chief Justice of the Supreme Court shall be appointed to office by the Riigikogu, on the proposal of the President of the Republic. Justices of the Supreme Court shall be appointed to office by the Riigikogu, on the proposal of the Chief Justice of the Supreme Court.

IV. POWERS

Constitutional Court Review

Preventive review:

Article 107 of the Constitution: The President of the Republic may refuse to proclaim a law passed by the Riigikogu and, within fourteen days after its receipt, return the law, together with his or her reasoned resolution, to the Riigikogu for a new debate and decision. If the Riigikogu again passes the law which is returned to it by the President of the Republic, unamended, the President of the Republic shall proclaim the law or shall propose to the Supreme Court to declare the law unconstitutional. If the Supreme Court declares the law constitutional, the President of the Republic shall proclaim the law.

A posteriori review:

Abstract review:

- Article 152 of the Constitution: The Supreme Court shall declare invalid any law or other legislation that is in conflict with the provisions and spirit of the Constitution.
- Article 142 of the Constitution: If the legislation is not brought into conformity with the Constitution or the law within twenty days, the Chancellor of Justice shall propose to the Supreme Court to declare the legislation invalid.

Other powers

Electoral matters:

Article 83 of the Constitution: The Chairman of the Riigikogu, acting as President of the Republic, does not have the right, without the consent of the Supreme Court, to declare extraordinary elections to the Riigikogu or to refuse to proclaim laws.

Other matters with which the Court is charged by the Constitution or statute:

- Article 64 of the Constitution: The authority of a member of the Riigikogu shall terminate prematurely: if the Supreme Court decides that he or she is incapable of performing his or her duties for an extended period. The President of the Republic may refuse to proclaim a law passed by the Riigikogu and, within fourteen days after its receipt, return the law, together with his or her reasoned resolution, to the Riigikogu for a new debate and decision. If the Riigikogu again passes the law which is returned to it by the President of the Republic, unamended, the President of the Republic shall proclaim the law or shall propose to the Supreme Court to declare the law unconstitutional. If the Supreme Court declares the law constitutional, the President of the Republic shall proclaim the law.
- Article 85 of the Constitution: Criminal charges may be brought against a judge during his or her term of office only on the proposal of the Supreme Court, and with the consent of the President of the Republic.
- Article 83 of the Constitution: If the President of the Republic is incapable of performing his or her duties for an extended period as decided by the Supreme Court, or if he or she is temporarily unable to perform them as in the cases specified by law, or if his or her powers have terminated prematurely, then his or her duties shall temporarily transfer to the Chairman of the Riigikogu.

SOURCES:

http://www.nc.ee/?id=181

https://www.constituteproject.org/constitution/Estonia_2011?lang=en

(58)

DOSSIER OF THE COUNCIL OF CONSTITUTIONAL INQUIRY OF THE FEDERAL DEMOCRATIC REPUBLIC OF ETHIOPIA

STATE: The Federal Democratic Republic of Ethiopia
TITLE: The Council of Constitutional Inquiry
YEAR OF FOUNDATION: 1994
SEAT: Adis Abeba

I. CHRONICLE

Date and context of establishment:
Para. 1 Article 83 of the Constitution: The Council of Constitutional Inquiry was established by the Constitution from 1994.

II. STANDARD LEGAL REFERENCE

Constitution of the Federal Democration Republic of Ethiopia: 1994

III. COMPOSITION AND ORGANIZATION

Composition
The number of judges:
Para. 2 Article 82 of the Constitution: Eleven members comprising: The President of the Federal Supreme Court, who shall serve as its President; The Vice-President of the Federal Supreme Court, who shall serve as its Vice-President; Six legal experts, who shall have proven professional competence and high moral standing; Three persons designated by the House of the Federation from among its members..

Electoral/appointment body:
Para. 2 Article 82 of the Constitution: Six legal experts are appointed by the President of the Republic on recommendation by the House of Peoples' Representatives, who shall have proven professional competence and high moral standing. Three persons are designated by the House of the Federation from among its members.

IV. POWERS

Other powers

Other matters with which the Court is charged by the Constitution or statute:
Article 84 of the Constitution: The Council of Constitutional Inquiry shall have powers to investigate constitutional disputes. Should the Council, upon consideration of the matter, find it necessary to interpret the Constitution, it shall submit its recommendations thereon to the House of the Federation. Where any Federal or State law is contested as being unconstitutional and such a dispute is submitted to it by any court or interested party, the Council shall consider the matter and submit it to the House of the Federation for a final decision. When issues of constitutional interpretation arise in the courts, the Council shall: Remand the case to the concerned court if it finds there is no need for constitutional interpretation; the interested party, if dissatisfied with the decision of the Council, may appeal to the House of the Federation.

and Submit its recommendations to the House of the Federation for a final decision if it believes there is a need for constitutional interpretation.

SOURCES:

https://www.constituteproject.org/constitution/Ethiopia_1994?lang=en

(59)

DOSSIER OF THE SUPREME COURT OF THE REPUBLIC OF FIJI

STATE: Republic of Fiji
TITLE: The Supreme Court
YEAR OF FOUNDATION: 2009
SEAT: Suva[57]

I. CHRONICLE

Position in the hierarchy of courts:
Para. 3a Article 98 of the Constitution: The Supreme Court is the final appellate Court.

II. STANDARD LEGAL REFERENCE

Fiji has had four constitutions:

- 1970 Constitution of Fiji
- 1990 Constitution of Fiji
- 1997 Constitution of Fiji
- 2013 Constitution of Fiji

III. COMPOSITION AND ORGANIZATION

Composition
Electoral/appointment body:
Para. 2 Article 106 of the Constitution: The Judges of the Supreme Court are appointed by the President on the recommendation of the Judicial Services Commission following consultation by it with the Attorney-General.

57 http://www.judiciary.gov.fj/

IV. POWERS

Constitutional Court Review

A posteriori review:

Concrete review:

Para. 5 Article 91 of the Constitution: The Governent's Cabinet may seek an opinion from the Supreme Court on any matter concerning the interpretation or application of this Constitution. Para. 3b Article 98 of the Constitution: The Supreme Court has exclusive jurisdiction, to hear and determine appeals from final judgments of the Court of Appeal, and original jurisdiction to hear and determine constitutional questions referred under Section 91(5) of the Constitution. The Supreme Court may review any judgment, pronouncement or order made by it.

V. NATURE AND EFFECTS OF DECISIONS

Finality:

Para. 3a Article 98 of the Constitution: The Supreme Court is the final appellate court.

Binding force:

Erga omnes:

Para. 6 Article 98 of the Constitution: Decisions of the Supreme Court are binding on all other courts of the State.

SOURCES:

https://www.constituteproject.org/constitution/Fiji_2013?lang=en

(60)

DOSSIER OF THE CONSTITUTIONAL LAW COMMITEE OF THE REPUBLIC OF FINLAND

STATE: Republic of Finland
TITLE: Supreme Court
YEAR OF FOUNDATION:
SEAT: Helsinki[58]

I. CHRONICLE

Similarly to other Nordic countries, Finland has eschewed establishing a constitutional court in favour of establishing a Constitutional Law Committee. This committee, established in 1906, has been empowered to review constitutionality under section 74 of the Constitution

II. STANDARD LEGAL REFERENCE

Constitution of the Republic of Finland: 1999, rev. 2011

III. COMPOSITION AND ORGANIZATION

Composition

Fifteen of the Finnish Parliament committees are special committees, while the Grand Committee deals with EU affairs, but also has a wider range of tasks. As Finland does not have a constitutional court, the role of the Constitutional Law Committee is to oversee constitutional affairs.

58 http://korkeinoikeus.fi/en/index/supremecourt/premises.html

Constitutional Court Review

Committee whose principal function is to issue statements on bills sent to it for consideration and on the constitutionality of other matters and their bearing on international human rights instruments.

The Constitutional Law Committee drafts the Constitution as well as legislation closely connected to it, such as the legislation pertaining to autonomy of Åland, election, citizenship, language and defence. The Constitutional Law Committee also deals with matters having to do with the alleged malfeasance of a minister, the reports of the Chancellor of Justice and the Parliamentary Ombudsman and the Government Annual Report.

Furthermore, the Committee conducts an assessment of those who have registered an interest in the position of Parliamentary Ombudsman and Deputy Parliamentary Ombudsman for purposes of the election of these officials that is held in a plenary session

SOURCES:

https://books.google.si/books?isbn=9287157006

http://korkeinoikeus.fi/en/index/supremecourt/history.htmlhttps://www.constituteproject.org/constitution/Finland_2011?lang=en

https://www.eduskunta.fi/EN/lakiensaataminen/valiokunnat/perustuslakivaliokunta/Pages/default.aspx

www.academia.edu/.../On_the_Role_of_the_Constitutional_Law_Com...

DOSSIER OF THE CONSTITUTIONAL COUNCIL OF THE FRENCH REPUBLIC

STATE: French Republic
TITLE: The Constitutional Council
YEAR OF FOUNDATION: 1958
SEAT: Paris

I. CHRONICLE

Date and context of establishment:
The Constitutional Council was established by the by the Constitution of the Fifth Republic adopted on 4 October 1958.[59]

Position in the hierarchy of courts:
The Constitutional Council is not a Supreme Court that is hierarchically superior to the Conseil d'État or the Cour de Cassation.[60]

II. STANDARD LEGAL REFERENCE

Constitution of the Fifth Republic adopted on 4 October 1958, with amendments

59 http://www.conseil-constitutionnel.fr/conseil-constitutionnel/english/presentation/general-presentation/general-presentation.25739.html

60 http://www.conseil-constitutionnel.fr/conseil-constitutionnel/english/presentation/general-presentation/general-presentation.25739.html

III. COMPOSITION AND ORGANIZATION

Composition

The number of judges:

Article 56 of the Constitution: Nine members.

Electoral/appointment body:

The Court members:

Article 56 of the Constitution: Three of its members shall be appointed by the President of the Republic, three by the President of the National Assembly and three by the President of the Senate.

The term of office:

Article 56 of the Constitution: Nine years.

The Court President:

The term of office:

Article 56 of the Constitution: Nine years.

IV. POWERS

Constitutional Court Review

Preventive review:

Article 61 of the Constitution: Institutional Acts, before their promulgation, Private Members' Bills mentioned in Article 11 of the Constitution before they are submitted to referendum, and the Rules of Procedure of the Houses of Parliament shall, before coming into force, be referred to the Constitutional Council, which shall rule on their conformity with the Constitution.

Other powers

Electoral matters:

Article 58 of the Constitution: The Constitutional Council shall ensure the proper conduct of the election of the President of the Republic. The Constitutional Council shall rule on the proper conduct of the election of Members of the National Assembly and Senators in disputed cases. It shall examine complaints and shall proclaim the results of the vote.

Referendums:
Article 60 of the Constitution: The Constitutional Council shall ensure the proper conduct of referendum proceedings as provided for in Articles 11 and 89 of the Constitution and in Title XV of the Constitution and shall proclaim the results of the referendum.

Other matters with which the Court is charged by the Constitution or statute:

- Article 7 of the Constitution: Should the Presidency of the Republic fall vacant for any reason whatsoever, or should the Constitutional Council on a referral from the Government rule by an absolute majority of its members that the President of the Republic is incapacitated, the duties of the President of the Republic, with the exception of those specified in Articles 11 and 12 of the Constitution, shall be temporarily exercised by the President of the Senate or, if the latter is in turn incapacitated, by the Government. In the case of a vacancy, or where the incapacity of the President is declared to be permanent by the Constitutional Council, elections for the new President shall, except in the event of a finding by the Constitutional Council of force majeure, be held no fewer than twenty days and no more than thirty-five days after the beginning of the vacancy or the declaration of permanent incapacity. In the event of the death or incapacitation in the seven days preceding the deadline for registering candidacies of any of the persons who, fewer than thirty days prior to such deadline, have publicly announced their decision to stand for election, the Constitutional Council may decide to postpone the election. If, before the first round of voting, any of the candidates dies or becomes incapacitated, the Constitutional Council shall declare the election to be postponed. In the event of the death or incapacitation of either of the two candidates in the lead after the first round of voting before any withdrawals, the Constitutional Council shall declare that the electoral process must be repeated in full; the same shall apply in the event of the death or incapacitation of either of the two candidates still standing on the second round of voting. All cases shall be referred to the Constitutional Council in the manner laid down in the second paragraph of Article 61 of the Constitution or in that laid down for the registration of candidates in the Institutional Act provided for in Article 6 of the Constitution. The Constitutional Council may extend the time limits set in paragraphs three and five above, provided that polling takes place no later than thirty-five days after the decision of the Constitutional Council. If the implementation of the provisions of this paragraph results in the postponement of the election beyond the expiry of the term of the President in office, the latter shall remain in office until his successor is proclaimed.

Finality:

Article 62 of the Constitution: No appeal shall lie from the decisions of the Constitutional Council.

Binding force:

Erga omnes:

Article 62 of the Constitution: They shall be binding on public authorities and on all administrative authorities and all courts.

SOURCES:

http://www.conseil-constitutionnel.fr/conseil-constitutionnel/english/presentation/general-presentation/general-presentation.25739.html

https://www.constituteproject.org/constitution/France_2008?lang=en

(62)

DOSSIER OF THE CONSTITUTIONAL COURT OF THE GABONESE REPUBLIC

STATE: The Gabonese Republic
TITLE: The Constitutional Court
YEAR OF FOUNDATION: 1991
SEAT: Libreville

I. CHRONICLE

Date and context of establishment:
The idea of a constitutional judge was retained in Gabon from the beginning of national independence. Thus the Supreme Court instituted by the first fundamental law of the country, the Constitution of 21 February 1961, included among the four chambers of which it was constituted, a constitutional chamber.

But unlike the other three judicial, administrative and accounts chambers (current Judiciary, Administrative and Accounts Courts), which can be said that in 1990 they had almost reached the fullness of their jurisdiction, this constitutional chamber for not having It has often been asked that in its advisory role it has had a very limited activity with regard to the review of constitutionality.

The Constitutional Court, as it exists today, owes its advent to the National Conference of March-April 1990. It emphasized the need for effective control of constitutionality and proposed to this effect, in its Act No. 1, the abolition of the constitutional chamber in favor of a Constitutional Council.

The following year, the constituent did indeed create a real constitutional court and chose, to designate it, the name of Constitutional Court (Constitution of March 26, 1991, modified).

Position in the hierarchy of courts:
In the Gabonese judicial system, the Constitutional Court is hierarchically the highest court. This supremacy stems from the provisions of Article 92 of the Constitution, according to which the decisions of the Constitutional Court are binding on the public authorities, on all the administrative and jurisdictional authorities and on all natural and legal persons .

II. STANDARD LEGAL REFERENCE

Constitution of the Gabonese Republic: 1991, 1997

III. COMPOSITION AND ORGANIZATION

Composition
The number of judges:
Article 89 of the Constitution: Nine.

Electoral/appointment body:
Article 89 of the Constitution: The nine (9) members of the Constitutional Court are chosen as follows: three by the President of the Republic, one of which will be the President; three, by the President of the Senate; three, by the President of the National Assembly.

The Court members:
The term of office:
Article 89 of the Constitution: Seven years.

IV. POWERS

Constitutional Court Review

Preventive review:

Article 56 of the Constitution: If it appears, during the course of the legislative procedure, that a text or an amendment is not within the domain of the law, in the sense of Article 47 of the Constitution above, or exceeds the limits of legislative habilitation granted to the Government according to Article 52 of the Constitution, the Prime Minister may declare it irreceivable. The President of the concerned Chamber at the demand of one-fifth of its members also may declare a bill irreceivable. The disagreement is referred to the Constitutional Court, which must decide within a time period of eight days.

A posteriori review:

Abstract review:

Article 84 of the Constitution: The Constitutional Court decides obligatorily on the constitutionality of organic laws and laws before their promulgation, regulatory acts which touch upon the fundamental rights of the human person and public liberties.

Article 84 of the Constitution: The Constitutional Court decides obligatorily on the rules of the national assembly, of the National Council of Communication and of the Economic and Social Council before their effectuation, regarding their conformity to the Constitution.

Other powers

Jurisdictional disputes:

- Article 84 of the Constitution: The Constitutional Court decides obligatorily on conflicts of attribution between the institutions of the State.

Electoral matters:

- Article 84 of the Constitution: The Constitutional Court is seized, in the case of contestation of the validity of an election, by any voter, any candidate, any political party or the delegate of the Government under the conditions provided for by the organic law.
- Article 10 of the Constitution: If, before the first round, one of the candidates dies or finds himself incapacitated, the Constitutional Court shall pronounce the results of the election. In the case of death or incapacity of one of the two most favored candidates in the first round before eventual withdrawals, the Constitutional Court shall declare that a new set of elections must proceed; it shall be the same in the case of the death or incapacitation of one of the two candidates remaining in competition in the second round. The Constitutional Court may extend the periods provided, in conformity with Article 11 of the Constitution hereafter, as long as the balloting does not take place more than thirty five days after the date of the decision of the Constitutional Court. If the application of the provisions of the present Article have for effect the delay of the election to a date after the expiration of the mandate of the incumbent President, he shall continue to function until the election of his successor.
- Article 9 of the Constitution: The President of the Republic is elected by an absolute majority of the votes cast. If this is not obtained in the first round, there shall be a second round, the second Sunday following the proclamation of the results by the Constitutional Court.

Referendums:

Article 84 of the Constitution: The Constitutional Court decides obligatorily on the regularity of all political elections and operations of the referendum of which it proclaims the results.

Other matters with which the Court is charged by the Constitution or statute:

- Article 13 of the Constitution: The government submits cases of definitive incapacitation of the President of the Republic to the Constitutional Court. A majority of the Constitutional Court is required to establish the definitive incapacitation of the President of the Republic. If a majority is not obtained in the Constitutional Court, a majority of the members of the bureaus of Parliament meeting jointly may certify the definitive incapacitation of the President of the Republic. If there is a vacancy of the Presidency of the Republic or duly established definitive incapacitation of the President of the Republic, the functions of the President of the Republic, with the exception of those provided for in Articles 18, 19, and 116 of the Constitution, 1st paragraph, shall be provisionally exercised by the President of the Senate or, if he is incapacitated in his turn and this is duly ascertained by the Constitutional Court summoned in the same conditions as above, by the First Vice-President of the Senate.

SOURCES:

https://www.constituteproject.org/constitution/Gabon_1997?lang=en

DOSSIER OF THE SUPREME COURT OF THE REPUBLIC OF THE GAMBIA

STATE: Republic of Gambia
TITLE: The Supreme Court
YEAR OF FOUNDATION: 1851 and laer remodeled/reintroduced
SEAT: Banjul[61]

I. CHRONICLE

Position in the hierarchy of courts:
Para. 1 Article 126 of the Constitution: The Supreme Court shall be the final court of appeal Supreme Court for The Gambia and shall have such appellate and other jurisdiction as may be conferred on it by the Constitution or any other law.

II. STANDARD LEGAL REFERENCE

Constitution of the Republic of the Gambia: 1996, rev. 2004

III. COMPOSITION AND ORGANIZATION

Composition
The number of judges:
Para. 2 Article 125 of the Constitution: The Supreme Court shall be constituted by an uneven number of not less than five judges of the Court.

61 http://www.judiciary.gov.gm/contact-us

Constitutional Court Review

Preventive review:

Para. 1a Article 127 of the Constitution: For the interpretation or enforcement of any provision of this Constitution other than any provision of sections 18 to 33 or section 36 (5) of the Constitution (which relate to fundamental rights and freedoms).

A posteriori review:

Concrete review:

Para. 1b Article 127 of the Constitution: On any question whether any law was made in excess of the powers conferred by this Constitution or any other law upon the National Assembly or any other person or authority.

Other powers

Electoral matters:

- Para. 1c Article 127 of the Constitution: The Supreme Court has an exclusive original jurisdiction on any question as to whether or not any person was validly elected to the office of President or was validly elected to, or vacated his or her seat in, the National Assembly.
- Article 49 of the Constitution: Any registered political party which has participated in the Presidential election or an independent candidate who has participated in such an election may apply to the Supreme Court to determine the validity of the election of a President by filling a petition within ten days of the declaration of the result of the election.

Other matters with which the Court is charged by the Constitution or statute:

Article 127 of the Constitution: The Supreme Court has an exclusive original jurisdition on any question whether any official document should be produced, or its contents disclosed, in proceedings before a court where such production is resisted on the grounds that its production or the disclosure of its contents would be prejudicial to the security of the state or be injurious to the public interest. Where any question referred to in paragraphs (a), (b) or (d) of subsection (1) arises in any proceedings in any other court, that court shall stay its proceedings and refer the matter to the Supreme Court for its determination, and such other court shall give effect to any decision of the Supreme Court in the matter.

Finality:

Para. 1 Article 126 of the Constitution: The Supreme Court shall be the final court of appeal for The Gambia and shall have such appellate and other jurisdiction as may be conferred on it by this Constitution or any other law

Binding force:

Erga omnes:

Para. 2 Article 126 of the Constitution: All other courts shall be bound to follow the decisions of the Supreme Court on a matter of law.

SOURCES:

https://www.constituteproject.org/constitution/Gambia_2004?lang=en

DOSSIER OF THE CONSTITUTIONAL COURT OF GEORGIA

STATE: Georgia
TITLE: The Constitutional Court
YEAR OF FOUNDATION: 1996[62]
SEAT: Batumi

I. CHRONICLE

Date and context of establishment:
The Constitutional Court of Georgia was established in 1996, based on the Constitution which was adopted by the Parliament in August 1995.[63]

Position in the hierarchy of courts:
Article 83 of the Constitution: The Constitutional Court of Georgia shall be the judicial body of Constitutional review. Its authority, the procedures of its creation and activity shall be determined by the Constitution and the Organic Law.

II. STANDARD LEGAL REFERENCE

Constitution of Georgia: 1995, rev. 2013

III. COMPOSITION AND ORGANIZATION

Composition
The number of judges:
Para. 2 Article 88 of the Constitution: Nine judges.

62 http://www.constcourt.ge/en/court/brief-history

63 http://www.constcourt.ge/en/court/brief-history

Electoral/appointment body:

Para. 2 Article 88 of the Constitution: Three members are appointed by the President of Georgia, three members are elected by the Parliament by not less than three fifths of the number of the members of the Parliament on the current nominal list, three members are appointed by the Supreme Court. A candidate to the office of the President of the Court is nominated by an agreed proposal of the President of Georgia, the President of the Parliament of Georgia and the President of the Supreme Court of Georgia.

The Court members:

The term of office:

Para. 2 Article 88 of the Constitution: Ten years.

The Court President:

The term of office:

Para 2. Article 88 of the Constitution: Five years.

IV. POWERS

Constitutional Court Review

Preventive review:

Para. 4 Article 65 of the Constitution: If a constitutional claim or a submission has been lodged with the Constitutional Court, the respective treaty or international agreement shall not be ratified until the Constitutional Court passes its judgement.

A posteriori review:

Abstract review:

- Para. E Article 89 of the Constitution: consider constitutionality of international treaties and agreements;
- Para. A Article 89 of the Constitution: adjudicate upon the constitutionality of a Constitutional Agreement, law, normative acts of the President and the Government, the normative acts of the higher state bodies of the Autonomous Republic Abkhazia and the Autonomous Republic of Ajara.
- Para. F2 Article 89 of the Constitution: consider disputes on the constitutionality of normative acts in terms of the provisions defined by Chapter Seven-1 of the Constitution on the basis of a lawsuit brought by a self-government representative body - Sakrebulo;

- Para. F3 Article 89 of the Constitution: consider the compatibility of normative acts with Articles 82, 84, 86, 86-1, 87 and 90 of the Constitution based on the submission by the High Council of Justice.

Constitutional complaints:

- Para. F Article 89 of the Constitution: consider, on the basis of a claim of a person, constitutionality of normative acts in relation to fundamental human rights and freedoms enshrined in Chapter Two of the Constitution;

Jurisdictional disputes:

- Para. F1 Article 89 of the Constitution: consider dispute on violation of the Constitutional Law of Georgia on the Status of the Autonomous Republic of Ajara;
- Para. B Article 89 of the Constitution: consider dispute on competence between state bodies.

Electoral matters/Referendum:

-Para. D Article 89 of the Constitution: consider dispute on constitutionality of provisions on referenda and elections as well as dispute on constitutionality of referenda and elections held on the basis of these provisions.

Other powers

The unconstitutionality of acts and activities of political parties:

Para. C Article 89 of the Constitution: Consider constitutionality of formation and activity of political associations of citizens.

Charges against the President of the Republic:

Article 63 of the Constitution: In the cases provided for by Article 75(2) of the Constitution, Parliament acting with at least one third of the total number of MPs shall have the right to raise a question to remove the President of Georgia from office via impeachment. The issue shall be referred to the Constitutional Court of Georgia for decision. If the Constitutional Court by its conclusion confirms components of crime in the actions of the President or confirms that the President has violated the Constitution by his/her actions, Parliament shall consider and vote for the removal of President from office via impeachment within not later than 15 days after the Court conclusion has been submitted.

Other matters with which the Court is charged by the Constitution or statute:

- Para. G Article 89 of the Constitution: exercise other powers determined by the Constitution and the Organic Law of Georgia,

- Article 54 of the Constitution: The recognition or early termination of office of an MP shall be settled by Parliament. The decision of Parliament may be appealed to the Constitutional Court.

V. NATURE AND EFFECTS OF DECISIONS

Finality:

Para. 2 Article 89 of the Constitution: The judgment of the Constitutional Court shall be final.

SOURCES:

https://www.constituteproject.org/constitution/Georgia_2013?lang=en

(65)

DOSSIER OF THE FEDERAL CONSTITUTIONAL COURT OF THE FEDERAL REPUBLIC OF GERMANY

STATE: Federal Republic of Germany
TITLE: Federal Constitutional Court
YEAR OF FOUNDATION: 1949
SEAT: Karlsruhe[64]

I. CHRONICLE

Beside the Federal Constitutional Court there are constitutional courts of federal units separately established (see more on www.concourts.net).

II. STANDARD LEGAL REFERENCE

Constitution of the Federal Republic of Germany: 1949, rev. 2012.

III. COMPOSITION AND ORGANIZATION

Composition

Electoral/appointment body:

Para. 1 Article 94 of the Constitution: Half the members of the Federal Constitutional Court shall be elected by the Bundestag and half by the Bundesrat.

64 http://www.bundesverfassungsgericht.de/EN/Gebaeude/gebaeude_node.html;jsessionid=020F2476A94963DF9DC3E7C2EE11A823.2_cid392

Constitutional Court Review

A posteriori review:

Abstract review:

Para. 1 Article 93 of the Constitution: in the event of disagreements or doubts concerning the formal or substantive compatibility of federal law or Land law with this Basic Law, or the compatibility of Land law with other federal law, on application of the Federal Government, of a Land government, or of one fourth of the Members of the Bundestag; on the interpretation of this Basic Law in the event of disputes concerning the extent of the rights and duties of a supreme federal body or of other parties vested with rights of their own by this Basic Law or by the rules of procedure of a supreme federal body;

Concrete review:

Para. 2 Article 93 of the Constitution: At the request of the Bundesrat, a Land government or the parliamentary assembly of a Land, the Federal Constitutional Court shall also rule whether in cases falling under paragraph (4) of Article 72 of the Constitution the need for a regulation by federal law does not exist any longer or whether in the cases referred to in clause 1 of paragraph (2) of Article 125a of the Constitution federal law could not be enacted any longer. The Court's determination that the need has ceased to exist or that federal law could no longer be enacted substitutes a federal law according to paragraph (4) of Article 72 of the Constitution or clause 2 of paragraph (2) of Article 125a of the Constitution. A request under the first sentence is admissible only if a bill falling under paragraph (4) of Article 72 of the Constitution or the second sentence of paragraph (2) of Article 125a of the Constitution has been rejected by the German Bundestag or if it has not been considered and determined upon within one year, or if a similar bill has been rejected by the Bundesrat.

Other powers

Constitutional complaints:

Para. 1 Article 93 of the Constitution: On constitutional complaints, which may be filed by any person alleging that one of his basic rights or one of his rights under paragraph (4) of Article 20 or under Article 33, 38, 101, 103 or 104 of the Constitution has been infringed by public authority; on constitutional complaints filed by municipalities or associations of municipalities on the ground that their right to self-government under Article 28 of the Constitution has been infringed by a law; in the case of infringement by a Land law, however, only if the law cannot be challenged in the constitutional court of the Land.

Jurisdictional disputes:

Para. 1 Article 93 of the Constitution: On other disputes involving public law between the Federation and the Länder, between different Länder, or within a Land, unless there is recourse to another court;

Charges against the President of the Republic:

Article 61 : The Bundestag or the Bundesrat may impeach the Federal President before the Federal Constitutional Court for wilful violation of this Basic Law or of any other federal law. The motion of impeachment must be supported by at least one quarter of the Members of the Bundestag or one quarter of the votes of the Bundesrat. The decision to impeach shall require a majority of two thirds of the Members of the Bundestag or of two thirds of the votes of the Bundesrat. The case for impeachment shall be presented before the Federal Constitutional Court by a person commissioned by the impeaching body. If the Federal Constitutional Court finds the Federal President guilty of a wilful violation of this Basic Law or of any other federal law, it may declare that he has forfeited his office. After the Federal President has been impeached, the Court may issue an interim order preventing him from exercising his functions.

Electoral matters:

Para. 1 Article 93: On complaints of associations against their non-recognition as party for the election to the German Federal Assembly.

Other powers:

Article 84: Should any deficiencies that the Federal Government has identified in the execution of federal laws in the Länder not be corrected, the Bundesrat, on application of the Federal Government or of the Land concerned, shall decide whether that Land has violated the law. The decision of the Bundesrat may be challenged in the Federal Constitutional Court.

V. NATURE AND EFFECTS OF DECISIONS

Finality: X

SOURCES:

http://www.bundesverfassungsgericht.de/EN/Gebaeude/gebaeude_node.html;jsessionid=020F2476A94963DF9DC3E7C2EE11A823.2_cid392

https://www.constituteproject.org/constitution/German_Federal_Republic_2012?lang=en

(66)

DOSSIER OF THE SUPREME COURT OF THE REPUBLIC OF GHANA

STATE: The Republic of Ghana
TITLE: The Supreme Court
YEAR OF FOUNDATION: 1876, later remodeled/reintroduced
SEAT: Accra

I.CHRONICLE

The Supreme Court was established by the Supreme Court Ordinance (1876) as the highest tribunal in the Gold Coast (now Ghana) during the colonial era. Appeals from the Supreme Court went to the West African Court of Appeals (WACA) established in 1866. Ghana withdrew from WACA following independence. After the military coup d'état of February 24, 1966, the National Liberation Council (NLC), by the Courts Decree, 1966 (NLCD.84) abolished the Supreme Court and vested judicial power in two sets of courts: the Superior Court of Judicature and the inferior Courts. This was reversed by Article 102(4) of the 1969 constitution establishing the second republic. After the coup on January 13, 1972, the Supreme Court was again abolished by the National Redemption Council with the reason that the 1969 constitution had been suspended and so there was no need for a court to interpret and enforce it . Its functions were transferred to the Court of Appeal. This was again reverted by the 1979 constitution when the third republic was established on September 24, 1979. The Supreme Court was left intact after the December 31, 1981 coup by the Provisional National Defence Council, though it made changes to the court system by introducing public tribunals.

Position in the hierarchy of courts:
Article 129 of the Constitution: The Supreme Court shall be the final court of appeal and shall have such appellate and other jurisdiction as may be conferred on it by this Constitution or by any other law.

II. STANDARD LEGAL REFERENCE

Constitution of the Republic of Ghana: 1992, rev. 1996

III. COMPOSITION AND ORGANIZATION

Composition

The number of judges:

Para. 2 Article 128 of the Constitution: Not less than five Supreme Court Justices.

IV. POWERS

Constitutional Court Review

A posteriori review:

Abstract review:

Para. 1 Article 130 of the Constitution: Subject to the jurisdiction of the High Court in the enforcement of the Fundamental Human Rights and Freedoms as provided in Article 33 of the Constitution, the Supreme Court shall have exclusive original jurisdiction in all matters relating to the enforcement or interpretation of this Constitution; and all matters arising as to whether an enactment was made in excess of the powers conferred on Parliament or any other authority or person by law or under this Constitution.

Other powers

Electoral matters:

Article 64 of the Constitution: The validity of the election of the President may be challenged only by a citizen of Ghana who may present a petition for the purpose to the Supreme Court within twenty-one days after the declaration of the result of the election in respect of which the petition is presented. A declaration by the Supreme Court that the election of the President is not valid shall be without prejudice to anything done by the President before the declaration. The Rules of Court Committee shall, by constitutional instrument, make rules of court for the practice and procedure for petitions to the Supreme Court challenging the election of a President.

Other matters with which the Court is charged by the Constitution or statute:

- Para. 4 Article 129 of the Constitution: For the purposes of hearing and determining a matter within its jurisdiction and the amendment, execution or the enforcement of a judgment or order made on any matter, and for the purposes of any other authority, expressly or by necessary implication given to the Supreme Court by this Constitution or any other law, the Supreme Court shall have all the powers, authority and jurisdiction vested in any court established by this Constitution or any other law.
- Article 132 of the Constitution: The Supreme Court shall have supervisory jurisdiction over all courts and over any adjudicating authority and may, in the exercise of that supervisory jurisdiction, issue orders and directions for the purpose of enforcing or securing the enforcement of its supervisory power.
- Para. 2 Article 130 of the Constitution: Where an issue that relates to a matter or question referred to in clause (1) of this Article arises in any proceedings in a court other than the Supreme Court, that court shall stay the proceedings and refer the question of law involved to the Supreme Court for determination; and the court in which the question arose shall dispose of the case in accordance with the decision of the Supreme Court.
- Article 7 of the Constitution: The Supreme Court shall, on application by or on behalf of a person who has suffered any punishment or loss to which clause (6) of this Article relates, award him adequate compensation, which shall be charged on the Consolidated Fund, in respect of any suffering or loss incurred as a result of the punishment.
- Para. 3 Article 121 of the Constitution: Where there is a doubt as to the nature of a document such as is referred to in clause (2) of this Article, the Speaker or the National Security Council, as the case may be, shall refer the matter to the Supreme Court for determination whether the production, or the disclosure of the, contents, of the document would be injurious to the public interest or, as the case may be, prejudicial to the security of the State.

V. NATURE AND EFFECTS OF DECISIONS

Finality:

Para. 1 Article 129 of the Constitution: The Supreme Court shall be the final court of appeal and shall have such appellate and other jurisdiction as may be conferred on it by this Constitution or by any other law.

Binding force:

Erga omnes:

Para. 3 Article 129 of the Constitution: The Supreme Court may, while treating its own previous decisions as normally binding, depart from a previous decision when it appears to it right to do so; and all other courts shall be bound to follow the decisions of the Supreme Court on questions of law.

SOURCES:

https://www.constituteproject.org/constitution/Ghana_1996?lang=en

https://en.wikipedia.org/wiki/Supreme_Court_of_Ghana

(67)

DOSSIER OF THE SPECIAL HIGHEST COURT OF GREECE (THE HELLENIC REPUBLIC)

STATE: Greece/Hellenic Republic
TITLE: Special Highest Court
YEAR OF FOUNDATION: 1975
SEAT: Athens

I. CRONICLE

The history of the Supreme Special Court is quite short, as it was first founded by the Constitution of 1975. Its organisation and function is regulated by the article 100 of the Constitution of 1975/1986/2001 and the Law 345/1976. Germs of this Court exist in the article 73 of the Constitution of 1952 (providing for a special electoral court) and in the constitutions of the military junta (1967-1974), providing for a special court resolving the disputes between the Supreme Courts.

II. STANDARD LEGAL REFERENCE

Constitution of 1975/1986/2001 and the Law 345/1976

III. COMPOSITION AND ORGANIZATION

Composition

The number of judges:

Para. 2 Article 100 of the Constitution: The Court specified in paragraph 1 shall be composed of the President of the Supreme Administrative Court, the President of the Supreme Civil and Criminal Court and the President of the Court of Audit, four Councillors of the Supreme Administrative Court and four members of the Supreme Civil and Criminal Court. The Court shall be presided over by the President of the Supreme Administrative Court or the President of the Supreme Civil and Criminal Court, according to seniority.

Electoral/appointment body:
Para. 2 Article 100 of the Constitution: Judges are chosen by lot.

The Court members:
The term of office:
Para. 2 Article 100 of the Constitution: Two-year term.

IV. POWERS

Constitutional Court Review

Preventive review:
Para. 1f Article 100 of the Constitution: The settlement of controversies related to the designation of rules of international law as generally acknowledged in accordance with article 28 paragraph 1.

A posteriori review:
Concrete review:
Para. 1e Article 100 of the Constitution: Settlement of controversies on whether the content of a statute enacted by Parliament is contrary to the Constitution, or on the interpretation of provisions of such statute when conflicting judgments have been pronounced by the Supreme Administrative Court, the Supreme Civil and Criminal Court or the Court of Audit.

Other powers
Jurisdictional disputes:
Para. 1d Article 100 of the Constitution: Settlement of any conflict between the courts and the administrative authorities, or between the Supreme Administrative Court and the ordinary administrative courts on one hand and the civil and criminal courts on the other, or between the Court of Audit and any other court.

Charges against the Prime Minister or against any Minister of State:
Para. 1c Article 100 of the Constitution: Judgment in cases involving the incompatibility or the forfeiture of office by a Member of Parliament, in accordance with Article 55 paragraph 2 and Article 57 of the Constitution.

Electoral matters:

Article 58 of the Constitution: The hearing of objections raised against the validity of parliamentary elections and their verification concerning either electoral violations related to the conduct of the elections, or the lack of legal qualifications, is assigned to the Supreme Special Court of article 100 of the Constitution.

Referendums:

Para. 1b Article 100 of the Constitution: Verification of the validity and returns of a referendum held in accordance with Article 44 paragraph 2 of the Constitution.

V. NATURE AND EFFECTS OF DECISIONS

Finality:

Para. 4 Article 100 of the Constitution: The judgments of this Court shall be irrevocable.

SOURCES:

https://www.constituteproject.org/constitution/Greece_2008?lang=en

(68)

DOSSIER OF THE EASTERN CARIBBEAN SUPREME COURT OF GRENADA

STATE: Grenada
TITLE: The Eastern Caribbean Supreme Court[65]
YEAR OF FOUNDATION: The Eastern Carribean Supreme Court: 1967[66],
SEAT: Santa Lucia[67]

I. CHRONICLE

Date and context of establishment:
In 1967, the Organization of Eastern Caribbean States – namely Antigua, Anguilla, Dominica, Grenada, Saint Vincent, Saint Kitts & Nevis, and Saint Lucia – joined in a new "status of association" with the United Kingdom, in accordance with the West Indies Act of 1967. The Act provided for Her Majesty by Order in Council to establish common courts for the Associated States with "such jurisdiction and powers as may be so specified or determined." The West Indies Associated States Supreme Court Order duly followed and gave effect to Section 6 of the West Indies Act, permitting the establishment of common courts for the Associated States – "West Indies Associated States Supreme Court ".[68]

I.STANDARD LEGAL REFERENCE

Constitution of Grenada: 1973, reinst. 1991, rev. 1992.

65 Grenada is a part of the Eastern Caribbean Supreme Court. (https://www.eccourts.org/structure-of-the-court/)

66 https://www.eccourts.org/brief-history-of-the-court/

67 https://www.eccourts.org/brief-history-of-the-court/

68 https://www.eccourts.org/brief-history-of-the-court/

III. COMPOSITION AND ORGANIZATION

Composition

The number of judges:

The Eastern Caribbean Supreme Court consists of two divisions, a Court of Appeal and a High Court of Justice. The Court of Appeal judges are based at the Court's Headquarters in Castries, Saint Lucia where administrative and legal support is provided under the supervision of the Court Administrator and Chief Registrar respectively. The High Court Judges are each assigned to, and reside in, the various Member States. The High Court Registry is headed by a legally trained Registrar who coordinates the provision of the necessary administrative and legal support for the functioning of the High Court. The Eastern Caribbean Supreme Court is composed of the Chief Justice, who is the Head of the Judiciary, four (4) Justices of Appeal, nineteen (19) High Court Judges; and three (3) Masters.[69]

IV. POWERS

"Appeals to the Caribbean Court of Justice

104. (1) of the Constitution An appeal shall lie as of right to the Caribbean Court of Justice (which Caribbean Court of Justice may hereinafter in this Chapter VIIIA be referred to as "the Court") from decisions of the Court of Appeal in the following cases–

(a) final decisions in any civil proceedings where–

(i) the matter in dispute on appeal to the Court is of the prescribed value or upwards; or

(ii) the appeal involves directly or indirectly a claim to or a question respecting property or a right regarding any matter of the prescribed value or upwards;

(b) final decisions in proceedings for dissolution or nullity of marriage;

(c) final decisions in any civil or criminal proceedings which involve a question as to the interpretation of this Constitution;

(d) final decisions given in the exercise of the jurisdiction conferred upon the High Court relating to redress for a contravention of the provisions of this Constitution for the protection of fundamental rights and freedoms;*12 Bill*

69 https://www.eccourts.org/structure-of-the-court/

(e) final decisions given in the exercise of the jurisdiction conferred upon the High Court relating to the determination of any question for which a right of access to the High Court is expressly provided by this Constitution; and

(f) such other cases as may be prescribed by Parliament.

SOURCES:

https://www.eccourts.org/structure-of-the-court/https://www.eccourts.org/brief-history-of-the-court/

(69)

DOSSIER OF THE CONSTITUTIONAL COURT OF THE REPUBLIC OF GUATEMALA

STATE: Guatemala
TITLE: *Corte de Constitucionalidad*
YEAR OF FOUNDATION: 1964
SEAT: Guatemala city

I. CHRONICLE

Date and context of establishment: 1964
Position in the hierarchy of courts:

II. STANDARD LEGAL REFERENCE

Constitution 1986 (rev. 1993)

III. COMPOSITION AND ORGANIZATION

Composition
The number of judges:
consists of five titled magistrates each of whom will have his respective alternate. When it is seized with matters of unconstitutionality against the Supreme Court of Justice, the Congress of the Republic, or the President or Vice President of the Republic, the number of its members will be raised to seven, the other two magistrates being selected by lot from among the alternates. Article 269/1 of the Constitution

The Court members:
The term of office:
The magistrates serve in their functions five years Article 269/2 of the Constitution

The Court President:

The term of office:

The Presidency of the Court of Constitutionality will be filled by the same titled magistrates on a rotating basis changing every year, beginning with the eldest member, and following in descending order of age. Article 271 of the Constitution

Organization

Administrative autonomy:

it acts with independence from the other organisms of the State and exercises specific functions assigned to it by the Constitution and the law in the matter Article 268/1 of the Constitution

The budget:

The economic independence of the Court of Constitutionality will be guaranteed through a percentage of the revenues that correspond to the Judicial Organism. Article 268/2 of the Constitution

IV. POWERS

Constitutional Court Review

Preventive review:

To issue an opinion on the constitutionality of treaties, agreements, and bills of law at the request of any of the organisms of the State;Article 272/1e of the Constitution

A posteriori review:

Abstract review:

Actions against the laws, regulations or provisions of a general character which contain a partial or total absence of constitutionality will be heard directly by the Tribunal or Court of Constitutionality.Article 267 of the Constitution

To take cognizance in sole [unique] instance of the charges brought against the laws or provisions of a general character, challenges of partial or total unconstitutionality; Article 272/1a of the Constitution

Concrete review:

In concrete cases, in every process of whatever competence or jurisdiction, in any instance, and in cassation and even before sentence is decreed, the parties will be able to press as an action, exception, or incident the total or partial unconstitutionality of a law. The court will have to make a determination in that respect. Article 266 of the Constitution

To take cognizance on appeal of all the challenges against the laws charged with being unconstitutional in specific cases, in any trial, in cassation, or in the cases contemplated by the law in the matter; Article 272/1d of the Constitution

Other powers

Constitutional complaints: /

Jurisdictional disputes:

To take cognizance and resolve issues relating to any conflict of jurisdiction in matters of constitutionality; Article 272/1f of the Constitution

The unconstitutionality of acts and activities of political parties: /

Charges against the President of the Republic:

To take cognizance in sole instance in its status of Extraordinary Tribunal of Amparo, in amparo actions brought against... the President or Vice President of the Republic; Article 272/1b of the Constitution

Charges against the Prime Minister or against any Minister of State: /

Electoral matters: /

Referendums: /

Other matters with which the Court is charged by the Constitution or statute:

To compile the doctrine and constitutional principles that have been invoked with the purpose of resolving them through amparo and of unconstitutionality of the laws, keeping up to date the jurisprudential journal or gazette; Article 279/1g of the Constitution

To issue an opinion on the unconstitutionality of laws vetoed by the Executive alleging unconstitutionality; Article 279/1h of the Constitution

To act, render opinions [opinar], dictate, or take cognizance of those matters under its competence established in the Constitution of the Republic. Article 279/1i of the Constitution

Other forms of human rights protection:

Habeas corpus Article 263 of the Constitution

Amparo Article 264 of the Constitution

To take cognizance in sole instance in its status of Extraordinary Tribunal of Amparo, in amparo actions brought against the Congress of the Republic, the Supreme Court of Justice, the President or Vice President of the Republic; Article 279/1b of the Constitution

To take cognizance on appeal of all the amparos brought before any of the tribunals of justice. If the appeal were against an amparo decision of the Supreme Court of Justice, the Court of

Constitutionality shall be expanded by two members [vocales] in the form anticipated in Article 268 of the Constitution; Article 279/1c of the Constitution

Standing before the Constitutional Court
State bodies:
the request of any of the organisms of the State; 272/1e

Individuals: X

V. NATURE AND EFFECTS OF DECISIONS

Finality: /
Binding force:

SOURCES:

https://www.constituteproject.org/constitution/Guatemala_1993.pdf

(70)

DOSSIER OF THE CONSTITUTIONAL COURT OF THE REPUBLIC OF GUINEA

STATE: Republic of Guinea
TITLE: Cour Constitutionnelle
YEAR OF FOUNDATION: 1958
SEAT: Conakry

I. CHRONICLE

Date and context of establishment: 1958
Position in the hierarchy of courts:

II. STANDARD LEGAL REFERENCE

Constitution of 7 May 2010

III. COMPOSITION AND ORGANIZATION

Composition
The number of judges:
The Constitutional Court includes nine (09) members Article 100 of the Constitution

Electoral/appointment body: /
The Court members:
The term of office:
The duration of the mandate of the members of the Constitutional Court is nine years non-renewable, Article 101/1 of the Constitution

The Court President:

The term of office:

The President of the Constitutional Court is elected by his peers for a duration of nine-years non-renewable, Article 101/2 of the Constitution

Organization

Administrative autonomy:

The budget:

The credits necessary for the functioning of the Constitutional Court are inscribed in the national budget, Article 105 of the Constitution

IV. POWERS

Constitutional Court Review

Preventive review:

Article 80 of the Constitution: Within the eight clear [francs] days that follow the adoption of a law, the President of the Republic, at least one-tenth of the Deputies or the Independent National Institution for Human Rights, may refer the Constitutional Court to [the matter] of a recourse looking to [visant] have it control the conformity of the law with the Constitution

the constitutionality of the laws before their promulgation; Article 94 of the Constitution

Other powers

Jurisdictional disputes:

the conflicts of attributions between the constitutional organs; Article 94 of the Constitution

Electoral matters:

Article 29 of the Constitution

The candidatures are presented at the Greffe [Registry] of the Constitutional Court forty days at least and sixty days at most before the date of the ballot. No candidature is receivable if it is not presented by a legally constituted political party. Each party may only present one sole candidacy. Thirty-nine days before the ballot, the Constitutional Court orders [arrête] and publishes the list of the candidates. The electors are then convoked by decree Article 30 of the Constitution

In the case of death or of definitive incapacity declared by the Constitutional Court of a candidate figuring on the list specified in Article 29, the Constitutional Court decides, if there is need, to reopen the time periods during which new candidatures can be deposited. In this case a new date of the ballot is established within the conditions specified in Article 28 of the Constitution.

Article 33 of the Constitution

...Constitutional Court proclaims the President of the Republic elected.

Article 93 of the Constitution

In the case of dispute [contestation], the Constitutional Court decides within the three days that follow its referral [to the matter]. Its order carries [emporte] proclamation or annulment of the election.

The Constitutional Court is the competent jurisdiction in... electoral matters...

It sees to the regularity of the national elections and of the referendums of which [dont] it proclaims the definitive results.

Article 94 of the Constitution

the electoral disputes [contentieux] of the national elections;

Referendums:

It sees to the regularity of the national elections and of the referendums of which [dont] it proclaims the definitive results. Article 93/3 of the Constitution

Standing before the Constitutional Court

State bodies: X

Individuals:

Any pleader [plaideur] may raise the exception of unconstitutionality of a law before any jurisdiction Article 96/3 of the Constitution

V. NATURE AND EFFECTS OF DECISIONS

Finality:

The jurisprudence of the Constitutional Court, in this matter, prevails [a primauté] over that of the other jurisdictional orders. Article 96/6 of the Constitution

Ex officio:

The organic laws are obligatorily submitted by the President of the Republic to the Constitutional Court before their promulgation. Article 95/1 of the Constitution

Obligatory opinions on the conformity of international treaties with the Constitution:

The international engagements specified in Article 150 of the Constitution *(international engagement contains a clause contrary to the Constitution)* are deferred before ratification to the Constitutional Court, either by the President of the Republic, or by the President of the National Assembly or by one Deputy. Article 97/1 of the Constitution

SOURCES:

https://www.constituteproject.org/constitution/Guinea_2010.pdf?lang=en

(71)

DOSSIER OF THE COURT OF APPEAL OF THE COOPERATIVE REPUBLIC OF GUYANA

STATE: Republic of Guyana
TITLE: Court of Appeal
YEAR OF FOUNDATION: 1980
SEAT: North Cummingsburg

I. CHRONICLE

Date and context of establishment 1980
The 1980 constitution established the judiciary as an independent branch of the government with the right of judicial review of legislative and executive acts.

Position in the hierarchy of courts

II. STANDARD LEGAL REFERENCE

Constitution 1980

III. COMPOSITION AND ORGANIZATION

Composition
The number of judges:
The Judges of the Court of Appeal shall be the Chancellor, who shall be the President of the Court of Appeal, the Chief Justice and such number of Justices of Appeal as may be prescribed by Parliament. (Article 124 of the Constitution)

Electoral/appointment body:
(1) The Chancellor and the Chief Justice shall be appointed by the President acting after consultation with the Minority Leader. (Article 127 of the Constitution)

The Judges, other than the Chancellor and the Chief Justice, shall be appointed by the President, acting in accordance with the advice of the Judicial Service Commission. (Article 128 of the Constitution)

IV. POWERS

Constitutional Court Review

Concrete review:

(1) An appeal to the Court of Appeal shall lie as of right from decisions of the High Court in the following cases, that is to say -- (a) final decisions in any civil or criminal proceedings on questions as to the interpretation of this Constitution; and (b) final decisions given in exercise of the jurisdiction conferred on the High Court by Article 153 of the Constitution (which related to the enforcement of fundamental rights and freedoms). (Article 133 of the Constitution)

Other powers

Electoral matters:

(3) An appeal shall lie to the Court of Appeal -- (a) from the decision of a Judge of the High Court granting or refusing leave to institute proceedings for the determination of any question referred to in paragraph (1); (b) from the determination by the High Court or any such question, or against any order of the High Court made in consequence of such determination. (Article 163 of the Constitution)

The Court of Appeal shall have exclusive jurisdiction to hear and determine any question as to the validity of an election of a President in so far as that question depends upon the qualification of any person for election or the interpretation of this Constitution; and decision of that Court under this paragraph shall be final. ((Article 177 of the Constitution)

V. NATURE AND EFFECTS OF DECISIONS

Finality:

...final decisions in any civil or criminal proceedings on questions as to the interpretation of this Constitution. (Article 133 of the Constitution)

SOURCES:

http://parliament.gov.gy/constitution.

(72)

DOSSIER OF THE CONSTITUTIONAL COUNCIL OF THE REPUBLIC OF HAITI

STATE: Haiti
TITLE: Konsèy konstitisyonèl
YEAR OF FOUNDATION: (not founded yet)
SEAT: (not founded yet)

I. CHRONICLE

Date and context of establishment
Position in the hierarchy of courts

II. STANDARD LEGAL REFERENCE

Constitution 1987 with amendments

III. COMPOSITION AND ORGANIZATION

Composition
The number of judges:
The Constitutional Council is composed of nine (9) members (Article 190bis-1 of the Constitution)

Electoral/appointment body:
of which three (3) are designated by the Executive Power, three (3) by the National Assembly with the majority of two-thirds (2/3) of the members of each of the two Chambers, and three (3) by the Superior Council of the Judicial Power. (Article 190bis-1 of the Constitution)

The Court members:

The term of office:

The duration of the mandate of the members of the Constitutional Council is of nine (9) years and is not renewable. The Constitutional Council renews itself by thirds every three (3) years. (Article 190ter-2 of the Constitution)

The Court President:

The term of office:

The President of the Constitutional Council is elected by his peers for a duration of three (3) years (Article 190ter-2 of the Constitution)

IV. POWERS

Constitutional Court Review

Preventive review:

The Constitutional Council sees to and decides when it is referred to a matter:

- on the constitutionality of the laws before their promulgation;
- on the constitutionality of the internal regulations of the Senate and of the Chamber of Deputies before their implementation
- on the orders

For the same purposes, the laws in general may be referred to the Constitutional Council, before their promulgation, by the President of the Republic, the President of the Senate, the President of the Chamber of Deputies, a group of fifteen (15) Deputes or of (10) Senators. (Article 190ter-5 of the Constitution)

A posteriori review:

Abstract review:

Concrete review:

When on the occasion of a pending legal proceeding before a jurisdiction, an exception of unconstitutionality is raised, the Constitutional Council may be referred to the matter on remand from the Court of Cassation. If the provision is declared unconstitutional, the Constitutional Council returns it to the Parliament which decides sovereignly on the case. The new provision is promulgated. (Article 190ter-8 of the Constitution)

The Constitutional Council is called to decide on the conflicts which oppose the Executive Power and the Legislative Power or the two branches of the Legislative Power.(Article 190ter-7 of the Constitution)

The unconstitutionality of acts and activities of political parties: /
Charges against the President of the Republic: /
Charges against the Prime Minister or against any Minister of State: /
Electoral matters: /
Referendums: /
Standing before the Constitutional Court
State bodies: x
Individuals: /

V. NATURE AND EFFECTS OF DECISIONS

Finality:
Its decisions are not susceptible to any recourse. (Article 190bis of the Constitution)

SOURCES:
https://www.constituteproject.org/constitution/Haiti_2012.pdf?lang=en

(73)

DOSSIER OF THE SUPREME COURT OF THE REPUBLIC OF HONDURAS

STATE: Honduras
TITLE: Corte Suprema de Justicia de Honduras
YEAR OF FOUNDATION: 1880
SEAT: Tegucigalpa

I. CHRONICLE

Date and context of establishment 1880
Position in the hierarchy of courts:
The Supreme Court of Justice is the highest court; its jurisdiction includes the whole of the State and has its seat in the capital, but you can change temporarily, when so determined, at any other part of the territory (Article 308 of the Constitution)

II. STANDARD LEGAL REFERENCE

Constitution 11 January 1982 (2005)

III. COMPOSITION AND ORGANIZATION

Composition
The number of judges:
The Supreme Court of Justice, shall consist of fifteen (15) Judges. (Article 308 of the Constitution)

Electoral/appointment body:
Judges of the Supreme Court of Justice, will be elected by the National Congress, with the vote in favor of the two-thirds of the totality of its members, from a slate of candidates not less than three by each of the judges to choose. (Article 311 of the Constitution)

The Court members:

The term of office:

- The period of the Judges of the Supreme Court of Justice will be of seven (7) years from the date on which provide the promise of Law may stand for reelection. (Article 314 of the Constitution)

The Court President:

The term of office:

The President of the Supreme Court of Justice remain in office for a period of seven (7) years and may be re-elected. (Article 315)

Organization:

- The Supreme Court of Justice will be organized in chambers, one of which is the Constitutional. (Article 316 of the Constitution)

IV. POWERS

Constitutional Court Review

Preventive review:

A posteriori review:

Abstract review:

- Laws may be declared unconstitutional by reason of form or content. The Supreme Court of Justice is the knowledge and the resolution originating and exclusive in the field and must give the requirements of the final judgments. (Article 184 of the Constitution)

Concrete review:

- declared unconstitutional a law and repeal may be sought, for whom it considers injured in its direct, personal and legitimate: 1. By way of action to be open to the Supreme Court of Justice; 2. By way of exception, which may oppose to any judicial proceedings ; (Article 185 of the Constitution)

Any power or authority can take lawsuits pending or open trials closed, except in cases tried in criminal matters that may be reviewed at any time in favor of the prisoners, to request of these, of any person, the Public Ministry or ex officio. Any person aggrieved that had been a part in the process, or with the right to be called to participate in it, you can sue the revision of judgments in civil matters within a period of six (6) months since the day that having done the last notification was upheld the judgment. The action of revision shall be exercised exclusively before the Supreme Court of Justice. The law shall regulate the cases and the form of revision. (Article 185 of the Constitution)

Other powers

Constitutional complaints: .

- The State recognizes the guarantee of Habeas Corpus or staff, and of Habeas Data. As a result in the Habeas Corpus or Staff, any person aggrieved or any other in behalf of it has the right to promote; and in the Habeas Data can only promote the person whose personal data or relatives in files, public records or private as follows. (Article 182 of the Constitution)

The State recognizes the guarantee of amparo. (Article 183 of the Constitution)

Other matters with which the Court is charged by the Constitution or statute:

If the veto was founded in the bill is unconstitutional , may not be subject to a new debate without hearing before the Supreme Court of Justice, it delivered its opinion in the term that the National Congress will bring (Article 216 of the Constitution)

- created the Council of the Judiciary whose members are appointed by the Supreme Court of Justice. The Law brought his organization, its scope and powers. (Article 317 of the Constitution)

Standing before the Constitutional Court

State bodies:

Individuals:

any person aggrieved or any other in behalf of it (Article 182 of the Constitution)

V. NATURE AND EFFECTS OF DECISIONS

Finality:

The Supreme Court of Justice is the knowledge and the resolution originating and exclusive in the field and must give the requirements of the final judgments (Article 184 of the Constitution)

Ex officio:

Also the court that known at any judicial procedure, it may request ex officio the declaration of the constitutionality of a Law and its repeal before passing resolution. (Article 184. paragraf 3 of the Constitution)

SOURCES:

http://www.icla.up.ac.za/images/un/use-of-force/latin-america-caribbean/Honduras/Constitution%20 Policies%20Honduras%201982.pdf

DOSSIER OF THE COURT OF FINAL APPEAL OF THE HONG KONG SPECIAL ADMINISTRATIVE REGION

STATE: Hong Kong Special administrative region of the People's Republic of China
TITLE: Court of Final Appeal
YEAR OF FOUNDATION: 1990
SEAT: Hong Kong

I. CHRONICLE

Date and context of establishment:
The Basic Law of the Hong Kong Special Administrative Region of the People's Republic of China is the constitutional document of the Hong Kong Special Administrative Region. Being a national law of the People's Republic of China, the Basic Law was adopted on 4 April 1990 by the Seventh National People's Congress and signed by President Yang Shangkun. The Basic Law came into effect on 1 July 1997 when sovereignty over Hong Kong was transferred from the United Kingdom to the People's Republic of China, replacing the Hong Kong's colonial constitution comprising the Letters Patent and the Royal Instructions. Before 1 July 1997, Hong Kong was a British Dependent Territory, and the power of final adjudication on the laws of Hong Kong was vested in the Judicial Committee of the Privy Council in London. The Basic Law was drafted according to the Sino-British Joint Declaration signed between the Chinese and British governments on 19 December 1984. The Basic Law stipulates the basic policies of China towards the Hong Kong Special Administrative Region. As stipulated in the Joint Declaration and following the one country, two systems principle, socialism practised in the PRC would not be extended to Hong Kong. Instead, Hong Kong would continue its capitalist system and way of life for 50 years after 1997. The Hong Kong Basic Law sets out the sources of law, the relationship between the Hong Kong SAR and the Central Government, the fundamental rights and freedoms of Hong Kong residents, and the structure and functions of the branches of local government, and it provides for the amendment and interpretation of the Basic Law. The courts of Hong Kong are given the power to review acts of the executive or legislature and declare them invalid if they are inconsistent with the Basic Law. The source of authority for the Basic Law is somewhat controversial,[citation needed] with most Chinese legal scholars[who?] arguing that

the Basic Law is a purely domestic legislation deriving its authority from the Constitution of the People's Republic of China, and with some legal scholars arguing that the Basic Law derives its authority directly from the Sino-British Joint Declaration.[citation needed] The argument is relevant in that it affects the level of authority that the PRC has in making any changes to the Basic Law. It is also essential in determining the Hong Kong courts' jurisdiction in issues related to the PRC domestic legislations.

Constitutional basis is provided with Article 31 of the Constitution of the People's Republic of China: The state may establish special administrative regions when necessary. The systems to be instituted in special administrative regions shall be prescribed by law enacted by the National People's Congress in the light of the specific conditions.

Position in the hierarchy of courts:

The court has the power of final adjudication with respect to the law of Hong Kong as well as the power of final interpretation over local laws including the power to strike down local ordinances on the grounds of inconsistency with the Basic Law. The power of final interpretation of national law including the Basic Law is vested in the Standing Committee of the National People's Congress of China (NPCSC) by virtue of Article 158 of the Basic Law and by the Constitution of the PRC, however national laws which are not explicitly listed in Annex III of the Basic Law are not operative in Hong Kong.

Article 19 of the Basic Law: (1) The Hong Kong Special Administrative Region shall be vested with independent judicial power, including that of final adjudication.

(2) The courts of the Hong Kong Special Administrative Region shall have jurisdiction over all cases in the Region, except that the restrictions on their jurisdiction imposed by the legal system and principles previously in force in Hong Kong shall be maintained.

(3) The courts of the Hong Kong Special Administrative Region shall have no jurisdiction over acts of state such as defence and foreign affairs. The courts of the Region shall obtain a certificate from the Chief Executive on questions of fact concerning acts of state such as defence and foreign affairs whenever such questions arise in the adjudication of cases. This certificate shall be binding on the courts. Before issuing such a certificate, the Chief Executive shall obtain a certifying document from the Central People's Government.

Art 80 of the Basic Law: The courts of the Hong Kong Special Administrative Region at all levels shall be the judiciary of the Region, exercising the judicial power of the Region.541.

Article 81 of the Basic Law: (1) The Court of Final Appeal5413, the High Court, district courts, magistrates' courts, and other special courts shall be established in the Hong Kong Special Administrative Region. The High Court shall comprise the Court of Appeal and the Court of First Instance.

(2) The judicial system previously practised in Hong Kong shall be maintained except for those changes consequent upon the establishment of the Court of Final Appeal of the Hong Kong Special Administrative Region.

Article 82 of the Basic Law: The power of final adjudication of the Hong Kong Special Administrative Region shall be vested in the Court of Final Appeal of the Region, which may as required invite judges from other common law jurisdictions to sit on the Court of Final Appeal.

II. STANDARD LEGAL REFERENCE

The Basic Law of the Hong Kong Special Administrative Region of the People's Republic of China, adopted on April 4, 1990

III. COMPOSITION AND ORGANIZATION

Composition

The number of judges:

Electoral/appointment body:

APPOINTMENT BASED SYSTEM (Without the Participation of a Representative Body):

Article 88 of the Basic Law: Judges of the courts of the Hong Kong Special Administrative Region shall be appointed by the Chief Executive on the recommendation of an independent commission composed of local judges, persons from the legal profession and eminent persons from other sectors.

The Court members:

The term of office:

The Chief Justice and permanent judges shall vacate their offices when they attain the age of 65, but there is no retiring age for non-permanent judges.

The term of office:

20 (permanent and non-permanent judges)

The qualifications and the required professional experience of constitutional court judges:

Article 90 of the Basic Law: (1) The Chief Justice of the Court of Final Appeal and the Chief Judge of the High Court of the Hong Kong Special Administrative Region shall be Chinese citizens who are permanent residents of the Region with no right of abode in any foreign country. (...)

Article 92 of the Basic Law: Judges and other members of the judiciary of the Hong Kong Special Administrative Region shall be chosen on the basis of their judicial and professional qualities and may be recruited from other common law jurisdictions.

Incompatibilities:
Article 85 of the Basic Law: The courts of the Hong Kong Special Administrative Region shall exercise judicial power independently, free from any interference. (...)

Immunities:
Article 85 of the Basic Law: (...) Members of the judiciary shall be immune from legal action in the performance of their judicial functions.

Release from office prior to the expiration of the term:
Article 89 of the Basic Law: (1) A judge of a court of the Hong Kong Special Administrative Region may only be removed for inability to discharge his or her duties, or for misbehaviour, by the Chief Executive on the recommendation of a tribunal appointed by the Chief Justice of the Court of Final Appeal and consisting of not fewer than three local judges.

(2) The Chief Justice of the Court of Final Appeal of the Hong Kong Special Administrative Region may be investigated only for inability to discharge his or her duties, or for misbehaviour, by a tribunal appointed by the Chief Executive and consisting of not fewer than five local judges and may be removed by the Chief Executive on the recommendation of the tribunal and in accordance with the procedures prescribed in this Law.

Article 90 of the Basic Law: (...) (2) In the case of the appointment or removal of judges of the Court of Final Appeal and the Chief Judge of the High Court of the Hong Kong Special Administrative Region, the Chief Executive shall, in addition to following the procedures prescribed in Articles 88 and 89 of this Law, obtain the endorsement of the Legislative Council and report such appointment or removal to the Standing Committee of the National People's Congress for the record.

IV. POWERS

Constitutional Court Review

A posteriori review:
Abstract review:

The Court of Final Appeal has the power of final adjudication with respect to the law of Hong Kong as well as the power of final interpretation over local laws including the power to strike down local ordinances on the grounds of inconsistency with the Basic Law. The power of final interpretation of national law including the Basic Law is vested in the Standing Committee of the National People's Congress of China (NPCSC) by virtue of Article 158 of the Basic Law and by the Constitution of the PRC, however national laws which are not explicitly listed in Annex III of the Basic Law are not operative in Hong Kong.

Article 158 of the Basic Law: (1) The power of interpretation of this Law shall be vested in the Standing Committee of the National People's Congress.

(2) The Standing Committee of the National People's Congress shall authorize the courts of the Hong Kong Special Administrative Region to interpret on their own, in adjudicating cases, the provisions of this Law which are within the limits of the autonomy of the Region.

(3) The courts of the Hong Kong Special Administrative Region may also interpret other provisions of this Law in adjudicating cases. However, if the courts of the Region, in adjudicating cases, need to interpret the provisions of this Law concerning affairs which are the responsibility of the Central People's Government, or concerning the relationship between the Central Authorities and the Region, and if such interpretation will affect the judgments on the cases, the courts of the Region shall, before making their final judgments which are not appealable, seek an interpretation of the relevant provisions from the Standing Committee of the National People's Congress through the Court of Final Appeal of the Region. When the Standing Committee makes an interpretation of the provisions concerned, the courts of the Region, in applying those provisions, shall follow the interpretation of the Standing Committee. However, judgments previously rendered shall not be affected.

(4) The Standing Committee of the National People's Congress shall consult its Committee for the Basic Law of the Hong Kong Special Administrative Region before giving an interpretation of this Law.

SOURCES:

Full Text: The Practice of the One Country, Two Systems Policy in the Hong Kong Special Administrative Region . Xinhua News Agency; and

Beijing's 'White Paper' Sets Off a Firestorm in Hong Kong, http://sinosphere.blogs.nytimes.com/2014/06/11/beijings-white-paper-sets-off-a-firestorm-in-hong-kong/?mwrsm=Email

Constitutional Remedies under the Basic Law, The Focus, Basic Law Bulletin Issue 13 - December 2011, http://www.doj.gov.hk/eng/public/basiclaw/basic13_2.pdf;

The Basic Law A Decade On: Implementation Challenges and Future Outlook, The Focus, Basic Law Bulletin Issue No. 10, December 2007, http://www.doj.gov.hk/eng/public/basiclaw/basic10_3.pdf

(75)

DOSSIER OF THE CONSTITUTIONAL COURT OF HUNGARY

STATE: Republic of Hungary
TITLE: Magyarország Alkotmánybírósága
YEAR OF FOUNDATION: 1 January 1990
SEAT: Budapest

I. CHRONICLE

Date and context of establishment

In January 1989, the Parliament decided on the establishment of a constitutional court, however, its structure and competences were formed later on by the trilateral political negotiations. Accordingly, the Parliament implemented Art. 32/A. into the Constitution in October 1989, regulating a new institution of Hungarian public law: the Constitutional Court. The Act XXXII. of 1989 on the Constitutional Court was adopted on 19 October 1989 and entered into force on 30 October. On 23 November 1989 the Parliament elected the first five judges of the Court, which could commence its operation on 1 January 1990. Five additional members were elected by the new, freely elected Parliament in mid-1990.

The Constitutional Court had an important role in the new democracy: it was one of the guarantees of the rule of law by practicing constitutional review of legal provisions. Most of the petitions aimed at posterior constitutional review, and were submitted by individuals. The Court performed also ex ante reviews which had outstanding political and constitutional importance.

Position in the hierarchy of courts

The Constitutional Court is the principal organ for the protection of the Fundamental Law. The Constitutional Court is seated in Budapest. The Court has an important role in protecting the democratic State governed by the rule of law, the constitutional order, the rights guaranteed in the Fundamental Law and in safeguarding the inner coherence of the legal system. The competence, organisation and operation of the Constitutional Court are regulated by Act n. CLI of 2011.

II. STANDARD LEGAL REFERENCE

Constitution 2011 (am. 2013)

III. COMPOSITION AND ORGANIZATION

Composition

The number of judges: 8.

The Constitutional Court shall be a body composed of fifteen members.. (Article 24 of the Constitution)

Electoral/appointment body:

The National Assembly shall: shall elect the members and the President of the Constitutional Court (Article 1 of the Constitution)

The Court members:

The term of office:

Each elected for twelve years (Article 24 of the Constitution)

The Court President:

The term of office:

The National Assembly shall, with the votes of two-thirds of the Members of the National Assembly, elect a member of the Constitutional Court to serve as its President until the expiry of his or her term of office as judge of the Constitutional Court. (Article 24 of the Constitution)

IV. POWERS

Constitutional Court Review

Preventive review:

The National Assembly may, upon the motion submitted before the final vote by the initiator of the Act, by the Government or by the Speaker of the National Assembly, send the adopted Act to the Constitutional Court for an examination of its conformity with the Fundamental Law. The National Assembly shall decide on the motion after the final vote. If the motion is adopted, the Speaker of the National Assembly shall forthwith send the adopted Act to the Constitutional Court for an examination of its conformity with the Fundamental Law. (Article 6 of the Constitution) Constitutional Court: a. shall examine adopted Acts not yet published for conformity with the Fundamental Law; (Article 24 of the Constitution)

A posteriori review:

Abstract review:

The Constitutional Court may review the Fundamental Law or the amendment of the Fundamental Law only in relation to the procedural requirements laid down in the Fundamental Law for its making and promulgation. (Article 24 of the Constitution)

Constitutional Court shall examine any legal regulation for conflict with any international treaties; (Article 24 of the Constitution)

Concrete review:

Constitutional Court: b. shall, at the initiative of a judge, review the conformity with the Fundamental Law of any legal regulation applicable in a particular case with priority but within ninety days at the latest; c. shall, on the basis of a constitutional complaint, review the conformity with the Fundamental Law of any legal regulation applied in a particular case; d. shall, on the basis of a constitutional complaint, review the conformity with the Fundamental Law of any judicial decision; (Article 24 of the Constitution)

Other powers

Constitutional complaints:

Shall, on the basis of a constitutional complaint, review the conformity with the Fundamental Law of any legal regulation applied in a particular case; (Article 24, section 2, paragraf c of the Constitution)

Charges against the President of the Republic:

The Constitutional Court shall have the power to conduct the impeachment procedure.

If, as a result of the procedure, the Constitutional Court establishes the responsibility of the President of the Republic under public law, it may remove the President of the Republic from office. (Article 13 of the Constitution)

Other matters with which the Court is charged by the Constitution or statute:

At the motion of the Government - submitted after obtaining the opinion of the Constitutional Court -, the National Assembly shall dissolve representative bodies the operation of which is in conflict with the Fundamental Law. (Article 35 of the Constitution)

As long as the state debt exceeds half of the Gross Domestic Product, the Constitutional Court may, within its powers set out in Article 24(2)b) to e) of the Constitution, review the

Acts on the central budget, the implementation of the central budget, central taxes, duties and contributions, customs duties and the central conditions for local taxes for conformity with the Fundamental Law exclusively in connection with the rights to life and human dignity, to the protection of personal data, to freedom of thought, conscience and religion, or the rights related to Hungarian citizenship, and it may annul these Acts only for the violation of these rights. The Constitutional Court shall have the unrestricted right to annul also Acts having the above subject matters, if the procedural requirements laid down in the Fundamental Law for the making and promulgation of those Acts have not been met. (Article 37 of the Constitution)

Standing before the Constitutional Court
State bodies: X
Individuals: X

V. NATURE AND EFFECTS OF DECISIONS

Finality: X
Binding force:X

SOURCES:

https://www.constituteproject.org/constitution/Hungary_2013.pdf?lang=en
http://hunconcourt.hu/

(76)

DOSSIER OF THE SUPREME COURT OF THE REPUBLIC OF INDIA

STATE: Republic of India
TITLE: Supreme Court of India
YEAR OF FOUNDATION: 1 October 1937 (1950)
SEAT: New Delhi

I. CHRONICLE

Date and context of establishment 1937 (1950)
Position in the hierarchy of courts

II. STANDARD LEGAL REFERENCE

Constitution, 26 January 1950

III. COMPOSITION AND ORGANIZATION

Composition
The number of judges:
There shall be a Supreme Court of India consisting of a Chief Justice of India and, until Parliament by law prescribes a larger number, of not more than seven other Judges. (Article 124 of the Constitution)

Electoral/appointment body:
Every Judge of the Supreme Court shall be appointed by the President by warrant under his hand and seal on the recommendation of the National Judicial Appointments Commission (Article 124 of the Constitution)

The Court members:
The term of office:
and shall hold office until he attains the age of sixty-five years: (Article 124 of the Constitution)

IV. POWERS

Constitutional Court Review

Preventive review:

(1) If at any time it appears to the President that a question of law or fact has arisen, or is likely to arise, which is of such a nature and of such public importance that it is expedient to obtain the opinion of the Supreme Court upon it, he may refer the question to that Court for consideration and the Court may, after such hearing as it thinks fit, report to the President its opinion thereon. (Article 143 of the Constitution)

A posteriori review:
Abstract review:
Concrete review:

An appeal shall lie to the Supreme Court from any judgment, decree or final order of a High Court in the territory of India, whether in a civil, criminal or other proceeding, (if the High Court certifies under Article 134A of the Constitution) that the case involves a substantial question of law as to the interpretation of this Constitution.(Article 132 of the Constitution). (1) An appeal shall lie to the Supreme Court from any judgment, decree or final order in a civil proceeding of a High Court in the territory of India 5[if the High Court certifies under Article 134A of the Constitution] (a) that the case involves a substantial question of law of general importance; and (b) that in the opinion of the High Court the said question needs to be decided by the Supreme Court.] (a) that the case involves a substantial question of law of general importance; and (b) that in the opinion of the High Court the said question needs to be decided by the Supreme Court.] (2) Notwithstanding anything in Article 132 of the Constitution, any party appealing to the Supreme Court under clause (1) may urge as one of the grounds in such appeal that a substantial question of law as to the interpretation of this Constitution has been wrongly decided. (Article 133 of the Constitution). (1) An appeal shall lie to the Supreme Court from any judgment, final order or sentence in a criminal proceeding of a High Court in the territory of India if the High Court— (a) has on appeal reversed an order of acquittal of an accused person and sentenced him to death; or (b) has withdrawn for trial before itself any case from any court subordinate to its authority and has in such trial convicted the accused person and sentenced him to death; or (c) 1[certifies under

Article 134A of the Constitution] that the case is a fit one for appeal to the Supreme Court: (Article 134 of the Constitution).

Other powers

Jurisdictional disputes:

Subject to the provisions of this Constitution, the Supreme Court shall, to the exclusion of any other court, have original jurisdiction in any dispute— (a) between the Government of India and one or more States; or (b) between the Government of India and any State or States on one side and one or more other States on the other; or (c) between two or more States (Article 131 of the Constitution).

Other matters with which the Court is charged by the Constitution or statute:

Parliament may by law confer on the Supreme Court power to issue directions, orders or writs, including writs in the nature of habeas corpus, mandamus, prohibition, quo warranto and certiorari, or any of them, for any purposes other than those mentioned in clause (2) of Article 32 of the Constitution (Article 139 of the Constitution).

Standing before the Constitutional Court

State bodies:

Individuals: X

V. NATURE AND EFFECTS OF DECISIONS

Binding force:

Erga omnes:

The law declared by the Supreme Court shall be binding on all courts within the territory of India. Article 141 The law declared by the Supreme Court shall be binding on all courts within the territory of India. (Article 141).

SOURCES:

http://lawmin.nic.in/olwing/coi/coi-english/coi-4March2016.pdf

(77)

DOSSIER OF THE CONSTITUTIONAL COURT OF THE REPUBLIC OF INDONESIA

STATE: Republic of Indonesia
TITLE: Mahkamah Konstitusi Republik Indonesia
YEAR OF FOUNDATION: 13 August 2003
SEAT: Jakarta

I. CHRONICLE

Date and context of establishment 2003

Position in the hierarchy of courts

The independence of the Constitutional Court is guaranteed by the Constitution as set forth in Article 24 of the 1945 Constitution which reads as follows: *"The judicial power shall be independent and shall posses the power to organize the judicature in order to enforce law and justice"*. The aforementioned provision is reaffirmed in Article 2 of the Constitutional Court Law which reads as follows, *"Constitutional Court is a state institution which executes independent judiciary functions to hold trials in order to enforce law and justice"*. (www.venice.coe.int/WCCJ/Rio/Papers/INA_Mahfud_E.pdf)

II. STANDARD LEGAL REFERENCE

Constitution 1945 (2002)

III. COMPOSITION AND ORGANIZATION

Composition

The number of judges:

The Constitutional Court shall be composed of nine persons (Article 24 of the Constitution)

Electoral/appointment body:
and who shall be confirmed in office by the President, of whom three shall be nominated by the Supreme Court, three nominated by the DPR, and three nominated by the President. (Article 24 of the Constitution)

IV. POWERS

Constitutional Court Review

Preventive review:
A posteriori review:
Abstract review:

(1) The Constitutional Court ... ...shall have the final power of decision in reviewing laws against the Constitution. (Article 24 of the Constitution)

Concrete review:

(1) The Constitutional Court shall possess the authority to try a case at the first and final level... (Article 24 of the Constitution)

Other powers

Jurisdictional disputes:
determining disputes over the authorities of state institutions whose powers are given by this Constitution (Article 24C of the Constitution)

The unconstitutionality of acts and activities of political parties:
deciding over the dissolution of a political party (Article 24C of the Constitution)

Charges against the President of the Republic:
(2) The Constitutional Court shall possess the authority to issue a decision over an opinion of the DPR concerning alleged violations by the President and /or Vice-President of this Constitution. (Article 24C of the Constitution)

(1) Any proposal for the dismissal of the President and/or the Vice-President may be submitted by the DPR to the MPR only by first submitting a request to the Constitutional Court to investigate, bring to trial, and issue a decision on the opinion of the DPR either that the President and/or Vice-President has violated the law through an act of treason, corruption, bribery, or other act of a grave criminal nature, or through moral turpitude, and/or that the President and/or VicePresident no longer meets the qualifications to serve as President and/or VicePresident. (Article 7B of the Constitution)

Electoral matters:
deciding disputes over the results of general elections Article 24C of the Constitution)

Standing before the Constitutional Court
State bodies: x
Individuals: x

V. NATURE AND EFFECTS OF DECISIONS

Finality:
(1) The Constitutional Court shall possess the authority to try a case at the first and final level and shall have the final power of decision in reviewing laws against the Constitution. (Article 24C of the Constitution)

SOURCES:

http://www.ilo.org/wcmsp5/groups/public/---ed_protect/---protrav/---ilo_aids/documents/legaldocument/wcms_174556.pdf

(78)

DOSSIER OF THE GUARDIAN COUNCIL OF THE ISLAMIC REPUBLIC OF IRAN

STATE: Islamic Republic of Iran
TITLE: Shora-ye Negahban-e Qanun-e Assassi
YEAR OF FOUNDATION: 1979
SEAT: Tehran

I. CHRONICLE

Date and context of establishment 1979
Position in the hierarchy of courts
The Council of Guardians also functions similar to a constitutional court. The authority to interpret the constitution is vested in the Council. Interpretative decisions require a three-quarters majority. The Council does not conduct a court hearing where opposing sides are argued.

II. STANDARD LEGAL REFERENCE

Constitution 1982 (1989)

III. COMPOSITION AND ORGANIZATION

Composition
The number of judges:
The Guardian Council has the following composition:

1. Six just Islamic jurisprudents who are conscious of the issues and needs of the time. These are selected by the leader.
2. Six legal scholars (hoquqdan), specialized in different fields of law, from among Muslim jurists who are presented by the head of the judiciary to the Islamic Consultative Assembly and are selected by the vote of the Assembly. (Article 91 of the Constitution)

Electoral/appointment body:
Six just Islamic jurisprudents.. .. are selected by the leader.

Six legal scholars (hoquqdan)... ... are selected by the vote of the Assembly. (Article 91 of the Constitution)

The Court members:

The term of office:
Members of the Guardian Council are selected for six years, but in the first term, once three years have passed, half of the members of the group will be changed by lottery and new members will be selected in their place (Article 92 of the Constitution)

IV. POWERS

Constitutional Court Review

Preventive review:

All legislation of the Islamic Consultative Assembly must be sent to the Guardian Council, which must evaluate it within ten days to assure its compatibility with the constitution and the Islamic criteria. The Council must return the legislation to the Assembly for reconsideration if it is incompatible; otherwise, the legislation can be executed. (Article 94 of the Constitution)

Electoral matters:
The Guardian Council is responsible for supervising the elections of the Leadership Council of Experts, the President of the Republic, the Islamic Consultative Assembly, and referrals to the public vote and referenda. Article 99 of the Constitution)

Other matters with which the Court is charged by the Constitution or statute:
At the time of war and military occupation of the country, upon the recommendation of the President of the Republic, and with the approval of three-fourths of all the representatives, and the confirmation of the Guardian Council, elections may be delayed for a specified period of time nationwide or in the occupied areas. In the event that a new Assembly is not formed, the previous Assembly shall continue its work (Article 68 of the Constitution) signing the appointment of the President of the Republic, after his election by the public. The qualifications of the candidates for presidency, with respect to the conditions set forth by the constitution, must be confirmed by the Guardian Council prior to the general elections and approved by the leader for the first term; (Article 110 of the Constitution)

The President of the Republic must take the following oath and add his signature to it at a session held at the Islamic Consultative Assembly in the presence of the head of the judiciary power and the members of the Guardian Council... (Article 121 of the Constitution).

SOURCES:

http://www.wipo.int/edocs/lexdocs/laws/en/ir/ir001en.pdf

https://en.wikipedia.org/wiki/Guardian_Council

DOSSIER OF THE FEDERAL SUPREME COURT OF THE REPUBLIC OF IRAQ

STATE: Republic of Iraq
TITLE: Al-Mahkamah al-'Ulyā
YEAR OF FOUNDATION: 2005
SEAT: Baghdad

I. CHRONICLE

Date and context of establishment 2005
Position in the hierarchy of courts
The Federal Supreme Court of Iraq (Arabic: المحكمة الاتحادية العليا, *Al-Mahkamah al-Ittihādiyah al-'Ulyā*) is the independent judicial body of Iraq that interprets the constitution and determines the constitutionality of laws and regulations. It acts as a final court of appeals, settles disputes among or between the federal government and the regions and governorates, municipalities, and local administrations, and settles accusations directed against the President, the Prime Minister and the Ministers. It also ratifies the final results of the general elections for the Council of Representatives.

II. STANDARD LEGAL REFERENCE

Constitution 2005

III. COMPOSITION AND ORGANIZATION

Administrative autonomy:
The Federal Supreme Court is an independent judicial body, financially and administratively (Article 92 of the Constitution)

Constitutional Court Review

Preventive review:

A posteriori review:

Abstract review:

Overseeing the constitutionality of laws and regulations in effect (Article 93 of the Constitution)

Concrete review:

Settling matters that arise from the application of the federal laws, decisions, regulations, instructions, and procedures issued by the federal authority. (Article 93 of the Constitution)

Other powers

Jurisdictional disputes:

Settling disputes that arise between the federal government and the governments of the regions and governorates, municipalities, and local administrations. (Article 93 of the Constitution)

Settling disputes that arise between the governments of the regions and governments of the governorates. Article 93 of the Constitution)

Charges against the President of the Republic:

Settling accusations directed against the President, the Prime Minister and the Ministers, and this shall be regulated by law (Article 93 of the Constitution)

Electoral matters:

Ratifying the final results of the general elections for membership in the Council of Representatives. (Article 93 of the Constitution)

Referendums:

Other matters with which the Court is charged by the Constitution or statute: Settling competency disputes between the federal judiciary and the judicial institutions of the regions and governorates that are not organized in a region. B. Settling competency disputes between judicial institutions of the regions or governorates that are not organized in a region. (Article 93 of the Constitution)

V. NATURE AND EFFECTS OF DECISIONS

Finality:
Decisions of the Federal Supreme Court are final and binding for all authorities. (Article 94 of the Constitution)

Binding force:
Erga omnes: and binding for all authorities (Article 94 of the Constitution)

SOURCES:

http://www.iraqinationality.gov.iq/attach/iraqi_constitution.pdf
https://en.wikipedia.org/wiki/Federal_Supreme_Court_of_Iraq

(80)

DOSSIER OF THE SUPREME COURT OF THE REPUBLIC OF IRELAND

STATE: Republic of Ireland
TITLE: Cúirt Uachtarach na hÉireann
YEAR OF FOUNDATION: 29 December 1937
SEAT: Dublin

I. CHRONICLE

Date and context of establishment 1937
Position in the hierarchy of courts:
The Court of Final Appeal shall be called the Supreme Court. (Article 34 of the Constitution)

II. STANDARD LEGAL REFERENCE

Constitution 1937, 2002

III. COMPOSITION AND ORGANIZATION

Composition
The Supreme Court is composed of the Chief Justice of Ireland, who is President of the Court, and nine ordinary Judges. In addition the President of the Court of Appeal is *ex officio* a member of the Supreme Court. The President of the High Court is also an *ex officio* member of the Supreme Court.

The Court usually sits with a composition of three or five Judges and, exceptionally, seven Judges. When hearing cases concerning the constitutional validity of an Act of the Oireachtas (parliament) the Constitution requires that the Court consists of a minimum of five Judges. This requirement also applies when the Court is requested to give an opinion on the constitutional validity of a Bill adopted by the Oireachtas when referred to it by the President of Ireland under

Article 26 of the Constitution. A minimum of five Judges is also required should the Court have to determine, pursuant to Article 12 of the Constitution, whether the President has become permanently incapacitated.

In addition to those cases in which it is required by the Constitution, a court composed of five Judges, or exceptionally seven Judges, will sit for appeals involving questions of law of particular importance or complexity. Where an insufficient number of Judges of the Supreme Court are available the Chief Justice may request any ordinary Judge of the High Court to sit as a member of the Supreme Court for the hearing of a particular appeal.

Interlocutory applications and procedural matters or issues may be determined by the Chief Justice sitting alone or another judge of the Supreme Court nominated by the Chief Justice.

Electoral/appointment body:

The judges of the Supreme Court, the Court of Appeal, the High Court and all other Courts established in pursuance of Article 34 hereof shall be appointed by the President. (Article 35 of the Constitution)

IV. POWERS

Constitutional Court Review

Preventive review:

The President may, after consultation with the Council of State, refer any Bill to which this Article applies to the Supreme Court for a decision on the question as to whether such Bill or any specified provision or provisions of such Bill is or are repugnant to this Constitution or to any provision thereof. (Article 26 of the Constitution)

A posteriori review:

Abstract review:

Concrete review:

The Supreme Court shall, subject to such regulations as may be prescribed by law, have appellate jurisdiction from a decision of the Court of Appeal if the Supreme Court is satisfied that- i the decision involves a matter of general public importance, or ii In the interests of justice it is necessary that there be an appeal to the Supreme Court (Article 34 of the Constitution)

Other powers

Charges against the President of the Republic:

The President shall hold office for seven years from the date upon which he enters upon his office, unless before the expiration of that period he dies, or resigns, or is removed from office, or becomes permanently incapacitated, such incapacity being established to the satisfaction of the Supreme Court consisting of not less than five judges. (Article 12 of the Constitution)

Standing before the Constitutional Court

State bodies:

Individuals: x

V. NATURE AND EFFECTS OF DECISIONS

Finality:

The decision of the Supreme Court shall in all cases be final and conclusive. (Article 34 of the Constitution).

Erga omnes:

The decision of the Supreme Court shall in all cases be final and conclusive. (Article 34 of the Constitution).

SOURCES:

http://www.taoiseach.gov.ie/eng/Publications/Publications_Archive/Publications_for_2002/November%202002%20Version%20Constitution.pdf

http://www.supremecourt.ie/

(81)

DOSSIER OF THE CONSTITUTIONAL COURT OF THE ITALIAN REPUBLIC

STATE: Italian Republic
TITLE: Corte costituzionale della Repubblica Italiana
YEAR OF FOUNDATION: 1956
SEAT: Rome

I. CHRONICLE

Date and context of establishment 1956
Position in the hierarchy of courts

II. STANDARD LEGAL REFERENCE

Constitution 1947 (2012)

III. COMPOSITION AND ORGANIZATION

Composition
The number of judges:
The Constitutional Court shall be composed of fifteen judges (Article 135 of the Constitution)

Electoral/appointment body:
a third nominated by the President of the Republic, a third by Parliament in joint sitting and a third by the ordinary and administrative Supreme Courts Article 135 of the Constitution)

The Court members:

The term of office:
Judges of the Constitutional Court shall be appointed for nine years, beginning in each case from the day of their swearing in, and they may not be re-appointed Article 135 of the Constitution)

The Court President:
The term of office:
The Court shall elect from among its members, in accordance with the rules established by law, a President, who shall remain in office for three years and may be re-elected, respecting in all cases the expiry term for constitutional judges (Article 135 of the Constitution)

IV. POWERS

Constitutional Court Review

Preventive review:
A posteriori review:
Abstract review:

The Constitutional Court shall pass judgement on: controversies on the constitutional legitimacy of laws and enactments having force of law issued by the State and Regions; (Article 134 of the Constitution)

The Government of the Republic may submit the constitutional legitimacy of the regional statutes to the Constitutional Court within thirty days of their publication (Article 123 of the Constitution)

The Government may question the constitutional legitimacy of a regional law before the Constitutional Court within sixty days from its publication, when it deems that the regional law exceeds the competence of the Region (Article 127 of the Constitution)

A Region may question the constitutional legitimacy of a State or regional law or measure having the force of law before the Constitutional Court within 35 sixty days from its publication, when it deems that said law or measure infringes upon its competence. (Article 127 of the Constitution)

Concrete review:

Other powers
Constitutional complaints: /

Jurisdictional disputes:
The Constitutional Court shall pass judgement on: conflicts arising from allocation of powers of the State and those powers allocated to State and Regions, and between Regions (Article 134 of the Constitution)

Charges against the President of the Republic:
The Constitutional Court shall pass judgement on: ... charges brought against the President of the Republic (Article 134 of the Constitution)

Charges against the Prime Minister or against any Minister of State:
The Constitutional Court shall pass judgement on: and the Ministers, according to the provisions of the Constitution.

V. NATURE AND EFFECTS OF DECISIONS

Finality:
No appeals are allowed against the decision of the Constitutional Court. (Article 137 of the Constitution)

SOURCES:

http://www.senato.it/documenti/repository/istituzione/costituzione_inglese.pdf
https://www.cortecostituzionale.it/default.do

(82)

DOSSIER OF THE CONSTITUTIONAL COURT OF THE STATE OF JAPAN

STATE: Japan
TITLE: Saikō-Saibansho
YEAR OF FOUNDATION: 1947
SEAT: Tokyo

I. CHRONICLE

Date and context of establishment 1947

The first Western-style supreme court in Japan was the Supreme Court of Judicature (大審院 *Dai-shin'in*) organized by the Ministry of Justice in 1875. This court was composed of 120 judges in both civil and criminal divisions. Five judges would be empaneled for any given case. The criminal division of the court was the court of first instance for crimes against the Emperor (e.g. *lèse majesté*) and for high crimes against public order.

The statute creating the Court was abolished in 1947, and the modern Supreme Court was formed that year under the constitution of 1947.

Position in the hierarchy of courts

II. STANDARD LEGAL REFERENCE

Constitution 1947

III. COMPOSITION AND ORGANIZATION

Composition

The number of judges:

The Supreme Court shall consist of a Chief Judge and such number of judges as may be determined by law (Article 79 of the Constitution)

Electoral/appointment body:
all such judges excepting the Chief Judge shall be appointed by the Cabinet. (Article 79 of the Constitution)

The Emperor shall appoint the Chief Judge of the Supreme Court as designated by the Cabinet. (Article 6 of the Constitution)

The Court members:

The term of office:
The appointment of the judges of the Supreme Court shall be reviewed by the people at the first general election of members of the House of Representatives following their appointment, and shall be reviewed again at the first general election of members of the House of Representatives after a lapse of ten (10) years, and in the same manner thereafter. (Article 79 of the Constitution)

IV. POWERS

Constitutional Court Review

Preventive review:

A posteriori review:

Abstract review:

The Supreme Court is the court of last resort with power to determine the constitutionality of any law, order, regulation or official act. (Article 81 of the Constitution)

Concrete review:

The Supreme Court is the court of last resort with power to determine the constitutionality of any law, order, regulation or official act. (Article 81 of the Constitution)

V. NATURE AND EFFECTS OF DECISIONS

Finality:
The Supreme Court is the court of last resort with power to determine the constitutionality of any law, order, regulation or official act. (Article 81 of the Constitution)

SOURCES:

http://japan.kantei.go.jp/constitution_and_government_of_japan/constitution_e.htm

http://www.courts.go.jp/english/

(83)

DOSSIER OF THE CONSTITUTIONAL COURT OF THE HASHEMITE KINGDOM OF JORDAN

STATE: The Hashemite Kingdom of Jordan
TITLE: Constitutional Court
YEAR OF FOUNDATION: 2012
SEAT: Amman

I. CHRONICLE

Date and context of establishment 2012
Position in the hierarchy of courts

II. STANDARD LEGAL REFERENCE

Constitution 1952 with amendments
Law No. 15 of 2012 (Jordan) Issued on 16/06/2012 CONSTITUTIONAL COURT LAW

III. COMPOSITION AND ORGANIZATION

Composition
The number of judges:
and shall be composed of nine members at least inclusive of the President (Article 59 of the Constitution)

Electoral/appointment body:
to be appointed by the King (Article 59 of the Constitution)

The Court members:

The term of office:
The term of membership in the Constitutional Court shall be six years non-renewable (Article 59 of the Constitution)

Organization
Administrative autonomy:
shall be considered as an independent and separate judicial body (Article 58 of the Constitution)

IV. POWERS

Constitutional Court Review

A posteriori review:
Abstract review:

The Constitutional Court shall have the competence of oversight on the constitutionality of the applicable laws and regulations (Article 59 of the Constitution)

Concrete review: In the case viewed by courts, any of the parties of the case may raise the issue of the nonconstitutionality; the court shallif it finds that the plea is serious-refer it to the court specified by the law for the purposes of the determination of its referral to the Constitutional Court. (Article 60 of the Constitution)

Other matters with which the Court is charged by the Constitution or statute:
The Constitutional Court shall have the right to interpret the provisions of the Constitution if such is requested therefrom by a decision issued by the Council of Ministers or by a decision taken by either House of the Parliament by majority; (Article 59 of the Constitution)

Standing before the Constitutional Court
State bodies:
The following entities- for limitation- shall the right to directly challenge at the Constitutional Court the constitutionality of the applicable laws and regulations: a- The Senate. b- The House of Representatives. c- The Council of Ministers. (Article 60 of the Constitution)

Individuals: /

Finality:
its judgments shall be final (Article 59 of the Constitution)

Binding force:
its judgments... ...and binding on all authorities and on all (Article 59 of the Constitution)

SOURCES:

http://cco.gov.jo/Portals/0/constitution_en.pdf

http://www.cco.gov.jo/Documents-of-the-Court/The-Law-of-the-Constitutional-Court

DOSSIER OF THE CONSTITUTIONAL COUNCIL OF THE REPUBLIC OF KAZAKHSTAN

STATE: Republic of Kazakhstan
TITLE: Constitutional Council of the Republic of Kazakhstan
YEAR OF FOUNDATION: 29 December 1995
SEAT: Astana

I. CHRONICLE

Date and context of establishment

The beginning of creation of constitutional control institute in Kazakhstan is connected with introduction in 1989 of addition into the Constitution of Kazakh Soviet Socialist Republic of 1978 providing establishment of Committee of the constitutional supervision which, however, hasn't been created.

Later the Constitutional law of the Republic of Kazakhstan of December 16, 1991 About the state independence of the Republic of Kazakhstan established that the supreme body of judicial protection of the Constitution is the Constitutional Court of the Republic of Kazakhstan. The Constitutional Court has begun to work in 1992 when the laws About the Constitutional Court of the Republic of Kazakhstan and About the Constitutional Legal Proceedings have been adopted, and the chairman and ten judges of the Constitutional Court were elected.

On August 30, 1995 according to the adopted new Constitution of the Republic of Kazakhstan the quasi-judicial authority of the constitutional control - the Constitutional Council has been founded.

Position in the hierarchy of courts

According to article 1 of the Constitutional law About the Constitutional Council of the Republic of Kazakhstan , the Constitutional Council as the state body, providing the rule of the Constitution of the Republic of Kazakhstan in all territory of the republic, when implementation its powers is independent and independent of state bodies, organizations, officials and citizens, submits only to the Constitution of the Republic and can't proceed from political and other reasons, carries out the powers, being guided by the Constitution of the Republic and the

Constitutional law, abstaining from establishment and research of other questions in all cases when it enters a competence of the courts or other state bodies.

II. STANDARD LEGAL REFERENCE

Constitution 1995

III. COMPOSITION AND ORGANIZATION

Composition

The number of judges:

The Constitutional Council of the Republic of Kazakhstan shall consist of seven members (Article 71 of the Constitution)

Electoral/appointment body:

Two members of the Constitutional Council shall be appointed by the President of the Republic, on two members shall be appointed accordingly by the Senate and the Majilis. (Article 71 of the Constitution)

The Court members:

The term of office:

whose powers shall last for six years (Article 71 of the Constitution)

IV. POWERS

Constitutional Court Review

Preventive review:

1. consider the laws adopted by Parliament with respect to their compliance with the Constitution of the Republic before they are signed by the President;

3.consider the international treaties of the Republic with respect to their compliance with the constitution, before they are ratified (Article 72 of the Constitution)

A posteriori review:

consider the decisions adopted by the Parliament and its Chambers to their compliance with the Constitution of the Republic (Article 72 of the Constitution)

Other powers

Charges against the President of the Republic:

1. The President of the Republic of Kazakhstan may be prematurely released from office in the case of continued incapacity to perform his duties due to illness. In this case the Parliament shall form a commission consisting of equal numbers of deputies from each Chamber and specialists of the respective areas of medicine. The decision of premature release based on the conclusion of the commission and that of the Constitutional Council confirming observance of the established constitutional procedures shall be adopted at a joint sitting of the Parliament's Chambers by the majority of no less than threefourths from the total number of deputies of each Chamber.
2. The President of the Republic shall bear responsibility for the actions performed while exercising his duties and only in the case of high treason may be discharged from office by Parliament. The decision to bring an accusation and conduct its investigation may be adopted by the majority of the deputies of the Majilis at the initiative of no less than onethird of the total number of its deputies. Investigation of the accusation shall be organized by the Senate and by the majority of votes of the total number of the deputies of the Senate its results are transferred for consideration at a joint session of the Parliament's Chambers. The final decision of this issue shall be adopted at a joint session of the Parliament's Chambers by the majority of no less than threefourths of the total number of the deputies of each Chamber, provided the Supreme Court concludes the validity of the accusation and conclusion by the Constitutional Council that the established constitutional procedures were observed. The failure to arrive at a final decision within two months from the moment of the accusation shall result in the recognition that the accusation against the President of the Republic is rejected. Rejection of the accusation of the President of the Republic in perpetration of high treason at any stage shall result in premature termination of the powers of the deputies of the Majilis who initiated the consideration of this issue (Article 47 of the Constitution)

Electoral matters:

decide on the correctness of conducting the elections of the President of the Republic, deputies of Parliament...; (Article 72 of the Constitution)

Referendums:

decide on the... ...and conducting an allnation referendum in case of dispute; (Article 72 of the Constitution)

Standing before the Constitutional Court

State bodies:

The Constitutional Council by appeal of the President of the Republic of Kazakhstan, the chairperson of the Senate, the Chairperson of Majilis, not less than onefifth of the total number of deputies of Parliament, the Prime Minister shall (Article 72 of the Constitution);

The courts shall have no right to apply laws and other regulatory legal acts infringing on the rights and liberties of an individual and a citizen established by the Constitution. (Article 78 of the Constitution)

V. NATURE AND EFFECTS OF DECISIONS

Finality:

Constitutional Council... ...and not subject to appeal. (Article 74 of the Constitution)

Binding force:

Erga omnes:

Decisions of the Constitutional Council shall come into effect from the day they are adopted, shall be binding on the entire territory of the Republic... (Article 74 of the Constitution)

SOURCES:

http://users2.unimi.it/dirpubesteuropa/2015/03/constitution-of-the-republic-of-kazakhstan/

http://www.ksrk.gov.kz/eng/index.php

(85)

DOSSIER OF THE SUPREME COURT OF THE REPUBLIC OF KENYA

STATE: Republic of Kenya
TITLE: Supreme Court of Kenya
YEAR OF FOUNDATION: 1963
SEAT: Nairobi

I. CHRONICLE

Date and context of establishment 1963
The Supreme Court is the highest Court in the Judiciary while the lowest Court is the Magistrates court.

Position in the hierarchy of courts
The court hears and determines cases relating to presidential elections. It hears appeals on cases that have been concluded by the Court of Appeal, issues advisory opinions on matters concerning County Governments, in any cases involving the interpretation or application of the Constitution and in matters of general public importance.

Further, the Supreme Court hears appeals from any other court or tribunal as prescribed by national legislation and determines the validity of a declaration of a state of emergency.

II. STANDARD LEGAL REFERENCE

Constitution 2010

III. COMPOSITION AND ORGANIZATION

Composition

The number of judges:

There is established the Supreme Court, which shall consists of:

(a) the Chief Justice, who shall be the president of the court;

(b) the Deputy Chief Justice, who shall:

  (i) deputise for the Chief Justice; and

  (ii) be the vice-president of the court; and

(c) five other judges (Article 163 of the Constitution)

IV. POWERS

Constitutional Court Review

Concrete review:

Appeals shall lie from the Court of Appeal to the Supreme Court—

(a) as of right in any case involving the interpretation or application of this Constitution; and

(b) in any other case in which the Supreme Court, or the Court of Appeal, certifies that a matter of general public importance is involved, subject to clause (Article 163 of the Constitution)

Other powers

Electoral matters:

A person may file a petition in the Supreme Court to challenge the election of the President-elect within seven days after the date of the declaration of the results of the presidential election. (Article 140 of the Constitution)

Standing before the Constitutional Court

State bodies: X

Individuals: X

SOURCES:

http://www.kenyalaw.org/lex/actview.xql?actid=Const2010

(86)

DOSSIER OF THE HIGH COURT OF THE REPUBLIC OF KIRIBATI

STATE: Republic of Kiribati
TITLE: High Court of Kiribati
YEAR OF FOUNDATION: 1995
SEAT: Betio Island

I. CHRONICLE

Date and context of establishment 1995
Position in the hierarchy of courts

II. STANDARD LEGAL REFERENCE

Constitution 1995 (2010)

III. COMPOSITION AND ORGANIZATION

Composition
The number of judges:
The judges of the High Court shall be the Chief Justice and such number of other judges, if any, as may be prescribed. (Article 80 of the Constitution)

Electoral/appointment body:

1. The Chief Justice shall be appointed by the Beretitenti, acting in accordance with the advice of the Cabinet tendered after consultation with the Public Service Commission.
2. The other judges of the High Court, if any, shall be appointed by the Beretitenti, acting in accordance with the advice of the Chief Justice sitting with the Public Service Commission.

(Article 81 of the Constitution)

Constitutional Court Review

Preventive review:

The High Court shall have jurisdiction to make a declaration as to whether any Bill referred to it by the Beretitenti under section 66(5) of the Constitution, if assented to, would be inconsistent with this Constitution. (Article 88 of the Constitution)

A posteriori review:

Concrete review:

1. Subject to the provisions of this Constitution, if any person alleges that any provision of this Constitution (other than Chapter II of the Constitution) has been contravened and that his interests are being or are likely to be affected by such contravention, then, without prejudice to any other action with respect to the same matter which is lawfully available, that person may apply to the High Court for a declaration and for relief under this section.
2. The High Court shall have jurisdiction, in any application made by any person under the preceding subsection or in any other proceedings lawfully brought before the Court, to determine whether any provision of this Constitution (other than Chapter II) has been contravened and to make a declaration accordingly: (Article 88 of the Constitution)

Other powers

Electoral matters:

1. The High Court shall have jurisdiction to hear and determine any question whether— a. any person has been validly elected as a member of the Maneaba ni Maungatabu; or b. any elected member of the Maneaba has vacated his seat therein or is required by virtue of section 58 of the Constitution to cease to perform his functions as a member.

2. An application to the High Court for the determination of— a. any question under paragraph (a) of the preceding subsection may be made by any person entitled to vote in the electoral district, and at the election, to which the application relates or by any person who was a candidate in that district at that election or by the Attorney-General; b. any question under paragraph (b) of the preceding subsection may be made by any person entitled to vote at an election in the electoral district for which the member concerned was returned or by any elected member of the Maneaba or by the Attorney-General: Provided that if such an application is made by a person other than the Attorney-General, the Attorney-General may intervene and may then appear or be represented in the proceedings (Article 60 of the Constitution)

Other matters with which the Court is charged by the Constitution or statute:
The High Court shall have jurisdiction to hear and determine any question whether any person has been validly declared to be the nominated member or the nominated member has vacated his seat in the Maneaba or is required by virtue of the preceding subsection and section 58 of the Constitution to cease to perform his functions as a member. (Article 117 of the Constitution)

Standing before the Constitutional Court

State bodies:
Provided that the following authorities only are entitled to make application to the High Court under this subsection— a. the Beretitenti, acting in accordance with the advice of the Cabinet; b. the Attorney-General; and c. the Speaker

Individuals:
The High Court shall have jurisdiction, in any application made by any person... (Article 88 of the Constitution)

SOURCES:

https://www.constituteproject.org/constitution/Kiribati_1995.pdf?lang=en

DOSSIER OF THE CONSTITUTIONAL COURT OF THE REPUBLIC OF KOSOVO

STATE: The Republic of Kosovo
TITLE: The Constitutional Court
YEAR OF FOUNDATION: 2009
SEAT: Prishtina

I. CHRONICLE

Date and context of establishment 2009
Position in the hierarchy of courts
The Constitutional Court is an independent organ in protecting the constitutionality and is the final interpreter of the Constitution (Article 4 of the Constitution).

Article 112 of the Constitution [General Principles]

1. The Constitutional Court is the final authority for the interpretation of the Constitution and the compliance of laws with the Constitution.
2. The Constitutional Court is fully independent in the performance of its responsibilities.

II. STANDARD LEGAL REFERENCE

The constitution was signed on 7 April 2008 at 13:00 local time at the national library in Prishtina. The constitution was ratified on 9 April and came to effect on 15 June 2008

III. COMPOSITION AND ORGANIZATION

Composition
The number of judges:
The Constitutional Court shall be composed of nine (9) judges who shall be distinguished jurists of the highest moral character, with not less than ten (10) years of relevant professional

experience. Other relevant qualifications shall be provided by law. Principles of gender equality shall be respected. (Article 114 of the Constitution).

Electoral/appointment body:
Judges shall be appointed by the President of the Republic of Kosovo upon the proposal of the Assembly and shall serve for a non-renewable mandate of nine (9) years (Article 114 of the Constitution).

The National Assembly make proposals (Article 65), appointment by the President of the State (Article 84 of the Constitution)

The Court members:
The term of office:
The Court President:
The President and Deputy President of the Constitutional Court shall be elected from the judges of the Constitutional Court by a secret ballot of the judges of the Court for a term of three (3) years. Election to these offices shall not extend the regular mandate of the judge (Article 114 of the Constitution).

Organization
Administrative autonomy:
Article 115 of the Constitution [Organization of the Constitutional Court]

1. The Constitutional Court shall determine its internal organization, rules of procedure, decision-making processes and other organizational issues pursuant to law.
2. The Constitutional Court shall publish an annual report.

IV. POWERS AND APPLICANTS (STANDING)

Article 113 of the Constitution [Jurisdiction and Authorized Parties]

1. The Constitutional Court decides only on matters referred to the court in a legal manner by authorized parties.

2. The Assembly of Kosovo, the President of the Republic of Kosovo, the Government, and the Ombudsperson are authorized to refer the following matters to the Constitutional Court:

(1) the question of the compatibility with the Constitution of laws, of decrees of the President or Prime Minister, and of regulations of the Government;
(2) the compatibility with the Constitution of municipal statutes.

3. The Assembly of Kosovo, the President of the Republic of Kosovo and the Government are authorized to refer the following matters to the Constitutional Court:

(1) conflict among constitutional competencies of the Assembly of Kosovo, the President of the Republic of Kosovo and the Government of Kosovo;
(2) compatibility with the Constitution of a proposed referendum;
(3) compatibility with the Constitution of the declaration of a State of Emergency and the actions undertaken during the State of Emergency;
(4) compatibility of a proposed constitutional amendment with binding international agreements ratified under this Constitution and the review of the constitutionality of the procedure followed;
(5) questions whether violations of the Constitution occurred during the election of the Assembly.

4. A municipality may contest the constitutionality of laws or acts of the Government infringing upon their responsibilities or diminishing their revenues when municipalities are affected by such law or act.

5. Ten (10) or more deputies of the Assembly of Kosovo, within eight (8) days from the date of adoption, have the right to contest the constitutionality of any law or decision adopted by the Assembly as regards its substance and the procedure followed.

6. Thirty (30) or more deputies of the Assembly are authorized to refer the question of whether the President of the Republic of Kosovo has committed a serious violation of the Constitution.

7. Individuals are authorized to refer violations by public authorities of their individual rights and freedoms guaranteed by the Constitution, but only after exhaustion of all legal remedies provided by law.

8. The courts have the right to refer questions of constitutional compatibility of a law to the Constitutional Court when it is raised in a judicial proceeding and the referring court is uncertain as to the compatibility of the contested law with the Constitution and provided that the referring court's decision on that case depends on the compatibility of the law at issue.

9. The President of the Assembly of Kosovo refers proposed Constitutional amendments before approval by the Assembly to confirm that the proposed amendment does not diminish the rights and freedoms guaranteed by Chapter II of the Constitution.

Additional jurisdiction may be determined by law.

Other powers

Charges against the President of the Republic:

The President of the Republic of Kosovo may be dismissed by the Assembly if he/she has been convicted of a serious crime or if she/he is unable to exercise the responsibilities of office due to serious illness or if the Constitutional Court has determined that he/she has committed a serious violation of the Constitution (Article 91 of the Constitution).

Standing before the Constitutional Court

State bodies:

In the event the Municipal Assembly chooses not to reconsider its act or decision, or the Vice President deems the result, upon reconsideration, to still present a violation of a constitutionally guaranteed right, the Vice President may submit the matter directly to the Constitutional Court, which may decide whether or not to accept the matter for review (Article 62 of the Constitution).

The President of the State (Article 84 of the Constitution), the Government (Article 93 of the Constitution)

Individuals: X

V. NATURE AND EFFECTS OF DECISIONS

Binding force:

Erga omnes:

Article 116 of the Constitution [Legal Effect of Decisions]

1. Decisions of the Constitutional Court are binding on the judiciary and all persons and institutions of the Republic of Kosovo.
2. While a proceeding is pending before the Constitutional Court, the Court may temporarily suspend the contested action or law until the Court renders a decision if the Court finds that application of the contested action or law would result in unrecoverable damages.
3. If not otherwise provided by the Constitutional Court decision, the repeal of the law or other act or action is effective on the day of the publication of the Court decision.
4. Decisions of the Constitutional Court are published in the Official Gazette.

SOURCES:

http://www.gjk-ks.org/?cid=2,1

(88)

DOSSIER OF THE SUPERIOR CONSTITUTIONAL COURT OF THE STATE OF KUWAIT

STATE: State of Kuwait
TITLE: Superior Constitutional Court
YEAR OF FOUNDATION: 1973
SEAT: Kuwait City

I. CHRONICLE

Date and context of establishment 1973
Position in the hierarchy of courts
The Superior Constitutional Court is the highest level of the Kuwaiti judiciary..

II. STANDARD LEGAL REFERENCE

Constitution 1961-1962: On November 1, 1962, the draft constitution was approved by the then Amir, late Sheikh Abdallah Al-Salem Al-Saba; reinstated in 1992

Law No. 14 of 1973 establishing the Constitutional Court

III. COMPOSITION AND ORGANIZATION

Composition
The number of judges: 5
Electoral/appointment body:
Are chosen by the Judicial Council by secret election, and one reserve member who is appointed by decree. Although judges of the other courts may be non-Kuwaiti, judges of the Constitutional Court must be Kuwaiti nationals.

According to the provisions of (Article 173 of the Constitution), the law shall specify the competent judicial body for settling disputes pertaining to the constitutionality of laws and regulations and define its powers and method of challenging and procedures to be followed before the said body.

It shall also specify the consequences of judgment regarding unconstitutionality.

The Law No. 14 of 1973 established the Constitutional Court, which has exclusive jurisdiction to interpret the constitutionality of legislation and it is empowered to review electoral contestations. An important guide to the judiciary in rendering opinions about legislation is the Explanatory Note stating the intentions of the legislature that frequently accompany legislative acts.

Constitutional Court Review

A posteriori review:

Concrete review:

The Superior Constitutional Court interpreted the constitution and dealt with disputes related to the constitutionality of laws, statutes and by-laws, as well as election disputes.

Other powers

Electoral matters:

The Superior Constitutional Court interpreted the constitution and dealt with disputes related to the constitutionality of laws, statutes and by-laws, as well as election disputes.

SOURCES:

http://www.nyulawglobal.org/globalex/Kuwait.html

DOSSIER OF THE CONSTITUTIONAL CHAMBER OF THE SUPREME COURT OF THE KYRGYZ REPUBLIC (KYRGYZSTAN)

STATE: The Kyrgyz Republic (Kyrgyzystan)
TITLE: The Supreme Court (The Constitutional Chamber of The Supreme Court)
YEAR OF FOUNDATION: 2010
SEAT: Bishkek city

I. CHRONICLE

Date and context of establishment 2010

Position in the hierarchy of courts

The Supreme Court shall be the highest body of judicial power in respect of civil, criminal, administrative as well as other cases; it shall revise the court rulings of local courts upon appeals of the participants in the judicial process in accordance with procedures established by the law. (Article 96 of the Constitution).

The Constitutional Chamber of the Supreme Court of the Kyrgyz Republic is the highest judicial authority which independently performs the constitutional oversight by way of constitutional legal proceedings.

The Constitutional Chamber shall act as part of the Supreme Court (Article 93 of the Constitution).

II. STANDARD LEGAL REFERENCE

The current constitution of Kyrgyzstan was passed by referendum on June 27, 2010, replacing the previous constitution

Composition

Article 97 of the Constitution

1.The Constitutional Chamber of the Supreme Court shall be a body which shall perform constitutional oversight.

The number of judges: ?

Electoral/appointment body:

Article 97 of the Constitution

2.Any citizen of the Kyrgyz Republic who is not younger than 40 years of age and not older than 70 years of age, has higher legal education and not less than 15 years of experience in legal profession may be the judge of the Constitutional Chamber of the Supreme Court.

The Court members:

The term of office:3

The Court President:

Article 97 of the Constitution

The judges of the Constitutional Chamber of the Supreme Court shall elect the chairperson and deputy chairperson from amongst them for the term of 3 years.

One and the same person may not be elected the chairperson or deputy chairperson of the Constitutional Chamber of the Supreme Court for two consecutive terms.

The term of office: 3

Organization

The composition and the procedures of formation of the Constitutional Chamber of the Supreme Court, election and dismissal of chairpersons, deputy chairpersons of the Constitutional Chamber as well as the procedure of administering constitutional justice shall be defined in the constitutional law.(Article 97 of the Constitution)

Administrative autonomy:

The State shall ensure funding and appropriate conditions for the functioning of courts and the activities of judges.

The funding of courts shall be at the expense of the national budget and should ensure the possibility of full and independent administration of justice. (Article 98 of the Constitution)

The jurisdiction, organization and procedure of activity of the Supreme Court of the Kyrgyz Republic shall be established by the Constitution of the Kyrgyz Republic, constitutional laws on status of courts and judges, procedural laws and by this Law. The Supreme Court of the Kyrgyz

Republic shall have the right to enact Regulations on Supreme Court of the Kyrgyz Republic referred to the internal issues of its activity which were not regulated by the law of the Kyrgyz Republic. (Article 3 of the Constitution) .

The budget:

The budget of the judicial system shall be drawn up independently by the judiciary and shall be included in the national budget upon agreement with the executive and legislative branches of power. (Article 98 of the Constitution)

Funding of the Supreme Court of the Kyrgyz Republic shall be made as a rule from the resources of the Republican budget under separate item, and must provide the possibility of complete and independent conduct of legal procedures in accordance with the Constitution of the Kyrgyz Republic and with this Law. (Article 13 of the Constitution)

IV. POWERS

Constitutional Court Review

Article 97 of the Constitution: The Constitutional Chamber of the Supreme Court:

1) shall declare unconstitutional laws and other regulatory legal acts in the event that they contradict the Constitution;

2) shall conclude on the constitutionality of international treaties not entered into force and to which the Kyrgyz Republic is a party;

3) shall conclude on the draft law on changes to the present Constitution.

Everyone shall have the right to challenge the constitutionality of a law or another regulatory legal act in case he/she believes that these acts violate rights and freedoms recognized in the Constitution.

Standing before the Constitutional Court

State bodies:

Article 101 of the Constitution

A court shall not have the right to apply a legal and regulatory act which is in contradiction with the present Constitution.

In the event that during examination of a case in any judicial instance, there arises a question concerning the constitutionality of the law or other legal and regulatory act on which ruling of the case shall be based, the court shall send an inquiry to the constitutional Chamber of the Supreme Court.

Individuals:
Everyone shall have the right to challenge the constitutionality of a law or another regulatory legal act in case he/she believes that these acts violate rights and freedoms recognized in the Constitution. (Article 97 of the Constitution)

V. NATURE AND EFFECTS OF DECISIONS

Finality:
Article 97 of the Constitution: The ruling of the Constitutional Chamber of the Supreme Court shall be final and shall be not subject to appeal.

In the event that the Constitutional Chamber of the Supreme Court determines unconstitutionality of laws or provisions thereof, such laws shall be repealed on the territory of the Kyrgyz Republic, the same applies to other regulatory legal acts based on such laws and provisions thereof declared unconstitutional with the exception of court rulings.

Court rulings based on provisions of laws declared unconstitutional, shall be revised by courts in each concrete case upon appeals of citizens whose rights and freedoms were affected.

SOURCES:

www.legislationline.org/documents/id/5045
http://constpalata.kg/en/about/

(90)

DOSSIER OF THE NATIONAL ASSEMBLY STANDING COMMITTEE OF THE LAO PEOPLE'S DEMOCRATIC REPUBLIC

STATE: Lao People´s Democratic Republic
TITLE: The National Assembly Standing Committee
YEAR OF FOUNDATION: 1991
SEAT: Vientiane

I. CHRONICLE

Date and context of establishment 1991

Position in the hierarchy of courts

Article 56 of the Constitution

The National Assembly Standing Committee is the permanent body of the National Assembly, and is to carry out duties on behalf of the National Assembly during the recess of the National Assembly.

II. STANDARD LEGAL REFERENCE

The constitution was adopted on August 14, 1991; rev.2003

III. COMPOSITION AND ORGANIZATION

IV. POWERS

Constitutional Court Review

The National Assembly Standing Committee has the following rights and duties:

1. To prepare for the National Assembly sessions and to ensure that the National Assembly implements its work plan;

2. To interpret and explain the provisions of the Constitution and the laws;

3. To oversee the activities of the executive organs, the people's courts and the [Office of the] Public Prosecutor during the recess of the National Assembly;

4. To appoint, transfer or remove judges of the people's courts at all levels and of the military courts;

5. To summon the National Assembly into session; [and]

6. To exercise such other rights and perform such other duties as provided by the laws.(Article 56 of the Constitution)

SOURCES:

https://www.constituteproject.org/constitution/Laos_2003.pdf?lang=en

http://www.na.gov.la/index.php?option=com_content&view=article&id=62&Itemid=147&lang=en

(91)

DOSSIER OF THE CONSTITUTIONAL COURT OF THE REPUBLIC OF LATVIA

STATE: Republic of Latvia
TITLE: The Constitutional Court
YEAR OF FOUNDATION: 1996
SEAT: Riga

I. CHRONICLE

Date and context of establishment
Constitutional Court of the Republic of Latvia is an independent court, which was established in 1996 on basis of amendments in law On Judicial Power and in the Constitution of Latvia made in 1994

Position in the hierarchy of courts
In Latvia, there shall be a Constitutional Court, which, within its jurisdiction as provided for by law, shall review cases concerning the conformity of laws with the Constitution, as well as other cases conferred within the jurisdiction thereof by law. (Article 85 of the Constitution)

II. STANDARD LEGAL REFERENCE

The Constitution was adopted by the people of Latvia, in their freely elected Constitutional Assembly of Latvia on 15 February 1992 and entered into force on 7 November 1922 (reinst. 1991, rev 2014)

III. COMPOSITION AND ORGANIZATION

Composition

The number of judges:

The Constitutional Court is comprised of seven Justices, who are confirmed into office by the majority vote of the Saeima – with at least 51 votes. Three Justices of the Constitutional Court are confirmed upon the proposal by at least ten members of the Saeima, two – upon the proposal by the Cabinet of Ministers, and two – upon the proposal of the Plenary Session of the Supreme Court.

Electoral/appointment body:

The Saeima shall confirm the appointment of judges to the Constitutional Court for the term provided for by law, with a majority of the votes of not less than fifty-one members of the Saeima. (Article 85 of the Constitution)

The Court members:

The term of office: 10

The Court President:

The term of office: 3

IV. POWERS

Constitutional Court Review

Preventive review:

...2) conformity of international agreements signed or entered into by Latvia (also until the confirmation of the relevant agreements in the Saeima) with the Constitution;

A posteriori review:

Abstract review:

Acording to the Section 16 of the Constitutional Court Law the Constitutional Court shall adjudicate matters regarding:

1) conformity of laws with the Constitution;

2) conformity of international agreements signed or entered into by Latvia (also until the confirmation of the relevant agreements in the Saeima) with the Constitution;

3) conformity of other laws and regulations or parts thereof with the norms (acts) of a higher legal force;

4) conformity of other acts of the Saeima, the Cabinet, the President, the Speaker of the Saeima and the Prime Minster, except for administrative acts, with law;
5) conformity with law of such an order with which a Minister authorised by the Cabinet has suspended a decision taken by a local government council;
6) conformity of Latvian national legal norms with those international agreements entered into by Latvia that is not in conflict with the Constitution.

Concrete review:

The Constitutional Court, within the jurisdiction established by the Satversme of the Republic of Latvia and Constitutional Court Law, hears cases on the compliance of laws and other regulatory enactments with the Satversme, as well as other cases placed in its jurisdiction.

Other powers

Constitutional complaints:

Any person, who considers that his or her fundamental rights included in the Satversme of the Republic of Latvia have been infringed upon by a law or other regulatory enactment, may submit a constitutional complaint or an application to the Constitutional Court

Jurisdictional disputes:

In difference to other courts, the essence of adjudication of justice at the Constitutional Court solving of special or specific disputes regarding the compliance of legal norms with norms of higher legal force.

Standing before the Constitutional Court

State bodies:

Decisions in court proceedings may be made only by bodies upon which jurisdiction regarding such has been conferred by law, and only in accordance with procedures provided for by law.

Individuals: X

SOURCES:

http://www.saeima.lv/en/legislation/constitution
http://www.satv.tiesa.gov.lv/en/

(92)

DOSSIER OF THE CONSTITUTIONAL COUNCIL OF THE LEBANESE REPUBLIC

STATE: Lebanon
TITLE: The Constitutional Council
YEAR OF FOUNDATION: 1993
SEAT: Beirut

I. CHRONICLE

Date and context of establishment
The Constitutional Council was established by virtue of Law 250 of 14/7/1993.

Position in the hierarchy of courts
Article 19 (As amended by the Constitutional Law of October 17, 1927 and the Constitutional Law of September 21, 1990)

A Constitutional Council shall be established to supervise the constitutionality of laws and to arbitrate conflicts that arise from parliamentary and presidential elections. The President of the republic, the speaker of Parliament, the Prime Minister, along with any ten Members of Parliament, have the right to refer to this Council matters that relate to the constitutionality of laws. The officially recognized heads of religious communities have the right to refer to this Council laws relating to personal status, the freedom of belief and religious practice, and the freedom of religious education.

The rules governing the organization, operation, composition of the Council and referral thereto shall be decided by a special law.

II. STANDARD LEGAL REFERENCE

The Constitution of Lebanon was adopted on 23 May 1926. (rev. 2004)

III. COMPOSITION AND ORGANIZATION

Composition

The number of judges:

The Council shall consist of ten members.

Electoral/appointment body:

The Council shall consist of ten members: five appointed by Parliament by an absolute majority and five appointed by the Council of Ministers by a two-thirds majority of the members of the Government.

IV. POWERS

Constitutional Court Review

A posteriori review:

Abstract review:

The Constitutional Council has the power to review the constitutionality of laws and to resolve electoral disputes (Article 19 of the Constitution)

Other powers

Electoral matters:

According to Article 19 of the Constitution and Article 23 of the law establishing the Constitutional Council, the council is competent to judge the disputes concerning the elections of the President of the Republic and the Head of Parliament.

SOURCES:

http://www.wipo.int/edocs/lexdocs/laws/en/lb/lb018en.pdf

http://www.cc.gov.lb/fr

(93)

DOSSIER OF THE HIGH COURT OF THE KINGDOM OF LESOTHO

STATE: Lesotho
TITLE: The High Court
YEAR OF FOUNDATION: 1984
SEAT: Maseru

I. CHRONICLE

Date and context of establishment 1984
Position in the hierarchy of courts
Article 119. of the Constitution: Establishment of High Court

(1) There shall be a High Court which shall have unlimited original jurisdiction to hear and determine any civil or criminal proceedings and the power to review the decisions or proceedings of any subordinate or inferior court, court-martial, tribunal, board or officer exercising judicial, quasi-judicial or public administrative functions under any law and such jurisdiction and powers as may be conferred on it by this Constitution or by or under any other law.
(2) The judges of the High Court shall be the Chief Justice and such number, of other judges (hereinafter referred to as the puisne judges) as may be prescribed by Parliament:
Provided that the office of a puisne judge shall not be abolished while there is a substantive holder thereof.
(3) The High Court shall be a superior court of record and, save as otherwise provided by Parliament, shall have all the powers of such a court.

II. STANDARD LEGAL REFERENCE

Constitution, adopted 1996, amendments (1996, 1997, 1998, 2001)

III. COMPOSITION AND ORGANIZATION

Composition

The number of judges: 2.

Electoral/appointment body:

Article 120 of the Constitution: Appointment of judges of High Court

(1) The Chief Justice shall be appointed by the King acting in accordance with the advice of the Prime Minister.

(2) The puisne judges shall be appointed by the King, acting in accordance with the advice of the Judicial Service Commission.

The Court members:

The term of office:

Article 121 of the Constitution: Tenure of office of Chief Justice and other judges of High Court

(1) Subject to the provisions of this section, a person holding the office of Chief Justice or other judge of the High Court shall vacate that office when he attains the prescribed age.

IV. POWERS

Constitutional Court Review

A posteriori review:

Concrete review:

Article 128 of the Constitution: Reference to High Court in cases in subordinate courts etc. involving interpretation of Constitution

(1) Where any question as to the interpretation of this Constitution arises in any proceedings in any subordinate court or tribunal and the court or tribunal is of the opinion that the question involves a substantial question of law, the court or tribunal may, and shall, if any party to the proceedings so requests, refer the question to the High Court.

(2) Where any question is referred to the High Court in pursuance of this section, the High Court shall give its decision upon the question and the court or tribunal in which the question arose shall dispose of the case in accordance with that decision or, if that decision is the subject of an appeal under section 129 of the Constitution, in accordance with the decision of the Court of Appeal.

SOURCES:

http://www.unesco.org/education/edurights/media/docs/5f117d45be0d3d8ed8e573ee1db7db551ad68565.pdf

https://www.lesotholii.org/courtnames/high-court

(94)

DOSSIER OF THE SUPREME COURT OF THE REPUBLIC OF LIBERIA

STATE: Republic of Liberia
TITLE: The Supreme Court of Liberia
YEAR OF FOUNDATION: 1839, 1984
SEAT: Monrovia

I. CHRONICLE

Date and context of establishment
The court was originally authorized by the 1839 Constitution of the American Colonization Society signed on January 5, 1839. Subsequent constitutions continued to authorize a Supreme Court, with the 1984 Constitution as the most recent version. Powers and structure of the court are determined by Article VII of the 1984 constitution.

Position in the hierarchy of courts
The Supreme Court of Liberia is the highest judicial body.

II. STANDARD LEGAL REFERENCE

The current constitution, which came into force on 6 January 1986, replaced the Liberian Constitution of 1847, which had been in force since the independence of Liberia

III. COMPOSITION AND ORGANIZATION

Composition
The number of judges: 5
The Supreme Court shall comprise of one Chief Justice and four Associate Justice. Article 67 of the Constitution

Electoral/appointment body:
The Chief Justice and Associate Justice of the Supreme Court shall, with the consent of the Senate, be appointed and commissioned by the President. Article 68 of the Constitution

The Court members:
The term of office:
70 years of age

IV. POWERS

Constitutional Court Review

A posteriori review:
Abstract review:

The Supreme Court shall be final arbiter of constitutional issues and shall exercise final appellate jurisdiction in all cases whether emanating from courts of record, courts not of record, administrative agencies, autonomous agencies or any other authority, both as to law and fact except cases involving ambassadors, ministers, or cases in which a country is a party. In all such cases, the Supreme Court shall exercise original jurisdiction. The Legislature shall make no law nor create any exceptions as would deprive the Supreme Court of any of the powers granted herein. Article 66 of the Constitution

Other powers
Electoral matters:
c. The Elections Commission shall, within thirty days of receipt of the complaint, conduct an impartial investigation and render a decision which may involve a dismissal of the complaint or a nullification of the election of a candidate. Any political party or independent candidate affected by such decision shall not later than seven days appeal against it to the Supreme Court. Article 83 of the Constitution

The Supreme Court exercises original jurisdiction in cases involving ambassadors, ministers, and cases in which a country is a party.

Other matters with which the Court is charged by the Constitution or statute:
The Supreme Court shall from time to time make rules of court for the purpose of regulating the practice, procedures and manner by which cases shall be commenced and heard before it and all other subordinate courts. It shall prescribe such code of conduct for lawyers appearing before it and all other subordinate courts as may be necessary to facilitate the proper discharge of the

court's functions. Such rules and code, however, shall not contravene any statutory provisions or any provisions of this Constitution. Article 75 of the Constitution

V. NATURE AND EFFECTS OF DECISIONS

Finality:

Judgements of the Supreme Court shall be final and binding and shall not be subject to appeal or review by any other branch of Government. Nothing in this Article shall prohibit administrative consideration of the Justiciable matter prior to review by a court of competent jurisdiction. Article 65 of the Constitution

Binding force:

Erga omnes:

Judgements of the Supreme Court shall be final and binding and shall not be subject to appeal or review by any other branch of Government. Nothing in this Article shall prohibit administrative consideration of the Justiciable matter prior to review by a court of competent jurisdiction. Article 65 of the Constitution

SOURCES:

www.parliament.am/library/sahmanadrutyunner/liberia.pdf

http://judiciary.gov.lr/supreme-court/

(95)

DOSSIER OF THE SUPREME COURT OF LIBYA

STATE: Libya
TITLE: The Supreme Court
YEAR OF FOUNDATION: 1951
SEAT: Tripoli

I. CHRONICLE

Date and context of establishment 1951

Position in the hierarchy of courts

The highest court is the Supreme Court, located in Tripoli, whose members are appointed by the General People's Congress.

II. STANDARD LEGAL REFERENCE

The Libyan Constitution was brought into force on 7 October 1951, amendment 2011, rev.2012

III. COMPOSITION AND ORGANIZATION

Composition

The number of judges:

The Supreme Court was located in Tripoli and comprised five chambers: civil and commercial, criminal, administrative, constitutional, and sharia. A five-judge panel sat in each chamber.

Electoral/appointment body:

Members are appointed by the General People's Congress.

IV. POWERS

Constitutional Court Review

Other powers

Constitutional complaints:

The Supreme Court is the court of first instance for the following: • Claims of the unconstitutionality of any legislation brought before the court by anyone, who has a direct, personal interest • Any legally essential matter concerning the Constitution or its interpretation, which arises in any case being heard by any court.

Jurisdictional disputes:

The Supreme Court is the court of first instance for the following: Conflicts of jurisdiction between courts and any exceptional judicial authority. Any dispute concerning the execution of two conflicting final judgements issued by a court and an exceptional judicial authority.

V. NATURE AND EFFECTS OF DECISIONS

Finality:

The court shall be the final appellate body for cases emanating from lower courts.

SOURCES:

https://www.constituteproject.org/constitution/Libya_2011.pdf

DOSSIER OF THE STATE COURT OF THE PRINCIPALITY OF LIECHTENSTEIN

STATE: Principality of Liechtenstein
TITLE: State Court of the Principality of Liechtenstein
YEAR OF FOUNDATION: 1921
SEAT: Vaduz

I. CHRONICLE

Date and context of establishment
The Constitution of 5th October 1921 brought the State Court into being, although not yet in fully functioning form as it lacked one particular act of law.

Position in the hierarchy of courts
The judges, within the lawful limits of their powers and when engaged in judicial proceedings, shall, in the exercise of their judicial office, be independent. Their decisions and judgements shall be accompanied by the grounds for such. The influence of nonjudicial bodies on these decisions and judgements is only permissible to the extent expressly provided for by the Constitution (Article 12 of the Constitution).

II. STANDARD LEGAL REFERENCE

The Constitution of Liechtenstein was promulgated on 5 October 1921 (rev.2003).

III. COMPOSITION AND ORGANIZATION

Composition

The number of judges:
The State Court shall consist of five judges and substitutes appointed by the Prince Regnant (Article 96 of the Constitution).

Electoral/appointment body:
The President of the State Court and the majority of the judges must possess Liechtenstein citizenship. Furthermore, the provisions of Article 102 of the Constitution apply mutatis mutandis.

The Court members:
The term of office:
The President of the State Court and the majority of the judges must possess Liechtenstein citizenship. (Article 105 of the Constitution)

The Court President:
The term of office:
For the selection of judges, the Prince Regnant and the Diet shall refer to a joint commission chaired by the Prince, who shall have a casting vote. He may appoint as many members to this body as the Diet delegates representatives. The Diet shall appoint one member for each electoral group represented in it. The Government shall appoint the member of the Government responsible for supervising the administration of justice. The commission's deliberations shall be confidential. The commission may only recommend candidates to the Diet with the Prince's assent. If the Diet chooses the recommended candidate, he or she shall be appointed a judge by the Prince.

Organization
Administrative autonomy:
The whole administration of justice shall be carried out in the name of the Prince Regnant and the People by responsible judges appointed by the Prince Regnant (Article 11 of the Constitution). The decisions of the judges in the form of judgments shall be delivered and drawn up "in the name of the Prince and the People. (Article 95 of the Constitution)

IV. POWERS

Constitutional Court Review
A State Court shall be established by a special law as a court of public law to protect rights accorded by the Constitution, to decide in conflicts of jurisdiction between the law courts and the administrative authorities and to act as a disciplinary court for members of the Government. (Article 104 of the Constitution)

Abstract review:

The said court shall also have jurisdiction to determine whether laws and treaties are in conformity with the Constitution and whether Government regulations are in conformity with the laws; in such eases it may declare their annulment.(Article 104 of the Constitution).

Other powers

Electoral matters:

Finally, the Court shall also act as an electoral tribunal. Article 104 Finally, it shall also act as an electoral tribunal. (Article 104 of the Constitution)

Complaints relating to elections shall be referred to the State Court.

The Diet shall adjudicate on the validity of the election of its members and of the election as such on the basis of the election records and, if applicable, of the decision of the State Court (validation procedure) (Article 59 of the Constitution)

Jurisdictional disputes:

A State Court shall be established by a special law as a court of public law to protect rights accorded by the Constitution, to decide in conflicts of jurisdiction between the law courts and the administrative authorities and to act as a disciplinary court for members of the Government. (Article 104 of the Constitution).

SOURCES:

hrlibrary.umn.edu/research/liechtenstein-constitution.pdf

DOSSIER OF THE CONSTITUTIONAL COURT OF THE REPUBLIC OF LITHUANIA

STATE: Republic of Lithuania
TITLE: Constitutional Court
YEAR OF FOUNDATION: 1992
SEAT: Vilnius

I. CHRONICLE

Date and context of establishment
Is a special court established by the Constitution of the Republic of Lithuania of 1992; it began the activities after the adoption of the Law on Constitutional Court of the Republic of Lithuania on February 3, 1993.

Position in the hierarchy of courts
The Constitutional Court shall decide whether the laws and other acts of the Seimas are not in conflict with the Constitution and whether the acts of the President of the Republic and the Government are not in conflict with the Constitution or laws.

The status of the Constitutional Court and the procedure for the execution of its powers shall be established by the Law on the Constitutional Court of the Republic of Lithuania. (Article 102 of the Constitution)

II. STANDARD LEGAL REFERENCE

The Constitution was approved in a referendum on 25 October 1992 (rev.2012)

Composition

The number of judges:

The Constitutional Court shall consist of 9 judges (Article 103 of the Constitution)

Electoral/appointment body:

The Seimas shall appoint candidates for justices of the Constitutional Court from the candidates, three each submitted by the President of the Republic, the President of the Seimas, and the President of the Supreme Court, and appoint them as justices.

The Seimas shall appoint the President of the Constitutional Court from among its justices upon the submission by the President of the Republic. (Article 103 of the Constitution)

The Court members:

The term of office:

The Constitutional Court shall consist of 9 justices, each appointed for a single nine-year term of office. Every three years, one-third of the Constitutional Court shall be reconstituted. The Seimas shall appoint candidates for justices of the Constitutional Court from the candidates, three each submitted by the President of the Republic, the President of the Seimas, and the President of the Supreme Court, and appoint them as justices. (Article 103 of the Constitution).

IV. POWERS

Constitutional Court Review

The Constitutional Court does not perform any preliminary judicial review of laws. The Constitutional Court decides the constitutionality issues of enacted laws and other legal acts (a posteriori control).

The Constitutional Court examines a case only when the subjects prescribed by the Constitution address the Constitutional Court with a petition requesting for the determination of the conformity of a law or a legal act with the Constitution.

A posteriori review:

Abstract review:

The Constitutional Court shall also consider if the following are not in conflict with the Constitution and laws:

1.acts of the President of the Republic;

2.acts of the Government of the Republic.(Article 106 of the Constitution).

Charges against the President of the Republic:

The Constitutional Court shall present conclusions:

> 4.whether concrete actions of Members of the Seimas and State officials against whom an impeachment case has been instituted are in conflict with the Constitution (Article 106 of the Constitution)
>
> :

Electoral matters:

The Constitutional Court shall present conclusions:...

> 1.whether there were violations of election laws during elections of the President of the Republic or elections of members of the Seimas ...(Article 106 of the Constitution)

The Seimas may request a conclusion from the Constitutional Court, and in cases concerning Seimas elections and international treaties, the President of the Republic may also request a conclusion.

Other matters with which the Court is charged by the Constitution or statute:

The Constitutional Court shall present conclusions:...

> 2.whether the state of health of the President of the Republic allows him to continue to hold office; (Article 106 of the Constitution)

Standing before the Constitutional Court

State bodies:

The Government, not less than 1/5 [one-fifth] of all the Members of the Seimas, and the courts, shall have the right to apply to the Constitutional Court concerning the acts specified in the First Paragraph of Article 105 of the Constitution.

Not less than 1/5 [one-fifth] of all the Members of the Seimas and the courts shall have the right to apply to the Constitutional Court concerning the conformity of acts of the President of the Republic with the Constitution and the laws.

Not less than 1/5 [one-fifth] of all the Members of the Seimas, the courts, as well as the President of the Republic, shall have the right to apply to the Constitutional Court concerning the conformity of acts of the Government with the Constitution and the laws.

The presentation by the President of the Republic for the Constitutional Court or the resolution of the Seimas asking for an investigation into the conformity of an act with the Constitution shall suspend the validity of the act.

The Seimas may request a conclusion from the Constitutional Court, and in cases concerning Seimas elections and international treaties, the President of the Republic may also request a conclusion. (Article 106 of the Constitution)

The Constitutional Court shall have the right to refuse to accept a case for consideration or to prepare a conclusion if the application is based on non-legal reasoning. (Article 105 of the Constitution)

Finality:

The Constitutional Court's decisions defined by the Constitution as falling within the Constitutional Court's competence are final and not subject to appeal.

Binding force:

Erga omnes:

Rulings of the Constitutional Court have the power of law and are obligatory for all institutions of authority, courts, all enterprises, establishments and organisations, officials and citizens (erga omnes). Obligatory opinions on the conformity of international treaties with the Constitution:

The Constitutional Court shall present conclusions:

....3.whether international treaties of the Republic of Lithuania are not in conflict with the Constitution...(Article 106 of the Constitution)

SOURCES:

https://www.constituteproject.org/constitution/Lithuania_2006.pdf?lang=en

DOSSIER OF THE CONSTITUTIONAL COURT OF THE GRAND DOUCHY OF LUXEMBURG

STATE: Grand Duchy of Luxembourg
TITLE: The Constitutional Court
YEAR OF FOUNDATION: 12. 3. 2009
SEAT: Luxemburg

I. CHRONICLE

Date and context of establishment 2009
Position in the hierarchy of courts

II. STANDARD LEGAL REFERENCE

Constitution of 2009

III. COMPOSITION AND ORGANIZATION

Composition
The number of judges:
The Constitutional Court consists of one Chamber which sits with five magistrates. Article 95 The Constitutional court is composed of the President of the Superior Court of Justice, the President of the Administrative Court, two councillors of the Court of Cassation and of five magistrates appointed by the Grand Duke, on the joint advice of the Superior Court of Justice and of the Administrative Court (Article 95 of the Constitution)

Electoral/appointment body:
The Constitutional court is composed of the President of the Superior Court of Justice, the President of the Administrative Court, two councillors of the Court of Cassation and of five

magistrates appointed by the Grand Duke, on the joint advice of the Superior Court of Justice and of the Administrative Court (Article 95 of the Constitution)

Organization

Administrative autonomy:

The organization of the Constitutional Court and the manner of the exercise of its attributions, are regulated by the law. (Article 95 of the Constitution)

IV. POWERS

Constitutional Court Review

The Constitutional Court decides, by means of opinion [arrt], on the conformity of laws with the Constitution. (Article 95 of the Constitution)

Preventive review:

The Constitutional Court may be referred to [a matter], under title of preliminary opinion [titre prejudiciel]. Following the modalities to be determined by the law, by any jurisdiction to decide on the conformity of the laws, with the exception of the laws concerning the approval of treaties, with the Constitution. (Article 96 of the Constitution)

A posteriori review:

Concrete review:

The Constitutional Court conducts concrete constitutional reviews*a* posteriori and cases are referred to it for preliminary rulings, while the Council of State has an *a priori* control in the context of its consultative role.

Other powers

Constitutional complaints:

The Constitutional Court serves as the main body for the protection of the Constitution, its tasks being the review of the constitutionality of statutes, and the protection of constitutional order and fundamental rights guaranteed by the Constitution.

Standing before the Constitutional Court

State bodies: Yes

Individuals: Yes

Obligatory opinions on the conformity of international treaties with the Constitution:

The Court has no jurisdiction on the constitutionality of treaties or legislation enacted to implement treaties.

SOURCES:

www.legilux.public.lu/leg/textescoordonnes/recueils/Constitution/

(99)

DOSSIER OF THE COURT OF FINAL APPEAL OF MACAO

STATE: Macao Special administrative region of the People's Republic of China
TITLE: The Court of Final Appeal
YEAR OF FOUNDATION: 1999
SEAT: Macau

I. CHRONICLE

Date and context of establishment:
The Basic Law of the Macau Special Administrative Region of the People's Republic of China is the Constitution of Macau. It was adopted on March 31, 1993 by National People's Congress and signed by President of the People's Republic of China Jiang Zemin, and came into effect on December 20, 1999. Macau has special administrative region status, which provides constitutional guarantees for implementing the policy of one country, two systems and the constitutional basis for enacting the Basic Law of the Macau Special Administrative Region. The Macau Special Administrative Region is directly under the authority of the central government of China in Beijing, which controls the foreign policy and defense of Macau but otherwise grants the region a high degree of autonomy. Constitutional basis for special administrative region status of Macau is provided with Article 31 of the Constitution of the People's Republic of China: "The state may establish special administrative regions when necessary. The systems to be instituted in special administrative regions shall be prescribed by law enacted by the National People's Congress in the light of the specific conditions."

The Basic Law of Macau is modelled upon the Basic Law of Hong Kong, although it is not totally equal, as it namely is influenced by the Portuguese Constitution in some points as, for example, in some norms concerning fundamental rights.

Position in the hierarchy of courts:
The Court of Final Appeal is the supreme body in the hierarchy of courts, exercising the ultimate judgment of the Macao Special Administrative Region conferred by the Basic Law. The Basic Law of Macao provides for three-level system of courts in Macao Special Administrative Region including the Court of Final Appeal, the Intermediate Court and lower courts (courts of first instance). This framework of judicial system defined by the Basic Law derives from previous

judicial system of Macao which was mainly based on Portuguese legal tradition (civil law). Till 1991 Macau judicial system was a sub-judiciary district of the judicial framework of the Portuguese legal system and was affiliated to the Judiciary District of Lisbon. In 1999, the Higher Court of Justice (Superior Court of Justice) of Macau replaced the role of Court of Appeal of the Judiciary District of Lisbon.

Article 19 of the Basic Law: "The Macao Special Administrative Region shall be vested with independent judicial power, including that of final adjudication. The courts of the Macao Special Administrative Region shall have jurisdiction over all cases in the Region, except that the restrictions on their jurisdiction imposed by the legal system and principles previously in force in Macao shall be maintained. The courts of the Macao Special Administrative Region shall have no jurisdiction over acts of state such as defence and foreign affairs. The courts of the Region shall obtain a certificate from the Chief Executive on questions of fact concerning acts of state such as defence and foreign affairs whenever such questions arise in the adjudication of cases. This certificate shall be binding on the courts. Before issuing such a certificate, the Chief Executive shall obtain a certifying document from the Central People's Government."

Article 84 of the Basic Law: "The primary courts, intermediate courts and Court of Final Appeal shall be established in the Macao Special Administrative Region. The power of final adjudication of the Macao Special Administrative Region shall be vested in the Court of Final Appeal of the Region. The structure, powers and functions as well as operation of the courts of the Macao Special Administrative Region shall be prescribed by law."

II. STANDARD LEGAL REFERENCE

The Basic Law of the Macau Special Administrative Region of the People's Republic of China, adopted on March 31, 1993, entered into force on December 20, 1999

The Basic Law of the Judicial Organization

III. COMPOSITION AND ORGANIZATION

Composition

The number of judges: 3

Electoral/appointment body:

APPOINTMENT BASED SYSTEM (Without the Participation of a Representative Body):

Article 87 of the Basic Law: "Judges of the courts of the Macao Special Administrative Region at all levels shall be appointed by the Chief Executive on the recommendation of an independent commission composed of local judges, lawyers and eminent persons.(...)"

Article 88 of the Basic Law: "The presidents of courts of the Macao Special Administrative Region at all levels shall be chosen from among judges and appointed by the Chief Executive. The President of the Court of Final Appeal of the Macao Special Administrative Region shall be a Chinese citizen who is a permanent resident of the Region."

The qualifications and the required professional experience of constitutional court judges:

Article 87 of the Basic Law: "(...) Judges shall be chosen on the basis of their professional qualifications. Qualified judges of foreign nationality may also be employed."

Incompatibilities:

Article 89 of the Basic Law: "(...) During the term of his or her office, a judge shall not concurrently assume other public or private posts, nor shall he or she assume any post in organizations of a political nature."

Immunities:

Article 89 of the Basic Law: "(...) Judges shall be immune from legal action for discharging his or her judicial functions.(...)"

Release from office prior to the expiration of the term:

Article 87 of the Basic Law: "(...) A judge may only be removed for inability to discharge his or her functions, or for behavior incompatible with his or her post, by the Chief Executive on the recommendation of a tribunal appointed by the President of the Court of Final Appeal and consisting of not fewer than three local judges. The removal of the judges of the Court of Final Appeal shall be decided on by the Chief Executive upon the recommendation of a review committee consisting of members of the Legislative Council of the Macao Special Administrative Region. The appointment and removal of the judges of the Court of Final Appeal shall be reported to the Standing Committee of the National People's Congress for the record."

Article 88 of the Basic Law: "(...)The appointment and removal of the President of the Court of Final Appeal shall be reported to the Standing Committee of the National People's Congress for the record."

Constitutional Court Review

A posteriori review:

Abstract review:

Article 143 of the Basic Law: "The power of interpretation of this Law shall be vested in the Standing Committee of the National People's Congress. The Standing Committee of the National People's Congress shall authorize the courts of the Macao Special Administrative Region to interpret on their own, in adjudicating cases, the provisions of this Law which are within the limits of the autonomy of the Region. The courts of the Macao Special Administrative Region may also interpret other provisions of this Law in adjudicating cases. However, if the courts of the Region, in adjudicating cases, need to interpret the provisions of this Law concerning affairs which are the responsibility of the Central People's Government, or concerning the relationship between the Central Authorities and the Region, and if such interpretation will affect the judgments in the cases, the courts of the Region shall, before making their final judgments which are not appealable, seek an interpretation of the relevant provisions from the Standing Committee of the National People's Congress through the Court of Final Appeal of the Region. When the Standing Committee makes an interpretation of the provisions concerned, the courts of the Region, in applying those provisions, shall follow the interpretation of the Standing Committee. However, judgments previously rendered shall not be affected. The Standing Committee of the National People's Congress shall consult its Committee for the Basic Law of the Macao Special Administrative Region before giving an interpretation of this Law."

Other powers

Constitutional complaints:

Yes, as provided by Article 44. of the Basic Law of the Judicial Organization. The Court of Final Appeal is competent also to decide in habea corpus matters.

Jurisdictional disputes:

Yes, as provided by Article 44. of the Basic Law of the Judicial Organization, the Court of Final Appeal is competent to decide in conflicts of jurisdiction between different courts of the same instance and different instances.

Charges against the President of the Republic:

Article 71 of the Basic Law: The Legislative Council of the Macao Special Administrative Region shall exercise the following powers and functions: (...) (7) If a motion initiated jointly by one-third of all the members of the Legislative Council charges the Chief Executive with serious breach of law or dereliction of duty and if he or she refuses to resign, the Council may, by a resolution, give a mandate to the President of the Court of Final Appeal to form an independent investigation committee to carry out investigation. If the committee considers the evidence sufficient to substantiate such charges, the Council may pass a motion of impeachment by a two thirds majority of all its members and report it to the Central People's Government for decision; (...)

Other matters with which the Court is charged by the Constitution or statute:
In accordance with Article 44 of the Basic Law of the Judicial Organization the Court of Final Appeal is competent to try cases of alleged breaches of law committed by judges and prosecutors.

SOURCES:

The Basic Law of the Macau Special Administrative Region of the People's Republic of China, adopted on March 31, 1993, entered into force on December 20, 1999, http://www.imprensa.macau.gov.mo/bo/i/1999/leibasica/index_uk.asp

http://www.court.gov.mo/pt/subpage/tui

(100)

DOSSIER OF THE CONSTITUTIONAL COURT OF THE REPUBLIC OF MACEDONIA

STATE: Republic of Macedonia
TITLE: The Constitutional of Macedonia
YEAR OF FOUNDATION: 1963, reintroduced 17.11.1991,
SEAT: Skopje

I. CHRONICLE

Date and context of establishment

The Constitution of the Socialist Republic of Macedonia of 1963 established the Constitutional judiciary in Macedonia.

In circumstances when former Yugoslavia was a federatively defined society, and Macedonia was its federative unit, the Constitutional Court of Macedonia, as an independent organ of the Republic protecting the constitutionality and legality, started its work on February 15, 1964. The Constitution defined its position and competence whereas the Law on Constitutional Court of Macedonia of 1963 regulated the procedure and legal effects of its decisions.

Confirming the statehood and sovereignty of the Republic of Macedonia, the citizens of the Republic of Macedonia expressed their own will and gave their vote for the Republic of Macedonia to be constituted as a sovereign and independent country at the referendum held on September 8, 1991 and this was constitutionally and legally concluded by bringing of the Constitution of the Republic of Macedonia on November 17, 1991.

According to the Constitution, the social economic and political system of the Republic is based on the principle of rule of law, human rights and freedoms, separation of power, market economy and other fundamental values of the modern democratic society.

The Constitution establishes the Constitutional Court of the Republic of Macedonia as an organ of the Republic which protects the constitutionality and legality as well as fundamental freedoms and rights of the individual and citizen (Article 108 of the Constitution).

Position in the hierarchy of courts

Considered through the prism of the relationships of different bearers of power in organization of the state government, the Constitutional Court, in accordance with its constitutional status, does not belong in the system of separation of power, but is a special constitutional body with a status, composition, organization and competences properly defined within the Constitution itself. Organizationally and functionally it does not descend from the legislative organ, nor it is accountable to. The protection of the constitutionality and legality does not represent any exercise of state power and is an autonomous and independent function; therefore, its exercising is beyond any form of established relationships between the legislative and executive power. In accordance with this, the Constitutional Court is one of the factors for implementation of the Constitution and with this it realizes the relationships defined by the Constitution as content of the organization of power.

The constitutional status of the Constitutional Court enables the court to distance itself from any political authority while performing its constitutional/judicial function, especially from a political authority presently in power, and continually and persistently perform the duty in its jurisdiction independently of the changes of the bearers of power. Regardless of the intensity and the scope of performing its functions, the Constitutional Court is constantly active in guaranteeing the protection of the constitutionality and legality. Thus, this organ becomes a guarantee for enabling the rule of law and is a real society factor in implementing the Constitution and eliminating the arbitrary and free interpretation, realization and implementation of the Constitution and laws.

II. STANDARD LEGAL REFERENCE

Constitution of the Republic of Macedonia (amendments 1992-2005), rev.2011

III. COMPOSITION AND ORGANIZATION

Composition

The number of judges:

The Constitutional Court consists of nine judges (Article 109 of the Constitution). The Assembly of the Republic of Macedonia elects the judges of the Constitutional Court from the rank of outstanding members of the legal profession for a term of nine years without the right to reelection (Article 68 of the Constitution).

Electoral/appointment body:

The Assembly of the Republic of Macedonia elects the judges of the Constitutional Court from the rank of outstanding members of the legal profession for a term of nine years without the right to reelection (Article 68 of the Constitution).

The Court members:

The term of office: 9

The Court President:

The Constitutional Court elects a President from its own ranks for a term of three years without the right to reelection.

The term of office: 3

Organization

Administrative autonomy:

The budget:

An addition necessary to the foundations of the Constitutional Court's autonomy, which arise from its position in the constitutional system and the manner judges are elected, is providing financial independence of the Court from other organs of the state authorities which determine and execute the budget. Moreover, financial matters pertaining to the Constitutional Court have negative influence on its role as a whole. Namely, the independent and autonomous position of the Court determined by the Constitution would be more complete and realistic provided it had greater financial independence. At present, the assets of the Constitutional Court are provided by the Budget of the Republic of Macedonia without any greater influence by the Court.

IV. POWERS

Constitutional Court Review

Preventive review:

Exception to the rule that the Court only controls valid acts is given in the Rules of Procedure which anticipates the possibility of the Court to decide on the constitutionality and legality of a normative act not in force since the commencement of procedure assessing its constitutionality and legality.

A posteriori review:

The control over the constitutionality and legality of normative acts is an abstract one, a posteriori, and it is applicable only on valid acts.

Abstract review:

Control over the constitutionality and legality

Within the framework of this competence, the Constitutional Court decides on the conformity of regulations with the Constitution and laws, as well as the constitutionality of the programs and statutes of political parties and associations of citizens.

Besides laws, collective agreements and programs and statutes of political parties whose identification is rather simple, different other normative acts regulating certain issues in a general way (books of rules, decrees, decisions, etc. of state organs and local self-government organs or organizations having public mandates) may be challenged before the Court. The Court accepts the competence over an act even when it does not satisfy the form of regulations, but obviously regulates certain issues in a general way.

Within the framework of this competence, the Court may decide on the constitutionality and legality of an act as a whole or in its certain parts and articles, which depends on the indications in the initiative and by its own judgment. (Article 110 of the Constitution).

Other powers

Constitutional complaints:

Protection of freedoms and rights of the individual and citizen.

According to the Constitution, the Constitutional Court protects the freedoms and rights of the individual and citizen regarding the freedom of conviction, conscience, thought and public expression, political association and activities, and prohibition of discrimination among citizens on grounds of sex, race, religious, national, social and political affiliation.

Different from abstract normative control, subject to evaluation within this competence are individual acts and activities of the organs of the public authority which the citizens consider to violate some of the declared constitutional rights. Besides the directness of the request (constitutional complaint) for protection of rights violated by an individual act or actions, the second characteristic of this competence is that the subject for challenge may not only be an administrative act, but also a court decision at any instance.

Regardless of the fact that introduction of this competence with the Constitution of 1991 was a significant novelty in the tradition of constitutional judiciary in the Republic of Macedonia, its restrictiveness only to the three already mentioned groups of freedoms and rights becomes a serious obstacle for more serious direct Court protection of other constitutional freedoms and rights of the individual and citizen.

Jurisdictional disputes/Deciding on conflict of competence

In order to fulfill this classical competence of the constitutional judiciary, the Constitutional Court decides on conflict of competences among the bearers of legislative, executive and judiciary power, as well as on conflict of competences between the organs of the Republic and the units of the local self-government. Focused on protection of the principle of separation of powers and of the local self-government, as fundamental values of the constitutional system of the Republic of Macedonia, this competence may be established equally in the case of positive and/or negative conflict of competences among the organs. In practice, however, rarely are these disputes commenced, but the Court very often decides on this type of conflicts by controlling the constitutionality of normative acts decreeing competences to organs, which, according to the Constitution, do not belong to them.

Charges against the President of the Republic/Deciding on accountability of the President of the Republic

Upon proposal of the Assembly of the Republic of Macedonia, the Constitutional Court decides on the accountability of the President of the Republic in case of violation of the Constitution and laws in exercising his/her rights and duties. The Assembly enacts the proposal for commencing the procedure by a two-thirds majority vote of the representatives. Provided that the Constitutional Court by a majority of vote of the judges considers the President accountable, the office of the President is ceased by the force of the Constitution (Article 87 of the Constitution)

Other matters with which the Court is charged by the Constitution or statute:

The Constitutional Court, by official duty, determines the conditions under which the office of the President of the Republic is ceased. They are: death, resignation, permanent inability to perform his/her duties and termination of the mandate by the force of the Constitution (for instance, expiring of the term he/she has been elected for). This competence is significant not only for creating conditions for election of a new president, but also because the ceased presidential office activates the provision under which the office president of the Republic will be carried out by the President of the Assembly up till the election of a new president.

The Constitutional Court also decides on immunity of the President of the Republic of Macedonia as well as on immunity of the Court judges. (Article 82 of the Constitution)

Standing before the Constitutional Court

State bodies: X

Individuals: X

Every citizen may invoke the protection of freedoms and rights determined by the Constitution before the regular courts, as well as before the Constitutional Court of Macedonia, through a procedure based upon the principles of priority and urgency. Judicial protection of the legality of individual acts of state administration, as well as of other institutions carrying out public mandates, is guaranteed. A citizen has the right to be informed on human rights and basic freedoms as well as actively to contribute, individually or jointly with others, to their promotion and protection (Article 50 of the Constitution).

Common characteristic of the decisions repealing or annulling normative acts or declaring unconstitutionality or illegality during the time of validity is their erga omnes effect. Otherwise, Court decisions activate legal effect upon their publication in the "Official Gazette of the Republic of Macedonia . (Article 112 of the Constitution)

The legal effect of the repealing decisions is ex nunc, meaning that the repealed normative act is only eliminated from the legal system, but the Court decision does not give grounds for intervention in individual acts and relationships arising from its application before the repeal. Yet, enforcement of individual acts brought upon an normative act which has been repealed by Court decision, shall not be allowed, and have the enforcement already started, it shall be terminated. The annulling effect of the decision is ex tunc and aims not only to eliminate the unconstitutional or unlawful normative act from the legal system, but also to allow the possibility for changing individual act brought upon it, at any time from the day it has entered into force. The retroactive effect of the repealing decision is conditioned with presenting the legal interest of the subjects in changing individual acts within six months after the day of the publication of the Court decision and the organ that issued it has the duty to change it.

A decision by virtue of which the Constitutional Court decides on the competence conflict among certain organs is another type of decision and it only determines the organs responsible to decide on certain legal matters. Its effect is limited to the organs involved in competence conflict as well as to any entity not being able to exercise certain right or interest in particular matter due to the conflict.

Decisions on protection of freedoms and rights violated by individual act or action determine whether there is violation of freedoms and rights and, dependent on this, the Court shall either annul the individual act, that is forbids the action, or deny the request. The effect of the decision is inter partes. In the decision, the Court shall determine the manner the consequences will be eliminated from the application of individual acts.

Decisions on accountability of the President of the Republic and the conditions that cease his/her office have determining character and their consequences are determined with the Constitution as referred in chapter IV.

Finality/Binding force:

Although the Constitutional provisions, according to which Constitutional Court decisions are final and executive, do not need additional support, yet, execution of Court decisions is a matter which, as in other countries, is not solely entrusted to the will of the subjects in the legal system. According to the Rules of Procedure, the Constitutional Court follows the execution of decisions and, if necessary, may ask the Government to safeguard the execution.

Obligatory opinions on the conformity of international treaties with the Constitution:

Preventative control is not specified in the Constitution as a possibility, not even for international agreements. The status of the international agreements in the legal system, in reference to the Constitutional Court's competence is rather vague and in current practice the Court does not regard them as being subject to constitutional/judiciary evaluation.

SOURCES:

http://www.ustavensud.mk/domino/WEBSUD.nsf

(101)

DOSSIER OF THE HIGH CONSTITUTIONAL COURT OF THE REPUBLIC OF MADAGASCAR

STATE: Republic of Madagascar
TITLE: High Constitutional Court
YEAR OF FOUNDATION: 1959 (remodeled 1975, 1991)
SEAT: Antananarivo

I. CHRONICLE

Date and context of establishment 1959 (remodeled 1975, 1991)

Position in the hierarchy of courts

The Constitutional High Court is autonomous and reviews laws, decrees, and ordinances and monitors elections and certifies their results. A military court has jurisdiction over all cases that involve national security

II. STANDARD LEGAL REFERENCE

The current Constitution of Madagascar was, according to the national electoral commission, endorsed by a majority of voters in the constitutional referendum held on 14 November 2010.

III. COMPOSITION AND ORGANIZATION

Composition

The number of judges:

The High Constitutional Court is composed of nine members. (Article114 of the Constitution)

Electoral/appointment body:

Three of the members are appointed by the President of the Republic, two are elected by the National Assembly, two by the Senate, and two are elected by the Supreme Council of the Magistrature.

The President of the High Constitutional Court is elected by and from among the members of that Court.

The Court members:

The term of office:

Their mandate is of seven (7) years non-renewable. (Article 114 of the Constitution)

IV. POWERS

Constitutional Court Review

A posteriori review:

Abstract review:

In addition to the issues that are directed to it by other Articles of the Constitution, the High Constitutional Court, within the conditions established by an organic law:

1°.decides on the conformity with the Constitution of the treaties, of the laws, of the ordinances, and of the autonomous regulations;

2°.rules on the conflicts of competence between two or more Institutions of the State or between the State and one or more Decentralized Territorial Collectivities or between two or more Decentralized Territorial Collectivities;

3°.decides on the conformity with the Constitution and with the organic laws, of the deliberations and of the regulatory acts adopted by the Decentralized Territorial Collectivities (Article 116 of the Constitution)

Electoral matters:

In addition to the issues that are directed to it by other Articles of the Constitution, the High Constitutional Court, within the conditions established by an organic law: 4°.decides on the disputes of the operations of referendum, of the election of the President of the Republic and of the elections of the Deputies and Senators. (Article 116 of the Constitution)

Referendums:

In addition to the issues that are directed to it by other Articles of the Constitution, the High Constitutional Court, within the conditions established by an organic law:

4°.decides on the disputes of the operations of referendum, of the election of the President of the Republic and of the elections of the Deputies and Senators;

5°.proclaims the official result of the presidential and legislative elections and of the consultations by referendum. (Article 116 of the Constitution)

V. NATURE AND EFFECTS OF DECISIONS

Finality:

In the matter of electoral dispute and of direct popular consultation, the High Constitutional Court renders orders.

In the other matters falling into its competence, except in the case specified in Article 119 of the Constitution, it renders decisions.

The orders and decisions of the High Constitutional Court are substantiated; they are not susceptible to any recourse. They impose themselves on all the public powers as well as on the administrative and jurisdictional authorities. (Article 120 of the Constitution)

SOURCES:

https://www.constituteproject.org/constitution/Madagascar_2010.pdf?...

http://www.hcc.gov.mg/

(102)

DOSSIER OF THE HIGH COURT OF THE REPUBLIC OF MALAWI

STATE: Republic of Malawi
TITLE: The High Court
YEAR OF FOUNDATION: 1970
SEAT: Blantyre

I. CHRONICLE

Date and context of establishment 1970
Position in the hierarchy of courts
Article 108. 1 of the Constitution:There shall be a High Court for the Republic which shall have unlimited original jurisdiction to hear and determine any civil or criminal proceedings under any law.

Article 108. 2 of the Constitution: The High Court shall have original jurisdiction to review anylaw, and any action or decision of the Government, for conformity with the Constitution, save as otherwise provided by the Constitution and shall have such other jurisdiction and powers as may be conferred on it by the Constitution orany other law.

II. STANDARD LEGAL REFERENCE

In the Constitution, unless the context otherwise requires— appointed day means 18th May, 1994, being the date on which this Constitution shall come into operation. (Article 215 of the Constitution)

III. COMPOSITION AND ORGANIZATION

Composition/ Electoral/appointment body:
Article 109 of the Constitution: The Judges of the High Court shall be such number of judges, not being less than three, as may be prescribed by an Act of Parliament.

The number of judges: 3
The Court members:
Article 111.2.of the Constitution: All other judges shall be appointed by the President on the recommendation of the Judicial Service Commission.

The term of office:
Article 119. 1. Subject to this section, a person holding the office of Judge shall vacate that office on attaining the age prescribed

The Court President:
Article 111. 1 of the Constitution: The Chief Justice shall be appointed by the President and confirmed by the National Assembly by a majority of twothirds of the members present and voting.

IV. POWERS

The High Court of Malawi has unlimited original jurisdiction to hear and determine any civil or criminal proceedings. It has a General Division which may also hear appeals from subordinate courts, and a Commercial Division, dealing with commercial or business cases.

Constitutional Court Review
Most High Court cases are heard before a single judge, without a jury, but cases on constitutional matters must be heard by three judges.

SOURCES:

http://www.parliament.am/library/sahmanadrutyunner/malavi.pdf
https://www.malawilii.org/

(103)

DOSSIER OF THE FEDERAL COURT OF MALAYSIA

STATE: Malaysia
TITLE: The Federal Court
YEAR OF FOUNDATION: 1957, 1994
SEAT: Palace of Justice, Putrajaya, FT

I. CHRONICLE

Date and context of establishment
The court was established during Malaya's independence in 1957 and received its current name in 1994.

Position in the hierarchy of courts
The Federal Court of Malaysia (Malay: Mahkamah Persekutuan Malaysia) is the highest court and the final appellate court in Malaysia.

II. STANDARD LEGAL REFERENCE

Federal Constitution of Malaya 1957

III. COMPOSITION AND ORGANIZATION

Composition
The number of judges: 11
Electoral/appointment body:
All judges are appointed by the Yang di-Pertuan Agong on the advice of the Prime Minister of Malaysia

The Court members:

The term of office:

Compulsory retirement at age 65

IV. POWERS

Constitutional Court Review

There shall be a court which shall be known as the Mahkamah Persekutuan (Federal Court) and shall have its principal registry at such place as the Yang di-Pertuan may determine, and the Federal Court shall have the following jurisdiction, that is to say:

a.jurisdiction to determine appeals from decisions of the Court of Appeal, of the High Court or a judge thereof;

b.such original or consultative jurisdiction as is specified in Articles 128 and 130 of the Constitution; and

c.such other jurisdiction as may be conferred by or under federal law. (Article 121 of the Constitution)

Concrete review:

The Federal Court shall, to the exclusion of any other court, have jurisdiction to determine in accordance with any rules of court regulating the exercise of such jurisdiction-

a.any question whether a law made by Parliament or by the Legislature of a State is invalid on the ground that it makes provision with respect to a matter with respect to which Parliament or, as the case may be, the Legislature of the State has no power to make laws (Article 128 of the Constitution)

Other powers

Jurisdictional disputes:

The Federal Court shall, to the exclusion of any other court, have jurisdiction to determine in accordance with any rules of court regulating the exercise of such jurisdiction-

b.disputes on any other question between States or between the Federation and any State (Article 128 of the Constitution).

V. NATURE AND EFFECTS OF DECISIONS

Finality:

The Federal Court of Malaysia (Malay: Mahkamah Persekutuan Malaysia) is the final appellate court in Malaysia.

SOURCES:

http://www.agc.gov.my/agcportal/uploads/files/Publications/FC/Federal%20Consti%20(BI%20text).pdf

(104)

DOSSIER OF THE SUPREME COURT OF THE REPUBLIC OF MALDIVES

STATE: The Republic of Maldives
TITLE: The Supreme Court
YEAR OF FOUNDATION: 18. 9. 2008
SEAT: Male

I. CHRONICLE

Date and context of establishment

With the Constitution of 2008, the Maldivian Judiciary has entered a new phase of transformation and progress. Under the Constitution, the Maldivian Judiciary is as independent as it has ever being, and the current Constitution established, for the first time in the history of the Maldives, a Supreme Court, and declared it the highest institution of the Maldivian Judiciary.

Position in the hierarchy of courts

The Supreme Court, sitting together in session, shall have sole and final jurisdiction to determine all disputes concerning the qualification or disqualification, election, status, of a presidential candidate or running mate or removal of the President by the People's Majlis. Article 113 of the Constitution

a. The judicial power is vested in the Supreme Court, the High Court, and such Trial Courts as established by law.

b. The Supreme Court shall be the highest authority for the administration of justice in the Maldives. Article 141 of the Constitution

II. STANDARD LEGAL REFERENCE

Constitution 2008

Composition

The number of judges:

The Supreme Court shall consist of an uneven number of Judges. Article 144 of the Constitution

Electoral/appointment body:

The President as the Head of State shall appoint the Chief Justice, after consulting the Judicial Service Commission and confirmation of the appointee by a majority of the members of the People's Majlis present and voting. Article 147 of the Constitution

a. The President as the Head of State shall appoint the Judges of the Supreme Court, after consulting the Judicial Service Commission and confirmation of the appointees by a majority of the members of the People's Majlis present and voting. Article 148 of the Constitution

The Court members:

The term of office:

c. Judges shall be appointed without term, but shall retire at the age of seventy years.

d. Notwithstanding Article (c), for a period of fifteen years from the commencement of the Constitution, Judges may be appointed for a fixed term of not more than five years, as specified in the terms of their appointment.

IV. POWERS

Constitutional Court Review

The People's Majlis may by resolution refer to the Supreme Court for hearing and consideration important questions of law concerning any matter, including the interpretation of the Constitution and the constitutional validity of any statute. The Supreme Court shall answer the questions so referred and shall provide the answers to the People's Majlis, giving reasons for its answers. The opinion shall be pronounced in like manner as in the case of a judgment on appeal to the Supreme Court. Article 95

Preventive review:

When deciding a constitutional matter within its jurisdiction, a court:

a.may declare that any statute, regulation or part thereof, order, decision or action of any person or body performing a public function that is inconsistent with the Constitution is invalid to the extent of the inconsistency; and b.may in connection with a declaration pursuant to Article (b) make any order that is just and equitable, including:

1.an order providing just compensation for any damage sustained by any person or group of persons due to any statute, regulation or action that is inconsistent with the Constitution; or

2.an order suspending the declaration of invalidity (of a statute, regulation or action due to inconsistency with the Constitution) for any period and on any conditions, to allow the competent authority to correct the defect:

c.may make an order limiting the retrospective effect of a declaration of invalidity of a statute, regulation or part thereof, order, decision or action of any person or body performing a public function that is inconsistent with the Constitution.

Jurisdictional disputes:

a. The Supreme Court and the High Court shall have jurisdiction to enquire into and rule on the constitutional validity of any statute or part thereof enacted by the People's Majlis. Article 143 of the Constitution

b. In any matter before them, all courts have jurisdiction to determine matters concerning the interpretation and application of any provision of the Constitution, and this shall not be deemed contrary to Article (a).

The unconstitutionality of acts and activities of political parties:

Any question concerning the qualifications or removal, or vacating of seats, of a member of the People's Majlis shall be determined by the Supreme Court. Article 74 of the Constitution

Electoral matters:

Any question concerning the qualifications or removal, or vacating of seats, of a member of the People's Majlis shall be determined by the Supreme Court. Article 74 of the Constitution

Other matters with which the Court is charged by the Constitution or statute:

a. A Judicial Service Commission composed of the following persons, shall be appointed within thirty days of the commencement of this Constitution:

1.a Judge of the Supreme Court other than the Chief Justice, elected by the Judges of the Supreme Court; Article 281

Standing before the Constitutional Court

State bodies: X

Individuals:X

Everyone related to a matter has the right to appeal a conviction and sentence, or judgement or order in a criminal or civil matter. Article 56 of the Constitution

Finality:

c. The Supreme Court shall be the final authority on the interpretation of the Constitution, the law, or any other matter dealt with by a court of law. Article 154 of the Constitution

:

SOURCES:

www.majlis.gov.mv/en/wp-content/uploads/Constitution-english.pdf

(105)

DOSSIER OF THE CONSTITUTIONAL COURT OF THE REPUBLIC OF MALI

STATE: Republic of Mali
TITLE: The Constitutional Court
YEAR OF FOUNDATION: 1994
SEAT: Bamako

I. CHRONICLE

Date and context of establishment
Constitutional Court was formally established on 9 March 1994

Position in the hierarchy of courts
The Constitutional Court shall be the judge of the constitutionality of the law and it shall guarantee the fundamental rights of the human person and civil liberties.

It shall be the regulatory organ of the operation of the institutions and activities of the Public Authorities. Article 85 of the Constitution

II. STANDARD LEGAL REFERENCE

Constitution of 1992 with amendments

III. COMPOSITION AND ORGANIZATION

Composition
The number of judges:
The Constitutional Court consists of nine members who carry the title of Councilor with a mandate of seven years renewable one time. Article 91 of the Constitution

Electoral/appointment body:
The President of the Constitutional Court shall be elected by his peers. Article 92

The Court members:
The nine members of the Constitutional Court shall be designated as follows:

- three shall be named by the President of the Republic of which at least two shall be jurists;
- three shall be named by the President of the National Assembly of which at least two shall be jurists;
- three Magistrates shall be designated by the High Council of the Judiciary. Article 91 of the Constitution

The term of office:
Seven years renewable one time. Article 91 of the Constitution

The Court President: President of the Constitutional Court shall be elected by his peers. Article 92 of the Constitution

IV. POWERS

Constitutional Court Review

Preventive review:
International engagements described in Articles 114 to 116 of the Constitution shall be deferred before their ratification to the constitutional court, either by the President of the Republic, the Prime Minister, the President of the National Assembly or by one tenth of the Deputies, the President of the High Council of Territorial Units or by one tenth of the National Councilors.

The constitutional court verifies, within one month, if these engagements contain a clause contrary to the Constitution. Article 90 of the Constitution

The Constitutional Court shall obligatorily decide upon:

the constitutionality of organic laws and laws before their promulgation, regulatory acts touching upon the fundamental rights of the human person and civil liberties;

interior regulations of the National Assembly, of the High Council of Territorial Units and of the Economic, Social and Cultural Council before they come into application when their conformity with the Constitution comes into question;

Jurisdictional disputes:
Conflicts between the institutions of the State regarding attribution;

Electoral matters:
the regularity of all elections and operations of referendum of which it proclaims the results. Article 86 of the Constitution

The Constitutional Court shall resolve, in the case of contested validity of an election, by any elector, any candidate, any political party or delegate of the Government, within the conditions preordained by an organic law. Article 87 of the Constitution

V. NATURE AND EFFECTS OF DECISIONS

Finality:
The decisions of the Constitutional Court shall not be subject to any recourse. Article 94 of the Constitution

SOURCES:

https://www.constituteproject.org/constitution/Mali_1992.pdf?lang=en

DOSSIER OF THE CONSTITUTIONAL COURT OF THE REPUBLIC OF MALTA

STATE: The Republic of Malta
TITLE: Constitutional Court
YEAR OF FOUNDATION: 1964
SEAT: Valetta

I. CHRONICLE

Date and context of establishment 1964
The Constitutional Court came into being as a Superior Court with the 1964 Independence Constitution. Originally it was composed of five Judges, including the Chief Justice as President and a Vice-President. In 1974 it was reduced to three Judges, and the post of Vice-President was abolished. It is today composed of the Chief Justice as President and two other Judges.

Position in the hierarchy of courts
The Constitutional Court is the highest court in the Maltese hierarchical judicial system.

II. STANDARD LEGAL REFERENCE

The current Constitution of Malta was adopted as a legal order on 21 September 1964 (rev 2014)

III. COMPOSITION AND ORGANIZATION

Composition
The number of judges:
It is composed of the Chief Justice as President and two other Judges.

Electoral/appointment body:

1.The judges of the Superior Courts shall be appointed by the President acting in accordance with the advice of the Prime Minister. Article 96 of the Constitution

The Court members:

The term of office:

1.Subject to the provisions of this Article, a judge of the Superior Courts shall vacate his office when he attains the age of sixty-five years. Article 97 of the Constitution

IV. POWERS

Constitutional Court Review

The Constitutional Court is not bound by the case law of the European Court of Human Rights, however, as the European Convention is also part of our law, it will surly influence the course of the action of the Constitutional Court.

A posteriori review:

Abstract review:

The jurisdiction of the Constitutional Court is appellate in cases involving violations of human rights, interpretation of the Constitution and invalidity of laws.

Concrete review:

The Constitutional Court has both an original and an appellate jurisdiction. As an appellate court it hears appeals from decisions of other courts on questions relating to the interpretation of the Constitution and on the validity of laws, as well as appeals from decisions on alleged breaches of fundamental human rights.

Other powers

Constitutional complaints:

Any person who alleges that any of the Human Rights and Fundamental Freedoms, has been, is being or is likely to be contravened in relation to him, or such other person as the Civil Court, First Hall, in Malta may, without prejudice to any other action with respect to the same matter that is lawfully available, apply to the Civil Court, First Hall, for redress. The Civil Court, First Hall, shall have original jurisdiction to hear and determine any such application and may make such orders, issue such writs and give such directions as it may consider appropriate for the purpose of enforcing, or securing the enforcement, of the Human Rights and Fundamental Freedoms to the enjoyment of which the person concerned is entitled:

Electoral matters:
The Constitutional Court decides questions concerning the validity of the election of members of the House of Representatives, the requirement in certain cases for a member to vacate his seat in the said House, and the validity of the election of the Speaker from among persons who are not members of the House.

It has jurisdiction in deciding on the validity or otherwise of a general election which has been suspended by the Electoral Commission, for example where it is believed that illicit practices have occurred.

V. NATURE AND EFFECTS OF DECISIONS

Binding force:
The decision in the Constitutional proceedings will be binding on the court which referred the question, be it a court of first or second instance.

Erga omnes:
In the case of a pronouncement on the constitutionality of a legislative act the effects are erga omnes.

Inter partes:
The decisions of the Constitutional Court bind the parties involved - inter parties.

SOURCES:

http://www.justiceservices.gov.mt/downloaddocument.aspx?app=lom&itemid=8566&l=1

(107)

DOSSIER OF THE COMMONWEALTH SUPREME COURT OF THE COMMONWEALTH OF THE NOTHERN MARIANA ISLANDS

STATE: Commonwealth of the Northern Mariana Islands
TITLE: Commonwealth Supreme Court
YEAR OF FOUNDATION: 1 May 1989
SEAT: Saipan

I. CHRONICLE

Date and context of establishment 1989
Position in the hierarchy of courts:
Article IV., section 1 of the Constitution: The judicial power of the Commonwealth shall be vested in a judiciary of the Northern Mariana Islands which shall include those trial and appeals courts established by the legislature under this article

Section 3. of the Constitution: Commonwealth Supreme Court. The Commonwealth Supreme Court shall hear appeals from final judgments and orders of the Commonwealth superior court. The Supreme Court shall have all inherent powers, including the power to issue all writs necessary to the complete exercise of its duties and jurisdiction under this constitution and the laws of the Commonwealth.

Article IV, section 3 of the Constitution: The legislature may establish a Commonwealth appeals court to hear those appeals from judgments and orders of the Commonwealth trial court.

II. STANDARD LEGAL REFERENCE

Constitution 1978 with amendments

III. COMPOSITION AND ORGANIZATION

Composition

The number of judges:

The Supreme Court shall consist of a chief justice and at least two associate justices. The Legislature may increase the number of justices when necessary.

Electoral/appointment body:

Article IV., section 4 of the Constitution: The governor shall appoint judges of the Commonwealth courts with the advice and consent of the senate.

The Court members: /

The Court President: /

Organization

Administrative autonomy:

The budget:

Article X., section 8 of the Constitution: The Department of Finance or its successor department shall control and regulate the expenditure of public funds.

IV. POWERS

Constitutional Court Review /

> **Preventive review:** /
> **A posteriori review:** /
> **Abstract review:** /
> **Concrete review:** /

Other powers

Constitutional complaints: /

Jurisdictional disputes:

Article IV., section 2 of the Constitution: The Commonwealth trial court shall have original jurisdiction in all cases in equity and in all cases at law which involve land in the Commonwealth, and in all other civil actions

The unconstitutionality of acts and activities of political parties: /

Charges against the President of the Republic: /

Charges against the Prime Minister or against any Minister of State:
Article II., Section 8 of the Constitution: The legislature may impeach those executive and judicial officers of the Commonwealth subject to impeachment under this Constitution. The house of representatives may initiate impeachment proceedings by the affirmative vote of two-thirds of its members and the senate may convict after hearing by the affirmative vote of two-thirds of its members'

Article III., section 19 of the Constitution: The governor and lieutenant governor are subject to impeachment as provided in article II, section 8, of this Constitution for treason, commission of a felony, corruption or neglect of duty.

Electoral matters: /
Referendums: /
Other matters with which the Court is charged by the Constitution or statute:
Article IV., section 6 of the Constitution: Judges are subject to impeachment as provided in article II, section 8, of this Constitution for treason, commission of a felony, corruption or neglect of duty.

Standing before the Constitutional Court /
State bodies:
Individuals: X

V. NATURE AND EFFECTS OF DECISIONS

Finality: /
Binding force: /
Erga omnes: /
Inter partes: /
Ex officio: /
The legislative omissions: /

SOURCES:

https://en.wikisource.org/wiki/Constitution_of_the_Commonwealth_of_the_Northern_Mariana_Islands
http://www.refworld.org/docid/3ae6b5450.html
http://cnmilaw.org/cnmiconstitution.html

DOSSIER OF THE HIGH COURT OF THE REPUBLIC OF THE MARSHALL ISLANDS

STATE: Republic of the Marshall Islands
TITLE: The High Court
YEAR OF FOUNDATION: 1.May. 1979
SEAT: Majuro

I. CHRONICLE

Date and context of establishment 1. May 1979
Position in the hierarchy of courts
Section 3 of the Constitution:
The High Court
1. The High Court shall be a superior court of record having general jurisdiction over controversies of law and fact in the Republic of the Marshall Islands; shall consist of a Chief Justice, and such number of other judges as may from time to time be prescribed by Act, shall have original jurisdiction over cases duly filed in the High Court; and shall have appellate jurisdiction over cases originally filed in subordinate courts; and, unless otherwise provided by law, shall have jurisdiction to review the legality of any final determination by a government agency at the behest of any party aggrieved by such determination.

II. STANDARD LEGAL REFERENCE

Constitution of Republic of the Marshall Islands (amendments through 1995)

III. COMPOSITION AND ORGANIZATION

Composition

The number of judges:

Section 3 of the Constitution:

2. At any time when the judges of the Supreme Court and of the High Court number 4 or more, any judge of the High Court may convene a bench of 3 judges to decide any case in the High Court's jurisdiction, if the convening judge has determined that the case involves either a substantial question of law as to the interpretation or effect of a provision of this Constitution or any other matter of public importance; and, if an insufficient number of judges of the High Court is available, then, without, prejudice to the appellate jurisdiction of the Supreme Court in relation to that case, the remaining members of the bench shall be judges of the Supreme Court.

IV. POWERS

·

Constitutional Court Review

Section 2 of the Constitution: The High Court may, on its own motion or on application of any party to the proceedings, remove to the Supreme Court any question arising as to the interpretation or effect of the Constitution in any proceedings of the High Court, other than proceedings set down for trial before a bench of 3 judges.

In any case in which a question has been removed to the Supreme Court, it shall determine that question and either dispose of the case or remand it to the High Court for disposition consistent with the Supreme Court's determination.

V. NATURE AND EFFECTS OF DECISIONS

SOURCES:

https://www.constituteproject.org/constitution/Marshall_Islands_1995.pdf?lang=en

(109)

DOSSIER OF THE CONSTITUTIONAL COUNCIL OF THE ISLAMIC REPUBLIC OF MAURITANIA

STATE: Islamic Republic of Mauritania
TITLE: The Constitutional Council
YEAR OF FOUNDATION: 2007
SEAT: Nouakchott

I. CHRONICLE

Date and context of establishment
The judicial organisation of Mauritania is currently regulated by Ordinance n 2007/012 of 8 February 2007.

Position in the hierarchy of courts
Article 88 of the Constitution: A law shall determine the rules of organization and functioning of the Constitutional Council, the procedure to befollowed before it, including the deadlines set for referred disputes.

II. STANDARD LEGAL REFERENCE

Mauritania's current constitution was adopted on 12 July 1991, amended 2006, 2012

III. COMPOSITION AND ORGANIZATION

Composition
Article 82 of the Constitution: The office of member of the Constitutional Council are incompatible with membership of the Government or Parliament. Other incompatibilities shall be determined by organic law.

The number of judges:

Article 81 of the Constitution: The Constitutional Council consists of six (6) members, whose mandate lasts nine (9) years and not renewable. The Constitutional Council is renewed by thirds (1 / 3) every three years.

Electoral/appointment body:

The Court members:

Three members are appointed by the President of the Republic, two by the Speaker of the National Assembly and the Chairman of the Senate.

The term of office: 9

Members of the Constitutional Council must be older than thirty five (35) years at least.

They may not belong to the governing bodies of political parties.

They enjoy parliamentary immunity.

The Court President:

The President of the Constitutional Council is appointed by the President of the Republic among the members nominated by it. It has a casting vote in case of a tie.

IV. POWERS

Constitutional Court Review

Preventive review:

Article 67 of the Constitution: Organic laws will be promulgated until the Constitutional Council has declared their conformity with the Constitution.

Article 86 of the Constitution: The organic laws, before promulgation of regulations and parliamentary assemblies before their implementation, must be submitted to the Constitutional Council, which decides on their compliance with the Constitution.

For the same purpose, the laws may be referred to the Constitutional Council before their promulgation by the President of the Republic, Speaker of the National Assembly, the President of the Senate or the third (1 / 3) Members of the Assembly national or the third (third) component of the senators in the Senate.

In the cases mentioned in the two preceding paragraphs, the Constitutional Council must rule within a period of one (1) month.

However, at the request of the President of the Republic, in case of emergency, this period is reduced to eight (8) days.

In these cases, referral to the Constitutional Council shall suspend the period of enactment.

Electoral matters:
Article 49 of the Constitution: The Constitutional Council rules in case of dispute over the legality of the election of parliamentarians and their Eligibility.

Article 83 of the Constitution: The Constitutional Council shall ensure the regularity of the election of the President of the Republic.

It examines the claims and announce the election results.

Article 84 of the Constitution: The Constitutional Council rules, if contested, the regularity of the election of deputies and senators.

Records of applications are received by the Constitutional Council rules on their legality and announce the election results Article 26 of the Constitution – presidential elections)

Referendums:
Article 85 of the Constitution: The Constitutional Council shall ensure the regularity of referendums and announce the results.

Other matters with which the Court is charged by the Constitution or statute:
Article 40 of the Constitution: In case of vacancy or incapacity declared permanent by the Constitutional Council, the President of the Senate as acting President of the Republic for the current business.

Article 58 of the Constitution: The declaration of war was authorized by Parliament.

Article 59 of the Constitution: Matters other than those in the field of law fall within the regulatory power.

The Acts of Parliament in such matters may be changed by decree, if the Constitutional Council declares that they are regulatory in nature under the preceding paragraph.

V. NATURE AND EFFECTS OF DECISIONS

Binding force/Erga omnes:
Article 87 of the Constitution: A provision declared unconstitutional may not be promulgated or implemented.

The decisions of the Constitutional Council are protected by the authority of res judicata.

The decisions of the Constitutional Council are not subject to appeal.

They apply to public authorities and all administrative and judicial authorities.

Obligatory opinions on the conformity of international treaties with the Constitution:

Article 79 of the Constitution: If the Constitutional Council, the President of the Republic or the President of the National Assembly or the Senate President or the third (third) of the deputies or senators, said that international agreement contains a clause contrary to the Constitution, authorization to ratify or approve it may only occur after revision of the Constitution.

SOURCES:

http://www.wipo.int/edocs/lexdocs/laws/en/mr/mr019en.pdf

(110)

DOSSIER OF THE SUPREME COURT OF THE REPUBLIC OF MAURITIUS

STATE: Republic of Mauritius
TITLE: Supreme Court
YEAR OF FOUNDATION: It was established in its current form in 1850 (rev. 2011)
SEAT: Port-Louis

I. CHRONICLE

Date and context of establishment 1850(2011)
Position in the hierarchy of courts
There shall be a Supreme Court for Mauritius which shall have unlimited jurisdiction to hear and determine any civil or criminal proceedings under any law other than a disciplinary law and such jurisdiction and powers as may be conferred upon it by this Constitution or any other law. Article 76 of the Constitution

II. STANDARD LEGAL REFERENCE

Constitution of 1968 with amendments

III. COMPOSITION AND ORGANIZATION

Composition
The number of judges:
Subject to section 77 of the Constitution, the judges of the Supreme Court shall be the Chief Justice, the Senior Puisne judge and such number of Puisne Judges as may be prescribed by Parliament Article 76 of the Constitution

Electoral/appointment body

1. The Chief Justice shall be appointed by the President acting after consultation with the Prime Minister.
2. The Senior Puisne Judge shall be appointed by the President, acting in accordance with the advice of the Chief Justice.
3. The Puisne Judges shall be appointed by the President, acting in accordance with the advice of the Judicial and Legal Service Commission. Article 77 of the Constitution

The Court members:
The term of office:
A judge of the Supreme Court holds office until retirement at the age of 62.

IV. POWERS

Section 83 of the Constitution :Original jurisdiction of Supreme Court in constitutional questions

Constitutional review
Concrete review

Section 84 of the Constitution Reference of constitutional questions to Supreme Court

(1) Where any question as to the interpretation of this Constitution arises in any court of law established for Mauritius (other than the Court of Appeal, the Supreme Court or a court martial) and the court is of opinion that the question involves a substantial question of law, the court shall refer the question to the Supreme Court.

(2) Where any question is referred to the Supreme Court in pursuance of this section, the Supreme Court shall give its decision upon the question and the court in which the question arose shall dispose of the case in accordance with that decision or, where the decision is the subject of an appeal to the Court of Appeal or the Judicial Committee, in accordance with the decision of the Court of Appeal or, as the case may be, of the Judicial Committee.

Other powers
Constitutional complaints

(1) Subject to sections 41(5), 64(5) and 101(1) of the Constitution, where any person alleges that any provision of this Constitution (other than Chapter II) has been contravened and that his interests are being or are likely to be affected by such contravention, then, without prejudice to any other action with respect to the same matter which is lawfully available, that person may apply to the Supreme Court for a declaration and for relief under this section.

(2) The Supreme Court shall have jurisdiction, in any application made by any person in pursuance of subsection (1) or in any other proceedings lawfully brought before the court, to determine whether any provision of this Constitution (other than Chapter II) has been contravened and to make a declaration accordingly:

Provided that the Supreme Court shall not make a declaration in pursuance of the jurisdiction conferred by this subsection unless it is satisfied that the interests of the person by whom the application under subsection (1) is made or, in the case of other proceedings before the court, a party to these proceedings, are being or are likely to be affected.

(3) Where the Supreme Court makes a declaration in pursuance of subsection (2) that any provision of the Constitution has been contravened and the person by whom the application under subsection (1) was made or, in the case of other proceedings before the court, the party in those proceedings in respect of whom declaration is made, seeks relief, the Supreme Court may grant to that person such remedy, being a remedy available against any person in any proceedings in the Supreme Court under any law for the time being in force in Mauritius, as the court considers appropriate.

(4) The Chief Justice may make rules with respect to the practice and procedure of the Supreme Court in relation to the jurisdiction and powers conferred on it by this section (including rules with respect to the time within which applications shall be made under subsection (1)).

(5) Nothing in this section shall confer jurisdiction on the Supreme Court to hear or determine any such question as is referred to in section 37 or paragraph 2(5), 3(2) or 4(4) of the First Schedule otherwise than upon an application made in accordance with that section or that paragraph, as the case may be.

Standing before the constitutional court:
State bodies: X
Individuals: X

V. NATURE AND EFFECTS OF DECISIONS

Finality:
The Supreme Court of Mauritius is the highest court of Mauritius and is the final court of appeal in the Mauritian judicial system.

SOURCES:

http://mauritiusassembly.govmu.org/English/constitution/Pages/default.aspx

(111)

DOSSIER OF THE SUPREME COURT OF JUSTICE OF THE NATION OF THE UNITED MEXICAN STATE

STATE: United Mexican State
TITLE: Supreme Court of Justice of the Nation
YEAR OF FOUNDATION: 1824 (reintroduced many times)
SEAT: Mexico City

I. CHRONICLE

Date and context of establishment 1824, remodeled many times
Position in the hierarchy of courts
The judicial power of the United Mexican States is vested in a Supreme Court of Justice, an Electoral Court, specialized circuit courts, unitary circuit courts and the district courts. Article 94 of the Constitution

II. STANDARD LEGAL REFERENCE

The constitution was adopted by the Constitutional Congress on 5 February 1917 (with amendments)

III. COMPOSITION AND ORGANIZATION

Composition
The number of judges:
The Supreme Court of Justice of the Nation shall consist of 11 Justices and shall work at plenary meetings or at courtrooms. Article 94 of the Constitution

Electoral/appointment body: For appointment of a Justice of the Supreme Court, the President of the Republic shall submit a list of three candidates to the Senate, who should present before the Senate. Within a 30-day period, the Senate shall choose one of the candidates by the vote of two thirds of the present members of the Senate. This period may not be extended. Should the Senate not decide within such term, then the President of the Republic shall appoint one person from the list he has proposed. Article 96 of the Constitution

The term of office:
Judges of the SCJN are appointed for 15 years

The Court President:
The term of office:
Every four years, the Supreme Court of Justice, in plenary meeting, shall appoint a president for the Supreme Court from among its members. The President of the Supreme Court cannot be reelected for the next immediate term. Article 97 of the Constitution

The President of the Court to serve a four-year period; a given minister may serve more than one term as president, but not in consecutive periods.

Organization
Administrative autonomy:
The budget:
The Supreme Court of Justice shall propose its own budget, and the Federal Judicial Council shall propose the budget for the rest of the federal judicial branch, but complying with the provisions established in the Article 99 of the Constitution, paragraph seventh, of this Constitution. These budgets shall be submitted by the President of the Supreme Court of Justice in order to include them into the Nation's federal budget. The President of the Supreme Court of Justice shall manage the Supreme Court's internal affairs. Article 100 of the Constitution

IV. POWERS

Constitutional Court Review

A posteriori review:
Concrete review:
The Supreme Court of Justice may, by its own motion or by motion of the collegiate circuit court, the Attorney General in the issues that concern to the Public Prosecution Service, or by the Federal Executive through its Legal Government Counselor, hear direct constitutional adjudications given that are considered important or transcendental (Article 94 of the Constitution)

Standing before the Constitutional Court

State bodies:

About constitutional disputes, except for those referring to electoral matters, between:

a.The Federal Government and one state or the Federal District.

b.The Federal Government and one municipal authority.

c.The Executive Power and the Congress of the Union; the President of the Republic and any of the Houses; or the President of the Republic and the Permanent Committee, acting as federal bodies or as Federal District's bodies.

d.Two states.

e.A state and the Federal District.

f.The Federal District and a municipal council.

g.Two municipal councils belonging to different states.

h.Two powers belonging to the same state about the constitutionality of their acts or regulations.

i.A state and one of its municipal councils, about the constitutionality of their acts or regulations.

j.A State and a municipal government belonging to another State, about the constitutionality of their acts or general norms.

k.Two governmental bodies belonging to the Federal District Government, about the constitutionality of their acts or general norms.

l.Two autonomous constitutional entities or between one autonomous constitutional entity and the Federal Executive or the Mexican Congress when the issue is related to the constitutionality of their acts or general norms. This Article is also applicable to the National Transparency Agency [organo garante] established in the 6th Article of the Constitution. Article 105 of the Constitution

II.

Unconstitutionality lawsuits directed to raise a contradiction between a general regulation and this constitution.

Unconstitutionality lawsuits shall be initiated within the 30 days after publication of the regulation, they shall be initiated by:

a.Thirty-three percent of the members of the House of Representatives against federal laws or laws enacted by the Congress and applicable to Federal District.

b.Thirty-three percent of the members of the Senate against federal laws or laws enacted by the Congress and applicable to Federal District, or against international treaties signed by the Mexican State.

c.The Executive Federal, through its Legal Government Counselor, against general norms of the federation or the federal entities.

d.Thirty-three percent of the members of a state legislature, against laws enacted by such state legislature.

e.Thirty-three percent of the members of the Federal District's Assembly of Representatives, against laws enacted by the Assembly.

f.The political parties registered before the National Electoral Institute, through their national leaders and against federal or local electoral laws; also, the state parties with local registration, through their leaders, only against laws enacted by the state legislature that granted them registration.

g.The National Human Rights Commission, against federal or state laws or laws enacted by the Federal District Government; as well as law against international treaties signed by the President of the Republic and approved by the Senate, which hamper the human rights system established in this Constitution and in the international treaties that Mexico has ratified. Likewise, the human right protection organs, equivalent to the National Commission for Human Rights in the federal entities against local legislation issued by the Local Congress and the Federal District Commission for Human Rights against the laws issued by the Federal District Legislative Assembly.

h.The National Transparency Agency [organo garante] established in the 6th Article of this Constitution against federal, local laws and laws of the Federal District, as well as international treaties signed by the Federal Executive and approved by the Senate when these diminish the right of access to information and the protection of personal data. Likewise, the local transparency agencies [organos garantes locales] may present an unconstitutional inquiry against the local laws enacted by the State Legislatures or the Federal District Transparency Agency can do so against the laws enacted by the Federal District Assembly.

i. The General Attorney in regard to the federal and local criminal laws and criminal procedure laws, as well as other issues related to his functions.

Individuals:

Article 107 of the Constitution

All controversies mentioned in the article 103 of the Constitution, except for electoral controversies, shall follow the legal procedures and formalities established by the statutory law, according to the following principles:

I. The constitutional adjudication (appeal on the grounds of unconstitutionality) shall be carried out at the request of the offended party. The offended party is the holder of an individual or collective right, which has been violated by the challenged act, affecting his/her legal framework, either directly or by the means of his/her special situation before the legal system.

Constitutional adjudications [amparo], constitutional controversies and unconstitutionality claims shall have priority when one of the chambers of the Congress, through its Speaker, or the President of the Republic, through its Legal Councilor, justifies the urgency on the basis of social interest or the law and order, in accordance with the regulatory laws (Article 94 of the Constitution

V. NATURE AND EFFECTS OF DECISIONS

Finality/Binding force:

The rulings taken by the Supreme Court of Justice, by a majority of eight vote, invalidating general provisions, shall have general compulsory effect; provided that the respective controversy is generated by the general provisions issued by a state or a municipal council, and which are challenged by the Federal Government; or by the general provisions issued by a municipal council and which has been challenged by the state; or in the cases indicated in paragraphs "c", "h" and "k". Article 105 of the Constitution

SOURCES:

http://www.wipo.int/wipolex/en/text.jsp?file_id=329447

DOSSIER OF THE SUPREME COURT OF THE FEDERATED STATES OF MICRONESIA

STATE: Federated States of Micronesia
TITLE: The Supreme Court
YEAR OF FOUNDATION: 1978
SEAT: Palikir

I. CHRONICLE

Date and context of establishment 1978
Position in the hierarchy of courts:
Article XI, Section 2 of the Constitution: The Supreme Court is a court of record and the highest court in the nation.

II. STANDARD LEGAL REFERENCE

Constitution of the Federated States of Micronesia: 1978, rev. 1990

III. COMPOSITION AND ORGANIZATION

Composition
The number of judges:
Article XI, Section 2 of the Constitution: Not more than 5 associate justices, at least three justice shall hear and decide appeals.

Electoral/appointment body:
Article XI, Section 3 of the Constitution: The Chief Justice and associate justices of the Supreme Court are appointed by the President with the approval of 2/3 of Congress.

Organization

The budget:

Article XI, Section 10 of the Constitution: The Congress shall contribute to the financial support of state judicial systems and may provide other assistance.

IV. POWERS

Constitutional Court Review

A posteriori review:

Concrete review:

Article XI, Section 7 of the Constitution: The appellate division of the Supreme Court may review cases heard in the national courts, and cases heard in state or local courts if they require interpretation of this Constitution, national law, or a treaty. If a state constitution permits, the appellate division of the Supreme Court may review other cases on appeal from the highest state court in which a decision may be had. When a case in a state or local court involves a substantial question requiring the interpretation of the Constitution, national law, or a treaty, on application of a party or on its own motion the court shall certify the question to the appellate division of the Supreme Court. The appellate division of the Supreme Court may decide on the case or remand it for further proceedings.

Other powers

Other matters with which the Court is charged by the Constitution or statute:

Article XI, Section 6 of the Constitution: The trial division of the Supreme Court has original and exclusive jurisdiction in cases affecting officials of foreign governments, disputes between states, admiralty or maritime cases, and in cases in which the national government is a party except where an interest in land is at issue. The national courts, including the trial division of the Supreme Court, have concurrent original jurisdiction in cases arising under this Constitution; national law or treaties; and in disputes between a state and a citizen of another state, between citizens of different states, and between a state or a citizen thereof, and a foreign state, citizen, or subject.

SOURCES:

https://www.constituteproject.org/constitution/Micronesia_1990?lang=en

(113)

DOSSIER OF THE CONSTITUTIONAL COURT OF THE REPUBLIC OF MOLDOVA

STATE: The Republic of Moldova
TITLE: The Constitutional Court of Moldova
YEAR OF FOUNDATION: 1995
SEAT: Chişinău

I. CHRONICLE

Date and context of establishment 1995
The Title V of the Constitution granted the Constitutional Court the status of sole authority of constitutional jurisdiction in the Republic of Moldova, independent of any other public authority and obeying only the Constitution, being the guarantor of the Constitution supremacy (Article 134 of the Constitution). Simultaneously, the Supreme Law expressly regulates its powers (Article 135 of the Constitution), the status of constitutional judges (Articles.137, 138, 139 of the Constitution) and the legal value of acts of the Constitutional Court (Article 140 of the Constitution).

Position in the hierarchy of courts
Article 134 of the Constitution

(1) The Constitutional court is the sole authority of constitutional jurisdiction in the Republic of Moldova.

(2) The Constitutional Court is independent of any other public authority and shall abide only by the Constitution.

(3) The Constitutional Court guarantees the supremacy of the Constitution, ascertains the enforcement of the principle of separation of the State powers into the legislative, executive and judiciary, and it guarantees the responsibility of the State towards the citizen and of the citizen towards the State.

II. STANDARD LEGAL REFERENCE

The current Constitution of Moldova was adopted on 29 July 1994 by the Moldovan Parliament (rev.2004)

III. COMPOSITION AND ORGANIZATION

Composition

Article 136 of the Constitution

Structure

(1) The Constitutional Court consists of 6 judges appointed for a 6-year term of office.

(2) Two judges shall be appointed by the Parliament, two -by the Government and two -by the Superior Council of Magistrates.

[Art. 136 para.(2) modified by the Law no.1115-XIV of 05.07.00, MO no. 88-90/28.07.00, art.661]

The number of judges: 6

Electoral/appointment body:

The Court members:

Article 136 of the Constitution

Structure

(2) Two judges shall be appointed by the Parliament, two -by the Government and two -by the Superior Council of Magistrates.

[Art. 136 para.(2) modified by the Law no.1115-XIV of 05.07.00, MO no. 88-90/28.07.00, art.661]

The term of office: 6

IV. POWERS

Article 135 of the Constitution

Powers

... (2) The Constitutional Court carries out its activity on the initiative brought forward

Constitutional Court Review

A posteriori review:

Abstract review:

Article 135 of the Constitution

Powers

(1) The Constitutional Court:

a) exercises, upon appeal, the review of constitutionality over laws and decisions of the Parliament, decrees of the President, decisions and ordinances of the Government, as well as over international treaties to which the Republic of Moldova is a party;

[Art. 135, para. (1) section a) modified by the Law no.1115- XIV of 05.07.00, MO no. 88-90/28.07.00, art.661] ...

Concrete review:

... g) solves the pleas of unconstitutionality of legal acts, as claimed by the Supreme Court of Justice;

Other powers

... b) gives the interpretation of the Constitution;

... c) formulates its position on initiatives aimed at revising the Constitution;

...

The unconstitutionality of acts and activities of political parties:

... h) decides over matters dealing with the constitutionality of a party.

Electoral matters:

e) confirms the results of parliamentary and presidential elections in the Republic of Moldova;

Article 79 of the Constitution

Validation of the Mandate and Taking the Oath

The Constitutional Court shall validate the result of election for the office of the President of the Republic of Moldova.

Article 62 of the Constitution

Validation of Mandate of the Member of Parliament

Upon the proposal submitted by the Central Electoral Commission, the Constitutional Court rules either on the validation of the mandate of the Member of Parliament, or on invalidation whenever electoral legislation has been infringed.

Referendums:

...d) confirms the results of republican referenda;

Other matters with which the Court is charged by the Constitution or statute:

f) ascertains the circumstances justifying the dissolution of the Parliament, the removal of the President of the Republic of Moldova or the interim office of the President, as well as the impossibility of the President of the Republic of Moldova to fully exercise his/her functional duties for more than 60 days;

[Art. 135, para.(1) section f) amended by the Law no.1115- XIV of 05.07.00, MO no. 88-90/28.07.00, art.661]

Article 90 of the Constitution

Vacancy of Office

(3) The impossibility of the President of the Republic of Moldova to exercise his/her duties for more than 60 days shall be confirmed by the Constitutional Court within 30 days from the date of the submission of application

9. Other forms of human rights protection

Standing before the Constitutional Court

State bodies:

Article 88 of the Constitution

Other Powers

The President of the Republic of Moldova also fulfils the following duties:

i) suspends the acts of the Government which are contrary to the legislation until the delivery of the final judgment of the Constitutional Court

V. NATURE AND EFFECTS OF DECISIONS

Finality/Binding force/Erga omnes:

Article 140 of the Constitution

Judgments of the Constitutional Court

(1) Laws and other normative acts or parts thereof become null and void from the moment of adopting by the Constitutional Court of the appropriate judgment to that effect.

(2) The judgments of the Constitutional Court are final and cannot be appealed against.

SOURCES:

http://www.constcourt.md/public/files/file/Actele%20Curtii/acte_en/MDA_Constitution_EN.pdf

(114)

DOSSIER OF THE SUPREME COURT OF THE PRINCIPALITY OF MONACO

STATE: Principality of Monaco
TITLE: The Supreme Court of Monaco
YEAR OF FOUNDATION: 1911
SEAT: Monaco Palace Justice

I. CHRONICLE

Date and context of establishment

From a historical point of view, the Monaco Supreme Court holds a very important place as it was established by the Constitution of 5 January 1911. It follows that it also confirms the establishment of the Supreme Court (Article 90 of the Constitution). More detailed rules concerning its organisation and operation were laid down by Sovereign Ordinance No. 2.984 of 16 April 1963.

Position in the hierarchy of courts

The Supreme Court is the highest court for judicial appeals and also interprets the constitution when necessary

Judicial power vests in the Prince, who, by the present Constitution, delegates its full exercise to the courts and tribunals.

Tribunals render justice in the name of the Prince. Article 88

II. STANDARD LEGAL REFERENCE

Constitution of 1911 as amended

Composition

The number of judges:

Supreme Court is composed of five full members and two substitute members. Article 89 of the Constitution

Electoral/appointment body:

The Supreme Courts members are appointed by the Prince, as follows:

One full member and one substitute member are introduced by the National Council from outside its members

One full member and one substitute member are introduced by the State Council from outside its members

One full member is introduced by the Crown Council from outside its members

One full member is introduced by the Court of Appeal from outside its members

One full member is introduced by the Civil Court of First Instance from outside its members.

The President of the Supreme Court is appointed by the Prince. Article 89 of the Constitution

The Court members:

The term of office:

The Supreme Court is made up of five full members and two alternate members appointed by the Prince for a period of four years, upon the proposal of the National Council, the Council of State, the Crown Council, the Court of Appeal and the Court of First Instance. Each of these institutions proposes a full member; only the National Council and the Council of State also propose an alternate member.

Autonomy of organization:

A sovereign order regulates the organisation and operations of the Supreme Court, especially relevant to the required qualifications of its members, incompatibilities regarding them as well as their status, the turnover of the administrative section's members, the procedure to follow before the Court, effects of petitions and awards, procedure and effects of conflicts of jurisdiction, as well as necessary transitional measures.

Constitutional Court Review

Concrete review

The Supreme Court rules on applications for annulment, determination of validity and compensation in connection with breaches of constitutional rights and freedoms, arising primarily from the law, namely the legislation expressing, under Article 66 of the Constitution, the agreement of the Prince and the National Council.

A. In constitutional matters, the Supreme Court rules in sovereign fashion over:

1.Compliance of the National Councils rules of procedure with constitutional and, if need be, legislative provisions under the conditions prescribed by Article 61 of the Constitution

2.Appeals on petitions for annulment, petitions to review validity and actions for damages arising from violations of these rights and freedoms prescribed in chapter III of the Constitution, and which are not referred to in subsection B of the present Article

B. In administrative matters, the Supreme Court rules in sovereign fashion over:

1.Proceedings for annulment of ultra vires decisions taken by various administrative authorities or Sovereign Ordinances to enforce laws, and the award of related damages

2.Appeals by way of quashing decisions of last resort taken by administrative jurisdictions

3.Appeals for interpretation and petitions to review the validity of decisions of various administrative authorities or Sovereign Ordinances to enforce laws

Article 91 of the Constitution

Other powers

Jurisdictional disputes:

The Supreme Court rules over conflicts of jurisdiction. Article 91 of the Constitution

SOURCES:

http://en.gouv.mc/Government-Institutions/Institutions/Constitution-of-the-Principality

DOSSIER OF THE CONSTITUTIONAL COURT OF MONGOLIA

STATE: Mongolia
TITLE: The Constitutional Tsets (Court) of Mongolia
YEAR OF FOUNDATION: 1992 (2001)
SEAT: Ulan Bator

I. CHRONICLE

Date and context of establishment: 1992 (2001)
Position in the hierarchy of courts:
The Constitutional Tsets (Court) of Mongolia shall be the competent organ with powers to exercise supreme supervision over the enforcement of the Constitution, to make a conclusion on the breach of its provisions, and to decide constitutional disputes, and is the guarantor for strict observance of the Constitution.

II. STANDARD LEGAL REFERENCE

Mongolia's Constitution of 1992 with Amendments through 2001

III. COMPOSITION AND ORGANIZATION

Composition
The number of judges: 9
The Court members/Electoral body:
The Members of the Constitutional Tsets shall be appointed by the State Great Hural (Parliament) for a term of six years, upon the nomination proposals of three of them by the State Great Hural (Parliament), other three by the President, and another three by the Supreme Court.

A Member of the Constitutional Tsets (Court) shall be a citizen of Mongolia, who attained the age of forty years, having a high qualifications in law and politics.

The Court President:
A Chairperson [Chief Justice] of the Constitutional Tsets

The term of office:
A Chairperson [Chief Justice] of the Constitutional Tsets (Court) shall be elected from amongst its nine Members for a term of three years, by a majority of their votes. He/she may be re-elected once.

Organization
Administrative autonomy: /
The budget:
Article 48 of the Constitution: The courts shall be financed from the State budget. The State shall ensure the economic guarantees for the operations of courts.

Administrative services:
Article 53 of the Constitution:The administration of justice shall be conducted in the Mongolian language.

IV. POWERS

Constitutional Court Review

A posteriori review:
Article 66 of the Constitution: 1.The Constitutional Tsets (Court) shall examine and decide disputes regarding a breach of the Constitution, on its own initiative pursuant to the petitions or information from citizens, and/or at the request by the State Great Hural (Parliament), the President, the Prime Minister, the Supreme Court and the Prosecutor General.

Abstract review:
Article 66 of the Constitution: 2. The Constitutional Tsets (Court) shall make conclusions based the grounds prescribed in Section 1 of this Article and submit its conclusions to the State Great Hural (Parliament), on the following issues under a dispute: • Constitutional court powers 1. On whether or not the laws, decrees or other decisions by the State Great Hural (Parliament) or by the President, as well as any Government (Cabinet) decisions and international treaties to which Mongolia is a Party, are in conformity with the Constitution;

Other powers

The unconstitutionality of acts and activities of political parties: /

Charges against the President of the Republic:

Article 66 of the Constitution: 2. The Constitutional Tsets (Court) shall make conclusions based the grounds prescribed in Section 1 of this Article and submit its conclusions to the State Great Hural (Parliament), on the following issues under a dispute: 3. On whether or not the President, the Speaker or members of the State Great Hural (Parliament), the Prime Minister or the members of the Government (Cabinet Ministers), the Chief Justice of the Supreme Court, or the Prosecutor General, have committed a breach of the Constitution; 4. On whether or not there is justification for removal of the President, the Speaker of the State Great Hural (Parliament) and the Prime Minister, and for recall of the members of the State Great Hural (Parliament).

Charges against the Prime Minister or against any Minister of State:

Article 66 of the Constitution: 2. The Constitutional Tsets (Court) shall make conclusions based the grounds prescribed in Section 1 of this Article and submit its conclusions to the State Great Hural (Parliament), on the following issues under a dispute: 3. On whether or not the President, the Speaker or members of the State Great Hural (Parliament), the Prime Minister or the members of the Government (Cabinet Ministers), the Chief Justice of the Supreme Court, or the Prosecutor General, have committed a breach of the Constitution; 4. On whether or not there is justification for removal of the President, the Speaker of the State Great Hural (Parliament) and the Prime Minister, and for recall of the members of the State Great Hural (Parliament).

Electoral matters:

Article 66 of the Constitution:2. The Constitutional Tsets (Court) shall make conclusions based the grounds prescribed in Section 1 of this Article and submit its conclusions to the State Great Hural (Parliament), on the following issues under a dispute: 2. On whether or not the national referendums or any decisions by the Central Electoral Authority regarding the elections to the State Great Hural (Parliament) or its Members as well as the Presidential elections, are in conformity with the Constitution;

Referendums:

A national referendum on the issue of proposed amendments or changes to the Constitution may be conducted with a supporting vote of at least two thirds by the members of the State Great Hural (Parliament). A referendum shall be conducted in accordance with the grounds in Clause 16 of Section 1 of Article Twenty Five of the Constitution

Other matters with which the Court is charged by the Constitution or statute:
Article 68: 1. Any proposed amendments or changes to the Constitution shall be initiated by the competent organs or officials with the right to legislative initiative, and such proposals may be submitted by the Constitutional Tsets (Court) to the State Great Hural (Parliament).

V. NATURE AND EFFECTS OF DECISIONS

Finality:
A decision by the Constitutional Tsets (Court) shall become effective and enter into force immediately upon its commencement.

If the Constitutional Tsets (Court) made a decision that the laws, decrees or other decisions of the State Great Hural (Parliament) and by the President, as well as the Government (Cabinet) decisions and the international treaties to which Mongolia is a State Party, are not in conformity with the Constitution, then such laws, decrees, instruments of ratification, or decisions shall be considered null and void.

SOURCES:

https://www.constituteproject.org/constitution/Mongolia_2001.pdf?lang=en
http://www.conscourt.gov.mn/

(116)

DOSSIER OF THE CONSTITUTIONAL COURT OF MONTENEGRO

STATE: Montenegro
TITLE: Constitutional Court
YEAR OF FOUNDATION: 2007
SEAT: Podgorica

I. CHRONICLE

Date and context of establishment: 2007
Position in the hierarchy of courts:
Like many other countries Montenegro has adopted the European continental model of constitutional judiciary based on Kelsen theory. The Constitutional Court is established as the highest constitutional body, sui generis, whose responsibilities include protection of the supremacy of the Constitution or the constitutional order and protection of the human rights and freedoms guaranteed by the Constitution and confirmed and published international treaties.

II. STANDARD LEGAL REFERENCE

Constitution of 2007

III. COMPOSITION AND ORGANIZATION

Composition
The number of judges: 7
The Court members:
Article 153 of the Constitution: Composition and election: The Constitutional Court judge shall be elected for the period of twelve years., The person enjoying reputation of a renowned legal

exert, with minimum 15 years of experience in this profession may be elected to the position of the Constitutional Court judge.

The term of office: 12
The Court President:
The President of the Constitutional Court
The term of office:
Article 153 pf the Constitution: The President of the Constitutional Court shall be elected for amongst the judges for the period of three years.The President and the judge of the Constitutional Court shall not discharge duties of a Member of the Parliament or other public duties or professionally perform some other activity.

IV. POWERS

Constitutional Court Review

Preventive review: /
A posteriori review:
Abstract review:
Article 149 of the Constitution: The Constitutional Court shall decide on the following: 1. Conformity of laws with the Constitution and confirmed and published international agreements; 2. Conformity of other regulations and general acts with the Constitution and the law"

Other powers
Constitutional complaints:
Article 149 of the Constitution: The Constitutional Court shall decide on the following: 3. Constitutional appeal due to the violation of human rights and liberties granted by the Constitution, after all other efficient legal remedies have been exhausted,

Jurisdictional disputes:
Article 149 of the Constitution: The Constitutional Court shall decide on the following: 5. The conflict of responsibilities between courts and other state authorities, between state authorities and local self-government authorities, and between the authorities of the local self-government units

The unconstitutionality of acts and activities of political parties:

Article 149 of the Constitution: The Constitutional Court shall decide on the following: 6. Prohibition of work of a political party or a non-governmental organization

Charges against the President of the Republic:

Article 149 of the Constitution: The Constitutional Court shall decide on the following: 4. Whether the President of Montenegro has violated the Constitution

Charges against the Prime Minister or against any Minister of State: /

Electoral matters:

Article 149 of the Constitution: The Constitutional Court shall decide on the following: 7. Electoral disputes and disputes related to the referendum, which are not the responsibility of other courts"

Referendums:

Article 149 of the Constitution: The Constitutional Court shall decide on the following: 7. Electoral disputes and disputes related to the referendum, which are not the responsibility of other courts

Other matters with which the Court is charged by the Constitution or statute:

Article 149 of the Constitution: 9. Performs other tasks stipulated by the Constitution.

Article 154 of the Constitution: Cessation of duty: "The Constitutional Court may decide that the President or the judge of the Constitutional Court that penal action has been initiated against shall not perform the duty for the period of duration of that action."

Standing before the Constitutional Court

State bodies:

Article 149 of the Constitution: The Constitutional Court shall decide on the following: 5. The conflict of responsibilities between courts and other state authorities, between state authorities and local self-government authorities, and between the authorities of the local self-government units, 8. Conformity with the Constitution of the measures and actions of state authorities taken during the state of war or the state of emergency

Individuals:

Article 150 of the Constitution: Initiation of the procedure to assess constitutionality and legality: Any person may file an initiative to start the procedure for the assessment of constitutionality and legality.

Ex offo:
The Constitutional Court itself may also initiate the procedure for the assessment of constitutionality and legality.

V. NATURE AND EFFECTS OF DECISIONS

Finality:
Article 151 of the Constitution: Decision of the Constitutional Court: The Constitutional Court shall decide by majority vote of all judges. The decision of the Constitutional Court shall be published. The decision of the Constitutional Court shall be generally binding and enforceable. When necessary, the Government shall secure the enforcement of the decision of the Constitutional Court."

Binding force:
The decision of the Constitutional Court shall be generally binding and enforceable.

SOURCES:

https://www.constituteproject.org/constitution/Montenegro_2007.pdf
http://www.ustavnisudcg.co.me/engleska/aktuelnostie.htm

(117)

DOSSIER OF THE CONSTITUTIONAL COURT OF THE KINGDOM OF MOROCCO

STATE: The Kingdom of Morocco
COURT TITLE: The Constitutional Court
YEAR OF FOUNDATION: 2011
SEAT: Rabat

I. CHRONICLE

Date and context of establishment:2011
Position in the hierarchy of courts:
Article 107 of the Constitution: The judicial power is independent of the legislative power and of the executive power. The King is the guarantor of the independence of the judicial power.

II. STANDARD LEGAL REFERENCE

Constitution of 2011

III. COMPOSITION AND ORGANIZATION

Composition
The number of judges: 12
The Court members:
Article 130 of the Constitution: The Constitutional Court is composed of twelve members appointed for a mandate of nine years non-renewable. Six members are designated by the King, of which one member is proposed by the Secretary General of the Superior Council of the Ulema, and six members are elected, half by the Chamber of Representatives, [and] half by the Chamber of Councilors from among the candidates presented by the Bureau of each Chamber, at the end of a vote by secret ballot and with the majority of two-thirds of the members composing

each Chamber. The members of the Constitutional Court are chosen from among the notable persons disposing of a high attainment of knowledge [formation] in the juridical domain and of a judicial competence, doctrinal or administrative, having exercised their profession for more than fifteen years, and recognized for their impartiality and their probity.

The Court President:

The term of office:

Article 130 of the Constitution: The President of the Constitutional Court is appointed by the King, from among the members composing the Court.

Organization:

Article 131 of the Constitution: An organic law determines the rules of organization and of functioning of the Constitutional Court, as well as the procedure which is followed before it and the situation of its members. It determines equally the incompatible functions, of which[,] notably[,] are those relative to the liberal professions, establishes the conditions of the two first triennial renewals and the modalities of replacement of the members impeached [empeches], [who] have resigned, or [who] have died in the course of the mandate."

IV. POWERS

Constitutional Court Review

Preventive review:

Article 132 of the Constitution: The Constitutional Court exercises the attributions which are devolved on it by the Articles of the Constitution and the provisions of the organic laws. The organic laws before their promulgation and the regulations of the Chamber of Representatives and of the Chamber of Councilors, before their implementation, must be submitted to the Constitutional Court which decides on their conformity to the Constitution. To the same ends, the laws, before their promulgation, may be deferred to the Constitutional Court by the King, the Head of Government, the President of the Chamber of Representatives, the President of the Chamber of Councilors, or by one-fifth of the members of the Chamber of Representatives or forty members of the Chamber of Councilors. In the case provided for in the second and third paragraphs of this Article, the Constitutional Court decides within a time of one month counting from its referral to [the matter]. However, at the demand of the government, if there is urgency, this time is reduced to eight days. In these same cases, the referral of [the matter] to the Constitutional Court suspends the time period for promulgation.

A posteriori review: /
Abstract review: /
Concrete review: /

Other powers
Constitutional complaints: /
Jurisdictional disputes: /
The unconstitutionality of acts and activities of political parties:
Article 133 of the Constitution: The Constitutional Court is competent to take cognizance of a pleading [exception] of unconstitutionality raised in the course of a process, when it is maintained by one of the parties that the law on which the issue of the litigation depends, infringes the rights and freedoms guaranteed by the Constitution. An organic law establishes the conditions and modalities of application of this Article.

Charges against the President of the Republic: /
Charges against the Prime Minister or against any Minister of State: /
Electoral matters:
Article 132 of the Constitution: It decides, moreover, on the regularity of the election of the members of Parliament and of the operations of referendum. Article 132 of the Constitution: It decides on the regularity of the election of the members of the Parliament within a time of one year, counting from the date of expiration of the legal time of recourse. However, the Court can decide beyond this time, by substantiated decision, in the case where the number of recourses or their nature requires it.

Referendums:
Article 132 of the Constitution: It decides, moreover, on the regularity of the election of the members of Parliament and of the operations of referendum.

Standing before the Constitutional Court
State bodies: X

V. NATURE AND EFFECTS OF DECISIONS

Finality:
Article 134 of the Constitution: A provision declared unconstitutional on the foundation of Article 132 of this Constitution may not be promulgated or implemented. A provision declared unconstitutional on the foundation of Article 133 of the Constitution is abrogated counting from

the date specified by the Constitutional Court in its decision. The decisions of the Constitutional Court are not susceptible to any recourse. They impose themselves on the public powers and on all the administrative and jurisdictional authorities.

SOURCES:

https://www.constituteproject.org/constitution/Morocco_2011.pdf?lang=en

DOSSIER OF THE CONSTITUTIONAL COUNCIL OF THE REPUBLIC OF MOZAMBIQUE

STATE: The Republic of Mozambique
TITLE: Constitutional Council
YEAR OF FOUNDATION: 2004
SEAT: Maputo

I. CHRONICLE

Date and context of establishment: 2004
Position in the hierarchy of courts:
Article 223 of the Constitution: Categories of Courts 1. In the Republic of Mozambique, there shall be the following courts: a. the Supreme Court; b. the Administrative Court; c. the courts of justice. 2. There may be administrative courts, labour courts, fiscal courts, customs courts, admiralty courts, arbitration courts and community courts. 3. The powers, organisation and functioning of the courts referred to in the preceding paragraph shall be established by law, which may provide for a hierarchical order among courts from provincial courts to the Supreme Court. 4. The courts of justice shall have common jurisdiction in civil and criminal matters and shall exercise their jurisdiction over all areas not assigned to other jurisdictional orders. 5. At first instance, there may be courts of special jurisdiction and specialized courts to adjudicate particular matters. 6. The establishment of courts with exclusive jurisdiction to try specific categories of crimes shall not be permitted, subject to the provisions on courts martial.

Article 241 of the Constitution: Definition: 1. The Constitutional Council is a sovereign public office with special jurisdiction to administer justice in matters of a legal-constitutional nature. 2. The law shall determine the organisation, the functioning, the procedures for scrutiny and control of constitutionality and of the legality of normative acts, and all other powers of the Constitutional Council.

II. STANDARD LEGAL REFERENCE

Constitution of 2004 with amendments through 2007

III. COMPOSITION AND ORGANIZATION

Composition
The number of judges: 7
The Court members/Electoral body:
Article 242 of the Constitution: Composition: 1.The Constitutional Council shall consist of seven judges of appeal, appointed in the following manner: a. one judge of appeal, who shall be the President of the Constitutional Council, appointed by the President of the Republic; b. five judges of appeal appointed by the Assembly of the Republic according to principles of proportional representation; c. one judge of appeal appointed by the Superior Council of the Judiciary. 2. Judges of the Constitutional Council shall be appointed for renewable terms of five years and they shall enjoy a guarantee of independence, security of tenure, impartiality and unaccountability. 3. At the time of their appointment, Judges of the Constitutional Council shall be of at least thirty-five years of age and shall have at least ten years of professional experience in the judiciary or in practice at the bar or in teaching law

IV. POWERS

Constitutional Court Review

Preventive review: /
A posteriori review:
Article 244 of the Constitution: The Constitutional Council shall have power to: a. evaluate and declare the unconstitutionality of laws and the illegality of normative acts of State offices;

Concrete review:
Article 247 of the Constitution: 1. Supreme Court decisions harmonising questions of law and other decisions made on grounds of unconstitutionality must be referred to the Constitutional Council in the following cases: a. in the event of a refusal to apply any rule on grounds of its unconstitutionality; b. when the Attorney General of the Republic or the Public Prosecution Service requests an abstract evaluation of the constitutionality or legality of a rule whose application has been refused, on grounds of unconstitutionality or illegality, by judicial decision

from which there is no appeal. 2. The law shall regulate the rules on admissibility of appeals contemplated in this provision.

Other powers

Jurisdictional disputes:

Article 244 of the Constitution: The Constitutional Council shall have power to: b. settle conflicts of jurisdiction between the sovereign public offices;"

The unconstitutionality of acts and activities of political parties:

Article 244 of the Constitution: The Constitutional Council shall also: e. decide, in the last instance, on the legality of the establishment of political parties and coalitions, as well as evaluate the legality of their names, acronyms and symbols, and order their dissipation in the terms of the Constitution and the laws; f. adjudicate actions contesting elections and the deliberations of political parties, as well as the legality of their names, acronyms and symbols; g. adjudicate actions concerning disputes about the terms of office of deputies; h. adjudicate actions concerning incompatibilities established in the Constitution and in the law.

Charges against the President of the Republic:

Article 244 of the Constitution: The Constitutional Council shall also: a. verify the legal prerequisites required of candidates for the office of President of the Republic; b. pronounce upon the permanent incapacity of the President of the Republic; c. verify the death and the divestiture of the President of the Republic;

Charges against the Prime Minister or against any Minister of State:/

Electoral matters:

Article 244 of the Constitution: The Constitutional Council shall also: d. evaluate electoral complaints and appeals in the last instance, and validate and proclaim electoral results, in the terms of the law;

Referendums:

Article 244 of the Constitution: The Constitutional Council shall have power to: c. make prior evaluations of the constitutionality of referenda.

Other matters with which the Court is charged by the Constitution or statute:

Article 244 of the Constitution: The Constitutional Council shall exercise such other powers as may be assigned to it in terms of the law.

Standing before the Constitutional Court

Article 245 of the Constitution: Request for Evaluation of Unconstitutionality: 2. The following may request the Constitutional Council to pronounce upon the unconstitutionality of laws, or on the illegality of normative acts of State offices: a. the President of the Republic; b. the President of the Assembly of the Republic; c. at least one third of the deputies of the Assembly of the Republic; d. the Prime Minister; e. the Attorney General of the Republic; f. the Ombudsman; g. two thousand citizens. 3. The law shall establish rules on the admission of actions for the evaluation of unconstitutionality.

V. NATURE AND EFFECTS OF DECISIONS

Finality:

Article 245 of the Constitution: Request for Evaluation of Unconstitutionality: The Constitutional Council shall with, general binding force, evaluate and pronounce upon the unconstitutionality of laws and the illegality of other normative acts of State offices, at any time during which they are in force.

Binding force:

Article 248 of the Constitution: Judgements Binding and Unappealable: 1. Judgements of the Constitutional Council shall be binding on all citizens, institutions and other legal persons, they shall not be subject to appeal and they shall prevail over other decisions. 2. A person who fails to comply with the judgements referred to in this article shall be guilty of the criminal offence of contempt, unless a more serious crime applies. 3. The decisions of the Constitutional Council shall be published in the Boletim da República.

SOURCES:

https://www.constituteproject.org/constitution/Mozambique_2007.pdf?lang=en

(119)

DOSSIER OF THE CONSTITUTIONAL COURT OF THE REPUBLIC OF THE UNION OF MYANMAR

STATE: Republic of the Union of Myanmar
TITLE: Constitutional Tribunal of the Union
YEAR OF FOUNDATION: 2011
SEAT: Ottarathiri Township, Naypyidaw Union Territory

I. CHRONICLE

Date and context of establishment:
2011 Formation of Constitutional Tribunal of the Union: In accordance with the provisions stated in Article 320 of the Constitution of the Republic of the Union of Myanmar, Article 9 (d) of the Union Government Law and Article 3 of the Constitutional Tribunal of the Union, Constitutional Tribunal of the Union has been formed.

Position in the hierarchy of courts:
Article 293 of the Constitution. Courts of the Union are formed as follows : (a) Supreme Court of the Union, High Courts of the Region, High Courts of the State, Courts of the Self-Administered Division, Courts of the SelfAdministered Zone, District Courts, Township Courts and the other Courts constituted by law; (b) Courts-Martial; (c) Constitutional Tribunal of the Union.

Article 294 of the Constitution. In the Union, there shall be a Supreme Court of the Union. Without affecting the powers of the Constitutional Tribunal and the Courts-Martial, the Supreme Court of the Union is the highest Court of the Union."

II. STANDARD LEGAL REFERENCE

Constitution of the Republic of the Union of Myanmar 2008

III. COMPOSITION AND ORGANIZATION

Composition

The number of judges: 9

The Court members/Electoral body:

Article 321 of the Constitution. The President shall submit the candidature list of total nine persons, three members chosen by him, three members chosen by the Speaker of the Pyithu Hluttaw and three members chosen by the Speaker of the Amyotha Hluttaw, and one member from among nine members to be assigned as the Chairperson of the Constitutional Tribunal of the Union, to the Pyidaungsu Hluttaw for its approval.

Article 334 of the Constitution. (a) The Chairperson and members of the Constitutional Tribunal of the Union may be impeached on any of the following reasons : (i) high treason; (ii) breach of any of the provisions under the Constitution; (iii) misconduct; (iv) disqualification of the qualifications of member of the Constitutional Tribunal of the Union prescribed under Section 333 of ; (v) inefficient discharge of duties assigned by law. Article 146 (b) of the Constitution: If the Chairperson or any member of the Constitutional Tribunal of the Union is to be impeached, it shall be done so in accord with the impeachment provisions as prescribed under Section 302 of the Chief Justice of the Union or a Judge of the Supreme Court of the Union.

Article 336 of the Constitution. The formation and communication of the Constitutional Tribunal of the Union, duties, powers and rights of the Chairperson and members of the Tribunal shall be prescribed by law.

The Court President: the Chairperson

Article 327 of the Constitution. The President shall appoint the Chairperson and members of the Constitutional Tribunal of the Union approved by the Pyidaungsu Hluttaw .

IV. POWERS

Constitutional Court Review

Preventive review: /

A posteriori review:

Article 322 of the Constitution. The functions and the duties of the Constitutional Tribunal of the Union are as follows : (a) interpreting the provisions under the Constitution; (b) vetting whether the laws promulgated by the Pyidaungsu Hluttaw, the Region Hluttaw, the State Hluttaw or the Self-Administered Division Leading Body and the Self-Administered Zone Leading Body are in conformity with the Constitution or not;

Other powers

Jurisdictional disputes:

Article 322 of the Constitution. The functions and the duties of the Constitutional Tribunal of the Union are as follows : (c) vetting whether the measures of the executive authorities of the Union, the Regions, the States, and the Self-Administered Areas are in conformity with the Constitution or not; (d) deciding Constitutional disputes between the Union and a Region, between the Union and a State, between a Region and a State, among the Regions, among the States, between a Region or a State and a Self-Administered Area and among the Self-Administered Areas; (e) deciding disputes arising out of the rights and duties of the Union and a Region, a State or a Self-Administered Area in implementing the Union Law by a Region, State or Self-Administered Area;

Charges against the President of the Republic:

Article 322 of the Constitution. The functions and the duties of the Constitutional Tribunal of the Union are as follows : (f) vetting and deciding matters intimated by the President relating to the Union Territory;

Other powers:

Article 322 of the Constitution. The functions and the duties of the Constitutional Tribunal of the Union are as follows : (g) functions and duties conferred by laws enacted by the Pyidaungsu Hluttaw.

Standing before the Constitutional Court

State bodies:

Article 325 of the Constitution. The following persons and organizations shall have the right to submit matters directly to obtain the interpretation, resolution and opinion of the Constitutional Tribunal of the Union : (a) the President; (b) the Speaker of the Pyidaungsu Hluttaw; (c) the Speaker of the Pyithu Hluttaw; (d) the Speaker of the Amyotha Hluttaw; (e) the Chief Justice of the Union; (f) the Chairperson of the Union Election Commission.

Article 326 of the Constitution. The following persons and organizations shall have the right to submit matters to obtain the interpretation, resolution and opinion of the Constitutional Tribunal of the Union in accord with the prescribed procedures : (a) the Chief Minister of the Region or State; (b) the Speaker of the Region or State Hluttaw; (c) the Chairperson of the Self-Administered Division Leading Body or the Self-Administered Zone Leading Body; (d) Representatives numbering at least ten percent of all the representatives of the Pyithu Hluttaw or the Amyotha Hluttaw.

V. NATURE AND EFFECTS OF DECISIONS

Finality:
Article 324 of the Constitution. The resolution of the Constitutional Tribunal of the Union shall be final and conclusive.

Binding force:
Article 323 of the Constitution. In respect of the said dispute, the resolution of the Constitutional Tribunal of the Union shall be applied to all cases.

SOURCES:

http://www.burmalibrary.org/docs5/Myanmar_Constitution-2008-en.pdf

http://www.myanmarconstitutionaltribunal.org.mm/en

(120)

DOSSIER OF THE SUPREME COURT OF THE NAGORNO – KARABAKH REPUBLIC (REPUBLIC OF ARTSAKH)

STATE: Nagorno – Karabakh Republic
TITLE: The Supreme Court
YEAR OF FOUNDATION: 2006
SEAT: Stepanakert

I. CHRONICLE

Date and context of establishment: 2006
Position in the hierarchy of courts:
Article 108 of the Constitution.:1. In the Nagorno Karabakh Republic justice shall be administered by the courts, in accordance with the Constitution and the laws.

2. Justice is realized by the constitutional, civil, criminal and other means of trial prescribed by law.

3. Judiciary is independent.

Article 109 of the Constitution.: 1. The judicial system of the Nagorno Karabakh Republic is composed of the first instance court of general jurisdiction, the courts of appeal, and the Supreme Court as well as specialized courts as stipulated by law.

2.The establishment of extraordinary courts is prohibited.

3.. The jurisdiction of the courts, their formation and activities are prescribed by the Constitution and laws.

3. The final verdicts of the courts are adopted in the name of the Nagorno Karabakh Republic.

II. STANDARD LEGAL REFERENCE

Constitution of the Nagorno Karabakah Republic 2006

III. COMPOSITION AND ORGANIZATION

Composition

The number of judges:

The Court members:

Article 110 of the Constitution. .1. Judges are appointed for life. A judge may hold office until the age of 65. 2. Powers of a judge are suspended only by the Constitution and in accordance with the cases and procedures stipulated by law.

The Court President:

Article 113 of the Constitution: 4. The president of the Supreme Court and other judges are appointed by the National Assembly at the recommendation of the President of the Republic.

IV. POWERS

Constitutional Court Review

Preventive review:

Article 114 of the Constitution.: 1.2 shall decide, prior to the ratification of an international treaty, whether the obligations assumed therein are in conformity with the Constitution;

A posteriori review:

Article 114 of the Constitution.: 1. The Supreme Court administers Constitutional justice. The Supreme Court by procedures stipulated by law:

1.1 shall decide on whether the laws, the resolutions of the National Assembly, the orders and decrees of the President of the Republic, the resolutions of Government, the Prime Minister, local self-government bodies are in conformity with the Constitution;

Other powers

Jurisdictional disputes: /

The unconstitutionality of acts and activities of political parties:

Article 114 of the Constitution.: 1.9 shall decide on the suspension or prohibition of a political party in cases as stipulated by law.

Charges against the President of the Republic:

Article 114 of the Constitution.: 1.6 shall determine whether there are grounds for the removal of the President of the Republic.

1.7 shall determine whether the President of the Republic is incapable of continuing to perform his/her duties.

Electoral matters:

Article 114 of the Constitution.: 1.4 shall rule on disputes concerning the decision adopted on election of the President of the Republic and election of the Deputies.

1.5 shall ascertain the existence of insurmountable obstacles facing a presidential candidate or the elimination of such obstacles;

Referendums:

Article 114 of the Constitution.: 1.3 shall rule on disputes concerning referenda;

Other matters with which the Court is charged by the Constitution or statute:

Article 114 of the Constitution.: 1.8 shall determine whether there are grounds for the removal of a member of the Supreme Court, his/her initiation of administrative or criminal proceedings or arrest through the judicial process;

Standing before the Constitutional Court

State bodies:

Article 114 of the Constitution.: 2. As stipulated by point 1 of the issues by Constitution and law, the Supreme Court may hear cases submitted by;

2.1 President of the Constitution for the cases specified in points 1.1, 1.2, 1.3,
1.8, and 1.9.

2.2 The National Assembly for the cases specified in points 1.3, 1.6, 1.8, and 1.9.

2.3 At least one-fifth of the members of the National Assembly in cases as specified by points 1.1 and 1.3.

2.4 The Government in cases as specified in points 1.1, 1.7, 1.9.

2.5 Local self-government bodies in cases when their constitutional rights have been violated by the normative acts of the state bodies in accordance with the Constitution...

2.7 The courts and Prosecutor General in the conduct of specific cases, constitutionality of the normative acts.

2.8 The Ombudsman points itemized in 1.1, in accordance with the cases specified in Chapter II of the Constitution.

2.9 The Presidential candidates and members of the National Assembly within the parameters of the points 1.4 and 1.5.

Individuals:

Article 114 of the Constitution.: 2. As stipulated by point 1 of the issues by Constitution and law, the Supreme Court may hear cases submitted by; ....

2.6 Everyone in cases stipulated by law......

V. NATURE AND EFFECTS OF DECISIONS

Finality:

Article 114 of the Constitution.: 4.The Decisions and conclusions shall be final and shall come into force following the publication thereof. , The Supreme Court may adopt a decision stipulating a later term for invalidating a normative act or a separate provision contradicting the Constitution . If the decision of the court is negative, the issue shall be removed from the scope of competence of the relevant body.

SOURCES:

http://www.nkr.am/en/constitution/9/

(121)

DOSSIER OF THE SUPREME COURT OF THE REPUBLIC OF NAMIBIA

STATE: Republic of Namibia
TITLE: The Supreme Court of Namibia
YEAR OF FOUNDATION: 1990
SEAT: Windhoek

I. CHRONICLE

Date and context of establishment: 1990
Position in the hierarchy of courts:
Article 79 of the Constitution

(1) The judicial power shall be vested in the Courts of Namibia, which shall consist of:

(a) a Supreme Court of Namibia;

(b) a High Court of Namibia;

(c) Lower Courts of Namibia.

(2) The Courts shall be independent and subject only to this Constitution and the law.

(3) No member of the Cabinet or the Legislature or any other person shall interfere with Judges or judicial officers in the exercise of their judicial functions, and all organs of the State shall accord such assistance as the Courts may require to protect their independence, dignity and effectiveness, subject to the terms of this Constitution or any other law.

(4) The Supreme Court and the High Court shall have the inherent jurisdiction which vested in the Supreme Court of South-West Africa immediately prior to the date of Independence, including the power to regulate their own procedures and to make court rules for that purpose.

II. STANDARD LEGAL REFERENCE

The Constitution of the Republic of Namibia 1990

Composition

The number of judges:

The Court members:

Article 79 of the Constitution:

(1) The Supreme Court shall consist of a Chief Justice and such additional Judges as the President, acting on the recommendation of the Judicial Service Commission, may determine.

(2) The Supreme Court shall be presided over by the Chief Justice and shall hear and adjudicate upon appeals emanating from the High Court, including appeals which involve the interpretation, implementation and upholding of this Constitution and the fundamental rights and freedoms guaranteed thereunder. The Supreme Court shall also deal with matters referred to it for decision by the Attorney-General under this Constitution, and with such other matters as may be authorised by Act of Parliament.

(3) Three (3) Judges shall constitute a quorum of the Supreme Court when it hears appeals or deals with matters referred to it by the Attorney-General under this Constitution: provided that provision may be made by Act of Parliament for a lesser quorum in circumstances in which a Judge seized of an appeal dies or becomes unable to act at any time prior to judgment.

(4) The jurisdiction of the Supreme Court with regard to appeals shall be determined by Act of Parliament.

IV. POWERS

Constitutional Court Review

Preventive review: /

A posteriori review: /

Other powers

Constitutional complaints: /

Jurisdictional disputes:

Article 138 of the Constitution:

(3) Pending the enactment of the legislation contemplated by Article 79 of the Constitution hereof:

(a) the Supreme Court shall have the same jurisdiction to hear and determine appeals from Courts in Namibia as was previously vested in the Appellate Division of the Supreme Court of South Africa;

(b) the Supreme Court shall have jurisdiction to hear and determine matters referred to it for a decision by the Attorney-General under this Constitution;

(c) all persons having the right of audience before the High Court shall have the right of audience before the Supreme Court;

The unconstitutionality of acts and activities of political parties: /
Charges against the President of the Republic: /
Charges against the Prime Minister or against any Minister of State: /
Electoral matters: /
Referendums: /
Other matters with which the Court is charged by the Constitution or statute: /
Standing before the Constitutional Court
State bodies: X
Individuals: X

V. NATURE AND EFFECTS OF DECISIONS

Binding force:
Article 81 of the Constitution: A decision of the Supreme Court shall be binding on all other Courts of Namibia and all persons in Namibia unless it is reversed by the Supreme Court itself, or is contradicted by an Act of Parliament lawfully enacted.

SOURCES:

http://www.orusovo.com/namcon/
http://www.servat.unibe.ch/icl/wa00000_.html

(122)

DOSSIER OF THE SUPREME COURT OF THE REPUBLIC OF NAURU

STATE: Republic of Nauru
TITLE: Supreme Court of Nauru
YEAR OF FOUNDATION: 1968
SEAT: Yaren

I. CHRONICLE

Date and context of establishment: 1968
Position in the hierarchy of courts:
Article 48 of the Constitution: (1.) There shall be a Supreme Court of Nauru, which shall be a superior court of record.(2.) The Supreme Court has, in addition to the jurisdiction conferred on it by this Constitution, such jurisdiction as is prescribed by law.

II. STANDARD LEGAL REFERENCE

Constitution of the Republic of Nauru 1968

III. COMPOSITION AND ORGANIZATION

Composition
The number of judges:
The Court members/Electoral body:
Article 49 of the Constitution: (1.) The Supreme Court consists of a Chief Justice and such number, if any, of other judges as is prescribed by law.(2.) The judges of the Supreme Court shall be appointed by the President.

IV. POWERS

Constitutional Court Review

Preventive review: /

A posteriori review:

Article 54 of the Constitution: (1.) The Supreme Court shall, to the exclusion of any other court, have original jurisdiction to determine any question arising under or involving the interpretation or effect of any provision of this Constitution. (2.) Without prejudice to any appellate jurisdiction of the Supreme Court, where in any proceedings before another court a question arises involving the interpretation or effect of any provision of this Constitution, the cause shall be removed into the Supreme Court, which shall determine that question and either dispose of the case or remit it to that other court to be disposed of in accordance with the determination.

Other powers
Constitutional complaints: /
Jurisdictional disputes:
The unconstitutionality of acts and activities of political parties:
Charges against the President of the Republic: /
Charges against the Prime Minister or against any Minister of State: /
Electoral matters: /
Referendums: /
Other matters with which the Court is charged by the Constitution or statute:
Standing before the Constitutional Court
State bodies: X
Individuals: X

V. NATURE AND EFFECTS OF DECISIONS

Finality: /
Binding force: /
Ex officio: /
The legislative omissions: /

SOURCES:

http://www.naurugov.nr/parliament-of-nauru/constitution-of-nauru.aspx

(123)

DOSSIER OF THE SUPREME COURT OF THE FEDERAL DEMOCRATIC REPUBLIC OF NEPAL

STATE: Federal Democratic Republic of Nepal
TITLE: Supreme Court
YEAR OF FOUNDATION: 1956
SEAT: Ram Shah Path, Kathmandu

I. CHRONICLE

Date and context of establishment 1956
Position in the hierarchy of courts:
Article 127 of the Constitution. Courts: 1. There shall be the following courts in Nepal: a. Supreme Court, b. High Court, and c. District Court 2. In addition to the courts referred to in Clause (1), other institutions may be established according to the need to adopt other means of alternatives of dispute resolution or judicial bodies to adjudicate cases at the local level according to the law.

Article 128 of the Constitution: Supreme Court: 1. There shall be a Supreme Court in Nepal. 2. The Supreme Court shall be the Court of Record. Unless otherwise provided in this Constitution, all other courts and judicial institutions shall be under the Supreme Court. The Supreme Court shall have the final power to interpret the Constitution and law.

Article 137 of the Constitution. Formation of the Constitutional Bench: 1. There shall be a Constitutional Bench in the Supreme Court. The Bench shall comprise of the Chief Justice and other four Justices appointed by the Chief Justice on the recommendation of Judicial Council.

II. STANDARD LEGAL REFERENCE

Constitution of Nepal 2015

Composition

The number of judges:

Maximum of 20 Justices in the Supreme Court

The Court members:

Article 129 of the Constitution. Appointment and qualifications of Chief Justice and Justices of the Supreme Court: 1. In addition to the Chief Justice of Nepal, there shall be maximum of 20 Justices in the Supreme Court. In case the number of the Justices is inadequate because of the increase of number of cases at the Supreme Court, a maximum of ten temporary Justices may be appointed for a certain period.

The term of office/Electoral bodies:

Article 129 of the Constitution. Appointment and qualifications of Chief Justice and Justices of the Supreme Court: 2. President shall appoint a Chief Justice on the recommendation of Constitutional Council and Justices of the Supreme Court on the recommendation of Judicial Council. 3. Any person who has worked as a Judge of the Supreme Court for at least three years is eligible for appointment as Chief Justice of the Supreme Court. 5. Any Nepali citizen who holds a bachelor degree of law and has worked as Chief Judge or Judge of the High Court for seven years or has practiced law for at least fifteen years as a law graduate senior advocate or advocate or has worked for at least fifteen years in the judicial or legal field or has worked as a gazetted officer first class or above of the judicial service for at least twelve years is eligible for appointment as a Judge of the Supreme Court.

Article 137 of the Constitution. Formation of the Constitutional Bench: 1. There shall be a Constitutional Bench in the Supreme Court. The Bench shall comprise of the Chief Justice and other four Justices appointed by the Chief Justice on the recommendation of Judicial Council.

Organization

Administrative autonomy: Article 128 of the Constitution. Supreme Court: 3. The Supreme Court may inspect, supervise and give necessary directives to courts and other judicial institutions falling under its jurisdiction on matters relating to judicial administration or management.

Article 136 of the Constitution. Responsibility of the Chief Justice: The Chief Justice shall have the ultimate responsibility to make the administration of justice effective of the Supreme Court and other courts under its jurisdiction or other judicial institutions.

Constitutional Court Review

Preventive review: /
A posteriori review: /

Other powers

Constitutional complaints:

Article 133 of the Constitution. Jurisdiction of the Supreme Court: 1. Any Nepali citizen may file a petition in the Supreme Court to have any law or any part thereof declared void on the ground of inconsistency with this Constitution because it imposes an unreasonable restriction on the enjoyment of the fundamental rights conferred by this Constitution or on any other ground, or any law formulated by the Provincial Assembly is inconsistent with the law formulated by Federal Parliament or any law formulated by Municipal Assembly or Village Assembly is inconsistent with the law formulated by Federal Parliament or Provincial Assembly, and extra -ordinary power shall rest with the Supreme Court to declare that law void either ab initio or from the date of its decision if it appears that the law in question is inconsistent.

Other forms of human rights protection:

Article 133 of the Constitution. Jurisdiction of the Supreme Court: 2. The Supreme Court shall, for the enforcement of the fundamental rights conferred by this Constitution, for the enforcement of any other legal right for which no other remedy has been provided or for which the remedy even though provided appears to be inadequate or ineffective, or for the settlement of any constitutional or legal question involved in any dispute of public interest or concern, have the extraordinary power to issue necessary and appropriate orders to enforce such rights or settle the dispute. 3. For this purpose, the Supreme Court may, with a view to imparting full justice and providing the appropriate remedy, issue appropriate orders and writs including the writs of habeas corpus, mandamus, certiorari, prohibition and quo warranto. Provided that, except on the ground of absence of jurisdiction, the Supreme Court shall not, under this Clause, interfere with the internal affairs of the Federal Parliament and, the proceedings and decisions of the Federal Parliament concerning violation of its privileges and any penalties imposed thereof. 4. The Supreme Court shall have jurisdiction to hear original and appellate cases, to review its own judgments or interim order, to examine decision referred for confirmation, review cases or hear petitions. Such review shall be done by judge other than the one involved in original verdict. 5. The Supreme Court shall hear appeal of cases that have been initiated and executed by the High Court, a subject of public interest litigation including a question related to the interpretation of the constitution and law or a case referred by the High Court along with its opinion that it would be appropriate for the Supreme Court to decide on it. 6. Other rights and procedural of the Supreme Court shall be as per the Federal law.

Jurisdictional disputes:
Article 137 of the Constitution. 2. The Bench under clause (1) shall hear and decide on the following cases in addition to the petitions filed according to clause (1) of Article (133): a. Related to disputes over the jurisdiction between the Federation and Province, among Provinces, between a Province and local level and among the local levels (of government),

Electoral matters:
Article 137 of the Constitution. 2. The Bench under clause (1) shall hear and decide on the following cases in addition to the petitions filed according to clause (1) of Article (133): b. Related to disputes concerning the election of members of the Federal Parliament or Provincial Assembly, and ineligibility of the member of the Federal Parliament or Provincial Assembly.

Referendums: /
Other matters with which the Court is charged by the Constitution or statute:
Article 138 of the Constitution. Annual report 1. Each year, the Supreme Court, Judicial Council and Judicial Service Commission shall present its annual report to the President, and the President through the Prime Minister shall submit such reports before the Federal Parliament.

Standing before the Constitutional Court
State bodies: X
Individuals: X

V. NATURE AND EFFECTS OF DECISIONS

Finality: /
Binding force: /
Ex officio: /
The legislative omissions: /

SOURCES:

https://www.constituteproject.org/constitution/Nepal_2015.pdf?lang=en

DOSSIER OF THE SUPREME COURT OF THE KINGDOM OF NETHERLANDS

STATE: Kingdom of the Netherlands
TITLE: Supreme Court of the Netherlands
YEAR OF FOUNDATION: 1838
SEAT: Hague

I. CHRONICLE

Date and context of establishment: 1838
Position in the hierarchy of courts:
Article 116 of the Constitution: 1. The courts which form part of the judiciary shall be specified by Act of Parliament. 2. The organisation, composition and powers of the judiciary shall be regulated by Act of Parliament. 3. In cases provided for by Act of Parliament, persons who are not members of the judiciary may take part with members of the judiciary in the administration of justice. 4. The supervision by members of the judiciary responsible for the administration of justice of the manner in which such members and the persons referred to in the previous paragraph fulfil their duties shall be regulated by Act of Parliament.

II. STANDARD LEGAL REFERENCE

Constitution of 2008

III. COMPOSITION AND ORGANIZATION

Composition
The number of judges:

The Court members/Electoral body:

Article 118 of the Constitution: 1. The members of the Supreme Court of the Netherlands shall be appointed from a list of three persons drawn up by the Lower House of the States General

The Court President: /

IV. POWERS

Constitutional Court Review

Preventive review: /

A posteriori review: /

Article 120 of the Constitution: The constitutionality of Acts of Parliament and treaties shall not be reviewed by the courts.

Other powers

Constitutional complaints: /

Jurisdictional disputes:

Article 118 of the Constitution: 2. In the cases and within the limits laid down by Act of Parliament, the Supreme Court shall be responsible for annulling court judgments which infringe the law (cassation).

The unconstitutionality of acts and activities of political parties: /

Charges against the President of the Republic: /

Charges against the Prime Minister or against any Minister of State:

Article 119 of the Constitution: Present and former members of the States General, Ministers and State Secretaries shall be tried by the Supreme Court for offences committed while in office. Proceedings shall be instituted by Royal Decree or by a resolution of the Lower House.

Electoral matters: /

Referendums: /

Other matters with which the Court is charged by the Constitution or statute:

Article 118 of the Constitution: 3. Additional duties may be assigned to the Supreme Court by Act of Parliament.

V. NATURE AND EFFECTS OF DECISIONS

Finality: /
Binding force: /
Ex officio: /
The legislative omissions: /

SOURCES:

https://www.government.nl/documents/regulations/2012/10/18/the-constitution-of-the-kingdom-of-the-netherlands-2008
www.hogeraad.nl

(125)

DOSSIER OF THE (COMMON) COURT OF JUSTICE OF ARUBA (THE NETHERLANDS)

STATE: Aruba - constituent country within the Kingdom of the Netherlands
TITLE: Common Court of Justice
YEAR OF FOUNDATION: 1951
SEAT: Oranjestad

I. CHRONICLE

Date and context of establishment 1951
Position in the hierarchy of courts
Common Court of Justice for Aruba, Curaçao, Bonaire, St Eustatius and Saba. Jurisdiction, including appeal, lies with the Common Court of Justice of Aruba and the Supreme Court of Justice in the Netherlands.

The judiciary shall have jurisdiction on disputes involving the suffrage and other fundamental rights, the legal status of public servants and the levying and collection of taxes, provided that the jurisdiction on these matters has not been entrusted by Land Ordinance to another judicial organ. ... (Article VI.3 of the Constitution)

II. STANDARD LEGAL REFERENCE

Constitution 1986

III. COMPOSITION AND ORGANIZATION

Judges for both first instance cases and on appeal are taken from a single pool of judges. The Courts of first instance sit as a single judge, while the appeal session are headed by a 3-judge panel. Judges that took part in at case at the lower level may not participate in a case at this level.

The court primarily hears disputes in first instance and on appeal of these six islands, and is on the same level as similar courts in the Netherlands. Since 2012, the court has also been authorized to hear inquiry procedures originated on Curaçao, of a type that would be heard in the Netherlands by the Enterprise Chamber in Amsterdam.

The Court has seats in courthouses located on Aruba, Curaçao, and Sint Maarten, and also is authorized to hold sessions on Bonaire, Sint Eustatius and Saba.

Most decisions of the court of appeal may be appealed in cassatie to the Supreme Court of the Netherlands in The Hague. Decisions of the Supreme Court are final and do not address the facts of the case, but only points of law: whether the decision was based on the right legal grounds and properly motivated. The legal basis for those appeals is the Regulation of 20 July 1961, Stb. 1961, 212, titled the Cassatieregeling Nederlandse Antillen (Appeals Regulations of the Netherlands Antilles), later renamed Cassatieregeling Nederlandse Antillen en Aruba .

One distinction between the appeals procedure in the Netherlands and that of the Caribbean territories is that when a judgment of a Netherlands court is overturned by the Supreme Court, the case is generally remanded to a different court at the lower level for purposes of rendering a new decision. Because the Joint Court is the only court at its level, it will rehear its own cases after being overruled. Another distinction is that clients may be represented by lawyers of the Caribbean islands, rather than lawyers registered with the court of The Hague.

SOURCES:

http://www.worldstatesmen.org/Aruba_const.pdf
http://constitutions.unwomen.org/en/search?keywords=judicial
https://en.wikipedia.org/wiki/Constitution_of_Aruba

(126)

DOSSIER OF THE (COMMON) COURT OF JUSTICE OF CURAÇAO (THE NETHERLANDS)

STATE: Country of Curaçao - constituent country within the Kingdom of the Netherlands
TITLE: Common Court of Justice
YEAR OF FOUNDATION: 2010
SEAT: Wilemstad

I. CHRONICLE

Date and context of establishment
Position in the hierarchy of courts
Common Court of Justice for Aruba, Curaçao, Bonaire, St Eustatius and Saba. Jurisdiction, including appeal, lies with the Common Court of Justice of Aruba and the Supreme Court of Justice in the Netherlands.

The judiciary shall have jurisdiction on disputes involving the suffrage and other fundamental rights, the legal status of public servants and the levying and collection of taxes, provided that the jurisdiction on these matters has not been entrusted by Land Ordinance to another judicial organ. ... (Article VI.3 of the Constitution)

II. STANDARD LEGAL REFERENCE

Constitution 2010
See DOSSIER OF THE (COMMON) COURT OF JUSTICE OF ARUBA

III. COMPOSITION AND ORGANIZATION

IV. POWERS

V. NATURE AND EFFECTS OF DECISIONS

SOURCES:

https://en.wikipedia.org/wiki/Constitution_of_Cura%C3%A7ao

(127)

DOSSIER OF THE CONSTITUTIONAL COURT OF SINT MAARTEN (THE NETHERLANDS)

STATE: Sint Maarten
TITLE: The Constitutional Court of Sint Maarten
YEAR OF FOUNDATION: 2010
SEAT: Philisburg

I. CHRONICLE

Date and context of establishment:
The Constitutional Court of St. Maarten was established on the initiative of St. Maarten's government itself and is a unique institution within the Kingdom. The constitutional court was establisment 17 November 2010.

Position in the hierarchy of courts
National ordinance Constitutional Court(Dutch: *Landsverordening Constitutioneel Hof*) forms the legal basis for the constitutional court. It was approved by the Island Council of Sint Maarten before Sint Maarten obtained the status of country within the Kingdom as part of the dissolution of the Netherlands Antilles and entered into force when Sint Maarten obtained that status on 10 October 2010.

II. STANDARD LEGAL REFERENCE

The Constitution of Sint Maarten (Dutch: Staatsregeling van Sint Maarten) was unanimously adopted by the Island Council of Sint Maarten on 21 July 2010

III. COMPOSITION AND ORGANIZATION

Composition

The number of judges:

The Constitutional Court shall consist of three members, including a president and a vice president, and three deputy members. Para.1 Article 128 of the Constitution

Electoral/appointment body:

The members and deputy members of the Court shall be appointed by national decree Para.2 Article 128 of the Constitution

The president and vice president of the Constitutional Court shall be appointed by national decree from among members of the Constitutional Court, on nominations by the Court. Para.25 Article 128 of the Constitution

The Court members:

The term of office: 10 years

The Court President:

The term of office: 10 years

Organization

Administrative autonomy:

The budget:

The Constitutional Court's budget in the state budget is part of the budget of the Ministry of Justice and hence apportioned by the minister of justice. https://www.transparency.nl/

IV. POWERS

Constitutional Court Review

The task of the Court is to assess the compatibility of a legal regulation that has been ratified but has not taken effect as referred to in Article 81(g) of the Constitution, with the exception of uniform national ordinances, 81(h), 81(i) and 81(j) of the Constitution, with the Constitution. Assessment shall not take place if the provision of the Constitution does not lend itself for assessment. (Para., Article 127 of the Constitution)

Preventive review:

A posteriori review:

Abstract review:

Concrete review:

Other powers

Constitutional complaints:

Request for constitutional compliance can only be made by the ombudsman on the basis of incompatibility with the constitution. https://www.transparency.nl

V. NATURE AND EFFECTS OF DECISIONS

SOURCES:

http://www.sintmaartengov.org/government/AZ/laws/Organic%20Laws/AB%201_Staatsregeling.pdf
https://en.wikipedia.org/wiki/Constitutional_Court_of_Sint_Maarten

(128)

DOSSIER OF THE HIGH COURT OF NEW ZEALAND

STATE: New Zealand
TITLE: The High Court of New Zealand
YEAR OF FOUNDATION: 1.1.2004
SEAT: Wellington

I. CHRONICLE

Date and context of establishment

The High Court of New Zealand is a superior court established in 1841.It was originally called the 'Supreme Court of New Zealand', but was renamed in 1980 to make way for the naming of a new Supreme Court of New Zealand,[3] which first met in 2004. The Supreme Court was established 1 January 2004.

Supreme Court means the Supreme Court of New Zealand established by section 6 of the Supreme Court Act 2003.

This section establishes as the court of final appeal for New Zealand a court of record called the Supreme Court of New Zealand. Subpart 2/ Article 6

Position in the hierarchy of courts

The Supreme Court is the highest court in New Zealand and our final appeal court.

II. STANDARD LEGAL REFERENCE

Supreme Court Act 2003.

III. COMPOSITION AND ORGANIZATION

Composition

The number of judges: 5

Electoral/appointment body:

The Supreme Court comprises—

(a) the Chief Justice; and

(b) not fewer than 4 nor more than 5 other Judges, appointed by the Governor-General as Judges of the Supreme Court. (Supreme Court Act 2003)

The Court members:

The term of office:

A Judge of the Supreme Court holds office until he or she ceases to hold office as a permanent Judge of the High Court. Article 22

IV. POWERS

Constitutional Court Review

The Supreme Court can hear and determine an appeal by a party to a civil proceeding in the High Court against any decision made in the proceeding, unless—

a.an enactment other than this Act makes provision to the effect that there is no right of appeal against the decision; or

b.the decision is a refusal to give leave or special leave to appeal to the High Court or the Court of Appeal; or

c.the decision was made on an interlocutory application.

Other powers

Constitutional complaints:

The Supreme Court can hear and determine an appeal by a party to a civil proceeding in the Court of Appeal against any decision made in the proceeding, unless—

(a) an enactment other than this Act makes provision to the effect that there is no right of appal against the decision; or

(b) the decision is a refusal to give leave or special leave to appeal to the Court of Appeal.

Other matters with which the Court is charged by the Constitution or statute:

The Supreme Court can also remit a proceeding that began in a New Zealand court to any New Zealand court that has jurisdiction to deal with it. Article 26

The Supreme Court can hear and determine appeals authorised by—

a.Part 6 of the Criminal Procedure Act 2011; or

b.section 10 or 10 A of the Court Martial Appeals Act 1953. Article 10

Standing before the Constitutional Court
State bodies: Yes
Individuals: Yes

V. NATURE AND EFFECTS OF DECISIONS

The judgment of the Supreme Court must be in accordance with the opinion of a majority of the Judges hearing the proceeding concerned.

If the Judges are equally divided in opinion, the decision appealed from or under review is taken to be affirmed. Article 31

Finality:
The right to appeal New Zealand court decisions to the Judicial Committee of the Privy Council in the United Kingdom was abolished in 2004 when the Supreme Court was set up.

However, the Privy Council may still hear and determine appeals in certain proceedings that existed before 1 January 2004. Information about this provision can be found in the Senior Courts Act 2016 Subpart7/ Article 31

Binding force
This Act binds the Crown.

SOURCES:

https://www.courtsofnz.govt.nz/the-courts/high-court

(129)

DOSSIER OF THE CONSTITUTIONAL CHAMBER OF THE SUPREME COURT OF THE REPUBLIC OF NICARAGUA

STATE: Nicaragua
TITLE: The Constitutional Chamber of the Supreme Court of Nicaragua
YEAR OF FOUNDATION: The Constitution of Nicaragua was reformed due to a negotiation of the executive and legislative branches in 1995. The reform of the 1987 Sandinista Constitution gave extensive new powers and independence to the National Assembly, including permitting the Assembly to override a presidential veto with a simple majority vote and eliminating the president's ability to pocket veto a bill. Constitution was revised 2014.
SEAT: Managua

I. CHRONICLE

Date and context of establishment 1995 (2014)
Position in the hierarchy of courts
The courts of law form a unitary system whose highest organ is the Supreme Court of Justice... . Article 159 of the Constitution

II. STANDARD LEGAL REFERENCE

Constitution 1995 with amendments

III. COMPOSITION AND ORGANIZATION

Composition
The number of judges:
The Supreme Court of Justice shall consist of sixteen magistrates ... (Para 1) Article 163 of the Constitution

The Supreme Court of Justice shall be composed of Chambers which shall consists of no less than three magistrates each, for terms of two and a half years, namely: the constitutional chamber, the civil, penal and administrativ3e law chambers and the others determined by law. (para. 2) Article 163 of the Constitution

Electoral/appointment body:

The Supreme Court of Justice shall consist of sixteen magistrates elected by the National Assembly for a term of five years. Article 163 of the Constitution

The magistrates sitting in each chamber shall elect by majority vote their President. Article 163 of the Constitution

The Court members:

The term of office:

The term of the magistrates of the Supreme Court of Justice is five years. Article162 of the Constitution

The Court President:

The term of office:

They elect their President and Vice President among themselves, by a majority of votes cast and for a term of two and a half years. (Para.4 163 of the Constitution)

Organization

Administrative autonomy:

The administration of justice shall be organized and shall function with popular participation as determined by the law (para.2) Article 166 of the Constitution

The budget:

The Judicial Power shall receive no less than four percent of the General Budget of the Republic. Article 159 of the Constitution

IV. POWERS

Other powers

Constitutional complaints:

To consider and determine amparo proceedings brought for violation of the rights established in the Constitution in accordance with the Law on Constitutional Justice. (Para.3) Article 164 of the Constitution

Jurisdictional disputes:

The Court in full attendance shall hear and resolve the petitions of unconstitutionality, the disputes concerning distribution of powers and constitutionality between the branches of government, and disputes on constitutionality between the central government and the municipal governments of the Autonomous Regions on the Caribbean Coast. Article 163

To consider and determine ordinary and extraordinary remedies against decisions of the courts of law of the Republic in accordance with the procedures established by law. Article164 of the Constitution

To consider and resolve in final instance administrative conflicts between organs of the public administration and between the latter and individuals.

To consider and resolve in final instance disputes that may occur between municipalities or between them and organs of the Central Government. Para 9,10) Article 164 of the Constitution

V. NATURE AND EFFECTS OF DECISIONS

SOURCES:

https://www.constituteproject.org/constitution/Nicaragua_2014.pdf?lang=en

(130)

DOSSIER OF THE CONSTITUTIONAL COURT OF THE REPUBLIC OF NIGER

STATE: Republic of Niger
TITLE: The Constitutional Court
YEAR OF FOUNDATION: 1999
SEAT: Niamey

I. CHRONICLE

Date and context of establishment: 1999
Position in the hierarchy of courts:
The Constitutional Court is the jurisdiction competent in constitutional and electoral matters. Article 120 of the Constitution

II. STANDARD LEGAL REFERENCE

Constitution 1999

The Republic of Niger has had seven constitutions, two substantial constitutional revisions, and two periods of rule by decree since its independence from French colonial rule in 1960.

The Constitution of the Republic of Niger was adopted on July 18, 1999 and promulgated by Decree No. 99-320/PCRN of August 9, 1999.

III. COMPOSITION AND ORGANIZATION

Composition
The number of judges:
The Constitutional Court includes seven (07) members aged forty (40) years at least.

It is composed of:

Two (2) notable persons with a great professional experience in juridical or administrative matters, of which one (1) is proposed by the President of the Republic and one (1) is proposed by the Bureau of the National Assembly;
two (2) magistrates elected by their peers, of which one (1) is of the first grade and one (1) is of the second grade;
one (1) lawyer with at least ten (10) years of exercise of the profession, elected by his peers;
one (1) professor-researcher holder of a doctorate in public law, elected by his peers;
one (1) representative of the associations of defense of human rights and of promotion of democracy, holder at least of a diploma of the third cycle in public law, elected by the singular or the plural collectives of these associations.

The members of the Constitutional Court are appointed for six (6) years by decree of the President of the Republic. Article 121 of the Constitution

Electoral/appointment body:
The members of the Constitutional Court are appointed for six (6) years by decree of the President of the Republic. Article 121 of the Constitution

The Court members:
The term of office:
The members of the Constitutional Court are appointed for six (6) years by decree of the President of the Republic. Article 121 of the Constitution

The Court President:
The term of office:
The President of the Constitutional Court is elected by his peers for a period of three (3) years renewable. Article 123 of the Constitution

Organization
Administrative autonomy: X
The budget: X

IV. POWERS

Constitutional Court Review
General
The Constitutional Court is the jurisdiction competent in constitutional and electoral matters. It is charged with deciding on the constitutionality of the laws, of the ordinances as well as of

the conformity of international treaties and agreements with the Constitution. • International law • Legal status of treaties It interprets the provisions of the Constitution. Article 120 of the Constitution

The Constitutional Court decides by order, on:

the constitutionality of the laws;

the Internal Regulations of the National Assembly before their application and their modifications;

the conflicts of attribution between the Institutions of the State.

The Constitutional Court is competent to decide on any question of interpretation and of application of the Constitution. Article 126 of the Constitution

Other powers

The unconstitutionality of acts and activities of political parties:

If the Constitutional Court referred to the matter by the President of the Republic, by the president of the National Assembly, by the Prime Minister or by one-tenth (1/10) of the Deputies, has declared that an international agreement contains a clause contrary to the Constitution, the authorization to ratify it can only intervene after revision of the Constitution. Article 170 of the Constitution

Charges against the President of the Republic:

After the ceremony of investiture and within a time period of forty-eight (48) hours, the President of the Constitutional Court receives the declaration, written on the honor, of the assets of the President of the Republic.

This declaration is subject to an annual updating and one at the cessation of the functions. The initial declaration and the updates are published in the Journal Officiel and by the way of the press.

A copy of the declaration of the President of the Republic is communicated to the Court of Accounts and to the tax services.

The gaps between the initial declaration and the annual updates must be duly justified. The Constitutional Court has all powers of evaluation in this domain.

The Court of Accounts is also charged with controlling the declaration of assets as received by the Constitutional Court. Article 51 of the Constitution

In the case of impeachment of the President of the Republic before the High Court of Justice, his interim is assured by the President of the Constitutional Court who exercises all the functions of President of the Republic, with the exception of those mentioned in Article 59 and in paragraph 8 of this Article of the Constitution. He may not stand as a candidate in the presidential elections. Article 53 of the Constiution

Electoral matters:

The Constitutional Court controls the regularity of the presidential and legislative elections. It examines the claims, decides on the disputes of the presidential and of the legislative elections and proclaims the results of the ballots. It decides on the regularity of the referendum and proclaims their results of them. Article 127 of the Constitution

It controls the regularity, the transparency and the honesty of the referendum, and of the presidential and legislative elections. It is the judge of the electoral disputes and proclaims the definitive results of the elections. Article 120 of the Constitution

Referendums:

It interprets the provisions of the Constitution. It controls the regularity, the transparency and the honesty of the referendum... Article 120 of the Constitution

Other matters with which the Court is charged by the Constitution or statute:

The refusal of the President of the Republic to obey an order of the Constitutional Court that declares a violation by him of the provisions of this Constitution is liable to the same consequences as the absolute impediment.

The absolute impediment is declared by the Constitutional Court, referred to the matter by the National Assembly, deciding by a majority of two-thirds (2/3) of its members.

In the case of death, the vacancy is declared by the Constitutional Court, referred to the matter by the Prime Minister or by a member of the Government.

In the case of resignation, the vacancy is declared by the Constitutional Court, referred to the matter by the resigning President of the Republic. Article 53 of the Constitution

The Constitutional Court is equally competent to decide on the cases specified in the Articles 6, 53, 54, 60, 67, 86, 103 and 110 of the Constitution. Article 129 of the Constitution

V. NATURE AND EFFECTS OF DECISIONS

Obligatory opinions on the conformity of international treaties with the Constitution:

If the Constitutional Court referred to the matter by the President of the Republic, by the president of the National Assembly, by the Prime Minister or by one-tenth (1/10) of the Deputies, has declared that an international agreement contains a clause contrary to the Constitution, the authorization to ratify it can only intervene after revision of the Constitution. Article 170 of the Constitution

SOURCES:

https://www.constituteproject.org/constitution/Niger_2010.pdf

(131)

DOSSIER OF THE SUPREME COURT OF THE FEDERAL REPUBLIC OF NIGERIA

STATE: Federal Republic of Nigeria
TITLE: The Supreme Court of Nigeria
YEAR OF FOUNDATION: 1979 (1999)
SEAT: Abuja

I. CHRONICLE

Date and context of establishment:
The coinage Supreme Court was first used in 1863 by the colonial administration through the enactment of the Supreme Court Ordinance No. II which established it as a colony with civil and criminal jurisdiction. The 1979 Constitution in its Section 210 (1) of the 1999 Nigerian Constitution clearly gave it the name Supreme Court of Nigeria. The Court operates as the apex Court on matters involving both Federal and State Laws.

Position in the hierarchy of courts:
The Supreme Court of Nigeria (SCN), is the highest court in Nigeria

II. STANDARD LEGAL REFERENCE

Nigeria has had a series of constitutions. The current constitution was enacted on 29 May 1999, inaugurating the Nigerian Fourth Republic

III. COMPOSITION AND ORGANIZATION

Composition
The number of judges:
The Supreme Court of Nigeria shall consist of-

a.the Chief Justice of Nigeria; and

b.such number of Justices of the Supreme Court, not exceeding twenty-one, as may be prescribed by an Act of the National Assembly. Article 230 of the Constitution

Presently the Supreme Court is made up of the Chief Justice and Sixteen (16) other Justices. http://supremecourt.gov.ng/

Electoral/appointment body:

The appointment of a person to the office of Chief Justice of Nigeria shall be made by the President on the recommendation of the National Judicial Council subject to confirmation of such appointment by the Senate. Para 1. Article 231 of the Constitution

The appointment of a person to the office of a Justice of the Supreme Court shall be made by the President on the National Judicial Council subject to confirmation of such appointment by the senate. Para.2 Article 232 of the Constitution

The Court members:

The term of office:

They are required to retire after a mandatory service age of 70. http://supremecourt.gov.ng/

I. POWERS

Other powers

Constitutional complaints:

Any right of appeal to the Supreme Court from the decisions of the Court of Appeal conferred by this section shall be exercisable in the Case of civil proceedings at the instance of a party thereto, or with the leave of the Court of Appeal or the Supreme Court at the instance of an person having an interest in the matter, and in the case of criminal proceedings at the instance of an accused person, or subject to the provisions of this Constitution and any powers conferred upon the Attorney-General of the Federation or the Attorney-General of a state to take over and continue or to discontinue such proceedings, at the instance of such other authorities or persons as may be prescribed. (Para.5 Article 231 of the Constitution)

The Supreme Court shall have jurisdiction, to the exclusion of any other court of law in Nigeria, to hear and determine appeals from the Court of Appeal. (Para. 1 Article 233 of the Constitution)

Jurisdictional disputes:

The Supreme Court shall, to the exclusion of any other court, have original jurisdiction in any dispute between the Federation and a state or between states if and in so far as that dispute involves any question (whether of law or fact) on which the existence or extent of a legal right depends. (Para. 1 Article 232 of the Constitution)

The unconstitutionality of acts and activities of political parties: X
Charges against the President of the Republic: X
Charges against the Prime Minister or against any Minister of State: X
Electoral matters:
An appeal shall lie form decisions of the Court of Appeal to the Supreme Court as of right in the following cases-

e.decisions on any question-

i.whether any person has been validly elected to the office of President or Vice-President under this Constitution,

ii.whether the term of office of office of President or Vice-President has ceased,

iii.whether the office of President or Vice-President has become vacant.Para.2 Article 233 of the Constitution

Referendums: X
Standing before the Constitutional Court
State bodies: /
Individuals:
Any right of appeal to the Supreme Court from the decisions of the Court of Appeal conferred by this section shall be exercisable in the Case of civil proceedings at the instance of a party thereto, or with the leave of the Court of Appeal or the Supreme Court at the instance of an person having an interest in the matter, and in the case of criminal proceedings at the instance of an accused person, or subject to the provisions of this Constitution and any powers conferred upon the Attorney-General of the Federation or the Attorney-General of a state to take over and continue or to discontinue such proceedings, at the instance of such other authorities or persons as may be prescribed. (Para.5 Article 231 of the Constitution

V. NATURE AND EFFECTS OF DECISIONS

Binding force:
Erga omnes:
The decisions of the Supreme Court shall be enforced in any part of the Federation by all authorities and persons, and by courts with subordinate jurisdiction to that of the Supreme Court. (Para 1. Article 287 of the Constitution)

Ex officio: X

The legislative omissions: X

SOURCES:

http://www.nigeria-law.org/ConstitutionOfTheFederalRepublicOfNigeria.htm

(132)

DOSSIER OF THE COURT OF APPEAL OF NIUE

STATE: Niue
TITLE: The Court of Appeal of Niue
YEAR OF FOUNDATION: 1992
SEAT: Alofi

I. CHRONICLE

Date and context of establishment 1974
The Court of Appeal of Niue is a superior Court of record and was created in the 1992 amendments to the Constitution Act. http://www.paclii.org/nu/other/niue-high-court-bench-book-2004.pdf

Position in the hierarchy of courts
There shall be a Court of Appeal of Niue, which shall be a superior Court of record. (Para.1, Article 52 of the Constitution)

II. STANDARD LEGAL REFERENCE

The Niue Constitution Act 1974 and the Constitution of Niue came into force on 19th October 1974; amended 1992, 2007 (2016)

III. COMPOSITION AND ORGANIZATION

Composition
Subject to Articles 53 and 54 of the Constitution, the Judges of the Court of Appeal shall be –

(a) The Chief Justice and other Judges of the High Court who shall be a member of the Court by virtue of their office; and

(b) Such other persons, possessing such qualifications as shall be prescribed by Act, as may from time to time be appointed by the Governor-General acting on the advice of the Cabinet tendered to him by the Premier.

The number of judges:

Any three Judges of the Court of Appeal may at any time in Niue or beyond Niue, exercise all the powers of the Court: Provided that the Court may have its judgment delivered by any one of the Court's members who is available, and, if there is no such member, then through the Registrar of the Court of Appeal. Para.1 Article 53 of the Constitution

Electoral/appointment body:

Niue chief justice appointed by the governor-general on the advice of the Cabinet and tendered by the premier; other judges appointed by the governor-general on the advice of the Cabinet and tendered by the chief justice and the minister of justice; judges serve until age 68

The Court members:

The term of office:

judges serve until age 68

The Court President:

The term of office:

judges serve until age 68

IV. POWERS

Other powers

Jurisdictional disputes:

Subject to the provisions of this Constitution, the Court of Appeal shall have jurisdiction to hear and determine any appeal from a judgment of the High Court. Para.1 Article 56 of the Constitution

Subject to the provisions of this Constitution, and such time limits as may be prescribed by enactment within which an appeal shall be commenced, and except where under any Act a judgment of the High Court is declared to be final, an appeal shall lie to the Court of Appeal from a judgment of the High Court-

V. NATURE AND EFFECTS OF DECISIONS

Finality:

Except as provided in subclause (2) of this Article, or as may be provided by enactment, the determination of the Court of Appeal shall be final. Para.1 Article 55 of the Constitution

SOURCES:

http://www.google.si/url?sa=t&rct=j&q=&esrc=s&source=web&cd=3&ved=0ahUKEwj-8u3A1JXXAhVLmBoKHTnnB38QFgg2MAI&url=http%3A%2F%2Fwww.paclii.org%2Fnu%2Flegis%2Fconsol_act%2Fcon231.rtf&usg=AOvVaw14khDcXGkX3EMPeAt1n5dJ

(133)

DOSSIER OF THE CONSTITUTIONAL COURT OF THE TURKISH REPUBLIC OF NORTHERN CYPRUS

STATE: Turkish Republic of Northern Cyprus
TITLE: The Supreme Court
YEAR OF FOUNDATION: 1983
SEAT: North Nicosia

I. CHRONICLE

Date and context of establishment 1983
Position in the hierarchy of courts
The Supreme Court is the highest court in Northern Cyprus. The Supreme Court shall carry out the functions of the Constitutional Court, the Supreme Council the Court of Appeal and the High Administrative Court. (3) The Supreme Court, sitting with the President and four Judges, shall have jurisdiction to act as the Constitutional Court. The two last appointed judges of the Supreme Court shall act as the alternate judges. (Para.2,3) Article 143 of the Constitution

II. STANDARD LEGAL REFERENCE

The Constitution of the Northern Cyprus was prepared by the Constituent Assembly of Northern Cyprus after the declaration of independence on 15 November 1983

III. COMPOSITION AND ORGANIZATION

Composition
The number of judges:
The Supreme Court of the Turkish Republic of Northern Cyprus shall be composed of a President and seven judges. In the absence of the President the most senior judge shall act in his place. Article 143 of the Constitution

Electoral/appointment body:
The appointments of the president and judges of the Supreme Court are subject to the approval of the President of the Republic.

IV. POWERS

Constitutional Court Review

Preventive review:
International treaties which have been duly put into operation shall have the force of law. Recourse cannot be made to the Supreme Court sitting as the Constitutional Court in respect of such treaties on the grounds of unconstitutionality. Article 90 of the Constitution

A posteriori review:
Concrete review:
The Constitutional Court shall have jurisdiction to adjudicate finally on a recourse made in connection with any matter relating to any conflict or contest of power or competence arising between State organs. (Para.1) Article145 of the Constitution

Other powers

Charges against the President of the Republic:
The Constitutional Court, sitting as the Supreme Council, shall within the framework of legislation in force, have jurisdiction to try the President of the Republic, the Prime Minister and the Ministers, for any offence committed by them. The duties of the Prosecuting Officer at the Supreme Council shall be performed by the Attorney-General or the Deputy Attorney-General. The judgments of the Supreme Council shall be final. Article 144 of the Constitution

Charges against the Prime Minister or against any Minister of State:
The Constitutional Court, sitting as the Supreme Council, shall within the framework of legislation in force, have jurisdiction to try the President of the Republic, the Prime Minister and the Ministers, for any offence committed by them. The duties of the Prosecuting Officer at the Supreme Council shall be performed by the Attorney-General or the Deputy Attorney-General. The judgments of the Supreme Council shall be final. Aricle 144 of the Constitution

Other matters with which the Court is charged by the Constitution or statute:
The Supreme Court shall make Rules of Court under the provisions of this Constitution and of the laws, for regulating the practice and procedure of itself and of any other court. (2) Without

prejudice to the generality of paragraph (1) of this Article the Supreme Court may make Rules of Court for the following purposes: (a) for regulating the court sittings and allocating duties to judges for any purpose ; (b) for the determination by summary proceedings of any appeal or other proceedings which appear to the Supreme Court or such other court before which such proceedings are pending to be frivolous or vexatious or to have been instituted for the purpose of delaying the course of justice ; (c) for prescribing forms and fees in respect of proceedings in the courts and regulating the cost of, and expenses incidental to, any such proceedings ; (d) for prescribing and regulating the composition of the registries of the courts and the powers and duties of the public personnel working in the courts ; (e) for prescribing the time within which any requirement of the Rules of Court is to be complied with. Article 154 of the Constitution

V. NATURE AND EFFECTS OF DECISIONS

Finality:

The Supreme Court shall have exclusive jurisdiction to adjudicate finally on all matters prescribed by the provisions of this Constitution, the laws and the Rules of Court. (Pra.1) Article144 of the Constitution

Binding force:

Erga omnes:

The provisions of the Constitution shall be the fundamental legal principles binding the legislative, executive and judicial organs, the administrative authorities of the State and individuals. Para.2 Article 7 of the Constitution

SOURCES:

https://www.embargoed.org/downloads/TRNC_Constitution.pdf

(134)

DOSSIER OF THE SUPREME COURT OF THE KINGDOM OF NORWAY

STATE: Norway
TITLE: The Supreme Court of Norway
YEAR OF FOUNDATION: 1815
SEAT: Oslo

I. CHRONICLE

Date and context of establishment
The Supreme Court of Norway was established in 1815 on the basis of section 88 in the Constitution of the Kingdom of Norway

Position in the hierarchy of courts
The Supreme Court pronounces judgment in the final instance. Article 88 of the Constitution

Despite the founding fathers' ideological basis, the Supreme Court started very early to apply the Constitution as a part of positive law.

The Norwegian system of judicial review of the constitutionality of legislative norms is the second oldest in the World.

It has no explicit basis in the Constitution of 1814, but it grew out by court practice since around 1820 and the final decisions – mainly those of the Supreme Court – were systematically respected by the other constituted powers.

II. STANDARD LEGAL REFERENCE

The Constitution, as laid down on 17 May 1814 by the Constituent Assembly at Eidsvoll and subsequently amended, most recently in May 2016

III. COMPOSITION AND ORGANIZATION

Composition

The number of judges:

The Supreme Court shall consist of a President and at least four other Members. Article 88 of the Constitution

Today, there are 19 ordinary justices of the Supreme Court, and one Chief Justice. http://www.domstol.no

IV. POWERS

Constitutional Court Review

A posteriori review:

Abstract review:

Concrete review:

In matters before the courts, the courts have the right and duty to review whether laws and other decisions made by the State authorities are contrary to the Constitution. Article 89 of the Constitution

V. NATURE AND EFFECTS OF DECISIONS

Finality:

The Supreme Court pronounces judgment in the final instance. Article 88 of the Constitution

SOURCES:

http://www.uio.no/studier/emner/jus/jus/JUR1020/h12/undervisningsmateriale/jutintrolecture3ppt2012.pdf

(135)

DOSSIER OF THE SUPREME COURT OF THE SULTANATE OF OMAN

STATE: The Sultanate of Oman
TITLE: The Supreme Court
YEAR OF FOUNDATION: 1999
SEAT: Muscat

I. CHRONICLE

Date and context of establishment
The Royal Decree 90/1999 established the present structure of the judiciary in Oman. At the apex of the system is the Supreme Court.

Position in the hierarchy of courts
Royal Decree 93/99 establishes the Supreme Judicial Council, which will formulate the general policy of the Judiciary and ensure its independence and further development. The Council convenes under the chairmanship of His Majesty the Sultan.

II. STANDARD LEGAL REFERENCE

The Constitution of Oman was promulgated by the Royal Decree No. 101/96 on November 6, 1996. It has been amended once in 2011 by the Royal Decree No. 99/2011

III. COMPOSITION AND ORGANIZATION

Composition
The number of judges: 5
The Court members:

The term of office:
They shall be irremovable except in circumstances specified by the Law Article 60 of the Constitution

IV. POWERS

Other powers
Jurisdictional disputes:
The judiciary shall have a Supreme Council which shall supervise the proper functioning of the courts and the auxiliary bodies, and the Law shall prescribe its authorities with regard to the service affairs of judges and Public Prosecution. Article 66 of the Constitution

Electoral matters:
The supervision of the elections of Majlis Al Shura and the disposal of electoral challenges shall be undertaken by a supreme committee that enjoys independence and neutrality, and chaired by one of the deputy presidents of the Supreme Court. The Law shall prescribe the manner of its formation, its competences, and the regulations for its functions. Article 58 BIS14 of the Constitution

Referendums: x

V. NATURE AND EFFECTS OF DECISIONS

Finality:
The Supreme Court is the final appellate Court that is also in charge of uniting the legal principles.

SOURCES:

https://www.constituteproject.org/constitution/Oman_2011.pdf?lang=en

(136)

DOSSIER OF THE SUPREME COURT OF THE ISLAMIC REPUBLIC OF PAKISTAN

STATE: Islamic Republic of Pakistan
TITLE: The Supreme Court
YEAR OF FOUNDATION: 1956
SEAT: Islamabad

I. CHRONICLE

Date and context of establishment
The Supreme Court (SCOP), established in 1956,[7] is the apex court in Pakistan's judicial hierarchy.

Position in the hierarchy of courts
The Supreme Court (SCOP), established in 1956,[7] is the apex court in Pakistan's judicial hierarch.

II. STANDARD LEGAL REFERENCE

The Constitution of the Islamic Republic of Pakistan was approved by the Parliament on 10 April and ratified on 14 August 1973. (reinst. 2002, rev. 2015)

III. COMPOSITION AND ORGANIZATION

Composition
The number of judges:
The Supreme Court shall consist of a Chief Justice to be known as the Chief Justice of Pakistan and so many other Judges as may be determined by Act of Majlis-e-Shoora(Parliament) or, until so determined, as may be fixed by the President. Article 176 of the Constitution

Electoral/appointment body:
The Chief Justice of Pakistan shall be appointed by the President, and each of the other Judges shall be appointed by the President after consultation with the Chief Justice. Para.1 Article 177 of the Constitution

The Court members:
The Court consists of a Chief Justice and other judges, 30 appointed by the President as per procedure laid down in the Constitution. An Act of Parliament 31 has fixed the number of Judges at 17 i.e. Chief Justice and 16 judges. Article 175A, The Supreme Court Number of Judges Act (Act No. XXXIII) of 1997

The term of office:
A Judge of the Supreme Court shall hold office until he attains the age of sixty-five years, unless he sooner resigns or is removed from office in accordance with the Constitution. Article 179 of the Constitution

IV. POWERS

Other powers
...the Supreme Court shall have jurisdiction to hear and determine appeals from judgements, decrees, final orders or sentences of a High Court. Article 185 of the Constitution

Jurisdictional disputes:
The Supreme Court shall, to the exclusion of every other court, have original jurisdiction in any dispute between any two or more Governments.Explanation.-In this clause, Governments means the Federal Government and the Provincial Governments. Article 184 of the Constitution

The unconstitutionality of acts and activities of political parties: x
Charges against the President of the Republic: x
Charges against the Prime Minister or against any Minister of State: x
Electoral matters: x
Referendums: x
Other matters with which the Court is charged by the Constitution or statute:
If, at any time, the President considers that it is desirable to obtain the opinion of the Supreme Court on any question of law which he considers of public importance, he may refer the question to the Supreme Court for consideration.

The Supreme Court shall consider a question so referred and report its opinion on the question to the President. Article 186 of the Constitutution

If, at any time, the President considers that it is desirable to obtain the opinion of the Supreme Court on any question of law which he considers of public importance, he may refer the question to the Supreme Court for consideration.

The Supreme Court shall consider a question so referred and report its opinion on the question to the President. Article 186 A of the Constitution

The Supreme Court shall have power, subject to the provisions of any Act of Majlis-e-Shoora (Parliament) and of any rules made by the Supreme Court, to review any judgment pronounced or any order made by it. Article 188 of the Constitution

V. NATURE AND EFFECTS OF DECISIONS

Finality:

It is the Court of ultimate appeal and final arbiter of law and the Constitution. Its decisions are binding on all other courts.

Binding force:

Erga omnes:

Any decision of the Supreme Court shall, to the extent that it decides a question of law or is based upon or enunciates a principle of law, be binding on all other courts in Pakistan Article 189 of the Constitution

SOURCES:

http://www.pakistani.org/pakistan/constitution/

(137)

DOSSIER OF THE SUPREME COURT OF THE REPUBLIC OF PALAU

STATE: Republic of Palau
TITLE: The Supreme Court
YEAR OF FOUNDATION: 1981
SEAT: Koror

I. CHRONICLE

Date and context of establishment Palau
Supreme Court was created in 1981, pursuant to Article X of the Constitution.

Position in the hierarchy of courts
The Supreme Court of Palau is the highest court of Palau. The trial division of the Supreme Court shall have original and exclusive jurisdiction over all matters affecting Ambassadors, other Public Ministers and Consuls, admiralty and maritime cases, and those matters in which the national government or a state government is a party. Section 5 Article X

II. STANDARD LEGAL REFERENCE

The Constitution of Palau, Constitution of the Republic of Palau was adopted by the Palau Constitutional Convention from January 28 to April 2, 1979, ratified at the Third Constitution Referendum on July 9, 1980, and entered into force January 1, 1981. The Second Constitutional Convention certifies the proposed amendments to the Constitution of the Republic of Palau that were duly adopted by majority vote of the Delegates on July 15, 2005

III. COMPOSITION AND ORGANIZATION

Composition

The number of judges:

The Supreme Court shall be composed of a Chief of Justice and not less than three (3) nor more than six (6) Associate Justices, all of whom shall be members of both divisions. Section 2 Article X of the Constitution

Organization

Administrative autonomy:

The budget:

The Chief Justice shall prepare and submit through the President to the Olbiil Era Kelulau an annual consolidated budget for the entire unified judicial system. The national government shall bear the total cost of the system unless the Olbiil Era Kelulau requires reimbursement of appropriate portions of such cost by the state governments. Section 13 Article X of the constitution

IV. POWERS

Constitutional Court Review

Other powers

Jurisdictional disputes:

The appellate division of the Supreme Court shall have jurisdiction to review all decisions of the trial division and all decisions of lower courts. Section 6 Article X of the Constitution

Charges against the President of the Republic:

The trial division of the Supreme Court shall have original and exclusive jurisdiction over all matters affecting Ambassadors, other Public Ministers and Consuls, admiralty and maritime cases, and those matters in which the national government or a state government is a party

Charges against the Prime Minister or against any Minister of State:

The trial division of the Supreme Court shall have original and exclusive jurisdiction over all matters affecting Ambassadors, other Public Ministers and Consuls, admiralty and maritime cases, and those matters in which the national government or a state government is a party

Charges against judges:

A justice of the Supreme Court may be impeached only for the commission of treason, bribery, other high crimes, or improper practices, or on the grounds of his inability to discharge the functions of his office upon a vote of not less than two-thirds (2/3) of the members of each house of the Olbiil Era Kelulau. Section 10 Article X of the Constitution

SOURCES:

http://www.unesco.org/education/edurights/media/docs/c4679995d1bddd3ef509d-dc66c3cb38e80d492fe.pdf

(138)

DOSSIER OF THE HIGH CONSTITUTIONAL COURT OF THE STATE OF PALESTINE

STATE: State of Palestine
TITLE: The High Constitutional Court
YEAR OF FOUNDATION: 2016
SEAT: Ramala

I. CHRONICLE

Date and context of establishment 2016
Position in the hierarchy of courts
The judicial authority shall be an independent authority to be exercised by the Supreme Court and other Courts in accordance with this Basic Law and any other law. Article 108 of the Constitution

II. STANDARD LEGAL REFERENCE

Constitution 2003
Presidential decree on April 3 2016

III. COMPOSITION AND ORGANIZATION

Composition
The number of judges:
It shall be composed of nine judges appointed by the head of state and nominated by the council of ministers, and approved by the House of Representatives. Article 181 of the Constitution

Electoral/appointment body

It shall be composed of nine judges appointed by the head of state and nominated by the council of ministers, and approved by the House of Representatives. Article 181 of the Constitution

The Court members:

The term of office:

The judges shall be elected for one term of nine years that shall not be renewed or extended directly. Article 181 of the Constitution

The Court President:

The term of office:

The judges of the Constitutional Court shall elect one of them as a president for the court for a three year term. Article 182 of the Constitution

IV. POWERS

Constitutional Court Review

Preventive review:

The Constitutional Court shall examine the constitutionality of the following matters, pursuant to a request from the president of the state, or the Prime Minister, or the speaker of the House of Representatives, or ten members of the House of Representatives, or from the courts, the public prosecutor, or anyone whose constitutional rights have been violated: - The constitutionality of laws before they are promulgated, whenever requested by the president of the state provided the request was submitted within 30 days of referring to the head of state for ratification and promulgation; Article 185 of the Constitution

A posteriori review:

Abstract review:

- Deciding disputes related to the constitutionality of laws, ordinances, regulations, measures and decisions issued by the president or the council of ministers which have the force of law; Article 185 of the Constitution
- The constitutionality of signing treaties and the procedures of their implementation, and nullification of or some of its Articles if it contradicts with the Constitution or an international treaty

Other powers

Jurisdictional disputes:

- Interpretation of constitutional texts when a dispute arises over the rights, duties and competencies of the three branches, and in case of a jurisdictional dispute between the head of state and the prime minister Article 185 of the Constitution

The unconstitutionality of acts and activities of political parties:

Deciding problems that arise concerning the constitutionality of programs and activities of political parties and associations and the procedures of their dissolution and suspension and their conformity with the Constitution;

Other matters with which the Court is charged by the Constitution or statute:

Any other jurisdictions assigned to it by the Constitution. Article 185 of the Constitution

V. NATURE AND EFFECTS OF DECISIONS

Finality:

Judicial decisions of the Constitutional Court shall be final and may not be appealed in any manner and binding on all government authorities and natural and legal persons. Article 187 of the Constitution

SOURCES:

https://en.wikisource.org/wiki/Constitution_of_Palestine_(2003)#Chapter_Six_.E2.80.94_The_Judiciary_Branch

iuscomparatum.info/palestine-establishes-constitutional-court/

(139)

DOSSIER OF THE SUPREME COURT OF JUSTICE OF THE REPUBLIC OF PANAMA

STATE: Republic of Panama
TITLE: Supreme Court of Justice
YEAR OF FOUNDATION: 1886
SEAT: Panama

I. CHRONICLE

Date and context of establishment 1886
Position in the hierarchy of courts
The Supreme Court of Justice is the main judicial organization of Panama, located in Panama City. It is a court created according to the statutes of the Constitution to protect and safeguard the judicial rights of the country.

II. STANDARD LEGAL REFERENCE

Constitution 1972 with amendments

III. COMPOSITION AND ORGANIZATION

Composition/Electoral-appointment bod
Article 203 of the Constitution

The Supreme Court of Justice shall be composed of the number of Justices determined by law, to be appointed by decision of the Cabinet Council, subject to the approval of the Legislative Branch, for a ten year term. If the post of a Justice becomes permanently vacant during the course of a term, a new Justice shall be appointed to serve the remainder of said term.

Each Justice has an alternate (suplente), appointed in the same manner as the principal Justice and for the same term who shall replace him in the case of his absence in accordance with the law. Only career judges active in the Judicial Branch may be designated as alternates.

Every two years, two Justices shall be appointed, except in cases when, in view of the number of Justices currently serving on the Court, more than two or less than two Justices are appointed. When the number of Justices is increased, the necessary appointments to this effect shall be made and the respective law shall make the appropriate provisions in order to maintain the principle of successive appointments.

May not be appointed as Justice of the Supreme Court:

1 Persons who are exercising or have exercised the functions of principal or alternate member of the National Assembly during the constitutional term currently under way;

2 Persons who are exercising or have exercised command and jurisdictional functions in the Executive Branch during the constitutional term currently under way.

The Court shall be divided into Chambers, each with three permanent Justices.

The number of judges: 6

The Court members/Incompatibilities:

Article 212 of the Constitution

Officials in the Judicial Branch shall not participate in politics, except to vote in elections, nor practice law, nor commerce, nor hold any other remunerated position, except that which is provided in Article 208 of the Constitution.

Organization

Administrative autonomy:

The budget:

Article 214 of the Constitution

The Supreme Court of Justice and the Attorney General of the Nation shall formulate the respective Budgets of the Judicial Branch and the Public Ministry, and shall send them, at the proper time, to the Executive Branch, to be included in the projected General Budget of the public sector. The President of the Court and the Attorney General shall support all stages of their respective projected Budgets.

The Budgets of the Judicial Branch and of the Public Ministry shall not, together, be less than two percent (2%) of the current Central Government income.

However, when this amount is more than necessary to cover fundamental necessities proposed by the Judicial Branch and the Public Ministry, the Executive Branch shall include the excess in other areas of expenditures or investments in the projected Budget of the Central Government, in order that the National Assembly determine whatever is proper.

Constitutional Court Review

Abstract review

Article 206 of the Constitution

Among the constitutional and legal functions of the Supreme Court of Justice shall be the following:

To guard the integrity of the Constitution. For this purpose, and after hearing the opinion of the Attorney General of the Nation or the Solicitor General of the Administration, the Court in plenary session shall try and rule on cases concerning the unconstitutionality of laws, decrees, decisions, resolutions and other acts that for reasons of substance or form are challenged before it, by any person.

Concrete review

When during the proceedings of a case, the public official entrusted with the administration of Justice considers, or it is observed by one of the parties, that the legal or regulatory provision applicable to the case is unconstitutional, he/she shall submit the question to the cognizance of the Court in plenary session, except when the provision has already been the subject of a decision, and shall order a continuance of the case, until the question of constitutionality is decided.

The parties only shall be able to formulate such observations one time during the process of a case;

To exercise contentious-administrative jurisdiction (administrative litigation) over acts, omissions, faulty or deficient public services, resolutions and orders or provisions which are executed, adopted, issued, or committed in the performance or duties, or on the pretext of performing them, by National, Provincial, and Municipal Government Employees, as well as those of Autonomous and Semi-autonomous Public Entities. In such cases, the Supreme Court of Justice, after hearing the opinion of the Solicitor General of the Administration, shall have the power to annul the acts that have been accused of unlawfulness, reestablish the private rights violated, enact new provisions in lieu of those opposed, and render a judgment with regard to the meaning, applicability or legal validity of an administrative act.

Persons affected by the act, resolution, order or decision in question may resort to contentious-administrative jurisdiction; and any natural or juridical person, domiciled in the country may exercise popular action.

V. NATURE AND EFFECTS OF DECISIONS

Finality:

Article 207 of the Constitution

Neither writ of unconstitutionality, nor for constitutional guarantees (amparo) shall be admitted against the judgments of the Supreme Court of Justice or its Chambers.

The decisions issued by the Supreme Court in exercise of the powers conferred on it by this Article are final, definitive and binding, and must be published in the Official Gazette;

To investigate and try the members of the National Assembly. In order to carry out the investigation, the plenary of the Supreme Court of Justice shall appoint an investigating officer.

Standing before the constitutional court

State bodies: X

Individuals: X

SOURCES:

https://www.constituteproject.org/constitution/Panama_2004.pdf?lang=en

www.organojudicial.gob.pa/tribunales/corte-suprema-de-justicia/

(140)

DOSSIER OF THE SUPREME COURT OF THE INDEPENDENT STATE OF PAPUA NEW GUINEA

STATE: Papua New Guinea
TITLE: Supreme Court
YEAR OF FOUNDATION: 16.09.1975
SEAT: Port Moresby

I. CHRONICLE

Date and context of establishment:
The Supreme Court is established under Article. 160 of the constitution.

Position in the hierarchy of courts /

II. STANDARD LEGAL REFERENCE

Constittution 1975 with amendments

III. COMPOSITION AND ORGANIZATION

Composition
The number of judges:
Chief Justice, Deputy Chief Justice and 21 Judges.

Electoral/appointment body: /
The Court members: /
The term of office: /
The Court President: /
The term of office: /

Organization

Administrative autonomy: /

The budget: /

IV. POWERS

Constitutional Court Review

Preventive review: /

A posteriori review:

Abstract review: /

Concrete review:

The Supreme Court has a special responsibility for developing the underlying law, i.e. the common law of Papua New Guinea, having resort to those rules of local custom in various regions of the country which may be taken to be common to the whole country. The responsibility has been given additional express warrant in the Underlying Law Act, 2000 which purports to mandate greater attention by the courts to custom and the development of customary law as an important component of the underlying law. In practice the courts have found great difficulty in applying the vastly differing custom of the many traditional societies of the country in a modern legal system and the development of the customary law according to indigenous Melanesian conceptions of justice and equity has been less thorough than may have been anticipated in 1975; the Underlying Law Act does not yet appear to have had significant effect Papua New Guinea's Constitution purports to adopt the principle of the separation of powers, enunciated in US jurisprudence in an environment where the three branches of government are indeed separate, the executive not being responsible to the legislature. In PNG as in Australia, the principle is in fact somewhat artificially defined simply to mean that the judiciary is independent from executive interference, as established by the English *Bill of Rights*, 1689; however, the principle does not extend, as was established in Australia during the early years of the Australian federation, to preventing the courts from rendering advisory opinions to the executive; nor are there any implications with respect to the quasi-judicial function of administrative tribunals, also an issue at one time in Australia

Other powers

Constitutional complaints: /

Jurisdictional disputes: /

The unconstitutionality of acts and activities of political parties: /

Charges against the President of the Republic: /

Charges against the Prime Minister or against any Minister of State: /

Electoral matters: /

Referendums: /

Other matters with which the Court is charged by the Constitution or statute:

Other forms of human rights protection /

Standing before the Constitutional Court

State bodies: X

Individuals: X

V. NATURE AND EFFECTS OF DECISIONS

Finality:

Its own decisions are binding on the lower courts as are the decisions of the English superior courts prior to PNG's independence, which are deemed to be part of PNG's underlying law. Decisions of the pre-Independence Supreme Court of PNG are deemed to be foreign law, equivalent in authority to decisions by any foreign court with a similar legal system, and of persuasive value only.

SOURCES:

http://www.wipo.int/wipolex/en/text.jsp?file_id=199188

(141)

DOSSIER OF THE SUPREME COURT OF JUSTICE OF THE REPUBLIC OF PARAGUAY

STATE: Republic of Paraguay
TITLE: Supreme Court of Justice (Constitutional Chamber)
YEAR OF FOUNDATION: 1992
SEAT: Asunción

I. CHRONICLE

Date and context of establishment 1992
Position in the hierarchy of courts:
The Costitution recognized the Supreme Court as the highest court of the Republic.

II. STANDARD LEGAL REFERENCE

Constitution 1992 with amendments

III. COMPOSITION AND ORGANIZATION

Composition
The number of judges: 9
Electoral/appointment body:
The Senate and the President of Paraguay select its nine ministers (judges) based on recommendations from a constitutionally created Consejo de la Magistratura (Council of Magistrates).

The Court members:
The term of office: /
The Court President:
The term of office: /

Organization

Administrative autonomy: /

The budget:

Independent, the organ of the State has the capacity to manage their own budgets, the budget should be approved by the Congress and the Comptroller General of the Republic (Article 249)

IV. POWERS

Constitutional Court Review

A posteriori review:

Abstract review: /

Concrete review:

Article 132 of the Constitution: Of Unconstitutionality

The Supreme Court of Justice has the faculty to declare the unconstitutionality of the juridical norms and of the judicial resolutions, in the manner and to the extent [alcances] established in this Constitution and in the law.

Article 260 of the Constitution: Of the Duties and of the Attributions of the Constitutional Chamber

[The following] are duties and attributions of the Constitutional Chamber:

1. to take cognizance [conocer] and to decide [resolver] on the unconstitutionality of the laws and of other normative instruments, declaring the inapplicability of the provisions contrary to this Constitution in each concrete case and in decision [fallo] that will only be effective in relation with that case, and
2. to decide on the unconstitutionality of the definitive or interlocutory sentences, declaring the nullity of those that result [as being] contrary to this Constitution.

The proceeding may be initiated by [an] action before the Constitutional Chamber of the Supreme Court of Justice, and by way [vía] of an excepción [pleadings of exception] in any instance, in which case the prior records [antecedentes] will rise [se elevarán] to the Court.

Other powers

Constitutional complaints: /

Jurisdictional disputes:

Exercise the supervision of all the bodies of the Judiciary and decide, in a single instance, conflicts of jurisdiction and competence in accordance with the law;

The unconstitutionality of acts and activities of political parties: hear and rule on unconstitutionality /

Charges against the President of the Republic: /
Charges against the Prime Minister or against any Minister of State: /
Electoral matters: /
Referendum: /
Other matters with which the Court is charged by the Constitution or statute:

1- Exercise the supervision of all the bodies of the Judiciary and decide, in a single instance, conflicts of jurisdiction and competence in accordance with the law;

2- To establish its own rules of procedure. Submit an annual report on the steps taken, the state and the needs of national justice to the executive and legislative branches;

3- To consider and decide in regular resources determined by law;

4- hear and resolve, in original instance, the habeas corpus, without prejudice to the competence of other judges or courts;

5- hear and rule on unconstitutionality;

6- To consider and decide on the appeal in the manner and extent established by law;

7- preventively suspend itself or at the request of the Trial Jury of Judges by an absolute majority of its members in the exercise of their functions, judicial magistrates prosecuted, until a final decision is rendered in the case;

8- Supervise institutes arrest and detention;

9- Understanding on conflicts of jurisdiction between the executive and departmental governments and between them and the municipalities, and

10- Other duties and powers established by this Constitution and laws.

(Article 259 of the Constitution).

Other forms of human rights protection /
Standing before the Constitutional Court
State bodies: X
Individuals: X

V. NATURE AND EFFECTS OF DECISIONS

Finality: /
Binding force: /

SOURCES:

https://www.constituteproject.org/constitution/Paraguay_2011.pdf?lang=en

http://www.pj.gov.py/

(142)

DOSSIER OF THE COSTITUTIONAL COURT OF THE REPUBLIC OF PERU

STATE: Peru
TITLE: Constitutional Court
YEAR OF FOUNDATION: 1980 (Court of Constitutional Guarantees)
1996 (Constitutional Court)
SEAT: Arequipa, but it has the power to hold hearings in any other city

I. CHRONICLE

Date and context of establishment:
1980 (Court of Constitutional Guarantees)
1996 (Constitutional Court)

Position in the hierarchy of courts:
It is an indipendent costitutional agency.

The Constitutional Court is entrusted with upholding the principle of constitutional supremacy, against the laws or acts of state bodies that seek to undermine it and intervenes to restore respect for the Constitution in general and constitutional rights in particular. The Court is the one specialized organ that is responsible for this type of enforcement. It has the authority to review the adequacy of laws, draft laws and decrees of the executive, conducting a review of the constitutionality of such acts.

According to Kelsen's model, the Constitutional Court acts as a negative legislator, lacking the power to make laws but with the power to repeal all or portions of the unconstitutional laws/acts. More recent theories argue that the task of the Constitutional Court strictly involves judicial functions and resolving constitutional disputes, which may include a review of the performance of the legislature, the protection of fundamental rights and the distribution of powers between the branches of government.

II. STANDARD LEGAL REFERENCE

Constitution 1993

III. COMPOSITION AND ORGANIZATION

Composition
The number of judges: 7
Electoral/appointment body:
The Court members:
The term of office: /
The Court President:
The term of office: /
Organization
Administrative autonomy:
The budget

IV. POWERS

Constitutional Court Review

Preventive review:
It has the authority to review the adequacy of laws, draft laws and decrees of the executive, conducting a review of the constitutionality of such acts.

A posteriori review: /
Abstract review:
Article 202 of the Constitution
•
It is the duty of the Constitutional Court:
To hear, in original jurisdiction, the writ of unconstitutionality...

Concrete review:

Other powers
Constitutional complaints: /

Jurisdictional disputes:

Article 202 of the Constitution

•

It is the duty of the Constitutional Court:

...

3. To hear disputes over jurisdiction or over powers assigned by the Constitution, in accordance with the law....

The unconstitutionality of acts and activities of political parties: /
Charges against the President of the Republic: /
Charges against the Prime Minister or against any Minister of State: /
Electoral matters: /
Referendums: /
Other matters with which the Court is charged by the Constitution or statute: /
Other forms of human rights protection

Article 202 of the Constitution

•

It is the duty of the Constitutional Court:

...2. To hear, as a court of last resort, orders refusing petitions of habeas corpus, amparo, habeas data, and mandamus....

Standing before the Constitutional Court

Article 203

The following are entitled to bring a writ of unconstitutionality:

1. The President of the Republic.
2. The Prosecutor General.
3. The Ombudsman.
4. Twenty-five percent of the legal number of congressmen.
5. Five thousand citizens, whose signatures shall be verified by the National Election Board. If the statute under question is a municipal ordinance, it may be challenged by one percent of citizens from the respective territorial division, provided that this percentage does not exceed the number of signatures cited above.
6. Regional presidents, with the advice and consent of the Regional Coordination Council or provincial mayors acting upon the consent of their councils, in matters within their jurisdiction.
7. Professional associations on matters within their fields.

State bodies: X

Individuals: X

V. NATURE AND EFFECTS OF DECISIONS

Finality/Binding force:

Article 204 of the Constitution

The ruling of the Constitutional Court declaring the unconstitutionality of a piece of legislation is published in the official gazette. The law becomes ineffective on the day following such publication.

The ruling of the Court declaring a statute to be, wholly or in part, unconstitutional does not have retroactive effects.

SOURCES:

https://ipfs.io/ipfs/QmXoypizjW3WknFiJnKLwHCnL72vedxjQkDDP1mXWo6uco/wiki/Constitutional_Tribunal_of_Peru.html

http://www.tc.gob.pe/

(143)

DOSSIER OF THE SUPREME COURT OF THE REPUBLIC OF PHILIPPINES

STATE: Republic of Philippines
TITLE: Supreme Court
YEAR OF FOUNDATION: 1945
SEAT: Manila

I. CHRONICLE

Date and context of establishment: 1987
Position in the hierarchy of courts
iIt is the highest court in the Philippines.

II. STANDARD LEGAL REFERENCE

Constitution 1987

III. COMPOSITION AND ORGANIZATION

Composition
The number of judges: 15
Electoral/appointment body:
Presidential appointment from the list of preferred nominees made by the Judicial and Bar Council

The Court members: /
The term of office: /
The Court President: /
The term of office: /

Organization

Administrative autonomy:
administrative supervision over all courts and the personnel thereof

The budget: /

IV. POWERS

Constitutional Court Review

Preventive review: /
A posteriori review:
Abstract review: /
Concrete review:

The powers of the Supreme Court are defined in Article VIII of the 1987 Constitution. These functions may be generally divided into two – judicial functions and administrative functions. The administrative functions of the Court pertain to the supervision and control over the Philippine judiciary and its employees, as well as over members of the Philippine bar. Pursuant to these functions, the Court is empowered to order a change of venue of trial in order to avoid a miscarriage of justice and to appoint all officials and employees of the judiciary. The Court is further authorized to promulgate the rules for admission to the practice of law, for legal assistance to the underprivileged, and the procedural rules to be observed in all courts.

The more prominent role of the Court is located in the exercise of its judicial functions. Section 1 of Article VIII of the Constitution contains definition of judicial power that had not been found in previous constitutions. The judicial power is vested in "one Supreme Court and in such lower courts as may be established by law." This judicial power is exercised through the judiciary's primary role of adjudication, which includes the "duty of the courts of justice to settle actual controversies involving rights which are legally demandable and enforceable, and to determine whether or not there has been a grave abuse of discretion amounting to lack or excess of jurisdiction on the part of any branch or instrumentality of the government."

The definition reaffirms the power of the Supreme Court to engage in judicial review, a power that had traditionally belonged to the Court even before this provision was enacted. Still, this new provision effectively dissuades from the easy resort to the political question doctrine as a means of declining to review a law or state action, as was often done by the Court during the rule of President Ferdinand Marcos. As a result, the existence of "grave abuse of discretion" on the part of any branch or instrumentality of the government is sufficient basis to nullify state action.

Other powers

Constitutional complaints: /

Jurisdictional disputes: /

The unconstitutionality of acts and activities of political parties:

As a result, the existence of "grave abuse of discretion" on the part of any branch or instrumentality of the government is sufficient basis to nullify state action

Charges against the President of the Republic: /

Charges against the Prime Minister or against any Minister of State: /

Electoral matters: /

Referendums: /

Other matters with which the Court is charged by the Constitution or statute: /

Other forms of human rights protection /

Standing before the Constitutional Court

State bodies: X

Individuals: X

V. NATURE AND EFFECTS OF DECISIONS

Finality:

there is no appeal, or any plain, speedy, and adequate remedy in the ordinary course of law

SOURCES:

http://www.officialgazette.gov.ph/constitutions/1987-constitution/

(144)

DOSSIER OF THE CONSTITUTIONAL TRIBUNAL OF THE REPUBLIC OF POLAND

STATE: Poland
TITLE: Constitutional Tribunal
YEAR OF FOUNDATION: 1982 – constitutional amendment established the Costitutional Tribunal; 1986 – the beginning of the activity
SEAT: Warsaw

I. CHRONICLE

Date and context of establishment 1982/1986
The Constitutional Tribunal (Polish: *Trybunał Konstytucyjny*) is the constitutional court of the Republic of Poland, a judicial body established to resolve disputes on the constitutionality of the activities of state institutions; its main task is to supervise the compliance of statutory law with the Constitution of the Republic of Poland. It has been established on 26 March 1982 by authoritarian communist government of the People's Republic of Poland during the time when communists drastically restricted normal life by introducing martial law in an attempt to crush political opposition.

Position in the hierarchy of courts:
The Constitutional Tribunal constitutes one of the formal guarantees of a state grounded on the rule of law.

II. STANDARD LEGAL REFERENCE

Constitution 1997 with amendments

III. COMPOSITION AND ORGANIZATION

Composition
The number of judges: 15
Electoral/appointment body:
Sejm RP

The Court members:
The term of office: 9 years
The Court President:
The term of office:
Organization
Administrative autonomy:
The budget:

IV. POWERS

Constitutional Court Review /

Preventive review: /
A posteriori review: /
Abstract review:

Article 188 of the Constitution. The Constitutional Tribunal shall adjudicate regarding the following matters:

1) the conformity of statutes and international agreements to the Constitution;
2) the conformity of a statute to ratified international agreements whose ratification required prior consent granted by statute;
3) the conformity of legal provisions issued by central State organs to the Constitution, ratified international agreements and statutes;

Concrete review:

Other powers
Constitutional complaints:
Article 188. The Constitutional Tribunal shall adjudicate regarding the following matters:
...;5) complaints concerning constitutional infringements, as specified in Article 79, para. 1.....

Jurisdictional disputes:
Article 188 of the Constitution:The Constitutional Tribunal shall settle disputes over authority between central concostitutional organs of the State

The Constitutional Court is a judicial body established to resolve disputes on the constitutionality of the activities of state institutions; its main task is to supervise the compliance of statutory law with the Constitution of the Republic of Poland.

The unconstitutionality of acts and activities of political parties:
Article 188 of the Constitution. The Constitutional Tribunal shall adjudicate regarding the following matters:

...4) the conformity to the Constitution of the purposes or activities of political parties;...

Charges against the President of the Republic: /
Charges against the Prime Minister or against any Minister of State: /
Electoral matters:
Three judges, appointed by the President of the Tribunal, serve as members of the National Electoral Commission (Act of 5 January 2011 Electoral Code).

Referendums: /
Other matters with which the Court is charged by the Constitution or statute:
Standing before the Constitutional Court
State bodies: X
Individuals: X

V. NATURE AND EFFECTS OF DECISIONS

Finality:
Article 190 of the Constitution

Judgments of the Constitutional Tribunal shall be of universally binding application and shall be final.

Judgments of the Constitutional Tribunal regarding matters specified in Article 188 of the Constitution, shall be required to be immediately published in the official publication in which the original normative act was promulgated. If a normative act has not been promulgated, then the judgment shall be published in the Official Gazette of the Republic of Poland, Monitor Polski.

A judgment of the Constitutional Tribunal shall take effect from the day of its publication, however, the Constitutional Tribunal may specify another date for the end of the binding force of a normative act. Such time period may not exceed 18 months in relation to a statute or 12 months in relation to any other normative act. Where a judgment has financial consequences not provided for in the Budget, the Constitutional Tribunal shall specify date for the end of the binding force of the normative act concerned, after seeking the opinion of the Council of Ministers.

A judgment of the Constitutional Tribunal on the non-conformity to the Constitution, an international agreement or statute, of a normative act on the basis of which a legally effective judgment of a court, a final administrative decision or settlement of other matters was issued, shall be a basis for re-opening proceedings, or for quashing the decision or other settlement in a manner and on principles specified in provisions applicable to the given proceedings.

Judgments of the Constitutional Tribunal shall be made by a majority of votes.

SOURCES:

http://www.sejm.gov.pl/prawo/konst/angielski/kon1.htm

(145)

DOSSIER OF THE TRIBUNAL COSTITUTIONAL OF THE PORTUGUESE REPUBLIC (PORTUGAL)

STATE: Portugal
TITLE: Tribunal constitucional
YEAR OF FOUNDATION: 1983
SEAT: Lisbon

I. CHRONICLE

Date and context of establishment:
The Costitutional Court was established by the passage of law no. 28/82 in 1983.

Position in the hierarchy of courts:
The Portuguese Constitution defines the Constitutional Court as a completely independent organ, that operates independently from the other branches of government, such as the Executive or the Legislative.

The most salient of the Constitutional Court's responsibilities is that of monitoring whether legal rules —particularly those set out in Laws and Executive Laws – comply with the Constitution. This is the Court's key task, and the one in which its role as 'guardian' or ultimate guarantor of the Constitution – entrusted to it by the Constitution itself – is clearest and most obvious to see.

II. STANDARD LEGAL REFERENCE

Constitution of 1983

Composition

The number of judges:

The court is composed by thirteen judges

Electoral/appointment body:

Election Based System:

Ten of them are elected by the Assembly of the Republic, the main legislative branch of the country, and they must be elected by two thirds majority of the members of the Assembly. The remaining three are elected by the already elected judges.

The qualifications and the required professional experience of constitutional court judges:

Of the thirteen judges, six must be chosen among the general court's judges, the remaining must have at least a degree in law.

IV. POWERS

Constitutional Court Review

Preventive review:

Prior review must be requested within eight days [counted without interruption – Articles 56(1) and 57(1) of the Law on the Tribunal Constitucional - LTC] of the date on which the document is received, in the event that the request is made by the President of the Republic or a Representative of the Republic, or of the date on which the President of the Assembly of the Republic informs the Prime Minister and the parliamentary groups that the decree in question has been sent to the President of the Republic for enactment as an organisational law, in the event that the request is made by the Prime Minister or one fifth of all the Members of the Assembly of the Republic. The Court has held that in the event that the request is made by a Representative of the Republic, the above deadline should be extended by the two days provided for by Article 56(4) of the LTC.

A posteriori review:

Abstract review:

The second way in which the Constitutional Court controls constitutionality is the so-called "successive abstract review". It is given this name because it is conducted independently of any concrete application (i.e. it is not called on in order to resolve a specific case or dispute) of the rule that is reviewed.

Concrete review:

The third way in which the Constitutional Court can be called on to control the constitutionality of legal rules is the so-called "concrete review", thus named precisely because it occurs in relation to the application by the courts of the rule in question to a concrete case.

Other powers

Constitutional complaints: NO

Charges against the President of the Republic:

Under the terms of the Constitution [Article 223(2)a and b] the Constitutional Court is responsible for verifying the death and declaring the permanent physical incapacity of the President of the Republic, situations in which he is temporarily prevented from performing his functions, the forfeiture of his office (for absenting himself from Portuguese territory without the consent of the Assembly of the Republic), or his removal from office (in the event that he is convicted of a crime committed in the performance of his functions).

These responsibilities – the procedure for which is regulated by Articles 86 to 91 of the LTC – are entrusted to the Court's Plenary. Depending on the specific circumstances, the proceedings must be initiated by the Attorney-General (cases involving the President of the Republic's death, permanent physical incapacity, or temporary incapacity), the President of the Assembly of the Republic (in the case of forfeiture of office), the President of the Supreme Court of Justice (in the case of removal from office), or the President of the Republic himself (if he is temporarily unable to perform his functions).

One key characteristic of these cases is their speed, which is clear from the fact that the deadlines by which the Court must take its decision are very short (see Articles 87 to 91 of the LTC).

Charges against the Prime Minister or against any Minister of State:

Electoral matters:

The Constitutional Court is the court of last instance in cases that seek to determine whether or not electoral procedural acts have been conducted properly and are valid, as laid down by law; appeals concerning elections to the Assembly of the Republic and the Legislative Assemblies of the autonomous regions; and suits involving the impugnation of elections that are subject to appeal, as laid down by law [Article 223(2)c, g and h of the Constitution].

In electoral matters the Constitutional Court intervenes either directly, or in appeals against the decisions of district courts. The Court's competence in electoral suits is generally exercised in plenary, and the procedure – which is regulated by the various electoral laws – is characterised by rules that impose the utmost speed.

Referendums:

The Constitutional Court is responsible for the prior review of the constitutionality and legality of national, regional and local referenda. This competence includes assessing the requirements concerning the applicable electorate [Article 223(2)f of the Constitution].

The President of the Republic must obligatorily submit the proposal for any national referendum to the Court [Article 115(8) of the Constitution]. The Court then has twenty-five days in which to review and assess it, although the President of the Republic can reduce this deadline for emergency reasons [Article 27 of Law no. 15-A/98 of 3 April 1998]

If the Court pronounces the proposal unconstitutional or illegal, the President of the Republic cannot promote the calling of the referendum. In this case he must return the proposal to the body that formulated it – the Assembly of the Republic or the Government – which can reconsider and reformulate it and expunge the defect in question (Article 28 of Law no. 15-A/98).

In the case of regional and local referenda the Constitutional Court is also called on to pronounce in advance on the referendum's constitutionality and legality. To this end the president of the body that decided to hold the consultation process is obliged to ask the Court to conduct the review. The procedure involved is regulated by the organisational laws governing the applicable systems (Article 105 of the LTC).

Organisational Law no. 4/2000 of 24 August 2000, which approved the legal system governing local referenda, states that the Constitutional Court has twenty-five days in which to conduct this verification and, in the event that it pronounces the decision to hold the referendum unconstitutional or illegal, to notify the president of the body that took the decision, so that the latter can reformulate it and expunge the defect in question (Articles 26 and 27).

The Constitutional Court exercises the abovementioned competences in plenary.

It should also be noted that the assembly which determines the overall results of national referenda sits at the Constitutional Court and is chaired by the Court's President; and that the Court's Plenary is responsible for deciding disputed appeals concerning allegations of irregularities during the voting or the operations to determine the results (Articles 163, 172, 174 and 175(4) of Law no. 15-A/98).

In relation to local referenda the Plenary of the Constitutional Court is responsible for deciding appeals concerning the decisions of polling stations and irregularities that are alleged to have occurred during the voting or the operations to determine the results (Articles 67, 151 and 153 of Organisational Law no. 4/2000).

Other matters with which the Court is charged by the Constitution or statute:

Under the terms of Articles 11-A and 106 to 110 of the LTC the Constitutional Court is responsible for receiving political officeholders' declarations of assets and income (the list of cases in which such declarations are required is set out by Article 4 of Law no. 4/83 of 2 April 1983, as amended by Law no. 25/95 of 18 August 1995), and verifying whether all those who are obliged to submit such declarations have done so.

In the event that a political officeholder does not submit his asset and income declarations within the legal deadline, the Court must notify him that he must do so. If the officeholder remains in breach of this requirement, the President of the Court then sends a certificate of this fact to the representative of the Public Prosecutors' Office, so that the latter can promote the application of the sanctions provided for by law [Article 109(1) of the LTC and Article 3 of Law no. 4/83].

The President of the Court must also inform the representative of the Public Prosecutors' Office of any communications and accusations that are made to him in relation to omissions or errors in such declarations [Article 6-A of Law no. 4/83].

There is free access to political officeholders' declarations of assets and income. However, when there are important grounds for doing so, a declarer can oppose dissemination, whereupon the Constitutional Court is responsible for determining whether or not the reason that is given is valid, and if and how dissemination should occur (Articles 5 and 6 of Law no. 4/83).

Individuals: NO

V. NATURE AND EFFECTS OF DECISIONS

The declaration of unconstitutionality and illegality:
When it comes to reviewing constitutionality, the Constitutional Court's responsibilities are not restricted to controlling legal rules. The Constitution – going beyond that which is customary in analogous documents – also gives the Court the power to examine cases involving unconstitutionality by omission; in other words, to "review and verify any failure to comply with this Constitution by means of the omission of legislative measures needed to make constitutional rules executable" (Article 283 of the Constitution).

The procedure that is followed in such cases is similar to that of the successive abstract review of constitutionality. However, given the great sensitivity surrounding both the problem of 'legislative omissions' and the Constitutional Court's fulfilment of this important responsibility, this process can only be initiated by the President of the Republic or the Ombudsman, or, in cases in which the rights of an autonomous region are at stake, the President of the Legislative Assembly in question.

If the Constitutional Court concludes that an omission does exist, it cannot draft the missing rule or rules, or even order the body with responsibility for doing so to draft them, inasmuch as either course would be contrary to its jurisdictional nature. The Court must restrict itself to ‘verifying’ that a case of unconstitutionality by omission exists, and to ‘informing’ the legislative body thereof.

The legislative omissions:

The declaration of unconstitutionality and illegality: When it comes to reviewing constitutionality, the Constitutional Court’s responsibilities are not restricted to controlling legal rules. The Constitution – going beyond that which is customary in analogous documents – also gives the Court the power to examine cases involving unconstitutionality by omission; in other words, to “review and verify any failure to comply with this Constitution by means of the omission of legislative measures needed to make constitutional rules executable” (Article 283 of the Constitution).

The procedure that is followed in such cases is similar to that of the successive abstract review of constitutionality. However, given the great sensitivity surrounding both the problem of ‘legislative omissions’ and the Constitutional Court’s fulfilment of this important responsibility, this process can only be initiated by the President of the Republic or the Ombudsman, or, in cases in which the rights of an autonomous region are at stake, the President of the Legislative Assembly in question.

If the Constitutional Court concludes that an omission does exist, it cannot draft the missing rule or rules, or even order the body with responsibility for doing so to draft them, inasmuch as either course would be contrary to its jurisdictional nature. The Court must restrict itself to ‘verifying’ that a case of unconstitutionality by omission exists, and to ‘informing’ the legislative body thereof.

VI PUBLICATION OF CONSTITUTIONAL COURT DECISIONS

http://www.tribunalconstitucional.pt/tc/en/home.html

SOURCES:

https://www.constituteproject.org/constitution/Portugal_2005.pdf
http://www.tribunalconstitucional.pt/tc/en/home.html

(146)

DOSSIER OF THE COSTITUTIONAL COURT OF THE PRIDNESTROVIAN MOLDAVIAN REPUBLIC

STATE: Pridnestrovian Moldovian Republic
TITLE: Constitutional Court
YEAR OF FOUNDATION: 1995
SEAT: Tiraspol

I. CHRONICLE

Date and context of establishment 1995
Position in the hierarchy of courts
The Constitutional Court of the Pridnestrovskaia Moldavskaia Respublica shall be an institute of constitutional control in the Pridnestrovskaia Moldavskaia Respublica. The Constitutional Court of the Pridnestrovskaia Moldavskaia Respublica shall guarantee supremacy of the Constitution of the Pridnestrovskaia Moldavskaia Respublica, ensure observance of the principle of separation of powers, and guarantee responsibility of the state before a citizen and a citizen before the state. (Article 86/1 of the Constitution)

II. STANDARD LEGAL REFERENCE

Constitution of 1995

III. COMPOSITION AND ORGANIZATION

Composition
The number of judges:
The Constitutional Court shall be composed of 6 (six) judges, including the Chairman of the Court. Article 86 of the Constitution.

A judge of the Constitutional Court shall be appointed for the term of seven years.

The powers of a judge of the Constitutional Court may be suspended or terminated only under the procedure stipulated by the constitutional law.

Electoral/appointment body:

Mixed system

The President of the Pridnestrovian Moldavian Republic, the Parliament, and the congress of judges of the Pridnestrovian Moldavian Republic each shall appoint two judges of the Constitutional Court.

Judges of the Constitutional Court shall be appointed from among individuals who reached the age of 40 by the day of their appointment and hold the office of a judge in other courts, as well as from among other individuals meeting the requirements of the second part of Article 82 of the Constitution. A person aged 58 and over may not be appointed a judge of the Constitutional Court (Article 86 of the Constitution)

The Court members:

The term of office: 7

The Court President:

Article 86 of the Constitution: The Chief Judge of the Constitutional Court shall be appointed from among the judges of the Constitutional Court under the procedure provided for by the Constitution.

The term of office: /

Organization

Administrative autonomy: /

The budget:

Budget of courts should enable them exercise their constitutional powers fully and independently; budgetary provision for organs of judicial power may not be less than that for other organs of state power in the Pridnestrovskaia Moldavskaia Respublica. Budget of courts may not be reduced during the current fiscal year without an agreement of highest organs of judicial power of the Pridnestrovskaia Moldavskaia Respublica, unless budget expenditures are cut out proportionately for all organs of state power.

IV. POWERS

Article 87 of the Constitution

The Constitutional Court of the Pridnestrovian Moldavian Republic shall decide only on law issues. Decisions of the Constitutional Court shall be approved by a majority of judges provided for by this Constitution.

Constitutional Court Review

Preventive review:

Article 87 of the Constitution

To exercise the constitutional control the Constitutional Court of the Pridnestrovian Moldavian Republic shall decide on: b) constitutionality of international treaties signed by the Pridnestrovian Moldavian Republic before their ratification or approval; c) unconformity of law (including the constitutional one) of the Pridnestrovian Moldavian Republic to universally recognized principles and norms of international law, or to regulations of a ratified international treaty of the Pridnestrovian Moldavian Republic; d) other cases stipulated by this Constitution.

A posteriori review: /

Abstract review:

Article 87 of the Constitution....

To exercise constitutional control, the Constitutional Court shall settle cases as to constitutionality of: a) laws (including constitutional ones) of the Pridnestrovian Moldavian Republic, as well as legal acts passed by the Parliament; b) legal acts of the President of the Pridnestrovian Moldavian Republic, of Ministries, Departments and other public authority, and local self-government of the Pridnestrovian Moldavian Republic;

Article 87 of the Constitution

To exercise constitutional control, the Constitutional Court shall settle cases as to constitutionality of: c) international treaties of the Pridnestrovian Moldavian Republic; d) law enforcement practice; e) resolutions and legal acts passed by elective organs and officials of local self-government.

Other powers

Constitutional complaints:

Article 87 of the Constitution

The Constitutional Court of the Pridnestrovian Moldavian Republic, proceeding from complaints about violation of constitutional rights and freedoms of citizens and requests from courts shall decide on the compliance of the law applied or due to be applied in a specific case with the Constitution of the Pridnestrovian Moldavian Republic; considers complaints of citizens about violations of human and civil rights arisen from application of a law or normative act.

Jurisdictional disputes:

Article 87 of the Constitution

To exercise constitutional control, the Constitutional Court shall settle cases as to constitutionality of: including as to settlement of disputes over jurisdiction between institutions of different power branches;

The unconstitutionality of acts and activities of political parties: Acts or their individual provisions recognized as unconstitutional according to subparagraphs a and b of paragraph 1, Article 87 of the Constitution, shall become null and void

Charges against the President of the Republic:

Article 87 of the Constitution

To exercise the constitutional control the Constitutional Court of the Pridnestrovian Moldavian Republic shall decide on: a) observation of the established procedure for bringing a charge against persons holding top public posts in the Pridnestrovian Moldavian Republic;

Charges against the Prime Minister or against any Minister of State: /

Electoral matters: /

Referendums: /

Other matters with which the Court is charged by the Constitution or statute: /

Other forms of human rights protection /

Standing before the Constitutional Court

State bodies:

Article 87 of the Constitution

.

At the request of the President of the Pridnestrovian Moldavian Republic, the Parliament, Plenums of the Supreme Court and the Court of Arbitration of the Pridnestrovian Moldavian Republic, or the Prosecutor General of the Pridnestrovian Moldavian Republic, the Constitutional Court of the Pridnestrovian Moldavian Republic shall resolve cases concerning constitutionality and exercise of the constitutional control in the cases and on the matters as provided by paragraphs 1 and 2 of this Article, shall give an obligatory interpretation of the Constitution and constitutional laws of the Pridnestrovian Moldavian Republic.

Individuals: X

Finality:

Article 88 of the Constitution

1. Decisions of the Constitutional Court of the Pridnestrovian Moldavian Republic shall be definitive. Acts or their particular provisions adjudged as unconstitutional according to subparagraphs "a" and "b" of paragraph 1, Article 87 of this Constitution, shall become loose force thereof. Recognition of an international treaty of the Pridnestrovian Moldavian Republic as unconstitutional shall lead to consequences stipulated by international law, the Constitution and law of the Pridnestrovian Moldavian Republic. Law enforcement deemed unconstitutional shall be subject to termination; the respective resolutions of state authority, local self-government and public officers should be reconsidered under the procedure prescribed by law.

2. The manner of establishment and activities of the Constitutional Court of the Pridnestrovian Moldavian Republic, the procedures observed by it and other matters shall be regulated by the constitutional law.

:

SOURCES:

https://en.wikisource.org/wiki/Constitution_of_the_Pridnestrovian_Moldavian_Republic

http://www.lact.ro/2013/10/07/constitution-of-the-pridnestrovian-moldavian-republic/

(147)

DOSSIER OF THE SUPREME COURT OF THE COMMONWEALTH OF PUERTO RICO

STATE: Commonwealth of Puerto Rico
TITLE: Supreme Court
YEAR OF FOUNDATION: 1952
SEAT: San Juan

I. CHRONICLE

Date and context of establishment: 1952
Position in the hierarchy of courts:
Article V, section 1 of the Constitution: The judicial power of Puerto Rico shall be vested in a Supreme Court, and in such other courts as may be established by law.

Article V, section 3 of the Constitution: The Supreme Court shall be the court of last resort in Puerto Rico

The Supreme Court of Puerto Rico (*Tribunal Supremo*) is the highest court of Puerto Rico, having judicial authority to interpret and decide questions of Puerto Rican law. The Court is analogous to one of the state Supreme Courts of the states of the United States; being the Supreme Court of Puerto Rico the highest state court and the court of last resort in Puerto Rico. Article V of the Constitution of Puerto Rico vests the judicial power on the Supreme Court.

II. STANDARD LEGAL REFERENCE

Constitution 1952

III. COMPOSITION AND ORGANIZATION

Composition
The number of judges:
Electoral/appointment body:
The number of Justices may be changed only by law upon request of the Supreme Court.

Organization
Administrative autonomy:
The budget:

IV. POWERS

Constitutional Court Review

Preventive review: /
A posteriori review: /
Abstract review:
Concrete review: /

Other powers
Constitutional complaints: /
Jurisdictional disputes: /
The unconstitutionality of acts and activities of political parties: /
Charges against the President of the Republic: /
Charges against the Prime Minister or against any Minister of State: /
Electoral matters: /
Referendums: /
Other matters with which the Court is charged by the Constitution or statute: /
Other forms of human rights protection: /
Standing before the Constitutional Court : /
State bodies: /
Individuals: X

Finality:
Binding force: /
Erga omnes: /
Inter partes: /
Ex officio: /
The legislative omissions: /

SOURCES:

http://www.constitution.org/cons/puertorico-eng.htm
https://en.wikipedia.org/wiki/Judiciary_of_Puerto_Rico

(148)

DOSSIER OF THE SUPREME CONSTITUTIONAL COURT OF THE STATE OF QATAR

STATE: Qatar
TITLE: Constitutional Court
YEAR OF FOUNDATION: 2009
SEAT: Doha

I. CHRONICLE

Date and context of establishment 2009
Article 140 of the Constitution

The law determines the judicial body competent to settle the disputes related to the constitutionality of the laws and regulations, defines its functions, the way to appeal, and the procedures to be followed before it. The law also defines the impact of a judgment of unconstitutionality.

Position in the hierarchy of courts
On September 27, 2009, Qatar's Constitutional Court began its work. Originally it was to begin functioning on October 1, 2008; administrative problems delayed the start date. It has jurisdiction over disputes concerning constitutional interpretations and is to make certain that legislation does not conflict with the constitution. The new court will rule on jurisdictional issues concerning lower courts. In addition, it has the power to appoint a court to adjudicate a specific issue.

The new court will also be an appellate court for cases in which lower courts' interpretations of laws are in dispute

II. STANDARD LEGAL REFERENCE

Constitution of 2004

III. COMPOSITION AND ORGANIZATION

IV. POWERS

Constitutional Court Review

According to the provisions of Article 140 of the Constitution, the law shall specify the competent judicial body for settling of disputes pertaining to the constitutionality of laws and regulations, define its powers and method of challenging and procedures to be followed before the said body. It shall also specify the consequences of judgment regarding unconstitutionality.

Other powers

Jurisdictional disputes:

According to the provisions of Article 138 of the Constitution, the law shall specify a competent judicial body for settling of Administrative Disputes of laws and regulations and define its powers. In 2008 law 12/2008 established the Supreme Constitutional Court.

The Constitutional Court was established by virtue of Law No. 6 of 2007 and forms a division of the Court of Cassation.

SOURCES:

https://www.constituteproject.org/constitution/Qatar_2003.pdf?lang=en

(149)

DOSSIER OF THE CONSTITUTIONAL COURT OF ROMANIA

STATE: Romania
TITLE: Constitutional Court
YEAR OF FOUNDATION: 1992
SEAT: Bucharest

I. CHRONICLE

Date and context of establishment 1992
Position in the hierarchy of courts
The Constitutional Court is the sole authority of constitutional jurisdiction in Romania, and it shall be independent of any other public authority. According to the law, the Constitutional Court competence cannot be contested by any public authority, the Court alone being entitled to decide thereupon.

To fulfil its functions as the "guarantor for the supremacy of the Costitution", the Court discharges the following powers prescribed by Article 146. of the Constitution.

II. STANDARD LEGAL REFERENCE

The Constitution of Romania 1991 with amendments
The Constitutional Court Act no. 233 of 21 November 1991

III. COMPOSITION AND ORGANIZATION

Composition
The number of judges: 9
Electoral/appointment body:
the President of Romania, the Chamber of Deputies and the Senate appointed one Judge each.

Election Based System:

The Costitutional Court shall be renewed by one third of its Judges every three years, when one Judge is appointed by each of the competent authorities. In the order to ensure application of the renewal scheme, the first Judges were appointed for respective periods of three, six and nine years, the competent authorities having appointed one Judge for each of these periods.

The qualifications and the required professional experience of constitutional court judges:

Judges must have a degree in Law, high professional competence and at least eighteen-years experience in the legal area or in the academic activities in Law.

Incompatibilities:

Immunities:

They enjoy immunity and cannot be held responsible for opinion and votes given in the adjudication of cases.

Proceedings

Hearing in plenum:

A quorum:

The quorum for the Plenum is two-thirds of the members. Judges sre bound to express their vote, whether affirmative or negative, and no abstention shall be allowed

IV. POWERS

Constitutional Court Review

Preventive review:

A posteriori review:

Abstract review: is regulated by the provisions under Article 146 a) first sentence of the Constitution and by Articles 15-18 of Law no. 47/1992

If the law is declared unconstitutional, pursuant to Article 147 (2) of the Constitution, Parliament must re-examine those provisions in order to bring them into line with the decision of the Constitutional Court.

Other powers

Jurisdictional disputes:

It resolves legal disputes of a constitutional nature between public authorities, at the request of the President of Romania, one of the Presidents of the two Chambers, the Prime Minister, or of the President of the Superior Council of Magistracy.

The unconstitutionality of acts and activities of political parties / Charges against the President of the Republic:

It gives the advisory opinion on the proposal to suspend the President of Romania from office

Electoral matters:

It guards the observance of the procedure for the election of the President of Romania and confirms the ballot returns; It ascertains the circumstances which justify the interim in the exercise of office of President of Romania, and reports its findings to Parliament and the Government

Referendums:

It guards the observance of the procedure for the organization and holding of a referendum, and confirms its returns.

The subject matter of the constitutional review provided under Article 23 of Law no.47/1992can only be laws for revision of the Constitution, i.e. constitutional laws, before submitting them for approval through the referendum.

This act shall become final following the referendum and shall enter into force on the day of publication in the Official Gazette of Romania, Part I, of the ruling of the Constitutional Court for confirmation of the results of the referendum.

Standing before the Constitutional Court

State bodies:

It resolves legal disputes of a constitutional nature between public authorities, at the request of the President of Romania, one of the Presidents of the two Chambers, the Prime Minister, or of the President of the Superior Council of Magistracy.

Individuals:

It checks on compliance with the conditions for the exercise of a legislative initiative by citizens

V. NATURE AND EFFECTS OF DECISIONS

Finality: X
Binding force: X

VI PUBLICATION OF CONSTITUTIONAL COURT DECISIONS

http://www.cdep.ro/pls/dic/site.page?id=371

SOURCES:

http://www.cdep.ro/pls/dic/site.page?id=371

(150)

DOSSIER OF THE CONSTITUTIONAL COURT OF THE RUSSIAN FEDERATION

STATE: Russian Federation
TITLE: Constitutional Court
YEAR OF FOUNDATION: 1991
SEAT: ST. Petersburg

I. CHRONICLE

Date and context of establishment 1991
The idea to create a special body, entrusted with overseeing the compliance with Basic Law, is attributed to Mikhail Gorbachev. He proposed to establish the Committee of Constitutional Supervision of the USSR.

The idea was implemented into legislation on December 1, 1988, when Article 125 of the Constitution of the USSR had been amended. The amendment stipulated that Committee of Constitutional Supervision (CCS) of the USSR was to consist of 23 experts in law and political science, it was also to include a representative from each of the 15 constituent republics; CCS was to be elected by the Congress of People's Deputies of the USSR.

Committee of Constitutional Supervision of the USSR was empowered to oversee the constitutionality of not only of enacted laws of the USSR, but also of legislative drafts as well as legal acts of the Prosecutor-General of the USSR, Supreme State Arbiter of the USSR and other normative acts.

In December 1991 the Committee of Constitutional Supervision of the USSR had voluntarily ceased its existence.

***

Amendment to the Russian Constitution, which was passed on December 15, 1990 for the first time mentioned the institution of the Constitutional Court. The amendment, approved by the Second Russian Congress of People's Deputies, stipulated that the Constitutional Court of Russia was to be elected by the Congress, while its operation was to be defined by a separate law.

On December 12, 1993 a new Constitution of Russia was adopted by a popular vote. Article 125 of the new Constitution established new legal framework for the operation of the Constitutional Court.

Beside the Federal Constitutional Court there are constitutional courts of federal units separately established (see more on www.concourts.net).

Position in the hierarchy of courts

The Constitutional Court of the Russian Federation is a judicial body of constitutional review, which independently exercises judicial power by means of constitutional judicial proceedings.

Powers, rules of the establishment and operation of the Constitutional Court are determined by the Constitution of the Russian Federation and the Federal Constitutional Law on the Constitutional Court of the Russian Federation.

II. STANDARD LEGAL REFERENCE

Constitution of 1993

III. COMPOSITION AND ORGANIZATION

Composition

The number of judges:

(Article 4 of the FCL)

The Constitutional Court consists of 19 judges.

Electoral/appointment body:

Appointed by the Federation Council upon nomination by the President of the Russian Federation. The Constitutional Court shall perform its functions provided that no less than three quarters of the total number of Judges are in office. The powers of the Constitutional Court are of unlimited duration.

The Court members:

The term of office:

Judges are appointed for an indefinite term of office, but are subject (except for the President of the Court) to the age limit of 70 years.

The Court President:

The term of office:

Organization

Administrative autonomy:

The budget:

IV. POWERS

Constitutional Court Review

Preventive review:

Decides on conformity with the Constitution of agreements between bodies of state power of the Russian Federation and international treaties pending their entry into force.

A posteriori review:

Abstract review:

Upon application by the President of the Russian Federation, the Federation Council or at least one fifth of its members, the State Duma or at least one of fifth of its members, Government of the Russian Federation, the Supreme Court of the Russian Federation and the Superior Court of Arbitration of the Russian Federation, legislative and executive bodies of the constituent entities of the Russian Federation decides on conformity with the Constitution of federal laws, normative acts, issued by the President, the Federation Council, the State Duma, Government of the Russian Federation and the constituent entities of the Russian Federation.

Concrete review:

Other powers

Constitutional complaints:

On complaints about violation of constitutional rights and freedoms of citizens, verifies the constitutionality of a law that has been applied in a specific case.

Jurisdictional disputes:

Decides disputes concerning competence between Federal bodies of state power, between Federal bodies of state power and constituent entities of the Russian Federation as well as between supreme bodies of state power of constituent entities of the Russian Federation, if such competence is defined by the Constitution and there are no alternative means to settle the dispute.

Charges against the President of the Republic:
Renders a declaratory judgment on the observance of a prescribed procedure for charging the President of the Russian Federation with high treason or with commission of other grave offense

Standing before the Constitutional Court
State bodies:
Upon application by the President of the Russian Federation, the Federation Council or at least one fifth of its members, the State Duma or at least one of fifth of its members, Government of the Russian Federation, the Supreme Court of the Russian Federation and the Superior Court of Arbitration of the Russian Federation, legislative and executive bodies of the constituent entities of the Russian Federation decides on conformity with the Constitution of federal laws, normative acts, issued by the President, the Federation Council, the State Duma, Government of the Russian Federation and the constituent entities of the Russian Federation.

Individuals: X

V. NATURE AND EFFECTS OF DECISIONS

Finality:
(Article 6 of the FCL)

Decisions of the Constitutional Court are obligatory throughout the territory of the Russian Federation for all representative, executive and judicial bodies of state power, local self-government, enterprises, agencies, organizations, public officials, citizens and their associations.

Decisions of the Constitutional Court are directly applicable, requiring no affirmation by any other body.

SOURCES:

http://www.constitution.ru/en/10003000-01.htm
http://www.ksrf.ru/en/Info/Pages/default.aspx

(151)

DOSSIER OF THE SUPREME COURT OF THE REPUBLIC OF RWANDA

STATE: Rwanda
TITLE: Supreme Court
YEAR OF FOUNDATION: 2003
SEAT: Kigali

CHRONICLE

Date and context of establishment 2003
The Supreme Court of Rwanda is the highest court of Rwanda, as defined by Article 143 of the 2003 Constitution of Rwanda. Article 144 of the Constitution determines that the Supreme Court is the highest jurisdiction in the country.

Position in the hierarchy of courts
Following the adoption of the new Rwandan constitution of 4 June 2003, enormous changes were made to the organization, functioning and jurisdiction of the Courts and the Judiciary in general.

Article 60 of the Constitution of the Republic of Rwanda of 4 June 2003, establishes the Judiciary as one of the three (3) independent arms of Government. Article 140 of the same Constitution establishes the exercise of Judicial Power under the Supreme Court and other Courts.

II. STANDARD LEGAL REFERENCE

Constitution of 2003

III. COMPOSITION AND ORGANIZATION

Article 60 of the Rwanda Constitution of 4 June 2003 established a united Supreme Court with no sections as the highest Court in the land. It is headed by a President assisted by a Vice-President and twelve (12) judges. The number of judges may be increased or reduced according to need. It further includes Court Registrars and other civil servants assigned to Court services.

Cases at the Supreme Court are normally presided over by three Judges, assisted by a Registrar.

However, depending on the importance of the case being tried, the number of Judges presiding may be more – 5, 7, 11 or 13.

Composition
The number of judges: 12
Electoral/appointment body:
The Court members:
The term of office:
The Court President:
The term of office:
Organization
Administrative autonomy:
The budget:
Supreme Court has both administrative and financial autonomy under Constitutional Provisions.

The Supreme Court has both administrative and financial autonomy. Its budget is consolidated and voted on by the Legislature.

IV. POWERS

On the jurisdictional level, the Supreme Court exercises ordinary and extraordinary powers. It rules.....

on:

- Appeals made against judgements rendered in the first instance by the HC , the Commercial High Court and the Military High Court;
- Appeals made against judgements rendered in the second instance by the HC when they fulfil conditions stipulated in article 43 of the code on organisation, functioning and jurisdiction of the Supreme Court;
- Criminal cases, in the first and last instance, involving the highest officials of the government;
- Petitions for presidential pardon or review of criminal cases.

Constitutional Court Review

On the jurisdictional level, the Supreme Court exercises ordinary and extraordinary powers. It rules....

Petitions on the unconstitutionality of laws, electoral disputes relating to the referendum and presidential and legislative elections;

Standing before the Constitutional Court

State bodies: X

Individuals: X

V. NATURE AND EFFECTS OF DECISIONS

SOURCES:

http://judiciary.gov.rw/about-us.html

https://www.constituteproject.org/constitution/Rwanda_2015.pdf?lang=en

(152)

DOSSIER OF THE NATIONAL COUNCIL OF THE SAHRAWI ARAB DEMOCRATIC REPUBLIC

STATE: Sahrawi Arab Democratic Republic
TITLE: National Council
YEAR OF FOUNDATION: 1976, 1991-1999
SEAT: El Aaiun
A constitution of the Sahrawi Arab Democratic Republic (SADR) was first promulgated in 1976, but it has been revised several times since then. The last major redrafting came in 1991, but this version was further changed by the Sahrawi National Council - the SADR's parliament in exile - in 1995 and 1999.

II. STANDARD LEGAL REFERENCE

Constitution 1976 with amendments

III. POWERS

Constitutional review
In addition to the areas reserved for organic laws under the Constitution, the National Council legislates through organic laws in the following areas:
- the organization of public services and their activities;
- the fundamental law of justice and the judiciary;
- the law concerning national security;
- the organic law must be subject to control to ensure the compatibility of the text with the Constitution

SOURCES:

https://en.wikipedia.org/wiki/Constitution_of_the_Sahrawi_Arab_Democratic_Republic
https://www.westernsahara-un.com/leadership-1/constitution/

(153)

DOSSIER OF THE SUPREME COURT OF THE FEDERATION OF SAINT CHRISTOPHER AND NEVIS, SAINT LUCIA AND SAINT VINCENT AND THE GRENADIES (WEST INDIES)

STATE: Federation of Saint Christopher and Nevis
TITLE: EASTERN CARRIBEAN SUPREME COURT (The Eastern Caribbean Supreme Court (ECSC) is a superior court of record for the Organisation of Eastern Caribbean States (OECS), including six independent states: Antigua and Barbuda, the Commonwealth of Dominica, Grenada, Saint Kitts and Nevis, Saint Lucia, Saint Vincent and the Grenadines and three British Overseas Territories (Anguilla, British Virgin Islands, and Montserrat). It has unlimited jurisdiction in each member State).
YEAR OF FOUNDATION: 1967
SEAT: Castries, St Lucia (quedquarters)

I. CHRONICLE

Date and context of establishment 1983
by the West Indies Associated States Supreme Court Order No. 223

Position in the hierarchy of courts

II. STANDARD LEGAL REFERENCE

Constitution of 1983

III. COMPOSITION AND ORGANIZATION

To be a judge or master of the Eastern Caribbean Supreme Court, a person must have served as a judge in a Commonwealth jurisdiction or be qualified to act as a lawyer in a Commonwealth jurisdiction. An appointee does not need to be a national, judge, or lawyer of a country within the jurisdiction of the Court. Judges are appointed by the Judicial and Legal Services Commission of the Caribbean Community.

High Court Judges and Masters are assigned to reside in and hear cases from a specific member state. It is common for judges to be asked to work in countries other than their home state. Judges are only occasionally assigned to reside in Montserrat and Anguilla—because of the small population of these countries, judges from the other jurisdictions hear cases that arise from these two jurisdictions. The Court of Appeal is itinerant and travels to the various countries to hear appeals.

Judges have life tenure but Justices of Appeal must retire when they are 65 and High Court Judges must retire when they are 62. Extensions of up to three years may be granted by the Judicial and Legal Services Commission only if all of the states agree to such an extension.

Composition

The number of judges:

The Eastern Caribbean Supreme Court is composed of the Chief Justice, who is the Head of the Judiciary, five (5) Justices of Appeal, High Court Judges; and High Court Masters, who are primarily responsible for procedural and interlocutory matters. The Court of Appeal judges are based at the Court's Headquarters in Castries, Saint Lucia where administrative and legal support is provided under the supervision of the Court Administrator and Chief Registrar respectively.

The High Court Judges are each assigned to, and reside in, the various Member States. The High Court Registry is headed by a legally trained Registrar who coordinates the provision of the necessary administrative and legal support for the functioning of the High Court. The High Court has 16 judges, two of whom are permanently resident in the country and sit in the court of summary jurisdiction.

Organization:

The Eastern Caribbean Supreme Court consists of two divisions, a Court of Appeal and a High Court of Justice.

The Court of Appeal is itinerant, traveling to each Member State and Territory, where it sits at various specified dates during the year to hear appeals from the decisions of the High Court and Magistrates Courts in Member States in both civil and criminal matters.

The Court of Appeal hears appeals from all subordinate courts (High Courts, Magistrates Courts and the Industrial Court in Antigua and Barbuda). Appeals from the Magistrates Courts might be heard from "any judgment, decree, sentence or order of a Magistrate in all proceedings." In respect of the High Court, the Court of Appeal has jurisdiction to hear and determine "any matter arising in any civil proceedings upon a case stated, or upon a question of law reserved by the High court or by a judge." This is, however, subject to "any power conferred in that behalf by a law in operation in that State." Subject to certain exceptions, the Court of Appeal is empowered to "hear and determine the appeal from any judgment or Order of the High Court in all civil proceedings." For the purposes of determining any issues incidental to an appeal and the remedies, execution, and enforcement of any judgment or order made thereto, the Court of Appeal is endowed with "all the powers, authority and jurisdiction of the High Court."

Each Member State has its own Court Office, which, in addition to the High Court Registry, houses the office of the local High Court judge(s). Filing in the Registries commences the proceedings in matters before the High Court in each of the nine territories and the Court of Appeal.

The trial Courts sit throughout the year. Criminal Assizes convene in each jurisdiction on specified dates.

IV. POWERS

Constitutional Court Review

The functions of the ECSC are as follows:

- To interpret and apply the laws of the various member states of the OECS;
- To decide cases of both civil and criminal matters;
- To hear appeals.

V. NATURE AND EFFECTS OF DECISIONS

SOURCES:

http://laws.gov.tt/pdf/App2.pdf

(154)

DOSSIER OF THE SUPREME COURT OF THE INDIPENDENT STATE OF SAMOA

STATE: Independent State of Samoa
TITLE: Supreme Court
YEAR OF FOUNDATION: 1960
SEAT: Apia

I. CHRONICLE

Date and context of establishment
There shall be a Supreme Court of Samoa, which shall be a superior Court of record (Article 65/1 of the Constitution).

Position in the hierarchy of courts

II. STANDARD LEGAL REFERENCE

Constitution 1960 with amendments

III. COMPOSITION AND ORGANIZATION

Composition
The number of judges:
Electoral/appointment body:
The Chief Justice of the Supreme Court shall be appointed by the Head of State, acting on the advice of the Prime Minister.

Organization

Administrative autonomy:

The budget:

The salaries of Judges of the Supreme Court to whom clause (1) of Article 68 of the Constitution applies shall be determined by Act and shall be charged on the Treasury Fund. The salaries of such Judges shall not be diminished during their period of office, unless as part of a general reduction of salaries applied proportionately to all persons whose salaries are determined by Act.

IV. POWERS

Subject to the provisions of this Constitution, the Court of Appeal shall have jurisdiction to hear and determine such appeals (including proceedings removed by order of the Supreme Court to the Court of Appeal) as may be provided by Article 80 of the Constitution.

Constitutional Court Review

A posteriori review:

Concrete review:

Each Judge of the Supreme Court or any 2 or more Judges may, in any part of Samoa and at any time or place, exercise all the powers of the Supreme Court.

Jurisdiction on constitutional questions –

(1) An appeal shall lie to the Court of Appeal from any decision of the Supreme Court in any proceeding, if the Supreme Court certifies that the case involves a substantial question of law as to the interpretation or effect of any provision of this Constitution.

(2) Where the Supreme Court has refused to give such a certificate, the Court of Appeal may, if it is satisfied that the case involves a substantial question of law as to the interpretation or effect of any provision of this Constitution, grant special leave to appeal from that decision.

(3) Where such a certificate is given or such leave granted, any party in the case may appeal to the Court of Appeal on the ground that any such question as aforesaid has been wrongly decided and, with the leave of that Court, on any other ground.

Other forms of human rights protection

Article 81 of the Constitution. Jurisdiction in respect of fundamental rights - An appeal shall lie to the Court of Appeal from any decision of the Supreme Court in any proceedings under the provision of Article 4 of the Constitution.

Standing before the Constitutional Court

State bodies: X

Individuals: X

V. NATURE AND EFFECTS OF DECISIONS

SOURCES:

http://www.wipo.int/wipolex/en/text.jsp?file_id=198467#LinkTarget_1833

(155)

DOSSIER OF THE HIGH COURT OF AMERICAN SAMOA

STATE: Territory of American Samoa
TITLE: High Court
YEAR OF FOUNDATION: 1921
SEAT: Fagatogo

I. CHRONICLE

Date and context of establishment: 1960

The High Court of American Samoa is a Samoan court and the highest court below the United States Supreme Court in American Samoa. The Court is located in the capital of Fagatogo. It consists of one chief justice and one associate justice, appointed by the United States Secretary of the Interior, holding office during good behavior and removable for cause.[1]

The High Court of American Samoa also has several Samoan associate judges who sit with the two justices. Normally, two associate judges will sit with the chief justice and associate justice on every case.

Position in the hierarchy of courts:
Article III., section1 of the Constitution: The judicial power shall be vested in the High Court, the District Courts, and such other courts as may from time to time be created by law

II. STANDARD LEGAL REFERENCE

Constitution 1960 with amendments

III. COMPOSITION AND ORGANIZATION

Composition
The number of judges: /

Electoral/appointment body:
Article III.,section 3 of the Constitution: The Secretary of the Interior shall appoint a Chief Justice of American Samoa and such Associate Justices as he may deem necessary. The Secretary of Interior may take into consideration any recommendation and advice by the Governor of American Samoa.

IV. POWERS

High Court had subject matter jurisdiction in case involving a contested senatorial election by county council where there was a case or controversy, it arose under the constitution, laws or treaties, and the cause was described in jurisdictional statutes. Meredith v. Mola, 4 ASR 773 (1973).

Constitutional Court Review /

Preventive review: /
A posteriori review: /
Abstract review: /
Concrete review: /

Other powers
Constitutional complaints: /
Jurisdictional disputes: /
The unconstitutionality of acts and activities of political parties: /
Charges against the President of the Republic: /
Charges against the Prime Minister or against any Minister of State: /
Electoral matters: /
Referendums: /
Other matters with which the Court is charged by the Constitution or statute:
Other forms of human rights protection
Standing before the Constitutional Court
State bodies: /
Individuals: X

V. NATURE AND EFFECTS OF DECISIONS

Finality: X
Binding force: /
Erga omnes: /
Inter partes: /

SOURCES:

http://unpan1.un.org/intradoc/groups/public/documents/UN-DPADM/UNPAN040209.pdf
https://en.wikipedia.org/wiki/High_Court_of_American_Samoa
https://ballotpedia.org/Article_III,_American_Samoa_Constitution

DOSSIER OF THE NATIONAL ASSEMBLY OF THE DEMOCRATIC REPUBLIC OF SAO TOME AND PRINCIPE

STATE: Democratic Republic of Sao Tome and Principe
TITLE: National Assembly
YEAR OF FOUNDATION: 1975 (rev. 1990)
SEAT: São Tomé

I. CHRONICLE

Date and context of establishment 1975
Position in the hierarchy of courts

II. STANDARD LEGAL REFERENCE

Constitution 1975

III. COMPOSITION AND ORGANIZATION

IV. POWERS

Article 111 of the Constitution: Oversight of constitutionality

1. In the deeds submitted to judgment, the courts cannot apply norms which infringe upon what is provided in the Constitution or in the principles consecrated therein.
2. The question of unconstitutionality may be raised obligingly by the court, by the Justice Department or by any of the parties.
3. Admitted a question of unconstitutionality, the case goes to the National Assembly, which will decide.

4. The decisions taken in the matter of unconstitutionality by the National Assembly shall have general binding force and shall be published in the Diario da Republica.

V. NATURE AND EFFECTS OF DECISIONS

SOURCES:

https://www.constituteproject.org/constitution/Sao_Tome_and_Principe_1990.pdf?lang=en

(157)

DOSSIER OF THE SUPREME COURT OF THE KINGDOM OF SAUDI ARABIA

STATE: Kingdom of Saudi Arabia
TITLE: Supreme Court
YEAR OF FOUNDATION: 2007
SEAT: Riyadh

I. CHRONICLE

Date and context of establishment 1992 (2007)
Position in the hierarchy of courts
The Saudi Arabian court system is regulated by the Law of Judiciary promulgated by Royal Decree No. M/78 on 19/09/1428H corresponding to 1 October 2007.

II. STANDARD LEGAL REFERENCE

Constitution 1992

III. COMPOSITION AND ORGANIZATION

Composition
The number of judges: 11 members

IV. POWERS

Constitutional Court Review The new Supreme Court will have a narrower writ, addressing administrative matters that will concentrate on the selection of judges, the setting up of tribunals, and other specialist courts to implement the King's, the Supreme Court will focus on selected cases that may require national attention recommendations.

The high court will firstly examine cases involving administrative appeals rulings, to handle disputes involving the rights of employees, compensation, contracts, disciplinary issues, administrative decisions, and the implementation of foreign regulations

According to the Saudi judicial system, there is only one Supreme Court in Saudi Arabia. This court oversees implementation of Islamic laws and decrees issued by the Saudi Monarch in conformity therewith in matters that lie within the jurisdiction of the general judiciary system.

The Supreme Court, in Riyadh, is the highest appellate court in Saudi Arabia. The jurisdiction of the Court is spelt out by Article 11 of the Law of Justice:

Reviewing judgments and decisions issued or supported by the appellate courts such as death, amputation, stoning or punishment.

Review judgments and decisions issued or supported by the appellate courts and related to cases not mentioned in the previous provision or to finalise matters without dealing with the merits of a case, if the reason of the objection to the judgment is the following:

- Inconsistence with Islamic Shari'ah laws and laws that the king shall issue that are
- not not inconsistent with Shari'ah laws.
- Issuing the judgment from a court that does not have a valid composition according to
- what is stated in this law and others.
- The judgment is issued by a non-competent panel or court.
- There is a fault in the case facts or description of the case.

V. NATURE AND EFFECTS OF DECISIONS

Finality:

Especially Article 5 of the Constitution identified the Supreme Judicial Council as the highest legal authority in Saudi Arabia.

SOURCES:

https://www.constituteproject.org/constitution/Saudi_Arabia_2005.pdf

(158)

DOSSIER OF THE CONSTITUTIONAL COUNCIL OF THE REPUBLIC OF SENEGAL

STATE: Republic of Senegal
TITLE: Constitutional Council
YEAR OF FOUNDATION: 1992
SEAT: Dakar

I. CHRONICLE

Date and context of establishment 1992
The Constitutional Council of Senegal was created in 1992 when the Supreme Court was abolished and replaced by three specialized bodies.

It was established by Law No. 92-23 of May 30, 1992, amended by Organic Law No. 99-71 of February 17, 1999.

Position in the hierarchy of courts
The Constitutional Council is a public institution in Senegal, the highest court in the judiciary. It has similarities with the French Constitutional Council.

II. STANDARD LEGAL REFERENCE

Constitution of 1959, 1960, 1963, 2001

III. COMPOSITION AND ORGANIZATION

Composition
The number of judges: 5
Article 89 of the Constitution: The Constitutional Council is composed of five members having one President, one Vice-President and three judges.

The Court members:

The term of office: 6

Article 89 of the Constitution: The duration of their mandates is of six years.

The Council is renewed every two years on the basis of the President or of two members other than the President, inthe order which results from the dates of the maturity [échéance] of their mandates.

Electoral/appointment body:

The members of the Constitutional Council are appointed by the President of the Republic.

The conditions to be fulfilled in order to be able to be appointed [as a] member of the Constitutional Council are determined by the organic law.

The mandate of the members of the Constitutional Council may not be renewed.

The functions of the members of the Constitutional Council may only be terminated before the expiration of their mandate on their demand or for physical incapacity, and within the conditions provide for by the organic law.

Members of the Constitutional Council are chosen among former Chief Presidents of the Supreme Court, President and former Presidents of the Council of State, Chief President and former Chief Presidents of the Court of Cassation, former Prosecutors General of the Supreme Court, Prosecutor General and former Prosecutors General of the Court of Cassation, former Division Presidents of the Supreme Court, Division Presidents and former Division Presidents of the State of Council, Presidents and former Presidents of Chamber in the Court of Cassation, former Chief Advocates General of the Supreme Court, Chief Advocate General and former Chief Advocates General of the Court of Cassation, Chief Presidents and former Chief Presidents of Courts of Appeal, and Prosecutors General and former Prosecutors General of Courts of Appeal.

Moreover, two Members of the Council out of the five may be chosen from Professors and former Professors at Law Faculties, State Inspectors General, and former State Inspectors General and Lawyers, providing they have at least 25 years of experience in the public service or have exercised their profession for at least 25 years.

Immunities:

Article 93 of the Constitution: Except in the case of flagrante delicto, the members of the Constitutional Council may only be prosecuted, arrested, detailed or judged in a criminal matter with the authorization of the Council and within the same conditions as the magistrates of the Supreme Court and of the Court of Accounts.

Organization

Article 94 of the Constitution: The organic laws determine the other competences of the Constitutional Council, of the Supreme Court and of the Court of Accounts[,] as well as their organization, the rules of appointment of their members and the procedure [to be] followed before them.

IV. POWERS

Constitutional Court Review

Abstract review

Article 92 of the Constitution: The Constitutional Council takes cognizance of the constitutionality of the laws, of the internal regulations of the assemblies and of the international commitments,

Article 92 of the Constitution: The Constitutional Council also controls the constitutionality of international laws and commitments.

Concrete review:

Article 92 of the Constitution: The Constitutional Council takes cognizance of the of the exceptions [pleadings] of unconstitutionality raised before the Supreme Court.

Other powers

Jurisdictional disputes:

Article 92 of the Constitution: The Constitutional Council takes cognizance of the conflicts of competence between the executive and the legislative,

Electoral matters:

The Constitutional Council receives applications to the Presidency of the Republic, draws up the list of candidates, adjudicates disputes arising from the election of the President of the Republic and Members of the National Assembly, and announces the results of the votes.

The President of the Republic takes the oath before the Constitutional Council, which notes his resignation, incapacity or death, or the resignation, incapacity or death of people replacing him under those conditions.

In national elections (presidential or legislative), the Constitutional Council receives the provisional results proclaimed by the Courts of Appeal, rules on the possible appeals and claims and proclaims the final results.

Referendums:
In addition, the Constitutional Council exercises its powers under Articles 46 and 47 of the Constitution when the President of the Republic decides to put a draft law to referendum or pronounces dissolution of the National Assembly.

Standing before the Constitutional Court
State bodies: X
Individuals: X

V. NATURE AND EFFECTS OF DECISIONS

Finality:
Article 92 of the Constitution: The decisions of the Constitutional Council are not susceptible to any way [voie] of recourse. They impose themselves on the public powers and on all the administrative and jurisdictional authorities. Decisions of the Constitutional Council are not subject to any remedy.

Binding force:
They impose themselves on the public powers and on all the administrative and jurisdictional authorities.

SOURCES:

https://www.constituteproject.org/constitution/Senegal_2009.pdf?lang=en
https://fr.wikipedia.org/wiki/Conseil_constitutionnel_(S%C3%A9n%C3%A9gal)

(159)

DOSSIER OF THE CONSTITUTIONAL COURT OF THE REPUBLIC SERBIA

STATE: Republic of Serbia
TITLE: Constitutional Court
YEAR OF FOUNDATION: 1963
SEAT: Belgrad

I. CHRONICLE

Date and context of establishment
The Constitutional Court of the Republic of Serbia commenced its work on 15 February 1964.

Position in the hierarchy of courts
The Constitutional Court has upon proclamation of the Constitution of the Republic of Serbia in 1990 acted within the framework of absence of division of powers, where the Parliament was the highest body of state power. The Constitutional Court of Serbia has through its presence and work contributed to the importance and contribution in preservation of the constitutional principles and legality.
Article 166 of the Constitution

The Constitutional Court shall be an autonomous and independent state body which shall protect constitutionality and legality, as well as human and minority rights and freedoms.

The Constitutional Court decisions are final, enforceable and generally binding.

II. STANDARD LEGAL REFERENCE

The Constitution of The Republic of Serbia 1990

Composition

The number of judges:

The Constitutional Court consists of 15 judges

Electoral/appointment body:

elected and appointed in the manner prescribed by the Constitution (the national Assembly) Article 99 of the Constitution

The Court President:

The term of office:

The Court shall adopt a decision on instituting the Court President election proceedings at least 30 days before the term of office of the President incumbent expires.

Incompatibilities:

A Constitutional Court judge may be dismissed if he/she becomes a member of a political party, violates the prohibition of conflict of interest, suffers permanent loss of ability to perform the duty of a Constitutional Court judge, or is convicted to a prison sentence or convicted for a punishable offence rendering them him/her unworthy to serve as a Constitutional Court judge. A justice of the Constitutional Court may not engage in another public or professional function or action, except for the professorship a law faculty in the Republic of Serbia, in accordance with the Law.

Immunities:

A justice of the Constitutional Court shall enjoy immunity as a deputy. The Constitutional Court shall decide on its immunity. (Article 172 of the Constitution)

Proceedings

Public hearing:

Summons to a public hearing shall include the subject matter of the public hearing and the date and venue where it shall be held.

The judge-rapporteur shall prepare a report for the public hearing which shall be distributed to all the parties to the proceedings and other participants thereto.

The report from paragraph 2 of this Article shall include, specifically: the content of the claim contained in the act aimed at instituting the proceedings; the content of the contested provisions of the general act the review of the constitutionality or legality of which has been requested; the constitutional issues which are the subject of the debate; expert opinion, if collected during the proceedings.

IV. POWERS

Constitutional Court Review

A posteriori review:

Abstract review:

The Constitutional Court shall decide on:

1. compliance of laws and other general acts with the Constitution, generally accepted rules of the international law and ratified international treaties,
2. compliance of ratified international treaties with the Constitution,
3. compliance of other general acts with the Law,
4. compliance of the Statute and general acts of autonomous provinces and local self-government units with the Constitution and the Law,
5. compliance of general acts of organisations with delegated public powers, political parties, trade unions, civic associations and collective agreements with the Constitution and the Law.

Concrete review: X

Other powers

Constitutional complaints:

Article 170 of the Constitution

A constitutional appeal may be lodged against individual general acts or actions performed by state bodies or organisations exercising delegated public powers which violate or deny human or minority rights and freedoms guaranteed.

Jurisdictional disputes:

The Constitutional Court shall:

1. decide on the conflict of jurisdictions between courts and state bodies,
2. decide on the conflict of jurisdictions between republic and provincial bodies or bodies of local self-government units,
3. decide on the conflict of jurisdictions between provincial bodies and bodies of local self-government units,

The unconstitutionality of acts and activities of political parties:
The Constitutional Court shall decide on the banning of a political party, trade union organisation or civic association.
Article 55 of the Constitution

Constitutional Court may ban only such associations the activity of which is aimed at violent overthrow of constitutional order, violation of guaranteed human or minority rights, or inciting of racial, national and religious hatred.

Judges of Constitutional Court, judges, public prosecutors, Defender of Citizens, members of police force and military persons may not be members of political parties.

Charges against the President of the Republic:
(Article 118 of the Constitution): The Constitutional Court shall have the obligation to decide on the violation of the Constitution, upon the initiated procedure for dismissal, not later than within 45 days.

Electoral matters:
The Constitutional Court shall decide on electoral disputes for which the court jurisdiction has not been specified by the Law,

Other matters with which the Court is charged by the Constitution or statute:
The Constitutional Court shall perform other duties stipulated by the Constitution. (Article 167 of th Constitution)
Article 44 of the Constitution

Constitutional Court may ban a religious community only if its activities infringe the right to life, right to mental and physical health, the rights of child, right to personal and family integrity, public safety and order, or if it incites religious, national or racial intolerance.

(Article 101 of the Constitution) Against the decision made in relation to confirmation of terms of office of deputies of the National Assembly, an appeal may be lodged before the Constitutional Court, which decides on it within 72 hours.

(Article 148 of the Constitution: The High Judicial Council shall pass a decision on termination of a judge's tenure of office. A judge shall have the right to appeal with the Constitutional Court against this decision. The lodged appeal shall not include the right to lodge a Constitutional appeal.
Article 155 of the Constitution

An appeal may be lodged with the Constitutional Court against a decision of the High Judicial Council, in cases stipulated by the Law.

Article 161 of the Constitution): Public Prosecutor and Deputy Public Prosecutor may lodge an appeal with the Constitutional Court against the decision on termination of their tenure of office. The lodged appeal shall not include the right to lodge a Constitutional appeal.

V. NATURE AND EFFECTS OF DECISIONS

Finality:
Decisions of the Constitutional Court are final, enforceable and universally binding.

Binding force:
Article 171 of the Constitution

Everyone shall be obliged to observe and enforce the Constitutional Court's decision.

The Constitutional Court shall regulate in its decision the manner of its enforcement, whenever deemed necessary.

Enforcement of the Constitutional Court's decisions shall be regulated by the Law.

VI PUBLICATION OF CONSTITUTIONAL COURT DECISIONS

The Official Gazette: Službeni glasnik RS
The Official Digest: X
Legal Journals: X
Electronic Publishing: X

SOURCES:

https://www.ilo.org/dyn/natlex/docs/ELECTRONIC/74694/119555/F838981147/SRB74694%20Eng.pdf
http://www.ustavni.sud.rs/page/home/en-GB

(160)

DOSSIER OF THE CONSTITUTIONAL COURT OF THE REPUBLIC OF SEYCHELLES

STATE: Republic of Seychelles
TITLE: Constitutional Court
YEAR OF FOUNDATION: 1903/1976/1993
SEAT: Victoria

I. CHRONICLE

Date and context of establishment 1903/1976/1993
Position in the hierarchy of courts
Supreme Court as Constitutional Court
Article 129 of the Constitution. (1) The jurisdiction and powers of the Supreme Court in respect of matters relating to the application, contravention, enforcement or interpretation of the Constitution shall be exercised by not less than two Judges sitting together.

> (2) Where two or more Judges sit together for the purposes of clause (1), the most senior of the Judges shall preside.
> (3) Any reference to the Constitutional Court in this Constitution shall be a reference to the Court sitting under clause(1).

II. STANDARD LEGAL REFERENCE

Constitution 1993

III. COMPOSITION AND ORGANIZATION

The Constitutional Court of Seychelles does not have its own premises. Its hearings take place in court room no.1 of the Supreme Court Building in Victoria. It is presided over by any 3 of the Supreme Court Judges.

Composition

The number of judges: 3

IV. POWERS

Constitutional court review

Constitutional questions before the Constitutional Court

Article 130 of the Constitution. (1) A person who alleges that any provisions of this Constitution, other than a provision of Chapter III, has been contravened and that the person's interest is being or is likely to be affected by the contravention may, subject to this article, apply to the Constitutional Court for redress.

(2) The Constitutional Court may decline to entertain an application under clause (1) where the Court is satisfied that the applicant has obtained redress for the contravention under any law and where the applicant has obtained redress in the Constitutional Court for any matter for which an application may be made under clause (1), a court shall not entertain any application for redress for such matter except on appeal from a decision of such court.

(3) Where the Constitutional Court on an application under clause (1) is satisfied that adequate means of redress for the contravention alleged are or have been available to the person concerned in any other court under any other law, the Court may hear the application or transfer the application to the appropriate court for grant of redress in accordance with law.

(4) Upon hearing an application under clause (1), the Constitutional Court may -

(a) declare any act or omission which is the subject of the application to be a contravention of this Constitution;

(b) declare any law or the provision of any law which contravenes this Constitution to be void;

(c) grant any remedy available to the Supreme Court against any person or authority which is the subject of the application or which is a party to any proceedings before the Constitutional Court, as the Court considers appropriate.

(5) Where the Constitutional Court makes a declaration under clause 4(b), the Court shall, subject to any decision in appeal therefrom, send a copy of the declaration to the President and the Speaker.

(6) Where in the course of any proceedings in any court, other than the Court of Appeal or the Supreme Court sitting as the Constitutional Court, or tribunal, a question arises with regard to whether there has been or is likely to be a contravention of this Constitution, other than Chapter III, the court or tribunal shall, if it is satisfied that the question is not frivolous or vexatious or has not already been the subject of a decision of the Constitutional Court or the Court of

Appeal, immediately adjourn the proceedings and refer the question for determination by the Constitutional Court.

(7) Where in an application under clause (1) or where a matter is referred to the Constitutional Court under clause (6), the person alleging the contravention or risk of contravention establishes a prima facie case, the burden of proving that there has not been a contravention or risk of contravention shall, where the allegation is against the State, be on the State.

(8) The Court in which the question referred to in clause (6) arose shall dispose of the case in accordance with the decision of the Constitutional Court, or if that decision is the subject of an appeal, in accordance with the decision of the Court of Appeal.

(9) Nothing in this article confers jurisdiction on the Constitutional Court to hear or determine a matter referred to it under Article 51(3) of the Constitution or Article 82(1) of the Constitution otherwise than upon an application made in accordance with Article 51 of the Constitution or Article 82 of the Constitution.

Standing before the Constitutional Court
State bodies: X
Individuals: X
The Constitutional Court hears petitions regarding breaches, potential or actual, of the Constitution of the Republic of Seychelles. Anyone who feels that their constitutional rights have or is likely to be breached can petition the court for redress. A litigant disatisfied with the decision of the Constitutional Court can appeal to the Court of Appeal.

V. NATURE AND EFFECTS OF DECISIONS

Finality: NO
A litigant disatisfied with the decision of the Constitutional Court can appeal to the Court of Appeal.

SOURCES:

http://greybook.seylii.org/w/se/CAP42#!fragment/zoupio-_Toc465957894/
KGhhc2g6KGNodW5rxIVhbsSHb3JUZXhoOnpvdXBpby1fVG9j
NDY1OTU3ODk0KSxub3Rlc1F1ZXJ5OicnLHNjcm9sbEPEiMSKOiFuxL plYXLEh8SyxLTEtsS4xYfFic-
SHU8SQdELEtl JFTEVWQU5DRSxoYWI6dMSgKSk=

DOSSIER OF THE SUPREME COURT OF THE REPUBLIC OF SIERRA LEONE

STATE: Republic of Sierra Leone
TITLE: The Supreme Court
YEAR OF FOUNDATION: 1991
SEAT: Freetown

I. CHRONICLE

Date and context of establishment: 1991, Constitution 1991
(Act No. 6 of 1991) (amended 2008, 2013)

Position in the hierarchy of courts:
The Supreme Court shall be the final court of appeal in and for Sierra Leone and shall have such appellate and other jurisdiction as may be conferred upon it by this Constitution or any other law (Para. 1 of Article 122 of the Constitution).

II. STANDARD LEGAL REFERENCE

Constitution 1991
(Act No. 6 of 1991) (amended 2008, 2013)

III. COMPOSITION AND ORGANIZATION

Composition
The number of judges:
The Supreme Court is composed of its president, at least four permanent judges and an appropriate number of other judges (Article 121 of the Constitution) - and such other Justices of the Superior Court of Judicature or of Superior Courts in any State practising a body of law similar

to Sierra Leone, not being more in number than the number of Justices of the Supreme Court sitting as such, as the Chief Justice may, for the determination of any particular cause or matter by writing under his hand, request to sit in the Supreme Court for such period as the Chief Justice may specify or until the request is withdrawn.

Electoral/appointment body:
The President shall, acting on the advice of the Judicial and Legal Service Commission and subject to the approval of Parliament, appoint the Chief Justice by warrant under his hand from among persons qualified to hold office as Justice of the Supreme Court (Para. 1 of Article 135 of the Constitution).

The other Judges of the Superior Court of Judicature shall be appointed by the President by warrant under his hand acting on the advice of the Judicial and Legal Service Commission and subject to the approval of Parliament (Para. 2 of Article 135 of the Constitution).

IV. POWERS

Constitutional Court Review
The Supreme Court has original and exclusive jurisdiction in all matters concerning the implementation of the Constitution as well as the power of constitutional review following the model of the American system of diffuse review (Article 124 of the Constitution). The Supreme Court is empowered in all matters relating to the enforcement or interpretation of any provision of this Constitution; and where any question arises whether an enactment was made in excess of the power conferred upon Parliament or any other authority or person by law or under this Constitution.

Additionally, where any question relating to any matter or question as is referred to in above section arises in any proceedings in any Court, other than the Supreme Court, that Court shall stay the proceedings and refer the question of law involved to the Supreme Court for determination; and the Court in which the question arose shall dispose of the case in accordance with the decision of the Supreme Court.

Other forms of human rights protection
The following proceedings may be also initiated before the Supreme Court: habeas corpus, certiorari, mandamus and prohibition (Article 125 of the Constitution). The Constitution also allows the popular complaint (Para. 1 of Article 127 of the Constitution).

Standing before the Constitutional/Supreme Court
State bodies: X

Individuals: X

The following proceedings may be also initiated before the Supreme Court: habeas corpus, certiorari, mandamus and prohibition (Article 125 of the Constitution). The Constitution also allows the popular complaint (Para. 1 of Article 127 of the Constitution).

V. NATURE AND EFFECTS OF DECISIONS

Finality:

The Court decisions are final and indisputable (Article 122 of the Constitution).

SOURCES:

http://www.sierra-leone.org/Laws/constitution1991.pdf

(162)

DOSSIER OF THE SUPREME COURT OF THE REPUBLIC OF SINGAPORE

STATE: Republic of Singapore
TITLE: The Supreme Court
YEAR OF FOUNDATION: 9 January 1970
SEAT: Singapore

I. CHRONICLE

Date and context of establishment: 1970
Constitution 9th August 1965 Original Enactment: S 1/63), amended many times until 2016.

Position in the hierarchy of courts:
Article 94. (1) of the Constitution: The Supreme Court shall consist of the Court of Appeal and the High Court with such jurisdiction and powers as are conferred on those Courts by this Constitution or any written law.

II. STANDARD LEGAL REFERENCE

Constitution 9th August 1965 Original Enactment: S 1/63), amended many times until 2016.

III. COMPOSITION AND ORGANIZATION

Composition
The number of judges:
Electoral/appointment body:
Article 95. (1) of the Constitution: The Chief Justice, the Judges of Appeal and the Judges of the High Court shall be appointed by the President if he, acting in his discretion, concurs with the advice of the Prime Minister.

The Supreme Court Bench consists of the Chief Justice, the Judges of Appeal, and Judges and Judicial Commissioners of the High Court. All members of the Bench are appointed by the President of Singapore if he, acting in his discretion, concurs with the advice of the Prime Minister.

The Court members:

The term of office:

Article 95 (3) of the Constitution: The office of a Judge of the Supreme Court shall not be abolished during his continuance in office.

Article 98 of the Constitution:

Subject to this Article, a person appointed as a Judge of the Supreme Court under Article 95(1) shall hold office until he attains the age of 65 years or such later time not being later than 6 months after he attains that age, as the President may approve.

Administrative autonomy:

Administration of the Supreme Court is managed by its registry,[1] which handles matters such as receiving and storing court documents filed in the court, and ensuring they are transmitted to judges for use during hearings.

IV. POWERS

Exclusion of judicial review has been attempted by the Parliament of Singapore to protect the exercise of executive power. Typically, this has been done though the insertion of finality or total ouster clauses into Acts of Parliament, or by wording powers conferred by Acts on decision-makers subjectively. Finality clauses are generally viewed restrictively by courts in the United Kingdom. The courts there have taken the view that such clauses are, subject to some exceptions, not effective in denying or restricting the extent to which the courts are able to exercise judicial review. In contrast, Singapore cases suggest that ouster clauses cannot prevent the High Court from exercising supervisory jurisdiction over the exercise of executive power where authorities have committed jurisdictional errors of law, but are effective against non-jurisdictional errors of law.

V. NATURE AND EFFECTS OF DECISIONS

SOURCE:

http://www.servat.unibe.ch/icl/sn__indx.html

DOSSIER OF THE CONSTITUTIONAL COURT* OF THE REPUBLIC OF SLOVAKIA

STATE: Republic of Slovakia
TITLE: The Constitutional Court
YEAR OF FOUNDATION: 1. 9. 1992
SEAT: Košice

I. CHRONICLE

Date and context of establishment:
The Constitutional Court of the Slovak Republic was established by Constitution of the Slovak Republic No. 460/1992.

Position in the hierarchy of courts :
Article 124 of the Constitution
The Constitutional Court shall be an independent judicial authority vested with the mandate to protect the constutionality.

II. STANDARD LEGAL REFERENCE

Constitution of the Slovak Republic (amendments 1998-2014)

III. COMPOSITION AND ORGANIZATION

Composition
The number of judges:
(Para. 1 of Article 134 of the Constitution)The Constitutional Court shall be composed of thirteen judges.

Electoral/appointment body:

Para. 2 of Article 134 of the Constitution) The judges of the Constitutional Court shall be appointed by the President of the Slovak Republic for a twelve-year term on a proposal of the National Council of the Slovak Republic. The National Council of the Slovak Republic shall propose double the number of candidates for judges that shall be appointed by the President of the Slovak Republic.

The Court members:
The term of office: 12
The Court President:
The term of office:
Organization
Administrative autonomy:
The tasks connected with the organisational, personal, administrative and technical aspects of the activity of the Constitutional Court are carried out by the Chancellery of the Constitutional Court. Details on the organisation and activity of the Chancellery of the Constitutional Court and on the status of its staff are set out in the Organisation schedule, approved by the Plenary Session of the Constitutional Court.

The budget:
The Constitutional Court manages its finances from the state budget as an independent budget category in accordance with law No. 523/2004 Coll. on budgetary rules as amended.

IV. POWERS

Constitutional Court Review

Preventive review:

The Constitutional Court shall not decide on conformity of a draft law or aproposal of other generally binding legal regulation with the Constitution, with an international treaty that was promulgated in the manner laid down by a law or with the constitutional law.

Article 125a of the Constitution:

(1) The Constitutional Court shall decide on the conformity of negotiated international treaties to which the assent of the National Council of the Slovak Republic with the Constitution and constitutional law is necessary.

(2) The President of the Slovak Republic or the Government may submit a proposal for a decision pursuant to paragraph 1 to the Constitutional Court prior to the presentation of a negotiated international treaty for discussion of the National Council of the Slovak Republic.

(3) The Constitutional Court shall decide on a proposal pursuant to paragraph 2 within a period laid down by a law; if the Constitutional Court holds in its decision that the international treaty is not in conformity with the Constitution or constitutional law, such international treaty cannot be ratified.

A posteriori review:

Abstract review:

The Constitutional Court shall decide on the conformity of

a) laws with the Constitution, constitutional laws and international treaties to which the National Council of the Slovak Republic has expressed its assent and which were ratified and promulgated in the manner laid down by a law,

b) government regulations, generally binding legal regulations of Ministries and other central state administration bodies with the Constitution, with constitutional laws, with international treaties to which the National Council of the Slovak Republic has expressed its assent and which were ratified and promulgated in the manner laid down by a law and with laws,

c) generally binding regulations pursuant to Article 68 of the Constitution, with the Constitution, with constitutional laws and with international treaties to which the National Council of the Slovak Republic has expressed its assent and which were ratified and promulgated in the manner laid down by a law, save another court shall decide on them,

d) generally binding legal regulations of the local bodies of state administration and generally binding regulations of the bodies of territorial self-administration pursuant to Article 71 para. 2 of the Constitution, with the Constitution, with constitutional laws, with international treaties promulgated in the manner laid down by a law, with laws, with government regulations and with generally binding legal regulations of Ministries and other central state administration bodies, save another court shall decide on them.

Concrete review: X

Other powers

Constitutional complaints:

Article 127 of the Constitution

(1) The Constitutional Court shall decide on complaints of natural persons or legal persons if they are pleading the infringement of their fundamental rights or freedoms, or human rights and fundamental freedoms resulting from the international treaty which has been ratified by the Slovak Republic and promulgated in the manner laid down by a law, save another court shall decide on protection of these rights and freedoms.

Jurisdictional disputes:

Article 126 of the Constitution

The Constitutional Court shall decide disputes over competency between the central state administration bodies save a law provides, that these disputes are to be decided by another state authority.

The unconstitutionality of acts and activities of political parties:

The Constitutional Court shall decide whether a decision dissolving a political party or movement or suspending political activities thereof is in conformity with the constitutional laws and other laws.

Charges against the President of the Republic:

The Constitutional Court shall decide on a prosecution by the National Council of the Slovak Republic against the President of the Slovak Republic in matters of wilful infringement of the Constitution or treason.

Electoral matters:

The Constitutional Court shall decide on a complaint against decision verifying or rejecting verification of the mandate of a Member of Parliament.

(2) The Constitutional Court shall decide whether the election of the President of the Slovak Republic, the elections to the National Council of the Slovak Republic, and the elections to local self-administration bodies have been held in conformity with the Constitution and the law.

Referendums:

The Constitutional Court shall decide on whether the subject of a referendumto be declared upon a petition of citizens or a resolution of the National Council of the Slovak Republic according to Article 95, para. 1 of the Constitution is in conformity with the Constitution or constitutional law.

Other matters with which the Court is charged by the Constitution or statute:

Article 127a of the Constitution

The Constitutional Court shall decide on complaints of the bodies of territorial self-administration against unconstitutional or unlawful decision or against other unconstitutional or unlawful action into the matters of self-administration, save another court shall decide on its protection.

Article 128 of the Constitution

The Constitutional Court shall give an interpretation of the Constitution or constitutional law if the matter is disputable. The judgement of the Constitutional Court on the interpretation of the Constitution or constitutional law shall be promulgated in the manner laid down for the promulgation of laws. The interpretation is generally binding from the date of its promulgation.

The Constitutional Court shall decide on whether a decision on declaring an exceptional state or an emergency state and other decisions connected to this decision were issued in conformity with the Constitution and constitutional law.

The Constitutional Court shall decide on complaints against the result of a referendum and complaint against the result of a plebiscite on the recall of President of the Slovak Republic.

Standing before the Constitutional Court

State bodies: Yes

Individuals: Yes

Article 130 of the Constitution

(1) The Constitutional Court shall commence proceedings upon a motion submitted by:

a) at least one-fifth of all Members of Parliament,

b) the President of the Slovak Republic,

c) the Government of the Slovak Republic,

d) a court,

e) the Attorney General and

f) everyone whose right is to be adjudicated in cases as provided in Articles. 127 and 127a of the Constitution

V. NATURE AND EFFECTS OF DECISIONS

Finality:

(Article 133 of the Constitution) There is no possibility of lodging an appeal against a decision of the Constitutional Court.

Binding force:

Erga omnes:

The valid judgement of the Constitutional Court shall be generally binding.

SOURCES:

https://en.wikipedia.org/wiki/Constitution_of_Slovakia

DOSSIER OF THE CONSTITUTIONAL COURT OF THE REPUBLIC OF SLOVENIA

STATE: Republic of Slovenia
TITLE: The Constitutional Court of the Republic of Slovenia
YEAR OF FOUNDATION: 5. 6. 1963, remodeled 1991
SEAT: Ljubljana

I. CHRONICLE

Date and context of establishment 1963;
The Constitution of the Socialist Republic of Slovenia of 1963 (Official Gazette SRS, No. 10/63) envisaged the first Slovenian (the then Republican) Constitutional Court; the former system of the constitutional review was modified and remodeled by the Constitution of the Republic of Slovenia (Official Gazette RS, Nos. 33/91, 42/97, 66/00, 24/03, 69/04, 68/06, 47/13, 75/16).

Position in the hierarchy of courts:
Article 1(1) of the Constitutional Court Act (Official Gazette RS, Nos. 15/94, 51/07, 64/07, 109/12) determines the position of the Constitutional Court considering the principle of separation of powers to the legislative, executive and judicial power[70]. Regarding the protection of constitutionality and legality as well as the protection of human rights and fundamental freedoms, the Constitutional Court has been acting as the highest body.

70 The constitutional position of the current Constitutional Court as an independent and autonomous body exercising constitutional review is regulated in more detail by the *Constitutional Court Act*, which entered into force on 2 April 1994. The amendments to the *Constitutional Court Act (Official Gazette RS*, No. 51/07 – ZUstS-A) entered into force on 15 July 2007. Later on the next amendment followed: *Official Gazette RS*, No. 109/12 - ZUstS-B). The first official consolidated text of the *Constitutional Court Act* was published in the *Official Gazette of the Republic of Slovenia*, No. 64/07. In the period between the adoption of the *Constitution* of 1991 and the adoption of the *Constitutional Court Act* of 1994 (*Official Gazette RS*, No. 15/94) the Constitutional Court worked on the basis of the former *Procedure Before the Constitutional Court Act* (*Official Gazette SRS*, Nos. 39/74 and 28/76), considering provisions of the *Constitutional Act* for the Implementation of the *Constitution of the Republic of Slovenia* (*Official Gazette* RS, No. 33/91).

II. STANDARD LEGAL REFERENCE

Constitution 1991, amendments 1997-2016

III. COMPOSITION AND ORGANIZATION

Composition
The number of judges: 9
Electoral/appointment body:
the National Assembly (based on the State President's list of candidates)

The Court members:
The term of office: 9
The Court President:
The term of office: (2X 3)
Organization
Administrative autonomy: X
The budget: Independent proponent (Article 8 of the Constitutional Court Act)

IV. POWERS

Constitutional Court Review

Preventive review:

Beside the prevailing system of repressive constitutional review, the preventive constitutional review has been adopted by the Constitutional Court but only in the adoption process for international agreements. In this case the Slovenian Constitutional Court performs a consultative function, although its opinion is obligatory, which gives to such opinions the force of decision (Article 160(2), Constitution; Article 70, Constitutional Court Act).

A posteriori review:
Abstract review: X
Concrete review: X

In the event that a court, in deciding upon any matter, concludes that a statute which it must apply is unconstitutional, it must stay the proceeding and refer the issue of the constitutional validity of the statute to the Constitutional Court. The original proceeding in the court may only be continued after the Constitutional Court has handed down its decision.

Other powers
Constitutional complaints: X
Jurisdictional disputes: X
The unconstitutionality of acts and activities of political parties: X
Charges against the President of the Republic: X
Charges against the Prime Minister or against any Minister of State: X
Electoral matters: X
Referendums: X
Other matters with which the Court is charged by the Constitution or statute: X
Standing before the Constitutional Court
State bodies: X
Individuals: X
Anyone (a natural person and/or a legal entity) who demonstrate legal interest may request the individual initiation of proceedings before the Constitutional Court (Article 162(2), Constitution; Article 24, Constitutional Court Act). Additionally, bodies, specified in Article 23.a of the Constitutional Court Act, may request the abstract (National Assembly, one third of deputies, National Council, Government) or concrete constitutional review (Ombudsman, Information commissioner, Bank of Slovenia, Court of Audit, State attorney general, representative body of local community, representative association of local community, national representative trade union – in connection with the concrete case they are dealing with). These bodies do not need to demonstrate their legal interest for commencing constitutional review.

V. NATURE AND EFFECTS OF DECISIONS

Finality: x
Binding force: x
Erga omnes: (abstract review decisions)x
Inter partes: (constitutional complaint decisions)x
Ex officio:
The Constitutional Court, though, is not the primary initiator of proceedings, because the initiation of proceedings still depends on an outside petitioner. However, as soon as the application has been filed with the Constitutional Court, the latter is free to act with reference to its opinion

on the integrity of the specific legal area, its involvement, and the reciprocal dependence of the respective legal measures[71].

71 According to Article 30 of the *Constitutional Court Act*, when deciding on the constitutionality and legality of statutes or general acts, including those issued in view of exercising public powers, the Slovenian Constitutional Court is not *in merito* bound by the proposal in the request or petition. The Constitutional Court may also evaluate the constitutionality and legality of other provisions of this or some other general act whereof the constitutionality or legality have not been challenged, if such provisions are mutually related or if this is absolutely necessary to resolve the case. According to Article 59(2) of the *Constitutional Court Act*, if the Constitutional Court in deciding a constitutional complaint, establishes that an individual act, thus retroactively abrogated, derived from an unconstitutional general act or general act issued for the exercise of public powers, it may abrogate such act with retroactive or prospective effect. When deciding a case relating to jurisdictional disputes, the Constitutional Court may issue a decision as to which body is empowered, and may also abrogate or annul, the general act, or the general act issued for the exercise of public powers, whereof unconstitutionality or illegality has been established (Article 60(4), *Constitutional Court Act*). AN: word 'deputies' should be replaced by 'judges' according to the amendment of the Constitution No. 146-IV 30.1.2014

History, http://www.gjk.gov.al/web/History_97_2.php

Constitutionnet - Constitutional history of Algeria, http://www.constitutionnet.org/country/constitutional-history-algeria

Ibid.

Annual Reports of the Constitutional Court, http://www.tribunalconstitucional.ad/memories

Constitutional history of Angola, http://www.constitutionnet.org/country/constitutional-history-angola

Ibid.

Nexus, Commonwealth Network, Legal System, http://www.commonwealthofnations.org/sectors-antigua_and_barbuda/business/legal/.

The Eastern Caribbean Supreme Court, https://www.eccourts.org/.

Nexus, Commonwealth Network, Legal System, http://www.commonwealthofnations.org/sectors-antigua_and_barbuda/business/legal/.

El tribunal, http://www.csjn.gov.ar/institucional/historia-de-la-corte-suprema/el-tribunal.

Los jueces de la corte suprema, http://www.csjn.gov.ar/institucional/historia-de-la-corte-suprema/los-jueces-de-la-corte.

Ibid.

Ibid.

Ibid.

Ibid.

Ibid.

The description of the Constitutional Court of the Republic of Armenia, http://concourt.am/english/cc/history.htm

Ibid.

High Court of Australia – Fact sheet 221, http://www.naa.gov.au/collection/fact-sheets/fs221.aspx.

VFGH, The History of the Constitutional Court: An Overview, https://www.vfgh.gv.at/verfassungsgerichtshof/geschichte/history_overview.en.html

The Constitutional Court of the Republic of Azerbaijan, About CC, http://www.constcourt.gov.az/cat/1

Ibid.

Ibid.

Ibid.

Ibid.

Ibid.

Ibid.

Ibid.

Ivory Coast court validates referendum on new constitution, https://www.reuters.com/ Article/us-ivorycoast-referendum/ivory-coast-court-validates-referendum-on-new-constitution-idUSKBN12Z2NC.

Creating the Republic of Croatia and establishing the constitutional court of the Republic of Croatia, https://www.usud.hr/en/history-and-development-croatian-constitutional-judicature.

Cuban Memories: the Cuban Constitution of 1940, then and today . Cuban Heritage Collection. University of Miami Libraries, http://library.miami.edu/chc/2010/10/14/cuban-memories-the-cuban-constitution-of-1940-then-and-today/.

Haken Ted, Celaya Miriam, Castellanos Dimas, Cuba, ABC-CLIO, 2013, p. 100-103.

CIA, The World Factbook, https://www.cia.gov/library/publications/the-world-factbook/fields/2094.html

Ibid.

Judicial system of Cuba, https://en.wikipedia.org/wiki/Judicial_system_of_Cuba

Haken Ted, Celaya Miriam, Castellanos Dimas, Cuba, ABC-CLIO, 2013, p. 102.

http://www.supremecourt.gov.cy/judicial/sc.nsf/DMLfaq_en/DMLfaq_en?OpenDocument

http://www.supremecourt.gov.cy/judicial/sc.nsf/DMLSCourt_en/DMLSCourt_en?OpenDocument

http://www.usoud.cz/en/history/

http://www.usoud.cz/en/history/

The Danish Supreme Court is not mentioned in its constitution.

http://www.supremecourt.dk/about/history/Pages/default.aspx

http://www.domstol.dk/om/otherlanguages/english/thedanishjudicialsystem/thesupremecourt/Pages/default.aspx

http://www.supremecourt.dk/about/history/Pages/default.aspx

http://www.domstol.dk/om/publikationer/HtmlPublikationer/Profil/Profilbrochure%20-%20UK/kap03.html

http://www.supremecourt.dk/about/staff/Pages/default.aspx

http://www.supremecourt.dk/about/staff/Pages/default.aspx

Commonwealth of Dominica is a part of the Eastern Caribbean Supreme Court. (https://www.eccourts.org/structure-of-the-court/)

https://www.eccourts.org/brief-history-of-the-court/

https://www.eccourts.org/brief-history-of-the-court/

https://www.eccourts.org/brief-history-of-the-court/

https://www.eccourts.org/structure-of-the-court/

http://www.sis.gov.eg/En/Templates/ Articles/tmp Articles.aspx?CatID=250#

http://www.csj.gob.sv/idioma.html

http://www.nc.ee/?id=181

http://www.nc.ee/?id=181

http://www.judiciary.gov.fj/

http://korkeinoikeus.fi/en/index/supremecourt/premises.html

http://www.conseil-constitutionnel.fr/conseil-constitutionnel/english/presentation/general-presentation/general-presentation.25739.html

http://www.conseil-constitutionnel.fr/conseil-constitutionnel/english/presentation/general-presentation/general-presentation.25739.html

http://www.judiciary.gov.gm/contact-us

http://www.constcourt.ge/en/court/brief-history

http://www.constcourt.ge/en/court/brief-history

http://www.bundesverfassungsgericht.de/EN/Gebaeude/gebaeude_node.html;jsessionid=020F2476A94963DF9DC3E7C2EE11A823.2_cid392

Grenada is a part of the Eastern Caribbean Supreme Court. (https://www.eccourts.org/structure-of-the-court/)

https://www.eccourts.org/brief-history-of-the-court/

https://www.eccourts.org/brief-history-of-the-court/

https://www.eccourts.org/brief-history-of-the-court/

https://www.eccourts.org/structure-of-the-court/

The constitutional position of the current Constitutional Court as an independent and autonomous body exercising constitutional review is regulated in more detail by the *Constitutional Court Act*, which entered into force on 2 April 1994. The amendments to the *Constitutional Court Act* (*Official Gazette RS*, No. 51/07 – ZUstS-A) entered into force on 15 July 2007. Later on the next amendment followed: *Official Gazette RS*, No. 109/12 - ZUstS-B). The first official consolidated text of the *Constitutional Court Act* was published in the *Official Gazette of the Republic of Slovenia*, No. 64/07. In the period between the adoption of the *Constitution* of 1991 and the adoption of the *Constitutional Court Act* of 1994 (*Official Gazette RS*, No. 15/94) the

The legislative omissions:

Article 48 of the Constitutional Court Act X

Obligatory opinions on the conformity of international treaties with the Constitution:

Beside the prevailing system of repressive constitutional review, the preventive constitutional review has been adopted by the Constitutional Court but only in the adoption process for international agreements. In this case the Slovenian Constitutional Court performs a consultative function, although its opinion is obligatory, which gives to such opinions the force of decision (Article 160(2), Constitution; Article 70, Constitutional Court Act).X

SOURCES:

www.us-rs.si

Constitutional Court worked on the basis of the former *Procedure Before the Constitutional Court Act* (*Official Gazette SRS*, Nos. 39/74 and 28/76), considering provisions of the *Constitutional Act* for the Implementation of the *Constitution of the Republic of Slovenia* (*Official Gazette RS*, No. 33/91).

According to Article 30 of the *Constitutional Court Act*, when deciding on the constitutionality and legality of statutes or general acts, including those issued in view of exercising public powers, the Slovenian Constitutional Court is not *in merito* bound by the proposal in the request or petition. The Constitutional Court may also evaluate the constitutionality and legality of other provisions of this or some other general act whereof the constitutionality or legality have not been challenged, if such provisions are mutually related or if this is absolutely necessary to resolve the case. According to Article 59(2) of the *Constitutional Court Act*, if the Constitutional Court in deciding a constitutional complaint, establishes that an individual act, thus retroactively abrogated, derived from an unconstitutional general act or general act issued for the exercise of public powers, it may abrogate such act with retroactive or prospective effect. When deciding a case relating to jurisdictional disputes, the Constitutional Court may issue a decision as to which body is empowered, and may also abrogate or annul, the general act, or the general act issued for the exercise of public powers, whereof unconstitutionality or illegality.

(165)

DOSSIER OF THE HIGH COURT OF SOLOMON ISLANDS

STATE: Solomon Islands
TITLE: The High Court
YEAR OF FOUNDATION: 31. 5. 1978
SEAT: Honiara

I. CHRONICLE

Date and context of establishment:
1978 NO. 783, The Solomon Islands Independence Order 1978

Position in the hierarchy of courts:
The High Court shall have jurisdiction, in any application made by any person in pursuance of the preceding subsection or in any other proceedings lawfully brought before the Court, to determine whether any provision of this Constitution (other than Chapter II) has been contravened.

II. STANDARD LEGAL REFERENCE

Constitution 1978, rev. 2009

III. COMPOSITION AND ORGANIZATION

Composition
The number of judges:
Electoral/appointment body:
Article 78 of the Constitution.-(1) The Chief Justice shall be appointed by the Governor-General, acting in accordance with the advice of the Judicial and Legal Service Commission.

(2) The puisne judges shall be appointed by the Governor-General, acting in accordance with the advice of the Judicial and Legal Service Commission.

The Court members:

The term of office:

A judge of the High Court shall hold office until he attains the age of sixty years.

IV. POWERS

Constitutional Court Review

A posteriori review:

Concrete review:

The High Court shall have jurisdiction, in any application made by any person in pursuance of the preceding subsection or in any other proceedings lawfully brought before the Court, to determine whether any provision of this Constitution (other than Chapter II) has been contravened.

Other powers

Constitutional complaints:

If any person alleges that any provision of this Constitution (other than Chapter II) has been contravened and that his interests are being or are likely to be affected by such contravention, then, without prejudice to any other action with respect to the same matter which is lawfully available, that person may apply to the High Court for a declaration and for relief under this section.

Standing before the Constitutional/High Court

State bodies: X

Individuals:

If any person alleges that any provision of this Constitution (other than Chapter II) has been contravened and that his interests are being or are likely to be affected by such contravention, then, without prejudice to any other action with respect to the same matter which is lawfully available, that person may apply to the High Court for a declaration and for relief under this section.

V. NATURE AND EFFECTS OF DECISIONS

SOURCES:

https://aceproject.org/ero-en/regions/pacific/SB/Solomon%20Islands%20Constitution%201978.pdf/view

(166)

DOSSIER OF THE CONSTITUTIONAL COURT OF THE FEDERAL REPUBLIC OF SOMALIA

STATE: The Federal Republic of Somalia
TITLE: The Constitutional Court
YEAR OF FOUNDATION: 1. 8. 2012 (Provisional Constitution)
SEAT: Mogadishu

I. CHRONICLE

Date and context of establishment:
1 August 2012, Provisional Constitution

Position in the hierarchy of courts:
The national court structure shall be of three levels, which are: (a) The Constitutional Court;

(b) The Federal Government level courts;

(c) The Federal Member State level courts. The highest court at the Federal Government level shall be the Federal High Court, whilst the highest court at the Federal Member State level shall be the Federal Member State High Court.

Any law, or administrative action that is contrary to the Constitution may be invalidated by the Constitutional Court, which has the authority to do so in accordance with this Constitution.

Legislation that has been challenged, in accordance with Clause 1 and 2 of this Article, must be presented to, and decided upon, only by the Constitutional Court.

II. STANDARD LEGAL REFERENCE

Constitution (provisional) of 2012

III. COMPOSITION AND ORGANIZATION

Composition

The number of judges:

This Constitution establishes the Constitutional Court, which is composed of five (5) Judges including the Chief Judge and the Deputy Chief Judge.

Electoral/appointment body:

The Judicial Service Commission shall nominate as judge of the Constitutional Court only persons of high integrity, with appropriate qualifications in law and Shari'a, and who are each highly competent in Constitutional matters.

(3) The Judicial Service Commission shall propose to the House of the People the person they want to be appointed as a Constitutional judge.

(4) If the House of the People of the Federal Parliament approves the name proposed in accordance with Clause 3 of this Article, the President of the Federal Republic shall appoint that Person as a judge of the Constitutional Court.

(5) From amongst their members, the Constitutional Court judges shall appoint the Chief Judge and Deputy Chief Judge.

IV. POWERS

Constitutional Court Review

Preventive review:

The Constitutional Court shall have the following exclusive powers:

Upon request from a member of the Council of Ministers, a committee from either one of the Houses, or ten members of either House of the Federal Parliament, to review draft legislation, and determine its compatibility with the Constitution;

A posteriori review:

Abstract review:

To hear and decide cases as stipulated in Article 86 of the Constitution concerning challenges to the constitutionality of a law passed by the Federal Parliament;

Concrete review:

If a case is presented before a court and the case concerns a constitutional matter, the court may refer the case to the Constitutional Court.

(a) Any court with judicial powers can decide on whether a matter brought before it is a constitutional matter or not, if this will not contradict the exclusive powers of the Constitutional Court, as stipulated in Article 109C of the Constitution;

(b) The Constitutional Court is the final authority in constitutional matters;

(c) The Constitutional Court shall have sole jurisdiction on matters of interpretation of the Constitution which have not arisen out of court litigation;

Other powers

Jurisdictional disputes:

To resolve any disputes between the Federal Government and the Federal Member State governments, or among the Federal Member State governments;

To hear and decide cases arising out of disputes between organs of the Federal Government, concerning their respective constitutional powers and duties;

Charges against the President of the Republic:

To hear and decide cases arising in terms of Article 92 of the Constitution concerning the impeachment trials of the President.

The motion for dismissing the President of the Federal Republic of Somalia may be introduced by no less than one-third (1/3) of the total membership of the House of the People of the Federal Parliament, and may be presented to the Constitutional Court, which shall preside over the case to see whether it has legal grounds.

Other matters with which the Court is charged by the Constitution or statute:

To hear and decide on cases that have been submitted to the Constitutional court resulting from matters stated in Article 109 (2) (c) of the Constitution, concerning matters of interpretation of the Constitution not arising out of Court litigation;

Standing before the Constitutional Court

State bodies: X

Individuals: X

(d) Any individual or group, or the government may submit a reference application directly to the Constitutional Court on matters concerning the public interest.

V. NATURE AND EFFECTS OF DECISIONS

The Constitutional Court shall determine the date from which the decision to void legislation shall come into effect.

In the case of legislation held to be unconstitutional, except in terms of Paragraph (b) of this Clause, taking into account the effect of the decision on the date of invalidation on the stakeholders and other social interests, the constitutional court may declare the legislation invalid from the time of enactment, or from the time of the judgment, or, to enable appropriate action pending invalidity, from a date specified in the future.

In the case of criminal legislation, if the effect of declaring the law invalid from the enactment date would be of benefit to a person who has been convicted through this unconstitutional legislation, the invalidity must be from the time of enactment.

SOURCES:

http://unpos.unmissions.org/LinkClick.aspx?fileticket=RkJTOSpoMME=

(167)

DOSSIER OF THE CONSTITUTIONAL COURT OF THE REPUBLIC OF SOUTH AFRICA

STATE: Republic of South Africa
TITLE: The Constitutional Court of the Republic of South Africa
YEAR OF FOUNDATION: 27. 4. 1994 (based on the 1993 Constitution), (new Constitution 1996, Amendments 1996-2016)
SEAT: Johannesburg

I. CHRONICLE

Date and context of establishment
The Constitutional Court was established in 1994 by South Africa's first democratic constitution - the interim constitution of 1993. The Court, the key institution of our constitutional democracy, continues to function under the final Constitution of 1996 of 18 December 1996, amended 1998 1999, 2001, 2002, 2003, 2005, 2007, 2008, 2009, 2013

Position in the hierarchy of courts:
The 1993 constitution, agreed upon at multiparty talks, ushered in a legal order based on the concept of constitutional supremacy. From 27 April 1994, the interim constitution became the law's touchstone. And the 11-person court it established became the highest legal authority in the land in all constitutional matters.

II. STANDARD LEGAL REFERENCE

1993 Constitution), (new Constitution 1996, Amendments 1996-2016)

III. COMPOSITION AND ORGANIZATION

Composition

The number of judges:

The Constitutional Court consists of the Chief Justice of South Africa, the Deputy Chief Justice and nine other judges.

Electoral/appointment body:

The other judges of the Constitutional Court are appointed by the President, as head of the national executive, after consulting the Chief Justice and the leaders of parties represented in the National Assembly

IV. POWERS

Constitutional Court Review

Preventive review:

If, after reconsideration, a Bill fully accommodates the President's reservations, the President must assent to and sign the Bill; if not, the President must either -

(a) assent to and sign the Bill; or (b) refer it to the Constitutional Court for a decision on its constitutionality. If, after reconsideration, a Bill fully accommodates the Premier's reservations, the Premier must assent to and sign the Bill; if not, the Premier must either -

(a) assent to and sign the Bill; or (b) refer it to the Constitutional Court for a decision on its constitutionality.

A posteriori review:

Abstract review:

The Constitutional Court

a. is the highest court in all constitutional matters;

b. may decide only constitutional matters, and issues connected with decisions on constitutional matters; and

c. makes the final decision whether a matter is a constitutional matter or whether an issue is connected with a decision on a constitutional matter.

Only the Constitutional Court may

a. decide disputes between organs of state in the national or provincial sphere concerning the constitutional status, powers or functions of any of those organs of state;

b. decide on the constitutionality of any parliamentary or provincial Bill, but may do so only in the circumstances anticipated in section 79 or 121of the Constitution;

c. decide applications envisaged in section 80 or 122 of the Constitution;

d. decide on the constitutionality of any amendment to the Constitution;

e. decide that Parliament or the President has failed to fulfil a constitutional obligation; or

f. certify a provincial constitution in terms of section 144 of the Constitution.

The Constitutional Court makes the final decision whether an Act of Parliament, a provincial Act or conduct of the President is constitutional, and must confirm any order of invalidity made by the Supreme Court of Appeal, a High Court, or a court of similar status, before that order has any force.

A constitutional matter includes any issue involving the interpretation, protection or enforcement of the Constitution.

If a provincial legislature has passed or amended a constitution, the Speaker of the legislature must submit the text of the constitution or constitutional amendment to the Constitutional Court for certification.

Concrete review:

The High Court of South Africa may decide— any constitutional matter except a matter that— (i) the Constitutional Court has agreed to hear directly in terms of section 167(6)(a) of the Constitution;

The Supreme Court of Appeal, the High Court of South Africa or a court of similar status may make an order concerning the constitutional validity of an Act of Parliament, a provincial Act or any conduct of the President, but an order of constitutional invalidity has no force unless it is confirmed by the Constitutional Court.

A court which makes an order of constitutional invalidity may grant a temporary interdict or other temporary relief to a party, or may adjourn the proceedings, pending a decision of the Constitutional Court on the validity of that Act or conduct.

(c) National legislation must provide for the referral of an order of constitutional invalidity to the Constitutional Court.

(d) Any person or organ of state with a sufficient interest may appeal, or apply, directly to the Constitutional Court to confirm or vary an order of constitutional invalidity by a court in terms of this subsection.

Other powers

Constitutional complaints:

National legislation or the rules of the Constitutional Court must allow a person, when it is in the interests of justice and with leave of the Constitutional Court

a. to bring a matter directly to the Constitutional Court; or

b. to appeal directly to the Constitutional Court from any other court.

Other matters with which the Court is charged by the Constitution or statute:
The signed copy of an Act of Parliament (or a provincial Act or a provincial Constitution) of is conclusive evidence of the provisions of that Act and, after publication, must be entrusted to the Constitutional Court for safekeeping.

Other forms of human rights protection

Standing before the Constitutional Court
State bodies:
(1) Members of the National Assembly may apply to the Constitutional Court for an order declaring that all or part of an Act of Parliament is unconstitutional.
(2) An application—
(a) must be supported by at least one third of the members of the National Assembly; and
(b) must be made within 30 days of the date on which the President assented to and signed the Act.
(3) The Constitutional Court may order that all or part of an Act that is the subject of an application in terms of subsection (1) has no force until the Court has decided the application if—
(a) the interests of justice require this; and
(b) the application has a reasonable prospect of success.
(4) If an application is unsuccessful, and did not have a reasonable prospect of success, the Constitutional Court may order the applicants to pay costs.

Members of the National Assembly may apply to the Constitutional Court for an order declaring that all or part of an Act of Parliament is unconstitutional. Members of a provincial legislature may apply to the Constitutional Court for an order declaring that all or part of a provincial Act is unconstitutional. If an application is unsuccessful, and did not have a reasonable prospect of success, the Constitutional Court may order the applicants to pay costs.

The President is responsible for— referring a Bill to the Constitutional Court for a decision on the Bill's constitutionality;

The Premier of a province, If, after reconsideration, a Bill fully accommodates the Premier's reservations, the Premier must assent to and sign the Bill; if not, the Premier must either— refer it to the Constitutional Court for a decision on its constitutionality.
(3) If the Constitutional Court decides that the Bill is constitutional, the Premier must assent to and sign it.

Members of a provincial legislature may apply to the Constitutional Court for an order declaring that all or part of a provincial Act is unconstitutional. If an application is unsuccessful, and did not have a reasonable prospect of success, the Constitutional Court may order the applicants to pay costs.

If a provincial legislature has passed or amended a constitution, the Speaker of the legislature must submit the text of the constitution or constitutional amendment to the Constitutional Court for certification.

Individuals:
National legislation or the rules of the Constitutional Court must allow a person, when it is in the interests of justice and with leave of the Constitutional Court

a. to bring a matter directly to the Constitutional Court; or

b. to appeal directly to the Constitutional Court from any other court.

V. NATURE AND EFFECTS OF DECISIONS

Finality: X
Binding force: X

SOURCES:

http://www.gov.za/documents/constitution/constitution-Republic-South-Africa-1996-1

(168)

DOSSIER OF THE CONSTITUTIONAL COURT OF THE REPUBLIC OF SOUTH KOREA (KOREA)

STATE: Republic of South Korea
TITLE: The Constitutional Court of the Republic of South Korea
YEAR OF FOUNDATION: 1988
SEAT: Seul

I. CHRONICLE

Date and context of establishment
Established and proclaimed on July 17, 1948, Founding Constitution stated in Chapter 5: "When the constitutionality of a law is at issue in a trial, the court shall request a decision of the Constitutional Committee, and shall rule according to the decision thereof." In 1960, the Constitution's Article 8 provided for a separate Constitutional Court. In 1962, the Constitution entrusted adjudication on the constitutionality of statutes, adjudication on dissolution of a political party, and election lawsuits to the Supreme Court. The Yusin Constitution and the Fifth Republic Constitution set up the Constitutional Committee once again. In response to the citizens' strong longing for democracy and assurance of basic rights, the ruling party and the opposition party agreed to provide for the establishment of a Constitutional Court in the revised constitution proclaimed on October 29, 1987.

Position in the hierarchy of courts :
The Constitutional Court of Korea is an independent and specialised court in South Korea, whose primary role is the reviewing of constitutionality under the Constitution of the Republic of Korea. The Constitution of Korea guarantees independent status and power to the Constitutional Court by having a separate chapter in the Constitution apart from the National Assembly, the Executive, and the Supreme Court. In line with the principle of separation of powers, the Constitutional Court exercises its authority along with the National Assembly, President, and the Supreme Court, making it on par with the other highest constitutional organs. The Constitutional Court, along with the ordinary courts, protects the Constitution through adjudication procedures. Jurisdiction belonging to the Constitutional Court all interpret and

apply the Constitution, aiming to solve constitutional conflicts and protect the Constitution from violation.

II. STANDARD LEGAL REFERENCE

Constitution 1987

III. COMPOSITION AND ORGANIZATION

Composition
The number of judges: 9
Electoral/appointment body:
Nine Justices serve on the court, all of whom are appointed by the President. Three of the positions are appointed directly by the President. Of the remaining six positions, three are appointed from candidates nominated by the Chief Justice of the Supreme Court, and three are appointed from candidates elected by the National Assembly. In addition, the head of the court is chosen by the President, with the consent of the National Assembly. Justices of the Constitutional Court are prohibited from joining political parties and engaging in political activities by Article 112(2) of the Constitution. In addition, Justices of the Constitutional Court are prohibited by law from running businesses, holding other public offices, and being otherwise employed.

The Court members:
The term of office: 6 years, re-election possible.

Justices serve renewable terms of six years, and are required to retire their posts at the age of 65, excepting the head of the Constitutional Court, who may serve until the age of 70.

The Court President:
The term of office: 6, re-election possible

Organization
Administrative autonomy:
The Constitutional Court Administration is responsible for the management of the general administrative affairs of the Constitutional Court. This Administration is composed of 1 Office, 2 Bureaus, and 1 Division. Specifically, these are the Planning & Coordination Office, the Judgment Affairs Bureau, the Judicial Records & Materials Bureau, and the General Services Division. The Secretary General, the Chief of the Administration takes responsibility for the affairs of the

Administration, directs and supervises the public officials under the direction of the President of the Constitutional Court.

IV. POWERS

Constitutional Court Review (Article 111 of the Constitution 1987)

A posteriori review:
Abstract review:
The Constitutional Court is competent to adjudicate the following matters:
The unconstitutionality of law upon the request of the courts;

Concrete review:

Other powers
Constitutional complaints:
The constitutional complaint is an adjudication system where anyone whose basic rights guaranteed under the Constitution has been infringed upon by the governmental power, can file a constitutional complaint. Anyone, including judicial persons may file a constitutional complaint.

Jurisdictional disputes: X
The unconstitutionality of acts and activities of political parties: X
Charges against the President of the Republic: X
Standing before the Constitutional Court
State bodies: X
Individuals: X

V. NATURE AND EFFECTS OF DECISIONS

Binding force:
Erga omnes: abstract review decisions X
Inter partes: constitutional complaint decisions X

SOURCES:

https://en.wikipedia.org/wiki/Constitutional_Court_of_Korea
http://www.servat.unibe.ch/icl/ks__indx.html
http://english.ccourt.go.kr/cckhome/eng/index.do

(169)

DOSSIER OF THE CONSTITUTIONAL COURT OF THE REPUBLIC OF SOUTH OSSETIA

STATE: Republic of South Ossetia
TITLE: The Constitutional Court of the Republic of South Ossetia
YEAR OF FOUNDATION: 2001
SEAT: Tskhinvali

I. CHRONICLE

Date and context of establishment
The Constitution of the Republic of South Ossetia was adopted by referendum on April 8, 2001. The previous constitution was adopted on November 2, 1993

Position in the hierarchy of courts:
Constitutional judiciary is a part of judicial branch (Para. 2. of Article 77 of the Constitution). Constitutional Court is empowered for constitutional review of all normative acts of the Republic of Ossetia (Para 1 of Article 82 of the Constitution).

II. STANDARD LEGAL REFERENCE

Constitution 1993, 2001

III. COMPOSITION AND ORGANIZATION

Composition
The number of judges: 5
Electoral/appointment body:
President of the Republic and the Parliament of the Republic

The Court members:
Term of office: 10
The Court President:
Term of office: 10
Organization
Administrative autonomy: X

IV. POWERS

Constitutional Court Review (Preventive review):
Treaties X

A posteriori review:
Abstract review: X
Concrete review: X

Other powers
Constitutional complaints: X
Jurisdictional disputes: X
Charges against the President of the Republic: X
Charges against the Prime Minister or against any Minister of State:
Other matters with which the Court is charged by the Constitution or statute: X
constitutional interpretation
Standing before the Constitutional Court
State bodies: X
Individuals: X

V. NATURE AND EFFECTS OF DECISIONS

Finality: X

SOURCES:

http://presidentruo.org/category/respublika/konstituciya/

(170)

DOSSIER OF THE SUPREME COURT OF THE REPUBLIC OF SOUTH SUDAN

STATE: Republic of South Sudan
TITLE: The Supreme Court of the Republic of South Sudan
YEAR OF FOUNDATION: 2011
SEAT: Juba

I. CHRONICLE

Date and context of establishment
Upon the Declaration of Independence and statehood of the Republic of South Sudan, on July 9, 2011, the President of the Government of Southern Sudan shall assent to and sign into law the amended Interim Constitution of Southern Sudan, 2005, after its adoption by the Southern Sudan Legislative Assembly, which shall thereafter be known as the Transitional Constitution of the Republic of South Sudan, 2011 (Article 201.1. of the Constitution). This Constitution shall remain in force until the adoption of a permanent constitution.

Position in the hierarchy of courts:
The Supreme Court shall be the custodian of this Constitution and the constitutions of the states (Article 126 of the Constitution).

II. STANDARD LEGAL REFERENCE

Transitional Constitution of the Republic of South Sudan, 2011

III. COMPOSITION AND ORGANIZATION

Composition
The number of judges: 11

Electoral/appointment body:
President of the Republic and the Parliament of the Republic

The Court members:
Term of office: permanent
The Court President:
Term of office: permanent
Organization
Administrative autonomy: X

IV. POWERS

Constitutional Court Review (Preventive review):

A posteriori review:
Abstract review: X
Concrete review: X

Other powers
Constitutional complaints:
individual complaints

Jurisdictional disputes: X
Charges against the President of the Republic: X
Charges against the Prime Minister or against any Minister of State: X
Cgarges against other State Officials: X
Other matters with which the Court is charged by the Constitution or statute:
X constitutional interpretation

Standing before the Constitutional/Supreme Court
State bodies: X
Individuals: X

V. NATURE AND EFFECTS OF DECISIONS

Finality: X

SOURCES:

https://www.constituteproject.org/constitution/South_Sudan_2011.pdf

(171)

DOSSIER OF THE CONSTITUTIONAL COURT OF THE KINGDOM OF SPAIN

STATE: Kingdom of Spain
TITLE: The Constitutional Court of Spain
YEAR OF FOUNDATION: 1980
SEAT: Madrid

I. CHRONICLE

Date and context of establishment
Constitution passed by the Cortes Generales in Plenary Meetings of the Congress of Deputies and the Senate held on October 31, 1978. Ratified by the spanish people in the referendum of December 7, 1978. Sanctioned by His Majesty the King before the Cortes on December 27, 1978. 3 October 1979: Public General Act authorising the creation of the Constitutional Court. 14 February 1980: Appointment of the first judges of the Constitutional Court.

Position in the hierarchy of courts :
The Constitutional Court is the supreme interpreter of the Spanish Constitution. It is unique in its order and holds jurisdiction over all of Spain, exercising the competences defined in Article 161 of the Constitution. The Constitutional Court is independent from all other constitutional bodies and is exclusively subject to the Spanish Constitution and to the Public General Act (Ley Orgánica) which regulates its functions.

The Court's competences are listed in Article 161 of the Constitution and are further developed in Article 2.1 of the Public Act that regulates this body. The list is open-ended, and it is expressly foreseen that the Court may be entrusted with other matters assigned to it by the Constitution or by other public general Acts.

II. STANDARD LEGAL REFERENCE

Constitution 1978

III. COMPOSITION AND ORGANIZATION

Composition
The number of judges: 12
Electoral/appointment body:
The King of Spain appoints them by Royal Decree, following a proposal made by the upper and lower House, (four members designated by the Congress and four by the Senate), two by the Government and two by the General Council of the Judiciary.

The Court members:
Term of office: 9
The Court President: 9
Organization
Administrative autonomy: X
The budget:
The Constitutional Court is independent in budgetary terms and its budget is included as section 04 of the Constitution in the statement of public expenditure of the National Budget.

IV. POWERS

Constitutional Court Review (Preventive review):
Treaties X

A posteriori review:
Abstract review: X
Concrete review: X

Other powers
Constitutional complaint: X
Jurisdictional disputes: X
Other matters with which the Court is charged by the Constitution or statute:
Reversal of decisions to uphold the Court's jurisdiction X

Standing before the Constitutional Court
State bodies: X
Individuals: X

V. NATURE AND EFFECTS OF DECISIONS

Finality: X

SOURCES:

http://www.tribunalconstitucional.es/en/tribunal/Pages/Tribunal.aspx

(172)

DOSSIER OF THE SUPREME COURT OF THE DEMOCRATIC SOCIALIST REPUBLIC OF SRI LANKA

STATE: Democratic Socialist Republic of Sri Lanka
TITLE: The Supreme Court of Sri Lanka
YEAR OF FOUNDATION: 1972
SEAT: Hultsdorf, Colombo

I. CHRONICLE

Date and context of establishment

The Constitution of the Democratic Socialist Republic of Sri Lanka has been the constitution of the island nation of Sri Lanka since its original promulgation by the National State Assembly on 7 September 1978. As of May 2015 it has been formally amended 19 times. The Supreme Court of Sri Lanka was created on 18 April 1801 with the Royal Charter of Justice of 1801 of King George the 3rd establishing the Supreme Courts of the Island of Ceylon by the British, who controlled most of the island at the time, excluding the inland territory of Kandy. This creation was repealed in 1833 and replaced by a new Charter covering the whole of the island. In 1972 the country gained its independence as Sri Lanka and adopted a new Constitution.

Position in the hierarchy of courts :

Article 118 of the Constitution - the Supreme Court is the highest and final superior court of record and is empowered to exercise original advisory and appellate judicial functions. It is also the final Court of Record and the Court of Appeal of Sri Lanka.

II. STANDARD LEGAL REFERENCE

Constitution 1978, with amendments

III. COMPOSITION AND ORGANIZATION

Composition
The number of judges:
The court consists of the Chief Justice and not less than six and not more than ten other Judges.

Electoral/appointment body:
The President of Sri Lanka is responsible for the appointment and removal of all the judges of the Supreme Court. The Supreme Court judges are appointed with the advice and consent of the Parliamentary Council.

The Court members:
Term of office: permanent
The Court President: permanent
Organization
Administrative autonomy: X

IV. POWERS

Constitutional Court Review (Preventive review):

A posteriori review:
Abstract review: X
Concrete review: X

Other powers
Constitutional complaint: individual complaints X
Electoral matters: X
Referendums: X
Other matters with which the Court is charged by the Constitution or statute:
Consultative jurisdiction (Article 129 of the Constitution) ¸ Jurisdiction in respect of any breach of the privileges of Parliament (Article 132 of the Constitution); Jurisdiction in respect of other matters which Parliament may by law vest or ordain X

Standing before the Constitutional /Supreme Court
State bodies: X
Individuals: X

V. NATURE AND EFFECTS OF DECISIONS

Finality: X

SOURCES:

http://www.parliament.lk/en/constitution/main

(173)

DOSSIER OF THE CONSTITUTIONAL COURT OF THE REPUBLIC OF SUDAN

STATE: Republic of Sudan
TITLE: The Constitutional Court of Sudan
YEAR OF FOUNDATION: 2005
SEAT: Khartoum

I. CHRONICLE

Date and context of establishment : 2005
The first permanent Constitution of Sudan was drafted in 1973. It incorporated the Addis Ababa Agreement (1972) ending the first Sudanese civil war. On 1 July 1998, a new constitution entered into forc e after being approved in the constitutional referendum. The current Interim National Constitution of the Republic of Sudan, 2005 (INC) was adopted on 6 July 2005.

Position in the hierarchy of courts :
The Constitutional Court shall be independent of Legislature and Executive and separate from the National Judiciary; the law shall determine its rules of procedure and execution of its judgements. The Constitutional Court shall be the custodian of this Constitution, the constitutions of southern Sudan and the States.

II. STANDARD LEGAL REFERENCE

Interim National Constitution of the Republic of Sudan, 2005

III. COMPOSITION AND ORGANIZATION

Composition
The number of judges: 9

Electoral/appointment body:

The President of the Constitutional Court shall be appointed by the President of the Republic with the consent of the First Vice President, from justices approved according to Article 121(1) of the Constitution herein. He/she shall be answerable to the Presidency.

All Justices of the Constitutional Court shall be appointed by the President of the Republic upon the recommendation of the National Judicial Service Commission and subject to approval by a two-thirds majority of all the representatives at the Council of States.

Southern Sudan shall be adequately represented in the Constitutional Court.

The Court members:
Term of office: 7, re-election possible
The Court President:
Term of office: 7, re-election possible
Organization
Administrative autonomy: X

IV. POWERS

Constitutional Court Review (Preventive review):

A posteriori review:
Abstract review: X
Concrete review: X

Other powers
Constitutional complaint: individual complaints X
Jurisdictional disputes: X
Charges against the President of the Republic: x
Charges against the Prime Minister or against any Minister of State: x
Charges against other State Officials: X
Other matters with which the Court is charged by the Constitution or statute:

-constitutional interpretation

-decide on appeals against the decisions of SouthernSudan Supreme Court on the Interim Constitution of Southern Sudan and the constitutions of Southern Sudan states;

Standing before the Constitutional /Supreme Court
State bodies: X

Individuals: X

V. NATURE AND EFFECTS OF DECISIONS

Finality: X

SOURCES:

https://www.constituteproject.org/constitution/Sudan_2005.pdf?lang=en

(174)

DOSSIER OF THE CONSTITUTIONAL COURT OF THE REPUBLIC OF SURINAME

STATE: Republic of Suriname
TITLE: The Constitutional Court of Suriname
YEAR OF FOUNDATION: 1987
SEAT: Paramaribo

I. CHRONICLE

Date and context of establishment : 1987
The current Constitution of Suriname was adopted on 30 September 1987, following a referendum. It marked the return to democracy after the Bouterse military dictatorship of the 1980s. There shall be a Constitutional Court which is an independent body.

II. STANDARD LEGAL REFERENCE

Constitution 1987

III. COMPOSITION AND ORGANIZATION

Composition
The number of judges: 5+3
The constitutional ourt shall be composed of a President, Vice-President and three members, who - as well as the three deputy members.

Electoral/appointment body:
President of the State: Judges shall be appointed for a period of five years at the recommendation of the National Assembly.

The Court members:
Term of office: 5
The Court President:
Term of office: 5
Organization
Administrative autonomy: X

IV. POWERS

Constitutional Court Review (Preventive review):
Treaties:X

A posteriori review:
Abstract review: X
Concrete review: X

Other powers
Constitutional complaint: individual complaints: X
Standing before the Constitutional /Supreme Court
State bodies: X
Individuals: X

V. NATURE AND EFFECTS OF DECISIONS

Binding force:
Erga omnes: X
Inter partes: X

SOURCES:

http://www.wipo.int/edocs/lexdocs/laws/en/sr/sr002en.pdf

(175)

DOSSIER OF THE HIGH COURT OF THE KINGDOM OF SWAZILAND

STATE: Kingdom of Swaziland
TITLE: The High Court of Swaziland
YEAR OF FOUNDATION: 2005
SEAT: Mbabane

I. CHRONICLE

Date and context of establishment : 2005
Position in the hierarchy of courts:
The Constitution introduces a clearly spelt out human rights component to the jurisdiction of the High Court. In section 151(2) of the Constitution the High Court is granted jurisdiction to enforce the fundamental human rights and freedoms guaranteed by the Constitution. Thus it can hear and determine any matter of a constitutional nature.

II. STANDARD LEGAL REFERENCE

Constitution 2005

III. COMPOSITION AND ORGANIZATION

Composition
The number of judges:
The High Court shall consist of the Chief Justice (ex officio) and not less than four judges of the High Court, plus such other justices of the superior courts of judicature as the Chief Justice may assign.

Electoral/appointment body:
The Chief Justice and the other Justices of the superior courts-shall be appointed by the King on the advice of the Judicial Service Commission.

The Court members:
Term of office: permanent
The Court President:
Term of office: permanent
Organization
Administrative autonomy: X

IV. POWERS

Constitutional Court Review (Preventive review):

A posteriori review:
Abstract review: X
Concrete review: X

Other powers
Constitutional complaint: individual complaints: X
Standing before the Constitutional /Supreme Court
State bodies: X
Individuals: X

V. NATURE AND EFFECTS OF DECISIONS

Finality: X
Binding force:
Erga omnes: X
Inter partes: X

SOURCES:

http://www.wipo.int/edocs/lexdocs/laws/en/sz/sz010en.pdf

DOSSIER OF THE SUPREME COURT OF THE KINGDOM OF SWEDEN

STATE: Kingdom of Sweden
TITLE: The Supreme Court of Sweden
YEAR OF FOUNDATION: 1789
SEAT: Stockholm

I. CHRONICLE

Date and context of establishment : 1789
Position in the hierarchy of courts:
The main role of the Supreme Court is to ensure uniformity, clarity and development of the law. This is done by establishing judicial precedents in leading cases thus ensuring guidance to the court of appeals and district courts.

Judicial review in Sweden is a constitutional provision, by which any Swedish court can declare an Act of the Parliament of Sweden to be in violation of the Constitution or a Government Ordinance to be in violation of laws passed by the Riksdag and thus inapplicable only if the error is manifest . This requirement of manifestness may, however, be removed as a result of a review of the Constitution which is currently underway. It has also become increasingly less relevant as many cases (such as the Åke Green case) are decided with primary reference to the European Convention rather than with reference to the rights provided by the Constitution itself. Since 1994, the Constitution has stipulated that no law or other regulation may violate the European Convention (Ch. 2, § 23).

Constitution, Article 14. If a court finds that a provision conflicts with a rule of fundamental law or other superior statute, the provision shall not be applied. The same applies if a procedure laid down in law has been disregarded in any important respect when the provision was made.

In the case of review of an act of law under paragraph one, particular attention must be paid to the fact that the Riksdag is the foremost representative of the people and that fundamental law takes precedence over other law.

II. STANDARD LEGAL REFERENCE

Constitution 1974

III. COMPOSITION AND ORGANIZATION

Composition
The number of judges: 16
Electoral/appointment body:
Judges are appointed by the government, but the court as an institution is independent of the Riksdag, and the Government is not able to interfere with the decisions of the court.

The Court members:
Term of office: permanent
The Court President:
Term of office: permanent
Organization
Administrative autonomy: X

IV. POWERS

Constitutional Court Review (Preventive review):
Traditionally, a more important check on the ability of the Riksdag to pass laws in violation of the rights provided by the Constitution has been the judicial preview exercised by the Council on Legislation, which, while not binding on the Riksdag, it is nevertheless often respected. Constitution, Article 20. There shall be a Council on Legislation which includes justices, or, where necessary, former justices of the Supreme Court and the Supreme Administrative Court, to pronounce an opinion on draft legislation.

Standing before the Constitutional /Supreme Court
State bodies: X
Individuals: X

V. NATURE AND EFFECTS OF DECISIONS

Finality: X
Binding force:
Erga omnes: X
Inter partes: X

SOURCES:

http://www.hogstadomstolen.se/The-Supreme-Court/

(177)

DOSSIER OF THE FEDERAL SUPREME COURT OF THE SWISS CONFEDERATION

STATE: Swiss Confederation
TITLE: Federal Supreme Court of Switzerland
YEAR OF FOUNDATION: 1874
SEAT: Lausanne

I. CHRONICLE

Date and context of establishment : 1874
The Constitution was adopted by popular vote on 18 April 1999. It replaced the prior federal constitution of 1874, which it was intended to bring up to date without changing it in substance.

Position in the hierarchy of courts:
The Federal Supreme Court is the final arbiter on disputes in the field of civil law (citizens-citizens), the public arena (citizen-state), as well as in disputes between cantons or between cantons and the Confederation. The Federal Court examines the uniform application of federal law by the cantonal and federal courts. It protects the rights that the citizen has according to the Federal Court.

II. STANDARD LEGAL REFERENCE

Constitution 1874, amended 1999

III. COMPOSITION AND ORGANIZATION

Composition
The number of judges: 38

Electoral/appointment body:
The federal judges are proposed by the Judicial Committee and elected by the United Federal Assembly (National Council and Council of States) for a term of office of six years. They can be re-elected an unlimited number of times until the age of 68. The Federal Supreme Court numbers 19 deputy judges, who are also elected by the Federal Assembly.

The Court members:
Term of office: 6, re-election possible
The Court President:
Term of office: 6, re-election possible
Organization
Administrative autonomy: X

IV. POWERS

According to the Constitution of Switzerland, the court has jurisdiction over violations of:
- federal law;
- public international law;
- inter-cantonal law;
- cantonal constitutional rights;
- autonomy of municipalities, and other guarantees granted by the Cantons to public corporate bodies; and
- federal and cantonal provisions concerning political rights.

Constitutional Court Review (Preventive review):

A posteriori review:
Abstract review: X
Concrete review: X

Other powers
Constitutional complaint: individual complaints: X
Standing before the Constitutional /Supreme Court
State bodies: X
Individuals: X

V. NATURE AND EFFECTS OF DECISIONS

Finality: X
Binding force:
Erga omnes: X
Inter partes: X

SOURCES:

http://www.bger.ch/

https://en.wikipedia.org/wiki/Federal_Supreme_Court_of_Switzerland

(178)

DOSSIER OF THE SUPREME CONSTITUTIONAL COURT OF THE SYRIAN ARAB REPUBLIC

STATE: Syrian Arab Republic
TITLE: Supreme Constitutional Court
YEAR OF FOUNDATION: 2012
SEAT: Damascus

I. CHRONICLE

Date and context of establishment : 2012
During the 2011–2012 Syrian uprising, a new constitution was put to a referendum. Amongst other changes,

- it abolished the old Article 8 of the Constitution which entrenched the power of the Ba'ath party. The new Article 8 reads: The political system is based on the principle of political pluralism, and rule is only obtained and exercised democratically through voting.
- in a new Article 88 of the Constitution, it introduced presidential elections and limited the term of office for the president to seven years with a maximum of one re-election.

The referendum resulted in the adoption of the new constitution, which came into force on 27 February 2012.

Position in the hierarchy of courts:
The Supreme Constitutional Court is an independent judicial body.

II. STANDARD LEGAL REFERENCE

Constitution 2012

III. COMPOSITION AND ORGANIZATION

Composition

The number of judges: 7

The Supreme Constitutional Court consists of at least seven members, one of them shall be named president in a decree passed by the President of the Republic.

President and members of the Supreme Constitutional Court shall be sworn in before the President of the Republic in the presence of the Speaker of the People's Assembly before they assume their duties.

Electoral/appointment body:
National Assembly
The Court members:
Term of office: 4, re-election possible
The Court President:
Term of office: 4, re-election possible
Organization
Administrative autonomy: X

IV. POWERS

Constitutional Court Review (Preventive review):
X laws, bylaws etc.

A posteriori review:
Abstract review: X
Concrete review: X

Other powers
Charges against the President of the Republic: X
Electoral matters: X
Standing before the Constitutional /Supreme Court
State bodies: X
Individuals: /

Finality: X
Binding force:
Erga omnes: abstract review decisions
Inter partes: concrete review decisions

SOURCES:

http://www.ilo.org/wcmsp5/groups/public/---ed_protect/---protrav/---ilo_aids/documents/legaldocument/wcms_125885.pdf

(179)

DOSSIER OF THE SUPREME CONSTITUTIONAL COURT OF THE SYRIAN KURDISTAN (ROJAVA, ROJAVA CANTONS)

STATE: Syrian Kurdistan (Rojava, Rojava Cantons)
TITLE: Supreme Constitutional Court
YEAR OF FOUNDATION: 2014
SEAT: Rojava

I. CHRONICLE

Date and context of establishment : 2014
The Constitution of Rojava or Constitution of the Rojava Cantons, officially titled Charter of the Social Contract, is the provisional constitution of the self-proclaimed autonomous region of Syria known as Rojava. It was adopted on 29 January 2014, when the Democratic Union Party (PYD), claiming to represent the Rojavans, declared the three Rojavan cantons it controls autonomous from the Syrian government.

Position in the hierarchy of courts:
Distinct and separate from the court system, the Constitutional Court renders decisions on compatibility of acts of government and legal proceedings with the constitution of Rojava (called the Social Contract).

II. STANDARD LEGAL REFERENCE

Constitution 2014

III. COMPOSITION AND ORGANIZATION

Composition
The number of judges: 7

Electoral/appointment body:
The National Assembly shall ratify the appointment of members of the Supreme Constitutional Court.

The Court members:
Term of office: 4, 1re-election possible
The Court President:
Term of office:4, 1 re-election possible
Organization
Administrative autonomy: X

IV. POWERS

Constitutional Court Review (Preventive review): laws X

A posteriori review:
Abstract review: X
Concrete review: X

Other powers
Charges against the President of the Republic: X
Other matters with which the Court is charged by the Constitution or statute:
charter's interpretation X

Standing before the Constitutional /Supreme Court
State bodies: X
Individuals: /

V. NATURE AND EFFECTS OF DECISIONS

Finality: X

SOURCES:

https://en.wikipedia.org/wiki/Constitution_of_Rojava
https://civiroglu.net/the-constitution-of-the-rojava-cantons/

(180)

DOSSIER OF THE CONSTITUTIONAL COURT OF TAIWAN (REPUBLIC OF CHINA - ROC)

STATE: Taiwan (Republic of China)
TITLE: Constitutional Court (Council of Grand Justices)
YEAR OF FOUNDATION: 1948
SEAT: Taipei

I. CHRONICLE

Date and context of establishment : 1948
The Constitution of the Republic of China is the fundamental law of the Republic of China (ROC), which since 1949 only controls the free area of the Republic of China , which is essentially the island of Taiwan and some minor outlying islands, the only territories not lost to the Chinese Communists in the Chinese Civil War and of which whether Taiwan was even legally transferred to the ROC from Japan is disputed. It was adopted by the National Constituent Assembly on 25 December 1946, and went into effect on 25 December 1947

Position in the hierarchy of courts:
As the only organ that is explicitly empowered by the Constitution to interpret the Constitution and render a uniform interpretation of statutes or regulations (the latter function was exercised by the Judicial Yuan-the Supreme Court in practice-before the promulgation of the Constitution), the Council of Grand Justices occupies a conspicuous position in the structure of the government.

II. STANDARD LEGAL REFERENCE

Constitution 1946

III. COMPOSITION AND ORGANIZATION

Composition
The number of judges: 17
Electoral/appointment body:
appointed by the president after the National Assembly approves nominees

The Court members:
Term of office: 9, re-election possible
The Court President:
Term of office: 9, re-election possible
Organization
Administrative autonomy: X

IV. POWERS

Constitutional Court Review

A posteriori review:
Abstract review: X
Concrete review: X

Other powers
Constitutional complaint: individual complaints: X
The unconstitutionality of acts and activities of political parties: X
Charges against the President of the Republic: X (+vice-president)
Other matters with which the Court is charged by the Constitution or statute:
charter's interpretation X

Other forms of human rights protection
Standing before the Constitutional /Supreme Court
State bodies: X
Individuals: X

V. NATURE AND EFFECTS OF DECISIONS

Finality: X

SOURCES:

http://www.parliament.am/library/sahmanadrutyunner/Taiwan.pdf

(181)

DOSSIER OF THE CONSTITUTIONAL COURT OF THE REPUBLIC OF TAJIKISTAN

STATE: Republic of Tajikistan
TITLE: Constitutional Court of the Republic of Tajikistan
YEAR OF FOUNDATION: 1995
SEAT: DUŠANBE

I. CHRONICLE

Date and context of establishment :
On November 6, 1994, for the first time in the social and the political life of Tajik people, the Constitution of independent state of Tajikistan was adopted through a national referendum.

It should be noted that the institution of constitutional control in the Republic of Tajikistan originated in 1990 with the establishment of the Committee for Constitutional Supervision of the Republic of Tajikistan, the creation of which was dictated by the needs of the social and political development, as well as, the need to create the newest institute in the system of state authorities. The named Committee accomplished the supervision in the field of observance and implementation of the norms of the Constitution and later played an important role in the establishment of the Constitutional Court of the Republic of Tajikistan.

The history of the functioning of the Constitutional Court of the Republic of Tajikistan is determined by the Decree of the President of the Republic of Tajikistan on May 15, 1995 № 238 "On the organizational activities of the Constitutional Court of the Republic of Tajikistan" and the Constitutional Law of the Republic of Tajikistan on November 3, 1995 № 84 "On the Constitutional Court of the Republic of Tajikistan."

Position in the hierarchy of courts:
The Constitution of the Republic of Tajikistan created a real legal basis for formation and development of a number of new state and political institutions, including the Constitutional Court of the Republic of Tajikistan, as a specialized body of the constitutional control.

II. STANDARD LEGAL REFERENCE

Constitution 1994 with amendments

Decree of the President of the Republic of Tajikistan on May 15, 1995 № 238 "On the organizational activities of the Constitutional Court of the Republic of Tajikistan

Constitutional Law of the Republic of Tajikistan on November 3, 1995 № 84 "On the Constitutional Court of the Republic of Tajikistan."

III. COMPOSITION AND ORGANIZATION

Composition
The number of judges:
7; the Constitutional Court is composed of seven members: the Chairman, Deputy-Chairman and five judges, one of whom is the representative Gorno-Badakhshan Autonomous Region.

Electoral/appointment body:
National Assembly (nominated by the president of the state)

The Court members:
Term of office: 10
The Court President:
Term of office: 10
Organization
Administrative autonomy: X

IV. POWERS

Constitutional Court Review (Preventive review): treaties X

A posteriori review:
Abstract review: X
Concrete review: X

Other powers
Constitutional complaint: individual complaints: X
Jurisdictional disputes: X

Referendums: X
Standing before the Constitutional court:
State bodies: X
Individuals: X

V. NATURE AND EFFECTS OF DECISIONS

Finality: X
Binding force:
Erga omnes: abstract review decisions X
Inter partes: inidividual complains X

SOURCES:

http://www.constcourt.tj/eng/index.php?option=com_content&view= Article&id=13&Itemid=4
http://www.constcourt.tj/eng/index.php?option=com_content&view= Article&id=174:the-constitutional-law-of-the-republic-of-tajikistan-on-constitutional-court-of-the-republic-of-tajikistan-&catid=2:documents&Itemid=3

(182)

DOSSIER OF THE SPECIAL CONSTITUTIONAL COURT OF THE UNITED REPUBLIC OF TANZANIA

STATE: United Republic of Tanzania
TITLE: The Special Constitutional Court of the United Republic of Tanzania
YEAR OF FOUNDATION: 1977
SEAT: Dodoma

I. CHRONICLE

Date and context of establishment :
The Constitution of Tanzania, formally Constitution of the United Republic of Tanzania and also known as Permanent Constitution or Fourth Constitution of Tanzania, was ratified in 1977. Before the current establishment, Tanzania has had three constitutions: the Independence Constitution (1961), the Republican Constitution (1962), and the Interim Constitution of the United Republic of Tanganyika and Zanzibar (1964).

Position in the hierarchy of courts:
There is hereby established the Special Constitutional Court of the United Republic whose jurisdiction, constitution and procedure shall be asstipulated in the provisions of Articles 126, and 128 of the Constitution.

II. STANDARD LEGAL REFERENCE

Constitution 1977 with amendments

III. COMPOSITION AND ORGANIZATION

Composition

The number of judges:

The Special Constitutional Court shall consist of members of whom one half shall be appointed by the Government of the United Republic and the other half shall be appointed by the Revolutionary Government of Zanzibar.

Organization

Administrative autonomy: X

IV. POWERS

The sole function of the Special Constitutional Court of the United Republic is to hear and give a conciliatory decision over a matter referred to it concerning the interpretation of this Constitution where such interpretation or its application is in dispute between the Government of the United Republic and the Revolutionary Government of Zanzibar.

Other matters with which the Court is charged by the Constitution or statute:

consultative function XX

V. NATURE AND EFFECTS OF DECISIONS

Finality: X

SOURCES:

http://www.judiciary.go.tz/downloads/constitution.pdf

(183)

DOSSIER OF THE CONSTITUTIONAL COURT OF THE KINGDOM OF THAILAND

STATE: Kingdom of Thailand
TITLE: The Constitutional Court of Tailand
YEAR OF FOUNDATION: 1997-2007
SEAT: Bangkok

I. CHRONICLE

Date and context of establishment : 1997-2007
The Constitutional Court is an independent Thai court originally founded under the 1997 Constitution with jurisdiction over the constitutionality of parliamentary acts, royal decrees, draft legislation, as well as the appointment and removal of public officials and issues regarding political parties. The current court was established by the 2007 Constitution and is part of the judicial branch of the Thai national government.

Position in the hierarchy of courts:
After the Constitutional Court was abolished by the Council for Democratic Reform and was replaced by the Constitutional Tribunal under the 2006 Constitution, the 2007 Constitution reestablishes the Constitutional Court and makes various changes to it. The Court is back with greater vigor and is also empowered to introduce to the National Assembly the draft laws concerning the Court itself

II. STANDARD LEGAL REFERENCE

Constitution 1997, 2006, 2007

III. COMPOSITION AND ORGANIZATION

Composition
The number of judges: 9
The Constitutional Court consists of the President and eight judges of the Constitutional Court to be appointed by the King upon advice of the Senate from the following persons:

(1) three judges of the Supreme Court of Justice holding a position of not lower than judge of the Supreme Court of Justice and elected at a general meeting of the Supreme Court of Justice by secret ballot;
(2) two judges of the Supreme Administrative Court elected at a general meeting of the Supreme Administrative Court by secret ballot;
(3) two qualified persons in law who having orientated knowledge and experience in this field and having been selected under section 206;
(4) two qualified persons in political science, public administration or other social sciences who having orientated knowledge and experience in the administration of State affairs

Electoral/appointment body:
Appointed by the King upon advice of the Senate.

The Court members:
Term of office: 9, no re-election
The Court President:
Term of office: 9 no re-election
Organization
Administrative autonomy: X

IV. POWERS

Constitutional Court Review (Preventive review): laws X; treaties X
A posteriori review:
Abstract review: X
Concrete review: X
Other powers
Constitutional complaint: X
Jurisdictional disputes: X
The unconstitutionality of acts and activities of political parties: X
Electoral matters: X

Other matters with which the Court is charged by the Constitution or statute: emergency decree reviewX

Standing before the Constitutional /Supreme Court

State bodies: X

Individuals: X

V. NATURE AND EFFECTS OF DECISIONS

Finality: X

Binding force: X

Erga omnes: abstract review X

Inter partes: individual complaint X

SOURCES:

https://en.wikipedia.org/wiki/Constitutional_Court_of_Thailand

https://www.unodc.org/tldb/pdf/Thailand_const_2007.pdf

(184)

DOSSIER OF THE SUPREME COURT OF JUSTICE OF THE DEMOCRATIC REPUBLIC OF EAST TIMOR – LESTE (EAST TIMOR)

STATE: East Timor
TITLE: Supreme Court of Justice
YEAR OF FOUNDATION: 22/3-2002
SEAT: Dili

I. CHRONICLE

Date and context of establishment: 2002
Position in the hierarchy of courts:
The Supreme Court of Justice is the highest court of law and the guarantor of a uniform enforcement of the law, and has jurisdiction throughout the national territory. It is also incumbent on the Supreme Court of Justice to administer justice on matters of legal, constitutional and electoral nature.

II. STANDARD LEGAL REFERENCE

Constitution 2002

III. COMPOSITION AND ORGANIZATION

Composition:
The Court members:
The Supreme Court of Justice shall consist of career judges, magistrates of the Public Prosecution or jurists of recognised merit in number to be established by law, as follows:

a) One elected by the National Parliament;
b) And all the others designated by the Superior Council for the Judiciary.

Only career judges or magistrates of the Public Prosecution or jurists of recognised merit of East Timorese nationality may become members of the Supreme Court of Justice. The Superior Council for the Judiciary is the organ of management and discipline of the judges of the courts and it is incumbent upon it to appoint, assign, transfer and promote the judges.

The Superior Council for the Judiciary shall be presided over by the President of the Supreme Court of Justice and shall have the following members:

a) One designated by the President of the Republic;

b) One elected by the National Parliament;

c) One designated by the Government;

d) One elected by the judges of the courts of law from among their peers;

The Court President:
The President of the Supreme Court of Justice shall be appointed by the President of the Republic from among judges of the Supreme Court of Justice for a term of office of four years.

IV. POWERS

Court Review:

Preventive review:

1. The President of the Republic may request the Supreme Court of Justice to undertake an anticipatory review of the constitutionality of any statute submitted to him or her for promulgation.
2. The preventive review of the constitutionality may be requested within twenty days from the date on which the statute is received, and the Supreme Court of Justice shall hand down its ruling within twenty-five days, a time limit that may be reduced by the President of the Republic for reasons of emergency.

A posteriori review:

Abstract review:

Declaration of unconstitutionality may be requested by:

a) The President of the Republic;

b) The Speaker of the National Parliament;

c) The Prosecutor-General , based on the refusal by the courts, in three concrete cases, to apply a statute deemed unconstitutional;

d) The Prime Minister;

e) One fifth of the Members of the National Parliament;

f) The Ombudsman.

1. The Supreme Court of Justice has jurisdiction to hear appeals against any of the following court decisions:

a) Decisions refusing to apply a legal rule on the grounds of unconstitutionality;

b) Decisions applying a legal rule the constitutionality of which was challenged during the proceedings.

2. An appeal under paragraph (1) (b) may be brought only by the party who raised the question of unconstitutionality.

3. The regime for filing appeals shall be regulated by law.

3. If the Supreme Court of Justice rules that the statute is unconstitutional, the President of the Republic shall submit a copy of the ruling to the Government or the National Parliament and request the reformulation of the statute in accordance with the decision of the Supreme Court

1. The legal system of East Timor shall adopt the general or customary principles of international law.

2. Rules provided for in international conventions, treaties and agreements shall apply in the internal legal system of East Timor following their approval, ratification or accession by the respective competent organs and after publication in the official gazette.

3. All rules that are contrary to the provisions of international conventions, treaties and agreements applied in the internal legal system of East Timor shall be invalid.

of Justice.

Charges against the President of the Republic:

The veto for unconstitutionality of a statute from the National Parliament that has been submitted for promulgation can be circumvented under section 88, with the necessary adaptations.

Referendums:

1. Voters who are registered in the national territory may be called upon to express their opinions in a referendum on issues of relevant national interest.

2. A referendum shall be called by the President of the Republic, following a proposal by one third, and deliberation approved by a two thirds majority, of the Members of the National Parliament, or following a well-founded proposal by the Government.

3. Matters falling under the exclusive competence of the Parliament, the Government and the Courts as defined by the Constitution shall not be the subject of a referendum.

4. A referendum shall only be binding where the number of voters is higher than half of the registered electors .

5. The process of a referendum shall be defined by law.

Standing before the Constitutional /Supreme Court

Declaration of unconstitutionality may be requested by:

a) The President of the Republic;

b) The Speaker of the National Parliament;

c) The Prosecutor-General , based on the refusal by the courts, in three concrete cases, to apply a statute deemed unconstitutional;

d) The Prime Minister;

e) One fifth of the Members of the National Parliament;

f) The Ombudsman.

SOURCES:

https://www.constituteproject.org/search?lang=en

(185)

DOSSIER OF THE OF THE CONSTITUTIONAL COURT OF THE TOGOLESE REPUBLIC (TOGO)

STATE: Togolese Republic
TITLE: Constitutional Court
YEAR OF FOUNDATION: 1997
SEAT: Lomé

I. CHRONICLE

Date and context of establishment: 1997
Position in the hierarchy of courts:
Article 99: The Constitutional Court is the highest jurisdiction of the State in constitutional matters. It is [the] judge the constitutionality of the law and it guarantees the fundamental rights of the human person and of the public freedoms. It is the regulatory organ of the functioning of the institutions and of the activity of the public powers. ž Article 120: The Supreme Court is the highest jurisdiction of the State in judicial and administrative matters.

II. STANDARD LEGAL REFERENCE

Constitution 1992 with amendments

III. COMPOSITION AND ORGANIZATION

Composition:
The number of judges:
Article 100 of the Constitution:' The Constitutional Court is composed of nine (09) members appointed for seven (7) years renewable

Electoral/appointment body:

Article 100 of the Conetitution: Three (3) are appointed by the President of the Republic of which one (1) on the basis of their juridical competence. Three (3) are elected by the National Assembly with the majority of two-thirds (2/3) of its members. They must be chosen [from] outside of the deputies. One among them must be designated on the basis of their juridical competence. Three (3) are elected by the Senate with the majority of two-thirds (2/3) of its members. They must be chosen [from] outside of the senators. One among them must be designated on the basis of their juridical competence.

The Court members: /

The Court President:

Article 101 of the Constitution: The President of the Constitutional Court is appointed by the President of the Republic from among the members of the Court for a time period of seven (7) years. He has preponderant vote in case of a tie.

IV. POWERS

Constitutional Court Review

Preventive review:

Article 104 of the Constitution: It is the judge of the constitutionality of the laws. The laws may, before their promulgation, be deferred to the Constitutional Court by the President of the Republic, the Prime Minister, the President of the National Assembly or one-fifth (1/5) of the members of the National Assembly. To the same ends, the organic laws, before their promulgation, and the internal regulations of the National Assembly and of the Senate, those of the High Authority of Audiovisual and of Communications [Haute Autorité de l'Audiovisuel et de la Communication] and of the Economic and Social Council, before their application, must be submitted to it.

Article 139 of the Constitution: When the Constitutional Court, referred to [the matter] by the President of the Republic, by the Prime Minister or by the President of the National Assembly, has declared that an international commitment contains a clause contrary to the Constitution, the authorization to ratify it or to approve it may only intervene after the revision of the Constitution.

Other powers

Constitutional complaints: /

Jurisdictional disputes: /

The unconstitutionality of acts and activities of political parties: /

Charges against the President of the Republic: /

Charges against the Prime Minister or against any Minister of State: /

Electoral matters:

Article 104 of the Constitution: The Constitutional Court judges the regularity of the referendum consultations, [and] of the presidential, legislative and senatorial elections. It decides on the challenges to these consultations and elections.

Referendums: Article 104 of the Constitution: The Constitutional Court judges the regularity of the referendum consultations, [and] of the presidential, legislative and senatorial elections. It decides on the challenges to these consultations and elections.

Other matters with which the Court is charged by the Constitution or statute:

Article 103 of the Constitution: The functions of members of the Constitutional Court are incompatible with the exercise of any elective mandate, of any public, civil or military office, of any professional activity as well as of any function of national representation. An organic law determines the organization and the functioning of the Constitutional Court, the procedure to be followed before it, notably the time periods for referral [of matters] to it, as well as the immunities and the disciplinary regime of its members.

V. NATURE AND EFFECTS OF DECISIONS

Finality:

Article 106: The decisions of the Constitutional Court are not susceptible to any recourse. They impose themselves on the public powers and on all the civil, military and jurisdictional authorities.

SOURCES:

https://www.constituteproject.org/search?lang=en

(186)

DOSSIER OF THE SUPREME COURT OF TONGA

STATE: Kingdom of Tonga
TITLE: Supreme Court
YEAR OF FOUNDATION: 1988 (Amendment 3, 2010)
SEAT: Nuku'alofa

I. CHRONICLE

Date and context of establishment: 1988
Position in the hierarchy of courts:
Article 84 of the Constitution: (1) The judicial power of the Kingdom shall be vested in the superior courts of the Kingdom (namely the Court of Appeal, the Supreme Court, and the Land Court) and a subordinate court namely the Magistrate's Court. (2) The Judiciary of the Kingdom shall comprise – (a) the Lord President of the Court of Appeal and Judges of the Court of Appeal; (b) the Lord Chief Justice, who shall be the professional Head of the Judiciary, and Judges of the Supreme Court; (c) the Lord President of the Land Court and Judges of the Land Court; and (d) the Chief Magistrate and the Magistrates.

The Supreme Court shall have jurisdiction in all cases in Law and Equity arising under the Constitution and Laws of the Kingdom (except cases concerning titles to land which shall be determined by a Land Court subject to an appeal to the Privy Council in matters relating to hereditary estates and titles or to the court of appeal in other land matters) and in all matters concerning Treaties with Foreign States and Ministers and Consuls and in all cases affecting Public Ministers and Consuls and all Maritime Cases. (Law 95 of 1916; Act 75 of 1942; Amended by Act 12 of 1990).

II. STANDARD LEGAL REFERENCE

Constitution 1975 (188) with amendments

III. COMPOSITION AND ORGANIZATION

Composition

The number of judges: /

Electoral/appointment body:

appointed from time to time by the King with the consent of the Privy Council

The Court President:

The Supreme Court shall consist of a judge called the Chief Justice

IV. POWERS

Constitutional Court Review

Preventive review:

Article 82 of the Constitution: Chief Justice may suspend laws: The present law shall be in force until repealed by the Legislative Assembly excepting such laws as are at variance with this Constitution. And it shall be lawful for the Chief Justice to suspend the operation of any law passed by the Legislative Assembly or Privy Council which is at variance with the Constitution until the next meeting of the Legislative Assembly. (Law 6 of 1903. S. 341.)

Other powers

Constitutional complaints:

Article 91 of the Constitution: Appeals from Supreme Court: (1) Subject to the provisions of any Act of the Legislative Assembly relating to appeals to the Court of Appeal, a party to any proceedings in the Supreme Court or Land Court (excepting matters relating to the determination of hereditary estates and titles) who is aggrieved by a decision given in those proceedings by that Court, or a judge thereof, sitting in first instance, may appeal to the Court of Appeal against such decision. (Amended by Act 12 of 1990) (2) Except as may be provided by any Act of the Legislative Assembly, or by rules in respect of limited classes of appeals, no appeal shall be finally determined by less than three members of the Court of Appeal. (Added by Act 13 of 1966.)

Jurisdictional disputes: /

The unconstitutionality of acts and activities of political parties: /

Charges against the President of the Republic: /

Charges against the Prime Minister or against any Minister of State:
Article 75 of the Constitution: Impeachment: It shall be lawful for the members of the Legislative Assembly to impeach any Privy Councillor, Minister, Governor, or Judge for any of the following offences— Breach of the laws or the resolutions of the Legislative Assembly, maladministration, incompetency, destruction or embezzlement of Government property, or the performance of acts which may lead to difficulties between this and another country. (Law I of 1914.).The Chief Justice shall preside but if the Chief Justice is impeached the King shall appoint some other member of the Assembly to preside.

Electoral matters: /
Referendums: /
Other matters with which the Court is charged by the Constitution or statute:
Article 93of the Constitution: Legal opinions: The judges shall give opinions upon important or difficult matters when requested so to do by the King the Cabinet or the Legislative Assembly.

Article 96 of the Constitution: Court fees:'The Legislature shall determine the fees payable to the various Courts. The Registrar of the Supreme Court shall keep the Court records.

SOURCES:

http://www.parliament.gov.to/parliamentary-business/documents/constitution-of-tonga

(187)

DOSSIER OF THE SUPREME COURT OF THE REPUBLIC OF TRINIDAD AND TOBAGO

STATE: Republic of Trinidad and Tobago
TITLE: Supreme Court - San Fernando, Supreme Court - Tobago
YEAR OF FOUNDATION: 1976
SEAT: San Fernando-Tobago; Scarabourgh-Tobago

I. CHRONICLE

Date and context of establishment : 1976
Position in the hierarchy of courts:
Article 99 of the Constitution: There shall be a Supreme Court of Judicature for Trinidad and Tobago consisting of a High Court of Justice (hereinafter referred to as the High Court) and a Court of Appeal with such jurisdiction.

Article 100 of the Constitution: (1) The Judges of the High Court shall be the Chief Justice, who shall be ex officio a Judge of that Court, and such number of Puisne Judges as may be prescribed. (2) The High Court shall be a superior court of record and save as otherwise provided by Parliament, shall have all the powers of such a court, including all such powers as are vested in the Supreme Court of Trinidad and Tobago immediately before the commencement of this Constitution.

II. STANDARD LEGAL REFERENCE

Constitution ,1976 with amendments

III. COMPOSITION AND ORGANIZATION

Composition :
Article 100 of the Constitution: The Judges of the High Court shall be the Chief Justice, who shall be ex officio a Judge of that Court, and such number of Puisne Judges as may be prescribed'

Other powers

Constitutional complaints:

Article 101 of the Constitution: (2) The Court of Appeal shall be a superior court of record and, save as otherwise provided by Parliament, shall have all the powers of such a court.

Jurisdictional disputes:

Article 108 of the Constitution: An appeal to the Court of Appeal shall be as of right from decisions of the High Court in the following, among other cases, that is to say: (a) any order or decision in any civil or criminal proceedings on questions as to the interpretation of this Constitution; (b) any order or decision given in exercise of the jurisdiction conferred on the High Court by section 14 of the Constitution (which relates to redress for contravention of the provisions for the (c) any order or decision given in the determination of any of the questions for the determination of which a right of access to the High Court is guaranteed by sections 4(a) and 5(1) of the Constitution; (d) any order or decision of the High Court granting or refusing leave to institute proceedings for the determination of any question referred to it under section 52 of the Constitution or determining any such question (which relates to the appointment, qualification, election or membership of a Senator or a member of the House of Representatives, as the case may be); (e) any order or decision of a Court in the exercise of its jurisdiction to punish for contempt of court, including criminal contempt.

The unconstitutionality of acts and activities of political parties:/

Charges against the President of the Republic: /

Charges against the Prime Minister or against any Minister of State: /

Electoral matters: /

Referendums: /

Other matters with which the Court is charged by the Constitution or statute:

Other forms of human rights protection:/

SOURCES:

http://www.ag.gov.tt/Features/Constitution-of-T-T

(188)

DOSSIER OF THE CONSTITUTIONAL COURT OF TUNISIA

STATE: Republic of Tunisia
TITLE: Constitutional Court
YEAR OF FOUNDATION: until 2017 not established
SEAT: until 2017 not established

I. CHRONICLE

Date and context of establishment:
until 2017 not established
Three years ago (2014), the Tunisian Parliament voted for a constitution that foresees a new Constitutional Court. Until today (2017) that Court has not been established, leaving a critical gap in the country's system of democratic checks and balances.

Position in the hierarchy of courts:
Article 118: The Constitutional Court is an independent judicial body, composed of 12 competent members

II. STANDARD LEGAL REFERENCE

Constitution 2014

III. COMPOSITION AND ORGANIZATION

Composition
The number of judges:
Article 118of the Constitution: The Constitutional Court is an independent judicial body, composed of 12 competent members

Electoral/appointment body:

Article 118 of the Constitution: The President of the Republic, the Assembly of the Representatives of the People, and the Supreme Judicial Council shall each appoint four members, three quarters of whom must be legal specialists. The nomination is for a single nine-year term. One-third of the members of the Constitutional Court shall be renewed every three years.

The Court President:

Article 118 of the Constitution: Members of the Court elect a President and a Vice President of the Court from amongst its members who are specialists in law

IV. POWERS

Constitutional Court Review:

Preventive review:

Article 120: The Constitutional Court is the sole body competent to oversee the constitutionality of the following:

-Draft laws, upon the request of the President of the Republic, the Head of Government, or thirty members of the Assembly of the Representatives of the People. The request shall be filed within seven days from the Assembly's ratification of the draft law or ratification of a draft law in a modified version, after it has been returned from the President of the Republic.

-Treaties presented to it by the President of the Republic before the draft law approving them is signed.Laws referred to it by courts as a result of a request filed by a court, in the case of the invocation of a claim of unconstitutionality by one of the parties in litigation, in accordance with the procedures established by law.An unconstitutional draft law shall be referred to the President of the Republic who refers it to the Assembly of the Representatives of the People for a second reading in accordance with the Constitutional Court's decision. The President of the Republic shall, before signing the draft law, resubmit it to the Constitutional Court to reconsider and rule on its constitutionality.

Other powers

Constitutional complaints:/

Jurisdictional disputes: /

The unconstitutionality of acts and activities of political parties:/

Charges against the President of the Republic: /

Charges against the Prime Minister or against any Minister of State:/

Electoral matters:

Article 126 of the Constitution: The elections commission, named the Supreme Independent Elections Commission, is responsible for the management and organization of elections and referenda, supervising them in all their stages, ensuring the regularity, integrity, and transparency of the election process, and announcing election results.

Referendums: /

Other matters with which the Court is charged by the Constitution or statute:

Article 144 of the Constitution: The Speaker of the Assembly of the Representatives of the People shall submit all propositions to amend the Constitution to the Constitutional Court to ensure that such propositions do not affect any provision that cannot be amended in accordance with this Constitution.

Other forms of human rights protection:

Article 128 of the Constitution: The Human Rights Commission oversees respect for, and promotion of, human freedoms and rights, and makes proposals to develop the human rights system. It must be consulted on draft laws that fall within the domain of its mandate.

Standing before the Constitutional Court

State bodies: X

SOURCES:

https://www.constituteproject.org/constitution/Tunisia_2014.pdf

DOSSIER OF THE CONSTITUTIONAL COURT OF THE REPUBLIC OF TURKEY

STATE: Republic of Turkey
TITLE: Constitutional Court
YEAR OF FOUNDATION: 1961
SEAT: Ankara

I. CHRONICLE

Date and context of establishment:
The Turkish Constitutional Court was established by the 1961 Constitution. It was modeled on the European constitutional justice practice. Like most European Constitutional Courts, it exercises a posteriori control of the consistency of the laws with the Constitution.

The Turkish Constitutional Court began to carry out its activities upon the enactment of the Law on the Establishment and Judgment Procedures of the Constitutional Court (No 44, 22 April 1962). The power to review the constitutionality of laws was endowed solely with the Constitutional Courtby the 1961 Constitution.

Position in the hierarchy of courts:
The system of constitutional review established by the 1961 Constitution was preserved in the 1982 Constitution with a few changes. In the 1982 Constitution, the Constitutional Court, being one of the highest constitutional organs, is on a par with the Grand National Assembly and the Executive and placed as the first judicial organ among the High Courts . Articles 146-153 of the Constitution lay down in detail the composition, duties, working methods of the Constitutional Court and other issues concerning constitutional review. The Constitutional Court carried out its duties until 2011 according to the Law No 2949 (dated 10 November 1983).

Since the composition, powers and structure of the Court were changed considerably by the constitutional amendments in 2010, a new law was enacted in 2011. The new Law on Establishment and Rules of Procedures of the Constitutional Court (No 6216, 30 March 2011), spelling out the provisions of the Constitution, stipulates its organization, independence, proceedings, disciplinary infractions and disciplinary proceedings. The Law No 6216 vested in the

Plenary of the Court the authority to regulate its rules. Therefore, the more detailed rules on the organization and procedure of the Constitutional Court are established by the Rules of Procedure of the Court.

II. STANDARD LEGAL REFERENCE

Constitution 2010

III. COMPOSITION AND ORGANIZATION

Composition
Article 149 of the Constitution: The Constitutional Court consists of two sections and the General Assembly. The sections convene under the chairpersonship of the deputy president with the participation of four members. The General Assembly shall convene with the participation of at least twelve members under the chairpersonship of the President of the Constitutional Court or a deputy president designated by the President.

The number of judges: 17
Electoral/appointment body:
Article 146 of the Constitution: The Grand National Assembly of Turkey shall elect, by secret ballot, two members from among three candidates to be nominated by and from among the president and members of the Court of Accounts, for each vacant position, and one member from among three candidates nominated by the heads of the bar associations from among self-employed lawyers.The President of the Republic shall appoint three members from High Court of Appeals, two members from Council of State, one member from the High Military Court of Appeals, and one member from the High Military Administrative Court from among three candidates to be nominated, for each vacant position, by their 74 respective general assemblies, from among their presidents and members; three members, at least two of whom being law graduates, from among three candidates to be nominated for each vacant position by the Council of Higher Education from among members of the teaching staff who are not members of the Council, in the fields of law, economics and political sciences; four members from among high level executives, self-employed lawyers, first category judges and public prosecutors or rapporteurs of the Constitutional Court.The members of the Constitutional Court shall be elected for a term of twelve years. A member shall not be re-elected. The members of the Constitutional Court shall retire when they are over the age of sixty-five.

The Court members:
Article 146 of the Constitution: The Constitutional Court shall be composed of seventeen members

The Court President:
Article 146 of the Constitution: The Constitutional Court shall elect a president and two deputy presidents from among its members for a term of four years by secret ballot and by an absolute majority of the total number of its members. Those whose term of office ends may be re-elected.

Organization
Administrative autonomy: X
The budget: X

POWERS

Constitutional Court Review

A posteriori review:
Article 148 of the Constitution: The Constitutional Court shall examine the constitutionality, in respect of both form and substance, of laws, decrees having the force of law and the Rules of Procedure of the Grand National Assembly of Turkey, and decide on individual applications. Constitutional amendments shall be examined and verified only with regard to their form. However, decrees having the force of law issued during a state of emergency, martial law or in time of war shall not be brought before the Constitutional Court alleging their unconstitutionality as to form or substance.

Other powers
Constitutional complaints:
Article 149 of the Constitution: The General Assembly shall hear the cases and applications concerning political parties, actions for annulment and objection, and trials where the Constitutional Court acts as the Supreme Court; the sections shall take the decision on individual applications

Jurisdictional disputes:
Article 149 of the Constitution: The Constitutional Court shall examine cases without holding a hearing, except where it acts as the Supreme Court. Nonetheless, it may be decided to hold a hearing for individual applications. If a court hearing a case finds that the law or the decree having the force of law to be applied is unconstitutional, or if convinced of the seriousness of a

claim of unconstitutionality submitted by one of the parties, it shall postpone the consideration of the case until the Constitutional Court decides on the issue.

Other matters with which the Court is charged by the Constitution or statute:
Article 148 of the Constitution: The Constitutional Court in its capacity as the Supreme Court shall try, for offences relating to their functions, the President of the Republic, the Speaker of the Grand National Assembly of Turkey, members of the Council of Ministers; presidents and members of the Constitutional Court, High Court of Appeals, Council of State, High Military Court of Appeals, High Military Administrative Court, High Council of Judges and Prosecutors, Court of Accounts, and Chief Public Prosecutors and Deputy Public Prosecutors.

The Constitutional Court shall also perform the other duties given to it by the Constitution.

V. NATURE AND EFFECTS OF DECISIONS

Finality:
Article 153 of the Constitution: The decisions of the Constitutional Court are final. Decisions of annulment shall not be made public without a written justification

Where necessary, the Constitutional Court may also decide on the date on which the annulment decision shall come into effect. That duration shall not be more than one year from the date of publication of the decision in the Official Gazette.

Binding force:
Article 153 of the Constitution: Decisions of the Constitutional Court shall be published immediately in the Official Gazette, and shall be binding on the legislative, executive, and judicial organs, on the administrative authorities, and on persons and corporate bodies.

SOURCES:

http://constitutionalcourt.gov.tr/inlinepages/legislation/TurkishConstitution.html

(190)

DOSSIER OF THE PARLIAMENT (MEJLIS) OF THE REPUBLIC OF TURKMENISTAN:

STATE: Republic of Turkmenistan
TITLE: Parliament (Mejlis)
YEAR OF FOUNDATION: 1992
SEAT: Ashgabat

I. CHRONICLE

Date and context of establishment : 1992
Position in the hierarchy of courts:

II. STANDARD LEGAL REFERENCE

Constitution 1992 with amendments
Article 63 of the Constitution

III. POWERS

Mejlis:..................

1. Enacts laws, makes amendments and additions to the Constitution and laws, monitors their performance and their interpretation;...............
5. Determines whether to hold national referendums;................
9. Determines conformity to or divergence from the Constitution and the normative-legal Acts by the state authorities and administration (government);

....

10. Ratifies and denounces international treaties;.

SOURCES:

https://www.constituteproject.org/constitution/Turkmenistan_2008.pdf?lang=en

(191)

DOSSIER OF THE HIGH COURT OF TUVALU:

STATE: Tuvalu
TITLE: High Court
YEAR OF FOUNDATION: 1986
SEAT: Funafuti

I. CHRONICLE

Date and context of establishment : 1986
Position in the hierarchy of courts:
Article 5: " The High Court has the jurisdiction in relation to the interpretation, application and enforcement of this Constitution conferred by – (a) section 14 (Parliamentary declaration of purpose); and (b) Division 5 of Part II (Enforcement of the Bill of Rights); (c) section 131 (constitutional interpretation), and otherwise by law."

Article 119: " The judicial system of Tuvalu consists of – (a) the Sovereign in Council (as provided for in Division 4); and (b) the Court of Appeal for Tuvalu (as provided for in Division 3); and (c) the High Court of Tuvalu (as provided for in Division 2); and (d) such other courts and tribunals as are provided for by or under Acts of Parliament."

II. STANDARD LEGAL REFERENCE

Constitution 1986

III. COMPOSITION AND ORGANIZATION

Composition
The number of judges:
Article 123 of the Constitution: If the Cabinet is satisfied that the appointment of an additional Judge is necessary for the proper performance of the functions of the High Court, the Head of State, acting in accordance with the advice of the Cabinet given after consultation with the Chief

Justice, may appoint a person to be a Judge of the High Court – (a) for such period; or (b) in relation to such matters, as is or are specified in the instrument of his appointment.

Electoral/appointment body:
Article 122 of the Constitution: (2) The Chief Justice shall be appointed by the Head of State, acting in accordance with the advice of the Cabinet, for such period as is specified in the instrument of his appointment

Organization
Administrative autonomy:
Article 48 of the Constitution: (1) Her Majesty Queen Elizabeth II, by the grace of God Queen of the United Kingdom of Great Britain and Northern Ireland and of Her Other Realms and Possessions, Head of the Commonwealth, Defender of the Faith, having at the request of the people of Tuvalu graciously consented, is the Sovereign of Tuvalu and, in accordance with this Constitution, the Head of State (2) The Royal Style and Titles are as determined by Act of Parliament. Article 50 of the Constitution: In addition to the other functions of the office, the office of Head of State is a symbol of the unity and identity of Tuvalu, and the Head of State is entitled to proper respect accordingly.

Article 54 of the Constitution: (1) An office of Governor-General of Tuvalu is established. (2) The Governor-General is the representative of the Sovereign.

Article 61 of the Constitution: (1) The executive authority of Tuvalu is primarily vested in the Sovereign, and in the Governor-General as the representative of the Sovereign.

The budget:
Article 165 of the Constitution: Notwithstanding anything in this Constitution (other than section 169 (remuneration of certain officials)), the raising and spending of money by the Government (including the imposition of taxation and the raising of loans) is subject to authorization and control by Parliament, and shall be regulated by an Act of Parliament.

IV. POWERS

Constitutional Court Review :
Subject to subsection (2), the High Court has original jurisdiction to determine any question as to the interpretation or application of this Constitution. (2) Where – (a) any question as to the interpretation or application of this Constitution arises in any proceedings in a subordinate court; and (b) that court is of the opinion that the question involves a substantial question of

law, the court may, and shall if a party to the proceedings so requests, refer the question to the High Court for determination.

Other powers

Jurisdictional disputes:

Article 130 of the Constitution: (1) The High Court has jurisdiction – (a) in relation to Part II (Bill of Rights) of this Constitution - as provided by Division 5 (Enforcement of the Bill of Rights) of that Part; and (b) in relation to questions as to membership of Parliament - as provided by section 100 (questions as to membership of Parliament); and (c) in relation to other questions as to the interpretation or application of this Constitution - as provided by section 131 (constitutional interpretation); and (d) in relation to appeals generally - as provided by section 132 (appellate jurisdiction of the High Court); and (e) in other matters - as provided for by sections 14(3) (which relates to the effect of Parliamentary declarations of purpose) and 133 (other jurisdiction, etc., of the High Court), and otherwise in this Constitution. (2) Subject to any Act of Parliament providing for the jurisdiction of two or more members of the High Court sitting together, the jurisdiction of the High Court may be exercised by the Chief Justice or a single Judge.

Article 132 of the Constitution: The High Court has such jurisdiction to determine appeals from decisions of subordinate courts as is provided for by this Constitution or by or under Acts of Parliament.

Article 133 of the Constitution: The High Court has such other jurisdiction, power and authority as are conferred by or under Acts of Parliament.(1) The High Court has original jurisdiction – (a) to determine any application made under section 38 (application for enforcement of the Bill of Rights); and (b) to determine any question referred to it under section 39 (questions as to the Bill of Rights arising in subordinate courts), and may make any orders, issue any writs and give any directions that it thinks appropriate for enforcing or securing the enforcement of this PArticle (2) The High Court may refuse to exercise its powers under subsection (1) if it is satisfied that adequate means of redress for the alleged contravention are or have been reasonably available to the person concerned under any other law.

(1) The High Court has jurisdiction to determine, in accordance with law, any question whether – (a) a candidate has been validly elected as a member of Parliament; or (b) a member of Parliament has vacated his seat, or is required by section 98 (vacation of seat on sentence) to cease to perform his functions as a member; or (c) the seat of a member has been declared vacant in accordance with any Act of Parliament or Rules of Procedure of Parliament provided for by section 97 (disclosure of interest); or (d) the seat of a member has been declared vacant in accordance with section 99 (recall of incapacitated member). (2) There is no appeal from a decision of the High Court in proceedings under subsection (1).

The unconstitutionality of acts and activities of political parties: /

Charges against the President of the Republic: /

Charges against the Prime Minister or against any Minister of State: /

Electoral matters: /

Referendums: /

Other matters with which the Court is charged by the Constitution or statute:

Other forms of human rights protection:/

SOURCES:

http://www.ilo.org/dyn/natlex/docs/ELECTRONIC/3899/95791/F656430737/TUV3899.pdf

(192)

DOSSIER OF THE CONSTITUTIONAL COURT/COURT OF APPEAL OF THE REPUBLIC OF UGANDA:

STATE: Republic of Uganda
TITLE: Court of Appeal
YEAR OF FOUNDATION: 1996
SEAT: Kampala

I. CHRONICLE

Date and context of establishment:
The Constitutional Court/ Court of Appeal of Uganda came into being following the promulgation of the 1995 Constitution, and the enactment of the Judicature Statute, 1996.

Article 134 of the Constitution established the structure of the Court of Appeal.

The Court of Appeal is the second highest court in the land. While presiding over matters , it is duly constituted when it consists of an odd number of not less than three (3) justices of the Court of Appeal. It is this court that constitutes itself into a Constitutional Court in accordance with the Constitution to hear constitutional cases.

Position in the hierarchy of courts :
Article 126 of the Constitution: Judicial power is derived from the people and shall be exercised by the courts established under this Constitution in the name of the people and in conformity with law and with the values, norms and aspirations of the people. In the exercise of judicial power, the courts shall be independent and shall not be subject to the control or direction of any person or authority.

Article 129 of the Constitution: (1) The judicial power of Uganda shall be exercised by the courts of judicature which shall consist of— (a) the Supreme Court of Uganda; (b) the Court of Appeal of Uganda; (c) the High Court of Uganda; and (d) such subordinate courts as Parliament may by law establish, including qadhis' courts for marriage, divorce, inheritance of property and guardianship, as may be prescribed by Parliament. (2) The Supreme Court, the Court of Appeal and the High Court of Uganda shall be superior courts of record and shall each have all the powers of such a court. (3) Subject to the provisions of this Constitution, Parliament may make provision for the jurisdiction and procedure of the courts.

Article 137 of the Constitution: (1) Any question as to the interpretation of this Constitution shall be determined by the Court of Appeal sitting as the constitutional court.

II. STANDARD LEGAL REFERENCE

Constitution 1995

III. COMPOSITION AND ORGANIZATION

Composition

The number of judges: 5

The Court members:

Article 135 of the constitution: (1)The Court of Appeal shall be duly constituted at any sitting if it consists of an uneven number not being less than three members of the court

IV. POWERS

Other powers

Charges against the President of the Republic:

The Chief Justice shall, within seven days after receipt of the notice transmitted under clause (3) of this article, constitute a tribunal comprising three justices of the Supreme Court to investigate the allegation in the notice and to report its findings to Parliament stating whether or not there is a prima facie case for the removal of the President

Referendums:

Other matters with which the Court is charged by the Constitution or statute: Article 137 of the Constitution: (3) A person who alleges that— (a) an Act of Parliament or any other law or anything in or done under the authority of any law; or (b) any act or omission by any person or authority, is inconsistent with or in contravention of a provision of this Constitution, may petition the constitutional court for a declaration to that effect, and for redress where appropriate. (4) Where upon determination of the petition under clause (3) of this article the constitutional court considers that there is need for redress in addition to the declaration sought, the constitutional court may— (a) grant an order of redress; or (b) refer the matter to the High Court to investigate and determine the appropriate redress. (5) Where any question as to the interpretation of this Constitution arises in any proceedings in a court of law other than a field court martial, the court— (a) may, if it is of the opinion that the question involves a substantial question of law; and (b) shall, if any party to the proceedings requests it to do so, refer the question to the constitutional court for decision in accordance with clause (1) of this article. (6) Where any question is referred to the constitutional court under clause (5) of this article, the constitutional court shall give its decision on the question, and the court in which the question arises shall dispose of the case in accordance with that decision. (7) Upon a petition being made or a question being referred under this article, the Court of Appeal shall proceed to hear and determine the petition as soon as possible and may, for that purpose, suspend any other matter pending before it.

Article 131 of the Constitution: (2) When hearing appeals from decisions of the Court of Appeal sitting as a constitutional court, the Supreme Court shall consist of a full bench of all members of the Supreme Court; and where any of them is not able to attend, the President shall, for that purpose, appoint an acting justice under article 142(2) of this Constitution

V. NATURE AND EFFECTS OF DECISIONS

Finality:

The Supreme Court shall be the final court of appeal.

SOURCES:

http://www.parliament.go.ug/new/images/stories/constitution/Constitution_of_Uganda_1995.pdf

https://www.judiciary.go.ug/data/smenu/77//Court%20of%20Appeal.html

(193)

DOSSIER OF THE CONSTITUTIONAL COURT OF UKRAINE

STATE: Ukraine
TITLE: Constitutional Court
YEAR OF FOUNDATION: 1996
SEAT: Kiev

I. CHRONICLE

Date and context of establishment :
Constitutional Court of Ukraine (Constitution 1996, Articles 147-153)

Position in the hierarchy of courts:
Article 147 of the Constitution: The Constitutional Court of Ukraine is the sole body of constitutional jurisdiction in Ukraine.

II. STANDARD LEGAL REFERENCE

Constitution 1996

III. COMPOSITION AND ORGANIZATION

Composition
The number of judges: 18
Electoral/appointment body:
The President of Ukraine, the Verkhovna Rada of Ukraine and the Congress of Judges of Ukraine each appoint six judges to the Constitutional Court of Ukraine.

The Court President:

The Chairperson of the Constitutional Court of Ukraine is elected by secret ballot only for one three-year term at a special plenary meeting of the Constitutional Court of Ukraine from among the judges of the Constitutional Court of Ukraine.

IV. POWERS

Constitutional Court Review :

The Constitutional Court of Ukraine decides on issues of conformity of laws and other legal acts with the Constitution of Ukraine and provides the official interpretation of the Constitution of Ukraine and the laws of Ukraine.

Article 150 of the Constitution: The authority of the Constitutional Court of Ukraine comprises:

> 1) deciding on issues of conformity with the Constitution of Ukraine (constitutionality) of the following:laws and other legal acts of the Verkhovna Rada of Ukraine; acts of the President of Ukraine; acts of the Cabinet of Ministers of Ukraine; legal acts of the Verkhovna Rada of the Autonomous Republic of Crimea.
>
> These issues are considered on the appeals of: the President of Ukraine; no less than forty-five People's Deputies of Ukraine; the Supreme Court of Ukraine; the Authorised Human Rights Representative of the Verkhovna Rada of Ukraine; the Verkhovna Rada of the Autonomous Republic of Crimea;
>
> 2) the official interpretation of the Constitution of Ukraine and the laws of Ukraine;On issues envisaged by this Article, the Constitutional Court of Ukraine adopts decisions that are mandatory for execution throughout the territory of Ukraine, that are final and shall not be appealed.

Other powers

Constitutional complaints: /

Jurisdictional disputes: /

The unconstitutionality of acts and activities of political parties: /

Charges against the President of the Republic:

On the appeal of the Verkhovna Rada of Ukraine, the Constitutional Court of Ukraine provides an opinion on the observance of the constitutional procedure of investigation and consideration of the case of removing the President of Ukraine from office by the procedure of impeachment.

Electoral matters: /

Referendums: /

Other matters with which the Court is charged by the Constitution or statute: /

Standing before the Constitutional Court

State bodies: X

Individuals: X

V. NATURE AND EFFECTS OF DECISIONS

Laws and other legal acts, or their separate provisions, that are deemed to be unconstitutional, lose legal force from the day the Constitutional Court of Ukraine adopts the decision on their unconstitutionality.

SOURCES:

https://web.archive.org/web/20061127211741/http://www.venice.coe.int/site/dynamics/N_Country_ef.asp?C=47&L=E

https://web.archive.org/web/20061125050625/http://www.venice.coe.int/docs/2006/CDL(2006)070-e.asp

http://www.ccu.gov.ua/en

(194)

DOSSIER OF THE SUPREME COURT OF THE UNITED ARAB EMIRATES

STATE: United Arab Emirates

TITLE: Supreme Court of the Union

YEAR OF FOUNDATION: 1971 (2004)

SEAT: Abu Dabi

The Supreme Court of the Union shall convene in the capital of the Union.

It may, exceptionally, convene when necessary in the capital of any one of the Emirates.

I. CHRONICLE

Date and context of establishment :

The Supreme Court of the Union

Position in the hierarchy of courts:

Article 94 of the Constitution: Justice is the basis of authority. Judges shall be independent and shall be subordinate to no authority but the law and their own consciences in the performance of their duties. Article 95 of the Constitution: The Union shall have a Supreme Court of the Union and Union Courts of the First Instance as explained hereinafter.

Article 102 of the Constitution: The Union shall have one or more Union Courts of the First Instance which shall sit in the permanent capital of the Union or in the capitals of some of the Emirates, in order to exercise the judicial powers within the sphere of their jurisdiction in the following cases:— 1. Civil, commercial and administrative disputes between the Union and individuals whether the Union is plaintiff or defendant. 2. Crimes committed within the boundaries of the permanent capital of the Union, excepting such matters as are reserved for the Supreme Court of the Union under Article 99 of the Constitution. 3. Personal status actions, civil actions, commercial actions and other actions between individuals which arise in the permanent capital of the Union.

II. STANDARD LEGAL REFERENCE

Constitution 1971 with amendments

III. COMPOSITION AND ORGANIZATION

Composition

The number of judges:

The Supreme Court of the Union shall consist of a President and a number of Judges, not exceeding five in all

Electoral/appointment body:

appointed by decree, issued by the President of the Union after approval by the Supreme Council.

The Court members:

The Court President:

IV. POWERS

Constitutional Court Review

A posterior review:

Article 99 of the Constitution:

(2) Examination of the constitutional legality of Union laws, if they are challenged by one or more of the Emirates on the grounds of violating the Constitution of the Union. Examination of the constitutional legality of legislation promulgated by one of the Emirates, if it is challenged by one of the Union authorities on the grounds of violation of the Constitution of the Union or of Union laws.

(3) Examination of the constitutional legality of laws, legislation and regulations generally, if such a request is remitted to it by any State Court during a case under consideration before it. The Court aforesaid shall be bound to accept the ruling of the Supreme Court of the Union in this case

(4) Interpretation of the provisions of the Constitution, when so requested by any authority of the Union or by the Government of any Emirate. Any such interpretation shall be considered binding on all.

Other powers

Constitutional complaints: /

Jurisdictional disputes:

Article 99 of the Constitution: (1) Miscellaneous disputes between member Emirates in the Union, or between any one Emirate or more and the Government of the Union, whenever such disputes are remitted to the Court on the basis of a request from any one of the interested parties.

(7) Conflict of jurisdiction between the Union judicial authorities and the local judicial authorities in the Emirates.

(8) Conflict of jurisdiction between the judicial authority in one Emirate and the judicial authority in another Emirate, and the classification of the principles relating thereto in a Union law.

(9) Any other jurisdiction stipulated in this Constitution, or which may be assigned by a Union law.

The unconstitutionality of acts and activities of political parties: /

Charges against the President of the Republic: /

Charges against the Prime Minister or against any Minister of State:

Interrogation of Ministers and senior officials of the Union appointed by decree concerning their actions in the conduct of their official duties on the basis of a request by the Supreme Council and in accordance with the relevant law.

Electoral matters: /

Referendums: /

Other matters with which the Court is charged by the Constitution or statute: /

V. NATURE AND EFFECTS OF DECISIONS

Finality:

The judgements of the Supreme Court of the Union shall be final and binding upon all.

SOURCES:

https://www.constituteproject.org/constitution/United_Arab_Emirates_2004.pdf

(195)

DOSSIER OF THE SUPREME COURT OF THE UNITED STATES OF AMERICA

STATE: United States of America
TITLE: Supreme Court
YEAR OF FOUNDATION: 1789
SEAT: Washington D.C.

I. CHRONICLE

Date and context of establishment :
The Supreme Court of the United States is the highest federal court of the United States. Established pursuant to Article Three of the United States Constitution in 1789, it has ultimate (and largely discretionary) appellate jurisdiction over all federal courts and state court cases involving issues of federal law plus original jurisdiction over a small range of cases. In the legal system of the United States, the Supreme Court is generally the final interpreter of federal law including the United States Constitution, but it may act only within the context of a case, in which it has jurisdiction. The Court does not have power to decide political questions, and its enforcement arm is in the executive rather than judicial branch of government.

According to federal statute, the Court normally consists of the Chief Justice of the United States and eight associate justices who are nominated by the President and confirmed by the Senate. Once appointed, justices have lifetime tenure unless they resign, retire, or are removed after impeachment (though no justice has ever been removed). In modern discourse, the justices are often categorized as having conservative, moderate, or liberal philosophies of law and of judicial interpretation. Each justice has one vote, and it is worth noting while a far greater number of cases in recent history have been decided unanimously, decisions in cases of the highest profile have come down to just one single vote, thereby exposing the justices' ideological beliefs that track with those philosophical or political categories. The Court meets in the Supreme Court Building in Washington, D.C.

Position in the hierarchy of courts:

Article III., section 1 of the Constitution: The judicial Power of the United States, shall be vested in one Supreme Court, and in such inferior Courts as the Congress may from time to time ordain and establish.

In the United States, judicial review is the ability of a court to examine and decide if a statute, treaty or administrative regulation contradicts or violates the provisions of existing law, a State Constitution, or ultimately the United States Constitution. While the U.S. Constitution does not explicitly define a power of judicial review, the authority for judicial review in the United States has been inferred from the structure, provisions, and history of the Constitution.

Two landmark decisions by the U.S. Supreme Court served to confirm the inferred constitutional authority for judicial review in the United States: In 1796, *Hylton v. United States* was the first case decided by the Supreme Court involving a direct challenge to the constitutionality of an act of Congress, the Carriage Act of 1794 which imposed a carriage tax The Court engaged in the process of judicial review by examining the plaintiff's claim that the carriage tax was unconstitutional. After review, the Supreme Court decided the Carriage Act was constitutional. In 1803, *Marbury v. Madison* was the first Supreme Court case where the Court asserted its authority for judicial review to strike down a law as unconstitutional. At the end of his opinion in this decision

The text of the Constitution does not contain a specific reference to the power of judicial review. Rather, the power to declare laws unconstitutional has been deemed an implied power, derived from Article III and Article VI of the Constitution.

The provisions relating to the federal judicial power in Article III of the Constitution state:

> The judicial power of the United States, shall be vested in one Supreme Court, and in such inferior courts as the Congress may from time to time ordain and establish. . . . The judicial power shall extend to all cases, in law and equity, arising under this Constitution, the laws of the United States, and treaties made, or which shall be made, under their authority. . . . In all cases affecting ambassadors, other public ministers and consuls, and those in which a state shall be party, the Supreme Court shall have original jurisdiction. In all the other cases before mentioned, the Supreme Court shall have appellate jurisdiction, both as to law and fact, with such exceptions, and under such regulations as the Congress shall make.

The Supremacy Clause of Article VI of the Constitution states:

> This Constitution, and the Laws of the United States which shall be made in Pursuance thereof; and all Treaties made, or which shall be made, under the Authority of the United States, shall be the supreme Law of the Land; and the Judges in every State shall be bound thereby, any Thing in the Constitution or Laws of any State to the Contrary notwithstanding. . . . [A]ll executive and

> judicial Officers, both of the United States and of the several States, shall be bound by Oath or Affirmation, to support this Constitution.

The power of judicial review has been implied from these provisions based on the following reasoning. It is the inherent duty of the courts to determine the applicable law in any given case. The Supremacy Clause says [t]his Constitution is the supreme law of the land. The Constitution therefore is the fundamental law of the United States. Federal statutes are the law of the land only when they are made in pursuance of the Constitution. State constitutions and statutes are valid only if they are consistent with the Constitution. Any law contrary to the Constitution is void. The federal judicial power extends to all cases arising under this Constitution. As part of their inherent duty to determine the law, the federal courts have the duty to interpret and apply the Constitution and to decide whether a federal or state statute conflicts with the Constitution. All judges are bound to follow the Constitution. If there is a conflict, the federal courts have a duty to follow the Constitution and to treat the conflicting statute as unenforceable. The Supreme Court has final appellate jurisdiction in all cases arising under the Constitution, so the Supreme Court has the ultimate authority to decide whether statutes are consistent with the Constitution.

II. STANDARD LEGAL REFERENCE

Constitution 1789 with amendments

III. COMPOSITION AND ORGANIZATION

Composition
The number of judges:
Electoral/appointment body: the President of State
The Court members: 9
Organization
Administrative autonomy: X
The budget: X

IV. POWERS

Constitutional Court Review:

Repressive review: X

Other powers
Constitutional complaints: /
Jurisdictional disputes: /
The unconstitutionality of acts and activities of political parties: /
Charges against the President of the Republic:
Article II, section 4 of the Constitution: The President, Vice President and all Civil Officers of the United States, shall be removed from Office on Impeachment for, and Conviction of, Treason, Bribery, or other high Crimes and Misdemeanors.

Charges against the Prime Minister or against any Minister of State: /
Electoral matters: /
Referendums: /
Other matters with which the Court is charged by the Constitution or statute:
Article III., section 2 of the Constitution: The judicial Power shall extend to all Cases, in Law and Equity, arising under this Constitution, the Laws of the United States, and Treaties made, or which shall be made, under their Authority;-to all Cases affecting Ambassadors, other public ministers and Consuls;-to all Cases of admiralty and maritime Jurisdiction;-to Controversies to which the United States shall be a Party;-to Controversies between two or more States;-between a State and Citizens of another State;-between Citizens of different States;-between Citizens of the same State claiming Lands under Grants of different States, and between a State, or the Citizens thereof, and foreign States, Citizens or Subjects. In all Cases affecting Ambassadors, other public Ministers and Consuls, and those in which a State shall be Party, the Supreme Court shall have original Jurisdiction. In all the other Cases before mentioned, the Supreme Court shall have appellate Jurisdiction, both as to Law and Fact, with such Exceptions, and under such Regulations as the Congress shall make.

SOURCES:

https://www.constituteproject.org/constitution/United_States_of_America_1992?lang=en
https://www.supremecourt.gov/

DOSSIER OF THE SUPREME COURT OF THE UNITED KINGDOM

STATE: United Kingdom of Great Britain and Northern Ireland
TITLE: Supreme Court
YEAR OF FOUNDATION: 1215 (2014)
SEAT: London

I. CHRONICLE

Date and context of establishment: 1215 (2014)
Position in the hierarchy of courts:
Article 92.1 of the Constituional Reform Act: Judicial power within the United Kingdom is vested in the courts in accordance with this Constitution.

Historically, the House of Lords held several judicial functions. Most notably, until 2009 the House of Lords served as the court of last resort for most instances of UK law. Since 1 October 2009 this role is now held by the Supreme Court of the United Kingdom.

The Constitutional Reform Act 2005 resulted in the creation of a separate Supreme Court of the United Kingdom, to which the judicial function of the House of Lords, and some of the judicial functions of the Judicial Committee of the Privy Council, were transferred. In addition, the office of Lord Chancellor was reformed by the act, removing his ability to act as both a government minister and a judge. This was motivated in part by concerns about the historical admixture of legislative, judicial, and executive power. The new Supreme Court is located at Middlesex Guildhall.

Unlike the United States and some other jurisdictions, English law does not permit judicial review of primary legislation (laws passed by Parliament), except in a few cases where primary legislation is contrary to EU law or the European Convention on Human Rights. A person wronged by an Act of Parliament therefore cannot apply for judicial review unless this is the case, but may still argue that a body did not follow the Act.

II. STANDARD LEGAL REFERENCE

Constitutional Reform Act 2005

III. COMPOSITION AND ORGANIZATION

Composition

The number of judges:

10 or more if is prescribed by Act of Parliament

Electoral/appointment body:

Art 96.2 of the Constitutional Reform Act: The Justices of the Supreme Court shall be selected from persons: who have served as judges of a superior court within the United Kingdom; or who, in the opinion of the United Kingdom Judicial Appointments Commission, have shown outstanding distinction in the practice or teaching of law in the United Kingdom.

IV. POWERS

Abstract review

Article 98 of the Constitutional Reform Act:

> The Supreme Court has original and exclusive jurisdiction: in any proceedings brought by the Government of the United Kingdom seeking a ruling that any Assembly Act is wholly or partly invalid under this Constitution. Has appellate jurisdiction in: the interpretation and effect of this Constitution, any proceedings alleging a contravention of the Bill of Rights, the validity, interpretation and effect of Acts of Parliament and subordinate legislation thereunder; any proceedings giving rise to a question of law in relation to which uniformity throughout the United Kingdom or in more than one jurisdiction within the United Kingdom is, in the opinion of the Supreme Court, desirable; the validity of any executive decision or act of the Government of the United Kingdom or of any public body exercising powers under this Constitution or an Act of Parliament; the interpretation and effect of the laws of the European Community and any other international treaties. The Supreme Court may, on the invitation of the country or territory in question, exercise the jurisdiction in relation to appeals from countries or territories outside the United Kingdom which, immediately prior to the coming into force of this Constitution, was exercised by the Judicial Committee of the Privy Council.

Other powers
Constitutional complaints: /
Jurisdictional disputes:
Article 98 of the Constitutional Reform Act: Has appellate jurisdiction in any dispute in which nations or regions are opposing parties, or in which the United Kingdom and a nation or region are opposing parties;

The unconstitutionality of acts and activities of political parties: /
Charges against the President of the Republic: /
Charges against the Prime Minister or against any Minister of State: /
Electoral matters: /
Referendums: /
Other matters with which the Court is charged by the Constitution or statute: /
Other forms of human rights protection: /
Standing before the Constitutional Court
State bodies: X
Individuals: X

V. NATURE AND EFFECTS OF DECISIONS

Finality:
Article 100.1 of the Constitutional Reform Act: Any decision of the Supreme Court (including a decision that it has jurisdiction to hear an appeal) is final and conclusive.

Binding force:
Article 100.2 of the Constitutional Reform Act: Until overruled by a subsequent decision of the Supreme Court, a decision of the Supreme Court is binding on all other courts in the United Kingdom.

SOURCES:

http://www.ippr.org/files/images/media/files/publication/2014/01/the-constitution-of-the-united-kingdom_1991-2014_1420.pdf?noredirect=1
https://en.wikipedia.org/wiki/Judicial_review_in_English_law

(197)

DOSSIER OF THE SUPREME COURT OF THE ORIENTAL REPUBLIC OF URUGUAY

STATE: Oriental Republic of Uruguay
TITLE: Supreme Court
YEAR OF FOUNDATION: 1907
SEAT: Montevideo

I. CHRONICLE

Date and context of establishment : 1907
Position in the hierarchy of courts :
Article 233 of the Constitution: The Judicial Power shall be vested in the Supreme Court of Justice and in the Tribunals and Courts as prescribed by law.

II. STANDARD LEGAL REFERENCE

Constitution 1830 with amendments

III. COMPOSITION AND ORGANIZATION

Composition
The Supreme Court is composed of five members, named Ministers of the Supreme Court:

The number of judges: 5
Electoral/appointment body:
Article 236 of the Constitution: The members of the Supreme Court of Justice shall be appointed by the General Assembly by a two-thirds vote of its full membership.

Organization

Administrative autonomy:

The budget:

The judiciary of Uruguay is possibly the most independent in Latin America, in part due to having its own budget.

IV. POWERS

Constitutional Court Review :

Preventive review: /

A posteriori review:

Article 256 of the Constitution: Laws may be declared unconstitutional by reason of form or content, in accordance with the provisions of the following articles.

Article 257 of the Constitution: The Supreme Court of Justice has original and exclusive jurisdiction in the hearing and decision of such matters; and must render its decision in accordance with the requirement for final decisions.

Article 239.1 of the Constitution: Try all violators of the Constitution, without exception; offenses against the law of nations and cases in admiralty; questions relating to treaties, pacts and conventions with other States; and take cognizance of cases involving diplomatic Representatives in such cases as are contemplated in international law.

Other powers

Constitutional complaints: /

Jurisdictional disputes: /

The unconstitutionality of acts and activities of political parties: /

Charges against the President of the Republic: /

Charges against the Prime Minister or against any Minister of State: /

Electoral matters: /

Referendums: /

Other matters with which the Court is charged by the Constitution or statute:

Article 239 of the Constitution: 2. Exercise directive, corrective, advisory, and economic supervision over the Tribunals, Courts and other dependencies of the Judicial Power;

4. With the approval of the Chamber of Senators, or during its recess with that of the Permanent Commission, appoint the citizens who shall compose the Appellate Tribunals, 5. Appoint the Lawyer Judges [jueces letrados] of all grades and classes, an absolute majority of all members of the Supreme Court being required in each case. 6. Appoint the permanent Official

Defenders and Justices of the Peace by absolute majority of all members of the Supreme Court of Justice. 7. Appoint, promote, or remove, by a vote of four of its members, the employees of the Judicial Power, in accordance with the provisions of Articles 58 to 66, wherever pertinent

Other forms of human rights protection: /

V. NATURE AND EFFECTS OF DECISIONS

Finality:
Article 259 of the Constitution: The decision of the Supreme Court of Justice shall refer exclusively to the concrete case and shall have effect solely on the proceedings for which it was rendered.

SOURCES:

https://www.constituteproject.org/constitution/Uruguay_2004?lang=en
http://www.poderjudicial.gub.uy/

(198)

DOSSIER OF THE CONSTITUTIONAL COURT OF THE REPUBLIC OF UZBEKISTAN

STATE: Republic of Uzbekistan
TITLE: Constitutional Court
YEAR OF FOUNDATION: 1992 (2011)
SEAT: Tashkent

I. CHRONICLE

Date and context of establishment :
The Constitutional Court of Uzbekistan was created after the nation declared its independence. The court functions as a "body of judicial authority that hears the cases relating to the constitutionality of acts passed by the legislative and executive branches." On August 31, 1991 the Uzbek people realized their inalienable right to self-determination, and so Islam Karimov declared their independence. Statehood was gained peacefully, and the Constitution was adopted on December 8, 1992. It created a separation of powers among a strong presidency, the *oliy majlis* (or parliament), and a judiciary.

Position in the hierarchy of courts :
Article 107 of the Constitution: The judicial system in the Republic of Uzbekistan shall consist of the Constitutional Court of the Republic of Uzbekistan, the Supreme Court of the Republic of Uzbekistan, the Higher Economic Court of the Republic of Uzbekistan, the Supreme Courts of the Republic of Karakalpakstan on civil and criminal cases, the Economic Court of the Republic of Karakalpakstan.

II. STANDARD LEGAL REFERENCE

Constitution 1992 with amendments

III. COMPOSITION AND ORGANIZATION

Composition
The number of judges: ?
Electoral/appointment body:
Elected from political and legal scholars

The Court members:
The Chairman, Deputy Chairman and judges of the Constitutional Court including a representative from the Republic of Karakalpakstan.

Article 108 of the Constitution: No member of the Constitutional Court, including the Chairman, shall have the right to simultaneously serve as a deputy.

The Chairman and members of the Constitutional Court may not be members of political parties and movements nor hold any other paid posts.

Judges of the Constitutional Court shall have the right of immunity.

Judges of the Constitutional Court shall be independent in their work and subordinate solely to the Constitution of the Republic of Uzbekistan.:

Organization
Administrative autonomy: /
The budget: /

IV. POWERS

Constitutional Court Review

Preventive review: /
A posteriori review:
Article 109. 3 of the Constitution: Interpret the norms of the Constitution and laws of the Republic of Uzbekistan.

Article 109 of the Constitution: The Constitutional Court of the Republic of Uzbekistan shall: 1. Define the compliance of the Constitution of the Republic of Uzbekistan, laws of the Republic of Uzbekistan and resolutions of the chambers of the Oliy Majlis of the Republic of Uzbekistan, decrees of the President of the Republic of Uzbekistan, enactments of the government and local bodies of state authority, interstate treaties and other obligations of the Republic of Uzbekistan, 2. conform the compliance of the Constitution of the Republic of Karakalpakstan to the Constitution of the Republic of Uzbekistan, laws of the Republic of Karakalpakstan – to laws of the Republic of Uzbekistan. 4. hear other cases relating to its competence in accordance with the Constitution and laws of the Republic of Uzbekistan.

Other powers
Constitutional complaints: /
Jurisdictional disputes: /
The unconstitutionality of acts and activities of political parties: /
Charges against the President of the Republic: /
Charges against the Prime Minister or against any Minister of State: /
Electoral matters: /
Referendums: /
Other matters with which the Court is charged by the Constitution or statute:
Article 109.4 of the Constitution: Hear other cases relating to its competence in accordance with the Constitution and laws of the Republic of Uzbekistan.

Other forms of human rights protection: /

V. NATURE AND EFFECTS OF DECISIONS

Finality:
Article 109 of the Constitution: Judgments of the Constitutional Court shall take effect upon publication. They shall be final and not subject to appeal.

SOURCES:

https://www.constituteproject.org/constitution/Uzbekistan_2011?lang=en#518
http://www.ksu.uz/en/page/index/id/8

(199)

DOSSIER OF THE SUPREME COURT OF THE REPUBLIC OF VANUATU

STATE: Republic of Vanuatu
TITLE: Supreme Court
YEAR OF FOUNDATION: 1980 (1983)
SEAT: Port Vila

I. CHRONICLE

Date and context of establishment : 1980 (1983)
Position in the hierarchy of courts:
Article 49.1 of the Constitution:The Supreme Court has unlimited jurisdiction to hear and determine any civil or criminal proceedings, and such other jurisdiction and powers as may be conferred on it by the Constitution or by law.

II. STANDARD LEGAL REFERENCE

Constitution 1980 with amendments

III. COMPOSITION AND ORGANIZATION

Composition
The number of judges: 4
The Court consists of the Chief Justice and three puisne judges.

Electoral/appointment body:
Article 49.3 of the Constitution: The Chief Justice shall be appointed by the President of the Republic after consultation with the Prime Minister and the Leader of the Opposition.

With the exception of the Chief Justice, all members of the judiciary are appointed by the President of Vanuatu, who acts on the advice of the Judicial Service Commission, pursuant to Article 47(2) of the Constitution of Vanuatu). The Chief Justice is appointed by the President after consultation with the Prime Minister and the Leader of the Opposition, pursuant to Article 49(3) of the Constitution

Organization
Administrative autonomy:
The budget: /

IV. POWERS

The Supreme Court has unlimited jurisdiction to hear and determine civil and criminal proceedings. It has jurisdiction to hear questions concerning elections and similar matters; and it has jurisdiction to hear any grievances from citizens about emergency regulations made by the Council of Ministers. The Supreme Court has jurisdiction to hear civil and criminal appeals from a Magistrate's Court and to hear appeals from Island Courts as to ownership of customary land. Its decision in such cases is final.

Constitutional Court Review

Preventive review: /
A posteriori review: /
Abstract review: /
Concrete review:

Article 53.3 of the Constitution: When a question concerning the interpretation of the Constitution arises before a subordinate court, and the court considers that the question concerns a fundamental point of law, the court shall submit the question to the Supreme Court for its determination.

Other powers
Constitutional complaints:
Article 53.1 of the Constitution: Anyone who considers that a provision of the Constitution has been infringed in relation to him may, without prejudice to any other legal remedy available to him, apply to the Supreme Court for redress.

Jurisdictional disputes:

Article 53.2 of the Constitution: The Supreme Court has jurisdiction to determine the matter and to make such order as it considers appropriate to enforce the provisions of the Constitution.

The unconstitutionality of acts and activities of political parties:

Charges against the President of the Republic: /

Charges against the Prime Minister or against any Minister of State: /

Electoral matters:

Article 54 of the Constitution: The jurisdiction to hear and determine any question as to whether a person has been validly elected as a member of Parliament, the National Council of Chiefs, and a Local Government Council or whether he has vacated his seat or has become disqualified to hold it shall vest in the Supreme Court.

Referendums: /

Other matters with which the Court is charged by the Constitution or statute:

Article 72 of the Constitution. Complaints to Supreme Court concerning emergency refulations: Any citizen aggrieved by reason of regulations made by the Council of Ministers in accordance with Article 69 of the Constitution may complain to the Supreme Court which shall have jurisdiction to determine the validity of all or any of such regulations.

Article 94 of the Constitution: All legal proceedings, whether civil or criminal, pending immediately before the Day of Independence before any court in Vanuatu shall be disposed of on and after that day in accordance with general or specific directions given by the Supreme Court subject to any law which may be enacted for that purpose.'

Other forms of human rights protection:/

Standing before the constitutional court:

State bodies X

Individuals X

SOURCES:

https://www.constituteproject.org/constitution/Vanuatu_1983?lang=en

https://courts.gov.vu/about-us/supreme-court

(200)

DOSSIER OF THE SUPREME COURT OF THE VATICAN CITY STATE

STATE: Vatican City State
TITLE: Supreme Court
YEAR OF FOUNDATION: 1987 (2000)
SEAT: Vatican City

I. CHRONICLE

Date and context of establishment 1987 (2000)
Position in the hierarchy of courts :
Legislation (n° CXIX) enacted on November 21st 1987 vests judicial authority in a Judge, a Tribunal, an Appeals Court and a Supreme Court, which exercise their authority in the name of the Pope.

Specific responsibilities are established by the codes of civil and penal procedures currently in force in Vatican City.

II. STANDARD LEGAL REFERENCE

The Fundamental Law of Vatican City State, promulgated by Pope John Paul II on 26 November 2000

III. COMPOSITION AND ORGANIZATION

Composition
The Supreme Court consists of its president, who is by law the Cardinal Prefect of the Apostolic Signatura, currently Cardinal Dominique Mamberti since 2014, and two other cardinals, who are appointed by the President on a yearly basis and who also have to be members of the Signatura.

The number of judges: /
Electoral/appointment body: /
The Court members: /
The Court President: /

IV. POWERS

Constitutional Court Review

Preventive review: /
A posteriori review: /
Abstract review: /
Concrete review: /

Other powers
Constitutional complaints: /
Jurisdictional disputes: /
The unconstitutionality of acts and activities of political parties: /
Charges against the President of the Republic: /
Charges against the Prime Minister or against any Minister of State: /
Electoral matters: /
Referendums: /
Other matters with which the Court is charged by the Constitution or statute
Other forms of human rights protection: /
Standing before the Constitutional Court
State bodies: /
Individuals: /

V. NATURE AND EFFECTS OF DECISIONS

Finality: /
Binding force: /
Erga omnes: /
Inter partes: /
Ex officio: /
The legislative omissions: /

SOURCES:

http://www.vaticanstate.va/content/dam/vaticanstate/documenti/leggi-e-decreti/Normative-Penali-e-Amministrative/FundamentalLaw1.pdf

https://en.wikipedia.org/wiki/Law_of_Vatican_City

(201)

DOSSIER OF THE SUPREME TRIBUNAL OF JUSTICE OF THE BOLIVARIAN REPUBLIC OF VENEZUELA

STATE: Bolivarian Republic of Venezuela
TITLE: Supreme Tribunal of Justice
YEAR OF FOUNDATION: 1999 (2009)
SEAT: Caracas

I. CHRONICLE

Date and context of establishment : 1999 (2009)
Position in the hierarchy of courts:
Article 335 of the Constitution: The Supreme Tribunal of Justice shall guarantee the supremacy and efficacy of constitutional rules and principles; it shall be the supreme and ultimate interpreter of the Constitution and shall see to the uniform interpretation and application of the same. Interpretations established by the Constitutional Division concerning the contents or scope of constitutional rules and principles are binding on the other division of the Supreme Tribunal of Justice and on all of the other courts of the Republic.

Article 334 of the Constitution: All of the judges of the Republic, within their respective spheres of competence and in accordance with the provisions of this Constitution and law, are obligated to ensure the integrity of the Constitution.

In the event of incompatibility between the Constitution and a law or other juridical provision, the provisions of the Constitution shall prevail, being the responsibility of the courts to rule accordingly in any case, even ex officio.

The Constitutional Division of the Supreme Tribunal of Justice, as court of constitutional competence, shall have the exclusive power to declare the nullity of laws and other acts of organs exercising Public Power which are issued by way of direct and immediate implementation of the Constitution or have the status of law.

II. STANDARD LEGAL REFERENCE

Constitution 1999

III. COMPOSITION AND ORGANIZATION

Composition
The number of judges: 32
Electoral/appointment body:
Article 270 of the Constitution: The Committee on Judicial Nominations is a body charged with advising the Judicial Power on the selection of candidates for designation as justices of the Supreme Tribunal of Justice.

The Court members: 32
Organization
Administrative autonomy:
The budget:
Article 267 of the Constitution: The Supreme Tribunal is also charged with preparing and implementing its own budget and that of the Judicial Power.

IV. POWERS

Constitutional Court Review

Preventive review:
Article 214 of the Constitution: When the President of the Republic considers that the law or any of its articles is unconstitutional, he shall be required to request a ruling from the Constitutional Division of the Supreme Tribunal of Justice, within the ten day period allowed the President for promulgating the law. The Supreme Tribunal of Justice shall reach a decision within 15 days of receipt of the communication from the President of the Republic. If the Tribunal declines to rule the provisions referred to it unconstitutional or fails to reach a decision within the aforementioned period, the President of the Republic must promulgate the law within five days of the Tribunal›s decision or the expiration of such term.

Article 336 of the Constitution: The following are functions of the Constitutional Division of the Supreme Tribunal of Justice:

.... (5) To verify, at the request of the President of the Republic or the National Assembly, the constitutionality of international treaties signed by the Republic, prior to ratification of the same.

A posteriori review:

Article 336 of the Constitution: The following are functions of the Constitutional Division of the Supreme Tribunal of Justice:

(1) To declare the nullity, in whole or in part, of national laws and other acts of National Assembly with the force of law, which are in conflict with this Constitution.

(2) To declare the nullity, in whole or in part, of state Constitutions and laws, municipal ordinances and other acts of the deliberating bodies of the States and Municipalities which are issued by way of direct and immediate implementation of the Constitution and are in conflict with the same.

(3) To declare the nullity, in whole or in part, of acts of the National Executive with the force of law, which are in conflict with this Constitution.

(4) To declare the nullity, in whole or in part, of acts issued by way of direct and immediate implementation of the Constitution by any other government organ exercising Public Power....

(6) To review in all cases, even ex officio, the constitutionality of decree of the President of the Republic decreeing states of exception....

(8) To resolve any conflicts existing between different provisions of law, and declare which of the same must prevail.

Concrete review:

Article 336 of the Constitution: The following are functions of the Constitutional Division of the Supreme Tribunal of Justice:

... (10) To review judgments embodying constitutional protective orders or control on the constitutionality of laws or juridical rules, handed down by the courts of the Republic, on the terms established by the pertinent organic law...

Other powers

Constitutional complaints: /

Jurisdictional disputes:

Article 336 of the Constitution: The following are functions of the Constitutional Division of the Supreme Tribunal of Justice:

(9) To resolve constitutional controversies arising between any of the organs of Public Power....

The unconstitutionality of acts and activities of political parties: /

Charges against the President of the Republic:

Article 266.2 of the Constitution: To rule as to whether or not there are grounds for impeaching the President of the Republic.

Charges against the Prime Minister or against any Minister of State: Article To rule as to whether or not there are grounds for impeaching the Vice President of the Republic; members of the National Assembly or the Supreme Tribunal of Justice itself, Ministers; the General Attorney; General Prosecutor; General Comptroller of the Republic, the People Defender; Governors; general officers and naval admirals of the National Armed Forces; or the heads of Venezuelan diplomatic missions.

Electoral matters: /

Referendums: /

Other matters with which the Court is charged by the Constitution or statute:

Article 336 of the Consitution: The following are functions of the Constitutional Division of the Supreme Tribunal of Justice:

... (11) Any other functions established by this Constitution or by law.

Other forms of human rights protection: amparo

Standing before the Constitutional Court

State bodies: X

Individuals: X

V. NATURE AND EFFECTS OF DECISIONS

Finality: X

Binding force: /

Erga omnes: /

Inter partes: /

Ex officio:

Article 336 of the Constitution: The following are functions of the Constitutional Division of the Supreme Tribunal of Justice:

--- (6) To review in all cases, even ex officio, the constitutionality of decree of the President of the Republic decreeing states of exception.

The legislative omissions:

Article 336 of the Constitution: The following are functions of the Constitutional Division of the Supreme Tribunal of Justice:

...(7) To declare the unconstitutionality of omissions on the part of the municipal, state, national or legislatures, in failing to promulgate rules or measures essential to guaranteeing compliance with the Constitution, or promulgating it in an incomplete manner; and to establish the time limit and, where necessary, guidelines for correcting the deficiencies.

SOURCES:

https://venezuelanalysis.com/constitution/title/5

https://www.constituteproject.org/constitution/Venezuela_2009?lang=en

(202)

DOSSIER OF THE STANDING COMMITEE OF THE NATIONAL ASSEMBLY OF THE SOCIALIST REPUBLIC OF VIETNAM

STATE: Socialist Republic of Vietnam
TITLE: Standing Committee of the National Assembly
YEAR OF FOUNDATION: 1992 (2013)
SEAT: Hanoi

I. CHRONICLE

Article 74 of the Constitution: The Standing Committee of the National Assembly has the following duties and powers:

1. To prepare for, to convene, and preside over the sessions of the National Assembly;
2. To enact ordinances on matters entrusted to it by the National Assembly; to interpret the Constitution, the law, and decree-laws;
3. To supervise the implementation of the Constitution, the law, the resolutions of the National Assembly, decree-laws, the resolutions of the Standing Committee; to supervise the activities of the Government, the Supreme People's Court, the Supreme People's Procuracy, State Audit, and other organs created by the National Assembly.
4. To suspend the execution of the formal written orders of the Government, the Prime Minister, the Supreme People's Court, the Supreme People's Procuracy that contravene the Constitution, the law, the resolutions of the National Assembly; to report the matter to the National Assembly for it to decide the abrogation of such orders in its nearest session; to repeal the written orders of the Government, Prime Minister, the Supreme People's Court, the Supreme People's Procuracy that contravene the decree-laws and resolutions of the Standing Committee;

II. STANDARD LEGAL REFERENCE

Constitution 2013

III. COMPOSITION AND ORGANIZATION

Composition

Article 73 of the Constitution:

1. The National Assembly's Standing Committee is its permanent Committee.

2. The National Assembly's Standing Committee is composed of the Chairman of the National Assembly, the Vice-Chairmen of the National Assembly, and the members.

3. The Number of members of the Standing Committee shall be determined by the National Assembly. A member of the Standing Committee cannot be at the same time a member of the Government.

4. The Standing Committee of each legislature shall fulfill its tasks and exercise its powers until the election by the new legislature of a new Standing Committee.

IV. POWERS

Other powers

Article 74 of the Constitution: the National Assembly's Standing Committee ha salso the following powers: 5. To direct, harmonize, and co-ordinate the activities of the Nationalities Council and the Committees of the National Assembly, to give guidance to, and to ensure good working conditions for the Assembly delegates.

6. To propose to the National Assembly on election, release from duty, removal from office of the State President, the Chairman of the National Assembly, the Vice-Chairmen of the National Assembly, and members of the Standing Committee of the National Assembly, Chairman of Nationalities Council, Chairmen of the Committees of the National Assembly, President of the National Council of Election, and Head of the State Audit.

7. To exercise supervision and control over, and to give guidance to the activities of the People's Councils; to annul wrong resolutions by the People's Councils of provinces and cities under direct central rule; to disband People's Councils of provinces and cities under direct central rule whenever such Councils cause serious harm to the interests of the people;

8. To decide on the establishment, merging, division, or adjustment of the boundaries of administrative units below the level of provinces and cities under direct central rule.

9. In cases where the National Assembly cannot meet, to decide on proclaiming the state of war, and report it to the National Assembly for decision at its nearest session;

10. To proclaim general or partial mobilization; to proclaim a state of emergency throughout the country or in a particular region;

11. To carry out the National Assembly's external relations;

12. To approve the proposals of appointment and release of ambassador extraordinary and plenipotentiary of Socialist Republic of Vietnam.

13. To organize a referendum as decided by the National Assembly.

SOURCES:

https://www.constituteproject.org/constitution/Socialist_Republic_of_Vietnam_2013?lang=en

DOSSIER OF THE SUPREME COURT OF THE REPUBLIC OF YEMEN

STATE: Republic of Yemen
TITLE: Supreme Court
YEAR OF FOUNDATION: 1991 (2001)
SEAT: Sana'a

I. CHRONICLE

Date and context of establishment : 1991 (2001)
Position in the hierarchy of courts:
The Supreme Court of the Republic is the highest judicial authority

II. STANDARD LEGAL REFERENCE

Constitution 20 February 2001

III. COMPOSITION AND ORGANIZATION le 152

The judiciary shall set up the supreme judicial council. The law shall organize it, stipulate its jurisdiction and system of nominating and appointing its members. The supreme judiciary council shall execute these guarantees for the judiciary in the fields of appointment, promotion, discharge and dismissal according to the law. The council shall study and approve the judicial budget in preparation for inserting it as one item within the overall budget of the State

Composition
The number of judges: /
Electoral/appointment body: /
The Court members: /

The Court President: /

Organization

Administrative autonomy:

The budget:

The judiciary shall set up the supreme judicial council. The law shall organize it, stipulate its jurisdiction and system of nominating and appointing its members. The supreme judiciary council shall execute these guarantees for the judiciary in the fields of appointment, promotion, discharge and dismissal according to the law. The council shall study and approve the judicial budget in preparation for inserting it as one item within the overall budget of the State.

IV. POWERS

Constitutional Court Review

Preventive review: /

A posteriori review:

Article 153 of the Constitution: a)Judge on cases and pleas that laws, regulations, by-laws and decisions are not constitutional.

Other powers

Constitutional complaints: /

Jurisdictional disputes:

Article 153 of the Constitution: b)Judge disputes over conflict of jurisdiction.

d)Rule on appeals of final judgments in civilian, commercial, criminal, personal and administrative disputes and disciplinary cases according to the law.

The unconstitutionality of acts and activities of political parties: /

Charges against the President of the Republic:

Article 153 of the Constitution: e) To try the President of the Republic, the Vice President according to the law.

Charges against the Prime Minister or against any Minister of State:

Article 152: e) To try the Prime Minister, his deputies, the ministers and their deputies according to the law.

Electoral matters: /

Referendums: /

Other matters with which the Court is charged by the Constitution or statute:
Article 153 of the Constitution: c) Investigate and give opinions regarding appeals referred by the House of Representatives which relate to its membership.

Other forms of human rights protection
Standing before the Constitutional Court
State bodies: /
Individuals: /

V. NATURE AND EFFECTS OF DECISIONS

Finality: /
Binding force: /
Erga omnes: /
Inter partes: /
Ex officio: /
The legislative omissions: /

SOURCES:

https://www.constituteproject.org/constitution/Yemen_2001?lang=en

(204)

DOSSIER OF THE CONSTITUTIONAL COURT OF THE REPUBLIC OF ZAMBIA

STATE: Republic of Zambia
TITLE: Supreme Court of Zambia
YEAR OF FOUNDATION: 2016
SEAT: Lusaka

I. CHRONICLE

Date and context of establishment: 2016
The Constitutional Court is a new Court which was established under Article 127 of the Constitution of Zambia (Amendment) Act, No. 2 of 2016 ("the Amendment Act"), which was assented to by the President of the Republic of Zambia on 5th January 2016.

Prior to Amendment Act coming into force, all Constitutional matters were dealt with primarily by the High Court of Zambia, with the possibility of such matters being taken to the Supreme Court on appeal.

Position in the hierarchy of courts:
jThe Constitutional Court, as established, is at the same level as the Supreme Court. This means that all decisions of the Constitutional Court are Final and a person dissatisfied with the decision of the Constitutional Court cannot appeal to any other Court.**dic 127**

Article 121 of the Constitution. The Supreme Court and Constitutional Court rank equivalently..

There is established the

II. STANDARD LEGAL REFERENCE

Constitution 2016

Composition
In terms of its composition, the Constitutional Court is supposed to have at least thirteen (13) Judges, that is the President of the Court, Deputy President and eleven (11) other Judges. (Article 129 of he Constitution)

The number of judges: 13
Electoral/appointment body:
The President:
The President presides over the Court and in her absence the Deputy President must preside over the Court. In the absence of the Deputy President the most senior Judge may preside over the Court.

Proceedings:
When hearing a substantive matter, the Constitutional Court has to comprise an uneven number of not less three judges except on interlocutory matters. This means that three Judges of the Court can hear and determine a matter. The full bench of the Constitutional Court is five Judges. All decisions of the Court are made by majority decision. (Article 129 of the Constitution)

IV. POWERS

Constitutional Court Review

Preventive review: /
A posteriori review:
Abstract review:

Article 128 of the Constitution. (1) Subject to Article 28, the Constitutional Court has original and final jurisdiction to hear—

(a) a matter relating to the interpretation of this Constitution;
(b) a matter relating to a violation or contravention of this Constitution;....
(e) whether or not a matter falls within the jurisdiction of the Constitutional Court.

Concrete review:

Article 128 of the Constitution: (2) Subject to Article 28 (2) of the Constitution, where a question relating to this Constitution arises in a court, the person presiding in that court shall refer the question to the Constitutional Court.

(3) Subject to Article 28, a person who alleges that—

(a) an Act of Parliament or statutory instrument;

(b) an action, measure or decision taken under law; or

(c) an act, omission, measure or decision by a person or an authority; contravenes this Constitution, may petition the Constitutional Court for redress.

(4) A decision of the Constitutional Court is not appealable to the Supreme Court.

However, since the referendum failed, enforcement of violation of Human Rights as enshrined in the Bill of Rights, that is under part three of the Constitution, will be within the Jurisdiction of the High Court in accordance with Article 28 of the Constitution of Zambia.

Other powers

Constitutional complaints: /

Jurisdictional disputes: /

The unconstitutionality of acts and activities of political parties: /

Charges against the President of the Republic: /

Charges against the Prime Minister or against any Minister of State: /

Electoral matters:

Article 128 of the Constitution. (1) Subject to Article 28, the Constitutional Court has original and final jurisdiction to hear—

....

(c) a matter relating to the President, Vice-President or an election of a President;

(d) appeals relating to election of Members of Parliament and councillors;

Referendums: /

Other matters with which the Court is charged by the Constitution or statute: /

Other forms of human rights protection: /

Standing before the Constitutional Court

State bodies: X

Individuals: X

V. NATURE AND EFFECTS OF DECISIONS

Finality:

The Constitutional Court, as established, is at the same level as the Supreme Court. This means that all decisions of the Constitutional Court are Final and a person dissatisfied with the decision of the Constitutional Court cannot appeal to any other Court. (Article 128 of the Constitution)

Binding force: /

Erga omnes: /

Inter partes: /

Ex officio: /

The legislative omissions: /

SOURCES:

https://www.constituteproject.org/constitution/Zambia_2009?lang=en

http://www.parliament.gov.zm/sites/default/files/documents/amendment_act/Constitution%20of%20Zambia%20%20%28Amendment%29%2C%202016-Act%20No.%202_0.pdf

(205)

DOSSIER OF THE CONSTITUTIONAL COURT OF THE REPUBLIC OF ZIMBABWE

STATE: Republic of Zimbabwe
TITLE: Constitutional Court
YEAR OF FOUNDATION: 2013
SEAT: Harare

I. CHRONICLE

Date and context of establishment: 2013
Position in the hierarchy of courts:
Article 162 of the Constitution: Judicial authority derives from the people of Zimbabwe and is vested in the courts, which comprise: the Constitutional Court, the Supreme Court, the High Court, the Labour Court, the Administrative Court, the magistrates courts, the customary law courts and other courts established by or under an Act of Parliament. The Constitutional Court is a superior court of record.

The highest court in the country is the Constitutional court which was introduced by the Constitution of Zimbabwe. This court is headed by the Chief Justice of the court and holds the maximum power and jurisdiction in the country. It has jurisdiction over alleged violations of fundamental rights which are guaranteed by and in the constitution of Zimbabwe.

II. STANDARD LEGAL REFERENCE

Constitution 1980 with amendments

III. COMPOSITION AND ORGANIZATION

Composition
The number of judges: 5

Electoral/appointment body:

The Court members:

The Chief Justice, the Deputy Chief Justice and five other judges of the Constitutional Court.

IV. POWERS

Constitutional Court Review

Preventive review:

Article 167 of the Constitution: a) Advise on the constitutionality of any proposed legislation, but may do so only where the legislation concerned has been referred to it in terms of this Constitution.

The Constitutional Court makes the final decision whether an Act of Parliament or conduct of the President or Parliament is constitutional, and must confirm any order of constitutional invalidity made by another court before that order has any force.

A posteriori review: /

Other powers

Constitutional complaints: /

Jurisdictional disputes:

Article 167 of the Constitution: b) decides only constitutional matters and issues connected with decisions on constitutional matters, in particular references and applications under section 131/b of the Constitution (refer a new Bill to the Constitutional Court for advice on its constitutionality), c) makes the final decision whether a matter is a constitutional matter or whether an issue is connected with a decision on a constitutional matter.

The unconstitutionality of acts and activities of political parties: /

Charges against the President of the Republic: /

Charges against the Prime Minister or against any Minister of State: /

Electoral matters:

Article 167 of the Constitution: b) hear and determine disputes relating to election to the office of President, c)hear and determine disputes relating to whether or not a person is qualified to hold the office of Vice-President

Referendums: /

Other matters with which the Court is charged by the Constitution or statute:

Article 167 of the Constitution: d) determine whether Parliament or the President has failed to fulfil a constitutional obligation.

Other forms of human rights protection: /

Standing before the Constitutional Court

State bodies: X

Individuals: /

V. NATURE AND EFFECTS OF DECISIONS

Finality: /

Binding force:

Article 167 of the Constitution: 1. a) is the highest court in all constitutional matters, and its decisions on those matters bind all other courts

Ex officio:

The legislative omissions: /

SOURCES:

https://www.constituteproject.org/constitution/zimbabwe_2013?lang=en

Ingram Content Group UK Ltd.
Milton Keynes UK
UKHW050929040423
419625UK00008B/683

9 781600 422973